From 1926 Britain fell into a condition of deep national crisis, which seemed to threaten its domestic stability and international power. By 1932 the effort to contain these problems had transformed British politics and policy. Strains produced by three-party politics, economic recession, and imperial difficulties resulted during 1931 in such a severe financial and political crisis that the Labour government collapsed and Conservative, Liberal and some Labour leaders joined together in a National government. Despite large public expenditure cuts and tax increases, and despite devaluation of sterling and a new crisis in the Indian Empire, this government obtained the greatest British election victory of modern times. The consequences were far-reaching: Indian constitutional reform, the onset of economic management, disintegration of the Liberal party, radicalisation of the Labour party, and the beginnings of a new interventionist Conservatism.

This book is the first to examine all aspects of the crisis together and in depth, using an extensive range of official, institutional, and personal papers. It demonstrates that a proper understanding of economic and imperial policies requires a sophisticated grasp of political processes. It shows how explanation of British political change must proceed by placing the power elites in their specific contexts, by exposing their beliefs, fears, objectives, and strategies, and by displaying their interactions. The Treasury, the Bank of England, big business, the TUC, and Keynes, as well as MacDonald, Baldwin, Lloyd George, Churchill, Mosley, and Chamberlain are seen tackling some of the most fundamental problems of the modern British state.

NATIONAL CRISIS AND NATIONAL GOVERNMENT

NATIONAL CRISIS AND NATIONAL GOVERNMENT

British politics, the economy and Empire, 1926–1932

PHILIP WILLIAMSON

Lecturer in History, University of Durham

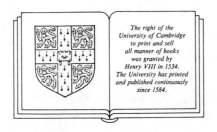

The right of the
University of Cambridge
to print and sell
all manner of books
was granted by
Henry VIII in 1534.
The University has printed
and published continuously
since 1584.

CAMBRIDGE UNIVERSITY PRESS

Cambridge
New York   Port Chester
Melbourne   Sidney

Published by the Press Syndicate of the University of Cambridge
The Pitt Building, Trumpington Street, Cambridge CB2 1RP
40 West 20th Street, New York, NY 10011–4211, USA
10 Stamford Road, Oakleigh, Victoria 3166, Australia

First published 1992

Printed in Great Britain at the University Press, Cambridge

A cataloguing in publication record for this book is available from the British Library

Library of Congress cataloguing in publication data
Williamson, Philip, 1953–
National crisis and national goverment: British politics, the economy and Empire,
1926–1932 / Philip Williamson.
p. cm.
Includes bibliographical references and index.
ISBN 0 521 36137 0
1. Great Britain – Politics and government – 1910–1936. 2. Great Britain – Economic
conditions – 1918–1945. 3. Great Britain – Colonies – History – 20th century. I. Title.
DA578.W45 91-2436
941.082-dc20 CIP

ISBN 0 521 36137 0 hardback

UP

For Jane

Contents

ix

Illustrations

Acknowledgements

Wherever access and time have allowed, this book is based upon original sources. For making these sources available, I am most grateful to the archivists and staff of the record offices, libraries, and other institutions given in the list of sources. For access to and permission to use papers still (or at the time) in private possession, and for hospitality while consulting these, I am especially grateful to the Rt. Hon. Julian Amery MP; Mr and Mrs William Bell; Mr Carron Greig; Mr George Lane-Fox; Viscount and Lady Simon; and Mrs Anne Stacey. Mrs Sheila Lochhead very kindly made her contemporary notes available to me, and gave permission to quote from the MacDonald papers.

For permission to quote from copyright material I am also grateful to Viscount and Lady Addison; Earl Baldwin; the Bank of England; the Trustees of the Beaverbrook Foundation; Mr Jonathan Benn; the University of Birmingham; the Trustees of the Bridgeman Family Papers; Lord Croft; the Dean and Chapter of Durham Cathedral; Sir Edward and Lady Ford; Mr John Grigg; the Earl of Halifax; the Clerk of Records, the House of Lords Record Office; Lord Kennet; Mr A. D. Maclean; the Trustees of the Malcolm MacDonald Papers and the University of Durham; Morgan Grenfell PLC; the Marquess of Reading; Viscount Runciman; and the Trustees of the Trevelyan Family Papers. Material from Crown Copyright records is quoted with permission of the Controller of HM Stationery Office. Documents in the Royal Archives have been used with the gracious permission of Her Majesty the Queen. I apologise to other owners of collections and copyright material whom I have been unable to consult. I also thank the Curator of the Bank of England for supplying photographs and permission to reproduce them, and Mr Ben Hopkins of the Hulton Picture Company for his patience and help in locating further illustrations.

For financial assistance I am very grateful to the Department of Education and Science; the Political Science Fund of the University of Cambridge; and the University of Durham Staff Travel and Research Fund. The Master and Fellows of Peterhouse, Cambridge also provided funds, but most of all a bracing intellectual atmosphere. I am also indebted to the Warden and Fellows of Nuffield College, Oxford, for electing me to a Prize Research Fellowship. Colleagues in the Durham History Department gave me much moral and practical support during dark times.

Important material was kindly obtained for me by Nigel Bowles, Kathleen Burk, Marguerite Dupree, David Dutton, Howell Harris, Andrew Jones, Sheila Lawlor, and Patrick Salmon. Peter Ghosh also supplied copies of documents, helped to locate books, and made innumerable stimulating comments. Professors R. S. Sayers and L. S. Pressnell offered valuable advice. Michael Brock, Roberta Dayer, Kenneth Morgan, John Turner, and the late Philip Williams read certain early drafts and influenced their shape. Peter Clarke and Michael Bentley made helpful criticisms as examiners of chapters 2–9 in earlier, thesis, form, and the latter commented on the penultimate draft. I also thank my colleagues, Anthony Fletcher, Ranald Michie, Howell Harris, and especially Duncan Bythell for their helpful comments on the typescript. I owe a special debt to Nigel Bowles both in this respect and for other great kindnesses.

Maurice Cowling provided the original inspiration for this book, and supervised its early stages. I am very grateful to him for encouragement and confidence over many years.

My parents gave me much support, but also showed a healthy impatience. Christine Woodhead has been research assistant, adviser, critic, proofreader, and a constant help.

Conventions and abbreviations

All significant participants and witnesses are identified in the Appendix.

Economic and financial statistics are for the most part those available to contemporaries rather than more accurate statistics which in some cases (notably for unemployment) have been re-calculated by economic historians.

For all primary and secondary sources, footnote references are given in the shortest form compatible with accuracy. Locations of documents, and full titles and details of publications, appear in the classified list of sources on pp. 542–56.

For literature noted in the introduction or receiving passing mention in chapters, and which did not constitute the sources used in this book, publication details are provided in the footnote references only.

Unless otherwise stated, the place of publication for all published material is London.

References to manuscript collections are shortened by omitting prefixes or collection numbers which will be obvious to those using the relevant record offices. It will be plain, for example, that references to all British Library collections are to ADD.MSS, those to the Lothian papers in the Scottish Record Office are to GD 40/17, and so on. In some cases collections were seen before they were fully listed, and it has not always been possible to give the detailed reference numbers they have since acquired. Reference numbers are not given for unpublished diaries, which are prominently located in their authors' collections.

References to the main J. R. MacDonald collection use the revised Public Record Office call numbers, which differ from earlier references given for example in David Marquand's biography: a conversion table is available in the PRO.

Wherever possible references are to the original document. If the source given is a collection other than that of the recipient, the document is usually a copy (generally carbons of outgoing letters).

Where diaries and private letters can also be seen in published form, a reference to the printed source – identified by either abbreviated title or the editor's name – is given in brackets. For example, the simple form 'Amery diary, 31 Oct. 1931' refers to material found only in the unpublished original, but 'Amery diary, 31 Oct. 1931 (*LSA* II, 217)' refers to the extract on page 217 in the second volume of the published edition. Another form would be 'Bridgeman diary, Sept. 1930 (Williamson, 239–40)'.

Where only a published edition has been seen, the reference is distinguished by the use of 'in'; for instance, 'Keynes memo, 21 July 1930, in *JMK* xx, 375', or 'Reith diary, 13 Oct. 1930, in Stuart, 164'.

Published editions of diaries and letters are listed under the name of the original writer (not the editor) in section 1 of the sources.

AC	Austen Chamberlain papers
app.	appendix
BIS	Bank for International Settlements
BoE	Bank of England papers
BoE Cte	Bank of England: Committee of Treasury minutes
CAB	Cabinet records
Cabinet	Cabinet conclusions (minutes)
ch.[s]	chapter[s]
col.[s]	column[s]
CP	Cabinet papers (memoranda)
DBFP	*Documents on British Foreign Policy 1919–1939*
EAC	Economic Advisory Council
EIA	Empire Industries Association
FBI	Federation of British Industries
FO	Foreign Office papers
FRBNY	Federal Reserve Bank of New York
FRUS	*Foreign Relations of the United States*
HC Deb	*House of Commons Debates*
HL Deb	*House of Lords Debates*
ILP	Independent Labour Party
IOR	India Office Records

JMK	*The Collected Writings of J. M. Keynes* (ed. Elizabeth Johnson and Donald Moggridge)
JRM	J. R. MacDonald papers (PRO collection)
LG	Lloyd George papers
LPACR	*Labour Party Annual Conference Report*
LPNEC	Labour Party National Executive Committee minutes
LSA	*The Leo Amery Diaries* (ed. John Barnes and David Nicholson)
Marquand	David Marquand, *Ramsay MacDonald*
m.	million[s]
MGC	Morgan Grenfell & Co. papers
NC	Neville Chamberlain papers
NCEO	National Confederation of Employers' Organisations
NLF	National Liberal Federation
NLS	National Library of Scotland
PEP	Political and Economic Planning
PLP	Parliamentary Labour Party minutes
PREM	Prime Minister's Private Office papers
q, qq	question[s]
RA GV	Royal Archives: King George V papers
SB	Stanley Baldwin papers
T	Treasury papers
tm	telegram
TUC	Trades Union Congress
TUCAR	*Trades Union Congress Annual Report*
TUCGC	Trades Union Congress General Council minutes
Webb Letters	*The Letters of Sidney and Beatrice Webb* (ed. Norman MacKenzie) – see under Passfield in Sources
WSC	*Winston S. Churchill* vol. v Companion volumes (ed. Martin Gilbert)

Introduction

These eventful years through which we are passing are not less
serious for us than the years of the Great War... We see our race
doubtful of its mission and no longer confident about its
principles, infirm of purpose, drifting to and fro with the tides
and currents of a deeply-disturbed ocean. The compass has
been damaged. The charts are out of date.
Winston Churchill, The Romanes Lecture, 19 June 1930[1]

The early 1930s were a pivotal period in modern British politics and
policy. It had already become painfully clear that Victorian and
Edwardian conditions of prosperity, progress, and imperial power
disrupted by the First World War could not be restored. Now the
deeper implications of this changed environment for the character of
British government became apparent, and could no longer be
evaded. The extension of the electorate, increased strength of the
Labour movement, and adjustments in the party system from 1918,
had also left unresolved problems about the role and finance of
government, and about the distribution of political power. Two
years of intense difficulty and uncertainty culminated in the greatest
peacetime crisis in Britain this century, that of August to October
1931. The longer-term effects were a new political pattern, new
bases for economic and imperial policy, and new conceptions about
the role of the state. These formed the political, administrative, and
intellectual context within which British policy was reshaped during
and after the Second World War.

During 1931 the party system underwent a major and lasting
reconstruction. The Labour party which MacDonald, Henderson,
Snowden, Clynes, and Thomas had made into a party of government

[1] 'Parliamentary Government and the Economic Problem', in Winston Churchill, *Thoughts
and Adventures* (1932), 240.

during the 1920s suffered a split leadership, a disastrous departure from office, and parliamentary devastation. Its expectation of steady political advance was destroyed, its strategies of 'gradualism' and accommodation to existing political conventions were discredited. The Liberal party, divided and weakened by the war and then reduced to third-party status in the early 1920s, had been surrendered acrimoniously by Asquith to Lloyd George and Samuel in 1926–7. After a period of revival it obtained its long-craved re-entry into government, only to disintegrate finally into three irreconcilable splinters and to disappear as a substantial parliamentary force. The Conservative party of Baldwin and Neville Chamberlain endured its own period of severe internal differences. It then obtained surprising allies in the two largest Liberal sections and three Labour leaders within a National government headed by the socialist, MacDonald. In a remarkable general election coup in October 1931 this National government obtained massive ascendancy over a newly radicalised Labour party led by Lansbury, Attlee, Cripps, Dalton, Morrison, and by the TUC leaders, Bevin and Citrine. The politics of 'national unity' had swamped the politics of 'socialism'.

Many political careers lay in ruins, including those not just of former Labour ministers and MPs but also, it seemed, of Lloyd George, Mosley, Amery, and Churchill. Of the three party leaders in the late 1920s – MacDonald, Baldwin, and Lloyd George – only Baldwin survived 1931 at the head of his party. The recurrent electoral uncertainty, parliamentary complications, and governmental instability of the three-party system of the 1920s had been replaced for the 1930s by the lesser insecurities of a two-bloc alignment of the 'National' allies as against the Labour party. This arrangement persisted despite subsequent differences within each bloc and cross-fertilisation between them during the international crisis of the late 1930s and in the war coalition of the early 1940s. Thereafter it solidified into the highly resilient two-party, Conservative–Labour, system which, despite challenges in the 1970s and 1980s, has survived into the present.

In economic policy, efforts made during the 1920s to restore the pre-1914 international financial and commercial system collapsed during 1931 and 1932. The gold standard – the regime of a stable pound and fixed exchange rates re-established in 1925 – had finally to be abandoned. After almost a hundred years, and following three decades of political assault inspired by Joseph Chamberlain, free trade was renounced and tariff protection imposed by Neville Chamberlain. In domestic finance, on the other hand, the 1931 crisis resulted in substantial reversion to pre-1914 conceptions of budgetary rectitude and fiscal apportionment between social classes. All classes were obliged to make some contribution towards balancing the budget, and the direct taxation net was spread more widely than ever before. Nevertheless the burden of impositions fell not so much progressively against wealth (through taxation) as regressively against lower incomes (through retrenchment). All unemployment benefits and state wages, salaries and fees were cut at a stroke. The growth of central government social service expenditure had been temporarily checked. Despite an unemployment rate of around 20 per cent the idea that government could and should spend substantial sums of money to create employment was defeated. Yet this victory for 'sound' public finance obscured important shifts in monetary, commercial, agricultural, and industrial policies towards state assistance and stimulus to private enterprise. Outside the government more explicit *dirigiste* ideas, of state management and planning, became deeply entrenched, while Keynes moved towards the full development of his theory and policy prescriptions.

Imperial relationships were also readjusted, in calculated relaxations of British control. The self-governing 'white' Dominions ceased to belong to the British Empire and became members of a British Commonwealth. As embodied in the 1931 Statute of Westminster this Commonwealth was regarded in Britain not as a retreat from Empire but as a British-led partnership. As trade and finance were considered to be the essential underpinnings for this new relationship, the establishment of an imperial preference system and a sterling bloc had profound political as well as economic significance. Meanwhile the British Empire in India – a miscellaneous collection of British provinces and dependent Native States, all still governed by some measure of autocracy – underwent a process of constitutional reform. This sought to establish, by means of Round Table conferences, a similar British-managed partnership based upon co-operation with moderate nationalists and princes in representative governments and an All-India Federation. These two movements, towards the British Commonwealth and Indian Federation, provoked the emergence of a new imperialist resistance, especially within the Conservative party. It therefore mattered a

great deal for the success of those two movements that the
Labour government was succeeded not by a Conservative government, heavily reliant upon diehard imperialist support, but by a
broad National coalition tipped towards moderate opinion.

These events of the early 1930s are not only important in
themselves. They are also important because since the late 1930s
they have been interpreted in ways which give them a special place
in common understandings of the shape of twentieth-century British
history. The Munich crisis, the Second World War, the Churchill
coalition, the Beveridge Report and the 'Keynesian' White Paper
on Employment Policy, the 1945 Labour election victory, and two
decades of 'full employment': these in various combinations cast a
dark shadow over the politics and policies of the 1930s. For
Churchill, 1931 was the beginning of the 'locust years'. In his
version of events, MacDonald 'brooded supinely' and Baldwin
'reigned placidly' at the head of a 'so-called National Government'
that 'steadfastly closed [its] eyes and ears' to the rise of the dictators
and challenges to British power.[2] More influential still have been
amalgams of this Churchillian view with either Labour or Keynesian
interpretations, or even a fusion of all three. Here criticism
broadened to include a supposed inertness in the face of depression
and mass unemployment, which seemed all of a piece with the foreign
policy record.[3] During the prosperous 1950s and 1960s such views
became standard. Robert Skidelsky, for instance, declared that the
failure of governments in the early 1930s to overcome the economic
problem 'helped create a mood of national self-doubt, of pessimism
regarding the future, in which appeasement could flourish'. The
'refusal to stand up to the dictators was part of the refusal to stand
up to unemployment'; it 'required Dunkirk to give the British faith
in themselves again'.[4]

Since the 1960s reassessments of appeasement and the economic
problems of the 1930s have qualified such interpretations, softening
their hard outlines. Yet the crucial events of the early 1930s which
were once seen as blighting the rest of that decade have not received
comprehensive examination. This does not mean that the period has

---

[2] Winston Churchill, *The Second World War, Vol. I: The Gathering Storm* (1948), 60–1, 64, 66,
also 71, 76–7, 80.

[3] For early versions see 'Cato' [Michael Foot, Peter Howard, and Frank Owen], *Guilty Men*
(1940), 16–26, and A. L. Rowse, *The End of an Epoch* (1947). The latter consists of essays
written between 1938 and 1946, whose heroes are Churchill, Keynes, and Bevin.

[4] Robert Skidelsky, *Politicians and the Slump. The Labour Government of 1929–1931* (1967), 386–7.

been neglected. On the contrary, certain aspects of it have attracted great controversy and historical scholarship of the highest quality.

For many years interest concentrated upon the 1931 political crisis. As its most spectacular features issued from a split within the Labour Cabinet, the principal problem seemed to be ascribing responsibility for that division. From the moment the Labour Cabinet fell and the National government was announced this question of responsibility became a central issue. Fought largely between members and former members of the Labour party, the debate was embittered by an election campaign and produced disclosures which meant that a great deal became known, or rather disputed, about Cabinet proceedings. As the Labour party was considerably more substantial and enduring than MacDonald's National Labour group, and seemed to receive justification in its political successes of the 1940s, the interpretations of its members became orthodox. Labour charges of a 'bankers' ramp'[5] – that British or American bankers had 'dictated' cuts in unemployment benefits and contrived the Labour government's downfall – and of various sorts of 'betrayal' of the Labour movement and the working class by Snowden, Thomas, and especially MacDonald, came to overshadow accusations that Henderson and his supporters had 'run away' from their ministerial responsibilities under pressure from TUC 'dictation'. MacDonald was said to have been perverted by deficient principles or seduced by an 'aristocratic embrace' into a long meditated desertion or 'plot' dating, perhaps, from his appeal in June 1929 for a 'Council of State', if not earlier. Sidney Webb's account published in 1932 became the first of a series of memoirs by ex-Cabinet ministers which combined selective amnesia with creative recollection. Herbert Morrison's were the most outrageous.[6] Labour intellectuals – Woolf, Laski, and Jennings – added the notion of a 'constitutional revolution', especially that the King had been responsible for, or had lent himself to 'undemocratic' action when he appointed a partyless MacDonald to head the

[5] This phrase was invented and used during the August 1931 crisis by the City and Night editors of the *Daily Herald*: see Francis Williams, *Nothing So Strange. An Autobiography* (1970), 101.

[6] Sidney Webb (Lord Passfield), 'What Happened in 1931: A Record', *Political Quarterly*, 3 (1932), 1–17. Morrison, a MacDonaldite up to October 1931, later resorted to outright fiction in order to present himself as a leading anti-MacDonaldite during the August crisis: see his 'recollections' recorded in Harold Nicolson, *King George the Fifth* [hereafter *George V*] (1952), 467; Herbert Morrison, *Government and Parliament* (1954), 78, and Herbert Morrison, *An Autobiography* (1960), 126–7.

National government.[7] The idea of a MacDonald 'plot' was reinforced by Snowden's *Autobiography*, where malice against MacDonald overshadowed malice against the Labour opponents, and by a bizarrely vicious account by MacDonald's former parliamentary private secretary.[8]

Such interpretations for long exercised an important influence upon Labour politics. In 1943 the Bank of England, dismayed to find Labour Cabinet ministers still perpetuating the 'bankers' ramp' accusation, compiled a detailed account of its own role during the crisis for non-attributable use in 'dispel[ling] misconceptions'.[9] The Bank nevertheless became the first institution nationalised by the 1945 Labour government, even though effective control of monetary policy had already passed to the Treasury in the immediate aftermath of the 1931 crisis. Fear of evoking unpleasant and damaging parallels with MacDonald's ' betrayal' inhibited Labour party leaders from resorting to cross-party co-operation in later periods of difficulty. Through such political obsessions and associated writings, the terms of the 1931 party conflict, however diluted or modified, for long determined the form of historical accounts. They were, at first, unshaken by Harold Nicolson's sensible account in his biography of King George V, based upon the Royal Archives and access to certain Cabinet papers and Bank of England documents.[10] If only because of the constrictions of abridged description, their residue can still be found in recent historical writings.

Reassessment was begun by Reginald Bassett, a MacDonaldite of 1931 writing as a political scientist in 1958. He understood that the key to an explanation of the 1931 crisis was a reliable, detailed narrative. He used this to explode the absurdities of earlier accounts,

---

[7] Leonard Woolf, 'A Constitutional Revolution', *Political Quarterly*, 2 (1931), 475–7; Ivor Jennings, 'The Constitution under Strain', ibid., 2 (1932), 194–205; Harold Laski, *The Crisis and the Constitution* (1932).

[8] Philip, Viscount Snowden, *An Autobiography* II, (1934), 929–58; L. MacNeill Weir, *The Tragedy of Ramsay MacDonald* (1938). Weir wrote his first draft during 1932, seeking material from Lloyd George (see Weir to Lloyd George, 21 June, 7 July 1932, and to Sylvester, 31 Aug. 1932, LG G/33/3/42, 43, 44). But Lloyd George was wary and offered little help, and Weir could find no publisher for such a strident attack until after MacDonald's death.

[9] BoE Cte, 10 March, 9 June, 11 Aug. 1943, and Norman to Sir Horace Wilson, 10 Aug. 1943, BoE G14/316. This activity was precipitated by statements made by the Home Secretary, Morrison (who during the 1931 crisis itself had given no sign of believing in any 'bankers' ramp'). The result was a 51-page memo by Thompson-McCausland, 'The Crisis of July–September 1931', used in chs. 8–11 below.

[10] Nicolson, *George V*, 455–69. For Nicolson being allowed to see the vital telegram of 23 August 1931 from New York bankers, see BoE Cte, 10 Aug. 1949, in BoE G14/316.

and to demonstrate that the differences between the two sections of the Labour Cabinet were much narrower than had been asserted.[11] However, as most documentary sources were then still unavailable, he could only speculate about motives. Following the opening of the public archives and with full access to MacDonald's papers, David Marquand's biography of MacDonald produced an impressive and convincing interpretation both of MacDonald himself and of his part in the crisis. He displayed not only MacDonald's vanity and disillusionment but also his sense of duty and honour, his courage, hard work, and resourcefulness, and his genuine attempts to get things done and prove the Labour party's 'fitness to govern'.[12] So far had rehabilitation of MacDonald proceeded that his Labour opponents now seemed neglected. A recent reappraisal of Henderson, however, has presented his actions as 'in the deepest sense, patriotic', in that his objective was to 'keep Labour moderate'.[13]

Accounts of the political crisis had long concentrated upon the Labour party. Autobiographies and biographies of Conservative and Liberal leaders and histories of their parties supplied important details, and showed how each had faced serious internal party problems after the inconclusive 1929 general election. Yet since from both Conservative and Liberal perspectives it seemed easy to regard entry into a National government as a straightforward matter of acting in the 'national interest', their role had not been treated as problematic. More recently, however, their activities have attracted detailed attention. One interpretation supposed that a Labour – Liberal failure to establish a parliamentary alliance enabled Neville Chamberlain successfully to mastermind a 'Conservative Party bid for power' in August 1931.[14] In contrast it has been argued that until a late stage no one could have expected advantage from joining a National government, and emphasis has been placed upon the importance of the Liberal leadership's role during its formation.[15] It

---

[11] R. Bassett, *Nineteen Thirty-One. Political Crisis* (1958). For his MacDonaldism, see Bassett to Allen, 29 Dec. 1931, in Martin Gilbert (ed.), *Plough My Own Furrow. The Story of Lord Allen of Hurtwood* (1965), 225–6.   [12] David Marquand, *Ramsay MacDonald* (1977).

[13] Andrew Thorpe, 'Arthur Henderson and the British Political Crisis of 1931', *Historical Journal*, 31 (1988), 117–39, at 123, 138–9. See also Andrew Thorpe, *The British General Election of 1931* (Oxford, 1991).

[14] John Fair, 'The Conservative Basis for the Formation of the National Government in 1931', *Journal of British Studies*, 19 (1980), 142–64, at 143; Fair, 'The Second Labour Government and the Politics of Electoral Reform, 1929–31', *Albion*, 13 (1981), 276–301.

[15] David Wrench, '"Cashing In": The Parties and the National Government August 1931–September 1932', *Journal of British Studies*, 23 (1984), 135–53.

has also been shown that Conservative leaders, far from seizing power in August 1931, wanted the Labour Cabinet to remain in office for the duration of the immediate financial crisis. Again, though, no special problem is seen about their ultimate decision: joining the National government seemed 'the only possible solution', a matter of 'patriotic duty'.[16]

Meanwhile, another form of interpretation had developed. Here the explanation for the Labour government's collapse lay not in the circumstances of the 1931 crisis, but in its longer-term failure since taking office in 1929 to tackle the economic problem effectively. This approach was foreshadowed as intra-party polemic by Woolf and Tawney, and as history by another Labour intellectual, Cole. For these, the failure was one of insufficient 'socialism'.[17] The approach received its fullest development in the writings of Skidelsky, but for him the failure lay in the nature of 'socialism'. He argued initially that 'socialism' had been 'Utopian' and 'nebulous', with 'nothing constructive to offer the present',[18] and later that it had been fatally rooted in orthodox nineteenth-century political culture and liberal economic assumptions, including that of the continuing viability of free-trade capitalism.[19] Both versions have great historiographical importance. The 'real story' of inter-war domestic politics becomes not the struggle between the political parties or between socialism and capitalism, but that between 'economic conservatives' and 'economic radicals'. It is assumed that 'all policies' turned upon the issue of mass unemployment. Effective means to create employment are said to have been available in 'interventionist' capitalism, as expressed in the ideas of Keynes and those politicians influenced by him.[20]

Skidelsky's approach broadened and deepened analysis, connected political with economic history, and exhumed two previously neglected 'Keynesian' programmes: Lloyd George's loan-financed public works schemes of 1929–30 and Mosley's national development

[16] Stuart Ball, 'The Conservative Party and the Formation of the National Government: August 1931', *Historical Journal*, 29 (1986), 159–82, at 162; Ball, *Baldwin and the Conservative Party. The Crisis of 1929–1931* (New Haven and London, 1988), chapter 9.

[17] Woolf, 'A Constitutional Revolution', 475: R. H. Tawney, 'The Choice Before the Labour Party', *Political Quarterly*, 3 (1932), 323–45; G. D. H. Cole, *History of the Labour Party From 1914* (1948), 255–8. [18] Skidelsky, *Politicians*, xii, 27, 394–5.

[19] Skidelsky, '1929–1931 Revisited', *Bulletin of the Society for the Study of Labour History*, 21 (1970), 6–7; Skidelsky, 'The Reception of the Keynesian Revolution', in Milo Keynes (ed.), *Essays on John Maynard Keynes* (Cambridge 1975), 89–107; and Skidelsky, *Oswald Mosley* (1975), 54–6.

[20] Skidelsky, *Politicians*, xi–xii, 387, and see Skidelsky 'Reception of the Keynesian Revolution', 95–102.

and international 'insulation' plans of 1930–31. At a time when Keynesian economics still seemed a body of almost self-evident truths, this emphasis upon the centrality of a 'Keynesian' solution to unemployment also pervaded the works of historians of economic policy.[21]

Ross McKibbin was the first to suggest that matters were more complicated. 'Keynesianism', he argued, did not offer a real choice because it had yet to become a coherent policy position, would have required fiscal and administrative leverage which the state did not then have, and, given the existing structure of power, would have faced insuperable political obstacles. In his view, the Labour government's effective choice lay only between drift and deflation. In clinging to the former it became so financially unorthodox that it helped manufacture its own collapse.[22] Thereafter, a broader debate about inter-war economic policy – stimulated by the 'end of Keynesianism' and radical changes in national policy during the late 1970s and 1980s – issued in a revisionism which from an economic direction gave analytical depth to what some had intuited from the political end. It has been argued that the unemployment problem was more diverse and more resistant to macroeconomic 'management' than Keynesians had supposed, and that if Lloyd George's and Mosley's public works programmes had been implemented their effect would have been limited, and possibly counter-productive.[23] It has also been argued that the Treasury's resistance to the claims of Keynes, Lloyd George, and Mosley was economically and politically intelligent, and emphasised that it had priorities other than reduction of unemployment.[24] Donald Moggridge, in a

---

[21] See, e.g., Donald Winch, *Economics and Policy* (1969), and Susan Howson and Donald Winch, *The Economic Advisory Council 1930–1939* (Cambridge, 1977); also W. H. Janeway, 'The Economic Policy of the Second Labour Government, 1929–31', (Cambridge Ph.D. thesis, 1971).

[22] Ross McKibbin, 'The Economic Policy of the Second Labour Government 1929–1931', *Past and Present*, 68 (1975), 95–123, reprinted in McKibbin, *The Ideologies of Class. Social Relations in Britain 1880–1950* (Oxford, 1990), 197–227.

[23] See esp. Alan Booth and Sean Glynn, 'Unemployment in the Interwar Period', *Journal of Contemporary History*, 10 (1975), 611–36; Sean Glynn and P. G. A. Howells, 'Unemployment in the 1930s', *Australian Economic History Review*, 20 (1980), 28–45; Sean Glynn and Alan Booth, 'Unemployment in Interwar Britain', *Economic History Review*, 26 (1983), 329–48; T. Thomas, 'Aggregate Demand in the United Kingdom 1918–45', in R. Floud and D. McCloskey (eds.), *The Economic History of Britain since 1700* (Cambridge, 1981), 332–46, and see the debate in Sean Glynn and Alan Booth (eds.), *The Road to Full Employment* (1987).

[24] Especially Roger Middleton, 'The Treasury in the 1930s', *Oxford Economic Papers*, 34 (1982), 48–77; Middleton, 'The Treasury and Public Investment', *Public Administration*, 61 (1983), 351–70, and Middleton, *Towards the Managed Economy* (1985); George Peden, 'The "Treasury View" on Public Works and Employment in the Interwar Period', *Economic History Review*, 37 (1984), 167–81.

Keynesian critique of monetary policy, nevertheless demonstrated that the Bank of England's position was more sensitive and sophisticated than Governor Norman's notorious evidence to the Macmillan Committee had suggested, a conclusion which R. S. Sayers elaborated and confirmed.[25] In a major riposte to the revisionist trend, Peter Clarke revealed how Keynes's challenges forced the financial authorities to examine their assumptions and reconstruct their justifications. He also made important methodological advances, showing that understanding demands attention to how the economic argument developed in specific contexts over time, and appreciation that in crucial aspects it was also a political argument.[26]

In contrast to the party-political and economic issues, imperial and international policies have aroused less scholarly controversy. Nevertheless work in this area has demonstrated that there was a fierce debate between internationalist and imperialist economic policies;[27] that earlier descriptions of the foundation of the British Commonwealth as deliberate constitutional 'evolution' towards independent states were a mythology;[28] and that the political and financial problems which Britain faced in India were partly self-inflicted.[29] These studies have added conceptions of a 'crisis' in Dominion relations and a 'crisis' of Indian unity to those 'crises' detected by other historians in domestic economic, sterling, and budget policies, within the Conservative, Liberal, and Labour parties, and of the party system as a whole. Almost as important, but generally overlooked, is Ronald Butt's view that 'a high tide of criticism of the existing parliamentary system occurred in 1929–31'.[30]

These various 'crises' in party politics, policy, and government have been studied in some depth, but due to the compartmentalisation of much historical interest they have also been studied more or less in isolation. Yet these problems did not bear upon contemporary political leaders in isolation, nor did they just happen

---

[25] Donald Moggridge, *British Monetary Policy 1924–1931* (Cambridge, 1972); R. S. Sayers, *The Bank of England 1891–1944* (Cambridge, 1976).

[26] Peter Clarke, *The Keynesian Revolution in the Making 1924–1936* (Oxford, 1988).

[27] E.g., Ian Drummond, *Imperial Economic Policy 1917–1939* (1974), and Robert Boyce, *British Capitalism at the Crossroads 1919–1932* (Cambridge, 1987).

[28] See esp. John Darwin, 'Imperialism in Decline? Tendencies in British Imperial Policy between the Wars', *Historical Journal*, 23 (1980), 657–79, and R. F. Holland, *Britain and the Commonwealth Alliance 1918–1939* (1981).

[29] R. J. Moore, *The Crisis of Indian Unity 1917–1940* (Oxford, 1974).

[30] Ronald Butt, *The Power of Parliament* (1967), 118.

to coincide: they became interconnected, and they reacted upon each other. They were parts of a general, delayed, aftermath of the First World War, representing the breakdown of the first attempts made between 1918 and 1925 to adjust to its multiple effects: the disruption of the nineteenth-century international economic and financial systems, a sharp increase in colonial nationalist feeling, and mass working-class enfranchisement and the possibility of socialist government. Between certain aspects of these problems there were substantive links. But connections were also created by politicians, as they took up particular issues in the course of advancing wider policy or party objectives.

As the economy failed to conform to pre-1914 patterns, as the principal imperial possessions declined to accept continued subordination, as the party system seemed locked in persistent compromises, and as political leaders tried to cope with the ensuing difficulties, there was a period of severe strains and deep uncertainty. It became apparent to a growing number of public figures that previous assumptions, arrangements, and expectations – Churchill's 'compass' and 'charts' – had become useless or obsolete. Increasingly it was thought and said that fundamental readjustments might have to be made. Doubts were even raised about the effectiveness of the institutions of government, including Parliament. The resulting atmosphere contributed to a transformation in British government, in its personnel, policy, power, and potential.

If these changes are to be understood, each important element in the political system – whether a party or a policy – has to be assessed in relation to the other important elements. From this perspective it is clear that although foreign policy, especially the issue of disarmament, was a large government concern and at an executive level mattered a great deal to MacDonald and Henderson, it did not form a central issue and had only marginal effects upon the course of political change. Consequently it makes only intermittent appearances in the present study.[31] On the other hand it becomes plain that the economic problem was not the all-engrossing issue it is often presumed to have been. Many politicians treated the Indian problem as almost as important, if not more so. Although it was possible to believe that the economy might soon recover, in India many lives were at immediate risk and loss of control there would be a permanent blow to British prestige and power. Contrary to

---

[31] For a valuable study of these aspects, see David Carlton, *MacDonald versus Henderson. The Foreign Policy of the Second Labour Government* (1970).

another common impression, it also becomes apparent that even within economic affairs unemployment was never the predominant issue around which all other policies turned. It was always a subordinate matter, secondary to a 'sound' currency, a balanced budget, debt management, industrial efficiency and business confidence, free trade or tariffs. Even trade unions considered employment subordinate to the maintenance of existing levels of wages and unemployment benefits.

One effect of studying different elements separately has been that each part has not always been fully understood. This is especially true where 'politics' and 'policy' overlap. For instance, as makers of Indian policy, Simon and Hoare have been criticised as 'trimmers...who placed personal and party considerations above principle'.[32] This statement may contain much truth, yet it is certain that Hoare, for instance, would never have steered the federation scheme past Conservative imperialists if he had not shown the closest attention to party management and his personal position. Misunderstanding is still more frequent in policy studies by economists and economic historians. A great deal of such literature on the interwar period rests upon an assumption that policy was, or should have been, determined by economic and financial experts on economic and financial merits. It can be granted that the financial authorities and economic interests helped to shape the culture of politics and government, and imposed certain constraints upon policy. Nevertheless, such literature fails either to grasp the primacy of politics in issues of government, or to display a genuine sense of the character of political activity.

Politics inevitably entered into the fundamental concerns of the experts. Clarke has shown how political prepossessions and participation crucially affected the development of Keynes's economic thinking, and similar things can clearly be said of the Treasury and the Bank of England.[33] Politics obviously became central at the level of economic and financial policy decisions – which, in most cases, were a matter of power relationships negotiated by politicians. These politicians had their own economic conceptions, however callow. More important, they also had constantly to concern themselves with other areas of policy, with the management of opinion, and

[32] Moore, *Crisis of Indian Unity*, 209.
[33] Clarke, *Keynesian Revolution*, esp. ch. 4, and see his earlier essay, 'The Politics of Keynesian Economics 1924–1931', in Michael Bentley and John Stevenson (eds.), *High and Low Politics in Modern Britain* (Oxford, 1983). For important comments about officials, see Middleton, 'The Treasury in the 1930s', 59–65.

with party objectives. Yet policy studies are often confined to the records of officials and economists, as if policy happened in a world divorced from that of politics, except for occasional, unpleasant, intrusions of some undefined 'political expediency'.[34] Alternatively, politics are reduced to a puppet show manipulated by officials, economists, and pressure groups.

In reality political activity was not some obscure monolithic force, but a matter of constantly shifting disagreement, debate, and persuasion over both fundamentals and details. It was not a passive reflection of 'interests' or inert implementation of advice, but a largely autonomous activity with its own complex priorities, procedures, and languages. So, for instance, if the unemployment policy debate of early 1929 is to be properly understood, it matters a great deal that it took place in the run-up to a general election. Similarly the introduction of protection will not be understood if it is assumed that politicians who had spent half a lifetime believing in tariff reform needed to be led in that direction by businessmen, officials, and economists.

A common distortion in the study of economic policy – rather than in the distinct study of the development of economic thinking – is that economists receive a prominence altogether disproportionate to their actual importance. In such works the only Henderson who appears to be significant is Hubert, the economist – not Arthur, the politician. Yet Arthur Henderson, despite being Foreign Secretary from 1929 to 1931, always had more weight than Hubert Henderson whenever he intervened in economic policy. More remarkable is the attention given to Keynes, which is on a scale explicable only in terms of his subsequent influence. Contemporary politicians might have considered that Keynes had valuable economic ideas, but within the whole context of assessing the practicality of policies – a judgement necessarily extending well beyond economics – he was of no more importance than, say, leading backbench MPs or the editors of *The Times*, *News Chronicle*, or *Daily Herald*. In this sense the space given to Keynes in the present study remains excessive. Nevertheless it seems justified for the negative purpose of

---

[34] To take only the most recent example, see the lists of what is considered relevant in W. R. Garside, *British Unemployment 1919–1939. A Study in Public Policy* (Cambridge, 1990), xiii–xiv: politics and party are not mentioned. For a politically more sophisticated approach, see Jim Tomlinson, *Public Policy and the Economy since 1900* (Oxford, 1990). See also Alan Booth and Sean Glynn, 'The Public Records and Recent British Economic Historiography', *Economic History Review*, 32 (1979), 303–15, for a dawning realisation of the limited usefulness of official records.

showing that his contributions to policy debate could be ambiguous or unhelpful, and that rejection of his views did not necessarily denote prejudice or stupidity. Then again, confusion arises if Keynes's ideas are assumed to be the standard for what constitutes economic 'radicalism', 'intervention', or 'management'.[35] Other versions existed, most notably Conservative imperial protectionism which offered an alternative, if much less sophisticated, political economy. By 1929 the real economic issues lay not between 'laissez-faire' and 'intervention', but between different forms and degrees of radical intervention.[36]

It is true that certain policies were treated as 'non-political', and left to the experts. Here non-political records obviously do provide most of the relevant source-material. Monetary policy is the chief example. Until August 1931 this almost never entered even into Cabinet deliberations, with the result that most political leaders remained ignorant of the issues and potentially at the mercy of officials. As Passfield said, notoriously, after suspension of the gold standard, 'nobody even told *us* we could do that'.[37] Yet such matters were 'non-political' only in the sense that they were taken out of politicians' hands. In a deeper sense these arrangements were highly political, representing the supremacy of a particular political-economic dispensation. This was true of the gold standard, and it can be seen again after 1931, when Conservative ministers placed tariffs and later unemployment relief in the hands of new 'non-political' agencies.

This book begins in 1926 and ends in 1932 not merely because that period encompasses the 1931 crisis, but because it has a distinct coherence. It stretches from the realisation that the gold standard was not operating smoothly to the establishment of new monetary arrangements, and from a free trade to a protectionist regime. The 1926 Imperial Conference defined the notion of Commonwealth, and that of 1932 determined its economic arrangements. Lord Irwin, the principal force behind Indian constitutional reform, became

[35] Alan Booth, 'Britain in the 1930s: A Managed Economy?', *Economic History Review*, 40 (1987), 499–522, develops this criticism.

[36] The point is forcefully made in Robert Self, *Tories and Tariffs. The Conservative Party and the Politics of Tariff Reform 1922–1932* (New York and London, 1986), xxiii–xxv. Skidelsky, 'Reception of the Keynesian Revolution', 102, and Skidelsky, *Mosley*, 56–8, had earlier accepted the salience of tariff reform before 1914, but ignored its inter-war Conservative manifestations.

[37] This is the version originally recorded in Dalton diary, 12 Jan. 1932. The phrase was then modified in the published source, Hugh Dalton, *Call Back Yesterday. Memoirs 1887–1931* (1953), 298, and is now usually rendered without the 'even'.

Viceroy in 1926; in 1932 the decisions were taken to persist with the process he had begun. The period also extends from one period of Conservative predominance to another.

A less obvious source of coherence, but in some senses the crucial one, is provided by the Liberal party. Except as generators of radical economic ideas Liberals are not often considered to be of much significance beyond 1924, when they failed to re-establish themselves as a party of government. It is generally said that their 'downfall' had already occurred, and that their attempted revival at the 1929 election was a failure. Yet being a self-sufficient party of government does not constitute the sole criterion of importance, nor is regaining such a position the only meaningful party aspiration. After Lloyd George became Liberal leader in 1926 the party enjoyed an increased share of the popular vote, and an advance from parliamentary powerlessness to possession of the balance of power. Later it became a major if divided partner in the National government. Even though the contests between the smaller and the two larger parties were unequal, the period from 1926 to 1932 was nonetheless one of genuine three-party politics. The existence of a 'hung' Parliament between the 1929 and 1931 elections had large consequences for the party struggle and for national policy.[38]

For the Conservative and Labour parties, the Liberal revival of the late 1920s greatly complicated the chief problem of modern government. This was the problem of obtaining sufficient assent from a mass electorate – largely poorly informed, and overwhelmingly working-class – for policies which were difficult to comprehend, which lacked a sensational appeal, or, most seriously, which might involve material sacrifice from large numbers of voters. Throughout the inter-war period there was much anxiety about whether democracy could be persuaded to face 'the truth', and be dissuaded from succumbing to irresponsible 'stunts'. The leaderships of both major parties initially reacted to the Liberal revival by compromising their own preferred policies and seeking to undercut it through appeals to moderate opinion. With the collapse of the Liberal party in 1931–2, they felt more freedom in asserting their own versions of radicalism.

Within the period 1926 to 1932 this book is organised around two shorter periods, which receive close examination as foci for the

---

[38] One common indication of inattention to the Liberals is that in accounts of the last weeks of the Labour government they are described as an 'opposition party', which altogether misunderstands the Liberal leadership's position.

several strands of exposition and argument. The importance of the
later sub-period, from mid July to late October 1931, is self-evident:
it was that of manifest financial and political crisis. Here explanation
demands detailed attention to chronology, as a series of major and
complex changes occurred in every part of the political system.
During those months nothing remained constant and predictable.
The sterling crisis, for instance, passed through several phases, while
attitudes towards the idea of 'national government' changed week
by week, and sometimes day by day.

The earlier sub-period, from October to early December 1930, has
not previously been regarded as one of general importance. Yet
during those months the notion of 'national crisis' took firm hold,
both as a description of substantive problems and as an instrument
in political conflict. This not only remained an ingredient in high
politics during the following year; it also created a wider public
atmosphere of 'crisis' which helped make the electorate so responsive
to the National government's appeal at the 1931 general election.
During this period too, the idea of 'national government' itself
became established, some ten months before the National government was actually formed.

These early coalition ideas have been treated in one of two ways,
either as evidence of a conspiracy or premeditated betrayal by
MacDonald or, more recently, as unimportant because having no
relevance to contemporary politics – 'the only national combinations formed in the autumn of 1930 were those scribbled on the backs
of menus at select dinner parties'.[39] Both views misunderstand the
character and significance of the 'national government' idea. In the
first place, the National government of August 1931 was not that
envisaged by any political leaders in autumn 1930. This was most
certainly true of MacDonald. Second, any serious consideration of
suspension of party conflict is an important indicator of severe strain
in the political system, particularly of a perceived gap between the
scale of policy problems and the ability of government to cope with
them. In this sense the discussions of autumn 1930 were similar to
those during the constitutional crisis of 1910 and the Irish crisis of
1914, or during the First World War crises of 1915 and 1916. Third,
these discussions were relevant even though they might appear to
have borne little relation to contemporary party positions. Politics

[39] Skidelsky, *Politicians*, 279; see also Ball, 'The Conservative Party and the Formation of the
National Government', 159–61, and Ball, *Baldwin*, 172–4. For a rather different, but still
sceptical, verdict, see Marquand, 574–80.

are not just about the present and the immediately foreseeable future, but also about the middle- and long-term futures. They operate simultaneously across several time-scales, and the politics of what might happen are as important as the politics of what is happening. Occasionally, when the future appears unusually uncertain, a large disjunction between present politics and future politics may seem probable. The 'national crisis' perceived in autumn 1930 was such an occasion: it was actually one of anticipated crisis, a fear that something might go very badly wrong and require extraordinary measures. Political leaders hoped that matters would remain stable and that government and party politics would continue safely within the bounds of reasonable calculation. But alongside these hopes there co-existed a politics of extreme uncertainty about the future. This led some politicians to consider contingency plans, just in case drastic and politically difficult action became necessary. Such ideas could remain dormant, yet retain a latent relevance. Even so, when the idea of 'national government' did eventually enter current politics, it did so in an unexpected manner.

The existence of 'national crisis' is a major theme of this book. Nevertheless the notions of 'national interest' or 'patriotism' are not offered as leading explanations for any of the responses to that condition. The difficulties of such notions are revealed by the fact that 'patriotism' can be used by one recent study to describe the actions of the Conservative leaders, and by another to describe those of Henderson. The same terminology might be applied to the Bank of England and the TUC, because during the 1931 crisis everyone saw themselves as acting patriotically, in the 'national interest'. What constituted this 'national interest' was itself central to the dispute. In contrast to the war crises of 1915, 1916, or 1940, no obvious agreed definition of the national interest existed. Defence of sterling might appear a strong candidate. Yet, if this makes Conservative leaders 'patriotic' in August 1931, it would be difficult to apply the same description to them a month later.

The point is not just that each party, institution, group, or individual had their own view of the national interest, but that each presumed an identity between their own higher interests and those of the nation. This book seeks to show how each tried to convert their own objectives into the policy of the nation, and how this competition issued in a major upheaval of politics and government.

PART I

Components of crisis

CHAPTER I

The erosion of Conservative predominance

The heat of the battle of to-day is not between H.M.G[overn-ment] and H.M.O[pposition]…It is comparatively unim-portant either to Baldwin or MacDonald or to the causes and interests they represent, whether the Tories remain in for another two or three years and get defeated at the next General Election, or whether the Labour Party takes office this year and gets defeated in a subsequent election. What is at stake is the continued existence of the Liberal Party and the continued power of Ll. George.

Beatrice Webb diary, 30 May 1929 (general election day)[1]

Despite the General Strike, British politics in the late 1920s were not conducted as an overt class struggle. Nor, despite persistent industrial stagnation and mass unemployment, were they really a policy struggle between 'economic radicals' and 'economic conservatives'.[2] Rather, as Beatrice Webb understood, they were a resumption of the party struggle of the 1924 Parliament – a conflict which turned upon the future of the Liberal party.

After the indecisive general election of December 1923 first Baldwin's Conservative government and then MacDonald's Labour government had suffered from the Liberal party's efforts to use its possession of the balance of power in the House of Commons as an instrument to re-establish itself as a party of government. This Liberal obstruction to Conservative ambitions to become the sole party of resistance and to Labour ambitions to become the sole party of progress resulted in tacit alliance between the Conservative and Labour leaderships to try and eradicate the Liberal party. Each engineered parliamentary opportunities to embarrass it; both established classless electoral appeals designed to win support for

---

[1] Printed in Cole, 193; MacKenzie IV, 171.   [2] Skidelsky, *Politicians*, xi, 51.

themselves from moderate, liberal, opinion. Behind the extrava-
gances of the 'red scare' which consumed the Labour government,
this was the real substance of the October 1924 general election. The
Conservative party won a parliamentary majority of over 200 seats.
The Labour party lost forty seats, but in gaining a million more votes
than at the 1923 election it displayed an enduring potential. The real
victim was the Liberal party: losing 1·3 million votes and 119 seats,
it was reduced to a powerless rump of just forty MPs. For Baldwin,
the chief beneficiary of the election, this result marked the beginning
of a new political era. Having, it seemed, witnessed 'the disappearance of the Liberal party', he now looked to 'the elimination
of the Communists by Labour' in order to create a future of safe
constitutional struggle between 'two Parties, the Party of the Right
and the Party of the Left', in which he assumed the balance of
advantages would favour the Conservative party.[3] MacDonald
might well have said the same, with the outcome reversed.

The political significance of the General Strike was twofold. As
much for MacDonald as for Baldwin, it appeared to produce the
welcome result of just such a defeat for militant trade unionism and
the far left (Baldwin's 'communists'), diverting labour politics back
into constitutional channels. But the second, unwelcome, result was
a Lloyd George-led Liberal revival, threatening the Conservative
and Labour division of the political world. It promised a great
increase in the number of awkward three-cornered constituency
contests: the final total of 447 in 1929 almost doubled that at any
previous general election. With the added complication of some
seven million new voters, increasing the electorate by a third –
chiefly the result of the 1928 equalisation of the franchise for women
– the electoral effects of a Liberal revival seemed likely to be as
unpredictable as they had been at the 1923 general election.

THE LIBERAL CHALLENGE

From 1924 Lloyd George had two consistent objectives. In the face
of Asquithian rancour dating from the Liberal split of 1916–23, one
aim was to capture control of the Liberal party. This was
accomplished after Asquith's condemnation first of the trade unions
and then of Lloyd George's criticism of the Conservative government
during the General Strike had dismayed most Liberals and

[3] Jones, *Whitehall Diary* I, 303, 4 Nov. 1924.

exposed the Asquithians' distance from most post-war Liberal thinking. In October, with Lloyd George capitalising upon this blunder and using his large personal political fund to buy out the near-bankrupt party organisation, Asquith preferred retirement to further humiliation. Lloyd George nevertheless wanted to unite the party and tried hard to be patient towards Asquith's followers, despite their formation in December 1926 of an anti-Lloyd Georgian Liberal Council. His acceptance of Samuel, an Asquithian sympathiser, as the new chairman of the party organisation was a genuine concession.

Lloyd George's other objective was to revive the Liberal party's power. To this he gave a great deal of time, effort, and money. Like all Liberals, he assumed that the party's authority and appeal lay in classlessness, disinterestedness, free trade, individualism tempered by a necessary collectivism, anti-socialism without reaction, and prudent progressivism. But he also understood that it was not sufficient for the Liberal party to be simply non-Conservative and non-Labour. A successful centre party could not be negative or neutral, but had to offer something positive, active, and solid. As the Liberal elite and parliamentary party were divided and likely to be obstructive, Lloyd George proceeded by independent initiatives. He personally sponsored a series of policy inquiries by Liberal businessmen, social investigators, and economists, mostly recruited from the Liberal Summer School and *Nation* groups, which included Layton, E. D. Simon, Muir, Keynes, Rowntree, and H. D. Henderson. The resulting reports, on *Coal and Power* (1924), *The Land and the Nation* and *Towns and the Land* (1925), *Trade Unionism and the Trade Union Bill* (1927) and *Britain's Industrial Future* (February 1928), represented an intellectually impressive body of new, radical, interventionist, economic ideas compatible with private enterprise.[4] In a striking pledge before the 1929 general election Lloyd George committed a Liberal government to reduce unemployment to 'normal proportions' within a year through public works, but without adding 'one penny' to taxation or rates. *We Can Conquer Unemployment* explained how: specific plans, with costings and manpower estimates, for two years of essential 'national development' financed by a £145m. loan secured on Road Fund revenues and some £70m. more in various other loans. Keynes and

---

[4] For a good examination, see Hart thesis, 'Decline of the Liberal Party', ch. 6.

H. D. Henderson supplied heavyweight economist support in their affirmative *Can Lloyd George Do It?*

From 1925 Lloyd George spent some £240,000 on a Land and Nation League. In late 1926 he gave £10,000 to the Industrial Inquiry, and sold his newspaper interests in order to provide the Liberal party machine with an election fund of £300,000 and a three-year subsidy of £30,000 per annum.[5] Samuel announced in January 1927 that 500 Liberal candidates would fight at the next general election – the largest number since the pre-war Liberal triumphs. The whole party organisation was resuscitated, propaganda was profuse, observers were sent to learn campaign methods from the 1928 American presidential election,[6] and intensive work was put into by-election campaigns. From March 1927 to March 1929 three seats were held and six won (five from the Conservative government) in a by-election revival which seemed to promise a large general election advance.[7]

It has often been assumed that these efforts should be interpreted as the unfolding of a coherent policy design, with *Britain's Industrial Future* leading naturally to *We Can Conquer Unemployment*; as a party strategy pitched consistently towards the radical left, and as an attempt to win a Liberal election majority – as a dash for a Liberal government. Yet each of these points, the last most of all, misunderstands Lloyd George's and other Liberal leaders' sense of the possibilities. For obvious reasons their public stance was that a Liberal victory (which within a three-party system would have required over 200 seats) was achievable. But privately they accepted that the 1924 election result had wrecked all hope of a foreseeable revival as an independent party of government: the electoral realities of Conservative and Labour competition were inexorable. In August 1925 Lloyd George's aim was 'a minimum of 100 Liberals in the next parliament'. By May 1928 he hoped for 100 or 120 MPs, by April 1929 for 80 to 100.[8] Samuel began as party chairman with a belief in a Liberal majority, but by July 1927 examination of the constituencies had disabused him. John Simon expected the party to

---

[5] Campbell, *Lloyd George*, 124, 196; Samuel in Perks to Rosebery, 9 Aug. 1927, Rosebery papers 10053. The *Daily Chronicle* newspaper group was sold for £2·8m.: see Nov. 1926 memos, LG G/15/7/5–7.

[6] West, *Lloyd George's Last Fight*, chs. 4–6.

[7] Hart thesis, 'Decline of the Liberal Party', 346–52, shows that in reality these by-election successes exaggerated the Liberal advance: but what mattered was the contemporary impression.

[8] Lloyd George to F. Stevenson, 20 Aug. 1925, in Taylor, 98; Dawson diary, 9 May 1928; Lady Hilton Young diary, 28 May 1928 (Kennet, 263); Clarke, *Diary*, 48, 18 April 1929.

win around 5 million votes, but still to come third.[9] During the general election campaign Keynes thought a 'miracle probable', but he meant only that Liberals might have 'more than 90 in the next House'.[10]

Liberal politics have to be understood within these expectations. If there was to be no Liberal government, what was the purpose of the Liberal revival? To this question there were three answers. For Keynes and other Liberal intellectuals the party constituted 'an almost perfect tabernacle for independent thought' and a 'method of bringing a sensible programme to the notice of the public and of politicians' – an instrument for advancing ideas in the confident expectation that one of the larger parties would 'steal them'.[11] That is to say, Keynes did not expect *Lloyd George* to 'do it' at all, but to alter the government agenda so that someone else might attempt to do so.

Lloyd George himself sometimes spoke in similar terms, of persuading other parties to adopt his programmes.[12] But he and other professional Liberal politicians hardly supposed that their role was to lead just a party of ideas. Nor would a party of ideas have required 500 candidates and an expensive election machine. Lloyd George possibly had a distant hope of forcing some reconstruction of the party system, making the Liberal party 'the rallying-point for men of all parties and of none'. Like all Liberals, he imagined that many politicians were in the 'wrong party' and that both 'moderate Labour' and 'progressive Conservatives' were closet Liberals.[13]

But the chief purpose of the Liberal revival was perfectly straightforward – to regain the balance of power in the House of Commons. This had always been the extent of Lloyd George's ambitions for the next general election,[14] and it was an objective about which Liberals could feel fairly confident. Around 80–120 MPs seemed the appropriate target because these would form a

[9] Scott diary, 22 July 1927 (Wilson, 487); Simon to Irwin, 18 Sept. 1928, Halifax papers 18/132. For similar Liberal headquarter forecasts, see West, *Lloyd George's Last Fight*, 35–6.

[10] Keynes to Garvin, 9 May 1929, Garvin papers. See also 'Liberalism and Labour', Feb. 1926, in *JMK* IX, 307.

[11] Keynes to Garvin, 9 Feb. 1928, and 'Liberalism and Industry', 5 Jan. 1927, in *JMK* XIX, 733, 640.

[12] E.g., Lloyd George to Scott, 10 Feb. 1926, LG G/17/11/19; interview, *The Times*, 13 March 1929.

[13] E.g., Lloyd George 'Foreword' to H. L. Nathan and H. H. Williams, *Liberal Points of View* (1927), 6; and for 'fluidity of parties', Scott diary, 13–14 Nov. 1925 (Wilson, 484).

[14] E.g., Scott diary, 14 Oct. 1927, 7 Dec. 1928 (Wilson, 491, 493); Lloyd George, 'Note of interview with Churchill', 18 Feb. 1929, LG G/4/4/23.

substantial bloc which no government could ignore. Five hundred candidates were nevertheless needed because the 1924 election (fought by only 339 Liberal candidates) appeared to demonstrate that voters would not return a large number of MPs unless they believed the party to be a serious contender for government office. 'People will only back a possible winner'.[15] So as many as four-fifths of Liberal candidates were lambs knowingly sent to slaughter for the party's greater good.

As there would not be a Liberal government to redeem election promises, the point of the celebrated detail of Liberal economic policies and the precision of Lloyd George's pledge was to create the same necessary illusion of the party's potential. This does not deny that Lloyd George 'believed' in the programmes. At some deep level he identified with the disadvantaged, assumed that the future lay with agricultural and industrial producers more than landlords, *rentiers*, and financiers, and had a radical's faith in selective state intervention together with a well-grounded conviction in his own unique capacity to get things done. But as a supreme political realist he understood that other parties had concerns and aims which meant they could never swallow Liberal programmes whole. Proposals forced upon, or implemented in co-operation with, another party would naturally be modified, diluted, truncated. Although Keynes had an intellectual commitment to defend the theoretical integrity and details of public loan finance for employment schemes – which he did with creative brilliance[16] – this must not obscure the propagandist purpose of *We Can Conquer Unemployment*, nor a context which determined that Lloyd George's attachment to its contents was necessarily – and given the Liberals' third-party status, unusually – conditional upon the party situation. The point is important for understanding not just Lloyd George's strategy before the 1929 election, but also what happened to the programme afterwards.

Moreover, party survival meant that economic programmes could not be the first priority. Obtaining the parliamentary balance of power at one election in itself offered nothing for the future, and the party could not afford indefinitely to finance 400 losing candidates.

---

[15] Lloyd George to F. Stevenson, 14 Aug. 1925, in Taylor, 88.

[16] See esp. Clarke, *Keynesian Revolution*, 83–102. There is continuing debate among economists about whether the *We Can Conquer Unemployment* programme could have fulfilled Lloyd George's pledge: for the most recent contributions see K. G. P. Matthews, 'Could Lloyd George Have Done It?', *Oxford Economic Papers*, 41 (1989), 374–407, and Garside, *British Unemployment*, 367–79. From a political perspective, however, such exercises are largely redundant.

Liberal leaders were haunted by the disastrous outcome of holding the balance in the 1924 Parliament. All were agreed that mistakes had been made, which must never be repeated. Never again would they vote 'blindfold' to install another party in office. The balance of power had to be converted into some real power by extracting terms for Liberal support, terms which would guarantee that the party gained some credit and advantage at succeeding elections.[17] Lloyd George's real ambition was 'to dictate the terms of [a] Treaty to the Government of the day'.[18] Given the imperative of securing continued Liberal party influence, this had to include electoral reform above all else.[19] Party policy was proportional representation, to convert the still substantial Liberal popular vote into a permanent and influential bloc of around 100 Liberal MPs.

Achievement of electoral reform was a constant priority. But in other respects the complexion of Liberal high politics and policy shifted repeatedly, because it depended largely upon the view taken of the potential for negotiation with either of the major parties. To avoid internal dispute and alienation of prospective Liberal voters the collective leadership's official line, reaffirmed at the October 1928 NLF conference, was that the Liberal party was and would remain a wholly independent party. There would, they said, be no pacts before the election and if a Liberal government could not be formed afterwards, the parliamentary leaders would decide upon the best course according to the merits of the situation.[20] Yet some effort to anticipate the election outcome was only sensible, so that policies and strategy might be pitched in an appropriate manner and perhaps make the result more certain. Lloyd George himself wanted a pre-election understanding about seats to ensure the return of as many Liberal MPs as possible, to be followed by a two-party coalition government.[21]

Lloyd George 'didn't mind who he combined with, Conservative

---

[17] See, e.g., Lloyd George in Scott diary, 27–30 Nov. 1924, 13–14 Nov. 1925, 22–3 July 1927, 14 Oct., 7 Dec. 1928 (Wilson, 470–1, 484, 488, 491, 493–4), and Lloyd George and Maclean in Maclean memo, Feb. 1929, Maclean papers c468/106–11.

[18] Lloyd George to F. Stevenson, 22 Jan. 1929, in Taylor, 114.

[19] Lloyd George in Scott diary, 7 Dec. 1928 (partly in Wilson, 493); Maclean memo, Feb. 1929, Maclean papers c468/106–11; and Lloyd George, 'Note of interview with Churchill', 18 Feb. 1929, LG G/4/4/23. See also Samuel to Lloyd George, 6 Oct. 1928, LG G/17/9/12, for 'the essentials of the situation'.

[20] Lloyd George, Samuel, and Hobhouse, 12 Oct., in *NLF Proceedings 1928*, 36–47.

[21] E.g., Scott diary, 7 Dec. 1928 (Wilson, 493–4): Lloyd George's denial here of wanting office for himself may be treated with the same scepticism as his occasional comments about resigning the parliamentary party leadership.

or Labour, only he would not swallow Protection for food on the one side or nationalization on the other'.[22] It would be easy to be cynical about this: readiness to move in either direction may appear characteristic of a notoriously agile political intelligence. But at least as important were the situational pressures upon him. Consistency – Asquith's parting injunction to his followers to 'look neither to the right nor the left, but keep straight on'[23] – was an unaffordable luxury for the leader of a third party who wanted it to remain an effective political force. As Liberal party ambitions were achievable only through effective manipulation of the balance of power, co-operation with another party was a matter of necessity. The choice of partner would depend upon the possibilities.

Lloyd George with other Liberal leaders had conspired with Conservatives to defeat the Labour government in 1924.[24] After Baldwin's concession to the TUC on 'Red Friday' in 1925, Lloyd George prepared for the possibility that a Conservative revolt might allow formation of an anti-socialist 'National government'.[25] But more often he thought Liberalism's best chance lay in co-operation with the Labour party, which was in opposition, electorally weaker, less experienced, and appeared most in need of policy assistance. Here his views coincided with those of his close adviser Kerr, of Scott and the *Manchester Guardian*, and of Keynes and other Liberal Summer School intellectuals, who saw the party's future in 'captur[ing] the Labour mind' for practical, efficient radicalism, and restoring the pre-war 'progressive alliance'.[26] By shifting 'definitely towards the Left' during 1926, with the land campaign establishing a rural appeal to complement Labour's urban appeal, Lloyd George thought he was becoming well placed to 'coordinate and consolidate all the progressive forces in the country'.[27] Trying to preserve that strategy in the face of Asquith's attack on the General Strike, Lloyd George was precipitated into the overture to Labour

[22] Lloyd George in Lady Hilton Young diary, 28 May 1928 (slightly modified in Kennet, 263). See also E. Haldane diary, 4 May 1928.

[23] Speech, *The Times*, 16 Oct. 1926.

[24] See, e.g., material in *WSC* v (1), 190–2, 208, 218; Hilton Young, and Hoare, to Lloyd George, 25 Sept., 7 Oct. 1924, LG G/10/14/15, G/19/18/1.

[25] Lloyd George to Garvin, 19 Aug. 1925, and Conway to Lloyd George, 20 Aug. 1925, LG G/8/5/1, G/30/4/32; Kerr to his mother, 30 Aug. 1925, Lothian papers 468/18; Garvin in Hudson to Gladstone, 14 Sept. 1925, Gladstone papers 46475/170–1.

[26] E.g., Kerr to Keynes, 25 Aug. 1927, Lothian papers 229/309–10; Scott to Hobhouse, 19 Nov. 1924, in Wilson, 469; Keynes, 'Liberalism and Labour', Feb. 1926, and 'Liberalism and Industry', 5 Jan. 1927, in *JMK* ix, 307–11, xix, 638–40.

[27] F. Stevenson diary, 1 April, 15 May 1926, in Taylor, 244, 245–6.

leaders for a 'parliamentary understanding'[28] which henceforth was to dog him with the accusation that he had wanted to join the Labour party. But apart from any other attachments, out of simple self-interest Lloyd George needed the Liberal party as a respectable, independent power base, and his unplanned success over Asquith appeared to make his strategy easier to advance. The Industrial Inquiry was to provide a further 'basis for co-operation with Labour',[29] and through Snowden, Haldane, Scott, and other intermediaries he sought an electoral understanding to improve Liberal prospects and prepare for an eventual 'united progressive party'.[30]

Whatever its other merits, however, *Britain's Industrial Future* had little political impact. This was due partly to excessively academic presentation, but mostly to another handicap: as with any third party policy, 'the chief difficulty [was] to make anybody pay attention to it'.[31] The audacity of *We Can Conquer Unemployment* eventually solved that problem, but this course was decided upon at a late stage and represented a defeat of the 1925–7 strategy.

Unemployment was just one among several possible election issues. For instance, during 1928 the Conservative government's most vulnerable point seemed to be a severe deterioration in Anglo-American relations, following the breakdown of the 1927 Geneva naval disarmament conference. The programme with which Lloyd George in August 1928 proposed to show that Liberals could 'lead the land out of its present difficulties' was an enormous NLF draft manifesto embracing the full range of Liberal policies and placing international peace before economic policy.[32] This draft was not dropped until March 1929. What first persuaded Lloyd George to consider something tougher and more focused was increasing evidence that a deal with the Labour leaders would be more difficult

[28] Henderson in MacDonald diary, 16 May 1926. Lloyd George's emissary was Kenworthy.
[29] See Scott to B. Hammond, 29 June 1926, Hammond papers 20/240c–d, commenting on a preliminary Inquiry meeting.
[30] E.g., Scott diary, 22–3 July, 14 Oct. 1927 (Wilson, 488–90, 491–2); Lloyd George to Scott, 11 Nov. 1926, and F. Stevenson to M. Richardson (of Labour Candidates Society), 8 Dec. 1926, LG G/17/11/27, G/31/1/62; E. Haldane diary, 4 May 1928. For Snowden, see below p. 41.
[31] Kerr to his mother, 2 Sept. 1928, Lothian papers 469/35. For reception of the industrial report, see, e.g., Keynes to his wife, 5 Feb. 1928, in *JMK* xix, 735, and Campbell, *Lloyd George*, 200–1.
[32] Lloyd George to Kerr, 11 Aug. 1928, and Kerr drafts with Lloyd George comments, all in LG G/12/5.

than anticipated. Although MacDonald was always considered an obstacle,[33] Snowden and other Labour leaders had seemed favourable. But when in September and October Labour ran candidates in hopeless by-election contests with no other purpose than that of spoiling Liberal candidates' chances, and when Lansbury as Labour party chairman denounced any association with Liberals, co-operation seemed impossible before the election and doubtful afterwards.[34]

For months this left Lloyd George 'fuddled' and uncertain about his 'plan of campaign'.[35] With most Liberal candidates now installed, it was too late to seek an alternative electoral understanding with Conservatives and the best course seemed to be to fight the election all out, in full independence. In these circumstances a radical employment policy was attractive as an appeal to voters 'regardless of parties', which evoked stirring comparisons with Lloyd George's success in war mobilization, and which he himself envisaged as a simple message of using slack times to prepare for future trade revival.[36] There is also evidence that the programme was produced hastily and in advance of the election campaign in order to pre-empt what was expected to be a similar Labour party initiative.[37]

Unemployment was Labour's own special ground. Liberal concentration upon that issue implied direct competition with the Labour party, exacerbating the problem of how to exploit the balance of power after the election. The obvious answer was to re-open the possibility of co-operation with Conservatives. In February 1929, after preparing other Liberal leaders for a change of tack,[38] Lloyd George approached Churchill and Horne, who as former ministers in his 1918–22 Coalition government seemed most likely to be amenable. Presenting himself now as 'all out against the Labour party', if the Conservative party lost its majority he wanted pressure brought upon Baldwin to remain in office and accept terms for

[33] Lloyd George to Scott, 19 Oct. 1927, in Wilson, 493.
[34] Lloyd George to F. Stevenson, 28 Sept. 1928, in Taylor, 108; and to Snowden, 3 Oct. 1928, LG G/18/7/6; Scott diary, 7 Dec. 1928 (Wilson, 493).
[35] Lloyd George to F. Stevenson, 31 Jan. 1929, in Taylor, 121.
[36] Rowntree to Lloyd George, 8 Feb. 1929, Rowntree papers; Lloyd George speech, *The Times*, 2 March 1929. *We Can Conquer Unemployment* was prepared by Rowntree, who also suggested the pledge.
[37] West, *Lloyd George's Last Fight*, 61–2. For Labour preparation of such a programme (though not in fact intended for publication), see below p. 40.
[38] Maclean memo, Feb. 1929, Maclean papers c468/106–11; Samuel memo, 13 Feb. 1929, Samuel papers A/72/1.

Liberal support. These terms were first, electoral reform, then free trade and government reconstruction. Loan-financed employment schemes came fourth.[39] Given that the Conservative election stance was still not settled the last condition was not incredible. Nevertheless unemployment policy was presented as a subordinate issue, and in proposing negotiations with Conservative leaders Lloyd George must certainly have expected the Liberal programme to be weakened. During the election campaign he declared Liberals to be as much anti-socialist as the Conservatives, and prepared for post-election negotiations by seeking anti-Labour newspaper support from Garvin and Rothermere.[40]

The Liberal leadership's politics were about survival – about the balance of power, co-operation with other parties, and electoral reform – and only conditionally about economic radicalism. Between these realities and the public rhetoric of party independence and potential Liberal government there was an extreme tension which aggravated the problems of holding together a divided and suspicious party. Such control would have required a degree of trust in the party leader which Lloyd George had long since forfeited. Distrust or hatred even prevented some from grasping that he shared their own objectives. Faced with the usual third-party dilemma of how to vote in parliamentary divisions Liberal MPs were frequently split three ways, between the Labour and Conservative lobbies and abstention. A few MPs defected to the Conservatives (Mond and Hilton Young), others to Labour (Benn and Kenworthy). But the chief problem was the Liberal Council.

In addition to earlier grievances, the Asquithians were outraged by Lloyd George's use of his personal fund first to run an independent land campaign and then to capture the party organisation. To them he was an unprincipled adventurer, a subvertor of Liberalism who had 'debauched' the party into 'a mere political machine…for the uneasy service of one man's wholly personal aims'.[41] They overreacted in May 1926 because they believed he was preparing to

---

[39] Lloyd George, 'Note of interview with Churchill', 18 Feb. 1929, LG G/4/4/23 (unaccountably attributed to Crozier in *WSC* v(1), 1426–7), and Churchill in Sanders diary, 29 April 1929, in Ramsden, 242. For Horne, see Jones, *Whitehall Diary* II, 174, 5 March 1929, and N. Chamberlain diary, 11 March 1929.

[40] Lloyd George speech, *Manchester Guardian*, 29 April 1929; F. Stevenson to Garvin, 27 April 1929, Garvin papers; Rothermere to Beaverbrook, tm 14 May 1929, Beaverbrook papers C/284. For Lloyd George maintaining cordial relations with a fiercely anti-socialist Rothermere, even during his leftward-looking phase, see 1925–8 correspondence in LG G/17/1.

[41] Johnstone to Beaverbrook, 26 Feb. 1929, Beaverbrook papers B/105.

join the Labour party. Thereafter they thought he intended to 'sell' the whole party to Labour.[42] Grey, Runciman, Maclean, Gladstone, Johnstone, Phillipps, Jones, and most other Asquithians formed the Liberal Council to keep Liberalism 'clean' and independent, to uphold traditional Liberal values, and to collect an Asquithian secret fund to secure the return of Liberal MPs hostile to Lloyd George.[43] Though they remained within the party, they ran separate by-election campaigns and repudiated the Lloyd George policy inquiries as 'the fatuous vanities of...long-haired political neurotics'.[44] Liberal policy was truly about peace, liberty, retrenchment, temperance, and free trade – which they expected to be the chief election issue.[45]

In Liberal Council conceptions, Lloyd George was the chief obstacle to Liberal recovery: 'the country wants Liberalism, but not L.G.'.[46] Yet despite themselves, most Asquithians were impressed by Liberal advances after 1926. They understood that the immediate objective could only be the balance of power – Maclean expected eighty MPs – and achievement of post-election co-operation with another party. Labour, as the other free-trade party, was their preference.[47] When they heard Lloyd George's unemployment policy, most were strong enough party men to appreciate that he offered Liberalism something special for the election, and so chose to join the bandwagon. They declined to be committed to his pledge, refused to sign a joint manifesto, and privately dismissed the proposed loan finance as fantastic. But they liked the idea that men should be employed rather than paid doles, and publicly Grey and Runciman supported the principle of Lloyd George's policy as 'absolutely right'.[48]

So when during spring 1929 Lloyd George described Liberals as a united party, the claim was not utterly absurd. They were in better

---

[42] Maclean to Gladstone, 11 May 1926, Gladstone papers 46474/45; Grey to H. D. Henderson, 30 May 1926, H. D. Henderson papers 21; Lady Oxford to Rosebery, 20 Feb. 1927, Rosebery papers 10127.

[43] Runciman, 'Secret Note', 1 Nov. 1926, and Johnstone to Runciman, 26 Feb. 1929, Runciman papers 204, 221; Gladstone to Maclean, 15 Dec. 1926, Gladstone papers 46474/192–4.

[44] Maclean to Gladstone, 7 Aug. 1927, Gladstone papers 46474/205.

[45] Gladstone to Samuel, 30 April 1927, Samuel papers A/155/vi/60; Runciman to Maclean, 18 Sept. 1928, Runciman papers 215, and Runciman speeches late 1928–Feb. 1929.

[46] Runciman to Foot, 3 Oct. 1928, Runciman papers 218.

[47] Maclean memo, Feb. 1929, Maclean papers c468/106–11.

[48] Runciman to his wife, and to Crook, 1 and 11 March 1929, and Jones to Runciman, 3 April 1929, Runciman papers 303, 221, 224. Runciman and Grey speeches, *Manchester Guardian*, 11 March, 11 April 1929. Phillipps, however, remained totally hostile.

WELSH WIZARDRY—A REVIVAL.

Sir Herbert Samuel } "OLD WIZARD, OLD WIZARD, WHITHER SO HIGH?"
Mr. Runciman
Mr. Lloyd George. "TO SWEEP THE COBWEBS OUT OF THE SKY."

1 'Welsh Wizardry – A Revival': Lloyd George, Sir Herbert Samuel, Walter Runciman, and *We Can Conquer Unemployment* (*Punch*, 13 March 1929)

condition than at any time since 1924, and presented to the other two parties a formidable electoral challenge. This was not just because the Liberal party seemed likely to achieve its leaders' objective of denying any party a parliamentary majority. Conservative and Labour each feared that the intervention of 500 Liberal candidates might wreck their own chances of forming the largest party.

LABOUR DILEMMAS

Dispute, division, and potential splits were facts of life in internal Labour politics. In the long aftermath of the first Labour government disagreement centred on such fundamentals as the role of parliamentary action, the transition from capitalism to socialism, the party's social base, and party independence. The Labour leadership's reactions to these differences explain the politics of the party's public policy in 1928–9, statements which in their economics have usually been compared unfavourably to *We Can Conquer Unemployment*. As the official opposition and prospective government, Labour's task was to overturn an enormous Conservative majority. Eight gains and six retentions in the thirty-seven by-elections from June 1926 to February 1929 indicated real electoral advance, but no landslide.

The TUC General Council had been cornered into unleashing the General Strike against its own better judgement. Revolutionary 'direct action' (always a minority passion) had been discredited in 1921 as it became apparent that capitalism was not on the point of collapse. Nevertheless the calculated use of the general strike threat was symptomatic of an important development: not so much a movement to the left as dissatisfaction with Labour party leaders. For Bevin, Pugh, Hicks, Swales, Citrine, and others – though not Thomas, Clynes, and Bondfield, who were also members of the party leadership – a party financed by the trade unions should be the agent of the unionised working classes, its political activities essential extensions of, but ultimately subordinate to, their specific economic and industrial concerns. The Labour party was 'their creation formed to serve [their] purposes'.[49] These assumptions had been shaken during the 1924 Labour government, when as ministers the party leaders denied the General Council privileged access to Cabinet business, threatened to use emergency powers against striking unions, and in policy and tactics seemed concerned with a 'national interest' and political constituency beyond those of the working classes. General Council militancy in 1925–6 manifested a

[49] Citrine notes, 'Cabinet making, 5 June 1929', Citrine papers 1/7/8, and see Citrine in B. Webb diary, 28 July 1927 (Cole, 148), and Bullock, *Bevin* I, 235–6, 243–5, 255–6.

belief that government policy could be influenced most reliably by deploying the trade unions' own resources rather than depending upon a distrusted party leadership, which anyway appeared powerless in the face of a huge Conservative majority. In this sense, the TUC's attitude was 'anti-political'.[50] Defeat in May 1926 meant that, for the time being at least, the strike threat was an unusable weapon,[51] that consultations on national industrial issues with leading employers – the Mond–Turner talks of 1928–9 – seemed an attractive alternative, and that renewed support for Labour party action became desirable in order to resist, and later seek repeal of, the miners' Eight Hours Act and the Trade Disputes Act.

This TUC shift restored the party leaders' sense of control. Yet General Council mistrust remained, as did its belief in the need for an autonomous TUC role in national affairs. Citrine even speculated that there might be advantages in the trade union movement disaffiliating from the Labour party. Together with Bevin, he extended General Council interests far beyond traditional trade union matters to those of high government concern – 'a definite and consistent "economic" policy', including 'political questions'.[52] In the long haul, the chief significance of the Mond–Turner talks lay not with any trade union 'corporatist' ambitions but with the stimulus those talks gave to General Council criticism of Treasury and Bank of England policies.

Like many TUC leaders, the ILP leaders believed that the Labour party was a specifically working-class party, and they too had been disappointed by the Labour government, particularly by its leaders placing parliamentary expediency before socialist commitment. For two ex-Cabinet ministers, Wheatley and Jowett, as much as for Maxton, the other Clydeside MPs, and Wise and Brockway, the experience of 1924 made the mechanisms for achieving socialism a pressing issue. Their answer in March 1926 was *Socialism in Our Time*. Co-authored by the economist Hobson and resting on his under-consumptionist theories, this proposed comprehensive nationalisation, planning, and increased direct taxation to ensure provision of 'a living wage' and family allowances as the first step towards removing poverty and unemployment and towards the rapid

---

[50] S. Webb to G. B. Shaw, 13 May 1926, in *Webb Letters* III, 264–5, and see Bullock, *Bevin* I, 260–1.

[51] Citrine in B. Webb diary, 28 July 1927 (Cole, 147; MacKenzie IV, 127).

[52] B. Webb diary, 28 July 1927 (Cole, 148); Citrine, *Men and Work*, 238–43; Bullock, *Bevin* I, 347–8, 386–7.

'realisation of a Socialist State'. This was an immediate programme, to be pursued in a 'militant' spirit by confrontation with the 'possessing classes' and 'capitalism'. It would be introduced at once by the next Labour government, even if it were in a parliamentary minority. The programme would be 'thrust into the forefront of practical politics', forcing the other parties to bear the responsibility for rejecting it and explaining themselves to a radicalised electorate.[53]

A variant upon this was provided by Mosley, who on joining the ILP and Labour party after the 1923 election had also latched upon the rapid transition from capitalism to socialism as the central issue. Where ILP leaders proposed a Hobsonian socialism he offered a Keynesian socialism: nationalisation of banks to create demand not by redistributive taxation but through credit expansion. His 1925 *Revolution by Reason* was accommodated within ILP policy, but as a member of a Labour National Executive programme committee in 1927–8 he offered a further version, and later joined with Trevelyan – another ex-Cabinet minister – in pressing for a published programme 'presenting in unmistakable terms the actual measures upon which a Labour government would at once embark'.[54]

Among the Labour party's big five leadership of MacDonald, Snowden, Henderson, Thomas, and Clynes – though not between MacDonald and Thomas – personal relationships had long been either cool or tense. After the 1924 government Snowden (like Bevin, the Clydesiders, Trevelyan, and Lansbury) had wanted MacDonald removed as party leader. Henderson (like the Webbs and many others) complained of his 'vanity', touchiness, aloofness, and enjoyment of 'smart' society.[55] But they agreed with MacDonald on the essentials of socialism, socialist strategy, and the Labour party's character. Even Thomas, Clynes, and Henderson – all trade unionists – believed in the priority of parliamentary and electoral activity over industrial action, of the party over the trade unions. Baldwin's 'surrender' to trade union pressure in 1925 had embarrassed them, and they had 'hate[d]' the General Strike.[56] MacDonald described himself as 'an unregenerate apostle of

---

[53] *Socialism in Our Time*, in Dowse, *Left in the Centre*, 212–25.
[54] Mosley to MacDonald, 8 Nov. 1927, JRM 1172; LPNEC, 2 May 1928.
[55] B. Webb diary, 8 Aug. 1925 (Cole, 67; MacKenzie IV, 53–4); Dalton diary, end 1927, 6 Feb. 1928 (Dalton, 175; Pimlott, 42).
[56] B. Webb diary, 8 Aug. 1925, 7 May 1926 (Cole, 67, 94; MacKenzie IV, 53, 78); Thomas in Lloyd George to F. Stevenson, 11 Aug. 1925, in Taylor, 84.

industrial peace'.[57] But if the TUC shift towards industrial appeasement after 1926 seemed a helpful development, Snowden at least remained 'indignant' at General Council 'political' statements and – with the presumed advantage reversed – shared Citrine's fantasy of party and trade union separation.[58]

The party leaders assumed evolutionary change and the Webbian 'inevitability of gradualness': socialism would not murder capitalism but emerge from it. For them social justice and economic efficiency through organisation, co-ordination, and application of science were the hallmarks of the modern world. Post-war company takeovers and mergers, producing large-scale corporate capitalism with ownership widely dispersed among shareholders and separated from management, were taken to be one set of proofs: capitalism was itself abolishing private enterprise – 'devouring its own children'. The 'logic of facts' was obliging Conservatives and Liberals themselves to accept a 'tentative, doctrineless socialism', embodied in social reform, municipal enterprise, and such public utilities as the Central Electricity Board. But those parties were too trammelled by 'meaningless social prejudices... obsolete class traditions' and 'old ideas' to achieve that 'transition to the twentieth century' which it was Labour's 'mission' to accomplish.[59]

Despite the concentration of Labour electoral support in coalfields, manufacturing areas, and among trade unionists, the party leaders also presented the Labour party as more than a working-class party. Except for a 'plutocracy' forming less than 10 per cent of the population, socialism was in the best interests of everyone – workers 'by hand or by brain', clerks, administrators, teachers, doctors, scientists, shopkeepers, small traders, farmers, as well as manual labourers.[60] 'Class psychology' was something which infected capitalist society and capitalist parties:[61] in contrast socialism was classless and authentically national. The Labour party would, and could only, succeed by resisting class feeling: rather than being 'the agent of this class or that', it appealed to 'men and women of goodwill in all classes'.[62]

---

[57] Article, *Socialist Review*, Jan. 1927.
[58] B. Webb diary, 22 Aug. 1927 (Cole, 151).
[59] *Labour and the Nation*, 6, 13, 23–4, and see also Snowden to Kerr, 27 Aug. 1927, Lothian papers 225/403–4, and MacDonald speech, *Daily Herald*, 14 Jan. 1929.
[60] *Labour and the Nation*, 5, 40.
[61] MacDonald diary, 5 Nov. 1924 (Marquand, 388).
[62] *Labour and the Nation*, 5, 40, 51.

Marching with history made good rhetoric and, with Labour support still at around 30 per cent of the electorate in the face of persistent Conservative success among the working classes, class-lessness or at least an appeal to progressive middle-class opinion constituted an electoral strategy. Nevertheless everything suggests that MacDonald and the others believed what they said. The TUC in 1925–6 and the ILP from 1924 offended by joining in the capitalist game of 'class war', which was negative and destructive whereas socialism was 'positive & constructive'.[63] The TUC was not thought to have any unique claim to represent the working class, as its membership comprised only around a quarter of the workforce. ILP leaders in assuming that 'the walls of capitalism' would fall 'by attack from outside' failed to grasp that 'change in…intellectual and moral desires' had to precede 'change in form',[64] and to understand that 'a modified capitalist system' was a large advance in the right direction.[65] Their desire for political confrontation before winning an electoral majority conflicted with that most fundamental Labour commitment, acceptance of parliamentary democracy. Worse, their activities upset potential Labour voters. For Snowden, who resigned from the ILP in 1927, they were 'fools doing their best to make the [Labour] party ridiculous'.[66] MacDonald, who tried to recapture the ILP from the Clydesiders, thought they frightened 'large numbers of people'.[67]

The ILP posed no threat to the party leadership since its influence was more than counterbalanced by the TUC, always suspicious of intellectual socialism and interference in wage matters. TUC hostility towards the ILP was confirmed by an abortive campaign by Maxton and Cook of the Miners Federation against the Mond–Turner talks as 'class collaboration'. Mosley, who had serious ambitions of Cabinet preferment from MacDonald, eventually conceded that the form of the party programme mattered less than winning power – passing from 'the test of words to the test of deeds'.[68] Nevertheless as the 1929 general election approached, party leaders wished to repair any damage inflicted upon moderate opinion by the General Strike and ILP agitation.

[63] MacDonald diary, 5 Nov. 1924 (Marquand, 388).
[64] MacDonald diary, 20 June 1926.
[65] Snowden in B. Webb diary, 22 Aug. 1925 (Cole, 70; MacKenzie IV, 57).
[66] Snowden to Addison, 7 Feb. 1928, Addison papers 95.
[67] MacDonald to Snowden, 25 Oct. 1928, JRM 1173.
[68] Mosley article, 25 July 1928, in Skidelsky, Mosley, 169.

MacDonald conceived his task to be 'quiet cautious leadership winning the trust of the people', in the belief that for the purpose of reviving Labour as a party of government 'confidence goes further than programmes'.[69] Reassurance was therefore a leading feature of the 1928 party statement, *Labour and the Nation.* Initiated by Henderson and drafted by MacDonald, this was intended as an updated version of the 1918 *Labour and the New Social Order* – a declaration of Labour principles and aims. It treated Conservative 'reaction' as the real threat to national well-being. It ridiculed the 'red bogy', presented socialism as a matter of practical experience, science, commonsense, and community service, and described its approach as 'experimental', as 'a peaceful revolution', acting with the consent of an electoral majority and using 'the ordinary machinery of democratic government'. It then described some sixty-five proposed Labour measures. Foreign policy – the chief area of Labour government success in 1924 – was prominent: restoration of Anglo-American friendship, disarmament, international arbitration, strengthening of the League of Nations. There would be national-isation of land, transport, electricity, and coal mines, and rationali-sation of manufacturing industries. The Bank of England was criticised for the time and manner of the return to the gold standard: it would become a public corporation, and its legacy of 'deflation' would be cured through central bank co-operation and an inquiry to recommend how domestic credit could be mobilised for national, rather than 'useless and socially injurious', purposes. There would be 'prudent and economical administration' of national finance, and taxation according to ability to pay yet without damaging production, through increased death duties, taxation of land values, and a surtax on substantial unearned incomes. A revised 1921 programme was offered for unemployment, which would be reduced by 'the restoration of normal trade' and expansion of overseas markets, but also by increase of the home market. Improved and extended unemployment insurance and better pensions would help raise purchasing power. A national economic committee and an employment and development board would develop national resources through diversified public works. The workforce would be reduced by a raised school-leaving age and early retirement pensions. As with the Liberal policies, free trade was assumed.

[69] MacDonald diary, Jan. 1928 (Marquand, 478).

Labour and the Nation was never conceived as an immediate
government programme. It avoided priorities and timetables
because of its propagandist purposes, and because Labour leaders –
unlike Lloyd George – were prospective ministers for whom, given
uncertainty about the conditions in which they might take office,
detailed public commitments would be imprudent. Webb admired
MacDonald's draft as 'properly vague'.[70] An immediate programme
was prepared, but privately by a parliamentary party committee of
Snowden (chairman), Graham, Shaw, and Webb. It had two
notable aspects. Firstly, compiled in early 1929 – before Lloyd
George's unemployment pledge – its proposed 'central feature' was
a 'great emergency programme' for unemployment. This included
slum clearance and re-housing to employ 100,000 'in a comparatively short time', road and bridge building to provide 120,000
jobs within twelve months, and unspecified numbers for drainage,
coastal works, and afforestation. Snowden 'showed no inclination to
be a stingy Chancellor', but was 'prepared to suspend, if necessary,
some of our financial orthodoxy'. He did not oppose state borrowing
in principle: there would be 'large public loans', including £100m.
secured on Road Fund revenues. To the probable charge that these
might injure national credit, the 'conclusive answer' would be that
trade depression and unemployment damaged it more.[71] This 'war
programme' was not quite so ambitous as *We Can Conquer
Unemployment*, its work-schemes and finance not so detailed, and it
lacked the *imprimatur* of an eminent economist. But its authors
expected to enter into possession of departmental and local authority
plans, and as they were not engaged in election propaganda their
stated objectives were arguably more realistic. In principle, these
Labour proposals were very similar to those subsequently published
by Lloyd George.

Secondly, the private programme assumed that the Labour party
would not have a full parliamentary majority. It was a programme
for a minority government. Despite a large loss of income due to the
Trade Disputes Act's political levy clauses, the party organisation
mounted a greater effort than for any previous general election, with

---

[70] S. Webb to B. Webb, 24 Feb. 1928, in *Webb Letters* III 296.

[71] 'Report of the Sub-Committee on the First Session's Administrative and Legislative
Programme', Passfield papers IV: 21. A later note ascribes this to 'early spring of 1929', but
for the accurate date see Dalton diary, 13 Feb. 1929 (Dalton, 182). For the description of
Snowden, see B. Webb diary, 12 Jan. 1929 (Cole, 188). Cf. Skidelsky, *Politicians*, 43–4, 68,
77, on Snowden and Labour policy.

fifty more candidates than in 1924. But it is doubtful whether Labour leaders ever expected to win a clear victory, first because the General Strike seemed likely to help sustain the anti-socialist vote, then because the 500 Liberal candidates threatened to divide the progressive vote. Snowden thought and implied publicly that there would be a combined Labour–Liberal majority. Henderson expected Labour to be the second party, as after the 1923 election.[72] MacDonald thought the by-elections showed 'plainly that the Government can be defeated but not that there can be an independent Labour government'.[73]

For some time the problem of how to proceed in these circumstances was a point of difference between MacDonald and other party leaders. None had any doubt that if opportunity allowed they should take and try to retain office for as long as possible, rejecting the ILP proposal of inviting defeat on a thoroughgoing socialist programme. Having demonstrated in 1924 that Labour was fit to govern they now wanted to take the next step in establishing a party of government, with what Snowden called a 'Parliament of achievement'. MacDonald had aspirations to 'transform' the office of Prime Minister so that he could 'drive policy'.[74] The issue was whether or not this required definite arrangements with the Liberal party. In 1925–6 one view was that temporary suspension of Labour party independence might result in eventual absorption of the Liberal remnant, and that a Lloyd George restored to radicalism and bearing a political fund, a national newspaper, and a substantial part of the Liberal electorate was an ally worth having. Snowden and Henderson encouraged Lloyd George's overtures around the time of the General Strike.[75] As Liberal recovery in 1927–8 weakened the prospects for a Labour majority Snowden, Thomas, and Henderson favoured a Labour–Liberal coalition after the election or at least, given doubts about whether the Labour party would accept that, some kind of 'concordat on policy'.[76] Snowden's belief that

---

[72] Snowden article, *Manchester Guardian*, 15 Sept. 1928, and Snowden to Lloyd George, 25 Sept. 1928, LG G/18/7/5; Henderson in B. Webb diary, 5 April 1927 (Cole, 137). The Webbs expected Conservatives to retain a small overall majority.

[73] MacDonald diary, 6 Nov. 1928.

[74] Snowden in Dalton diary, end 1927 (Dalton, 174); MacDonald diary, 7 Nov. 1928, 30 Jan. 1929 (Marquand, 484).

[75] Henderson in MacDonald diary, 16 May 1926; Snowden in F. Stevenson diary, 30 May 1926, in Taylor, 248.

[76] Henderson and Snowden in B. Webb diary, 5 April, 22 Aug. 1927 (Cole, 137, 151); Snowden and Thomas in Dalton diary, end 1927 (Dalton, 174); Snowden to Lloyd George,

such an arrangement might be advanced by MacDonald's replacement as party leader by himself probably contributed to two
public rows between them during 1927.[77]

MacDonald in contrast remained as hostile towards the Liberal
party as he had been during 1924, and repudiated all approaches
from Lloyd George's intermediaries.[78] His view throughout was that
Labour independence and the defeat of the Liberal party were the
surest path to Labour success. To assume the impossibility of a
Labour majority government was self-defeating: 'our immediate
duty is to place every obstacle we can in the way of the survival of
the three-party system' – to 'fight with every effort... to secure a
maximum success & face the situation which the ballot boxes
reveal'.[79] In this MacDonald was much closer to general Labour
sentiment than Henderson or Snowden. Lansbury's warning shot as
chairman of the October 1928 party conference that 'any attempt
by whomsoever made to unite with the decadent remains of
Liberalism is foredoomed to failure' gave MacDonald authoritative
party support.[80]

The consequences were far-reaching. Perhaps further influenced
by Snowden's knowledge of Lloyd George's subsequent switch
towards the Conservatives,[81] the parliamentary programme committee did not propose attempting any formal understanding with
Liberal leaders. It decided that although a minority Labour
government would be unable to press 'advanced Socialist proposals',
in particular coal nationalisation, there was within Labour policies
'much work of a useful character', particularly on unemployment,
which would secure parliamentary support. As in 1924 a Labour
government might, within limits, proceed independently by trusting
in the merits of its proposals and in divisions among its parliamentary
opponents.[82]

Lloyd George's unemployment pledge strengthened this stance.
When an advance leak of his proposals was received, the
parliamentary leaders concluded, accurately, that the policy could

---

25 Sept. 1928, LG G/18/7/5, and see Snowden article, *Pall Mall Magazine*, republished in
Manchester Guardian, 15 Sept. 1928.   [77] See Marquand, 468–9, 475–7.
[78] E.g., MacDonald diary, 16 May 1926; Scott diary, 4 March 1925, 22–3 July, 14 Oct. 1927
(Wilson, 478, 489–90, 492).
[79] MacDonald diary, 6 Nov. 1928 (Marquand, 483).   [80] *LPACR 1928*, 152.
[81] B. Webb diary, 12 Jan. 1929 (Cole, 188).
[82] 'Report of Sub-Committee on the First Session's Administrative and Legislative
Programme' [Feb. 1929], Passfield papers IV:21; Dalton diary, 13 and 14 Feb. 1929
(Dalton, 182–3).

barely be distinguished from their own.[83] When the character of his campaign was revealed, it appeared to be a direct threat to Labour chances of forming a government. As such it alienated even Snowden, previously Lloyd George's closest Labour sympathiser, while Lansbury and other Labour MPs privately assisted the Conservative *Morning Post*'s attempts to smear Lloyd George with the accusation that he had tried to join Labour in 1926.[84] More generally, the obvious Labour response was to treat his campaign as a simple election stunt. The public works proposals were not attacked but presented as self-evident and as 'political robbery', stolen from Labour's 1921 programme. The pledge – particularly the claim that the taxpayer would not pay 'a penny' – was dismissed as absurd and irresponsible; as yet another empty Lloyd George promise, like his shameful and broken 1918 pledges to create a 'land fit for heroes', and easily made because he knew there was no chance of a Liberal government.[85] Labour's best strategy was not to compete directly against this 'stunt', but to continue avoiding details and present itself as the responsible, statesmanlike party of social progress. On MacDonald's insistence the election manifesto contained nothing '"flashy" or "attractive"',[86] but paraphrased *Labour and the Nation* and emphasised the message 'no pledges we cannot fulfil'.

MacDonald had, then, prevailed in all respects. Reaction to the General Strike, to the ILP, and to Lloyd George had produced a Labour election platform calculated to appeal to central, moderate, opinion, as much anti-Liberal as it was anti-Conservative.

THE CONSERVATIVE RESPONSE

Despite the Conservative party's 1924 election triumph, neither Baldwin nor his colleagues supposed that the world had been made secure for Conservativism, constitutionalism, and capitalism.[87] The

---

[83] Greenwood to MacDonald, [Feb. 1929], enclosing Tawney to Henderson, 31 Jan. 1929, JRM 1174 (Marquand, 484).

[84] Peaker memos, 6 March–16 April 1929, Gwynne papers 20; see *Morning Post*, 22 May 1929. For Labour knowledge during the election campaign that Lloyd George had designs for a Conservative alliance, see MacDonald diary, 15 April 1929.

[85] E.g., speeches and articles by MacDonald and Snowden, *Daily Herald*, 2 and 4 March 1929; Snowden and Henderson speeches, *The Times*, 7 March, 12 April 1929.

[86] Dalton diary, 13 March 1929 (Dalton, 183).

[87] This section is based upon Williamson, 'Safety First' (which has fuller documentation), but contains more mature thoughts and fresh evidence. I am grateful to Peter Clarke for bringing further material to my attention.

Labour popular vote had increased, its potential remained enormous if class voting became more fully established, and there still seemed to be a powerful section of socialist or trade union 'extremists'. In the face of the Labour parliamentary leaders' calculated moderation, sustained Conservative success required consolidation of support among those liberal and uncommitted voters temporarily frightened in 1924 by imputations of Labour's 'bolshevik' sympathies. On the other hand, an election which had been won on anti-socialist scares might provoke a backlash of real socialism. It seemed clear that 'reaction [would] be fatal'.[88] One startling indication of Baldwin's liberal intent was the appointment of a free-trade ex-Liberal – Churchill – as Chancellor of the Exchequer. As Minister of Health a Unionist municipal collectivist – Neville Chamberlain – produced important social, housing, and administrative reforms. Contributory pensions for widows, orphans, and the elderly were considered a major achievement. Despite the heavy cost of persistent unemployment, no attempt was made to make the Unemployment Insurance Fund solvent through cuts in benefit payments or imposition of a means test. Instead the Fund was sustained by borrowing, with 'transitional benefit' – a state dole – being invented for those unemployed who had exhausted their insurance entitlement. Baldwin himself dispensed goodwill, reassurance, and a message about democratic duties, responsible leadership, mutual respect, community service, and shared interests which aimed to educate 'democracy' and bind together employer and employee, rich and poor, Church and Chapel.

Baldwin's preoccupations went beyond the constitutional and political. For him, preventing 'the class war becoming a reality'[89] was also at the heart of the economic problem. As the nation had rejected the Conservative remedy of tariffs in 1923, other medicine had to be tried. The return to the gold standard in 1925 would have happened anyway: it was 'an almost inevitable move on a course previously fixed and definitely set'[90] by Treasury, Bank of England, and government decisions since 1920, which the Labour and Liberal leaderships as much as Churchill, the Cabinet, and Conservative MPs – all inexperienced in this technical, 'non-political' area – assumed to be right even if a few had doubts about the timing. But it increased the pressure for, and was thought to facilitate, necessary

[88] A. Chamberlain to Baldwin, 31 Oct. 1924, SB 45/189–90.
[89] Baldwin in 1924, in Boothby, *I Fight to Live*, 36.
[90] Steel-Maitland memo, 'Unemployment', CP37(29), 16 Feb. 1929.

adjustments to the post-war patterns of international and domestic demand. Given private enterprise and strong trade unions, Baldwin understood that industrial peace and co-operation were pre-conditions for these shifts and improvements in production, management, work practices, and cost-competitiveness.

Baldwin's leadership from the high middle ground was often impressive and sometimes commanding. Nevertheless it exasperated many Conservative MPs and party activists. The Cabinet's policy and strategic concerns left its own party repeatedly disappointed or bewildered – in 1925 over reluctance towards industrial safeguarding, delays in anti-trade union legislation, and the coal subsidy. The General Strike and Trade Disputes Act assisted Conservative morale, but were serious setbacks to industrial conciliation and, with the coal lockout, weakened support in industrial areas and among moderate opinion. During 1927 the Cabinet was 'stuck in a glue-pot'.[91] The industrial disputes seemed to have checked revival in trade and employment. Private Cabinet encouragement of industrial rationalisation and the Mond–Turner talks would yield results only in the long term. Aside from exhortation to improve organisation and marketing there was nothing substantial to offer agricultural interests, among whom there was growing resentment. Factory, poor law and rating reform, and other proposed government legislation were important in themselves, but leaden or repellent in political effect.[92] Equalisation of the parliamentary franchise (the 'flapper vote') was disliked by many Conservatives, and Baldwin had difficulty overcoming party and Cabinet pressure for the reactionary step of making twenty-five rather than twenty-one the age-qualification for both men and women.[93] The party wanted House of Lords reform but was divided over method: Baldwin, who thought it provocative to non-Conservatives, annoyed the National Union by seizing the chance for indefinite postponement.[94] Gunboats to China, disputes with the USA, collapse of the Geneva conference and resignation of Cecil, the Arcos raid and severance of relations with Soviet Russia, forfeited confidence among peace, disarmament, and League of Nations opinion. One way or another, the government

[91] Baldwin in Reith diary, 4 Feb. 1928, in Stuart, 99.

[92] E.g., Davidson to Baldwin, 12 Dec. 1927, in Middlemas and Barnes, *Baldwin*, 507.

[93] National Union Central Council minutes, 1 March, 14 June 1927; 1922 Committee minutes, 12 April 1927; Amery diary, 13 April 1927 (*LSA* I, 504); Sanders diary, 25 and 27 April 1927, in Ramsden, 232.

[94] See National Union Executive and Central Council minutes, 14 and 28 Feb., 13 Nov., 11 Dec. 1928.

was both losing popular support and demoralising Conservatives. Ministers themselves were conscious of indecision and 'negativism', of politically and economically 'drifting on the rocks'.[95]

In this atmosphere the Cabinet began preparations for the general election. It knew there was much political ground to make up; but neither in 1927 nor during the run up to the election did ministers and party leaders believe there was a decisive movement against them. Presiding over an inflated parliamentary majority of 200, they both expected and knew they could afford to lose a good number of seats. Many of the fourteen by-election losses after the General Strike were ascribed to abnormal local or temporary conditions;[96] in any case nineteen other seats were held. Persistent criticism from the Beaverbrook and Rothermere mass-circulation newspapers – the principal media among non-Labour voters – was a serious problem, resulting largely from Baldwin's refusal to acknowledge the political pretensions of those particular 'press lords'. Negotiations with them in 1928 conducted by Davidson, the party chairman, and by Churchill showed only that the problem had to be lived with.[97] The 'flapper vote' was expected to cause damage in industrial seats,[98] but it was likely that more of these would fall to Labour in any event. Government leaders nevertheless assumed that they had done enough to prevent considerable increase of an alienated, socialist working-class, and that the activities of the TUC and ILP hindered large Labour advances among moderate opinion.

The greater electoral threat seemed to be the Liberal party. Like MacDonald, most Conservative leaders believed that in the natural course of events Liberalism would have disappeared, and that its revival was an artifice manufactured by Lloyd George's money.[99] Liberal policies could be regarded as stunts, safely ignored or easily disposed of. The real problems were the lavish by-election efforts and the 500 general election candidates which, by attracting new voters and some of those liberals and 'mugwumps' who had voted Conservative in 1924, might divide the anti-socialist vote and

---

[95] Percy, Amery, and Churchill to Baldwin, 2 and 10 April, 6 June 1927, SB 52/145, 28/251–62, 5/125–35 (last in *WSC* v(1), 1006–10).

[96] For North Hammersmith, Sanders diary, 9 June 1926, in Ramsden, 227: for others, see Williamson, 'Safety First', 391.

[97] Davidson to Baldwin, 13 Sept. 1928, and Davidson memos, 24 Sept., 30 Oct. 1928, Davidson papers; Churchill to Rothermere, 14 Nov., 2 Dec. 1928, in *WSC* v(1), 1376–7, 1386–7.

[98] For Central Office view, Sanders diary, 25 April 1927, in Ramsden, 232.

[99] E.g., N. Chamberlain, Davidson, and Hoare to Irwin, 12 Aug., 3 Dec. 1928, 21 Jan. 1929, Halifax papers 18/114a, 173, 205; Astor to Garvin, 22 May 1929, Astor papers.

prevent government retention of an independent majority. The loss of the Market Bosworth by-election in May 1927 to the Liberal party prompted the appointment of a party policy committee to prepare election policies for the remainder of the parliament and the manifesto.[100]

However, although the government felt itself in some electoral difficulty, it believed this to be containable. The eventual election slogan of 'Safety First' reflects that basic confidence, but it certainly did not represent lack of initiative or the inertia so prevalent in 1927. Three major policy developments were considered between then and the election. Rather, the Conservative election platform was modest because it was chosen within constraints which had more to do with party strategy than policy assumptions, and which continued to place accommodation of liberal opinion before satisfaction of Conservative party opinion.[101] Its genesis therefore reveals much about the Conservative leadership and about subsequent party difficulties. Attention was focussed throughout upon domestic issues. Continuing friction with the United States over disarmament and then the Kellogg Pact, international arbitration, and belligerent rights meant that it seemed best to say as little as possible about foreign policy.

Much of the policy committee's work was pre-empted by Churchill, who had proved to be an unusually political Chancellor of the Exchequer, resorting where necessary to juggling his figures and raiding non-recurrent capital funds to create a false appearance of budgetary balance. His concern was not simply to ensure a 'successful culmination of [the] Government in 1929'.[102] As an ex-Liberal and strong yet anxious anti-socialist, unlike Baldwin deeply mistrustful of the post-war democratic electorate, it seemed obvious to him that success could be achieved only by preserving 'the present cleavage between Socialism and anti-socialism'.[103] By this he meant retention of the liberal vote by resisting Conservative party attacks upon free trade. Opposition to further industrial safeguarding and imperial preference was also the test of his own influence within the government, yet he knew his free-trade attachments made him

---

[100] Davidson to Baldwin, 13 June 1927, SB 36/66–70. The committee's papers are in Worthington-Evans papers c895–6.

[101] Cf. the conventional view of Conservative politics before the 1929 election in J. Ramsden, *The Age of Balfour and Baldwin* (1978), 285–92.

[102] Churchill to Baldwin, 17 Dec. 1927, SB 5/138–89 (*WSC* v(1), 1138). For an important account of Churchill at the Treasury, see Short thesis, 'Politics of Personal Taxation', 208–35.   [103] Churchill memo, 12 Dec. 1927, in *WSC* v(1), 1129.

unpopular within the wider party and therefore vulnerable whenever
the next Cabinet reconstruction occurred. To secure his own
position and to stave off protectionism, he needed a bold initiative.
Boxed in by Treasury commitments to gold standard, debt
reduction, sound finance, and retrenchment, the best he could
propose was 'de-rating': a petrol tax to finance rate relief for
manufacturing industry, railways, canals and docks, and abolition of
already reduced agricultural rates.

Churchill pushed de-rating as a grandiose multi-purpose economic, financial, and political scheme. By reducing costs upon
production it would increase competitiveness, profitability, and
employment. It would dovetail with Chamberlain's proposed poor
law reform to produce a comprehensive reform of local government
structure and finance. It would also 'recover command of the public
mind' and lift the government 'above the ruck of current affairs'.[104]
On the whole, the Cabinet and party were convinced. It gave them
a great deal to say and suggest, even if the details were complex, if
the benefits would only accrue after the election, and if many
domestic rates would rise. Chamberlain's Local Government Bill
became the principal measure of the last session of the 1924
Parliament. All Conservatives regarded the policy as a major
constructive achievement. Some persuaded themselves that it might
be the election winner.[105]

Even so, de-rating did not puncture party pressure for further
protection and imperial preference. Its sources were partly the
economic interests of agrarian Conservatism and those industrialists
and distributors suffering from import competition, but mostly the
success of a generation of tariff reform propaganda in persuading
even Home Counties Conservatism that this was the constructive
answer to Liberalism and socialism, promising prosperity, employment, emigration, reduced direct taxation, selective social
reform, and continued imperial power. Agitation was sustained by
the Empire Industries Association and its parliamentary committee
of around 200 Conservative backbench MPs, which persuaded the
National Union to make repeated calls for extensions of industrial
safeguarding.[106]

[104] Churchill to Baldwin, 6 June 1927, SB 5/125–35 (*WSC* v(1), 1006–10).
[105] N. to I. Chamberlain, 4 Nov. 1928, NC 18/1/633; Macmillan to Cecil, 8 Nov. 1928, Cecil
papers 51166/79–80; Astor to Garvin, 22 and 24 May 1929, Astor papers.
[106] E.g., National Union Central Council minutes, 1 March, 28 June 1927, 28 Feb., 26 June
1928.

Inside the Cabinet the EIA MPs had support from Amery, a tariff reform ideologue for whom the policy was the specific against most economic, financial, and political ills, a necessary support for the trade balance, gold standard, and budget, and the antidote to socialism. Since 1924 he had fought a running battle against Churchill over imperial development and fiscal policy. In mid 1928 he thought 'the unripe fruit which resisted [Joseph Chamberlain's] picking 25 years ago is ripe and overripe and may come down at a touch from anyone who is prepared to pluck it'.[107] This optimism arose from an increase in unemployment which demonstrated that the slowness of trade recovery was not just a temporary consequence of the 1926 industrial disruptions. Cabinet policy reassessment in June and July 1928 produced early railways de-rating, a Baldwin appeal to employers to maintain jobs, assisted emigration, and a scheme for using existing public works to 'transfer' labour out of high unemployment areas.[108] None of this impressed Conservative MPs, the EIA demanded iron and steel safeguarding, while Amery pressed hard for establishing protection as the prime election issue.[109]

Apart from Churchill, most of the Cabinet – including Baldwin – shared Amery's belief that imperial protectionism was the radical solution to unemployment. But the experience of twenty-five years had not yet shown how a majority of voters could be persuaded to agree, and the electorate was now swollen by young women and mothers who might be especially susceptible to the free traders' cry that protection meant 'dear food'. No one supposed that Amery was a Joseph Chamberlain, capable of transforming public opinion.[110] No other minister was so doctrinaire – not even Neville or Austen Chamberlain – and none trusted Amery's judgement. Conservative leaders had become as gradualist about tariff reform as the Labour leaders had about socialism. All depended upon the right economic and electoral conditions. At this moment it seemed that protection would produce the result they most wanted to avoid, a real Liberal recovery like that at the 1923 election, enabling Labour to return to

---

[107] Amery to Maxse, 6 June 1928, Amery papers. For his broader views, see, e.g., Amery to Baldwin, 10 April 1927, SB 28/251–62 (Amery, *Political Life* II, 486–91).

[108] Cabinets 35, 36 and 40(28), 27 June, 4 and 23 July 1928; Amery diary, 27 June, 4 and 23 July 1928 (*LSA* I, 552, 553, 557). For labour transference as a modest success in easing labour mobility, see Lowe, *Adjusting to Democracy*, 208–9, 223.

[109] Details in Williamson, 'Safety First', 395–6.

[110] See Bridgeman to Oliver, 9 Aug. 1928, Bridgeman papers (Williamson, 216). Amery to Maxse, 6 June 1928, Amery papers, disclaims any such parallel.

government. In other words, the Cabinet majority stood somewhere between Amery and Churchill: 'unemployment was due to Free Trade and could only be cured by protection... [but] the essential thing was to say as little about it as possible and avoid letting protection become an issue at the election'.[111]

Baldwin acted with unusual firmness in rejecting the EIA request and muzzling Amery. Yet it was plainly desirable to offer something to prevent a party rebellion and encourage Conservative voters in industrial areas. The policy committee now provided a solution, which was usefully neither free trade nor yet protection: a simplification of safeguarding procedure after the election, open to all industries claiming unfair foreign competition, including iron and steel. Amery, the EIA MPs, and the party conference in September were unhappy and continued to argue the case,[112] but they had enough faith in the party's election prospects to choose not to rock the boat. Thus did Amery confirm that he was no Joseph Chamberlain.

De-rating, industrial transference, safeguarding and emigration, together supporting natural processes of adjustment and rationalisation, were thought to be good, solid policies which would retain the respect of much of the electorate. Yet their benefits for employment would be slow to take effect and in the meantime, during another hard winter of unemployment, they were old news and appeared insufficiently striking to make election success certain. Something fresh and more immediate seemed desirable, particularly once it became apparent that Lloyd George was preparing some dramatic initiative.[113] What emerged in February 1929 were proposals for loan-financed imperial and domestic development. Joynson-Hicks argued that 'L.G.'s thunder' could be 'stolen' with a programme of colonial and dominion development to stimulate emigration and demand for British manufactures, together with acceleration of existing road-building schemes. This idea evoked a good deal of support. Steel-Maitland offered more specific schemes and, anticipating Treasury objections, suggested a reconsideration of the assumptions of monetary and financial policy.[114] Amery

---

[111] Hailsham in Amery diary, 2 Aug. 1928 (*LSA* I, 561).

[112] See Williamson, 'Safety First', 395, 396–7.

[113] For attempts to breathe new life into safeguarding and emigration policies, see Williamson, 'Safety First', 397–9.

[114] Joynson-Hicks and Steel-Maitland memos, 'Unemployment', CP27, 37(29), 7 and 16 Feb. 1929. See Clarke, *Keynesian Revolution*, 54–8; Lowe, *Adjusting to Democracy*, 202–3; Garside, *British Unemployment*, 193–6.

resumed his attack upon Treasury control of finance for empire development. Davidson, wanting to demonstrate that the party was 'still full of energy', proposed a £100m.–£200m. loan secured on colonial revenues for an imperial policy to 'fire the imagination of the country'.[115] Neville Chamberlain, expecting empire development to become the issue of the future, decided that in a reconstructed Cabinet he wanted the Colonial Office rather than the Treasury.[116]

The Conservative government, then, had available its own loan-financed public works programme comparable to those of Lloyd George and the Labour leaders. It was also one which was distinctively Conservative. The proposed road works were only a modest (around £8m.) extension of the public-work schemes which all Cabinets since 1921 had accepted and financed by ordinary capital account borrowing. But empire development was of an altogether different order: it would appeal to the Conservative party as imperial and Chamberlainite, and could be presented elsewhere as a 'progressive' colonial reform as well as an industrial and employment policy.

In asking why this programme did not become the centre-piece of the Conservative election platform, part – but only part – of the answer is obviously financial. Treasury officials attacked large loan-financed works in principle as wasteful, 'nugatory', and harmful in employment terms because these would 'crowd out' private investment, and they defended sound credit policy as integral to the large economic and social benefits ascribed to the gold standard.[117] Churchill himself was placed in an awkward position: still anxious for a strong front against socialism, he sought a Conservative–Liberal understanding for the election, and responded positively to Lloyd George's overture on 18 February. He knew Lloyd George wanted loan-financed public works,[118] but he himself had developed doubts about the Treasury and Bank of England insistence upon financial rigour and deflation.[119] On the other hand, Churchill was not

---

[115] Amery diary, 22, 24, 27 Feb. 1929 (mostly in *LSA* 1, 589–90); Davidson to Baldwin, 19 Feb. 1929, Davidson papers.

[116] Amery diary, 27 Feb. 1929 (*LSA* 1, 590); N. Chamberlain diary, 11 March 1929.

[117] Treasury Note, CP53(29), 23 Feb. 1929, and see Clarke, *Keynesian Revolution*, 58–63.

[118] Sanders diary, 23 July 1929, in Ramsden, 239; Lloyd George, 'Note of interview with Churchill', 18 Feb. 1929, LG G/4/4/23 (misattributed in *WSC* v(1), 1426–7); Williamson, 'Safety First', 401–2.

[119] E.g., Churchill to Niemeyer, 20 May 1927, in *WSC* v(1), 996–9; Amery diary, 27 June 1928 (*LSA* 1, 552).

prepared to admit error by foresaking his positions of the previous four years, and lacked sufficient confidence on vital financial issues to resist his officials' advice. He also thought that Lloyd George could not have believed in his own programme – that it was an electioneering trick which would not prevent him coming to some arrangement after the election.[120] Churchill therefore came down strongly in support of his officials against 'unsound schemes'.[121]

Baldwin's reaction was to postpone decision and keep the matter in his own hands. This has been presented as a device to support Churchill and allow Joynson-Hicks's proposal to 'wither on the vine'.[122] But Baldwin's thinking was more complicated than that, for he soon planned a Cabinet reconstruction with the principal purpose of removing Churchill from the Treasury before the election.[123] There were two reasons for this, both the result of Lloyd George's unemployment pledge on 1 March.

Deeply hostile towards Lloyd George and any arrangement which might perpetuate Liberal party influence, Baldwin was worried both by the possibility that Lloyd George's campaign might secure Liberals the balance of power, and by evidence that he hoped for alliance between the Liberal and Conservative parties.[124] Churchill's demotion would have weakened the chief Conservative proponent of such an alliance and a potential challenger to Baldwin's own leadership if the election went wrong.[125] But secondly, the government needed some reply to Lloyd George, and empire development seemed a strong possibility. The further attraction of shifting Churchill was the removal of the principal Cabinet obstacle to that policy, and its appeal would be much increased if, as Baldwin

---

[120] Jones, *Whitehall Diary* II, 176, 6 March 1929; Sanders diary, 29 April 1929, in Ramsden, 243. Lloyd George had rejected Churchill's request for a deal on seats to prevent splits in the anti-socialist vote.

[121] Churchill note to CP53(29), 23 Feb. 1929; Clarke, *Keynesian Revolution*, 62–8.

[122] Clarke, *Keynesian Revolution*, 61. For repeated postponements, see Cabinets 9, 11, and 13(29), 26 Feb., 13 and 26 March 1929.

[123] Amery diary, 4 March 1929 (*LSA* I, 590–1); N. Chamberlain diary, 11 March 1929, referring to 5 March (for extract, *WSC* v(1), 1442–3). For earlier plans for Cabinet reconstruction (including a Churchill move) *after* the election, see also Williamson, 'Safety First', 403–4. Ironically in view of subsequent events, Baldwin proposed to send Churchill to the India Office.

[124] Lloyd George, 'Note of interview with Churchill', 18 Feb. 1929, LG G/4/4/23, has Churchill proposing to report their discussion to Baldwin. For awareness of the overture through Horne, see Baldwin and N. Chamberlain in N. Chamberlain diary, 11 March 1929.

[125] See Jones, *Whitehall Diary* II, 180, 5 March 1929, and N. Chamberlain diary, 11 March 1929, referring to 5 March (which mentions Churchill as a possible party leader).

intended, Churchill was replaced by Neville Chamberlain – an imperial development enthusiast and bitter anti-Lloyd Georgian.[126] Baldwin certainly shared Churchill's opposition to special development loans, but he agreed with Joynson-Hicks, Steel-Maitland, and Amery to the extent of insisting upon a more modest scheme funded from the capital account.

Churchill perhaps saved himself from demotion by overruling his officials and conceding future Treasury creation of a Colonial Development Fund.[127] In the event, however, imperial development was not made into the major election policy but placed below de-rating and alongside safeguarding, labour transference, emigration, slum clearance, and a range of social policies. There was also a more important reason for the abandonment of Cabinet reconstruction than Churchill's concession. Baldwin settled for a different response to Lloyd George. No Conservative leader was impressed by the substance of his programme: it was 'merely ridiculous'.[128] If Joynson-Hicks and Steel-Maitland did not, like most ministers, consider his financial proposals absurd, they agreed with them in thinking the employment schedules fallacious or impracticable. All riddled his programme with public criticism. Churchill – annoyed that Liberal persistence in running so many candidates would split the anti-socialist vote – did so as much as every other minister. The question was how to destroy it. Baldwin eventually decided that to compete against Lloyd George with some Conservative election 'stunt' was a mistake, and that the best course was to stress past achievements, understate future policy, and appeal for trust – 'Safety First' – as devices to highlight the dishonesty and irre-sponsibility of Lloyd George's 'stunt'.

Most leading Conservatives thought this an effective approach, especially in maximising Baldwin's popular appeal to average opinion as a man of truth, decency, and commonsense.[129] The Treasury critique of the Joynson-Hicks/Steel-Maitland proposals was now converted into a critique of Lloyd George's, used in

---

[126] I have dismissed the possibility that Baldwin wanted a new initiative on safeguarding or protection: this was against the grain of Baldwin's position since July 1928, and was not an issue among ministers at this time.

[127] See Churchill to Baldwin, 10 or 12 April 1929, SB 36/126–7 (*WSC* v(1), 1458); Baldwin speech, *The Times*, 19 April 1929.

[128] N. to H. Chamberlain, 2 March 1929, NC 18/1/645.

[129] See Williamson, 'Safety First', 405–8. For one probable source of the election strategy, see Bridgeman to Baldwin, 27 March 1929, SB 175/50–1 (Williamson, 218).

Churchill's budget speech as a definitive expression of the 'Treasury view', and then, together with other departments' criticisms of its administrative feasibility, was published in May as a White Paper intended finally to discredit the Liberal pledge. During the election campaign Conservative leaders and managers expected to retain an overall majority of between forty and eighty, while Baldwin thought there was 'no steam in the socialists' and relished 'the prospect of possibly laying out L. G., Rothermere, and Beaverbrook all at one go'.[130]

THE 1929 GENERAL ELECTION

Each party, then, had radical policies available: the Conservatives had imperial protectionism, Labour had nationalisation, and in early 1929 all three parties considered some form of loan-financed public works. Far from the Liberal party being the sole source of radical ideas at the 1929 election, it was the principal obstacle to Conservative and Labour adoption of their own versions of radicalism, as both Conservative and Labour leaders decided that the Liberal challenge could best be defeated by an appeal to moderate, liberal opinion. On the public works issue, neither had any belief in the detailed Liberal plans, and understood that Lloyd George's real purpose was a spoiling campaign to deny them an overall parliamentary majority. The effect was to sharpen hostility towards the Liberal party. Conservative and Labour leaders played down their own public works proposals in attempts to expose the Liberal programme as a mere election 'stunt', a tactic to which Lloyd George's record as Prime Minister during 1918–22 in presiding over the initial onset of mass unemployment made him peculiarly vulnerable. Where Labour offered 'no pledges we cannot fulfil', Conservatives offered 'performance' not 'promises'. Each concentrated their criticism more upon the Liberal party than upon each other, attacks in which Lloyd George's chief Conservative and Labour contacts, Churchill and Snowden – current and prospective Chancellors of the Exchequer – became particularly prominent. With Baldwin and MacDonald privately confirming to each other their refusals to co-operate with Lloyd George,[131] there was again, as

[130] N. to H. Chamberlain, 11 May 1929, NC 18/1/653. For Central Office predictions, Sanders diary, 29 April 1929, in Ramsden, 242; for others, Williamson, 'Safety First', 408.
[131] See MacDonald diary, 7 May 1929, for Baldwin 'determined in his lack of confidence in Ll. G.'.

in 1924, a tacit Conservative and Labour alliance against the Liberals.

The general election on 30 May was the first at which three parties each sponsored over 500 candidates. The Conservatives obtained the largest share of the popular vote, but lost 140 seats and were reduced to 260 MPs. Labour gained 126 seats and with a total of 287 MPs became the largest parliamentary party, but again lacked an independent House of Commons majority. The Liberals obtained more votes than ever before and recovered the parliamentary balance of power, but won only nineteen more seats than at the 1924 election. Despite its unemployment campaign it actually lost seats in industrial, high unemployment, areas to Labour. That Liberal gains were instead mostly in rural Conservative seats suggested that it had advanced on the slim basis of a protest vote against the Conservative government, rather than by re-establishing a genuine Liberal allegiance. To Labour and Conservative leaders and some Liberals, a Liberal parliamentary party of just fifty-nine MPs seemed to have little future. Both Conservative and Labour blamed the increased numbers of Liberal candidates for their own failure to obtain a clear majority.

In these circumstances, Lloyd George's ambition was frustrated: he was not consulted before either the Conservative government's resignation or the formation of a Labour government. Maliciously, most Conservative leaders wanted their government to face Parliament in order to fasten upon Liberals the odium of putting socialists back into office – a repeat of the 1924 tactic.[132] Baldwin insisted upon immediate resignation partly because he sensed future danger in appearing to frustrate the election verdict and to thwart the Labour party, but mostly because – in contrast – he thought Lloyd George might keep Conservative leaders suspended in office in order either to humiliate them or to intrigue with Churchill.[133] MacDonald, becoming Prime Minister for the second time, hoped for support from individual Liberal MPs, tried to persuade some to defect to Labour, and appointed one – Jowitt – as Attorney-

[132] Joynson-Hicks, Bridgeman, and N. Chamberlain to Baldwin, 31 May, 1 and 2 June 1929, SB 164/124, 36/191, 210/11; Amery diary, 3 June 1929 (*LSA* I, 596); Jones, *Whitehall Diary* II, 192–3, 20 June 1929.
[133] Stamfordham memos, 31 May, 2 June 1929, RA GV K2223/24, 30; Jones, *Whitehall Diary* II, 192–3, 20 June 1929 – including 'the Ll.G. obsession weighing heavily on [Baldwin's] mind'.

2 Ramsay MacDonald, Philip Snowden, and other ministers at 10 Downing Street, 10 June 1929

General.[134] Both Baldwin and MacDonald ignored the Liberal *party* in the hope that the strain of holding the balance of power would force its final disintegration and disappearance. That the 1929 Parliament had no clear party majority and that the two largest parties began it in a determinedly anti-Liberal mood were matters of the greatest consequence.

Despite the dominance of unemployment during the election campaign, neither MacDonald nor Baldwin expected the issue to dominate their attention thereafter. MacDonald consigned the issue to a new unemployment committee, and concentrated upon improving Anglo-American relations. Baldwin was on surer ground in expecting India to become a large issue, the Viceroy having given

---

[134] Kenworthy, *Sailors, Statesmen*, 281. For Labour interest in Liberal divisions, see, e.g., B. Webb diary, 1 and 6 June 1929 (Cole, 194, 197), and Dalton diary, 2 June 1929 (Dalton, 212).

him prior notice of a major initiative.[135] But neither anticipated the onset in autumn 1929 of the combination of economic and imperial difficulties which are the subject of the next chapter. These created parliamentary and party difficulties which made it impossible to continue ignoring the Liberals: these are examined in chapter 3. The effects are considered in chapter 4.

[135] Dawson to Irwin, 8 April 1929, Halifax papers 18/243. See Baldwin in *HC Deb*, 229, col. 63, 2 July 1929.

CHAPTER 2

Economic and imperial troubles

[T]he position of the country, either industrially or from the Budgetary point of view, has not been so serious for the last hundred years, and something will have to be done if...disastrous consequences are to be averted.

Snowden, addressing deputation from Association of
British Chambers of Commerce, 17 February 1931

We are...at the beginning of a disastrous & degrading period of the Empire. Of this there can be no doubt...Full-fledged democracy cannot rule an Empire or anything else. We are nearing the beginning of the end of all that you and I have worked for.

Lord Sydenham to Lord Lloyd, 10 August 1929[1]

THE SLUMP IN ECONOMIC AND FINANCIAL OPINION

The arrival of a democratic electorate and powerful Labour movement, followed in 1920 by the breaking of the post-war boom, resulted in the condition of the national economy and national finances becoming matters of public concern in a way which had never previously been the case. Given the structure of the British economy as the leading international supplier of financial services, investment, shipping, manufactures, and coal, it was assumed that Britain's prosperity and social stability depended upon eradicating the economic and financial effects of the Great War and restoring as much of the pre-war economic world as possible. The re-establishment of strict budget control, the return to sound money and stable exchange rates under the gold standard, and the political and financial stabilisation of continental Europe, had all been central to this effort. But by the late 1920s it was obvious that the

---

[1] For Snowden, memo in T172/1516; for Sydenham, Lloyd papers 13/19.

war had altered the economic world much more than had been anticipated. The great manufacturing industries, coal, agriculture, and shipping had suffered large falls in demand, the result of increased foreign competition, altered markets, and technological change. Particularly in the previously prosperous export sectors there were substantial business losses and large-scale unemployment. The trade deficit was larger and the balance of payments surplus smaller than before the war. As a financial centre London was rivalled by New York and, after 1926, by Paris. Both accumulated enormous gold reserves, both had large claims on London banks, and the existence of three financial powers rather than one brought new complications to the international financial system. Despite the efforts to remove wartime effects, the demands of government upon the international and national economies remained substantial. 'Laissez-faire' capitalism in its late nineteenth-century sense no longer existed. German payments of war reparations (which the French insisted upon) and Allied payments of war debts (on which the Americans insisted) distorted international capital and commercial movements. With the national debt increased twelve-fold, debt charges swallowed a third of budget expenditure. Social service expenditure had risen seven-fold. Budgets which before the war balanced at under £200m. now did so at over £750m. Taxes, rates, and contributions had all risen: income tax, which stood at 1s. 2d. in 1913, was from 1926 at 4s. Unemployment was chronic to the extent that the unemployment insurance system had ceased to be solvent, and had to be repeatedly topped up by borrowing. Despite unemployment and the defeat of the General Strike, average money wages were also higher than before the war. All other prices had been falling almost continuously since 1920.

These matters shaped the economic policy debate of the 1920s. Unemployment was the chief issue of the 1929 election because of its persistence, not because it was increasing. The Labour government took office at a time of comparative recovery, with trade and industrial production rising and unemployment, though still at 1·1m., falling. Most economic signals were so encouraging that the business world 'received the result of the general election...with almost complete equanimity'.[2] These relatively favourable economic circumstances contributed to MacDonald's initial decision to

[2] 'The State of Trade', *Economist* Monthly Supplement, 29 June 1929.

concentrate upon foreign policy. As late as September, the economic outlook still seemed 'distinctly promising'. In this phase the principal problems were the failure of unemployment to fall further, a weak pound, and gold reserve losses caused largely by the New York stock market boom. With the gold standard threatened, the Bank of England raised bank rate to $6\frac{1}{2}$ per cent, its highest level since 1921. This brought renewed criticism of the Bank, and Labour government fulfilment of its promised banking inquiry, with the appointment of the Macmillan Committee on Finance and Industry.

The Wall Street crash in October ended the monetary pressures and allowed reductions in bank rate, but it also accelerated collapses of international lending and commodity prices. The result was a deep world recession which inflicted almost immediate damage upon the British economy and upon the Labour government. When MacDonald created an Economic Advisory Council in December, this represented an acquiescence to the priority of the economic problem which had not been anticipated six months previously.

By October 1930 economic deterioration had been continuous and severe, had produced alarming financial results, and showed no sign of early abatement. Exports for the July to September quarter were 26 per cent less by value and 20 per cent by volume than the equivalent period in 1929.[3] Imports had not fallen so far, and, as the world recession had also depleted invisible foreign earnings, a large balance of payments deficit was in prospect. Wholesale prices had fallen 17 per cent and the cost of living 6 per cent, but wage rates remained virtually unchanged. Industrial production had fallen by 10 per cent, and profits had taken a 'marked downward movement', by around 7 per cent. Unemployment had risen against normal seasonal trends since February and in October reached 2·2m., almost 20 per cent of the insured workforce. The City was also suffering. Business decline had reduced the Stock Exchange to 'a state of idleness and despondency' and brought a 'headlong fall' in discount rates, from 6 per cent to almost 2 per cent. British government stocks had appreciated sharply, but only through the fall in yields elsewhere and lack of alternative investments, not from any satisfaction with government finance. Falling revenue and increased expenditure, particularly a doubling of the estimated cost of

---

[3] Statistics in this paragraph are mostly from *Board of Trade Journal*, Oct.–Nov. 1930; quotations are from various issues of the *Economist*, Sept. 1930–Feb. 1931.

'transitional' unemployment benefits – payments to those whose insurance entitlement was exhausted, which became a direct budget charge in March 1930 – indicated that there would be a serious budget deficit, while Unemployment Insurance Fund borrowing had apparently passed out of all control. The announcement on 28 October of a Royal Commission on Unemployment Insurance showed that no early decisions would be taken to curb this expenditure. It was evident that economically and financially 'the country [was] approaching an extremely difficult winter'.

The effects of this slump upon economic and financial opinion were dramatic. Sharp movements in attitude were apparent among all the leading economic interests and government financial advisers – agriculturalists, industrialists, trade unions, economists, City financiers, the Bank of England, and the Treasury. These movements imposed great demands upon the political parties. Yet a feature of each movement was increasing disillusionment with party politics as the means to resolve economic problems.

For agriculture, after nine years of bare profitability, the collapse of prices – cereals by as much as 25 per cent since October 1929 – was a disaster. In the agricultural community there was great bitterness. Successive governments had shrunk from assisting it by burdening the consumer with duties on foreign imports ('food taxes') or the taxpayer with subsidies. Consequently many landlords, farmers, and labourers had long blamed their difficulties as much upon 'political handicaps' as upon world market conditions.[4] They now attributed the price collapse to cheap imports, and considered protection the only remedy. After a government-convened conference of agricultural experts broke down in March 1930 because the Labour Cabinet rejected protective measures, the National Farmers' Union, agricultural workers' unions, and landowners' associations held joint 'non-political' mass meetings to call for 'the sinking of party differences' in saving agriculture from 'calamity'.[5] In the event the NFU and the agricultural workers' unions soon fell out over the best form of protection, and over NFU pressure for wage reduction. But a divided agricultural community was no easier than a united one for politicians to deal with. The NFU was particularly troublesome, distrusting Conservative leaders almost as much as the

[4] *NFU Yearbook 1930*, 396.
[5] Resolutions at agricultural meetings, *The Times*, 6 and 19 March, 7 and 14 April 1930.

Labour Cabinet and opposing agricultural marketing arrangements, which both parties favoured as a means to raise agricultural prices, as excessive interference in private enterprise.[6] It was plain both that agriculture had become a major problem, and that satisfying it without upsetting other sections of the electorate would be difficult.

Industrialist opinion had in the late 1920s been diverse. This was partly because there were two 'peak' organisations with separate responsibilities – the Federation of British Industries (economic and commercial) and the National Confederation of Employers' Organisations (labour and social). In addition the FBI was split and forced to be neutral over trade policy, and both organisations were divided over the Mond–Turner talks. Those 'industrial statesmen' who participated in the talks did not represent the smaller, more hard-pressed, employers who dominated the FBI and NCEO, and who opposed the erosion of managerial powers implied by co-operation with the TUC. The Mond group were 'blackleg employers'. In 1929 the FBI and NCEO rejected the Mond–Turner proposal for a permanent industrial council, and accepted only limited consultations with the TUC in the hope of exercising some influence with a Labour government.[7] But during 1930 employers' differences narrowed, opinion hardened, and consultation with the TUC withered.

One explanation for industrial stagnation which the Mond group and FBI leaders shared with the TUC was 'premature' return to the gold standard, causing international uncompetitiveness and tight, expensive credit. The FBI's remedy was central bank co-operation to ease the operation of the gold standard. But this approach expressed the views of the FBI's economic experts more than its general membership.[8] The Mond group's chief explanation was industrial inefficiency, for which its remedy was 'rationalisation' in the sense of amalgamation, modernisation, and labour redeployment. This had been its main concern in seeking TUC co-operation. But with the slump, 'rationalisation' came to mean scrapping excess capacity and reduction of the labour force, where the NCEO expected only obstruction from consultation with the TUC. The sole area of

---

[6] For long-running tensions between the NFU and party leaders, see Cooper, *British Agricultural Policy*, 67–9, 77–9, and chs. v–vii.

[7] For 'blacklegs', Lithgow, June 1928, in Tolliday, *Business, Banking, and Politics*, 102. Generally, see McDonald and Gospel, 'Mond-Turner Talks', 816–19, 822–6; Dintenfass, 'Politics of Producers' Co-operation', 76–92.

[8] Macmillan Committee *Evidence* I, 186–209, 20 March 1930; Holland, 'Federation of British Industries', 288–9.

successful consultation was the uncontentious one of stimulating intra-imperial trade, with a joint FBI–TUC memorandum of September 1930 urging the creation of 'Commonwealth economic machinery'.[9]

Most industrialists, however, had less sophisticated explanations and cruder solutions, which once pressed soon emasculated industrial co-operation. They believed the main cause of uncompetitiveness to be high wage and tax costs, and as prices collapsed from autumn 1929 this view was made increasingly explicit. Criticism focused on social service expenditure and especially upon unemployment insurance, as a cause of both high taxation and rigidity in wage-levels. From early 1930 government industrial advisers and employers' organisations argued against further social reform because additional 'unproductive' expenditure would be 'nothing short of disastrous'.[10] By October, as the prospective budget deficit threatened increased direct taxation, industrialists were attacking even existing social service expenditure as 'extravagant' and demanding retrenchment, with unemployment payments as the main target.[11]

This shift was accompanied by another of almost equal force. The recession destroyed many industrialists' lingering hopes that pre-war trade conditions would return, and as hope departed so did faith in free trade. This transformation manifested itself in increased membership and activity of protectionist associations, and in a poll of FBI members which in October 1930 resulted in its adoption of protection and imperial preference.

As with agriculturalists, these developments were accompanied for industrialists by considerable impatience with politicians. NCEO leaders deeply distrusted all governments, for in its view all tended to be 'socialistic' under pressures to conciliate the working classes in ways which reduced industrial initiative and efficiency.[12] The FBI wanted 'the restoration of British industry' treated as a matter 'lying outside the realm of party politics'.[13] The most striking expression of disillusionment – because also implying criticism of FBI and NCEO effectiveness – was Sir William Morris's formation in September

[9] *The Times*, 25 Sept. 1930; Dintenfass, 'Politics of Producers' Co-operation', 83–5.
[10] FBI Council statement, *The Times* 17 Feb. 1930; Balfour and Cadman EAC report, 2 May 1930, in Howson and Winch, *Economic Advisory Council*, 177–80.
[11] Balfour to MacDonald, 1 Oct. 1930, JRM 673; and for the NCEO, Rodgers, 'Employers' Organizations', 326–38.
[12] Rodgers, 'Employers' Organizations', 321, and see Lowe, *Adjusting to Democracy*, 83.
[13] FBI statements, *The Times*, 14 and 15 Oct. 1930.

1930 of the National Council of Industry and Commerce. This body of about 100 leading businessmen aimed to promote domestic protection, intra-imperial trade, and retrenchment. But it spoke also of 'the extravagance of successive Governments' and 'slavish adherence' to obsolete economic theories, of politicians putting 'party matters first and business afterwards', and of 'the necessity for...Government to be run on business lines'.[14]

For the TUC General Council, an education in high policy which had begun with the Mond–Turner talks was advanced by Bevin's membership of the Macmillan Committee and Bevin's and Citrine's of the EAC. But this did not alter the basis of their thinking: a denial that existing levels of working-class incomes, whether wages or unemployment benefits, were 'in any way' to blame for Britain's economic difficulties. To reduce them would be economically 'completely futile' because it would reduce consumption, and socially a 'monstrous injustice' while unearned incomes of *rentiers* remained untouched. A wage-cutting campaign would be resisted with 'all the means in their power'.[15] The TUC not only expected unemployment insurance benefits to be fully maintained; as unemployment mounted during 1930 they wanted unemployment insurance extended to agricultural workers, and expenditure on unemployment relief schemes increased.[16]

The General Council expected this expenditure to be met from general taxation: it simply ignored arguments that high taxation deterred industrial enterprise. Rather, it concerned itself with what it considered were the three explanations for Britain's economic difficulties. One was foreign competition and trade restrictions, in response to which it developed during 1930 the idea of a consolidated Commonwealth 'economic group'. This was manifested not only in the joint TUC–FBI proposal for bureaucratic encouragement of imperial trade, but also in acceptance of the desirability of physical re-direction of trade. Although adopted only after considerable dispute and on the understanding that general tariffs (affecting food prices) were unacceptable except as a final resort, this represented nevertheless an important departure from the TUC's traditional internationalism.[17] Another explanation was industrial inefficiency,

[14] NCIC and Morris statements, *The Times*, 19, 20, and 26 Sept. 1930.
[15] Macmillan Committee *Evidence*, II, 324–5, Nov. 1930.
[16] Bevin to MacDonald, 27 Aug. 1930, JRM 461; *TUCAR 1930*, 287–91, 2 Sept. 1930.
[17] General Council Economic Committee report, May–June 1930, and debate, 2 Sept. 1930, in *TUCAR 1930*, 208–17, 257–87.

on which there had been broad agreement with the Mond group. But just as the employers' interpretation of 'rationalisation' changed, so did that of the TUC. As the recession seemed to expose the consequences of capitalist 'anarchy', it argued that effective rationalisation meant 'socialisation': the creation of publicly owned utilities and a National Investment Trust.[18] A third explanation, which Bevin increasingly thought the most important, was monetary deflation. Here again there was a marked shift. In May 1930 TUC leaders argued for price stabilisation through international banking co-operation, but in the autumn, as this seemed increasingly unlikely, it wanted 'very careful consideration' given to devaluation.[19]

The TUC's thinking was ordered by its sense of social justice. If world conditions should make drastic British economic adjustments necessary, it wanted the burden spread equally to every class through devaluation rather than borne proportionately more heavily by those on lower incomes through tariffs. On no account should the burden be imposed solely on the working class through cuts in wages and unemployment insurance. For the present, TUC leaders felt that continued ' "footling about" ' in national policy was intolerable, and that 'the best brains in the country should be mobilised for really tackling the economic problem'.[20]

As Bevin knew, some of the best brains were already at work. With the Labour government's appointment of the Macmillan Committee and Economic Advisory Council, leading economists were given an unprecedented opportunity to interrogate the financial authorities and influence policy. The central figure was Keynes, who now became an adviser to MacDonald and the Labour Cabinet, moving away from the Liberal party. He was not involved when in summer 1930 Lloyd George again recruited experts, to re-cast *We Can Conquer Unemployment*. Despite Keynes's propaganda effort during the election campaign he was not really a committed party man: he had declined to stand as a Liberal candidate, and his commitments were rather to notions about the role of intellectual experts and to an

---

[18] Bevin to MacDonald, 27 Aug. 1930, JRM 461; Macmillan Committee *Evidence* II, 321–3, Nov. 1930.

[19] Macmillan Committee *Evidence* I, 307–12, II, 325, 2 May, Nov. 1930; and see Bevin at EAC 9th meeting, 7 Nov. 1930, and in Bullock, *Bevin* I, 428, 431–2.

[20] Macmillan Committee *Evidence* II, 325–6, Nov 1930; Bevin statement, Aug. 1930, in Bullock, *Bevin* I, 453; Beard (TUC president) 1 Sept. 1930, in *TUCAR 1930*, 72.

essentially non-party body of 'progressive' political and economic ideas. The Macmillan Committee and EAC replaced the Liberal party as his 'tabernacle' for developing these ideas, which Labour leaders, presiding over a minority government and perplexed by economic difficulties, might now be more inclined to 'steal'.[21] His co-pamphleteer, H. D. Henderson, who had been a Liberal candidate, made a similar transition, becoming EAC joint secretary.

Through the EAC Keynes hoped to inject into government 'the scientific spirit as distinct from the sterility of the purely party attitude', and he was instrumental in persuading MacDonald to 'magnify' its terms of reference beyond industrial policy to general economic policy.[22] When it became apparent that as a 'mixed body' containing businessmen the EAC could not reach agreement, Keynes persuaded MacDonald to appoint a committee of economists to produce 'an agreed diagnosis of our present problems and a reasoned list of the possible remedies'.[23] Keynes also ensured that the Macmillan Committee considered not simply industrial finance but monetary and economic fundamentals, and in early 1930 – as later with the economists' committee – he made a remarkable effort to convert it to his own new analysis, clarified and deepened since the election.

Keynes's explanations for the economic problem were monetary ones. The world recession resulted from a failure of international investment, and British difficulties from an overvalued sterling defended by high interest rates, which had strangled productive investment and forced price deflation yet failed to achieve an equivalent deflation of wages and other costs. Given Bank of England and Treasury attitudes and the genuine risks to financial confidence, he accepted that voluntary devaluation was not a realistic option – though he thought fear of enforced devaluation should not obstruct adoption of other remedies.[24] Like the TUC, and

[21] See above, p. 25. Examination of Keynes's political positions over the whole period 1926–32 gives more support for Freeden, *Liberalism Divided*, 164, than for Clarke, *Keynesian Revolution*, 80–1.

[22] Keynes memo, 'Economic General Staff', 10 Dec. 1929, in *JMK* xx, 22–7. For MacDonald's original idea of a body to stimulate industry, see Jones, *Whitehall Diary* II, 219–20, 224–5: 2, 9, and 16 Dec. 1929.

[23] Keynes to MacDonald, 10 July 1930, in *JMK* xx, 368–9. For differences see reports of Committee on the Economic Outlook (chaired by Keynes), 2 May 1930, in Howson and Winch, *Economic Advisory Council*, 174–80.

[24] Macmillan Committee private session, 28 Feb. 1930, and see also H. D. Henderson memo, 13 Oct. 1930, in *JMK* xx, 100, 453–4. For a fine exposition of Keynes's analysis and remedies, see Clarke, *Keynesian Revolution*, 107–17, 163–7, 183–7, 198–200.

primarily for reasons of social justice and political stability, he also rejected a policy of singling out wages for reduction. Within those constraints, his analysis licensed an 'eclectic programme' which, by appearing to accept 'suggestions from all quarters', he hoped might conjure up an economic and political consensus.[25] He even tried to persuade the Governor of the Bank of England. Central bank co-operation might obtain a resumption of international lending. But if that failed, the Bank of England should be 'very brave' and encourage London banks to lead the way, 'shaming or stimulating' the French and Americans to follow.[26] He advocated industrial rationalisation, a 'national treaty' for agreed, simultaneous, reductions in all incomes, and export bounties. His own favourite remained loan-financed public works, now primarily as a device to jump-start a cumulative revival of home investment. From February, he also increasingly favoured tariffs – not in a simple Conservative sense of industrial and agricultural protection, but for the macro-economic purposes of decreasing real wages, raising prices, increasing profits, and reviving business confidence. All these measures should be tried in some combination: the 'unforgivable attitude' was to be 'negative'.[27]

Perhaps Keynes and MacDonald seriously believed that agreement between leading economists could persuade the various economic interests, the Bank of England, the Treasury, and a parliamentary majority to accept effective expansionist policies. If so, the ambition received a severe blow with the completion of the EAC economists' committee report in October 1930. Only Stamp – despite being also a businessman and Bank of England director – fully accepted Keynes's analysis, and Keynes had to make considerable concessions to produce even partial agreement. H. D. Henderson, Pigou, and Robbins placed more emphasis than Keynes upon non-monetary explanations for the depression, lacked his faith in early recovery of international lending and prices, and thought the remedy lay much more directly in bringing costs into line with prices. Henderson, deeply pessimistic, thought that business and financial confidence had become the central problem, and that fear

---

[25] Keynes memo, 'The State of Trade', 21 July 1930, in *JMK* xx, 375–6; and see Keynes to Brand, 7 Sept. 1930, Brand papers 28, both as an example of his tactics and adding to his remedies of early 1930.

[26] Keynes to Norman, 22 May 1930, in *JMK* xx, 354.

[27] Keynes memo, 'The State of Trade', 21 July 1930, in *JMK* xx, 375.

of tax increases was destroying enterprise and might ultimately force abandonment of the gold standard, resulting in 'confusion and horror' and 'permanent impoverishment'. Accordingly he now renounced loan-financed works and saw no alternative but to agree with the 'ordinary...unintellectual businessman' and 'face the disagreeable reactionary necessity of cutting costs (including wages)...and [public] expenditure', particularly unemployment insurance.[28]

On the other hand, Henderson shared Keynes's conversion to tariffs, having already proposed them as a means to finance industrial rationalisation and balance the budget.[29] Otherwise, in a profession which had been almost completely Cobdenite, even stronger objection was taken to Keynes's support for tariffs than to his other proposals. Pigou thought it 'ungentlemanly' to do anything more than insert notes of dissent, but Robbins considered Keynes's draft report 'monstrous' and when Keynes tried to force his acquiescence they had a 'violent quarrel'.[30] Robbins insisted upon submitting a minority report, and mobilised Beveridge, Layton, Clay, and other economists into 'a sort of Committee of Public Safety' to prepare a defence of free trade for whenever Keynes made his views public. To more immediate effect, Robbins also alerted Labour ministers to the intensity of expert opposition to Keynes.[31] With the economics profession itself now sharply divided, from a government perspective Keynes's efforts had produced every bit as much 'sterility' as he detected in party politics.

Keynes was not altogether isolated, however. Mosley continued to borrow much from him. So too did Bevin. Keynes also had an ally in McKenna, former Chancellor of the Exchequer and another Macmillan Committee member, who was 'the one powerful champion of the new ideas [critical of Bank of England policy] speaking from an unchallengeable position in the City', having made the chairmanship of the Midland Bank 'a pulpit from which

[28] H. D. Henderson to Keynes, 30 May 1930, and 'The Drift of the Draft Report', 13 Oct. 1930, in *JMK* xx, 357–60, 452–6. For accounts of the economists' differences, see Skidelsky, *Politicians*, 207–15, and Howson and Winch, *Economic Advisory Council*, 60–70.

[29] H. D. Henderson, 'Industrial Reconstruction Scheme', 30 May 1930, JRM 455.

[30] Dalton diary, 23 Oct. 1930 (Pimlott, 122–4); Robbins to Cannan, 17 Oct., 10 Nov. 1930, Cannan papers 1030/197–8, 202–4.

[31] Clay to Lothian, 26 Sept. 1930, Lothian papers 247/101–2; Robbins to Cannan, 10 Nov. 1930, Cannan papers 1030/202–4; Beveridge diary, Oct. 1930–Jan. 1931 passim; Dalton diary, 23 and 29 Oct. 1930 (Pimlott, 122–4).

to instruct and educate public opinion'.[32] Like Keynes, McKenna attributed Britain's difficulties largely to sterling overvaluation, and wanted credit expansion while rejecting devaluation. For the world recession, however, he had a rather different explanation, shared with some other City financiers and derived principally from Strakosch and the League of Nations Gold Delegation. This blamed excessive American and French accumulation and 'sterilisation' of monetary gold, for which the remedy was international co-operation to economise on gold use and release funds for investment.[33] But most leading financiers supported Bank of England policy, believing the international gold standard to be the indispensable guarantee not just of the City's profits but of British economic stability. For them, gold maldistribution was only a secondary problem: the real explanation for the British and international problems were post-war distortions in production caused by economic nationalism and maladjustment of costs.

In one respect McKenna and other leading City financiers were agreed. As the recession intensified economic nationalism elsewhere, they submitted to a 'revolution in facts' and accepted domestic and imperial protectionism, as a means to defend the British industrial base and balance of payments which ultimately sustained the City's financial strength. Coming from a former citadel of free trade, the 'bankers' manifesto' of July 1930[34] indicated a shift even more portentous than those of the FBI, the TUC, and Keynes.

Above all, however, most City financiers believed the British malaise was high costs relative to other industrial nations. As a matter of public responsibility they responded to Bank of England and ministerial appeals to help finance industrial rationalisation. But they had little faith in this. To them the problem was not so much industrial inefficiency as a politically determined 'standard of wages, pensions and unemployment pay totally above' the country's 'real means'.[35] The price collapse meant that in autumn 1930 reduction of these costs, beginning with government retrenchment, was regarded as imperative. Another City banker on the Macmillan

---

[32] Keynes obituary of McKenna, 1943, in *JMK* x, 58.
[33] Williamson, 'Financiers', 117. For Strakosch and the Gold Delegation, see Boyce, *British Capitalism*, 42, 166–8, 289–90.
[34] See *The Times*, 4, 5, and 10 July 1930 (quotation from editorial, 5 July).
[35] Holland-Martin (president, Institute of Bankers; secretary, Bankers' Clearing House) speech, *The Times*, 6 Nov. 1930. For rationalisation, see, e.g., Burk, *Morgan Grenfell*, 96–7.

Committee, Brand, believed that without an international price rise
there was 'no alternative...to a direct attack on costs', including
wages, and that if not undertaken voluntarily 'then ultimately
economic forces...[would] bring it about, possibly as a result of a
really serious economic and financial crisis'.[36]

The principal City institution, the Bank of England, was not
monolithic: aside from Stamp, its directorate expressed a variety of
opinions on credit and trade policies.[37] During 1930, however, the
Bank's only important initiative was in industrial rationalisation.
The lack of more definite responses to the depression resulted from
the Governor's understanding of the Bank's functions and of
international conditions, and from political prudence. Norman
thought the Bank's role was more limited, and operated in a more
complicated world, than did Keynes, McKenna, and other critics.
Its responsibilities were maintenance of currency stability and
management of government debt, not industrial or employment
policies. It assumed that a well-ordered monetary system was the
fixed structure to which all other economic activities conformed to
their own benefit, and in supervising this system it considered itself
the trustee for 'all sections of the community, financial, commercial
and industrial', and as a non-political (because private) corporation
treating successive governments with 'complete impartiality'.[38] In
re-establishing the gold standard, its objectives had been to restore
general economic prosperity as well as the City's international role;
to re-establish an 'automatic' mechanism for economic adjustments,
and to retrieve monetary policy from political interference. But none
of these aims had been fully achieved, while sterling had come under
repeated pressures.

The Bank did not think the pound overvalued. Sterling suffered
strains not because Bank policy was mistaken but because of external
'abnormalities': the effects of reparations, war debts, foreign
undervaluations, and speculative movements of foreign balances. By
1930 it accepted that the return to gold had aggravated Britain's
industrial difficulties, but thought this was vastly outweighed by the
benefits of reattachment to the international system, and of small
importance compared to the damage caused by shifts in world

---

[36] Brand memo, 'Unemployment' [late 1930], Lothian papers 133/25–87.

[37] E.g., Blackett and Addis (for whom see Dayer, *Finance and Empire*, esp. 210–16) favoured
credit expansion; Anderson and Whigham signed the 'Bankers' manifesto'.

[38] Harvey to Keynes, 17 Dec. 1929, and to Newbold, 10 July 1930, BoE G3/208/268,
G3/209/185a; and see Macmillan Committee *Evidence*, qq 3, 454.

production and demand.[39] As for the world slump, Norman and his closest colleagues explained this as a combination of commodity overproduction, disequilibrium between national economies, and French and American monetary nationalism – their 'acquisitive and unnecessary' habits of hoarding gold rather than employing it for international investment.[40]

The Bank believed it had done everything within its power and more to assist British industry, and could do little alone to stimulate world economic recovery. From 1927 it had tried to shield the domestic economy from extraneous monetary pressures, avoiding bank rate increases whenever possible by market interventions and – as its critics suggested – seeking co-operation with foreign central banks. These seemed major departures from the ideal of an 'automatic' mechanism: sterling had become 'a more or less managed Currency'.[41] It had also attempted to remedy the monetary problems, urging economy in gold use and cancellation of reparations and war debts, and supporting creation of the Bank for International Settlements. But the Bank came up repeatedly against foreign obstruction: the French insisted upon reparations and the Americans on debt repayment, both rejected criticism of their gold policies, and the BIS was a disappointment, because 'dominated by American habits and French ideas'.[42] Even Stamp accepted that any British effort to convene an international gold conference would founder on American and French hostility. It was not obvious how these might be persuaded to increase their foreign lending, and if it were achieved French balances might be withdrawn from London, aggravating an existing tendency to lose gold.[43] Sterling defence also seemed to preclude London acting alone to expand international credit. Norman knew there were serious international problems, but he understood better than his critics that the obstacles to solving them were formidable. Then again, on the assumption that the slump also had non-monetary causes, it followed that banks alone could not supply all the remedies.

[39] See Williamson, 'Financiers', 112–13.

[40] Norman to Keynes, 20 May 1930, in *JMK* xx, 349; Kindersley speech, *The Times*, 20 Sept. 1930.

[41] Norman notes, summer 1928, in Clay, *Norman*, 310. For techniques, see Moggridge, *British Monetary Policy*, chs. 7–9; Sayers, *Bank of England*, 217–19, 224–5, 312, 331–47; and Clarke, *Central Bank Cooperation*, passim.

[42] Norman to Clegg, 10 Dec. 1930, BoE G3/197/581.

[43] Stamp at EAC 9th meeting, 7 Nov. 1930; Norman to Keynes, 20 May 1930, in *JMK* xx, 349.

The Bank considered that the domestic effects of its policy had been not deflationary but essentially neutral, neither causing serious harm to industry nor sheltering it from changes in world production and demand. Adjustment to those changes would have been necessary in any event: to suggest this was avoidable was a 'real disservice' to industry. Like Keynes, the Bank thought that adjustment had got 'jammed'. But unlike Keynes, it thought the causes and therefore the remedies were not really banking but industrial problems. The Bank had provided conditions in which adjustment should have occurred: credit expansion could not help industries made uncompetitive by high costs, though it could jeopardise confidence in sterling.[44] Yet even here the Bank had gone well beyond its traditional responsibilities. From 1928 Norman helped to arrange finance for industrial rationalisation, particularly in steel and cotton. In early 1930 he recruited wider City assistance through a Bankers Industrial Development Company (BIDCo), seeking to direct more investment towards domestic industries. He also helped promote hire purchase as a new device to stimulate demand.[45] But by autumn 1930 the Bank, like most City financiers, believed that the recession was undercutting the benefits of rationalisation. Despite defections by individual directors it still rejected protection, as evading the issue of adjustment. Rather, the Bank thought industry needed a more direct attack upon costs – upon wage and tax levels – and, still more fundamentally, the nation's return to a 'Calvinistic outlook'.[46]

So long as industry alone seemed in difficulty, Norman left these matters to industrialists, the Treasury, and politicians. Apart from the Bank's customary avoidance of direct interference in 'political' matters, he was sensitive to its delicate position under a Labour government. The Bank was 'impartial' within the parameters of private ownership and capitalism, but it was certainly not impartial towards 'socialism'. Its increased support for industrial rationalisation in 1929–30 was intended to pre-empt nationalisation:[47] the

[44] Macmillan Committee *Evidence*, qq 3336–47, 3458 (Norman, 26 March), 6672–5 (Niemeyer, 4 June), 7611–36, 7719–22 (Stewart, 3, 4 July, all 1930); Lubbock to Brand, 1 Jan. 1931, Brand papers 28; and see Clarke, *Keynesian Revolution*, 131–40.

[45] For industrial policy, see Sayers, *Bank of England*, ch. 14, and Tolliday, *Business, Banking and Politics*, chs. 7–11. For hire purchase, see BoE Cte, 13 Nov. 1929, and Norman to Smith, 13 Feb. 1930, BoE G3/197/69.

[46] Osborne memo, July 1930, in Clarke, *Keynesian Revolution*, 136.

[47] See, e.g., BoE Cte, 19 June 1929; Norman to Peacock, 23 Sept., 7 Oct. 1929, BoE G3/195/337, 364; also Tolliday, *Business, Banking and Politics*, 199–201, 208, 298.

Bank in effect operated an anti-socialist policy. Norman also feared an attempt to impose government control over the Bank itself, and so in summer 1929 went to extraordinary lengths to postpone a controversial bank rate increase and to avert a bank inquiry. The Macmillan Committee subjected the Bank's practical intuitions to interrogation on unfamiliar theoretical ground: Norman 'scarcely understood' what Keynes was saying, his evidence left a disastrous impression of ineptitude, and thereafter the Bank was hard pressed to explain itself.[48] A hostile report leading to government control seemed a real threat, so it was obviously sensible not to press unwelcome advice on industrial matters. But Norman's reticence would last only so long as domestic conditions did not affect the Bank's specific responsibility, sterling defence.

Like the Bank of England, the Treasury was only incidentally concerned with industrial or employment policies. Its functions were public finance: to raise revenue, preserve government credit, reduce the national debt, and prevent unlimited borrowing, chiefly through control of expenditure. These functions issued in conventions of 'sound finance', crucially that of a 'balanced budget', the purposes of which were as much political as economic – to check the inclination of politicians to seek popular support by spending money without imposing new taxation.[49] Treasury policy emerged from dialogue between senior officials and the Chancellor of the Exchequer. The officials were economic liberals who assumed the natural efficacy of capitalism; Snowden was socialist in moral aspiration but a tough-minded Radical within capitalism. Their ends were different but their means very similar. Snowden differed from Treasury officials in being committed to land taxation, in seeking to shift the burden of taxation towards the rich, and in his readiness, where budgetary balance and financial confidence allowed, to spend on social services and public works. Otherwise his radicalism was expressed in unshakeable attachment to free trade and low living costs, and to strict financial rectitude and monetary discipline.

Snowden appointed the Macmillan Committee because he believed some improvement could be made in capital investment in

---

[48] Harvey to Stewart, 11 April 1930, BoE G3/209/93, and see Clarke, *Keynesian Revolution*, chapter 6.
[49] See Skidelsky, *Politicians*, 15–16, and Middleton, 'The Treasury in the 1930s', 56–63.

industry and in small banking facilities,[50] not because he disagreed with monetary fundamentals or thought the Bank of England required early nationalisation. For him as for Treasury officials, the Bank had the enormous virtue of being free from direct political constraints in imposing unpalatable but necessary measures, whether bank rate increases or industrial rationalisation. Although privately they themselves deprecated bank rate increases which might hurt trade and arouse political criticism, their official view was that monetary policy was 'exclusively' a Bank of England matter, which did not necessarily impair trade and employment.[51] They were fully committed to the gold standard, both as an essential monetary control and, like balanced budgets, as a 'knave-proof' check upon political manipulation. To abandon it would, in Snowden's words, 'have disastrous consequences'.[52] Insofar as the Treasury accepted monetary explanations for British difficulties and the world recession, it agreed with the Bank in blaming them on inter-governmental debts and foreign monetary policies. Leith-Ross was influenced by gold maldistribution ideas and exasperated by the Bank's caution about international action; but neither he nor Snowden supposed that a British government initiative would be successful. There seemed little to do except hope for a chance to obtain cancellation of reparations and war debts, and for the 'education' of French and American opinion through Norman's efforts at the BIS.[53]

Within the Treasury, however, only Hawtrey, its house economist, proposed a purely monetary explanation and reflationary remedies.[54] But in this he had no influence. Treasury officials were highly sceptical about professional economists, believing them to operate in a 'world of abstractions' far from the real world (their own) of complex practical problems.[55] This was considered especially true of their principal adversary Keynes, whose work was closely followed but concluded to be 'all wrong' where it was not fluid and

[50] Norman to Fisher, 20 June 1929, and Harvey to Norman, 12 July 1929, BoE G3/195/217, G1/515.

[51] Macmillan Committee Evidence, q 5321 (Hopkins, 16 May 1930); Snowden in LPACR 1929, 227–8, 3 Oct.; Williamson, 'Financiers', 111, 114–15.

[52] Snowden at EAC 9th meeting, 7 Nov. 1930. For 'knave-proof', P. J. Grigg to Snowden, 11 Oct. 1929, T160/426/F11548.

[53] Leith-Ross, 'Possibilities of Government action in regard to the recent fall in world prices' [July 1930], and memo, 28 July 1930, JRM 257; Leith-Ross to McKenna, 1 Nov. 1930, T188/15B; Snowden at EAC 9th meeting, 7 Nov. 1930.

[54] See, e.g., Hawtrey memo, Macmillan Committee Evidence II, 315–21, July 1930.

[55] Leith-Ross, 'Assumptions of Mr Keynes', 28 March 1930, T175/26; Macmillan Committee Evidence, qq 5624–5 (Hopkins, 22 May 1930).

inconsistent.[56] For Snowden, Keynes's sophistry was confirmed by his adoption of tariffs. He treated the Keynes–Stamp economists' report with 'withering scorn', while regarding Robbins's minority report as 'a most trenchant reply'.[57]

For Treasury officials, Keynes's greatest offence was that he had inspired the loan-financed development programmes of Lloyd George and then of Mosley – what one official later called making 'economics into a *vade mecum* for political spivs'.[58] Some public works could be justified where public enterprise would not naturally operate, if they had genuine economic value and promised a financial return, and were funded through ordinary capital investment grants. In accordance with its pledges, the Labour Cabinet stepped up such work schemes by relaxing some of the financial criteria, and by October 1930 schemes costing some £140m. had been approved.[59] But Snowden now accepted that a special public loan was unnecessary because suitable schemes could be funded by conventional means, and undesirable because of its likely effects. The basic Treasury objection to a large development loan was that either it would be pure inflation, or it would 'crowd out' private investment and employment, and raise interest rates and therefore production costs. In either event, the employment created by such means would be temporary, 'artificial' and, in aggregate, negligible. To this were added the arguments first that massive, accelerated work schemes raised insuperable technical, administrative, and political difficulties – so that implementation might 'necessitate the substitution of autocracy for Parliamentary Government'[60] – and then, during 1930, that the Labour government's existing grant-aided schemes were exhausting the possibilities for productive work, with important financial consequences.

While Keynes, Lloyd George, and Mosley tended to assume that new, large-scale state borrowing was a straightforward technical operation, this conflicted with Treasury concerns and experience. There were repeated difficulties in managing existing government

[56] Leith-Ross to Jones, 27 March 1928, in Jones, *Whitehall Diary* II, 250; Leith-Ross, 'Notes on Keynes' Exposition', 28 March 1930, T175/26, and memo, 28 July 1930, JRM 257.
[57] Dalton diary, 29 Oct. 1930 (Pimlott, 124).
[58] P. J. Grigg, *Prejudice and Judgment*, 7.
[59] Middleton, 'Treasury and Public Investment', 361.
[60] N. W. Fisher (permanent secretary, Treasury) to Baldwin, in CP104(29), 2 April 1929. For development of Treasury thinking, see Clarke, *Keynesian Revolution*, 48–69, 149–56, revising Middleton, 'Treasury in the 1930s', and Peden, 'The "Treasury View"'.

debt; reduction of a floating debt of 'menacing proportions' and a large conversion of war loan to reduce the enormous burden of debt charges upon the budget were major objectives.[61] Officials were also acutely conscious of dependence upon financial market conditions and the perceptions of private institutions. As further public-work schemes could not satisfy the 'sound finance' test of being useful and remunerative, so – in increasingly serious financial conditions – a development loan would 'be almost universally regarded as the inauguration of an orgy of extravagance', shattering business and financial confidence.[62]

The 'Treasury view' was not merely that such programmes, even if practicable, would be 'dangerously counterproductive':[63] it was also that they were beside the point. British difficulties were mostly due to export uncompetitiveness caused by high costs, and the world recession to overproduction, so the main remedies were adjustment to shifts in world demand, increased efficiency, and reduced costs, including wages if necessary.[64] Snowden opposed cuts in real wages, but otherwise agreed. By rationalisation Britain could 'in substantial measure recapture export trade...and replace imported goods'.[65] Through temporary sacrifices producers could prepare for the inevitable trade recovery: he 'despair[ed]' at trade union refusals to postpone claims for improved living standards and to abandon restrictive practices.[66] Protection was self-defeating because agriculture had 'to set [its] house in order', while industries must be 'compel[led]...to make themselves efficient by expos[ure]...to the cold blast of reality'.[67]

From the belief that 'the salvation of industry [was] in the hands of industry itself',[68] it followed that maintenance of business confidence became a major consideration. Between June and October 1929 Snowden authorised increased expenditure on roads,

[61] For problems over debt maturities and Treasury bills, see Macmillan Committee *Evidence*, qq 5429–30 (Hopkins, 16 May 1930); for conversion, Howson, *Domestic Monetary Management*, 37–41, 71–3.

[62] Treasury note on Liberal proposals, Oct. 1930, PREM 1/108.

[63] Hopkins note concerning the Mosley memo, 1 Feb. 1930, T175/42.

[64] Leith-Ross, 'Assumptions of Mr Keynes', 28 March 1930, T175/26; Leith-Ross to Keynes, and to McKenna, 24 Oct., 1 Nov. 1930, T188/274, 15B.

[65] Snowden, 'Economic Outlook', 8 April 1930, EAC(H), copy in H. D. Henderson papers 1.

[66] B. Webb diary, 3 Aug. 1930 (Cole, 249; MacKenzie IV, 225); Snowden at EAC 9th meeting, 7 Nov. 1930, and speeches, *The Times*, 16 Oct., 24 Nov. 1930.

[67] Snowden to MacDonald, 24 Feb., 28 April 1930, JRM 243; Snowden, 'Agricultural Policy', CP 250(30), 17 July 1930.

[68] Snowden speech, *The Times*, 16 Oct. 1930.

pensions, housing, and unemployment insurance. But from October, when a large budget deficit was estimated, Snowden resisted plans for further new expenditure.[69] He wanted a strict budget balance in order to end Churchill's habit of raiding capital funds and to ease the problems of debt management.[70] Snowden's special attention to expenditure, however, arose from a belief that increased taxation would depress business 'psychology'. Snowden's April 1930 budget, though meeting the current deficit by an additional 6d. on income tax and increased surtax, was nevertheless designed to encourage 'a spirit of enterprise and confidence' among businessmen. He declared that 'in the absence of unforeseeable calamities or of heavy increases in expenditure... no further increases of taxation [would] need to be imposed next year'.[71]

Despite the considerable increase in expenditure and unforeseen fall in revenue by the autumn, Snowden meant to keep that pledge. The recession had made this seem imperative since 'the psychological effect of any increase in taxation [would] be very bad indeed': another 6d. on income tax would, he asserted, increase unemployment by 500,000.[72] Yet even with optimistic forecasting, the prospective deficits were £14·25m. for 1930 and £46m. for 1931.[73] The price fall had increased the real burden of debt charges, but market conditions were not yet favourable to war-loan conversion. Snowden was prepared to help avoid tax increases by resorting to Churchill's expedient of capital raids – 'criminal in ordinary circumstances but justifiable in this emergency' – but he also thought there was 'great justification' in the widespread demands for expenditure cuts.[74]

The chief cause of the prospective deficit was unemployment insurance expenditure. Like many businessmen, financiers, and economists, Treasury officials believed these payments aggravated industrial difficulties and unemployment, and 'demoralized' the workforce; they would have welcomed 'reform' in any event. But they were now alarmed by the size of the Unemployment Insurance

---

[69] Generally, Snowden, 'The Growth of Expenditure', CP344(29), 29 Nov. 1929. Objections to specific expenditures are prominent in the Cabinet and Treasury papers for October to December 1929.
[70] Snowden to Churchill, 23 Jan. 1930, T172/1690.
[71] Snowden in *HC Deb*, 237, col. 2681, 14 April 1930.
[72] Snowden speech, *The Times*, 16 Oct. 1930, and at EAC 9th meeting, 7 Nov. 1930.
[73] Hopkins to Snowden, 10 Oct., 4 Nov. 1930, T171/287.
[74] Snowden to MacDonald, 16 Aug., 9 Sept. 1930, JRM 676; Snowden speech, *The Times*, 16 Oct. 1930. The private correspondence corrects the interpretation of the public statement in Skidelsky, *Politicians*, 298.

Fund's deficit and even more by the soaring budget charge for transitional benefit. Snowden was just as worried. Like his officials, he thought the system was subject to considerable 'abuse' by employers and recipients, and that to have non-contributory transitional benefit alongside the contributory insurance scheme was an unjustifiable anomaly.[75] Since July Treasury and Ministry of Labour officials had searched for politically acceptable means of abolishing the transitional arrangements.[76] In mid October Snowden increased pressure for action not just by warnings to the Cabinet about the budget deficit, but also by an appeal to public opinion: at the Mansion House he spoke of the cost of unemployment 'distressing [him] almost beyond measure', and of 'the duty of Parliament to face up to this problem and to put the Insurance Fund upon an insurance basis'.[77] After the Cabinet postponed decision by appointing a Royal Commission, the Treasury attitude was that 'public opinion may speak before the Commission has spoken'.[78]

The effect of the slump upon the leading economic interests and policy advisers was, then, a marked shift or hardening of attitudes. Everyone hoped that economic recovery might be accelerated by some kind of international financial co-operation and reflation, but this lay beyond British power alone and depended upon the sceptical Americans and French. Otherwise, sharp polarisations were developing. For the TUC General Council all working-class incomes were inviolable and devaluation an acceptable option. The Bank of England and the City, the Treasury, and Snowden considered the gold standard a closed question and with industrialists thought that costs, including some or most working-class incomes, would have to be reduced. Farmers, industrialists, the TUC General Council, Keynes, and leading financiers wanted import controls or tariffs, but were opposed by Snowden and most economists. Keynes was trying to stitch together some agreement allowing expansionist measures, but without success. Any central ground which the Labour Cabinet might have successfully occupied was dissolving, with most opinion critical of either or both of the two major Labour economic commitments – to social service expenditure and free trade. From many perspectives government policies were thought to be worsening the recession. Yet lack of confidence in the Labour Cabinet was not

[75] Snowden at EAC 7th meeting, 24 July 1930; Hurst to Upcott, 14 July 1930, T175/31.
[76] Janeway thesis, 'Economic Policy of the Second Labour Government', 173.
[77] Cabinets 60, 61(30), 15 and 17 Oct. 1930; Snowden speech, The Times, 16 Oct. 1930.
[78] Hopkins to Snowden, 4 Nov. 1930, T171/287.

all to the benefit of other parties. Even Snowden, in appealing to public opinion and 'Parliament', implied that party politics had become an obstacle to effective policy.

THE EMPIRE IN DANGER

If the Labour government was unfortunate in taking office just before the onset of the world depression, its timing was no less unfortunate as regards the condition of the Empire. Faced with reduced financial and military capacity, stronger Dominion and Colonial nationalisms, and the United States' arrival as a world power, British policy-makers in the 1920s had convinced themselves that much of the substance of imperial control and external power could be sustained by calculated, limited, concession and compromise.[79] But they also believed that success depended firstly upon a high quality of imperial management, finely and flexibly balanced between firmness and conciliation, and secondly upon broad agreement between the leading elements of British political opinion, in order to contain both anti-imperial sentiment which might encourage nationalist movements and diehard resistance which might provoke them. To a large extent the party leaderships maintained such agreement through private negotiation between themselves, not least because they understood that imperial issues could present intractable parliamentary and party problems. Hence the Labour Cabinet's preference was for continuity of policy and co-operation in any new departures. Normally, when differences arose these occurred within and across parties. It was both a symptom and a further source of imperial difficulty that in 1929–30 party pressures jeopardised consensus between the party leaderships.

The election of a Labour government in itself heightened the sensitivities of imperialists towards particular imperial issues.[80] There were a number of secondary controversies. The peremptory removal of Lord Lloyd, High Commissioner in Egypt, in July 1929 for intransigence towards Egyptian nationalists, and the London Naval Treaty of April 1930, which limited warship construction, were regarded as triumphs by the Labour party and accepted by the Conservative and Liberal leaderships, but they annoyed Conservative imperialist diehards. An East African White Paper of June

[79] For valuable suggestions, see Darwin, 'Imperialism in Decline?', and Holland, *Britain and the Commonwealth Alliance*, chs. 2, 4.
[80] See, e.g., the second epigraph heading this chapter.

1930 declaring the paramountcy of native rights provoked such resistance from Kenyan settlers, the High Commissioner Grigg, and Conservative and Liberal sympathisers – who all wanted creation of a new white dominion – that the government was compelled in November to refer the matter to a joint select committee. A Palestine White Paper of October 1930, proposing restrictions on Jewish immigration and colonisation, aroused the international Zionist movement to charges that the Balfour Declaration and League of Nations Mandate had been infringed and the Conservative and Liberal leaderships to accusations of a 'breach of national faith', forcing the Cabinet to back down before a Commons debate in mid November.[81] These incidents were of cumulative importance in contributing in autumn 1930 to an atmosphere of deep uneasiness about the conduct of imperial policy. But the major problems concerned the Imperial Conference of October–November 1930 and Indian policy, on which a Round Table Conference had been summoned for mid November.

It has been seen that business and trade union opinion looked to imperial markets for a restoration of export trade and employment. But the concept of imperial economic unity had a further aspect: it was a central issue in the preservation of the self-governing Empire following the 1926 Balfour Report. By accepting the constitutional equality and autonomy of the Dominions, the Conservative government had intended to outflank secessionist movements and under the new guise of 'Commonwealth' enable the white Empire to be maintained through ties of sentiment, defence needs, and economic interest. For Britain, the Dominions' new status was a matter of internal imperial convenience, with the Empire remaining for all external purposes a single international entity, as symbolised by a unitary Crown. The Canadian, Australian, and especially Irish and South African governments, however, interpreted the Balfour Report to mean they had become independent international entities, for whom Commonwealth co-operation was a matter not of obligation but preference, with the corollary that the Crown was divisible. After 1926 Dominion self-assertion was accelerated in separate adhesion to international treaties and independent diplomatic representation. Common allegiance to the Crown began to

---

[81] See Baldwin/Amery/A. Chamberlain letter, Lloyd George speech, and Hailsham/Simon letter, *The Times*, 23 and 25 Oct., 4 Nov. 1930. For details of the incidents above, see Carlton, *MacDonald versus Henderson*, chs. 5, 6, 8; Gregory, *Sidney Webb and East Africa*, chs. 3–4; and Rose, *Gentile Zionists*, ch. 1.

seem fragile when separate Dominion legislation on the royal succession was proposed, and when from March 1930 the Australian government insisted against the King's wishes that an Australian judge, Sir Isaac Isaacs, be appointed Governor-General.[82] With the 1930 Imperial Conference arranged to complete implementation of the Balfour Report, the Irish and South African governments made it clear at a preparatory committee in late 1929 that they expected all remaining evidence of constitutional subordination to be removed. In August 1930 their plans included final confirmation of Dominion autonomy in a declaration of a right of secession from the Commonwealth.[83]

In reality strategic, financial, or internal domestic constraints meant that Dominion ministers had no intention of exercising that right.[84] But this was not obvious in Britain, where there was much dismay about Dominion attitudes. Some leading ministers, officials, and Conservative and Liberal politicians regarded secession as a serious possibility.[85] Labour government law officers, charged with legal implementation of the Balfour Report, were alarmed at the 'disjunctive tendencies' it had created.[86] The King and his private secretary, Stamfordham, 'very anxious' about the Crown's position and angry with the Balfour Report now that its implications were apparent, pressed Labour ministers for support in resisting the Australian appointment and South African and Irish demands.[87] MacDonald thought 'the structure of the Empire [was] threatened' because two alien 'states & peoples not belonging to [the] same stock or history' had been coerced into it. The 'British union' had ended in 1926, but it was necessary to prevent the world from understanding this and to maintain a Commonwealth 'group psychology'.[88]

Underlying these reactions was anxiety about the preservation of

---

[82] Nicolson, *George V*, 478–9, 485.
[83] Milligan (Irish External Affairs Minister) note of conversation with Hertzog (South African Prime Minister), 29 Aug. 1930, in Harkness, *Restless Dominion*, 263–8.
[84] Holland, *Britain and the Commonwealth Alliance*, 118–19, 126.
[85] Amery to Jowitt [Aug. 1930], and Hankey, and Thomas, to MacDonald, 10 and 11 Aug. 1930, all JRM 347; Holland, *Britain and the Commonwealth Alliance*, 117–18.
[86] Holland, *Britain and the Commonwealth Alliance*, 123–4; Sankey to MacDonald, 9 July 1930, JRM 347; Jowitt to Amery, 17 Sept. 1930, Amery papers.
[87] The King to MacDonald, 30 Nov. 1929, in Nicolson, *George V*, 485; reported in Henson journal, 6 April 1930, and in Lady Hilton Young diary, 27 July 1930. For pressure, Sankey diary, 21 July 1930; MacDonald diary, 17 April, 29 Oct. 1930; MacDonald to Stamfordham, 30 Oct. 1930, JRM 577.
[88] MacDonald diary, 9 Feb., 25 Aug., 28 Sept., 1 Oct., 13 Nov. 1930; MacDonald to Cecil, 7 Aug. 1930, Cecil papers 51081.

British power. This was thought to depend to a considerable extent upon a common imperial foreign policy. Yet like its Conservative predecessor the Labour government found its policies complicated, embarrassed, and sometimes obstructed by the Dominions, seeming to threaten 'chaos' in foreign relations. If it became apparent to foreign powers that Britain could no longer rely on Dominion support, its international influence would be crippled.[89] Ultimately, what everyone feared was the threat foreshadowed by the Chanak crisis – that in the event of war Britain might be disabled by lack of Dominion assistance.

In preventing the Irish and Afrikaners from dismantling the Commonwealth, one obvious strategy, employed at the 1929 committee, was to argue that constitutional changes required the consent of all Dominions.[90] If Britain was not to be isolated in exercising a veto, Canadian, Australian, and New Zealand support was needed. One method of securing that, and a second possible strategy for Commonwealth consolidation, was imperial economic integration. As within Britain, so in the Dominions, the economic slump had made this a central issue. Faced with balance of payments crises the Australian and Canadian governments had raised their tariffs, but they indicated that if their agricultural surpluses were given privileged access to the British market, they would allow reciprocal preferences on British manufactured goods. These initiatives resulted in economic policy supplanting constitutional questions as the dominant issue of the Imperial Conference. Bennett, the Canadian Prime Minister, came to London 'tremendously keen' to strengthen 'practical' imperial unity – prepared to resist further constitutional separation, but principally concerned to obtain reciprocal trade agreements.[91]

The Labour Cabinet was sympathetic towards certain aspects of imperial economic integration, particularly under the pressure of high unemployment. It retained the Empire Marketing Board and passed a Colonial Development Act largely prepared by the Conservative government. Thomas, while minister responsible for employment policy in 1929, visited Canada to promote emigration and trade. In response to the Australian and Canadian initiatives,

---

[89] MacDonald to Cecil, 7 and 13 Aug. 1930, and Cecil to MacDonald, 8 Aug. 1930, Cecil papers 51081. For example of Optional Clause controversy, see Holland, *Britain and the Commonwealth Alliance*, 95–101.

[90] E.g., Passfield in B. Webb diary, 20 Oct., 4 Nov. 1929 (Cole, 224, 227).

[91] Willingdon (Governor-General, Canada) to Bridgeman, 23 Sept. 1930, Bridgeman papers.

the Cabinet developed proposals for co-ordination of imperial production through 'rationalisation' and an 'imperial economic machinery'. But these were vague substitutes for definite proposals, and despite efforts by Thomas, now Dominions Secretary, a free-trade Cabinet majority led by Snowden refused to offer the Dominions preferential advantages, whether through tariffs, quotas, or bulk purchase. One free-trade argument was that bargaining for trade advantages produced not closer relations but antagonism:[92] on this occasion, however, it was resistance to imperial trade bargains which produced the friction.

At the Imperial Conference on 8 October Bennett offered reciprocal preferences based on a 10 per cent increase in Canadian tariffs on foreign goods. All British ministers, including Thomas, understood that in practice this represented little advantage to British exporters, certainly not enough in itself to make it worthwhile changing government policy. But Snowden's brutal rejection of the offer and all subsequent references to import controls caused great offence to Canadian and Australian delegates.[93] A Cabinet effort to mollify them with a conference committee to discuss a wheat quota misfired when the delegates concluded that British ministers were actually proposing one, and had to be disabused.[94] Further resentment was caused when Bennett's offer – made into a party issue through its acceptance by the Conservative leadership – was publicly dismissed by Thomas as 'humbug'. All that could be salvaged was agreement to reconsider the various proposals at an economic conference in Ottawa in 1931.

Acrimony and absence of definite agreements on economic relations aggravated differences over the other conference issue. MacDonald, Thomas, and Sankey, denied the positive instrument of economic integration, had no resource for preserving imperial unity except negative obstruction to radical constitutional demands. The Irish and South Africans were persuaded not to raise the secession issue, but they expected satisfaction of other claims and much resented British obstruction. The Canadians, retaliating for their rebuff on economic policy, switched course and supported them on

[92] For Dominion Office views, see Holland, *Britain and the Commonwealth Alliance*, 17–19, 110–12. For Cabinet divisions, see below pp. 97–8.

[93] MacDonald diary, 9, 13, and 17 Oct. 1930. For these issues, see Drummond, *Imperial Economic Policy*, 154–61.

[94] Cabinets 59, 63, 64, 67(30) of 9, 24, 28 Oct., 11 Nov. 1930; MacDonald diary, 26 and 28 Oct., 12 and 13 Nov. 1930.

most issues. So too did the Australians, annoyed about their Governor-Generalship, leaving British delegates little room for manoeuvre.[95] Frequently bad-tempered discussions, occasionally close to breakdown, produced agreement on major points of the Balfour and 1929 committee reports, but Labour ministers refused to renounce provisions which ultimately safeguarded the concept of the Commonwealth as a unitary state.[96]

The Conference was everywhere regarded as unfortunate. Agreement to the Statute of Westminster had not been balanced by a strengthening of mutual interests and imperial sentiment. Dominion ministers and politicians complained of British intransigence: Bennett spoke of getting other Dominion delegates to join in publicly 'condemning the MacDonald Government root and branch', and none had much hope for the Ottawa conference while the Labour government remained in power.[97] Most Conservative leaders had accepted constitutional separation as inevitable, but despaired at a 'heartbreaking loss' of 'an unparalleled opportunity' in economic relations.[98] The King and Stamfordham, obliged by a conference agreement on Governor-Generalships to accept the Australian nominee, thought Labour ministers had been weak and had 'pander[ed] in every way to the Dominions'.[99] Labour ministers had only the consolation that 'the Conference has come to an end but the Empire has not'.[100]

In India the difficulty was even greater, with more fundamental implications for the Empire. Since the Montagu Declaration of 1917 there had been broad acceptance of gradual Indian constitutional reform compatible with continued British control, and genuine consultation between party leaderships on policy essentials. Differences over degree and pace cut across the parties. Until late 1930 the spectrum of opinion among the effective policy-makers, from those wanting the most change to those wanting the least, was as follows: Irwin, the Viceroy and a Conservative, together with Benn, the Labour Secretary of State for India; then MacDonald and

---

[95] For details, Harkness, *Restless Dominion*, 192–9; Holland, *Britain and the Commonwealth Alliance*, 123–5.

[96] MacDonald diary, 13 Nov. 1930; Sankey diary, 14 Oct., 14 Nov. 1930.

[97] N. to H. Chamberlain, 15 Nov. 1930, NC 18/1/717, and see Harkness, *Restless Dominion* 222–3, and Holland, *Britain and the Commonwealth Alliance*, 126.

[98] A. Chamberlain to his wife, 15 Nov. 1930, AC 6/1/771.

[99] Stamfordham to Dawson, 4 Dec. 1930, Dawson papers; and see Crisp, 'Appointment of Sir Isaac Isaacs', and Nicolson, *George V*, 479–82.

[100] Sankey to Hankey, 12 Nov. 1930, in Roskill, *Hankey* II, 529.

Baldwin, then Lloyd George and two other Liberals, Simon, chairman of the 1927–30 Indian Statutory Commission, and Reading, Irwin's predecessor as Viceroy; and finally two Conservative ex-Indian Secretaries, Peel and Austen Chamberlain.

Irwin's Anglo-Catholic and patrician manner conveyed a sincerity and sympathy which impressed many Indians and gave him a British reputation for an inspired ability to manage Indian politicians.[101] He had wide Conservative connections, the 'immense confidence' of Baldwin, and a pivotal supporter in Dawson, editor of *The Times*.[102] Despite belonging to a different party he achieved a remarkable moral authority over Labour ministers, who found his 'wisdom & liberality striking' and formally 'congratulated themselves' that he was Viceroy.[103] All this equipped him to attempt a solution of the dilemma of Indian government: a British-controlled central executive denied adequate collaboration in provincial and central legislatures from Indian politicians with growing nationalist ambitions. The problem had been exacerbated in 1927–8 by resentment at the all-British membership of the Simon Commission, appointed to assess the possibilities for further constitutional reform. Moderate and extremist Indian political leaders had united in boycotting it and drafting their own constitution for a self-governing Indian Dominion. If Dominion status was not conceded by 31 December 1929, the Indian Congress threatened to seek full independence from the Empire through civil disobedience.

For Irwin, the problem was fundamentally 'psychological': the Indian politicians' 'inferiority complex', vanity, and mistrust. His answer was to establish trust, break what he considered to be the 'artificial' nationalist unity, and shift the moderates from resentful subordination to grateful co-operation.[104] To achieve these aims, Irwin had by mid 1929 two related proposals. The first was announcement of a round table conference, drawing British India politicians into the 'liberal method' of consultation on whatever the Simon Commission might recommend, yet simultaneously playing 'the card' of including the Indian princes as a conservative counter-

---

101 E.g., Dawson memo., Feb. 1929 in Wrench, *Dawson*, 271; Lloyd George to Irwin, 6 Aug. 1929, LG G/18/16/2; Benn to G. Stanley, 30 Jan. 1930, Stansgate papers 223/10/366–70.

102 Baldwin in Dawson to Irwin, 8 April 1929, Halifax papers 18/243.

103 MacDonald diary, 17 July 1929, and Cabinet 31(29), 26 July 1929, commenting on meetings while Irwin was on leave in London.

104 Irwin to Baldwin, 28 March 1929, SB 103/20–23, and reported in N. Chamberlain diary, 26 July 1929, and in Amery diary, 30 July 1929 (*LSA* II, 48).

weight.[105] The second was a declaration re-stating the ultimate
purpose of British policy, but replacing Montagu's 'responsible
government' with the term 'Dominion status'. To Irwin the value
of this term was its ambiguity, enabling the various strands of Indian
and British opinion to be knitted together. Indian nationalists and
British Labour would be impressed by its suggestion of ultimate self-
government on equal terms with the white Dominions, and Congress
would be persuaded to continue seeking its aims within the Empire.
Conservatives and Liberals would understand that Indian administrative, communal, strategic, and financial conditions made its
full attainment so distant and probably so impracticable that no
immediate change of real substance was intended.[106] Irwin himself
believed the outcome would be a solution acceptable to Indian
moderate leaders – 'Dominion status with reservations'.[107] He
assumed an early reform in central government, which by
'saddl[ing]' Indians with some 'real responsibility' for certain
departments would force them into close collaboration with British
officials, who would retain control of the key areas of law and order,
defence and foreign policy. It would be a constitutional 'facade'
which left 'the essential mechanism of power still in [British]
hands'.[108]

The Labour Cabinet gratefully embraced Irwin's conference and
declaration proposals as unexpected opportunities to display a major
initiative, and thereafter India was an issue on which the Labour
party remained securely united. Baldwin gave his personal assent
out of trust in Irwin, and a deep sense that some major readjustment
was necessary. But the aim of inducing a 'sedative effect' in India[109]
failed because all miscalculated the effect in Britain. The Liberal and
other Conservative leaders concurred in the proposed conference;
the trouble arose over the declaration. Part of this was about
procedure, since Simon in initially raising no objection and Baldwin
in giving assent had each assumed that the other approved of the
declaration.[110] The objections of substance originated with Reading.

---

[105] Irwin to Baldwin, 23 April 1929, Halifax papers 18/338. For the genesis of Irwin's
initiatives, see Moore, *Crisis of Indian Unity*, 42–59.
[106] Irwin memo, Sept. 1929, Templewood Indian papers 76/70–1; Irwin to Baldwin, 8 Oct.
1929, and memo, SB 103/108–9, 113–14; and see impression given to Salisbury, in Peele,
'A Note on the Irwin Declaration'.
[107] Irwin note, Nov. 1929, Baldwin papers 103/81–6.
[108] Irwin to Ormsby-Gore, 10 Jan. 1929, and to Dawson, 6 May 1929, Halifax papers 18/264,
349; and reported in Amery diary, 30 July 1929 (*LSA* II, 48).
[109] MacDonald to Baldwin, 19 Sept. 1929, SB 103/104–6.
[110] Details in Moore, *Crisis of Indian Unity*, 63–80.

For Reading, the ambiguity of the declaration was a source of danger. He thought Indian politicians would regard it as a change of policy, assume it meant constitutional advance was being accelerated, and, since it contained no explicit reference to conditions and reservations, would expect 'Dominion status' in the full sense of the Balfour Report. Alleviation of current 'temporary difficulties' was being purchased at the cost of 'grave troubles in the future'.[111] Coming from a former Viceroy, these views commanded considerable authority. They convinced Lloyd George and other Liberal leaders to refuse consent to the declaration. They also stiffened the instinctive opposition of Peel, Austen Chamberlain, Churchill, and other leading Conservatives, whom Baldwin was unable to restrain once it became known that the declaration had not received the Simon Commission's approval. Simon, now persuaded and 'much perturbed' by Reading's views, became even more 'rattled' when Baldwin had to withdraw assent, threatening the parliamentary consensus which underpinned his Commission.[112]

Irwin and the Cabinet rejected appeals for postponement from Reading, Lloyd George, Baldwin, and Simon, and the Irwin Declaration was published on 31 October 1929. The results were far-reaching. Among Conservatives and Liberals opposition to major constitutional advance in India hardened, producing unmeasured speeches in Parliament and sharp criticism of Baldwin for initially assenting to the declaration. Continued Conservative participation in the all-party approach to Indian policy plainly hung on the thread of Baldwin retaining his party leadership. In order to paper over the cracks – and assist Baldwin – the Cabinet felt obliged to be publicly explicit where Irwin had wanted silence, in stating that the declaration involved no change of policy.[113] Reading was mollified, while Simon laboured hard to suppress party recriminations and so preserve his Commission. Confidence in Irwin and Benn had, however, been badly shaken.

Confidence was further damaged by the reception of the initiatives in India.[114] Moderate as well as Congress leaders treated the purpose of the round table conference as the drafting of a Dominion constitution, to be implemented immediately. After Irwin denied

---

[111] Reading memo, 1 Oct. 1930, Reading Indian papers E238/57/29; and reported in Irwin note, 8 Oct. 1930, and in Peel to Baldwin, 23 Oct. 1929, SB 103/115–17, 61–2.
[112] Lane-Fox diary, 7, 29, and 30 Oct. 1929; Simon to Benn, 28 Oct. 1929, JRM 344.
[113] MacDonald diary, 10 Nov. 1929, for Baldwin requesting help; Baldwin-MacDonald correspondence, 11 Nov. 1929, JRM 344 (later published).
[114] See Gopal, *Viceroyalty of Irwin*, 50–88, and Moore, *Crisis of Indian Unity*, 98–102, 165–75.

3 The Return of the Indian Statutory Commission: Sir John Simon listening to
an Indian Address of Welcome at Victoria Station, May 1929

this in December, Congress resolved to boycott the conference and
to carry out its threat of civil disobedience in support of
independence. This went too far for moderate leaders, who later
accepted Irwin's invitations to the conference, seeming to fulfil the
Viceroy's hope of the emergence of a powerful moderate party. But
Gandhi's defiance of the Government of India in breaking the salt
laws in April 1930 evoked an enormous popular response for civil
disobedience. By linking the nationalist campaign to the issue of
economic exploitation he tapped many resentments, and the boycott
of British goods inflicted real damage. Soon an imperial nightmare
was being enacted, with widespread disregard for the law, outbreaks
of violence, evidence of communist conspiracy, seizures of arms, and
a loss of control on the North-West Frontier. Irwin and the Labour
Cabinet had to authorise repression, sealed with Gandhi's arrest in
May.

For Simon, the conclusions were obvious: Indian moderate
politicians had no real control, India remained very far from fitted
for full self-government, and the Irwin Declaration was a 'very

foolish...piece of bunkum'.[115] His Report, published in June, proposed full Indian self-government in the provinces, but recommended only a restructuring of the central legislature – with Federation as a distant prospect – and was silent on Dominion status. The provincial proposals enabled Simon to present the Report in liberal clothes, as 'an extremely progressive and advanced document'.[116] Many Conservatives had hesitations about these proposals, but in other respects the Report presented such a contrast to Irwin's and the Labour Cabinet's apparent intentions that it immediately commanded assent from almost all Liberals and Conservatives.

Irwin, however, drew different conclusions. He professed not to understand why his Declaration had aroused such an outcry in London.[117] He continued to believe in the Indian moderates: whatever their rhetoric, in practice they would accept 'Dominion status with safeguards'. As for Congress, its reaction was the result of renewed distrust of British intentions caused by Conservative and Liberal attacks upon his declaration.[118] Moreover, it was conventional Government of India wisdom that repression alone was no remedy, and could actually be counter-productive unless balanced by conciliation. He was appalled by the Simon Report's proposals for central government, which by not allowing Indian responsibility were 'quite unworkable', and at its 'very grave lack of imagination' in failing to mention Dominion Status which he feared would 'provoke an explosion' in India and wreck the proposed round table conference.[119] In order to reassure Indian opinion he sought to bypass the Report. He proposed that it should receive no Cabinet approval, that it should not be the sole agendum for the conference, that the British delegation should be solely ministerial – excluding Simon, all other Liberals, and Conservatives – and that his own declaration should be reiterated.[120]

[115] Simon note of conversation with MacDonald, 1 May 1930, Simon papers; Simon to Garvin, 1 May 1930, Simon Indian papers 24/10–12.

[116] Simon to Buchan, 2 July 1930, Tweedsmuir (Queens) papers.

[117] Irwin to Baldwin, 26 Nov. 1929, SB 103/79–80, attributes the outcry to a conspiracy against the Labour government and Baldwin.

[118] Irwin to Salisbury, 3 Dec. 1929, Halifax papers 18/402a, and material in Moore, *Crisis of Indian Unity*, 108.

[119] Irwin to Hoare, 10 June 1930, Templewood Indian papers 76/83–7; and to Benn, 19 June 1930, Halifax papers 6/33; Moore, *Crisis of Indian Unity*, 108, 115–17.

[120] Irwin reported in A. Chamberlain and Reading memos, June–July 1930, in AC 22/3/27–47, and Reading Indian papers E238/57/54–111.

These proposals, suggesting that Irwin preferred to appease law-breakers rather than accept an all-party parliamentary report, surprised and alarmed Liberal and Conservative leaders when they were consulted by MacDonald and Benn during June and July. Even Baldwin became concerned that Irwin was 'too incredulous of human baseness, & too sanguine of success, to be wholly adequate to the situation'.[121] On Austen Chamberlain's initiative, the Conservative leadership warned Irwin that acceptance of the Simon Report was the only means of avoiding the 'national disaster' of party division over India – although Baldwin made it plain to MacDonald that he rejected Chamberlain's view that the Report should be the sole conference topic. Reading thought Irwin's proposals 'very dangerous', suspected him of aiming to present the conference with a *fait accompli* agreed with Indians, and spoke of responsible government in the centre as 'fatal...because it would lead directly to fighting, bloodshed and perhaps the loss of India'. Simon, Reading, and Chamberlain argued that the safety of India depended on government demonstrating that there was some point at which it would stand firm.[122]

In the event, by threatening resignation[123] Irwin largely got his way. The Cabinet approved a reiteration of his declaration, MacDonald ensured that the conference was not tied exclusively to the Simon Report, and Simon resentfully accepted his own exclusion. But another damaging parliamentary debate revealing policy divergences was avoided only by the Cabinet conceding Conservative and Liberal representation at the conference. The divergences were now, however, substantial and in some cases bitter. Simon, feeling himself tricked and his report ignored, spoke of Irwin as 'incapable of constructive administration' and his policy as having 'utterly broken down'.[124] Reading and Austen Chamberlain had 'grave doubts' about the usefulness of the conference.[125] Irwin regarded Reading as 'reactionary' and Conservative leaders' attitudes as those of a 'super-ostrich'.[126] It was, however, an attitude

---

[121] Henson journal, 25 July 1930.

[122] See A. Chamberlain and Reading memos, June–July 1930, AC/22/3/27–47 and Reading papers E238/57/54–111. For Baldwin, see MacDonald to Irwin, 2 July 1930, Halifax papers 19/89. [123] Irwin to Baldwin, 6 July 1930, AC 22/3/39.

[124] Lady Lee diary, 1 July 1930 (Lee III, 1290); Lane-Fox diary, 29 Oct. 1930; Simon to Runciman, 18 Sept. 1930, Runciman papers 221.

[125] Respectively in Coatman to Irwin, 17 Oct. 1930, Halifax papers 19/149a, and in Henson journal, 30 July 1930.

[126] Irwin to Hoare, 5 Aug. 1930, Templewood Indian papers 76/92–3; and to Benn, 5 July 1930, JRM 344.

which continued to receive reinforcement, and not only from within the Conservative party.

The establishment of a diehard position was advanced from March 1930 by the formation of the Indian Empire Society. Describing itself as 'strictly non-party', its original membership consisted of retired Indian governors, army officers, and civil servants (including Lord Sydenham, Field-Marshal Jacob, General Knox MP, O'Dwyer, and Craddock), some former Conservative Cabinet ministers (Brentford, Carson, and Londonderry) with a sprinkling of Liberal and other Conservative peers and MPs. Its aims for India emphasised the maintenance of law and order and responsibility towards the 'oppressed classes', and its targets were the 'folly' and 'dereliction of duty' in 'raising false hopes'.[127] Resistance also had an obvious economic heartland in Lancashire, where cotton interests already suffering from Indian tariffs and the boycott of British cloth feared that a self-governing India would mean permanent loss of markets.

As the Round Table Conference approached there was ample reason to fear a disintegration of the all-party approach and confrontation between on the one hand Conservative and Liberal delegates, and on the other the Indian representatives. This seemed all the more likely because the Cabinet decided to impose no policy of its own but to act simply as arbiter.[128] For both proponents and opponents of major reform, what seemed at stake was the peace of India and its retention within the Empire. Given the Cabinet's performances at the Imperial Conference and in East African and Palestine policies, Conservative and Liberal politicians might doubt its ability to manage the situation. After Irwin declined an extension of his period of duty, there was certainly reason to doubt the Cabinet's sense when for party reasons it nominated as his replacement a politically obscure and inexperienced Labour peer, Gorell.[129] Ranged against the Labour government were both an increasingly powerful opinion that 'someone has got to stand up to the bowling these dangerous days if we aren't to go down in the East', and an impression, encouraged by the Imperial Conference, that 'the day[s] of the British Raj [were] over'.[130]

---

[127] Indian Empire Society aims, on its notepaper, and Lord Sumner (president) speech, *The Times*, 5 July 1930.　[128] Cabinet 46(30), 30 July 1930.

[129] Irwin to Hoare, 10 June 1930, Templewood Indian papers 76/83–87; Williamson, 'Party First', 87–93.

[130] Lloyd to Keyes, 2 Aug. 1929, in Halpern, *Keyes Papers* II, 259; Maharajah of Bikaner reported in MacDonald diary note, 16 Nov. 1930, JRM 1753.

CHAPTER 3

Government and party troubles

> Politics are in a more queer state than they have been in my day. Never seen such a mix up.
>
> Lloyd George to his wife, 20 February 1930[1]

THE SECOND LABOUR GOVERNMENT

Despite the Labour party's lack of an overall parliamentary majority its leaders agreed to form a government without seeking any arrangement with either of the other parties, and to proceed with the intention of spending at least two years in office.[2] Their ambition of demonstrating a Labour capacity for sustained achievement in government made it appear more desirable than ever to establish self-momentum, especially by resisting Liberal party attempts to use the balance of power to impose its policies. It also precluded alternatives proposed by ILP leaders, that they should either decline office until a socialist absolute majority had been obtained or else immediately introduce socialist measures to challenge 'capitalism' directly at a second election. MacDonald, approved by most Labour MPs, dismissed these ideas as respectively 'cowardly' and 'romantic'.[3] Neither Wheatley nor Jowett were included in the government.

The belief that a minority Labour government could survive largely on its own terms for a substantial period was based upon several calculations. It was thought that Liberal MPs would feel obliged to accept much Labour policy even without formal agreement, and that if Lloyd George did oppose the government on

---

[1] Morgan, *Family Letters*, 210.

[2] MacDonald diary, 1 June 1929, and statement, *The Times*, 3 June 1929; Snowden, *Autobiography* II, 759 (Snowden's suspicion, pp. 757–8, that MacDonald wanted some arrangement with Conservatives, may safely be disregarded).

[3] See account of Parliamentary Labour party meeting in Brockway, *Inside the Left*, 197–9.

non-socialist issues his party might well split to Labour's advantage. There seemed good reasons for believing that a Baldwin-dominated Conservative leadership would not enter into an opposition alliance with Lloyd George.[4] It was assumed that on great national issues there were areas where most MPs desired co-operation irrespective of party feeling, yet without abandoning party commitment – a conventional sentiment, by no means confined to MacDonald with his appeal to the Commons to consider itself a 'Council of State'.[5] Above all, Labour leaders felt confident of remaining in office by showing 'the country, all interests and all classes, that Labour can rule, and can rule successfully'.[6] All this meant that Labour leaders, supported by almost all party members, were content to postpone nationalisation and to achieve what they could within the checks and balances of ordinary parliamentary and government processes, certain that by doing so they could implement many essential 'socialistic' measures and believing that only when these had been accomplished and seen to be universally beneficial would 'socialism' become practicable. Except in rhetoric, few had ever supposed that any other course was possible.

In a mood of great confidence, the Cabinet authorised advances in all domestic departments and major initiatives in foreign and imperial policies. During its first five months it achieved a series of successes in these latter areas which seemed to vindicate Labour's claims to rule. Snowden's defence of Britain's share of reparations at the Hague Conference brought him great non-partisan acclaim, royal approval, and Freedom of the City. MacDonald visited the USA to resolve the naval dispute and restore cordial diplomatic relations, which according to Dalton gave him 'an eternal niche in the temple of history'.[7] Henderson as Foreign Secretary settled evacuation of the Rhineland, re-established relations with the USSR, removed Lord Lloyd and began negotiating an Egyptian treaty, and signed the League of Nations Optional Clause, accepting the principle of arbitration in all international disputes. In domestic affairs, however, the government was already experiencing difficulties in satisfying its supporters' expectations, implementing its

---

[4] For a private Baldwin assurance, confirming general experience, see below p. 119.

[5] *HC Deb*, 229, cols. 64–5, 2 July 1929. The absence of contemporary controversy, almost even of comment, about this statement, demonstrates that it was less novel than its subsequent notoriety suggests. See also below, pp. 142–3.

[6] MacDonald speech, *The Times*, 26 June 1929.

[7] Dalton diary, 1 Nov. 1929 (Dalton, 246).

own chosen policies, and reducing unemployment. From October 1929 successes (such as Greenwood's Pensions Act and Morrison's Road Traffic Act) were fewer, or partial (as with the London Naval Treaty), or precarious (as with India, given Liberal doubts), and these were overshadowed by the difficulties. Economic policies which were making little impression on Britain's own persistent problems now became overwhelmed by the world recession, while Snowden's tightened expenditure regime impeded emergency employment schemes and curtailed social policies. If not altogether impregnable,[8] Snowden's authority on financial questions was firm. But he was not a dictator: he tolerated the EAC and submission of other advice alternative to that of the Treasury. Rather, MacDonald, Thomas, and other key ministers shared or reached similar positions on national finance to those of Snowden, while the rest of the Cabinet, however much they 'hate[d]' his refusal of specific expenditures, considered that in general 'his logic seem[ed] unanswerable'.[9]

The central problem was unemployment. The government's original unemployment committee not merely failed to reduce unemployment: its members drew opposite conclusions from the experience.[10] Road, home, and colonial development works were greatly increased, mostly on a grant-aided basis, to an extent which Treasury officials had previously considered inadvisable. But Thomas, co-ordinating employment policy as Lord Privy Seal, soon decided that these and the party's other immediate remedies of early retirement pensions and increased school-leaving age could have little effect upon aggregate unemployment and might aggravate the problem by increasing the tax burden on production. Increasingly demoralised, he turned instead to the long-term remedies of assisting export revival, especially through industrial rationalisation. In contrast his assistants, Lansbury, Johnston, and Mosley, wanted more vigorous implementation of public works and other short-term remedies. Believing substantial export revival unlikely, Mosley in January 1930 proposed drastic administrative intervention and a Keynes/Lloyd George-style £200m. public loan for home development.

[8] For Snowden having to concede extension of the road-building programme in May 1930, see Janeway, thesis 'Economic Policy of Second Labour Government', 49. For unemployment insurance, see below, pp. 100–1.

[9] Lansbury to Mosley, 25 Sept. 1929, Lansbury papers 19.d.177.

[10] Details in Skidelsky, *Politicians*, 91–109, 167–82, 400–7.

Opposition to Mosley came not only from Snowden and the Treasury, but from other ministers associated with employment. Morrison, for instance, in stepping-up trunk road schemes had 'no complaint against the Treasury', but was impressed by the genuine practical and administrative obstacles to rapid action.[11] Mosley resigned after his programme was rejected in May. But the political damage of the government's inability to halt soaring unemployment was such that MacDonald was obliged to move Thomas, take personal charge of a new unemployment policy machinery, and order increased road-building and renewed attention to other public work schemes.[12]

These changes were essentially cosmetic. By mid 1930 MacDonald and the Cabinet doubted that much employment could be created so long as the world recession continued. In effect, the Mosley dispute and reassessment of public works resulted simply in more ministers learning what Thomas had already discovered. By June 1930, with unemployment almost at two million, government-assisted public works had at a cost of £44·3m. directly employed just 61,165 persons.[13] Oblivious in the face of overwhelming departmental counter-advice to Keynes's notion of home development as a device to reflate the whole economy; looking only at the immediate, limited, employment effects and so seeing no cause for an administrative revolution which it in any case lacked the political authority to attempt, the Cabinet interpreted these results as proof that the idea of public works as an unemployment 'cure' was 'humbug...superficial and ill-considered'.[14] Independently of Snowden and the Treasury, the new policy machinery concluded that any spectacular initiative by development loan or abandonment of the economic tests for work schemes would be self-defeating – a 'disastrous...shock to confidence'.[15] In September, with some £140m. worth of schemes approved, the Cabinet accepted the conclusion of Thomas's successor, Hartshorn, that there was little scope for new public works proposals. All that seemed possible was

---

[11] Morrison in Jones, *Whitehall Diary* II, 257, 19 May 1930. For the dispute over the 'Mosley memorandum' (CP31(30), 23 Jan. 1930) see Skidelsky, *Mosley*, 193–220. For Mosley's politics see below, pp. 145–9. [12] See Skidelsky, *Politicians*, 193–8.

[13] See Middleton, 'The Treasury and Public Investment', 361: assuming secondary effects, this figure might be raised to 183, 495.

[14] MacDonald to Newbold, 2 June 1930, in Marquand, 538, and see Cabinet 26(30), 8 May 1930.

[15] Anderson (head of unemployment policy secretariat) to MacDonald, and MacDonald to Anderson, 30 and 31 July 1930, JRM 462.

to accelerate implementation of already approved schemes. But obtaining this from local authorities remained a persistent problem, and the results were expected to be slight and temporary.[16]

Yet if public works appeared to offer little, industrial rationalisation involved the risks of difficulties with trade unions and more unemployment in the short term. Nevertheless it seemed essential to restore export competitiveness. Thomas, like Snowden, had thought that both to evade criticism from government supporters and to secure the necessary finance without budget and parliamentary complications, the most effective agencies to promote rationalisation were the Bank of England and BIDCo. Legislation was used only for the coal industry, where the government was committed to repeal the Eight Hours Act. But to reduce hours and regulate production without precipitating another ruinous confrontation between miners and owners over wage levels and organisation involved hard-won compromises. The results were prolonged parliamentary difficulties and recurrent disputes within the industry. Ministerial committees on the cotton and iron and steel industries proposed rationalisation schemes in summer 1930, but advance was obstructed in the first by pay and conditions disputes, and in the second by the owners' preference for protection. Frustration at the slow progress persuaded Graham and Attlee, Mosley's successor, that the government should take powers to impose rationalisation. But to Snowden, MacDonald, and Thomas it seemed obvious that this would provoke withdrawal of Bank of England assistance and City finance, and cause formidable parliamentary resistance. It was also obvious that, however achieved, rationalisation could make little impression on employment until world markets recovered.[17]

Other suggested employment policies included land settlement, reclamation, and food-import substitution. But success here was impeded by agriculture itself being in severe depression, while the Cabinet had great problems deciding upon an agricultural policy. The collapse of the agricultural experts conference wrecked an early opportunity for agreement with the agricultural community, and it was not until August 1930 that the Cabinet announced its own programme. This proposed action on agricultural marketing, small-holdings, allotments, land utilisation, and rural housing – a package

[16] Hartshorn, 'Unemployment Policy', CP293(30), 18 Aug. 1930; Cabinets 56, 70(30), 25 Sept., 26 Nov. 1930.
[17] MacDonald diary, 24 June, 14 Aug. 1930; Hartshorn, 'Unemployment Policy', CP293(30), 18 Aug. 1930.

which in the absence of other initiatives was offered from September as a new contribution to unemployment policy.[18] But on the main problem of the unprofitability of cereal-growing it merely postponed decision until the Imperial Conference economic deliberations. The delays arose chiefly because the agriculture ministers, Buxton and Addison, like the agricultural community, believed that no programme could succeed without some form of import control. Agriculture therefore raised in acute form the issue which also offered a possible way out of the impasse in industrial and employment policies, a device for strengthening the Empire, and a means of easing the budget problem.

Free trade was part of the baggage which the Labour party inherited from nineteenth-century radicalism. It had been considered essential for obtaining cheap food and decent real wages for the working classes and for maintaining international peace, and since 1918 had become a policy for restoring the world economy and recovering British export markets. Accordingly between September 1929 and February 1930 Graham negotiated through the League of Nations an international tariff truce, while Snowden announced that the safeguarding duties would lapse. The recession, however, had as persuasive an impact upon some Labour ministers as it did upon TUC leaders and City financiers. For these the preservation of domestic production, the chance of larger imperial markets, the maintenance or creation of employment, and the political advantage of major initiatives hitched to the protectionist bandwagons among most economic interests, seemed more pressing Labour objectives. From late 1929 Thomas, MacDonald, and Hartshorn were in turn converted to industrial protection.[19] In February 1930 MacDonald proposed a registration fee on grain imports, and from April Buxton and Addison were stubborn advocates of cereal quotas.[20] In June and August MacDonald, Thomas, Addison, and Hartshorn obtained Cabinet postponements of ratification of Graham's tariff truce.[21] From July MacDonald thought deteriorating budget prospects might force protection through the backdoor, and tried out the idea

---

[18] Snowden statement, *HC Deb*, 242, cols. 890–3, 1 Aug. 1930; MacDonald to Lloyd George, 12 Sept. 1930, PREM 1/108; MacDonald speech, 7 Oct. 1930, *LPACR 1930*, 183–4.

[19] Thomas in Amery diary, 4 Dec. 1929 (*LSA* II, 56–7) and in MacDonald diary, 22 Dec. 1929; MacDonald in Jones, *Whitehall Diary* II, 235, 14 Jan. 1930; Hartshorn, 'Unemployment Policy', CP293(30), 18 Aug. 1930, and in Dalton diary, 29 Oct. 1930.

[20] MacDonald to Snowden, Graham, Buxton, Addison, 24 Feb. 1930, JRM 244; Buxton, and Addison, to MacDonald, both 17 April 1930, JRM 243, 676.

[21] Cabinets 33, 49(30), 24 June, 6 Aug. 1930.

of a revenue tariff on Snowden and other ministers.[22] Addison and
Thomas both sought to use the Imperial Conference to push the
Cabinet into acceptance of import control.[23]

Here, then, was one area where Snowden came under sustained
challenge. Nevertheless he was able to exercise a Cabinet veto,
commanding support not just from Graham but Alexander,
Parmoor, Passfield, Shaw, Trevelyan, Benn, Clynes, and Henderson,[24] reinforced by general recognition that apostasy from free trade
was an immensely sensitive and difficult issue which would divide
junior ministers and backbench MPs. MacDonald could not force
the issue or remove Snowden without precipitating a Cabinet and
party crisis; in anxious financial conditions the acrimonious
departure of a Chancellor of the Exchequer, on whatever issue,
might damage national credit and business confidence. Snowden
was therefore able with 'hard dogmatism' to savage every proposed
import control. He forced tariff truce ratification through the
Cabinet in September.[25] Under pressure during the Imperial
Conference, he became 'impossible & obstinate' to the embarrassment of the whole Cabinet; even other free-trade ministers found
his threat to resign over a trivial issue incomprehensible.[26]

In October, with the Cabinet deadlocked over import controls
and the Imperial Conference yielding no tangible economic benefits,
with agricultural and industrial policies denied hope of early
stimulus and public works having negligible effect upon the
unemployment figures, with the Committee of Economists also
deadlocked and no early international action apparently possible,
ministers felt as if their 'heads were up against a brick wall'.[27] For
months they had excused themselves by arguing that the economic
problem had been transformed by causes beyond British control and
was now of 'a totally new character' to that existing when they had
taken office: rising unemployment was not their fault.[28] This was

[22] MacDonald diary, 22 July, 14 Aug., 16 Oct. 1930; MacDonald reported in Snowden,
Autobiography II, 923, and by Alexander in B. Webb diary, 21 Sept. 1930.
[23] For Thomas, Cabinet 36(30), 7 July 1930, and CP366(30), 27 Oct. 1930; for Addison,
speeches in *The Times*, 25 Aug., 15 Sept. 1930, and CP307(30), 15 Sept. 1930.
[24] See Alexander's list of 'ten stalwarts' in B. Webb diary, 21 Sept. 1930.
[25] MacDonald diary, 29 April 1930; Cabinet 50(30), 2 Sept. 1930; Snowden to MacDonald,
4 Sept. 1930, JRM 676.
[26] Sankey diary, 15 Oct. 1930; Henderson note, 16 Oct. 1930, JRM 1753; MacDonald diary,
passim for Oct. 1930; Cabinet 65(30) and committee notes, 29 Oct. 1930, in CAB 23/65;
P. J. Grigg, *Prejudice and Judgment*, 236–7.   [27] MacDonald diary, 9 Oct. 1930.
[28] E.g., Lansbury speech, *The Times*, 24 May 1930; MacDonald interview, *Daily Herald*,
6 June 1930; Hartshorn, *HC Deb*, 244, col. 162, 29 Oct. 1930.

true, but politically barren. It was of hardly more use saying that unemployment could be cured only under 'socialism',[29] since the Cabinet had no influence over foreign capitalists, the British electorate remained unconverted, and current conditions seemed to preclude a Labour government performance which might convert those voters. The Cabinet, apparently, could only persist with existing, patently inadequate, measures, and await a revival of economic activity. This made other ministers as concerned as Snowden with the condition of business confidence, with – for socialists – some ironic effects. MacDonald, for instance, complained during October that capitalist industrial leaders were showing insufficient enterprise.[30]

Inability to halt rising unemployment, Snowden's financial warnings, and concern about business confidence converged in October 1930 to make unemployment insurance a major Cabinet problem. It had been a difficulty from the beginning, especially since apart from financial worries ministers held an important idea in common with Conservatives, Liberals and, indeed, with much progressive opinion, as represented for instance by Beveridge and Cole.[31] While as socialists they wanted collective state assistance for those who under capitalism suffered deprivation through no fault of their own, they wanted equally to sustain individual self-help as the stimulus to that self-reliance and self-respect which socialism aimed to make available to all. Socialism did not mean public charity: it meant rescuing the poor from all dependency. In such terms provision of non-contributory transitional payments – always intended as a temporary expedient – alongside contributory benefits seemed anomalous and inequitable, threatening to demoralise those paying contributions and to discredit the whole system. Ministers also accepted the desirability of restoring the Insurance Fund to solvency, ending its need to borrow. Yet Labour party policy was to increase benefits, relax disallowance regulations, and make the system universal. The ultimate Labour party and TUC solution, financing the whole system from taxation, seemed impossible in current parliamentary and economic conditions. In July and

[29] Lansbury speech, *The Times*, 24 May 1930; MacDonald speech, *Manchester Guardian*, 27 May 1930.
[30] MacDonald to Runciman, 1 Oct. 1930, Runciman papers 225; to Balfour, 2 Oct. 1930, JRM 273, and speech, *The Times*, 7 Oct. 1930.
[31] See Harris, *Beveridge*, 353–7, and for Cole, Skidelsky, *Politicians*, 236–7.

October 1929 Snowden helped by increasing Exchequer contributions to the Fund and accepting transitional payments as a direct charge upon the budget. But under his expenditure restraint in late 1929 the Cabinet postponed increase of standard benefit payments and extension of insurance to agricultural workers, and it was only under intense party pressure that it conceded full abolition of the old disallowance test.[32]

Thereafter, the issue became whether existing unemployment payments could be preserved. From first taking office Margaret Bondfield as Minister of Labour feared that the system would escape all financial control, and repeatedly pressed the Cabinet to impose strict limits. She opposed abolition of claimants' responsibility to prove eligibility for benefits, and subsequently believed this had allowed substantial 'abuse' both by claimants (those who were not normally part of the workforce, including many married women) and by employers (those exploiting the system to organise short-time employment), with the result that the unemployment totals were artificially increased. In March she had to resort to a £10m. increase in the Unemployment Fund's borrowing powers, to a total of £50m. In July, with expenditure out of control and mounting Conservative and Liberal parliamentary criticism, she suggested a means test or transference of transitional claimants to local public assistance, the 'poor law'. All she obtained was another £10m. increase in borrowing, to a £60m. total. In October she proposed measures to prevent 'abuse' and among several possible solutions for the financial problem mentioned a cut in benefit rates to be justified by the fall in living costs.[33] By then MacDonald and Thomas as well as Snowden also believed that the cost and numbers of the unemployed had become excessively inflated, and agreed that some form of drastic action was financially and politically necessary.[34]

For most Cabinet members, however, the principle of 'work or adequate maintenance' was a fundamental party and moral commitment, making a means test or transference to the poor law highly objectionable and benefit cuts inconceivable. There was also dispute about the extent of 'abuse'. Henderson was particularly

---

[32] Cabinets 40, 43(30), 22 and 30 Oct. 1930.

[33] Bondfield to Snowden, 20 Sept. 1930, CAB 21/325; Bondfield, 'Unemployment Insurance', CP318(30), 10 Oct. 1930. For the Ministry of Labour as 'heroic' and Bondfield as 'consistent and courageous', see Lowe, *Adjusting to Democracy*, 134–5, 143–4, 152–4.

[34] MacDonald diary, 16 Oct. 1930; EAC 8th and 9th meetings, 11 Sept., 7 Nov. 1930. Generally, see Deacon, *In Search of the Scrounger*, 69–79.

emphatic in reminding ministers of party commitments.[35] Consequently the Cabinet simply failed to face up to the problem. It remained committed to 'sound finance' and a solvent Insurance Fund, but there was no agreement on how to accomplish these and decision was repeatedly postponed. Persuading the House of Commons to accept the increases in the Fund's borrowing powers and extensions of transitional arrangements was increasingly difficult, but was achieved in July by appointment of an all-party committee and in October – when another £10m. was obtained, increasing borrowing to £70m. – of the Royal Commission.

The intractability of economic and financial problems was not the only cause of ministerial lack of achievement. The Cabinet handicapped itself simply by trying to do too much. It was overburdened by business, the parliamentary timetable was repeatedly congested, and some legislation was ill-prepared or had to be postponed.[36] The Cabinet blamed much of the congestion upon parliamentary procedure, and in June decided to refer the problem to a Select Committee.[37] On the other hand, congestion of business became a useful excuse for postponing contentious issues, notably repeal of the Trade Disputes Act to which Liberals were hostile, and raising the school-leaving age, which involved new expenditure and the sensitive matter of assistance to denominational schools.

Postponements, incomplete implementation, or abandonment of party policies and failure to reduce unemployment caused bewilderment and anger within the Labour party. Relations between the Cabinet and some parts of the movement became badly strained. TUC leaders resented the ministerial attitude that the TUC was a 'sectional' interest towards which a Cabinet with 'national' responsibilities had to remain aloof, and was especially annoyed with its failure to consult them on industrial legislation.[38] There was no

---

[35] Dalton diary, 6 Nov. 1930 (Pimlott, 126).

[36] Jones to Bickersteth, 23 Dec. 1929, in Jones, *Whitehall Diary* II, 229; for congestion, Cabinets 53, 55(29), 17 and 23 Dec. 1929, and Cabinets 2, 10, 11, 12, 24, 32, 33, 41, 44, 53(30), 15 Jan., 12, 19, and 26 Feb., 30 April, 7 May, 4, 18, and 24 June, 16 and 23 July, 18 Sept. 1930. The number of bills both introduced and passed by this minority government during the 1929–30 session had been surpassed since 1918 only during the first session of the 1924 Conservative government, which had a massive majority: see D. Butler and J. Freeman, *British Political Facts* (1969 edn), 124.

[37] Cabinets 31, 32, 33(30), 4, 18, and 24 June 1930. The Select Committee on procedure was appointed in late November.

[38] For rejection of consultations, Henderson in Citrine notes, 'Cabinet making, 5 June 1929', Citrine papers I/7/8; Snowden, *Autobiography* II, 762; Cabinet 3(30) and Jones, *Whitehall*

contact between ministers and the General Council's increasingly crucial economic committee. Trade union MPs led the parliamentary party's successful agitation on the unemployment insurance disallowance test in late 1929, and TUC leaders bluntly expressed to ministers their dissatisfaction with unemployment policy.[39] The General Council, furious at the repeated postponements, pressed for Trade Disputes Act repeal through a re-formed Trade Union Group of some 150 MPs, and through the Labour National Executive and party conference. ILP leaders, annoyed by Wheatley's exclusion from the Cabinet,[40] were from the outset critical over a wide range of policy and from December 1929 abstained or voted against the government on unemployment insurance and other sensitive issues. By October 1930 they formed a group of seventeen MPs insistent upon rights of independence from Labour party discipline.[41] This added considerably to the government's parliamentary insecurity. From May Mosley formed another small group of parliamentary critics, and attempted to use the extra-parliamentary party to impose his policies upon the Cabinet.

To some extent these pressures could be ignored or contained. The TUC, the ILP, and Mosley's group were mutually antipathetic. Almost all other Labour MPs shared the Cabinet's deep resentment at the ILP's 'assumption of a special righteousness', and together with the National Executive co-operated in Henderson's efforts as party secretary to enforce the parliamentary party's standing orders.[42] Mosley was widely distrusted as an upper-class political adventurer, and was easily outmanoeuvred by Henderson within the parliamentary party.[43] But despite the whole Cabinet's dislike of the TUC General Council's 'arrogant claim[s]',[44] it was compelled to include Trade Disputes Act repeal in its parliamentary programme in October 1930. Criticisms from all three groups aggravated

Diary II, 236, both 16 Jan. 1930. For resentment, 'Report of Discussion in General Council', 22 Jan. 1930, Citrine papers III/1/13.

[39] TUCGC, 7 Nov. 1929; Hayday and 52 other MPs to PLP consultative committee [Nov. 1929], and Thorne (for Trade Union parliamentary group) to MacDonald, 3 Dec. 1929, both JRM 440. Bevin to MacDonald, 27 Aug. 1930, JRM 461.

[40] Wise reported in Garvin to Astor, 10 June 1930, Astor papers.

[41] See Middlemas, *The Clydesiders*, 236–47, especially for Clydeside purge of the ILP parliamentary group.

[42] Snell (chairman, PLP consultative committee) to MacDonald, 31 March 1930, JRM 1175; Dalton diary, 20 May 1930 (Pimlott, 111). For prolonged negotiations, see LPNEC from May 1930, and *LPACR 1931*, 293–6.

[43] For accounts of PLP meeting, see Skidelsky, *Politicians*, 185–6, and Dalton diary, 22 May 1930 (Pimlott, 112–14).

[44] Passfield memo on 1931 crisis [Sept. 1931], Passfield papers 26:34.

existing uneasiness throughout the Labour party. Ultimately party loyalty, recognition of economic and parliamentary difficulties, disbelief in ILP and Mosley alternatives, and the desire to deny office to the other parties kept discontent in check. But ministers were subjected to streams of complaint from the parliamentary party, the NEC and party committees on unemployment, education, agriculture, and industrial legislation. The near success of a Mosleyite motion at the party conference in October was understood not to be a vote for Mosley but an expression of discontent with government unemployment policy:[45] yet it was no less serious for that.

Ministers who had intended to achieve much in government had unexpectedly been faced with a real test of capacity to govern, and found the experience painful and demoralising. Labour watchwords, like 'work or maintenance', were discovered to involve embarrassment in practice. Policies proclaimed in opposition crumbled or seemed inappropriate in office. Sensitive socialist consciences were strained. Party criticisms shamed some ministers; others were annoyed that their problems were insufficiently appreciated. Several ministers were inadequate or difficult. Buxton was allowed to retire, Thomas was moved, Passfield's responsibilities were curtailed. Bondfield was tactless in sensitive dealings with the party. Trevelyan could not carry education business through the Cabinet (though he blamed obstruction by MacDonald). Ministerial representation in the Lords was weak in numbers and ability: Parmoor's performances as leader were lamentable. Resignation was resorted to only by Mosley, but Lansbury and Johnston thought about joining him,[46] and at various times Thomas, Parmoor, Snowden, Graham, and several junior ministers threatened to resign.[47] MacDonald made some changes in June 1930, but thought the party lacked sufficient

---

[45] The vote was 1,046,000 for consideration of Mosley's programme, 1,251,000 against: see Skidelsky, *Mosley*, 229–31. Beatrice Webb's often-quoted question, 'Has MacDonald found his superseder in OM?', was rhetorical and followed by reservations which showed she thought not: B. Webb diary, 29 May 1930 (Cole, 243–4; MacKenzie iv, 217–18), and similarly 14 Oct. 1930. Ministerial private papers give no sign that Mosley was considered a threat.

[46] MacDonald diary, 12 Dec. 1929. For MacDonald success in separating these two from Mosley, see Jones, *Whitehall Diary* ii, 256–60, 13, 19, 20 May 1930, and Dalton diary, 20–1 May 1930 (Pimlott, 110, 111).

[47] For Thomas, MacDonald diary, 17 Nov., 22 Dec. 1929, and Thomas–MacDonald correspondence, 19 and 21 Feb. 1930, Thomas papers U1625/c101–2. For Parmoor, B. Webb diary, 13 Aug. 1929 (Cole, 214), Dalton diary, 21–2 Aug. 1929, and Parmoor to MacDonald, 20 Sept. 1930, JRM 676. For Snowden, above p. 98. For Graham, MacDonald diary, 18 Nov. 1930. Other threats came from Susan Lawrence, Arnold, and Russell.

ministerial talent to allow major reconstruction. Some junior ministers were annoyed at this failure to take them at their own estimation.[48] MacDonald over-worked himself and provided little inspiration or cohesion; he was bad-tempered with complainants, tended to 'scold' backbenchers, and became aloof from most ministers. Yet he was thought to be too attached to Thomas.[49] With that exception, the frictions between MacDonald, Henderson, Snowden, and Thomas – the staple of Labour high politics – received further edge from MacDonald's initial attempt to exclude Henderson from the Foreign Office and patent lack of confidence in his conduct of policy, from Thomas's failure as unemployment minister, and from differences over protection and unemployment insurance. Graham replaced Clynes in the big five leadership, yet MacDonald considered him 'small and weak'. If the government's position had been stronger, he might have accepted Snowden's and Graham's resignations.[50] These ministerial tensions, sensed by Labour MPs and journalists, stimulated unsettling rumours of 'splits' and 'plots'.[51]

In October and November 1930, ministers already considering themselves overworked were faced by another overcrowded parliamentary timetable and the burden of the Imperial and Indian Conferences.[52] Divided one way over protection and another over unemployment benefit, apparently powerless to reduce or contain unemployment, and with a 'Jewish hurricane' blowing over Palestine policy, the Cabinet was 'at sixes and sevens'.[53] In prospect were a sharp winter increase in unemployment, a difficult budget, ILP revolts, and parliamentary difficulties over the Trade Union bill. The government's weak standing was reflected in poor by-election and municipal election results. In existing circumstances, escape by means of Cabinet resignation or parliamentary dissolution would be humiliating, was likely to result in a Labour electoral rout,

---

[48] There was particular trouble in October 1930, when Amulree was brought from outside the government to become Air minister after Thomson was killed in the R101 crash: Arnold, Ponsonby, and Russell all complained. Morrison repeatedly asked for promotion to the cabinet.

[49] See, e.g., MacDonald to Arnold, 31 Oct., 1930, JRM 676; Picton-Turbervill, *Life Has Been Good*, 178, 224; B. Webb diary, 23 Sept. 1929, 28 July, 7 Aug., 23 Nov. 1930.

[50] MacDonald diary, 28 Oct., 18 Nov. 1930.

[51] See Marquand, 576–7, and Dalton diary, 8 Nov. 1930 (Pimlott, 127).

[52] For complaints, Alexander in B. Webb diary, 21 Sept. 1930; Sankey diary, passim for Oct.–Nov. 1930; MacDonald diary, 19 Oct. 1930.

[53] Sankey diary, 17 and 19 Oct., 5 Nov. 1930: for Palestine, Passfield to B. Webb, 22, 27, and 28 Oct. 1930, Passfield papers II:3:(1):86–113, 115–16.

and might destroy what remained of Labour's credibility as a party of government.

The obvious course was to cling to office in the hope of surviving long enough to take advantage of any recovery in the world economy. This meant that something definite would now have to be done about strengthening the government's parliamentary position. During the 1929–30 session it had been defeated once on important detail, and several times only just escaped defeat on matters of confidence. The calculation that no Conservative–Lloyd George alliance would materialise had proved correct, and the position was eased by Conservative preoccupation with internal party disputes. But less came of the hopes of all-party co-operation: that on India was uncertain; the committee on unemployment insurance collapsed, and invitations in May for all-party consultations on agriculture and unemployment insurance were rejected by Conservative leaders. Despite MacDonald's encouragement to Liberal Council leaders,[54] Liberal party divisions had so far been insufficient to neutralise its possession of the balance of power. Once Coal and Unemployment Insurance Bills had first made parliamentary defeat a threat in December 1929, Lloyd George had been able to force ministers into negotiation on controversial legislation.

In an initial attempt to keep Liberals quiet the Cabinet agreed in July 1929 to an all-party committee on electoral practices, but without intending to allow any reform which might help them. In order to save the Coal Bill, however, leading ministers had in March 1930 to promise introduction of an electoral reform bill. Henderson was the most and MacDonald the least[55] willing to make arrangements with the Liberals: but all ministers concerned shared the desire to obtain Liberal parliamentary support at the smallest possible cost. They prolonged the negotiations and then offered only the alternative vote, considered less harmful to Labour interests than the Liberal demand of proportional representation. Even so, Henderson excepted, there was no regret when in May Labour National Executive opposition forced abandonment of the pro-

[54] MacDonald diary, 3 Dec. 1929, for Maclean and Runciman; and Beechman to Runciman, 18 Dec. 1929, Runciman papers 224, for MacDonald hoping for parliamentary co-operation with Liberal Council MPs.

[55] E.g., MacDonald diary, 18 March 1930, and memos, 4 Feb. 1930 and April or May 1930, JRM 1305, 1300, for opposition to electoral reform as an abandonment of Labour ambitions to replace Liberalism. See also Marquand, 526–33, 545–7, 564–8.

posal.[56] As Lloyd George then accepted the invitation to consultations on agriculture and unemployment, talks proceeded from June through the summer recess. But MacDonald, Snowden, Hartshorn, Addison, and Morrison did not expect that Lloyd George could help them with ideas; they no more believed in his unemployment programme now than they had done before the election.[57] For them the purpose of the consultations was to demonstrate that he had nothing practicable to offer, and that if he was serious about unemployment his only course was to support government proposals. By September, they believed this policy debate had been won.[58]

However, the approach of the parliamentary session, TUC pressure to repeal the Trade Disputes Act, and threats by Lloyd George made it increasingly difficult to string Liberals along without definite concessions. In August, it was agreed that Liberal leaders should be consulted before policies, bills, and parliamentary business were announced.[59] In September, the Cabinet authorised renewed negotiations on electoral reform.[60] In late October Lloyd George was consulted on the contents of the King's Speech, and at his insistence the promise of an electoral reform bill was added to it.[61]

These arrangements with Lloyd George were kept secret, in order to avoid difficulties with Labour party members liable to be literal about the party's independence, and who hated or distrusted Lloyd George, if not the whole Liberal party. The Cabinet tried to persuade itself that there was no 'general understanding'[62] and that it retained substantial freedom. Nevertheless, though unacknowledged and begrudged, it had been cornered into collaboration with

---

[56] LPNEC, 20 May 1930; MacDonald diary, 21 May 1930; and Dalton diary, 20 and 21 May 1930 (Pimlott, 109, 112). Fair, 'Politics of Electoral Reform', 287, erroneously states that the alternative vote was accepted.

[57] For ministerial reluctance to send papers and arrange meetings, and failure to give notice of their agricultural policy statement, see Lloyd George to MacDonald, 22 Aug., 23 Oct. 1930, PREM 1/108. For disbelief, Hartshorn-MacDonald exchange, 18 and 19 Aug. 1930, JRM 472.

[58] MacDonald to Hartshorn, 22 Sept. 1930, JRM 1308.

[59] Lothian note, 27 Aug. 1930, Lothian papers, 251/502-3; for parliamentary business, Hutchison to Lloyd George, 1 Oct. 1930, LG G/10/9/10, and Kennedy to MacDonald, 3 Oct. 1930, JRM 376; for bills, Cabinet 65(30), 29 Oct. 1930. For examples of consultation, Snowden, Trevelyan, and Bondfield in Cabinet 68(30), 17 Nov. 1930.

[60] 'Note of Discussion at Cabinet meeting', 25 Sept. 1930, CAB 23/90B; Snowden, Autobiography II, 883-5.

[61] MacDonald diary, 20 Oct. 1930; Cabinet 62(30), 22 Oct. 1930. See also Lothian to MacDonald, 21 Oct. 1930, JRM 378, sending a promised drafting proposal (unused) for the King's Speech.   [62] Cabinet 68(30), 17 Nov. 1930.

the Liberal party and concession to its electoral interests. The Labour party's central strategic commitment to party independence and the supersession of Liberalism, like the fundamental policy commitments to 'work and maintenance' and free trade, were now under serious threat.

LIBERALS AND THE BALANCE OF POWER

For Liberals, the meaning of the 1929 election result was ambiguous and yielded conflicting interpretations. Fifty-nine MPs seemed a poor return for the effort and expenditure of the previous two and a half years. To the NLF executive, it had been a 'lost battle'.[63] Many Liberals again became despondent about the party's future. Asquithians reverted to type and consoled themselves with a belief that Lloyd George had finally been discredited.[64] Sourness from them was only to be expected. But Jowitt's defection to the Labour government, Keynes's and H. D. Henderson's to the EAC, and various Liberal candidates to either Labour or Conservative, were even clearer expressions of disillusionment.

Lloyd George, Samuel, Simon, Sinclair, and other party leaders, however, found compensations and ground for optimism in the result. This was not simply a matter of making the best of the situation: their expectations had been lower than those of most party members, and their objectives had been substantially achieved. The Liberal party had obtained almost a quarter of the popular vote and regained the parliamentary balance of power. In similar terms to those of Asquith after the 1923 election, Lloyd George asserted privately as much as publicly that the increased poll was a 'remarkable achievement', showing that Liberals had 'very formidable support' in the country. 'There [was] not the slightest danger of the Party being wiped out.' Both 'Toryism and Socialism [had] been emphatically repudiated...by overwhelming majorities'; the 'mandate of the nation' was in reality a 'Liberal mandate'. The Liberal party's 'bargaining position [was] impregnable', the 'course of events in...Parliament [would] largely depend on [its] action',

---

[63] Wilson, *Downfall of the Liberal Party*, 348. For result interpreted as a defeat, see also Bentley, *Liberal Mind*, 114–16, and Thorpe, *British General Election*, 48–9.

[64] Lambert, and Runciman, to Gladstone, 3 June, 4 July 1929, Gladstone papers 46086/207, 214–15; Maclean, and Phillipps, to Gladstone, both 5 June 1929, ibid. 46474/211, 46475/312–13.

and it had a high proportion of talented and experienced MPs able
to provide 'the intellectual lead'.[65] That more Liberal MPs had not
been returned seemed in one sense a source of strength, for the large
disparity between the popular support and the parliamentary
representation for the Liberal party demonstrated that the electoral
system was a 'pure stultification of democracy'. Electoral reform was
now established as a major public issue.[66]

From this interpretation of the election result, Lloyd George drew
two conclusions. Firstly, under existing electoral arrangements it was
futile to continue financing the Liberal party on the scale of a major
party. Despite the uncertain parliamentary position he allowed his
subsidies to the party organisation to lapse, in order to force it to
become self-sufficient.[67] Muir, who became party chairman following Samuel's return to Parliament, soon made complaints
against the Lloyd George Fund similar to those of his Asquithian
predecessors before 1927, and pleaded inadequate finance to
maintain the electoral machine and candidatures.[68] But Lloyd
George remained unmoved, for his second conclusion was that to be
certain of obtaining electoral reform, either in the present or a
succeeding parliament, it was still more imperative than previously
that the balance of power should be used to achieve definite alliance
with another party. In looking to Liberal party survival, he now
'pinned his faith on electoral [re]form & future coalition'.[69]

The problem was that his electoral objective had not been
completely fulfilled. Even with the balance of power, a Liberal party
with under sixty MPs had less conviction as a parliamentary force
than it would have had with eighty or 100 MPs. Given the hostility

---

[65] Lloyd George to St. Davids, 13 June 1929, LG G/17/6/10, and reported in Garvin to
Astor, 5 June 1929, Astor papers; speeches, *The Times*, 14 June 1929 and *NLF Proceedings
1929*, 23–4, 4 Oct. See also Scott to Samuel, 10 July 1929, Samuel papers A/155/VII/145,
agreeing that 'Liberalism has conquered the country'; and Sinclair in Lockhart diary, 15
July 1929, in Young 1, 97.

[66] Lloyd George speech, *The Times*, 14 June 1929, and statement, *Manchester Guardian*, 1 June
1929. See also Simon to Irwin, 6 June 1929, Simon Indian papers 5/56–8, and article, *The
Sunday Times*, 9 June 1929; and Freeden, *Liberalism Divided*, 121, for electoral reform being
the dominant issue at the 1929 Liberal Summer School.

[67] The 1927–9 election subsidy ceased with the election. Lloyd George offered only to transfer
an unspecified sum for the next election to a committee chaired by Reading: Reading to
Grey, 10 Oct. 1929, Reading papers F118/127. Grants to party headquarters were
reduced, then stopped in June 1930: see Thorpe, *British General Election*, 57–8.

[68] Muir to Lloyd George, 23 July, 3 Dec. 1929, Lloyd George papers G/15/6/12, 16.

[69] Lloyd George in Morris-Jones diary, 20 Aug. 1929. See also Lloyd George to St. Davids,
13 June 1929, LG G/17/6/10, for getting electoral reform either from Labour or
Conservatives.

of the other two parties, the Liberal bargaining position was, in truth, far from 'impregnable'. The immediate aftermath of the election demonstrated that. Lloyd George in accordance with his February overture to Churchill was ready to negotiate terms for keeping the Conservative government in office, but was allowed no opportunity to do so.[70] Bringing either of the other parties to serious negotiations would be much more difficult and prolonged than he had anticipated.

For the next six months Lloyd George faced both ways, tried to meet all possibilities, and waited upon events. After the promised consultation with the parliamentary party, he publicly offered general support to the Labour government provided it pursued 'Liberal' policies and did not obstruct electoral reform.[71] That stance at least seemed consistent with the party's radical unemployment policy. But the election result meant that even more than before, Lloyd George could not afford that programme to be his principal concern. Privately he thought the best chance of agreement was still with the Conservative party, especially as Labour leaders were in a triumphant mood and, after the Conservative defeat, Baldwin might be weakened relative to Churchill.[72] In late June and July, with Churchill as intermediary, he sought Conservative co-operation in the electoral reform conference and offered Liberal support for a Conservative government in return for an electoral reform bill. In contrast to February and early June, his proposed terms no longer included acceptance of Liberal unemployment policies.[73] In the autumn, while still 'perplex[ed]' about the political prospects, he experimented with Egypt, Palestine, Russia, coal, India, and Ireland as issues on which to establish alliance with a Churchill-dominated Conservative party.[74]

[70] Hodgson memo, early June 1929, in Clarke *Diary*, 52–3.
[71] Maclean memo, 14 June 1929, Runciman papers 221; Lloyd George speeches, *The Times*, 14 June 1929, and *HC Deb*, 229, cols. 141–59, 3 July 1929.
[72] Lloyd George in Garvin to Astor, 5 June 1929, Astor papers.
[73] Churchill to Baldwin, 26 and 29 June 1929, SB 165/58–61 and 164/36 (*WSC* v(2), 8, 10–11); Amery diary, 27 June, 17 July 1929 (*LSA* II, 40, 45); and see Withers to Fry, 30 July 1929, SB 165/258.
[74] Lloyd George to Churchill, 16 Oct. 1929, LG G/4/4/24; reported in Irwin, and in A. Chamberlain, to Baldwin, 8 and 12 Oct. 1929, SB 103/108–9 and 116/29; MacDonald and Amery diaries, 26 Nov. 1929 (last in *LSA* II, 56); Lloyd George speeches, *The Times*, 5 and 19 Oct. 1929. Campbell, *Lloyd George*, 253–5, rightly states that no evidence exists of a 'coalitionist intrigue' over the Irwin Declaration. But this does not preclude the probability that Lloyd George wanted to push matters in that direction.

By December, however, events had clarified Lloyd George's thoughts. Baldwin had survived the Irwin Declaration controversy, and the Conservative party was moving towards protection, which remained anathema to many Liberals. In contrast the Labour government's failure on unemployment revealed a place for Liberal radicalism, and the Coal Bill – on which the Liberal policy of compulsory amalgamation of colliery companies was in advance of Cabinet policy – had forced ministers into negotiation. Despite the growing helplessness of the Labour government, or rather because its difficulties increasingly wore down ministerial resistance, Lloyd George was henceforth consistent in seeking Liberal objectives through the Labour Cabinet and in concentrating upon domestic issues.

From December 1929 to October 1930 there were four phases of Liberal–Labour negotiations. During the debates on the Coal Bill, Lloyd George tried both to bring it into conformity with Liberal policy and to use it to obtain a general alliance – but with pressure for the first purpose regulated to serve the second: it was a 'matter of tactics, not principle'.[75] He threatened to defeat the government, and in November, February, and March led Liberal MPs in divisions against the bill. At other times he was conciliatory, offering help with agricultural and unemployment policies 'regardless of party interests', and proposing to keep the government in office for two or three years in return for electoral reform and 'reasonable consultations'.[76] In public he declared that the two-party system had produced 'fumbling and failure'; that the three-party 'group system' had 'come to stay', and that in these new conditions 'traditional opposition' by Liberals would be 'unpatriotic' and would be best replaced by 'cooperation with the government of the day'.[77] In March the threats worked, with ministers accepting the preliminaries for an alliance. Liberals would provide support on similar lines to that given by the Irish and Labour parties to the pre-war Liberal government, provided an electoral reform bill was forced through Parliament as effectively as the 1912 Home Rule and 1913 Trade Unions Bills had been pressed. Again, Lloyd George did

---

[75] Lloyd George at parliamentary party meeting in Morris-Jones diary, 4 March 1930, and see also entry for 20 Feb. 1930.

[76] Lloyd George reported in Buxton to MacDonald, 6 Dec. 1929, JRM 672; in MacDonald diary, 27 Jan., 2, 3, and 20 Feb. 1930; and in Garvin to Astor, and Garvin to MacDonald, 16 Jan., 1 Feb. 1930, Astor papers and JRM 1515.

[77] Speech, *Manchester Guardian*, 21 Jan. 1930.

not require acceptance of the Liberal unemployment programme.[78] Using the delicate position of the Naval Conference as a pretext, he then persuaded the Liberal parliamentary party to abstain from further opposition to the Coal Bill.[79]

The second phase consisted of negotiations on the content of an electoral reform bill. Lloyd George believed 'the only chance for a revived Liberal party wd. be a measure of proportional representation',[80] so when ministers refused to offer anything more than the alternative vote he threatened them in May with parliamentary defeat. He was 'very much upset' when the Labour National Executive torpedoed the negotiations by rejecting even the alternative vote.[81] This did not, however, cause him to turn back towards the Conservatives: political circumstances were such that Liberals were 'bound to co-operate with' the government.[82] Instead, he took up the Cabinet's alternative of consultations on unemployment and agricultural policies. Having trounced Thomas, Buxton, and MacDonald for their ineffectiveness, Lloyd George now resumed the role of 'man of emergency' and breathed new life into *We Can Conquer Unemployment*. He spoke of a 'grave national crisis', drew parallels with his wartime crisis-management, demanded 'emergency measures', and, in contrast to the Conservatives, claimed for Liberals the 'patriotic' course of submerging 'party advantage' for 'the common good'.[83]

Lloyd George put considerable effort into this third phase, that of economic policy consultations. As with previous policy studies, he worked through members of his personal entourage (principally Rowntree and Kerr, now Lord Lothian) rather than party representatives.[84] They obtained departmental papers, cross-

---

[78] 'Basis for a Parliamentary understanding between the Government and the Liberal Party' [March 1930], unsigned but with Lloyd George amendments, LG G/84/11, and see MacDonald diary, 18 March 1930 (Marquand, 530–1).

[79] Morris-Jones diary, 18 March 1930; MacDonald and Dalton diaries, 18 March 1930 (respectively Marquand, 531; Pimlott, 98).

[80] Lloyd George at parliamentary party meeting, in Morris-Jones diary, 4 March 1930, and see Muir memo, 8 May 1930, Samuel papers A/73/10: 'the outlook for the Party is hopeless unless we get Proportional Representation'.

[81] MacDonald diary, 19 and 21 May 1930, and Henderson reported in Dalton diary, 21 May 1930 (Pimlott, 112).

[82] Lloyd George at parliamentary party meeting, in Morris-Jones diary, 27–8 May 1930. This position did not preclude trying to edge Conservatives towards accepting PR at the electoral reform conference: see Fair, 'Politics of Electoral Reform', 289.

[83] Speeches, *Manchester Guardian*, 30 June, 2 and 22 Sept., 18 Oct. 1930.

[84] See Morris-Jones diary, 21 July 1930 for the parliamentary party not even being consulted.

examined ministers and officials, and consulted professional experts
in order to criticise official opinion and overhaul the earlier land and
unemployment programmes.[85] The experience was, however, frus-
trating. They soon sensed that ministers treated the talks less
seriously than themselves. It also emerged that, whatever the claims
made before the general election, Liberal and ministerial plans for
land reclamation and settlement, agricultural marketing, road and
electrical development, and house-building were in fact similar 'in
principle'. This left only small or intangible differences over
telephone and regional development, the implementation time and
employment results of agreed work schemes, and, chiefly, the claim
that the government lacked the 'driving energy... which is essential
in [an] emergency'.[86]

Lloyd George's frustration was expressed in several ways. During
July he fired a warning shot by again bringing the government close
to Commons defeat, this time on the Finance Bill.[87] He was
'truculent' in exchanges with ministers, and in September
threatened (disingenuously) that 'the Tories were open to bargain
with him'.[88] In public he criticised the government's 'self-
complacent and stubborn ineptitude' and 'inertness', and the
'puny, pale and rickety' unemployment proposals in the King's
Speech, and warned MacDonald not to 'presume too much' on
Liberal dislike of the Conservative party.[89] In early November he
published a revised economic programme.

Like earlier versions, *How To Tackle Unemployment* contained
public works and agricultural improvement schemes, a national
development loan, incentives to industry, and empire development,
with defence of free trade. But in the face of the recession, shifts in
economic opinion, and detailed criticism by officials and ministers,
the emphasis had shifted markedly away from immediate loan-

---

[85] See mass of material in Lothian papers, 134–40, 250; in LG G/12/5, G/116, and in
PREM 1/108.

[86] Lloyd George to MacDonald, 22 Aug. 1930, and 'Memorandum on the Liberal Proposals
on Unemployment and Agriculture', introduction, early Oct. 1930, both PREM 1/108.
See also Lloyd George to F. Stevenson, 9 Aug. 1930, in Taylor, 130.

[87] For Lloyd George's motives, see Morris-Jones diary, 10 and 23 July 1930. For details,
Snowden, *Autobiography* II, 862–6.

[88] Hartshorn to MacDonald, and enclosure, 18 Aug. 1930, JRM 472; Lloyd George to
MacDonald, 22 Aug., 14 Sept., 23 Oct. 1930, PREM 1/108 (1st letter) and JRM 1308;
Snowden, *Autobiography* II, 883–4, and 'Note of Discussion at Cabinet meeting', 25 Sept.
1930, CAB 23/90B.

[89] Speeches, *Manchester Guardian*, 22 Sept., 27 Oct. 1930; *HC Deb*, 244, cols. 52–6, 29 Oct.
1930.

financed schemes towards long-term reconstruction. The retreat from the high claims of 1928–9 was even clearer in a new set of proposals: a national industrial conference to seek an all-round 10 per cent reduction in production costs, a new 'Geddes axe' committee to obtain similar cuts in government expenditure, and restoration of unemployment insurance to an insurance basis.[90]

In reality the Liberal leadership's policy was now not far removed from the position of the Cabinet and its official advisors. Nevertheless the new programme, like its accompanying public rhetoric, was intended to create an impression of distance from the Labour government. In this Lloyd George had several objectives. Despite the threats, these did not include alliance with Conservatives, who in October adopted full-blooded protection and who now plainly considered it unnecessary to concede electoral reform.[91] Rather, Lloyd George was trying to avoid implication in the government's failures, and to establish a Liberal claim at the next election to be more convincingly yet more responsibly radical than the Labour party. He was preparing also for the possibility that some crisis might occur, in which the advocates of drastic solutions might form the basis for a new coalition government.[92] More immediately, he was tightening the screw of Liberal pressure upon the Labour Cabinet.

By October 1930 this had been successful, and Liberal–Labour relations entered the fourth phase of secret alliance. Lloyd George's position was that Liberals now had no choice but to accept 'the lesser of two evils'. It was better to maintain a government in which they had 'very little confidence' than to put in another in which they could have 'no confidence at all'.[93] He had doubts about the Cabinet's Palestine and Indian policies, and its will to tackle the unemployment and financial problems. Nevertheless its free trade and agricultural policies were acceptable, it had submitted to effective consultations on parliamentary business, and TUC and Labour party pressure for a Trade Union Bill gave Liberals an even better lever than the Coal Bill. Above all, the Cabinet was at last prepared to 'save the Liberal party from extinction' by introducing

---

[90] For useful discussions, see Skidelsky, *Politicians*, 224–7 and, more critically, Hart thesis, 'Decline of the Liberal Party', 374–82, 392.

[91] See Grigg memo of talk with Lloyd George, 11 Nov. 1930, Altrincham papers: for a problem in interpreting this document, see note 105 below.

[92] See following chapter.

[93] Speech, *Manchester Guardian*, 27 Oct. 1930. See also Lloyd George reported in Lockhart diary, 5 Oct. 1930, in Young I, 128, and in Grigg memo, 11 Nov. 1930, Altrincham papers.

electoral reform. Pressure remained necessary in order to extract definite results, but it had become so important for Lloyd George to show some result that he was now willing to accept the less favourable method of the alternative vote.[94]

Lloyd George's further objective was to retain control of the Liberal party. Given the dilemma of choosing between the government and opposition division lobbies, any option he might have chosen would have involved risks of Liberal disagreement. But these risks had been greatly increased by the effect of the economic recession in polarising opinions on trade and financial issues, and by the policies or policy failures of the Labour government. The course he chose received firm support on free trade and electoral reform grounds from Samuel, now deputy Liberal leader,[95] from Beauchamp, the leader in the Lords, and from Muir. But whether he threatened or supported the Labour government, some Liberal MPs objected. Lloyd George's fundamental problem was that his strategy of forcing a party alliance demanded secret negotiations and tactical somersaults, which strained the confidence of followers who felt that experience gave them little cause to trust him. An increasing number of MPs complained that they 'never knew what LlG was going to do' and were being treated 'like children'.[96] From December 1929 the Liberal parliamentary party was split in the three crucial Commons votes designed to put pressure on the government. By July some Liberal MPs feared that the party was 'on the eve of disruption' or almost 'done for'.[97] In October it seemed that disintegration had begun.

Three sets of dissentients, of varying importance, had emerged. Those whom Lloyd George had least to worry about in the long run, because they were heading in the same direction, were MPs who wanted to keep the government in office but had failed to understand that this was his own aim, and so ignored the party whips and either voted for the government or abstained on sensitive divisions. These numbered around six, including a former Coalition Liberal, Edge

---

[94] Grigg memo of talk with Lloyd George, 11 Nov. 1930, Altrincham papers.
[95] Samuel led the detailed negotiations on the Coal Bill (as former chairman of the Coal Commission), and on electoral reform. Increasingly, his main concern was defence of free trade: see Samuel to Alexander, 10 Oct. 1930, Alexander papers, 5/2/22, and speech, *The Times*, 1 Nov. 1930.
[96] Various Liberal MPs in Morris-Jones diary, 25 March, 10, 21, and 23 July 1930; E. D. Simon in B. Webb diary, 29 March 1930.
[97] Morris-Jones, and Hutchison, Nathan, and Harris in Morris-Jones diary, 10 and 23 July 1930.

(who resigned as a party whip in February), and the progressive radicals Mander, Harris, and E. D. Simon.[98]

The effectiveness of a second group, the Liberal Council MPs, was impaired by their obsessive enmity towards Lloyd George and by policy commitments which increasingly pulled them in opposite directions. After the general election they had plotted Lloyd George's removal, having supposed that its result would persuade the party to repudiate dependence on him and his fund. But a Grey speech in January 1930 which was intended to spark off revolt[99] simply irritated most Liberals, impatient of Asquithian hatreds and their attachment to old-fashioned Liberal principles. Subsequently, Runciman, Maclean, Collins, and Jones considered themselves independent of the parliamentary leadership.[100] But along with Grey and other Council members their activities were largely confined to olympian statements on free trade and government retrenchment,[101] ignoring the dilemma implied by these commitments as between Labour and Conservative. Runciman, feeling 'repell[ed]' from the Liberal party by Lloyd George, might have joined the Conservative party but for protection. Instead, he felt stranded as 'a free trader...with no central party attachments', increasing his business involvements, accepting the task of reconstructing the Kylsant companies, and contemplating political retirement.[102] But if the Liberal Council had ceased to be a threat to Lloyd George's leadership, the defiance and despair of these experienced, talented, wealthy, traditional, Liberals contributed to a broader despondency within the party.

The last group to emerge was the most threatening, because it expressed outright an increasingly common view: that Lloyd

[98] For Mander as informant for Labour ministers and claims that regardless of Lloyd George up to a dozen Liberals would prevent the government's defeat, see Dalton diary, 11 March, 12 May, 15 July, 28 Oct., and 4 Nov. 1930 (Pimlott, 97, 98–9, 117, 124, 126). E. D. Simon was notable as the first Liberal publicly to advocate an import duty, which annoyed Liberals but which he evidently hoped Labour ministers would adopt: see speech, *The Times*, 4 Aug. 1930, and article 'Some Questions about Free Trade', *Political Quarterly*, I, Sept.–Dec. 1930.

[99] *The Times*, 15 Jan. 1930. For plotting, see correspondence in Gladstone and Runciman papers, June 1929–Jan. 1930.

[100] Runciman to Samuel, and to Hutchison, 5 March 1930, Runciman papers 221, 225.

[101] Manifesto on economy, Grey speech, and 'National Association of Merchants and Manufacturers' (including Grey, Runciman) statement, *The Times*, 16 and 31 July, 1 Sept. 1930. Liberal Council Free Trade Conference, *Manchester Guardian*, 14 Nov. 1930.

[102] Runciman to Fitzherbert Wright, 25 Nov. 1929, 27 Sept., 31 Oct. 1930, Runciman papers 221 (1st letter), and SB 31/78, 84. For proposed resignation of parliamentary seat, Tomkin to Runciman, 31 July 1930, Runciman papers 225.

George's strategy of keeping a discredited Labour government in office was discrediting the Liberal party and should be discontinued. The group included Lambert, Brown, Kedward, Murdoch Mac-Donald, and the chief whip, Hutchison. Most prominent was John Simon, not only for his specific grievance against the Cabinet's Indian policy but also because as a barrister who had denounced the General Strike as illegal, he was a leading opponent of repeal of the Trade Disputes Act.[103] These MPs considered that the government had 'proved a complete failure in almost all departments', was financially irresponsible, and had become 'a real danger to the country'.[104] They wanted the Liberal party to demonstrate its 'independence'. The weaknesses of this position were its corollaries: to defeat the Labour government would mean loss of the opportunity to save Liberal seats through electoral reform, and replacement of a free-trade government by a protectionist one. They themselves were only beginning to contemplate the obvious solution to this embarrassment, acceptance of import controls and some electoral understanding with the Conservatives. But Grigg, returning from the Governorship of Kenya in October with his own grievance against the Labour government's East African policy, already wanted to re-create the 1918–22 Liberal–Conservative Coalition. After a misconceived attempt to put Lloyd George in touch with Conservative leaders,[105] he transferred his attentions to Simon as potential Liberal coalition leader. Lloyd George had every reason to fear that, if economic deterioration continued, dislike of protection might cease to inhibit the development of a substantial Liberal breakaway movement.

Possession of the parliamentary balance of power had again inflicted major damage upon the Liberal party. Caught between a protectionist Conservative opposition and a free trade but prostrated Labour government, it had little effective freedom for manoeuvre. New divisions had emerged, and the splits and depression of MPs

---

[103] Simon in Garvin to Astor, 14 July 1930, Astor papers (for government defeat desirable on Indian grounds), and Simon to Lloyd George, 25 Oct. 1930, Simon papers.

[104] Hutchison to Lloyd George, 1 Oct. 1930 (2 letters), LG G/10/9/7, 10, and to Sinclair, 8 Oct. 1930, Thurso papers; Simon to Lloyd George, 25 Oct. 1930, Simon papers; Lambert letter, *The Times*, 24 Sept. 1930.

[105] For Grigg telling Conservatives that Lloyd George wanted a Liberal–Conservative alliance, see N. Chamberlain diary, 21–2 Nov., Lady Hilton Young diary, 22 Nov., and Amery diary, 30 Nov., all 1930 (last in *LSA* II, 138). But careful reading of Grigg memo of talk with Lloyd George, 11 Nov. 1930, Altrincham papers, shows Lloyd George disbelieving in such an alliance yet allowing Grigg to think otherwise in order not to alienate him.

added to the demoralisation of the party in the country, facing an electorate increasingly dissatisfied with the government and a Liberal party helping to keep it in office. It seemed that electorally, the party faced another 1924. Its electoral experts calculated it would lose twenty seats: even the alternative vote would bring a net gain of just fourteen seats.[106] Confidence in the party's future as a major electoral machine was lacking to the extent that even its leading members did not bother to help the party organisation or contribute to its funds. The party was nearly bankrupt, the organisation was 'going to pieces',[107] candidatures were falling, by-elections were left uncontested, and an exasperated Muir, declaring that 'the Party [might] as well be wound up', threatened in October to resign the party chairmanship.[108] In such conditions, a general election would plainly be disastrous. There seemed to be a ghastly race to achieve salvation through electoral reform before the Liberal party collapsed or was crushed.

Lloyd George tried various devices to hold the party together. He tried conciliation and stirring appeals to party unity and he tried the whip of party discipline, before resorting to subterfuge. No less than Labour ministers, party pressures obliged Lloyd George to deny the existence of a Liberal–Labour alliance. But in a division on the Address on 4 November, nine MPs defied the parliamentary party decision to abstain: Edge, Runciman, Maclean, and Collins voted with the government, Simon, Hutchison, Lambert, Kedward, and Murdoch MacDonald with the Conservatives. On the following day Hutchison resigned as chief whip and Simon publicly revealed his disagreement with Lloyd George.[109] The implications were not just critical for the Liberal party. How far and how soon these Liberal splits might develop was an uncertainty on which not only the Labour government's fate but also Conservative prospects seemed to depend.

---

[106] 'Forecast of next election', unsigned, 6 Nov. 1930, Samuel papers A/73/11.

[107] Morris-Jones diary, 23 July 1930. For details of organisational problems, see Thorpe thesis, 'General Election of 1931', 105–15.

[108] Muir memo, 29 Oct. 1930, and Muir to Sinclair, 3 Nov. 1930, both Thurso papers II/75/4.

[109] Hutchison to Lloyd George, 5 Nov. 1930, LG G/10/9/13; Simon to Lloyd George, 25 Oct. 1930, published in *The Times*, 6 Nov. 1930.

CONSERVATIVE DIVISIONS

The 1929 election defeat was a shock to Conservatives. A few party leaders thought it represented a substantial advance for 'socialism', even something like 'continental class hatred', and in its aftermath concluded that adequate resistance required 'co-operation and ultimate fusion' with the Liberal party.[110] This was true of Austen Chamberlain, Worthington-Evans, Cunliffe-Lister, and especially Churchill, who pressed for acceptance of Lloyd George's early proposal of a deal conditional on electoral reform.[111] But most Conservative leaders kept their heads: after all, their party had obtained a majority of the popular vote, and they understood that there was no marked 'conversion to socialism'.[112] With Liberal intervention prominent among alternative explanations for the large loss of seats, the many Conservatives who had long detested the Liberal party and Lloyd George in particular – 'Satan in British politics' – found much satisfaction in what they considered to be the failure of the Liberal revival and in the prospect of that party's disintegration.[113] Baldwin allowed Neville Chamberlain, Amery, and Salisbury to ensure that Conservatives entered the electoral reform conference without commitment, and within the conference Hoare tacitly co-operated with Labour representatives in bringing it to an inconclusive end a year later.[114] Baldwin also encouraged Liberal Council leaders to defy Lloyd George's leadership.[115] Towards the Labour government, the prevailing attitude among leading Conservatives was that to deny it a reasonable term of office might be counter-productive in strengthening the influence of the left; that as it was a minority government it could do 'nothing extreme'; and that tolerance was prudent because it might well fail.

---

[110] A. to I. Chamberlain, 6 June 1929, AC 5/1/475, and reported in Amery diary, 11 July 1929 (*LSA* II, 42–3).

[111] Churchill to Baldwin, 26 and 29 June 1929, SB 165/58–61, 164/36 (*WSC* v(2), 8, 10–11); Amery diary, 11 and 17 July 1929 (*LSA* II, 43, 45); Worthington-Evans to Hall, 4 June 1929, Worthington-Evans papers c896/197.

[112] N. Chamberlain diary, 8 June 1929.

[113] Quotation in Ormsby-Gore to Bridgeman, 2 June 1929, Bridgeman papers. Generally, see, e.g., Lane-Fox and Headlam diaries, 1 June 1929; Joynson-Hicks to Steel-Maitland, 2 June 1929, Steel-Maitland papers 251; N. Chamberlain diary, 8 June 1929.

[114] Amery diary, 11 and 17 July 1929 (*LSA* II, 43–4, 45); for Hoare's activities, see material for May to July 1930 in Templewood papers VI.2.

[115] See Baldwin references to Maclean and Runciman, in Devonshire to Fitzherbert Wright, 22 Dec. 1929, Runciman papers 357.

What would best stop the Labour advance was 'such a dose of Labour Government as will in turn disappoint and antagonise its supporters'.[116]

Baldwin, as an opponent of Conservative reaction and proponent of the need to 'educate' Labour and the electorate in democratic responsibilities, was especially concerned to demonstrate respect towards a Labour leadership which could not be suspected of harbouring dangerous ambitions. Privately he assured MacDonald that while conducting parliamentary opposition on conventional lines, 'he would not "worry"' him in office 'but would give fair play'.[117] Publicly he anticipated MacDonald's 'Council of State' appeal by promising no 'fractious opposition', and urging that national difficulties made it essential for all parties to 'face the world as a united Parliament'. This required 'self-control on both sides' – including the Conservative side. He was thinking particularly of the Indian issue. With a mind to the acute national and party embarrassments caused between 1912 and 1921 by the similar problem of Irish self-government, and for that reason wanting to keep the matter out of party politics and to support Irwin's policy of conciliation, he spoke of Indian policy as 'the supreme, the acid, and ultimate test' of Britain's fitness for 'democratic conditions'.[118] In some respects, the Labour government was perfectly tolerable. MacDonald's American visit and the Naval Treaty achieved what Baldwin would have attempted if he had remained in office. In other areas, including colonial development and industrial rationalisation, there was further continuity. When in December 1929 Churchill wished to join with Liberals in defeating the Coal Bill, Baldwin was 'very strongly and soundly against Parliamentary subtleties' and the whips allowed the government to survive through Conservative abstentions.[119]

None of this meant that Baldwin was not prepared to hit hard in obvious areas for Conservative criticism. From autumn 1929 like other Conservative leaders he made much of the government's inability to fulfil its 'lavish promises', reduce unemployment, and

---

[116] N. to I. Chamberlain, 2 June 1929, NC 18/1/656; N. Chamberlain diary, 8 June 1929.
[117] MacDonald diary, 4 June 1929.
[118] *HC Deb*, 229, col. 63, 2 July 1929, immediately preceding, and perhaps stimulating, MacDonald's appeal.
[119] Lane-Fox to Irwin, 22 Dec. 1929, Halifax papers 18/333. Some 30 Conservative MPs were absent from the crucial division; and similar circumstances again helped the government avoid defeat in February 1930.

assist agriculture, and of the damage that rising expenditure, 'political intervention' in the coal industry, and threatened abolition of safeguarding duties was causing to business confidence. In summer 1930, while ready to accept all-party consultation in order to spread responsibility on the highly delicate issue of unemployment insurance,[120] he agreed with other Conservative leaders in rejecting the Cabinet's efforts to use that device to evade discredit on the unemployment and agricultural issues.

Nevertheless Baldwin was not a vigorous opposition leader. Apart from his strategic concerns – allowing the Labour government time to fail and the Liberal party time to disintegrate – temperamentally he found it difficult to oppose for opposition's sake. Conscious that on trade policy Conservative views varied from 'coal black to jet white', with the Shadow Cabinet itself divided and uncertain,[121] and wishing to avoid repetition of his miscalculation in rushing a protection programme at the 1923 election, he did not want to move in advance of the emergence of a wider party and popular consensus. As economic conditions deteriorated he moved towards a programme of retrenchment, bolder industrial safeguarding, a guaranteed price for wheat, and imperial preference and 'cartelisation'. But he wanted the details left for further enquiry and cautious development,[122] because he was not deluded into thinking that the opinions of clamorous protectionists and party activists in the safe Conservative seats of Southern England were a reliable indication of the readiness of voters in the vital Midlands, Northern, and Scottish marginal seats to accept taxes on food imports. He also regarded the opposition of most leading Conservatives to the Irwin Declaration as 'unreasonable':[123] but if it temporarily 'made him feel the hopelessness of trying to liberalise the Tory Party',[124] he believed the objective so vital as to demand his persistence.

All this contributed to serious difficulties within the party. After the election defeat there was much gloom and a tendency to search for scapegoats other than just the Liberals. There were considerable rank-and-file complaints against the party organisation and its chairman, Davidson, a close friend of Baldwin. There was a

---

[120] Baldwin to Churchill, 19 July 1930, in *WSC* v(2), 171.
[121] Baldwin in Jones, *Whitehall Diary* II, 244, 9 Feb. 1930; Amery diary, 30 Jan. 1930 (*LSA* II, 59–60).
[122] N. Chamberlain to his wife, 25 Oct. 1929, NC 1/26/417; Wolmer to Selborne, 26 Jan. 1930, 2nd Selborne papers Add 5; Amery diary, 30 Jan. 1930 (*LSA* II, 59–60).
[123] Lane-Fox diary, 30 Oct. 1929, and Dawson diary, 2 Nov. 1929.
[124] Lytton to Irwin, 20 Nov. 1929, Halifax papers 18/309.

substantial accumulation of resentments at the 1924 government's failure to respond to party opinion on industrial safeguarding, agricultural assistance, the 'flapper vote', and retrenchment. There was much criticism of de-rating as lacking popular appeal, a reaction against the election platform as too negative, and a strong feeling that the defeat released the party from earlier pledges and accommodations, and demanded new initiatives. All these sentiments implied criticism of Baldwin, especially as so much of the party's election platform had rested upon his personal appeal. When he resisted rapid policy advance, appeared reluctant to attack the government, and seemed 'woolly and careless' in his manner of assenting to the Irwin Declaration,[125] criticism became explicit. By October 1929 the party seemed to be 'all to pieces', with 'everywhere & from all sides... depression, distrust & despair'.[126] The broad discontent was expressed in protectionist and imperial preference resolutions from local associations to the National Union, the formation by Moore-Brabazon of a defeated candidates' association, criticism at 1922 Committee meetings, and grumbling by Shadow Cabinet members.[127] Focus was provided by five individuals or groups.

The most prominent was Beaverbrook, a longstanding advocate of imperial trade unity and critic of Baldwin. He had 'rejoiced' at Baldwin's election setback,[128] and considered it an opportunity both to advance his own proposals and to regain the political influence he had enjoyed under Bonar Law. After approaches to Conservative leaders had revealed that he was still considered 'untouchable',[129] he called in July 1929 for free trade within the Empire and tariffs against foreign imports. Beginning as a campaign in his *Daily Express* newspaper group, this 'Empire Crusade' attracted considerable interest among industrialists and agriculturalists and pledges of support from discontented Conservative peers, MPs, candidates, and local association members. By the autumn the effects were so serious that Beaverbrook received approaches from party leaders concerned to prevent a rebellion. This encouraged him to intensify the pressure, in December establishing the Crusade as a definite organisation and appealing for members and funds. With extravagant flattery, he

[125] Lane-Fox to Irwin, 7 Nov. 1929, Halifax papers 18/292.
[126] N. to I. and H. Chamberlain, 22 and 26 Oct. 1929, NC 18/1/673-4.
[127] For a good detailed account of party mood, see Ball, *Baldwin*, 30-96.
[128] Beaverbrook to Birkenhead, 7 June 1929, Beaverbrook papers C/39.
[129] Beaverbrook to Rothermere, 3 July 1929, Beaverbrook papers C/284.

sought support from other newspaper proprietors and editors, and public commitments from protectionist politicians.[130] His consistent objective, as the central feature of Empire Free Trade, was acceptance of food taxes. Otherwise, he oscillated between threats and conciliation towards the Conservative party, never quite sure whether he wanted to force Baldwin's removal or to be accorded respect and influence by the existing leadership.

Rothermere had no such doubt. Though not a party Conservative, he had many reactionary views and had considered Baldwin's government 'semi-socialist'. His politics were erratic, affected by his desire to demonstrate the political power of the press in general and his *Daily Mail* in particular, and to avenge public attacks upon him by Baldwin in 1924.[131] He had encouraged Lloyd George before the election, and afterwards encouraged Beaverbrook's launch of the Empire Crusade.[132] After Baldwin denounced inaccurate *Daily Mail* criticism of his assent to the Irwin Declaration, Rothermere entered into alliance with Beaverbrook. 'Intoxicated with excitement',[133] he persuaded Beaverbrook to sponsor parliamentary candidates and in February to join in the formation of their own United Empire Party on the model of the Anti-Waste League of 1921–2, with the intention of embarrassing the Conservative party and provoking rebellion against Baldwin.[134] When in March Beaverbrook briefly reverted to conciliation with Baldwin, Rothermere continued the UEP on his own. The difference between them was that, while Beaverbrook was preoccupied with Empire Free Trade, Rothermere had doubts about food taxes and was as much concerned with 'no surrender' in India – the issue he considered to be 'Baldwin's Achilles Heel'.[135] Nevertheless their relations remained close. Together they ensured that the Conservative leadership suffered sustained criticism from the chief mass circulation newspapers read by Conservatives, and their intervention in a series of by-elections from May 1930 uncovered considerable seams of dissatisfaction among natural Conservative supporters.

[130] Beaverbrook to Rothermere, 30 Nov. 1929, to Gwynne of *Morning Post*, 1 Jan. 1930, and to Camrose of *Daily Telegraph*, 9 Jan. 1930, Beaverbrook papers C/284, C/149, C/78; Amery diary, 24 Nov. 1929 (*LSA* II, 55).
[131] See Cazalet diary, autumn 1929, in James, *Cazalet*, 126.
[132] E.g., Rothermere to Beaverbrook, 5 July 1929, Beaverbrook papers C/284.
[133] Elibank notes, 24 Feb. 1930, Elibank papers 25/74.
[134] Rothermere to Beaverbrook, 24 Jan., 4 Feb. 1930, Beaverbrook papers C/284. For Anti-Waste, see Cowling, *Impact of Labour*, 55–9.
[135] Rothermere to Beaverbrook, 4 Feb. 1930, Rothermere public statement and Beaverbrook reply, 7 March 1930, all Beaverbrook papers C/284.

Among a loosely associated body of parliamentary protectionists, Amery, released from the inhibitions of office, became the most prominent though not the most effective. He believed the election defeat vindicated his stance in 1928: from his particular perspective, the fundamental cause was 'a complete absence of a positive policy'. Almost immediately afterwards he resolved to form 'a small band' to drag the party towards the tariff reform dawn.[136] While still a minister he had encouraged Beaverbrook to mount a press campaign, advice he repeated in July 1929 only to have Beaverbrook pre-empt his own plans by creating the Empire Crusade.[137] Instead with Lords Lloyd and Melchett (formerly Mond), and a number of leading businessmen, he established the Empire Economic Union as simply a research and propaganda group. But as in 1928 his effectiveness was crippled by his desire to remain within the collective party leadership. In February 1930 he caused Baldwin some difficulty by publicly calling for food taxes at a moment of particular Beaverbrook–Rothermere pressure. But he was easily persuaded to patch up the difference,[138] and for his pains was excluded when a secret inner 'Business Committee' of party leaders was formed in March. For parliamentary purposes Amery, Melchett, and Lloyd also became active in the Empire Industries Association which – under Page Croft's chairmanship – pressed in early 1930 for the party leadership's acceptance of a policy of a 'free hand' to introduce protective measures. All the EIA and EEU leaders maintained close contact with Beaverbrook, but they regarded complete Empire Free Trade as utopian and argued instead for imperial preferences and quotas. They also disliked his attempted 'press dictation' and wanted the party to move under its own momentum, but as Baldwin continued to hold back on full protection through spring 1930 they became progressively disillusioned with him. In order to increase pressure the various advanced protectionists consolidated themselves in June into 'Imperial Economic Unity Groups' in both Houses. That in the Lords was organised by Melchett and Elibank (of the Empire Crusade executive), while the more important Commons group, which by September numbered

---

[136] Amery to Page Croft, 6 June 1930, Croft papers 1/2/12–13.
[137] Amery to Beaverbrook, 19 Nov. 1928, Beaverbrook papers C/5; Amery diary, 1, 10, 13, 18, and 19 July, 22, 24, and 25 Oct., 24 Nov. 1929 (partly in *LSA* II, 41, 42, 44–5, 46, 51, 52, 55).
[138] Amery speech, and Amery–Baldwin exchange, *The Times*, 8 and 12 Feb. 1930; Amery diary, 11 Feb. 1930 (*LSA* II, 62–3).

almost 100 MPs – about half the Conservative backbenchers – made its chairman, Page Croft, a powerful figure.[139]

Page Croft was also a member of the fourth focus of discontent, another group of backbench MPs. These were the 'diehards', the core of the party Right, about forty in number and headed by Gretton. From July to October 1929 they acted as a body 'aggrieved over the conduct and outcome of the General Election', which asserted that there was 'considerable discord' in the parliamentary party and wanted a party meeting in order to establish increased backbench influence over the leadership.[140] Thereafter, they complained of front bench timidity towards the Labour government, tried to persuade the 1922 Committee to act independently of the party whips, wanted advanced protection,[141] and were hostile to the Irwin Declaration and everything appearing to weaken British imperial control. They were particularly active during May 1930 in a movement to dissuade Baldwin from acquiescing in the Naval Treaty.[142] Although alone they posed no serious threat to Baldwin, at all moments of difficulty they were ready with deputations or motions which expressed the dissatisfaction of many more backbench MPs.

The final focus of discontent was Churchill. Though he became a member of the leadership's Business Committee, in some respects it was easy to think that he was ceasing to be important. Vigorous parliamentary performances during the six months after the election failed to re-establish a party reputation which he had lost as Chancellor of the Exchequer. His problem was that he remained attached to the essentials of free trade. This was not merely because free trade was his 'only' remaining conviction.[143] It was also central to his strategic preoccupations: he continued to want an anti-socialist alliance with Liberals, and feared that protection would result instead in a 'Lib–Lab block' supported by an 'electorate of consumers' hostile to food taxes, leaving Conservatives 'hopelessly

[139] For the development of this movement, see, e.g., Beaverbrook to Horne, 28 May 1930, and Elibank circular to Lords, 26 June 1930, Beaverbrook papers C/178, C/126; 1922 Committee, 30 June 1930; Page Croft letter, *The Times*, 18 Sept. 1930.

[140] Gretton to Baldwin, 25 July (containing backbench petition), 5 and 9 Oct. 1930, SB 164/66–7, 70–1; and see Grant Morden at 1922 Committee, 22 July 1929. For a good description of the Diehards, see Ball, *Baldwin*, 21–4.

[141] Heneage at 1922 Committee, 11 Nov. 1929; Gretton to Baldwin, 27 Jan. (with backbench petition), 6 Feb., 3 April 1930, SB 31/15–22, 25, 30–1.

[142] 1922 Committee, 5, 12, and 19 May 1930; Amery diary, 12 May 1930; Gretton to Beamish, 20 May 1930, and other material in Beamish papers 4/3; Headlam diary, 21 May 1930.   [143] Churchill in Nicolson diary, 23 Jan. 1930 (Nicolson I, 41).

excluded from Power'.[144] Lacking party support, he had little choice but to acquiesce in Baldwin's protectionist advances in early 1930. These left him 'very depressed' about the party's future and his own loss of influence and growing isolation, and inclined, in some moods, to resign himself solely to authorship.[145] Yet in another respect Churchill was very much attuned to Conservative feeling. From June 1929 he became increasingly convinced that the Empire was in danger. He was the leading critic of Lloyd's dismissal and the proposed Egyptian treaty. He was 'almost demented with fury' over the Irwin Declaration, and was prominent in opposing the Naval Treaty.[146] On one or more of these issues Churchill was aligned with most Conservative leaders, with the diehards and other back-benchers, and with many ordinary party members. On all he differed from Baldwin. But 'defence of Empire' not only offered him an opportunity of regaining a leading position: he also believed it was a means of cutting across differences over protection, re-uniting the Conservative party, and obtaining Liberal co-operation in defeating the Labour government. He looked especially to the Indian issue as 'a band of unity between the strong war-time forces and...the means of joint action'.[147] In June 1930 he had declared the economic difficulties to be the most serious problem since the war; but as the Round Table Conference approached his position became that India was 'the most serious of all our problems', and the one he 'care[d] more about...than anything else in public life'.[148]

In the face of party discontent and criticism, Baldwin's response was to cling on in the belief that he was the indispensable barrier to the Conservative party being wrecked by reaction, Lloyd George, and 'Press Lords', and that given time commonsense and decency would prevail. He convinced himself that the 'fuss' over the Irwin Declaration was largely a plot between Lloyd George and 'disloyal

[144] Churchill to Baldwin, 29 June 1929, SB 164/36, (*WSC* v(2), 11) and to N. Chamberlain, 5 July 1929, NC 7/9/30.
[145] N. to I., H., and I. Chamberlain, 22 and 29 March, 6 April 1930, NC 18/1/686, 687, 690; Lockhart diary, 23 Jan., 13 April, in Young I, 114, 118; MacDonald diary, 28 Sept. 1930.
[146] Hoare to Irwin, 13 Nov. 1929, Halifax papers 18/298, and Churchill to Baldwin, 17 May 1930, SB 117/53–4 (*WSC* v(2), 111, 156–7). See Headlam diary, 21 May 1930, for Churchill in the company of Gretton's group.
[147] Churchill to Sinclair, 8 Jan. 1931, Thurso papers II/85/3. See also Churchill to Irwin, 1 Jan. 1930, Halifax papers 19/1, and to Beaverbrook, 23 Sept. 1930, Beaverbrook papers C/86 (*WSC* v(2), 128, 185–6); speeches *The Times*, 17 Dec. 1929, 21 Aug., 8 Sept. 1930.
[148] 'Parliamentary Government and the Economic Problem', 19 June 1930, in Churchill, *Thoughts and Adventures*, 240; Churchill to Baldwin, 24 Sept. 1930, SB 104/51 (*WSC* v(2), 186); speech, *The Times*, 8 Sept. 1930.

colleagues' to remove him from the party leadership, and that Churchill could safely be left to make a fool of himself.[149] On protection and imperial preference he was obliged to advance more quickly than he liked, but his principal concern was to avoid the impression that policy was being imposed by Beaverbrook and Rothermere. Aside from deep personal animosity (to call them 'swine...was to libel a very decent, clean animal'), Baldwin considered the political aspirations of an irresponsible and capricious popular press to be 'the most obvious peril to democracy'.[150] He refused to have any dealings with the more erratic and megalomaniacal Rothermere. Towards Beaverbrook he shifted between his own inclination to fight back and party pressures to reach agreement, with the course punctuated by party meetings intended to restore party discipline. Baldwin met Beaverbrook to hear his ideas before the Albert Hall meeting in November 1929 which announced the first move towards an imperial trade policy. He gave Beaverbrook a private preview of his more detailed presentation of this policy at the Coliseum meeting in February 1930. After a further private discussion had revealed sharp differences and Beaverbrook had joined Rothermere in the United Empire party, Baldwin wanted to precipitate a series of by-elections in order to 'expose the real weakness of the Press Lords'.[151] When the Central Office advised that Conservative rank-and-file discontent was so severe that this tactic might in practice produce 'disastrous' results – even 'break [the party] up altogether'[152] – he hurriedly compromised with Beaverbrook on a policy of a national referendum on food taxes, announced at a Hotel Cecil meeting in March.[153] Beaverbrook, however, subsequently repudiated the referendum, resumed his alliance with Rothermere, and intervened in Conservative local associations. When leading protectionist MPs also began to repudiate the referendum, Baldwin at the Caxton Hall meeting in June shifted the issue to a constitutional question, making rejection

---

[149] Baldwin to Bridgeman to his mother, 23 Nov. 1929, Bridgeman papers (Williamson, 235); in MacDonald diary, 26 Nov. 1929 (for Lloyd George 'preparing again to lead my diehards'); and in Amery diary, 26 May 1930 (*LSA* II, 72).

[150] Jones, *Whitehall Diary* II, 153, 23 Oct. 1928: for 'swine', Headlam diary, 20 Feb. 1930.

[151] Amery diary, 24 Feb. 1930 (*LSA* II, 64); Davidson to Tyrrell, 9 March 1930, Davidson papers. See Baldwin to Simon, 19 Feb. 1930, Simon papers, for conviction that press power could be broken.

[152] Davidson to Baldwin, 26 Feb. 1930, Davidson papers.

[153] Amery diary, 3 March 1930 (*LSA* II, 65); Elibank notes, 3–4 March 1930, Elibank papers 25/74; speech, *The Times*, 5 March 1930.

of the 'preposterous and insolent demands' of press dictation and adherence to official party policy the test of loyalty to his leadership.[154]

The success of this tactic left Baldwin in a complacent mood about his own position. After attempts by Neville Chamberlain in July to reach a settlement with Beaverbrook and Rothermere had broken down, Baldwin 'rejoic[ed]' that the 'disgusting one-sided alliance' with 'the lunatics' had ended.[155] There remained, however, widespread party feeling that Baldwin was 'too timid, weak and pacifist', too reluctant to join in the party's 'general move to the right on all questions' and to take advantage of the 'landslide' to protection, as indicated by the bankers' manifesto.[156] The short-term success of staking his leadership upon the referendum policy was in the longer term dangerous. The confidence vote at the Caxton Hall was generally attributed to hostility to press dictation, not to satisfaction with party policy,[157] and about eighty MPs and candidates had supported a Gretton–Page Croft motion for a 'free hand'. The possibility of Baldwin being forced to resign, already discussed intermittently by the discontented, became a major issue in the autumn.

There was no shortage of candidates proposed or offering themselves as his successor. At various times Beaverbrook, Amery, Lloyd, Hailsham, Horne, and Neville Chamberlain were mentioned. Some were obviously handicapped by insufficiently broad support or membership of the Lords; but the more likely candidates were constrained from striking against Baldwin because of fear of seeming to advance the Press Lords' cause, thereby inviting continued press interference and splitting the party faithful. Horne, as an ex-Cabinet minister who had never been part of the Baldwin regime, was widely regarded as a strong candidate, even by leading members of that regime.[158] Emerging from political semi-retirement as the party

---

154 Speech, *The Times*, 25 June 1930.
155 Baldwin to Bridgeman, 9 Aug. 1930, Bridgeman papers. Beaverbrook's and Rothermere's principal interest in the negotiations appears to have been to persuade Chamberlain to remove Baldwin: see N. Chamberlain diary, 19–30 July 1930.
156 Ormsby-Gore to Irwin, 3 July 1930, Halifax papers 19/91a; A. to I. Chamberlain, 7 July 1930, AC 5/1/508.
157 Amery diary, 24 June 1930 (*LSA* II, 74); Headlam diary, 24 June 1930; Astor to Garvin, 24 June 1930, Astor papers.
158 N. to I. Chamberlain, 17 May 1930, and Hoare to N. Chamberlain, 8 Oct. 1930, NC 18/1/695, NC 8/10/8; Amery diary, 20 June, 20 July 1930 (*LSA* II, 73, 78); Ormsby-Gore to Irwin, 3 July 1930, Halifax papers 19/91a; Hannon to Beaverbrook, 12 Aug., 7 Oct. 1930, Beaverbrook papers C/154.

troubles developed in late 1929, he had become active around the Beaverbrook, Amery, Page Croft, and Gretton groups and taken the lead in enunciating a 'free hand' policy on protection.[159] Proof of his potential came in May when Baldwin invited him to join the Conservative front bench, but Horne rejected so obvious an attempt to neutralise his influence.[160] Nevertheless at the Caxton Hall meeting he felt obliged to take a leading part in supporting Baldwin's appeal for party unity as against Beaverbrook and Rothermere.[161]

Similar considerations affected Neville Chamberlain. As an impressive Minister of Health, he had been regarded as a strong contender for the succession even before the election. Afterwards he had been one of the first to call for an advance in imperial trade policy,[162] but unlike Amery his efforts to develop this were conducted wholly within the party's collective leadership. With a vigorous interest in policy-making, he supplanted Percy as chairman of the newly created Conservative Research Department and then, sharing the general dissatisfaction with Davidson, had removed him and become party chairman too. He had acted as an intermediary with Beaverbrook, with whose policy objectives, though not tactics, he had general sympathy. Assisted by his Research Department committees he developed policies of industrial tariffs and agricultural quotas designed not simply as protection but to stimulate rationalisation and marketing arrangements. He disliked the referendum, but like Baldwin thought it could not be abandoned at Beaverbrook's dictation.[163] He was himself exasperated by Baldwin's 'want of inspiration & decision', and knew that within the Business Committee Hoare, Cunliffe-Lister, and Austen Chamberlain – angry with Baldwin over India – were equally critical of his leadership.[164] Neville Chamberlain was also well-informed about party feeling. He feared that backbench agitation over the Naval Treaty was 'the first beginnings of a revolt'; in July he thought that if Baldwin would retire 'the whole party would heave a sigh of

---

[159] Hannon to Beaverbrook, 12 and 13 Dec. 1929, Beaverbrook papers C/154; Elibank notes, 27 Feb., 3 and 29 March 1930, Elibank papers 25/74; Horne speech, and announcement of joining EIA executive, *The Times*, 28 Feb., 6 March 1930.

[160] Horne to Baldwin, 13 May 1930, SB 165/195.

[161] *The Times*, 25 June 1930. For similar private activity, see, e.g., Amery diary, 22 May, 19 June 1930 (*LSA* II, 71, 72); and N. to H. Chamberlain, 21 June 1930, NC 18/1/701.

[162] Speech, *The Times*, 5 July 1929.   [163] N. Chamberlain diary, 22 June 1930.

[164] N. to H. Chamberlain, 13 and 26 Oct. 1929, 21 June 1930, NC 18/1/672, 674, 701; N. Chamberlain diary, 22 June 1930.

relief'.[165] He knew there were many who thought he should take the party leadership but was averse to any action which might be thought disloyal (he would not 'on any account play L. G. to [Baldwin's] Asquith'), and tried to persuade himself that he did not want the position and that, if Baldwin retired, he would readily serve under Horne.[166] From July, however, he was determined to use his strong party position to push Baldwin towards a bolder policy on protection, especially after a Rothermere UEP candidate polled unexpectedly well against an official Conservative in the Bromley by-election in early September. In a speech on 20 September he outlined his own 'unauthorised programme' of advanced protection and imperial preferences,[167] and obtained the assistance of Bridgeman, Baldwin's closest political friend, in persuading him that acceptance of this policy was the only means of keeping the party together.[168]

By now, however, the party leaders' concern to resist Beaverbrook and Rothermere had placed them seriously out of step with the prevailing movements in industrial, agricultural, and Conservative party opinion, including, now, that in northern constituencies. There was deep discontent throughout the local and provincial party organisation, with some associations close to revolt: Conservative MPs and Conservative grandees found that 'the Party [was] simply rotting before [their] eyes'.[169] At this point Page Croft's power as leader of the largest backbench group was felt. He told both Chamberlain and Bridgeman that loss of confidence in Baldwin had become irretrievable and was now 'positively dangerous to the party' itself: the party would not accept any policy from him, and unless he was removed there would be an open split, with a rank-and-file 'avalanche to the United Empire Party'.[170]

Bridgeman's reaction was dismissive. But as party chairman Neville Chamberlain was receiving many 'anti-Baldwin letters'

---

[165] N. to I. Chamberlain, 17 May, 26 July 1930, NC 18/1/695, 705.
[166] N. to H. Chamberlain, 26 Oct. 1929, 8 June 1930, and to I. Chamberlain, 17 May 1930, NC 18/1/674, 699, 695.
[167] *The Times*, 22 Sept. 1930; N. to H. or I. Chamberlain [21 Sept. 1930] – misplaced among 1931 letters at time of consultation.
[168] *The Times*, 22 Sept. 1930; N. to I. Chamberlain, 28 Sept. 1930, and Bridgeman to N. Chamberlain, 3 Oct. 1930, NC 18/1/711, 8/10/6; Bridgeman diary, Sept. 1930 (Williamson, 239–40).
[169] See Ball, *Baldwin*, 95–8, with quotation (Ormsby-Gore to Salisbury, 5 Oct. 1930) at 98.
[170] Page Croft to Bridgeman, 4 and 9 Oct. 1930, Bridgeman papers, and to N. Chamberlain, 6 Oct. 1930, NC 8/10/7.

from local association officers.[171] Consultation with Hoare and Austen Chamberlain confirmed his own view that Page Croft's implied threat could not be ignored. There was a real danger that if Baldwin remained a rebellion might erupt against the whole collective leadership and its policy: that 'unless something happen[ed] quickly, everything and everybody [would] collapse like a pack of cards', with the party 'going...over to Horne'.[172] In the belief that continued loyalty to Baldwin was making their own positions as precarious as his, the three now gave serious consideration to forcing Baldwin's resignation.[173]

Yet, although rank-and-file discontent was at least as serious as that which sparked the 1922 party revolt, Baldwin did not feel obliged to consider resignation. In the event the collective leadership held together, and after a short period of anxious calculation a 'high political' manoeuvre easily contained the 'low political' revolt.[174] What principally restrained the two Chamberlains and Hoare was the 'revolting' prospect that Baldwin's removal at this point would seem a triumph for Rothermere and Beaverbrook.[175] Then, fortuitously, Bennett's offer of reciprocal preferences at the Imperial Conference provided a 'Heaven-sent opportunity'[176] for the leadership to present a new policy successfully, without appearing to submit to newspaper dictation. On Neville Chamberlain's initiative, Baldwin accepted Bennett's offer and dropped the referendum. This was followed on 14 October by the Business Committee accepting Chamberlain's programme. Churchill, as a leading opponent of food taxes, was brought very close to breaking with the party leadership.[177] Baldwin and Chamberlain would have liked him to go over an issue on which he was so patently isolated, but for that very reason Churchill thought better of it.[178]

[171] Bridgeman to Page Croft, 8 and 11 Oct. 1930, Croft papers 1/5/25, 26–7; and to N. Chamberlain, 8 and 13 Oct. 1930, NC 8/10/9, 13 (latter in Williamson, 241–2). N. Chamberlain to Bridgeman, 5 Oct. 1930, Bridgeman papers, and Dawson diary, 6 Oct. 1930.

[172] Hoare to N. Chamberlain, 8 Oct. 1930, NC 8/10/8.

[173] A. to I. Chamberlain, 4 Oct. 1930, and N. to A. Chamberlain, 8 Oct. 1930, AC 5/1/516, 39/2/39; A. to N. Chamberlain, 9 Oct. 1930, NC 8/10/10.

[174] Cf. Ball, Baldwin, xiv–xvi, 96–7.

[175] A. to N. Chamberlain, 9 Oct. 1930, NC 8/10/10.

[176] N. to A. Chamberlain, 10 Oct. 1930, AC 58/75.

[177] N. Chamberlain to Bridgeman, 18 Oct. 1930, Bridgeman papers; Churchill to Baldwin, 14 Oct. 1930 (not sent), in WSC v(2), 191–3.

[178] Fulsome Baldwin and N. Chamberlain appeals for Churchill to remain (18 and 21 Oct. 1930, in WSC v(2), 193–4, 203–4), must be understood in the light of the assumption that

By these means the Conservative party acquired the main features of its policy for the next election. As well as retrenchment, reduction of direct taxation, and 'drastic reform' of unemployment insurance, these included an emergency tariff on manufactures, a wheat quota and duties on other agricultural produce, and a 'completely free hand' to negotiate preferences with the Dominions. The programme placed the party squarely with the dominant movement of opinion discontented with the Labour government, and enabled it to establish close contact with Dominion ministers, the NFU, the FBI, the NCIC, and other protectionist bodies.[179] It also satisfied the local Conservative associations and almost all protectionist politicians, with Melchett and Elibank notably expressing public agreement.

Contrary to the party leaders' expectations, however, it did not solve the problem of a revolt against Baldwin. Neville Chamberlain had acted in the belief that Baldwin could not remain much longer, but that the new policy would enable him to remain long enough to thwart the Press Lords and leave with dignity.[180] But discontent with his leadership remained strong, and was extended in criticism of his attachment to the 'old gang' of ex-Cabinet ministers. From mid October it was expressed within the National Union executive, in letters to the press, and in a Gretton–Page Croft group request for a party meeting.[181] It was fomented by attacks in the Rothermere newspapers and by Beaverbrook, who treated the new policy as inadequate and ran an Empire Crusade candidate against the official Conservative at the South Paddington by-election.

Baldwin, feeling that 'every crook in the country [was] out for [his] scalp', was now angry and itching for a fight.[182] With the Press Lords openly demanding his removal, Neville Chamberlain and the Business Committee agreed that Baldwin should fight back and that the new policy made it possible for him to confront his critics successfully. The announcement of another party meeting brought

he would go anyway, and the only half-hearted appeals at the Business Committee: see Baldwin to Irwin, 16 Oct. 1930, Halifax papers 19/147, and N. to H. Chamberlain, 18 Oct. 1930, NC 18/1/713.

[179] For Bennett, Scullin, and NFU deputation, N. to H. Chamberlain, 15 Nov. 1930, NC 18/1/717. For FBI, EEU, and NCIC co-operating in studying tariff schedules, and getting in touch with the Conservative Research Department, Amery diary, 18, 27, and 28 Oct., 28 Nov. 1930 (*LSA* II, 84, 86, 137); Amery to N. Chamberlain, 29 Nov. 1930, NC 7/2/50.

[180] N. Chamberlain to Bridgeman, 10 Oct. 1930, Bridgeman papers.

[181] National Union Executive Committee minutes, 14 Oct. 1930; Gretton letter, and report of request by 48 MPs, *The Times*, 18 and 24 Oct. 1930.

[182] Baldwin to Irwin, 16 Oct. 1930, Halifax papers 19/147.

the leadership issue to a head, creating conditions of such party turmoil and uncertainty that Derby, consulted as a leading representative of northern Conservatism, bluntly told Baldwin that he should resign.[183] But at a second Caxton Hall meeting on 30 October, Baldwin carried acceptance of the policy with only Beaverbrook dissenting. Then, with Hailsham now taking the role Horne had filled at the previous meeting in repudiating press dictation, a Gretton–Page Croft motion against his leadership was defeated by 462 votes to 116.[184]

Coming after a long period of mounting tension, this result was treated by Conservative leaders as a triumph. It appeared to neutralise the announcement on the following day that the Empire Crusade candidate had won at South Paddington. The number of dissidents was, however, substantial – even if they consisted of the individually unimpressive diehard MPs, peers, and candidates – and as after the first Caxton Hall meeting the result could be regarded as owing more to hostility to press dictation than to confidence in Baldwin. Moreover, the approach of the Indian Conference threatened further party trouble. The Conservative leaders had established a politically effective economic policy. Nevertheless, during a period when the government had severe difficulties, the chief opposition party was at first tearing itself apart and was then only doubtfully united. It did not look credible as a prospective government of national salvation, and this was increasingly being thought essential.

[183] Derby–Baldwin conversation reported in Derby to Baldwin, 28 Oct. 1930 (not sent), Derby papers, 920 Der(17) 33.
[184] *The Times*, 30 Oct. 1930.

CHAPTER 4

'National crisis'

It is clear that Britain is confronted with a grave emergency. It is equally clear that an election on party lines will not help us to meet it... I have met... not hundreds but thousands of men and women of every class and shade of opinion... They all say, if the right man were to appeal to the people of Britain to abandon party strife and come together and pull together until this emergency is over, he would receive overwhelming support from the whole mass of the people.

General J. B. Seely letter, *The Times*, 2 December 1930

THE ATMOSPHERE

During 1930 there developed a public view that Britain was falling into a dangerous condition: from September there was commonly said to be a 'crisis'. Such statements had two meanings. In one sense they expressed genuine anxiety about the accumulation of economic, financial, and imperial difficulties, all occurring during a period of minority government, with the Labour Cabinet widely thought to be ineffective and with the Conservative and Liberal parties each internally divided. Grave problems had arisen, yet the political system seemed in no condition to cope with them. It was unclear how the Labour government could find sufficient cohesion or wider support to impose the firm measures which seemed necessary to overcome or contain the policy difficulties; or alternatively, given Liberal possession of the parliamentary balance of power and Conservative divisions, how the Labour government could be defeated and an alternative government formed before the problems became very much worse. In another sense 'crisis' was said to exist because this and related terms were deliberately used to heighten tension, with the purpose of defending, or more often criticising and attempting to force changes in, existing policy or personnel. 'Crisis' terminology was a conventional instrument of political struggle: 'almost every year produced a "political crisis"'.[1] But now the accumulation of policy and party difficulties meant that its use became much more frequent. How far the cries of 'crisis' in late 1930 were description and how far rhetoric varied between different individuals or groups, and can be determined only by examining each in turn. What matters here is that the two usages fed upon each other, acquiring a momentum which generated an atmosphere of deep 'national crisis'. This 'national crisis' in turn had considerable effects upon political conduct.

With different emphases, the notion of crisis was expressed by all prominent interest groups, experts, officials, commentators, newspapers, and reviews, and across the whole range of political opinion. The NFU spoke of an agricultural 'emergency', the FBI of the industrial slump posing 'a grave national peril', the Institute of Bankers of the nation being on 'the road to destruction'.[2] Bevin declared that the 'terrible economic crisis' warranted government declaration of 'a state of national emergency'.[3] Keynes described the world slump as 'one of the greatest economic catastrophes in world history'.[4] Conservative leaders presented their new economic policy as a response to 'a national and an industrial crisis of the gravest character'.[5] The ILP and Mosley similarly addressed themselves to a 'grave national emergency'.[6] Gretton asserted that in his experience the party situation had 'never been so critical and at the same time chaotic'.[7] For Snowden, it was 'a hell of a time'.[8] The state of the Empire was integral to this crisis atmosphere. Horne spoke of possible imperial disintegration as a cause of approaching 'ruin'.[9] 'In [India] & in some other things of great importance', Grey could not 'see how the problems are to be solved'.[10] Comparisons with the Great War became commonplace. Austen

---

[1] Cowling, *Impact of Labour*, 9.

[2] NFU deputation, FBI resolution, Holland-Martin speech, *The Times*, 17 and 14 Oct. 1930, 6 Nov. 1930.

[3] Bevin to MacDonald, 27 Aug. 1930, JRM 461 (and see Bullock, *Bevin* I, 453).

[4] Keynes, 'The Great Slump of 1930', *Nation*, 20 Dec. 1930 (*JMK* IX, 127).

[5] Baldwin statement, *The Times*, 16 Oct. 1930, and N. Chamberlain speech, *HC Deb*, 244, col. 504, 3 Nov. 1930.

[6] Maxton motion at Labour party conference, *The Times*, 8 Oct. 1930; Mosley in *HC Deb*, 244, cols. 67–8, 29 Oct. 1930.

[7] Gretton to Tyrrell, 1 Nov. 1930, Gwynne papers 24.

[8] Snowden to MacDonald, 16 Aug. 1930, JRM 676.

[9] Horne speech, *The Times*, 24 Nov. 1930.

[10] Grey to Simon, 18 Oct. 1930, Simon papers.

Chamberlain and Churchill presented the Indian issue as the most serious problem since then; MacDonald and Lloyd George competed in claims that the economic and political position was the greatest crisis since 'the darkest hours of the War'.[11] To some, the situation was a fateful moment for British power. H. D. Henderson feared the 'opening phase of the decline and fall of Great Britain as a prosperous industrial country'.[12] Maclean spoke of Britain as on the same path of extravagant expenditure which had caused the fall of Rome, imperial Spain, and Tsarist Russia.[13] Churchill conceived a task of averting 'the decline and fall of the British Empire'.[14] Garvin, editor of *The Observer*, 'fe[lt]...that Götterdämmerung...[was] descending upon all British greatness'.[15] A few, like Percy, were influenced by literary notions of an imminent 'collapse of...western civilisation'.[16]

There was no shortage of proposed solutions for the substantive economic and imperial problems: land settlement, marketing, rationalisation, loan-financed development works, export revival, international monetary co-operation, tariff truce, quotas, tariffs, retrenchment; and Empire Free Trade, imperial economic unity, the Simon Report, Dominion status. More broadly, Churchill wanted 'a new and strong assertion of Britain's right to live and right to reign with her Empire splendid and united'. Bevin and the ILP wanted their own versions of 'socialism', Mosley the application of 'modern minds' to 'modern problems'.[17] From all quarters there were calls for 'urgent', 'drastic', or 'emergency' measures.

Yet despite this consensus about the existence of 'crisis' and need for firm action, there seemed to be a lack of governmental capacity, political will, or political agreement to enable effective implementation of any policy or combination of policies. This stimulated a view that the system of government was somehow inadequate and at

---

[11] A. to I. Chamberlain, 7 July 1930, AC 5/1/508; Churchill to Baldwin, 24 Sept. 1930, SB 104/51 (*WSC* v(2), 186); MacDonald to Lloyd George, and Lloyd George to MacDonald, 12 and 14 Sept. 1930, JRM 1308.
[12] 'The Background of the Problem', 18 Sept. 1930, in H. D. Henderson, *Inter-War Years*, 69.
[13] Maclean in *HC Deb*, 244, col. 109, 29 Oct. 1930.
[14] Churchill speech, *The Times*, 21 Aug. 1930.
[15] Garvin to Astor, 14 July 1930, Astor papers.
[16] Percy, *Democracy on Trial* (written late 1930), chap. II 'The Crisis of Western Civilisation', and esp. 16.
[17] Churchill to Beaverbrook, 23 Sept. 1930, Beaverbrook papers C/86 (*WSC* v(2), 185); Bevin to MacDonald, 27 Aug. 1930, JRM 461; Jowett motion, *HC Deb*, 244, col. 397, 31 Oct. 1930; Mosley speech, *HC Deb*, 244, col. 80, 29 Oct. 1930.

risk of becoming discredited. MPs from all parties spoke of 'public' disillusionment with Parliament and drew warning parallels with the slide of continental nations into dictatorship.[18] Grey thought 'the strain on Democratic Government [was] very great'.[19] Muir, Lloyd George, Churchill, Mosley, and Percy all declared that 'Parliament' or 'democracy' was 'on trial'.[20]

Such thinking produced extensive debate about the efficiency of government machinery. This debate has obvious parallels with those at other periods of severe policy strain during and after the Boer and Great Wars; it drew upon several traditions of criticism of 'congestion' of public business, of excessive centralisation and 'bureaucracy', and of 'Cabinet government'.[21] The 1930–1 debate was, however, notable because it developed in peacetime, because it focussed upon the treatment of economic issues, and because it attracted contributions from prominent individuals in each party, including party leaders and former Cabinet ministers. Jowett, Beatrice Webb, and Mosley, Muir and Lloyd George, Churchill and Percy deployed incisive criticism of an 'antiquated' constitutional machinery, and offered various proposals for radical reform: creation of parliamentary standing committees, devolution to 'functional' and regional assemblies, reconstruction of government departments, establishment of a smaller Cabinet on the wartime model.[22] 'Drastic reform' of House of Commons procedure became Liberal party policy.[23] Even Baldwin, a leading defender of existing arrangements, acknowledged that there was impatience with democratic institutions and that analyses of this condition were 'important and of some urgency' – though characteristically his own view was that the

---

[18] See, e.g., *HC Deb*, 244 for Elliot, W. J. Brown, and Hopkin-Morris, cols. 66, 118, 133, 29 Oct.; Brockway, col. 408, 31 Oct.; Eden, cols. 613–14, 3 Nov., all 1930.

[19] Grey to Simon, 18 Oct. 1930, Simon papers.

[20] Muir, *How Britain is Governed*, 325; Lloyd George article, *Daily Express*, 18 March 1930; 'Parliamentary Government and the Economic Problem', 19 June 1930, in Churchill, *Thoughts and Adventures*, 240; Mosley, *HC Deb*, 244, col. 69, 29 Oct. 1930; Percy, *Democracy on Trial*. [21] For background, see Butt, *The Power of Parliament*, chaps. 2–4.

[22] Their chief contributions were: ILP adoption of Jowett proposals, in Brockway, *Socialism Over Sixty Years*, 278–83, and *LPACR 1930*, 241–3, 9 Oct.; B. Webb, 'A Reform Bill for 1932', *Political Quarterly*, 2, Jan. 1931; Mosley speeches, *HC Deb*, 239, col. 1350, 28 May 1930, and *LPACR 1930*, 203, 7 Oct., and manifesto, *The Times*, 8 Dec. 1930; Muir, *How Britain is Governed*, and 'What is Wrong with the British System of Government?', *Nineteenth Century*, DCXLV, Nov. 1930; Lloyd George, article, *Daily Express*, 18 March 1930, interview, *Daily Herald*, 17 June 1930, and *HC Deb*, 244, cols. 53–4, 29 Oct. 1930; Churchill, 'Parliamentary Government and the Economic Problem', 19 June 1930, in *Thoughts and Adventures*, 229–41; Percy, *Democracy on Trial*.

[23] NLF resolution, *Manchester Guardian*, 18 Oct. 1930.

failure lay not in the machinery, but in 'faith'.[24] Some Labour
ministers had a speculative interest in the subject,[25] but having
directed their party towards constitutionalism and lacking a clear
parliamentary majority, in practice they had no desire to attempt
large reforms. Nevertheless in response to economic policy difficulties
the Cabinet introduced piecemeal innovations including the EAC
and Public Works Facilities Act, and in frustration at parliamentary
congestion appointed a Select Committee on Commons procedure.[26] From February to July 1931 this committee received
evidence from the leaders and chief whips of each party and from
Churchill, Mosley, Muir, Jowett, and Percy, ranging well beyond
procedure to the arguments for and against major institutional
change.[27]

In June 1931 Churchill called for 'co-operation of all parties in the
improvement of our parliamentary institutions'.[28] However, the
significance of this issue lay not in its having any practical result, but
as a measure of the prevailing sense of extraordinary political
difficulty. The cause of institutional reform was hampered by
differences between the proposals of its advocates. But more
decisively, most politicians and commentators thought such reform
unnecessary, because they found more obvious explanations for the
shortcomings of government and Parliament in the distribution of
power within the party system. For this problem, members and
supporters of each party naturally thought that the most obvious
and best solution was simply the establishment of a strong majority
government with effective policies, formed by their own party. But
in late 1930 the condition of every party meant it was open to doubt
whether the normal processes of party politics could soon produce a
competent and authoritative party government. Consequently,
across important sections of opinion anti-party sentiment increased
markedly.

As with government machinery, so with the party system there
was a long history of criticism – particularly, though not exclusively,
during wars and their immediate aftermaths. The nature of the

[24] Speech, 'Democracy, Old and New', *The Times*, 15 July 1930.
[25] E.g., Passfield speech, *The Times*, 20 March 1930; and Greenwood, Adamson, Alexander
in B. Webb diary, 15 Nov. 1929, 5 Feb., 21 Sept. 1930.
[26] In Cabinet, 'everybody [was] in favour of a drastic enquiry into the machinery of the
House of Commons': Jones, *Whitehall Diary* II, 265, 18 June 1930.
[27] See *Special Report from the Select Committee on Procedure on Public Business*, 7 Oct. 1931.
[28] *HC Deb*, 253, col. 109, 2 June 1931.

complaints in 1930 were those commonplace at most periods: that party competition generated spurious conflict and obstruction, where there might otherwise be agreement and action on the merits of issues; that it deterred politicians from 'facing the facts' and 'telling the truth' to the electorate. Now, however, the quantity of such criticism became unusually large, and a new element had developed. It appeared that the central political issues – already substantially altered by the war – were undergoing a further large shift and ceasing to correspond with a pattern of parties which, despite the rise of Labour and decline of the Liberals, remained rooted in pre-war or immediate post-war conditions. Opinion and party were becoming dissociated,[29] with important effects upon attitudes towards the party system. On the one hand substantial groups had emerged who felt that their views were not adequately represented within existing parties, and who appeared to provide material for effective independent political pressure: here, the Empire Crusade and United Empire party provided both evidence and example. On the other hand, under substantive pressures the public stances of some leading members of each established party on such matters as protection, imperial trade, retrenchment, and India were plainly converging, and appeared to create a possibility of cross-party co-operation.

It has been seen that agricultural organisations, the FBI, NCIC, TUC leaders, and Indian Empire Society all called for a 'non-party', 'business', or 'expert' approach on their special concerns.[30] Since each had definite policy preferences, this did not mean they lacked inclination towards a particular party – as indicated by the NFU, FBI, and NCIC contacts with the Conservative leadership once its protection policy was settled. But if in practice their 'non-party' appeals meant they wanted other parties to co-operate with the party which best represented their policy preferences, this was no less an expression of frustration with the party struggle and a contribution to an atmosphere favouring 'national' agreement. Some businessmen were more definitely critical of existing parties. Morris and other officers of the NCIC would have liked to establish

---

[29] For transformation of issues, see esp. Churchill, 'Parliamentary Government and the Economic Problem', and for mismatch between opinion and party, Keynes, 'Sir Oswald Mosley's Manifesto', *Nation*, 13 Dec. 1930 (*JMK* xx, 475–6).

[30] For other examples, see Engineering and Allied Employers' National Federation and National Citizens' Union (a rate- and tax-payers' organisation, successor of the Middle Class Union) statements, *The Times*, 4 and 6 Dec. 1930.

a business party, even a businessmen's government. Sceptical of the Conservative leadership's commitment to business interests, they proposed to run their own parliamentary candidates and in December established a local branch structure, the League of Industry, for that purpose[31] – though in the event Conservative policy denied it sufficient support to emulate the Empire Crusade and UEP. More representative of business attitudes was a group of old-fashioned Liberal businessmen led by Hugh Bell, Ernest Benn, Henry Bell, Cooper, and Lords Cowdray and Leverhulme, which published in July 1930 a manifesto complaining that 'large sections of serious citizens' – those supporting both free trade and re-trenchment – were 'excluded from and forgotten by the parties as at present constituted'. Many of the group had Liberal Council connections, but they declined to become a Council vehicle; and, finding that their emphasis upon retrenchment attracted con-siderable interest among protectionist businessmen, they decided to concentrate on that issue and organise a 'strictly non-party' movement of 'Friends of Economy'. Though denying any desire 'to complicate the political position still further', they planned a 'demonstration' in the City for January with the intention of influencing 'all parties'.[32] On that basis, they began with substantial success to recruit support from leading industrialists, financiers, retailers, and former public servants, and to seek speakers from each political party.

Calls for a 'non-party' approach to outstanding problems were also made or taken up by newspapers and journals of several different persuasions. The strongest critic of the party system was *The Week-end Review*. Its editor, Barry, and his staff were young radicals who felt themselves disfranchised by the Liberal party's decline, and who identified a new audience disillusioned no less by a political slump as by the economic slump. The *Review*'s message was self-consciously young, independent, progressive, and activist: politics were in a 'bad way' because the loss of the war generation had left the country under the leadership of a 'Monstrous Regiment of Old Men', wedded to nineteenth-century shibboleths and shirking the real economic issues. Each party had failed, and the country was

---

[31] Jarvie (NCIC secretary) at inaugural meeting, and NCIC statements, *The Times*, 26 Sept., 4 Oct., 8 Dec. 1930; Steel-Maitland to Jarvie [draft, Oct. 1930] and to Scott, 17 Oct. 1930, Steel-Maitland papers 629, 94/2.

[32] 'Manifesto on Economy', and announcement of the 'Friends', *The Times*, 16 July, 7 Aug. 1930. For origins of the movement, see E. Benn diary, 6, 7, 21, and 27 July 1930.

'sick of Parliament'. What was needed were 'an intelligent grasp of contemporary facts', and reconstruction, efficiency, planning, and positive, undoctrinaire, leadership.[33]

From these perspectives, *The Week-end Review* admired the programmes of Lloyd George and Mosley, encouraged contributions from 'progressives' in all three parties, and emphasised the similarities in their ideas. Challenged by Percy and other MPs to declare themselves, the *Review*'s staff offered its own programme for bringing together enlightened Conservatism, moderate Socialism, and constructive Liberalism. 'A National Plan' proposed, *inter alia*, a 'corporatist' reform of government machinery and retrenchment, tax reduction, industrial and imperial rationalisation, and planned trade.[34] Circulated to leading economists, bankers, industrialists, agriculturalists, editors, scientists, trade unionists, and 'progressive' politicians, the plan attracted a considerable amount of favourable comment.[35] The outcome was the formation in March 1931 of Political and Economic Planning, chaired by Blackett, a maverick Bank of England director and former Treasury official who considered a national plan 'vital' for escaping 'national collapse'.[36] Though PEP was a select research body of non-political experts rather than a political movement, its formation and the activities of *The Week-end Review* were important in revealing a convergence of progressive opinion and the possibilities for co-operation outside the existing party system.

The Observer was equally committed to promoting a non-party approach, but in contrast believed this must occur between the existing parties. It also differed in being conducted from a position of 'Progressive Independent Unionis[m]'.[37] Although its proprietor, Lord Astor, and his MP wife were formally Conservatives, their sympathy towards undoctrinaire constructive radicalism and imperi-

---

[33] 'New Lamps for Old' and 'The Tyranny of Idleness', *Week-end Review*, 1 and 8 Nov. 1930. For the review's origin, see Max Nicholson, 'The Proposal for a National Plan', in Pinder, *Political and Economic Planning*, 6.

[34] Nicholson, 'The Proposal for a National Plan', 6–7; Barry journal, 15 Feb. 1931; 'A National Plan for Great Britain', *Week-end Review* supplement, 14 Feb. 1931, and see PEP papers A/5/1, for a draft dated Nov. 1930.

[35] 'Comments on the National Plan', *Week-end Review*, 14 and 21 Feb. 1931. With various reservations those in favour included Percy, Mosley, Pugh, Duff Cooper, and Laski. For circulation list, see PEP papers A/5/1.

[36] *Week-end Review*, 14 Feb. 1931. For Blackett, see Sayers, *Bank of England*, 598. For PEP origins, see Kenneth Lindsay, 'PEP through the 1930s', in Pinder, *Political and Economic Planning*, 9–15.

[37] Astor to Garvin, 22 May 1929, and Garvin to Astor, 25 Feb. 1929, Astor papers.

alism of whatever party affiliation received public expression in the licence they allowed their editor, Garvin. As perhaps the leading political journalist of the day, Garvin's editorials and articles were 'read by all the political leaders of any note'.[38] During 1929–31 those who solicited his goodwill included Lloyd George, Reading, Simon, Beaverbrook, Wise of the ILP, Mosley, Alexander, Thomas, and MacDonald (who offered him a privy councillorship in December 1929). This influence arose from a stance which was independent, yet inclusive of aspects of each party. He was hostile to socialism where it meant punitive taxation, to liberalism where it meant free trade, and to conservatism where it meant reaction. Otherwise, his Unionism was a broad church embracing whatever seemed to advance the causes of domestic development, imperial integration, and Britain's international leadership.

Much of Garvin's message in late 1930 was what he had been declaring for years: doom-laden warnings about Britain's industrial and imperial decline, 'insuperable disgust' at the state of politics, his hope for some 'constructive revolution', admiration for Lloyd George, and advocacy of party alliances.[39] During and immediately after the 1929 election he wanted Conservatives and Liberals to merge in a 'National party'.[40] Thereafter Conservative anti-Liberalism and divisions over protection, the Labour government's foreign policy, a belief that MacDonald could best steer between Irwin and the reactionaries, and confidence that economic imperatives would force adoption of imperial protectionism all converted him to a Labour–Liberal alliance.[41] But by October 1930 his vision had become apocalyptic. There was now a condition not merely of 'national emergency' but of 'imperial emergency', with 'the drift to catastrophe' in India as the greatest danger.[42] The party 'dog-fight' was mostly to blame – a 'spectacle for ridicule and abhorrence' which was obstructing 'life or death' decisions on tariffs, imperial economic unity, retrenchment, and India. Now disillusioned with the Labour Cabinet for allowing Snowden to reduce the Imperial

[38] Lloyd George to F. Stevenson, 19 Aug. 1925, in Taylor, 93.
[39] E.g., Garvin to Lloyd George, 2 Nov. 1928, and to F. Stevenson, 29 April 1928, 25 April 1929, LG G/8/5/14–17; Garvin to Astor, 25 Feb., 25 April 1929, Astor papers.
[40] Garvin to Astor, letters passim for May–June 1929, Astor papers.
[41] Garvin to MacDonald, 20 July 1929 to 30 April 1930, JRM 1515; Garvin to Lloyd George, 29 June, 15 Nov. 1929, 5 March 1930, LG G/8/5/19, 21, 23.
[42] 'The Cabinet and the Crisis' and 'India: A Grave Warning', *Observer*, 19 Oct., 2 Nov. 1930.

Conference to a 'fiasco' and for its failure to impose retrenchment, his message was that the great issues should be lifted outside the 'party vortex' in a 'common national effort', mobilising 'peace-energy on a war-scale'.[43]

In campaigning for co-operation outside or between the parties, *The Observer* and *The Week-end Review* were remarkable only in making this their central editorial policy. *The Economist* – under Layton's editorship another journal seeking a place for Liberalism outside the Liberal party – found indications that 'the nation will not indefinitely submit to the domination of the party machine' and hoped for a 'non-party national policy in economic affairs'.[44] Gwynne, editor of the diehard Conservative *Morning Post*, campaigned for cross-party co-operation on imperial economic unity.[45] In December Dawson's *Times* agreed that a 'dislocated' party system was now 'incompetent' to deal with the 'grave emergency'. Although its long-term preference was for a Baldwin-led Conservative government, it was sufficiently sensitive to the prevailing atmosphere – and concerned to preserve all-party agreement on India – that for the meantime it called upon the Labour government to shift its domestic and imperial policies towards 'the highest common measure of agreement' – to adopt 'a national policy'.[46]

THE REACTIONS

In the last quarter of 1930, then, the political atmosphere became markedly more anxious and uncertain. A sense of crisis of wartime proportions prevailed, the adequacy of government machinery was under scrutiny, and extra-parliamentary criticism of the party system had intensified. Political leaders were increasingly being expected to take radical action to put their houses in order: to behave or to arrange themselves in a manner which would enable critical problems to be resolved on non-party or 'national' terms, or else to stand aside and allow 'experts' to settle them.

That certain matters of State were best handled outside party politics had long been accepted and practised by party leaders – from mutual concern for vital imperial, defence, diplomatic and financial interests, and in order to maintain continuity in national policy (as in tripartisan consultation on important Indian and

---

[43] Editorials and signed Garvin articles, *Observer*, passim for Oct.–Nov. 1930.
[44] 'Electoral Reform' and 'The Devil and the Deep Blue Sea', *Economist*, 2 Aug., 29 Nov. 1930.
[45] See below, p. 151.   [46] Editorial, 'A National Policy', *The Times*, 2 Dec. 1930.

Committee of Imperial Defence issues, and in monetary policy being treated as 'non-political'). The smooth conduct of parliamentary business depended upon routine co-operation between the rival whips' offices. That the areas of co-operation or collusion might be extended was a familiar idea to those having particular policy commitments or tactical interests. In such respects Baldwin's reference in June 1929 to a 'united Parliament' and MacDonald's to a 'Council of State' were perfectly conventional. Labour ministers – including those on the Labour left like Lansbury and Johnston – had not only accepted the conventional areas of co-operation as integral to the creation of a constitutional party: they also attempted to make increased resort to such arrangements, for three reasons. There was a simple socialist faith that dispassionate examination of the 'facts' produced socialistic conclusions, manifested for example in a party commitment to an all-party parliamentary approach towards unemployment policy.[47] There was the strategic concern to demonstrate the Labour party's determination to govern responsibly, and also a hope that a minority government might be maintained in office by spreading the onus for difficult decisions or the blame for any failures.[48] But in the most central and critical areas of policy existing all-party consultation was fragile or else by October 1930 attempts to extend it had failed, exactly because these were areas of considerable party sensitivity. The tripartisan approach on India was jeopardised by Liberal doubts and Conservative divisions over Irwin's policy; the three-party committee on unemployment insurance foundered on the refusal of most ministers to contemplate benefit cuts; the Cabinet's effort to 'rope...Conservatives and Liberals into the administration' of unemployment and agricultural policies[49] resulted, after Conservative refusal to participate, in the less useful and politically awkward consultations with the Liberals alone.

Despite these experiences, the atmosphere of crisis and extra-parliamentary criticism had become so substantial that all politicians

[47] *HC Deb*, 203, cols. 1152–96, 8 March 1927; Johnston, *Memoirs*, 96–7; Snowden article, *Reynolds News*, 24 March 1929; Lansbury speech, *The Times*, 21 Dec. 1929; Johnston to MacDonald, 24 Jan. 1930, CP33(30).

[48] MacDonald consulted both Baldwin and Lloyd George about the reports on Dominion Legislation and Palestine Disturbances, difficulties at the Naval Conference, and amendment of the League of Nations Covenant. A different device, with the same objective, was the joint select committee on East Africa.

[49] Johnston in Jones, *Whitehall Diary* II, 260, 20 May 1930.

felt obliged to offer some response to the appeals for 'non-party' action. The readiest answer was that their own party enunciated the true national policy. But for some members of all three parties, this alone seemed inadequate. Sharing the anxieties about economic, financial, or imperial conditions and the frustration at the state of party politics, these encouraged the idea of extending the area of co-operation. Such was Snowden's appeal for the assistance of 'Parliament' in achieving retrenchment. Churchill, Percy, Jowett, and Lloyd George proposed reforms of government machinery as a means to take crucial problems 'out of politics'. Grey, Horne, and Wedgwood became prominent in the Friends of Economy. In the Commons during late October and early November Lord Stanley, Wolmer, Hilton Young, Oliver Stanley, O'Connor, and Boothby from the Conservative benches and Cocks, Mosley, W. J. Brown, Philips Price, and Strachey from the Labour side all remarked upon a narrowing of party differences and consequent opportunity and desirability for a common policy.[50]

One obvious problem was the mechanism by which non-party action might be achieved. For some the answer seemed to be a national conference or council or 'sub-parliament'; the three-party representation at the Indian Round Table Conference seemed to provide a model for domestic policy.[51] As the proposed objective was usually acceptance of all-round reduction of costs (Keynes's 'national treaty'), it was generally suggested that such a conference might also include industrialists, trade unionists, bankers, distributors, and economists.[52] From October, this became Liberal party policy.[53] Labour ministers were however suspicious of proposals for co-operation coming from political rivals, and doubted the practicality of a formal conference. In late October the Cabinet considered a new appeal for co-operation on unemployment, but in view of the Conservative rejection of their previous invitation concluded that it would be futile and a gratuitous admission of

---

[50] *HC Deb*, 244, cols. 264, 536, 545, 548, and 695 for Lord Stanley, Cocks, Hilton Young, and Wolmer. For the rest, see below, note 71.

[51] See esp. Balfour proposal, below p. 150, and for a similar idea, Hankey memo, 'Unemployment. A Challenge to Defeatism', 19 Sept. 1930, CAB 63/43.

[52] E.g., F. Schuster (the banker) speech, and National Citizens' Union statement, *The Times*, 24 Oct., 6 Dec. 1930; and 'A National Emergency', *Economist*, 10 Jan. 1931. There is obvious similarity with the economic 'sub-parliament' or councils proposed by Churchill, Percy, Muir, and Beatrice Webb.

[53] Lloyd George speech at NLF conference, *Manchester Guardian*, 18 Oct. 1930, and *How to Tackle Unemployment*.

weakness.[54] Their answer to the Liberal proposal was that 'nothing effective could be looked for from a spectacular conference' of producers and economic experts.[55]

Another possible mechanism for achieving 'national' co-operation was coalition across or between the political parties. Obviously those calling for co-operation were not necessarily seeking such realignments. Their motivations were various but for the most part perfectly compatible with the maintenance and even advancement of distinctive party positions. When co-operation was genuinely desired, as by Snowden or the Friends of Economy, the intention might be broad agreement on specific issues without prejudice to other party interests. Co-operation proposals might also be attempts to relieve party or personal difficulties, like the Labour government's over unemployment or Churchill's over protection, or else efforts to embarrass opponents or gain influence over rivals, both concerns of Lloyd George. Nevertheless for some politicians the atmosphere of crisis and calls for co-operation – especially given the conditions of a hung parliament and party divisions[56] – made the idea of all-party coalition a matter for serious consideration. For a few, the situation seemed pregnant with potential for an altogether new political departure.

The first to plan a transformation of the party system was Mosley, who had always wanted more than was offered by conventional party politics. An ex-serviceman, self-consciously representative of the 'war generation', he believed the 'static' pre-war world had been replaced by 'a dynamic age of great and dangerous events', in which politics were constantly performed on the brink of 'crisis' and demanded youthful minds combining 'ruthless Realism', 'soaring Idealism', and a thirst for 'action'.[57] This conception of a new radicalism had carried him through phases as a Coalition Conservative, Cecilian independent, and Asquithian Liberal sympathiser to a position balanced between ILP activism, Keynesian economics, and cultivation of MacDonald. On entering the Labour government,

---

[54] Cabinet 62(30), 22 Oct. 1930. For origin of the proposal, see below, note 102.
[55] MacDonald at EAC 9th meeting, 7 Nov. 1930.
[56] See Thomas and Amery in Amery diary, 4 Dec. 1929 (*LSA* II, 57), and Churchill in Jones, *Whitehall Diary* II, 229, 23 Dec. 1929, for earlier speculations.
[57] This consistent view of politics as high drama can be traced through Mosley to Cecil, 17 April 1921, and 1922 election address, in Skidelsky, *Mosley*, 111, 117–18; Mosley, *Revolution by Reason*, 28–9, and Mosley articles, *Daily Express*, 19 Feb. 1929, *Labour Magazine*, May 1929, *Sunday Express*, 25 May 1930.

he thought that 'the age of youth has not quite arrived but events are travelling towards it with an extraordinary momentum'.[58] The rejection of his unemployment proposals, however, convinced him that Labour leaders were as wedded to pre-war ideas as those of other parties: he had 'misunderstood' them.[59]

In May 1930 Mosley expected an unemployment crisis in the winter which the existing government would be unable to contain: unless reconstructed the Labour party would, he asserted, be destroyed for a generation.[60] His resignation speech – a parliamentary triumph – was a long-premeditated claim to leadership close to the political centre.[61] Henceforth he spoke about 'emergency' conditions, argued for drastic reform of government machinery because 'the modern world is sick of words and demands action', and followed the prevailing shifts of opinion in moving rapidly towards imperial protectionism, thinly disguised as 'insulation'.[62]

These positions served the simultaneous development of two alternative strategies. The first was to capture the Labour party for his memorandum policy. Working with a parliamentary following consisting of his wife, Strachey, Bevan, Forgan, Oliver Baldwin (the Labour son of the Conservative leader), and W. J. Brown, and with Cook, secretary of the miners' union, he sought to give direction to the extra-parliamentary party's discontent and to force Mac-Donald's removal.[63] His second strategy was to create a 'national' alliance from 'dynamic' elements of all parties and of none. By the autumn he had established contact with the restless political spirits of the older generation – Lloyd George, Churchill, Beaverbrook, Rothermere, Garvin, and Lloyd – where his potential was registered in election to Churchill's Other Club.[64] His greater interest, however – and principal recommendation to these elders – lay in providing leadership for discontented, 'progressive', younger men. These

[58] Mosley to Garvin [10 June 1929], Garvin papers.
[58] Jones, *Whitehall Diary* II, 259, 20 May 1930.
[60] Lockhart diary, 13 and 20 May, in Young I, 121; B. Webb diary, 19 May 1930 (MacKenzie IV, 216); Lady Hilton Young diary, 3 June 1930.
[61] For his resignation being long contemplated, see, e.g., Dalton diary, 29 Jan., 12 March 1930 (Pimlott, 91, 98).
[62] Mosley articles, *Sunday Express*, 25 May 1930, and *Daily Herald*, 7 July 1930; speeches, *HC Deb*, 241, cols. 1347–57, 16 July 1930, *LPACR 1930*, 202, 7 Oct., and *The Times*, 20 Oct. 1930.
[63] See B. Webb diary, 19 May 1930. For apparent willingness to accept Henderson as leader, see Dalton diary, 1 Aug., 10 Nov. 1930. For Mosley's activities within the Labour party, see Skidelsky, *Mosley*, 221–4, 229–32, 236–7.
[64] Mosley, *My Life*, 275–7; Mosley to Garvin, 30 Oct. 1930, Garvin papers; Boothby to Mosley, autumn 1930, in N. Mosley, *Rules of the Game*, 151–3; Coote, *Other Club*, 67.

included Sinclair, Nicolson, Keynes,[65] the Conservative MP Allen, and especially a loosely associated 'young Conservative' group – Elliot, Oliver Stanley, Boothby, O'Connor, Moore-Brabazon, Macmillan, and Melchett's son, Mond. In common with Mosley, these 'young Conservatives' shared disillusionment with their party leaders, belief in the obsolescence of pre-war ideas, acceptance of state management as the engine of economic and social regeneration, and recognition that the existing ineffectiveness of parties was both a danger and an opportunity.[66] For some, contact with Mosley was long established. Through them Mosley obtained access to the Astors' political salon. Like Astor and Allen, some had their own interests in a 'Young Party' or 'activist' alliance.[67] Some had already joined Mosley in speculations on such themes as 'the decay of democracy and parliamentarianism' and 'whether it would be well to have a fascist coup'.[68] With Mosley, they contributed to and obtained stimulus from *The Week-end Review*. Though they would have preferred the ex-prime minister Lloyd George to the relatively inexperienced Mosley as leader of any new movement,[69] they responded positively to a revised Mosley diagnosis.

For Labour consumption Mosley continued to emphasise his original memorandum policy of loan-financed public works. But in a new memorandum circulated in October to his non-Labour associates as the prospectus for their 'contemplated movement', public works were downgraded to 'perhaps a minor matter in relation to the greater task' of 'insulation'. Other elements included Keynesian monetary reform, but also restoration of unemployment insurance to an actuarial basis and reduction of income tax. There was to be 'Caesarism' in India, and at home massive 'State action' through a small 'executive Cabinet' armed by a 'General Powers Bill' with all legislative power on economic matters, confining Parliament to a right of veto and involving 'a certain surrender of political liberty'. The overall theme was of a 'war situation'

[65] See Mosley to Keynes, 6 Feb. 1930, Jan. 1931, in *JMK* xx, 312–13, 482; Dalton diary, 2 and 29 Oct. 1930 (partly in Pimlott, 125), and Nicolson diary, 30 Nov. 1930 (Nicolson I, 61).

[66] For anti-Baldwinism, Jones, *Whitehall Diary* II, 274, 24 Oct. 1930, and Stanley in Hoare to N. Chamberlain, 8 Oct. 1930, NC 8/10/8. For economic ideas, see Boothby, Loder, Macmillan, and Stanley, *Industry and The State* (1927).

[67] See, e.g., Elliot, Boothby, Macmillan in memo, 'Discussion … at 30 St James Place', 5 Nov. 1929, and Allen to Blumenfeld, 28 May 1930, Beaverbrook papers C/235, B/123; Astor to Garvin, 15 July 1930, Astor papers; Macmillan in Nicolson diary, 2 July 1930 (Nicolson I, 51); Jones, *Whitehall Diary* II, 275, 26 Oct. 1930.

[68] Mosley, Stanley, Elliot, Moore-Brabazon, O'Connor, Boothby in Nicolson diary, 15 Feb. 1930.   [69] Jones, *Whitehall Diary* II, 275, 26 Oct. 1930.

requiring an authoritarian regime in order to achieve 'national Renaissance'.[70] The influence of Mussolini's example is obvious.

The various webs spun by Mosley were partially exposed during the Debate on the Address from late October, when Mosley, Strachey, Brown, Bevan, Elliot, Stanley, O'Connor, Boothby, and Mond made mutually supporting speeches – some certainly by prior arrangement – on the causes of the economic crisis and need for 'insulation'.[71] Believing that these speeches manifested 'for the first time a line up of youth against the old gangs in the demand for action', Mosley abandoned his first strategy of trying to capture the Labour party and concentrated upon creating a 'new party of younger Nationalists'.[72] What were ostensibly moves within the Labour party became in reality efforts to take Labour support into this new combination, and to uncover potential support elsewhere. His December manifesto, though signed only by Cook and sixteen Labour MPs, obtained favourable notices in *The Observer*, *The Week-end Review*, and other non-Labour journals,[73] and public encouragement from not just Elliot, Macmillan, Boothby, and Moore-Brabazon, but also Keynes, Amery, and Morris – who proposed combination with the NCIC to form 'a vigorous Industrial Party', aiming at a 'drastic revision' of national leadership.[74]

From one perspective, Mosley's activities can be seen as an intelligent exploration of new possibilities. Yet from another perspective it might be argued that they were miscalculations based on a misapprehension of political realities. He was undeterred by his small personal following and a succession of defeats within the Labour party, and he saw nothing incongruous in an assortment of

---

[70] 'Private & Confidential' memo, Oct. 1930, copies in Garvin and Astor papers, and Beaverbrook papers C/254. This was probably the document 'which is to unite Boothby, Macmillan, Stanley, etc. with ... Mosley in his scheme to save England' noted in Headlam diary, 15 Dec. 1930.

[71] *HC Deb*, 244, cols. 57–67 (Elliot), 67–81 (Mosley), 81–9 (Stanley), 109–19 (W. J. Brown), 169–74 (Strachey), all 29 Oct.; 234–40 (O'Connor), 30 Oct.; 578–89 (Boothby) and 607–11 (Mond), 3 Nov. 1930.

[72] Mosley to Garvin, 30 Oct. 1930, Garvin papers. Nicolson diary, 6 Nov. 1930 (Nicolson I, 59), and Bevan reporting Mosley in Dalton diary, 24 Nov. 1930 (Pimlott, 131). Cf. Skidelsky, *Mosley*, 236.

[73] Details, including effort to recruit Cole, Bevin, and ILP members, in Skidelsky, *Mosley*, 237–40, and see Nicolson diary, 30 Nov. 1930 (Nicolson I, 61) for hoping to get Stanley, Macmillan, and 'Keynes and other experts' to sign.

[74] Elliot, Moore-Brabazon, and Boothby letters, *The Times*, 11, 13, and 17 Dec. 1930; Macmillan in *Week-end Review*, 27 Dec. 1930; Keynes article, *The Nation*, 13 Dec. 1930 (JMK xx, 473–6); Amery speech, *The Times*, 9 Dec. 1930, and see Mosley cultivating him in Amery diary, 12 and 17 Dec. 1930 (*LSA* II, 144); Morris statement, *The Times*, 18 Dec. 1930.

contacts ranging from the Communist Cook to the near-fascist Morris. At every stage, however, Mosley's concern was not with immediate circumstances but with the near future. He acted in anticipation of a major policy collapse and failure of established parties – a breakdown which would liquefy existing affiliations and enable a new radical movement of previously disparate elements to erupt in the political centre. These notions also explain Mosley's decision to leave the Labour party and form the New party on 1 March 1931. His various contacts had a similar view of the possibilities, but most were not willing to declare themselves until an actual breakdown occurred. However, once Mosley had found a financial sponsor in Morris, he thought it worthwhile to form the vanguard of the coming political reconstruction. The only MPs to follow him were his wife, Strachey, Forgan, Oliver Baldwin, and one Conservative, Allen. But a movement which retained the friendly interest of Lloyd George, Churchill, Garvin, Beaverbrook, Rothermere, Sinclair, Cook, Keynes, and 'young Conservatives' had real potential.[75] Mosley would have agreed with Neville Chamberlain's verdict: that in the event of a financial crisis and Labour government collapse, Mosley and Lloyd George could become a 'dangerous' combination.[76]

Other advocates of coalition thought in terms of an arrangement between existing party leaders. From November 1930 Garvin became the foremost public campaigner for a 'national government' to 'heave the country clean out of the ruts'. His original idea was an emergency government to deal primarily with India, embracing MacDonald, Lloyd George, and Baldwin but led by the ex-Viceroy, Reading.[77] By February 1931 his ideas had broadened into an all-purpose permanent coalition including Lloyd George, Reading, Simon, Baldwin, Churchill, Beaverbrook, and Mosley, under MacDonald's leadership.[78] Astor, fearing 'a deadlock election or some catastrophe' forcing a choice between 'national government or national disaster', gave Garvin proprietorial and practical support.[79] Morris-Jones, a Liberal backbench MP who despaired of the Liberal

---

[75] For details of New party formation, Skidelsky, *Mosley*, 242–9. For Mosley's timing being dependent largely on funding, see Nicolson diary, 6 Nov. 1930 (Nicolson I, 59).

[76] N. to H. Chamberlain, 14 Feb. 1931, NC 18/1/726.

[77] Editorials, *Observer*, 9 and 23 Nov. 1930.

[78] Article, 'A Plague on Your Parties. A Plea for National Government', *Observer*, 22 Feb. 1931.

[79] Astor to O'Connor, 12 Feb. 1931, Astor papers 1066/1/82. The same file contains correspondence on a proposed research and publicity group to prepare a 'platform on which reasonable Conservatives, Liberals and Labourites might stand'.

party and wanted 'a new party – led by Lloyd George, Churchill and Mosley', gave notice on 19 November of a Commons motion on 'the Need for Better Co-operation among the Parties'. Although at first blush its gaucherie evoked mirth, MPs soon showed 'a great deal of interest'.[80] Other 'national government' appeals were made by Wardlaw-Milne MP, chairman of the Conservative Indian Affairs committee; by Felix Schuster, the banker; by Sir Frederick Lewis, the shipowner; and by Chilcott, a businessman and former Conservative MP.[81] General Seely, the Liberal War Secretary of the Curragh incident and Coalition Liberal minister 1918–19, as National Savings Committee chairman and a figure with wide financial, business, and social contacts pronounced in *The Times* of 2 December that a national government 'would receive over-whelming support from the whole mass of the people'.[82]

There were also private attempts to promote alliance between political leaders. John Buchan, the author, Conservative MP, friend and flatterer of the great, suggested a national government to MacDonald, Lloyd George, and probably others in September.[83] In late October he was the first to raise the idea in Parliament. With Stanley and Elliot he persuaded Horne in mid December to join in a well-publicised call for national consensus – an obvious kite.[84] Balfour, an industrialist member of the EAC, sent MacDonald in October an authoritative opinion that Britain was close to an economic 'debacle', which was circulated as a Cabinet paper. Its recommendations included, as a means to overcome political resistance to tariffs and retrenchment, 'a Round Table Conference on...Home Affairs' and 'some form of Coalition Government'.[85] Lady Londonderry, the Conservative political hostess and friend of MacDonald, urged him to 'join with [Baldwin] to "save the

---

[80] Morris-Jones diary, 4 and 19 Nov., 2 Dec. 1930; *HC Deb*, 245, col. 1439, 19 Nov. 1930; Morris-Jones, *Doctor in the Whips' Room*, 85.

[81] Wardlaw-Milne letter, F. Schuster and Lewis speeches, *The Times*, 21 and 24 Oct. 1930, 11 Feb. 1931. Chilcott articles in *The Whitehall Gazette*, Dec. 1930–April 1931, reprinted in Chilcott, *Political Salvation*. For Chilcott's dubious reputation, see Roskill, *Hankey* II, 420–3.

[82] Letter, *The Times*, 2 Dec. 1930, and see epigraph to this chapter.

[83] Buchan to MacDonald, 5 Sept. 1930, JRM 1400, and reported in Sinclair to Sylvester, 11 Sept. 1930, Thurso papers. The last makes it clear that the initiative came from Buchan, not Lloyd George: cf. Marquand, 564.

[84] *HC Deb*, 244, cols. 122–3, 29 Oct. 1930; *The Times* (and most major national and provincial newspapers), 17 Dec. 1930. For Buchan making good use of his experience here in the other side of his imaginative life, see the story 'The Rt. Hon. David Mayot', in John Buchan, *The Gap in the Curtain* (1932).

[85] Balfour to MacDonald, 1 Oct. 1930, JRM 673, circulated as CP330(30), 8 Oct. 1930.

country"'.[86] Wing Commander Louis Greig, a stockbroker, Gentleman Usher to the King, and another friend of MacDonald, not only made similar suggestions[87] but joined with Gwynne of *The Morning Post* as a self-appointed intermediary between MacDonald and Baldwin.[88]

Moreover, Seely's public appeal was an outcome of considerable private effort. On 29 October he held a dinner for those of his political friends whom he supposed 'could form a national government to cope with the present acute emergency'. The guests included MacDonald, Lloyd George, Reading, and their sons; Churchill, Horne, and Mond, with Lord Southborough as 'an exceptionally close friend' of the King.[89] Not all of these had advance notice of the dinner's purpose, but for three hours they considered Seely's proposal and agreed to continue the discussion at a further meeting.[90] In the meantime Seely established contact with Greig and Felix Schuster, and found support for his ideas from Brand, Kindersley, and 'other City pundits'.[91] The second dinner, on the day after Seely's appeal was published, was attended by MacDonald, Reading, Churchill, Horne, and, Lloyd George being ill, by his son Gwilym Lloyd George.[92]

Although Seely, Greig, Gwynne, Balfour, Buchan, Garvin, Morris-Jones, and the other various advocates of 'national government' were not themselves leading political figures, they were significant in that, with a freedom denied to politicians constrained

[86] MacDonald diary, 16 Dec. 1930, also 9 Nov. 1930. See Lady Londonderry letter, *The Times*, 19 Dec. 1930, supporting the Buchan/Stanley/Elliot/Horne appeal and, for friendship with MacDonald, Marquand, 405–6, 495–6, 687–92.

[87] Greig to MacDonald [?13 Oct., ?7 Nov., and ?14 Nov. 1930], JRM 676, 1176 (last two letters misplaced in 1931 file), and see Dalton diary, 16 Sept. 1931 (Pimlott, 156). For Greig's status, see Jones, *Whitehall Diary* II, 161, 5 Dec. 1930, and for acting as an intermediary between MacDonald and the Palace, Greig to Stamfordham, 4 June 1929, RA GV K2223/39.

[88] Gwynne to Greig, 2 Nov. 1930 (shown to MacDonald); MacDonald to Greig, 6 Nov. 1930 (shown by Gwynne to Baldwin); Baldwin reported in Gwynne to Greig, 11 Nov. 1930 (shown to MacDonald); MacDonald to Greig [11 Nov. 1930] (shown to Baldwin); Gwynne to Greig, 12 Nov. 1930; all Greig papers (copies in Gwynne papers 19). Gwynne to Tyrrell, 11 Nov. 1930, Gwynne papers 24, describes the exchanges.

[89] Seely to Reading, 8 and 26 Oct. 1930, Reading papers F118/98.

[90] The sources for the dinner are: Seely to Southborough, 26 Oct. 1930, Southborough papers 12; Southborough, Conway, and MacDonald diaries, 29 Oct. 1930 (latter in Marquand, 576, who on pp. 574, 579, predates Seely's elevation as Lord Mottistone by three years); seating plan and untitled record of the conversation in Mottistone papers 4/10 and 4/42 (latter misplaced in 1931 file: names are omitted, but discussants are identifiable by reference to the seating plan).

[91] Greig to MacDonald, [?13 Oct. 1930], JRM 676; F. Schuster to Seely, 5 Nov. 1930, Mottistone papers 4/14–15; Seely to Reading, 8 Nov. 1930, Reading papers F118/98.

[92] MacDonald diary, 4 Dec. 1930, referring to the 3rd (Marquand, 578).

by party pressures, they articulated a widespread opinion and by doing so inserted a new element into politics. Prompted by the public appeals and rumours of private 'intrigues', from mid November much of the political press debated the idea. *The Daily Herald*, suspecting anti-Labour objectives, rejected it. Otherwise, the general verdict was that 'national government' was desirable in principle but impracticable because party differences remained too wide.[93] *The Times*, though preferring MacDonald's 'council of state' notion as a more realistic objective, nevertheless accepted that Seely's appeal 'unquestionably' expressed what 'many people [were] thinking, saying and hoping'.[94] One way or another, the 'national government' idea had acquired sufficient plausibility to have entered serious political debate.

In one case the response was unequivocally positive, if necessarily kept under restraint. If a 'national government' was to become possible the attitude of the King, constitutionally responsible for the choice of Prime Minister, might be important and perhaps decisive. Although instinctively distrustful of the Labour party, the King and Stamfordham had dutifully displayed tolerance. They were impressed by the government's early American reparations and Indian successes, and they respected and liked Thomas, Snowden, and MacDonald.[95] But following sharp disagreements about Egypt and Russia, they considered Henderson a 'vain, stupid man', 'a damned ass',[96] and as the government got into difficulties during 1930 they became 'sarcastic' about other ministers.[97] Imperial affairs were their touchstone. For the King, Dominion relations had deteriorated to the point where he had 'to try to save my Empire',[98] and he and Stamfordham were astonished and dismayed by the Cabinet's nomination of Gorell for the Indian Viceroyalty. By the autumn they thought the government was generally 'incompetent'.[99] Yet they had little confidence in Baldwin's ability to restore

---

[93] E.g., 'The Devil and the Deep Blue Sea', *Economist*, 29 Nov. 1930. But the *Nation*, 15 Nov., 6 Dec. 1930, and *Week-end Review*, 22 Nov., 6 Dec. 1930, thought further economic deterioration might easily make coalition practicable.

[94] Editorial, 'A National Policy', *The Times*, 2 Dec. 1930.

[95] Stamfordham to Esher, 13 and 31 Aug. 1929, Esher papers 12/11; the King reported in Wigram to MacDonald, 16 Aug. 1929, JRM 4, in MacDonald diary, 5 Nov. 1929, in Henson journal, 6 April 1930, and in N. Chamberlain diary, 24 July 1930.

[96] The King in N. Chamberlain diary, 24 July 1930, and in Rose, *George V*, 369.

[97] The King in Chetwode to Irwin, 30 May 1930, Halifax papers 19/70, and in Henson journal, 6 April 1930.

[98] The King in N. Chamberlain to his wife, 24 July 1930, NC 1/26/431.

[99] Williamson, 'Party First', 93–5, 97; Dawson diary, 14 and 25 Nov. 1930.

order to the Conservative party and provide an alternative government.[100]

All this strengthened the King's and Stamfordham's inclination, natural in their position, to regard party politics with impatience. Despite the constraints of constitutional propriety, indications of their wishes surfaced. Balfour's letter, received as a Cabinet paper, gave them an opportunity to impress upon ministers their own view that 'the time has come when even emergency measures may be necessary in order to avert a calamity which...is not altogether incomparable with the Great War'.[101] It was on the King's suggestion that the Cabinet considered including in the King's Speech an appeal to 'all sections of Parliament' to 'unite' in treating unemployment 'on national as distinct from Party lines'.[102] By mid October Stamfordham had begun collecting opinions on 'what the King...ought to do if conditions go on as they are and parliamentary government becomes much more farcical'.[103] They possibly knew of the activities of Greig, a Royal Household member. They were certainly aware of Seely's, the King asking to see his appeal before publication and Stamfordham wishing him 'every success'.[104] There was little else they could do unless party leaders requested the King's constitutional services. He had no means of compelling ministers and party leaders to take a certain course of action, but could only attempt moral suasion if and when his advice was sought. Nevertheless it is clear that from November 1930 the King wanted a 'national government', and that if the opportunity arose he was ready to press for it.

Among political leaders the 'national government' idea had a mixed reception, and where it left an impression the effect was subtle. To most it seemed undesirable or impossible on policy or party grounds. The idea came from persons on the right, except for Mosley, and he was jumping rightwards. Collectively these wanted a 'national government' to impose an Indian settlement, but were indefinite as between the Simon and Irwin policies. More clearly,

[100] Stamfordham in Reith diary, 13 Oct. 1930, in Stuart, 164.
[101] King's minute on CP330(30), Oct. 1930, and Stamfordham (reporting the King) to MacDonald, 11 Oct. 1930, RA GV K2301/1, 4 (Nicolson, *George V*, 448).
[102] Stamfordham in Hankey to MacDonald, 20 Oct. 1930, JRM 278; Cabinet 62(30), 22 Oct. 1930; and for the Cabinet decision, see above, pp. 144–5.
[103] Reith diary, 13 Oct. 1930, in Stuart, 182.
[104] Seely to Reading, 28 Nov., 1 Dec. 1930, Reading papers F118/98; and see Smith in Dalton diary, 16 Sept. 1931 (Pimlott, 156).

they wanted protection. Consequently the idea evoked no interest in such doctrinaire free-traders as Snowden, Samuel, and Maclean. They also wanted retrenchment, particularly in unemployment payments. So to Henderson and most other Labour ministers it seemed hostile, especially as it implied that they were too inflexible, sectional, or feeble to cope with the situation. Yet the idea was not necessarily attractive to Conservatives, despite its congenial policy objectives. Its proponents thought primarily in terms of persons rather than parties – Greig, Gwynne, and Lady Londonderry wanted MacDonald to detach himself from Labour – but they all assumed that if essential policies were to be carried without damaging resistance and delays, a successor government would need substantial Labour and Liberal support. That is to say, they implied the inadequacy of Conservativism as a national force, or else the incapacity of existing Conservative leaders to act with sufficient decision.

Nevertheless, among those politicians with nostalgic interest in coalition, or who were frustrated, angry, or discontented with established party leadership, there existed material to sustain high-level discussion of 'national government'. A few, anxious about policy problems and exasperated by party difficulties, gave it serious thought. If the development of the 'national government' idea is to be understood, the character of this thinking needs definition. In later years Southborough supposed that Seely's dinner had given 'rise to what became the National Government', while Lloyd George teased Seely with the sobriquet 'Father of the National Government'.[105] Any such implication of direct connection between the discussions of autumn 1930 and subsequent events is certainly misleading. The dinner conversation, and the other public or private statements about 'national government', proceeded on the premise that the country was 'drifting to a cataclysm'.[106] Yet this did not mean that Seely's guests thought a cataclysm was inevitable. Whatever Seely and other self-appointed matchmakers thought they were doing, for those politicians who were interested 'national government' was not a plan or plot. Rather it was an idea which might possibly have service if economic or imperial conditions deteriorated further and if party conditions continued to frustrate effective action: it might then provide either an escape from a

---

[105] Southborough undated note on Seely to Southborough, 26 Oct. 1930, Southborough papers 12; Lloyd George in F. Stevenson diary, 18 Feb. 1934, in Taylor, 254.
[106] Seely memo [29 Oct. 1930], Mottistone papers 4/42.

political *impasse* or else an arrangement for coping with a real emergency. Their concern, like that of Mosley, was less with the immediate difficult conditions than with a potentially disastrous future. Even so, for them, 'national government' remained only one, extreme, possibility. As the idea related to a hypothetical situation, views varied according to opinions on the likelihood of a real *impasse* or emergency.

Lloyd George, as the former Coalition Prime Minister, might have been expected to take the most interest in revived coalitionism. He encouraged Buchan and Morris-Jones, and was interested by Garvin's articles; he listened to Mosley, had foreknowledge of Seely's purpose, and proposed that Henderson be invited to the second dinner.[107] Publicly he was preparing to become the 'man of emergency', in case such was to be required. For him 'national government' had become a possibility in reserve, dependent upon circumstances. Yet, as someone who had faced and surmounted genuine national and world crises, he had the experience to be sceptical and relaxed about the idea of 'crisis'. At the Seely dinner he surmised that any 'cataclysm' was still two or three years ahead.[108] By this he meant MacDonald to understand that there was time to avert collapse provided the Liberal–Labour alliance were consummated. That alliance remained his immediate objective.

Rather, the Liberal most interested in 'national government' was Reading. His interest was a reflection of his importance as an elder statesman, with immense experience as Liberal Cabinet minister, Lord Chief Justice, wartime ambassador in the United States, and Viceroy of India, who knew that the Round Table Conference had elevated him to a pivotal position in high politics. His anxieties about Indian policy were genuine, and he had extensive financial interests and connections which persuaded him that the economic situation really was precarious.[109] He was also Seely's and Garvin's candidate for the 'national government' premiership. From the start he collaborated with Seely, though with the natural caution and hesitation of the active politician. Unhopeful beforehand, he thought the dinner 'a great success... notwithstanding the absence of clear

---

[107] Buchan to MacDonald, 5 Sept. 1930, JRM 1400; Morris-Jones diary, 30 Oct., 29 Nov. 1930, and Morris-Jones, *Doctor in the Whips' Room*, 85; Mosley, *My Life*, 276–7, and for a Lloyd George/Mosley/Beaverbrook conclave, Amery diary, 12 Oct. 1930; Seely to Reading, 21 Oct. 1930, and Reading to Seely, 13 Nov. 1930, Reading papers F118/98.
[108] Seely memo [29 Oct. 1930], Mottistone papers 4/42.
[109] Seely memo [29 Oct. 1930], Mottistone papers 4/42.

cut conclusions', and agreed to host the second dinner because discussions 'must continue'.[110] He doubted the success of a public appeal, but only because he thought it premature: 'bad as things are, they would have to be worse before Parties could sink their differences'. Nevertheless, he persuaded Dawson to print Seely's statement.[111]

Reading's further interest, as one of the few who retained contacts with the various Liberal factions and who had repeatedly tried to mediate between them, was that coalition might help prevent Liberal party disintegration. Seeking to restrain Simon from further acts of rebellion on 27 November, he suggested that Simon should consider himself a candidate for high office in a 'national government'.[112] For Simon, a dissident still uncertain whether dissidence offered him a future, that idea had obvious attractions. So when on 1 December Neville Chamberlain asked him for help in defeating the Labour government, Simon proposed its replacement by a 'broad-bottomed administration' and suggested consultation with Reading.[113]

What Chamberlain actually had in mind – and therefore what he understood Simon to have said – was incorporation of Simon and other Liberal dissidents in a Conservative government.[114] As an inner member of the Conservative leadership, at this time he thought no further than that. Nor did Austen Chamberlain and Hailsham, despite their friendship with Chilcott and willingness to express broad sympathy for his ideas.[115] However, more detached Conservatives showed more interest in 'national government'. Horne, wanting to be part of whatever happened yet aspiring to the Conservative leadership, displayed calculated ambivalence. Though attending the Seely–Reading dinners, he expressed scepticism about their objective: his joint appeal with Elliot, Stanley, and Buchan reinforced the Seely and Mosley statements, yet in a deniable form.[116] Amery's naive and unmeasured public enthusiasm for

---

[110] Reading to Seely, 22 and 30 Oct. 1930, Mottistone papers 4/9, 12–13; Seely to Southborough, 26 Oct. 1930, Southborough papers 12. Reading is the 'very wise man' quoted in Seely's *Times* letter.

[111] Reading to Seely, 13 and 15 Nov. 1930, Reading papers F118/98.

[112] Simon memo, 27 Nov. 1930, Simon papers.

[113] Simon memo, 1 Dec. 1930, Simon papers; N. Chamberlain diary, 5 Dec. 1930.

[114] See below, pp. 175–6.

[115] A. Chamberlain 'Foreword', and Hailsham to Chilcott, 18 Jan. 1931, in Chilcott, *Political Salvation*, 11, 23.

[116] MacDonald diary, 4 Dec. 1930 (Marquand, 578); Horne in *Morning Post*, 17 Dec. 1930, denying an attempt to form a 'National bloc'.

Mosley's manifesto resulted from his doctrinaire protectionism: if there were 'any form of Coalition' that could introduce tariffs and imperial preference more rapidly and fully than 'any single party, by all means let us have it – and the sooner the better'. In existing conditions, however, he did not think this an immediate prospect.[117] Churchill flirted with Mosley and the 'national government' idea partly because he was becoming separated from other Conservative leaders and was on the look-out for alliances over India. In February 1931 he apparently expressed readiness to accept Reading's Indian policy 'in connection with a National Government'.[118] Another reason was an instinctive open-mindedness towards most possibilities.

This was also characteristic of Thomas. As a professional fixer who gravitated naturally towards the political centre and who had wide contacts in all three parties and in business, he responded to shifts in opinion even when (apparently) not directly approached. Conscious of failure as minister responsible for employment policy, he was now angry that the Cabinet had forced him into negativism towards the Dominions. Believing tariffs and retrenchment were inevitable but could wreck the Labour government, he was interested in means to smother, fudge, or escape the consequences. As early as July he gave Conservative acquaintances the impression that he and 'several... colleagues' were 'open' to coalition on an 'empire free trade' basis. The day after Seely's appeal, he told Amery that the country was 'not far from a general breakdown and a National Government'.[119]

MacDonald's perspective was similar to that of Thomas, but complicated by considerable psychological tensions. He was reluctant to delegate work, was excessively conscious of difficulties, and bore the responsibilities of office heavily. He thought imperial disintegration a real danger: in addition to anxieties about Indian civil disobedience and the burden of presiding over the Round Table Conference, he was 'worried to death' about the Dominions and Palestine.[120] He also thought the country was in danger of slipping into some economic or financial collapse. At Seely's dinner he

[117] Amery speech, *The Times*, 9 Dec. 1930.
[118] Garvin to Astor, 26 Feb. 1931, Astor papers. See also Seely memo [29 Oct. 1930], Mottistone papers 4/42; MacDonald diary, 4 Dec. 1930; and, for Churchill's rumoured participation in schemes for a 'National Party', Headlam diary, 21 Jan. 1931.
[119] Waring to Beaverbrook, 8 July 1930, Beaverbrook papers, C/320; Amery diary, 3 Dec. 1930 (*LSA* II, 139); and see above note 56.
[120] Passfield to B. Webb, 11 Nov. 1930, Passfield papers II:3:(1):92/120; also MacDonald diary, 26 Oct., 9, 13, and 16 Nov. 1930.

declared that 'a real disaster [was] impending'. In these conditions he believed national responsibility dictated extraordinary action, however regrettable – suspension of earlier promises and acceptance of temporary reduction in living standards through protection and retrenchment in social service expenditure.[121] He himself had no ideological inhibition about this. For him socialism meant organisation to establish 'cooperative independence', not a 'pauperising...extension of public charity'.[122] Like business leaders but also some progressive intellectuals, he thought unemployment insurance had become overextended and subject to much 'abuse' – 'doing great harm to the country' not just by its cost but by 'inflicting injury on the mentality of the people', even encouraging 'spongers'.[123] Yet his Cabinet would not 'face unpleasant facts & ... act unpleasantly'. On unemployment insurance it was 'against' him, and 'feeble'. On trade and imperial economic policies Snowden was 'impossible'. Henderson he suspected of plotting to replace him. Other ministers were inadequate or committed 'blunders'.[124] Before the election he had wanted to 'drive policy', but he now felt thwarted and denied control over his own government. Despite his life's work, he feared the fatal criticism was being substantiated: that, as presently composed, the Labour party was 'unfit to govern'.

The problem was not only at Cabinet level. Annoyed by TUC 'arrogance', ILP rebellions, and backbench criticism, there were times when he despaired of the whole party: it was 'being killed by its own internal troubles & its own self-criticism'.[125] Conservative and Liberal obstruction and a weak parliamentary position were further distractions: he was 'sick of the disgraceful show which parties [were] making'.[126] Overworked, frustrated, disillusioned, suspicious, depressed, anxious: in some moods he seemed close to a nervous breakdown and expressed a wistful desire to escape from his

---

[121] Seely memo [29 Oct. 1930], Mottistone papers 4/42. See also MacDonald diary, 14 Aug., 16 Oct. 1930 (first in Marquand, 555).

[122] MacDonald diary, 10 July 1929; MacDonald to K. Glasier, 18 Dec. 1929, JRM 1439. See also MacDonald diary, 17 Dec. 1929, and speech, 7 Oct. 1930, in Marquand, 525, 569.

[123] EAC 7th–10th meetings, 24 July, 11 Sept., 7 Nov., 11 Dec. 1930; MacDonald to Mosley, 30 Dec. 1929, in N. Mosley, Rules of the Game, 126.

[124] MacDonald notes, 9 and 16 Nov. 1930, JRM 1753 (Marquand, 577–8); MacDonald diary, 22 July, 30 Oct. 1930; Jones, Whitehall Diary II, 263, 3 June 1930.

[125] MacDonald diary, 14 Dec. 1930. See also note, 9 Nov. 1930 (Marquand, 577), and B. Webb diary, 31 May, 4 Oct. 1930.

[126] MacDonald to Greig, 6 Nov. 1930, Greig papers (copy in Gwynne papers 19). See also, e.g., MacDonald to Balfour, 2 Oct. 1930, JRM 673 (Marquand, 576), and MacDonald diary, 4 Nov. 1930.

current position,[127] encouraging ideas that he might accept the Viceroyalty of India, or a place in a 'national' or even Conservative government.[128]

Much of this arose, however, from MacDonald's self-pity, irritation, and exasperation under enormous executive and political pressures, and unburdening of his troubles to well-meaning but politically simple-minded friends. He had another, equally prominent, side: conscientious, tenacious, proud, certain of his own ability, and convinced that the Labour party he had tried to create and as it ought to be were indispensable to working-class and national interests. He thought the desperate national situation meant that a general election would be 'very bad' for the country, and should oblige all politicians to suspend partisanship and support the government of the day in nationally vital measures.[129] His real intention was to maintain the Labour Cabinet as long as possible, if necessary with a Liberal alliance, in the hope that it would face realities and take the hard decisions. For this purpose he wanted Conservatives and Liberals to cease exploiting national difficulties for their own advantage, and to support the Labour government in a 'council of state' spirit. It was in this sense that he responded favourably to the first mentions of 'national government' – seeking co-operation, but regarding actual coalition as impracticable.[130] He had no foreknowledge of the purpose of Seely's dinner, and, although 'he played somewhat gracefully with the notion, he had no intention of treating [national government] as one of politics "au sérieux"' and seemed unlikely to attend the second dinner.[131]

Then, in mid November, newspaper speculation about 'national government' and the Greig–Gwynne communication link with

---

[127] MacDonald diary, 19 Oct., 6 Nov. 1930, note 9 Nov. 1930, and MacDonald to Buchan, 8 Sept. 1930, JRM 1753, 1440 (Marquand, 575, 577). MacDonald was prone to depression, but this was especially noticeable in autumn 1930: see Nicolson diary, 5 Oct. 1930 (Nicolson I, 56–7), and Sankey diary, 15 and 23 Oct., 5 Nov. 1930.

[128] Greig to MacDonald, [?13 Oct. 1930], JRM 676; Gwynne to Greig, 2 Nov. 1930, Greig papers; Lady Londonderry in MacDonald note, 9 Nov. and diary, 16 Dec. 1930. See also Williamson, 'Party First', 98–9.

[129] MacDonald to Buchan, 8 Sept. 1930, and to Balfour, 2 Oct. 1930, JRM 1440, 673, and MacDonald note, 9 Nov. 1930 (Marquand, 575–7).

[130] MacDonald to Greig, 6 Nov. 1930, Greig papers (copy in Gwynne papers 19); MacDonald to Buchan, and to Balfour, 8 Sept., 2 Oct. 1930, JRM 1440, 673 (Marquand, 575–6).

[131] Reading to Seely, 30 Oct. 1930, Mottistone papers 4/12–13. MacDonald diary, 29 Oct. 1930, corrects the suggestion in Marquand, 579, that MacDonald had prior notice of the dinner's purpose.

Baldwin prompted MacDonald to think seriously about what his own position might be if the Labour government broke down over emergency measures which he himself considered necessary. One thought was to give independent support to the successor government, regardless of party consequences.[132] But from what Baldwin appeared to say to Gwynne there now seemed to be a Conservative willingness to compromise, which might allow formation of a 'national government' on terms favourable to Labour. By this MacDonald meant a 'combination...determined by a Parlty. situation not by design. With S.B. & the good honest Conservative I would co-operate in this crisis with pleasure & would be prepared to give them something.'[133] That is to say, MacDonald envisaged conditions of Labour government defeat or collapse but, contrary to subsequent accusations, he was not planning to abandon the Labour party. Such action would, it then seemed, leave him powerless, without any political base and serious claim to high office. Rather, he assumed a position where he remained prime minister at the head of most if not all Labour MPs, and in return for parliamentary support would admit some Conservative leaders into his Cabinet. On this understanding he wrote pleasant things about Conservatives to Greig for transmission to Baldwin, and accepted the invitation to Reading's dinner.[134] Then, on 1 December, he raised directly with Baldwin 'the possibility of...a national Govt'.[135]

Baldwin had built his career upon anti-coalitionism, and – even if he had wished it otherwise – with his leadership so recently threatened he could not afford any move which might compromise Conservative protection policy. He also expected no difficulty about establishing a strong Conservative government once the Labour government collapsed. If it would precipitate Liberal disintegration and hasten the government's defeat he was prepared to accommodate individual Liberals who accepted protection, but he saw no need for party alliances. He was interested in the Greig–Gwynne reports of MacDonald's demoralisation, and for obvious tactical reasons fostered this with messages feeding his self-pity – suggesting

---

[132] MacDonald note, 9 Nov. 1930, JRM 1753 (Marquand, 577).
[133] MacDonald to Greig [?10 or 11 Nov. 1930], Greig papers (copy in Gwynne papers 19).
[134] Ibid., and Reading to Seely, 13 Nov. 1930, Reading papers F118/98.
[135] MacDonald diary, 3 Dec. 1930 (Marquand, 578). The valuable interpretation in Marquand, 575–80, stresses suspicion of Henderson for the development of MacDonald's thinking, but discovery of the Greig/Gwynne/Baldwin link suggests stronger motivation.

that MacDonald did 'not quite realise the strength and ... malignity of the forces working against him'. This manoeuvre required Baldwin to humour the Greig–Gwynne notions, but he did not suppose there was anything in them.[136] His own answer to MacDonald's predicament, suggested at their 1 December meeting, was that he should remove himself to the Viceroyalty of India. In reply to MacDonald's mention of a 'national government', Baldwin rejected it as 'impossible' because of party differences over protection. Abruptly disillusioned about Baldwin's attitude, Mac-Donald could only agree.[137]

Speculation about 'national government' had become so intense by early December that each party leader felt obliged to respond publicly to it. All dismissed the idea but, acknowledging the strength of the underlying sentiment, they made what capital they could from doing so. Lloyd George said it was ruled out by Conservatives putting party before national interests, so the only alternative for true Liberals was to persuade the Labour government to accept Liberal policies. MacDonald spoke of it as a 'magnificent' but impractical idea, before appealing again for non-partisan treatment of the unemployment problem. Baldwin rejected it because the other parties failed to recognise the necessity for protection and because the Conservative party was the true national party.[138] Government and Conservative whips refused parliamentary time for Morris-Jones's motion.[139]

Baldwin meant what he said. But despite their public statements MacDonald and Lloyd George did not abandon the national government idea altogether. Nor did Reading, Simon, Thomas, Churchill, Amery, and the King. For them 'national government' remained a possible or desirable recourse in the event of a major policy or political collapse, where tariffs might not be the overriding issue or, alternatively, might become generally acceptable. The idea had been implanted, broadly favourable reactions had been exchanged, in certain circumstances figures who mattered were

---

[136] Gwynne to Greig, 11 Nov. 1930, Greig papers (copy in Gwynne papers 19). Baldwin led Gwynne to believe he would raise the matter with MacDonald, but failed to do so: see Gwynne to Greig, 12 Nov. 1930, Greig papers; Seely to Reading, 17 Nov. 1930, Reading papers F118/98; MacDonald diary, 13 Nov. 1930.

[137] MacDonald diary, 3 Dec. 1930 (partly in Marquand, 578).

[138] Lloyd George speech, *Manchester Guardian*, 6 Dec. 1930; MacDonald and Baldwin speeches, *The Times*, 13 Dec. 1930.

[139] *HC Deb*, 246, col. 853, 15 Dec. 1930; Morris-Jones, *Doctor in the Whips' Room*, 85.

prepared to revive the idea, and there was evidently substantial support for non-party or cross-party co-operation in many sections of opinion. 'National government' had entered the political repertoire and was available if the situation got very much worse, as many still feared it might.

PART II
Crisis avoided

CHAPTER 5

The impact of India

Irwin has worked a miracle.

Dalton diary, 6 March 1931

Baldwin is a very bad Parliamentary leader, but on the other hand his policy is nearer honesty & common sense than anybody else's. But the unfortunate thing is that we can't keep Humpty Dumpty from falling off the wall if he hasn't the natural balance.

F. S. Oliver to Dawson, 6 March 1931[1]

During the winter of 1930–1 some substantive policy problems did grow worse, but these and other pressures upon the Labour Cabinet were gradually eased through compromise, postponement, or evasion. With 'national government' disclaimed as an objective, party leaders tried to resolve parliamentary difficulties through more limited arrangements, and the government received further relief from renewed Conservative divisions. Consequently, from March onwards it seemed less likely that the 'national crisis' identified in the autumn of 1930 would develop into a real crisis.

INDIAN COMPROMISE

From November 1930 the tension was taken out of imperial policies. Palestine and Kenya ceased altogether to be problems, as Henderson negotiated with Weizmann an 'authoritative interpretation' – really a repudiation – of the Palestine White Paper, and the Conservative-dominated East Africa Select Committee buried the White Paper on Native Policy.[2] In the two most critical areas of Dominion relations

[1] Respectively Pimlott, 139, and Oliver papers.
[2] Rose, *Gentile Zionists*, 21–8; Gregory, *Sidney Webb and East Africa*, 128–36.

and Indian constitutional reform imminent difficulties receded, but in both cases the possibility of future trouble remained a significant element in political calculation. The Ottawa Imperial Economic Conference planned for August 1931 was postponed by the Canadian government in June because of political uncertainty in Australia and New Zealand.[3] This relieved the Labour government of imminent embarrassment on intra-imperial economic policies, but only deferred a threatened repetition of the October 1930 fiasco into 1932. The prospects changed most in Indian policy, through an unexpected and dramatic development in both Indian and British political opinion.

On the British side, the Labour government's deliberate abstention from positive leadership at the Round Table Conference meant that Reading became the crucial figure. From September 1930 his views advanced markedly from his inflexible stance of autumn 1929 and the summer months. For this there were several reasons. As the Conference approached he became sensitive to the danger of a 'sensational breakdown' which might drive Indian moderates into the arms of Gandhi and force Britain into the 'bankruptcy' of a 'reactionary policy'.[4] His fellow Liberal delegates, Foot, Hamilton, and Lothian, emphasised the opportunity offered by the Conference to display the continued relevance of Liberalism – 'the idealism of Fox, Gladstone, Campbell-Bannerman and the Parliament of 1906'.[5] These considerations together contributed to an accommodating disposition which was also appropriate both to the Liberal leadership's strategy towards the Labour government and to Reading's interest in 'national government'. Following the Lloyd George–MacDonald negotiations on a parliamentary alliance in October, Reading made it clear to MacDonald that 'he wanted to work with [the government]' on India.[6]

More particularly, Reading felt reassured by the Government of India's Dispatch on Constitutional Reform, which explained in detail the rationale of Irwin's objections to the Simon Report. It argued that concession of Indian responsibility at Delhi would replace a resented 'subordination' by a 'partnership' which would strengthen the central government. More important, it spelt out the 'safeguards' for continued British control: the reserved subjects of

---

[3] Cabinet 31 (31), 4 June 1931; Bennett statement in *The Times*, 8 June 1931.
[4] Haig, and Schuster, to Irwin, both 24 Oct. 1930, Halifax papers 19/153a, 153b.
[5] Lothian to Reading, 18 Nov. 1930, Reading Indian papers E238/563/62–7.
[6] MacDonald diary, 20 Oct. 1930.

defence, foreign policy, internal security, high finance, and the civil service; the Viceregal prerogatives; and the supremacy of Westminster.[7] For Reading, these safeguards represented the 'firm stand' lacking in July.[8]

Above all Reading was impressed by the 'new situation' produced by the Indian Princes.[9] Irwin's decision to play the 'card' of involving the Native States in the process of constitutional review succeeded to a degree not even he had anticipated. Everyone understood that the Princes' eventual role in any All-India solution was as conservative allies of the British, but at this moment they were a progressive force.[10] They had both a grievance and a fear; they resented British interference in their states, yet knew that self-government in British India would undermine their authority even more. Their solution was an All-India Federation, in which they might escape British control but be able to check nationalist radicalism.

Federation was not a new idea: the Simon Report had suggested it as a desirable development from its scheme of provincial autonomy. But hitherto the obstacles to its achievement, including doubts about whether Native States would accede, had seemed so great that it had been regarded as a distant prospect. Advocacy of federation by certain Princes and their ministers in autumn 1930, however, rapidly made it into an immediate policy. This dramatic shift occurred because, as a principle, federation seemed the 'solvent of all [conference] difficulties',[11] and could be interpreted in varying ways. Hindu Liberals saw it as an instrument for extracting early responsible government from the British. Muslims perceived a further advantage of protection against unbridled Hindu predominance. All three British party delegations recognised that federation would divert the Conference from possible confrontation into constructive discussion, and quickly agreed to consider it in committee. The deliberations of this Federal Structure Committee convinced Reading that it could be the device both to pacify India and to preserve British interests. On 5 January 1931 he 'crossed the Rubicon',[12] accepting central responsibility with safeguards on

[7] The Dispatch was circulated privately to Conference delegates in October and published in November: see Gopal, *Viceroyalty of Lord Irwin*, 95–6; Moore, *Crisis of Indian Unity*, 117.

[8] Haig, and Schuster, to Irwin, both 24 Oct. 1930, Halifax papers 19/153a, 153b.

[9] Schuster, and Reading, to Irwin, 20 and 21 Nov. 1930, Halifax papers 19/167, 167b.

[10] For much of this and the succeeding paragraph, see Moore, *Crisis of Indian Unity*, 25–33, 127–50.   [11] Haig to Irwin, 21 Nov. 1930, Halifax papers 19/168.

[12] Sankey note to M. MacDonald, 5 Jan. 1931, M. MacDonald papers 8/12/1.

federal terms. This speech was central to the conference's success, not least by placing pressure upon the Conservative delegation.

Like Reading, Conservatives sympathetic to some reform had been attracted initially to the federal idea as a means to 'damp down Indian devotion to Dominion Status'.[13] That the Conservative delegation advanced beyond this to a more positive position owed much to the largely fortuitous character of its composition. Baldwin decided that as party leader he should not lead the delegation, partly in order to exclude Lloyd George from the conference – where Baldwin thought his influence would be 'disastrous' – and partly because he wanted to remain free to defend his leadership.[14] Baldwin's vulnerability also meant that his original delegate choices reflected prevailing party opinion. Hailsham and Austen Chamberlain were 'very much against concessions' and shocked by what seemed to be Reading's 'complete surrender'.[15] But the first declined nomination because of private legal commitments, while the latter withdrew because – in an irony which Baldwin greatly enjoyed – Salisbury indicated that the Conservative right doubted his firmness, having never forgiven his signature of the Irish Treaty.[16] This enabled Baldwin to nominate Oliver Stanley, chosen as a rising figure but soon displaying 'liberal' inclinations, and Zetland, an ex-Indian governor who had implemented the 1919 reforms and who soon accepted that 'Federation [was] the only hope'.[17] Peel, put up early in the Conference to express the Conservative party perspective, was so obviously at odds with its mood that the rest of the Conservative delegation virtually repudiated him.[18] This left effective leadership to Hoare.

Recognising India in late 1929 as a major issue for the future, Hoare had chosen it as suitable material for his political ambition, ingratiating himself with Irwin and soliciting his services in

---

[13] Lane-Fox diary, 19 Nov. 1930; Hoare in Lane-Fox to Irwin, 19 Nov. 1930, Halifax papers 19/166e.

[14] Baldwin to Lloyd George, 2 Aug. 1930, LG G/1/15/1; and to Irwin, 16 Oct. 1930, Halifax papers 19/147.

[15] Lane-Fox to Irwin, 21 Aug. 1930, Halifax papers 19/120; A. to H. Chamberlain, 22 Nov. 1930, 9 Jan. 1931, AC 5/1/521, 525.

[16] Hailsham, and Salisbury to Baldwin, 1 Sept., 4 Aug. 1930, SB 104/45–6, 23–6; Baldwin to A. Chamberlain, 9 Aug. 1930, A. Chamberlain to Baldwin, 11 Aug. 1930, and A. to H. Chamberlain, 11 Aug. 1930, AC 22/3/17, 18, and 5/1/511; Baldwin to Irwin, 16 Oct. 1930, Halifax papers 19/147.

[17] Henson journal, 18 Nov. 1930. For Zetland as prospective Viceroy, see Williamson, 'Party First', 87–8.

[18] Lane-Fox, Schuster, and Coatman (enclosing report of Conservative–Liberal delegations meeting), respectively 19, 20, and 21 Nov. 1930, Halifax papers 19/166e, 167, 169.

persuading Baldwin to consider him as prospective Secretary of State for India.[19] Hoare's aims were in equal measure to encourage a settlement with Indians, to defend British interests, and to conciliate suspicious Conservative party opinion.[20] Supported by Zetland and Stanley, he produced a policy which followed the Conference trend but fell short of Reading's position, and which faced several ways – willing to consider federation, yet non-committal until a detailed scheme with British safeguards was known. As circumstances demanded, this could be presented as either an advance upon or a fulfilment of the Simon Report. It offered Indians the possibility of central responsibility yet suggested that 'the realities and verities of British control' would be retained, and left everything concrete to be settled, probably, by a Conservative government.[21] Exposure to hostile interrogation at party meetings in December meant that Hoare became more rigidly 'non-committal', but Reading's speech – threatening to isolate the Conservative delegation – was a further deterrent to 'non-possumus'.[22]

Conservative non-commitment enabled the Round Table Conference to end on 19 January with agreement on movement towards both limited central and full provincial responsibility, with details to be considered at a second conference in autumn 1931. Compared to the doubts and fears about India before the conference, 'the transformation [was] marvellous'.[23] The Labour government received an undeserved vindication of its decision to act merely as conference arbiters, and won an easy and much-needed success. MacDonald had established impressive control over the proceedings, repairing a reputation for diplomacy tarnished by the Imperial Conference. Sankey had been a successful chairman of the Federal Structure Committee and was given charge of preparing a Government of India Bill, work which he wished to complete, with important consequences for his future attachments. Moreover, pressure from the King, Stamfordham, Baldwin, Reading, Indian

[19] Hoare to Irwin, 28 Oct., 13 Nov., 24 Dec. 1929, 17 and 31 May, 15 July, 1 Aug. 1930, Halifax papers 18/287, 298, 339, and 19/61, 71, 100, 106.
[20] For observations (by non-politicians) of Hoare as excessively concerned with party opinion, see Haig, Coatman, and Hailey to Irwin, respectively 7 Nov., 19 Dec. 1930, 6 Jan. 1931, Halifax papers 19/161a, 189a, 201.
[21] Hoare reported in Lane-Fox to Irwin, 19 Nov. 1930, Halifax papers 19/166e, and in Amery diary, 23 Nov. 1930; Hoare memo, Dec. 1930, in Moore, *Crisis of Indian Unity*, 155–6.
[22] Dawson, and Haig, to Irwin, 2 and 6 Jan. 1931, Halifax papers 19/179b, 201.
[23] MacDonald diary, 15 Jan. 1931.

Princes, and a hostile press had saved the government from its own folly over the succession to Irwin, forcing abandonment of the unsuitable Gorell, and a safe appointment in the professional proconsul, Willingdon.[24]

Simon, ignored during the conference even by Liberal delegates, was sourly sceptical about the outcome.[25] Irwin, however, had embraced federation as the solution to the dilemmas of Indian government. Officials sent by him to London as Conference advisers had encouraged the Princes to bring it forward, had reassured Reading, and had helped draft MacDonald's much acclaimed closing address.[26] Once the Conference ended, Irwin moved rapidly to accomplish the result he most wanted: an end to civil disobedience. On 22 January he released Congress leaders from gaol, and on 17 February began negotiations with Gandhi. In the face of Conservative diehard criticism and doubts even among his ministerial, Liberal, and Conservative sympathisers at 'bargaining with sedition', the Irwin–Gandhi pact was concluded on 4 March. Gandhi gained an abrogation of coercion, a political amnesty, and enhanced status as a negotiating equal of the Viceroy. But many critics were disarmed and the doubters were ecstatically relieved by Irwin's success in obtaining an end both to civil disobedience and to the boycott of British goods, and Gandhi's acceptance of British 'safeguards' in any federal reform.

The pacification of India was a considerable achievement. It ended a prolonged period of strain upon the Government of India and within British politics, and strengthened confidence in Britain's imperial future. Yet, despite its importance, the achievement was fragile. India remained an open, if temporarily dormant, issue. Where the first Round Table Conference had papered over cracks with a general formula of federation, the second was likely to expose differences in interpretations of that formula. In India Willingdon, succeeding Irwin in April, felt he was 'sitting on a tinder box'. There were pinpricks from Congress extremists, which converted his own long-standing scepticism about Irwin's strategy into a belief that Congress acceptance of the settlement was hollow. There was also a 'desperately bad' Indian economic situation, as the political

---

[24] Williamson, 'Party First', 93–100, to which should be added Reading memo, 8 Dec. 1930, Reading Indian papers E238/106/108–9; Bikaner in Stamfordham to Dawson, 2 Dec. 1930, Dawson papers 75/76–8; Baldwin in Reith diary, 23 June 1938, in Stuart, 222.
[25] E.g., reported in Lane-Fox diary, 21 Jan. 1931.
[26] See Schuster, Haig, Hailey letters to Irwin, Oct. 1930–Jan. 1931, Halifax papers.

uncertainty exacerbated the effects of the world depression, producing a mounting budget deficit and severe exchange problems, which in turn made it difficult to obtain loan finance in London.[27] The Government of India tottered on the brink of a first-class financial crisis, facing the prospect either of rupee devaluation or imposing deflation and probably inflaming nationalist opinion.[28] On the other hand, its decision to raise cotton tariffs in January had threatened such damage to the Lancashire cotton industry that the Labour Cabinet felt obliged to object.[29] As expected, Irwin's insistence on the tariffs provoked a sharp movement of Lancashire business into support for the political opposition to Indian reform. That opposition, crystallising around the Indian Empire Society, prepared to renew its attack during the next conference. Its potential to disrupt the all-party approach on Indian policy had already been displayed at the end of the first conference, in contributing to Conservative party difficulties.

CONSERVATIVE REBELLION

After the Caxton Hall meeting of 30 October, Conservative leaders expected to be able to direct their party's energies towards defeat of the Labour government. Only Churchill, as an opponent of the Indian Conference, was prepared for substantial distraction from that objective. With agreement at last reached upon a protection and imperial trade programme, and with Baldwin having confronted and defeated critics of his leadership, there seemed by late November to be a 'miraculous' improvement in party morale and confidence.[30] Backbench MPs obtained a general impression from the constituencies that 'the feeling in favour of [Beaverbrook and Rothermere] & their agitation was dying down, & that the Party was rallying towards unity'.[31] The restoration of morale was aided by large Conservative successes in municipal elections, by victory over

---

[27] Willingdon to Baldwin, 8 June 1931, SB 105/47–8; and to Butler, 18 July, 12 Aug. 1930, Butler papers 53/97–101; to Lloyd, 4 April 1931, Lloyd papers 11/1; to Reading, 24 April 1931, Reading papers F118/106/45.

[28] See Moore, *Crisis of Indian Unity*, 211–14, and Tomlinson, 'Britain and the Indian Currency Crisis', 88–95. Government of India officials were already seriously considering voluntary devaluation: BoE Cte, 26 Nov. 1930.

[29] Cabinet 10(31), 28 Jan. 1931.

[30] Baldwin to the Davidsons, 27 Nov. 1930, in Davidson, *Memoirs of a Conservative*, 356; N. Chamberlain to Bridgeman, 18 Nov. 1930, Bridgeman papers.

[31] 1922 Committee, 24 Nov. 1930.

Labour at the Shipley by-election, by evidence of a Liberal split, and by the obvious floundering of the Labour Cabinet. For the first time since the general election, there appeared to be both opportunity and readiness to form a Conservative government.

From November Baldwin and Neville Chamberlain led a sustained onslaught upon the Labour government's economic and financial policies. The government was a 'colossal failure'; it had not merely failed to cure unemployment, but was making matters worse. By the tariff truce and rejection of Dominion trade offers, it had sacrificed industry to 'the ancient and obsolete... theories of Cobdenism', and 'statesmanship to prejudice'. The £46m. increase in taxation in the 1930 budget had 'knocked the life out' of industry, yet Education, Land Utilisation, and other bills involving additional expenditure were still being introduced. The government's 'cowardice' in postponing 'reform' of unemployment insurance abuses was a further deterrent to enterprise. Government intervention in industry had met its inevitable reward in coal industry disputes. Confidence was also threatened by the Trade Disputes Bill – a 'General Strike Enabling Bill'. Ministers failed to understand the gravity of the situation and lacked any constructive ideas. They were 'incompetent and incapable to an almost incredible extent', at their 'wit's end'. Baldwin rubbed in his 1929 election message, that the 'land of promise' was far from the 'land of performance', and claimed conclusive proof of 'the complete bankruptcy of socialism'.[32] Hailsham was particularly brutal: 'no government in history ha[d] done so much mischief in so little time'.[33] As acting Conservative leader in the Lords while Salisbury was ill in early 1931, he inflicted real damage by securing defeat of the Education Bill and mutilation of the Land Utilisation Bill.

There were no illusions about the difficulties to be faced by the next government. As already shown, behind Conservative rhetoric there was genuine belief in a national crisis: it was a 'damnosa hereditas'.[34] But, despite further economic deterioration during the winter, the inner party leadership still saw no point in 'national government' ideas.[35] Their position remained that protection and

---

[32] Baldwin speeches and statement, *The Times*, 10 and 26 Nov., 13 and 31 Dec. 1930, 17 Feb. 1931; N. Chamberlain speeches, ibid., 20 Nov. 1930, 9 Jan., 21 Feb. 1931, and in *HC Deb*, 244, cols. 503–5, 3 Nov. 1930.   [33] *The Times*, 4 Dec. 1930.

[34] N. to H. Chamberlain, 3 Jan. 1931, NC 18/1/722, and see Baldwin to Bridgeman, 16 Jan. 1931, Bridgeman papers.

[35] See dismissive references in N. Chamberlain to Bridgeman, 10 Jan. 1931, Bridgeman papers, and to H. Chamberlain, 1 March 1931, NC 18/1/728.

imperial economic unity would not just give immediate stimulation to the whole economy, but would command such widespread support – among the electorate, within other parties, and even from the TUC – as to ensure the establishment of a strong Conservative government. In readiness, Chamberlain appointed in December a Conservative Research Department committee under Cunliffe-Lister and including Amery and Lloyd to formulate detailed plans for implementing 'emergency' and 'scientific' tariffs.[36]

What changed in Conservative domestic policy during the winter was the priority given to retrenchment, since an embarrassing mishap in the parliamentary party's management revealed that the political significance of this issue had been seriously underestimated. On 10 December a Commons private members' economy debate collapsed through lack of a quorum. This attracted criticism from business opinion, the Conservative press and local associations of the Conservative leadership's apparent uninterest in retrenchment.[37] To counteract this 'very disastrous effect', Baldwin and Chamberlain immediately pledged that a Conservative government would give urgent attention to retrenchment,[38] and on 11 February the damage was repaired by a Commons motion censuring the Labour government on the issue. On Chamberlain's suggestion Baldwin thereafter presented Conservative party policy as a four-point programme of retrenchment, protection of the home market, help for agriculture, and development of imperial trade – in that order.[39]

The Conservative leadership, pushed by conservative opinion into switching its policy priorities, suddenly found itself able to exploit a powerful and strengthening agitation for retrenchment, now embracing ordinary taxpayers, industrialists, the City, the Friends of Economy, Treasury officials, readers of Rothermere newspapers, and non-party and cross-party as well as traditional Conservative opinion. But while this had considerable advantages, it also had obvious dangers. Unless skilfully presented, commitment to retrenchment and to defence of the direct taxpayer might saddle Conservatives with a reputation as the party of the reactionary and selfish wealthy and comfortable classes. By arousing widespread fear

[36] Amery diary, 3 Dec. 1930; Ramsden, *Making of Conservative Party Policy*, 52–3.
[37] E.g., *The Times*, 12 Dec. 1930; National Union Executive Committee minutes, 15 Jan. 1931.
[38] N. to H. Chamberlain, 14 Dec. 1930, NC 18/1/720; Baldwin speech and N. Chamberlain letter in *The Times*, 13 Dec. 1930.
[39] Baldwin speech, *The Times*, 7 March 1931. N. to I. Chamberlain, 7 March 1931, NC 18/1/729, and see his speeches in *The Times*, 21 Feb., 7 March 1931.

of cuts in the benefits of the unemployed, the wages of the employed labourer, and the salaries of the lower middle classes, it might lose support which Conservative leaders believed they were capturing with protection and imperial trade policies. It might even cost them their expected election victory; if not, it would still remain a delicate matter once a Conservative government was installed.[40]

Warnings about expenditure by Snowden and Hopkins were presented as proof that retrenchment was a national necessity, not a class interest. But what Conservative policy would involve in practice was left imprecise. Baldwin said that it did not 'necessarily' mean lower wages; it would do so only if protection were not introduced.[41] In terms of unemployment insurance, retrenchment meant ending 'abuses' and restoring the system to a 'proper insurance basis', with 'machinery' to provide for those losing their insurance entitlement.[42] However, although a Research Department committee determined that this machinery should be Public Assistance Committees and a means test (the old 'Poor Law' arrangements), this was not publicly stated, in order to avoid 'misrepresentation [by] the enemy'.[43] Conservative leaders, no less than MacDonald and Snowden, were waiting for the Royal Commission on Unemployment Insurance to relieve party responsibility for potentially unpopular cuts by providing 'impartial' justification and proposals.

Meanwhile, the Labour government was unexpectedly and frustratingly difficult to dislodge. In November 1930 and again in January 1931 an election seemed imminent as the government appeared about to collapse through incompetence, despair among its leaders, or divisions among its followers. During the second period Baldwin began planning ministerial appointments.[44] But Mac-Donald's persistence made it seem that the government could only be removed by decisive House of Commons defeat, which would

[40] See Morris-Jones diary, 10 Feb. 1931, for Kingsley Wood, a prospective Cabinet minister, asked privately about a Conservative government's attitude towards reduction of unemployment benefit: 'I question whether we could tackle it'.

[41] Baldwin speeches, *The Times*, 17 Feb., 7 March 1931.

[42] N. Chamberlain speeches, *The Times*, 9 Jan., 21 Feb. 1931.

[43] N. Chamberlain to Grigg, 16 Feb. 1931, Altrincham papers. For the unemployment insurance committee, see Ramsden, *Making of Conservative Party Policy*, 46–8. Significantly, little importance was attached to a CRD economy committee: see ibid., 54–5.

[44] Bridgeman, and Baldwin, to Davidson, 2 and 27 Nov. 1930, in Davidson, *Memoirs of a Conservative*, 352, 356; Worthington-Evans to 'John', 25 Nov. 1930, Worthington-Evans papers c897/280–1. N. Chamberlain, and Baldwin, to Bridgeman, 10 and 16 Jan. 1931, Bridgeman papers; A. Chamberlain to his wife, 19 Jan. 1931, AC 6/1/778.

require arrangement with all or some Liberal MPs. As the government appeared hopelessly discredited, Conservative leaders initially assumed that the Liberal leaders had no serious choice but to be pliable towards the Conservative party. In late November Grigg's reports of Lloyd George's disposition and a leaked account of the Liberal parliamentary party's rejection of a formal pact with the Cabinet persuaded Neville Chamberlain and other Conservative leaders – though not Baldwin – that Lloyd George was about to propose alliance with them.[45] At first even the introduction of an alternative vote bill was regarded less as evidence of a real Liberal–Labour alliance than as a Lloyd George trick to 'frighten' Conservatives into conceding better terms, particularly proportional representation.[46] On an assumption that Lloyd George and most other Liberal MPs would now feel compelled to swallow some form of protection, Amery, Hoare, and perhaps others were prepared to enter into negotiation with him. But Baldwin and Chamberlain remained cool towards any arrangement which would assist the Liberal party and Lloyd George, and neither felt able to afford any dilution of Conservative trade policy.[47] Their aim was to manoeuvre Liberal MPs into voting against the government, and then allow most of them to suffer the electoral penalty of their earlier support for it. To advance that end, the most they were prepared to do was to rescue complaisant Liberals by absorbing them into the Conservative party either directly or *via* some intermediate 'independent' grouping, on the model of their reception of Churchill and other 'Constitutionalists' in 1924.[48]

In approaching Simon on 1 December, Neville Chamberlain was therefore aiming to pre-empt an expected Lloyd George overture. He may have hoped that Simon could be persuaded to challenge Lloyd George for the Liberal leadership, in which case he was disappointed. But what Chamberlain did learn was perfectly satisfactory: that in order to eject the government Simon was prepared to contrive the Liberal party's destruction. He was not 'irreconcilable' on tariffs, would not insist upon electoral reform,

---

[45] N. Chamberlain diary, 21 and 23 Nov. 1930; N. to I. Chamberlain, 22 Nov. 1930, NC 18/1/718; Lady Hilton Young diary, 24 Nov. 1930; Amery diary, 30 Nov. 1930 (*LSA* II, 138); Baldwin to Davidson, 27 Nov. 1930, in Davidson, *Memoirs of a Conservative*, 356.

[46] N. to I. Chamberlain, 5 Dec. 1930, NC 18/1/719; N. Chamberlain diary, 6 Dec. 1930; Amery diary, 4 Dec. 1930 (*LSA* II, 143).

[47] Amery diary, 30 Nov. 1930 (*LSA* II, 138); Hoare in Lothian to Lloyd George, 3 Dec. 1930, Lothian papers 251/506–7.   [48] E.g., Baldwin speech, *The Times*, 13 Dec. 1930.

and wanted what the Conservative leaders could more easily concede – a guarantee of seats for himself and his supporters, and office in the next Conservative Cabinet. In light of this, it was easy for Chamberlain to disregard Reading, approached on Simon's suggestion the following day, when he raised tariffs as a difficulty and pressed for electoral reform.[49]

Thereafter leading Conservatives expected Simon to form an independent Liberal group, and did their utmost to assist him by embarrassing other Liberals. Over the next two months Simon received private encouragement, advice, and flattery, including that of Austen Chamberlain urging him to be like Joseph Chamberlain in 1886: 'not merely an outstanding Personality but a Force'.[50] Publicly Baldwin praised Simon's 'courageous opposition' to other Liberal MPs' 'bare-faced attempt to sacrifice the national interests for party gain'. Appeal was made to 'the more patriotically-minded Liberals in the country', and their party was characterised as betrayed by free trade and betraying individualism, left with a choice only between 'sudden death and death by slow poison'.[51] Neville Chamberlain concentrated upon 'bully[ing]' Liberal MPs over their most sensitive problem, their attitude to the Trade Disputes Bill, while Austen Chamberlain tried to incite Liberal Council leaders into demonstrating the sincerity of their professions about retrenchment.[52]

As it became evident from mid January that Lloyd George really was intent upon a 'corrupt bargain' with the Labour government, there was considerable Conservative shock and bitterness towards him and his followers.[53] Even former Coalitionists such as Austen Chamberlain, Horne, and Churchill now attacked him as a 'real danger to the country'.[54] Efforts were therefore intensified during February and March to prompt the formation of a definite Liberal

---

[49] N. to I. Chamberlain, 5 Dec. 1930, NC 18/1/719; N. Chamberlain diary, 5 Dec. 1930.

[50] A. Chamberlain to Simon, 16 Jan. 1931, Simon papers; A. Chamberlain to I. Chamberlain, and to his wife, 17 and 19 Jan. 1931, AC 5/1/527, 6/1/778; Hoare to Simon, 29 Jan. 1931, Simon papers.

[51] Baldwin statement, and speech, *The Times*, 31 Dec. 1930, 9 Jan. 1931.

[52] N. to I. Chamberlain, 23 Dec. 1930, NC 18/1/721, and speech, *The Times*, 9 Jan. 1931; A. Chamberlain letter, ibid. 28 Jan. 1931.

[53] N. to H. Chamberlain, 31 Jan. 1931, NC 18/1/724; Buchan to his wife, 28 Jan. 1931, Tweedsmuir (Queens) papers.

[54] Horne to Beaverbrook, 22 Jan. 1931, Beaverbrook papers C/178, and speech, *The Times*, 23 Jan. 1931; A. Chamberlain to his wife, and to I. Chamberlain, 22 Jan., 16 Feb. 1931, AC 6/1/781 and 5/1/530; Churchill, *HC Deb*, 247, cols. 696–7, 26 Jan. 1931.

breakaway group, with encouragement now given to Grigg as well as Simon.[55]

By the end of February, however, there was a more pressing concern in a renewed Conservative leadership crisis, which again threatened the party's capacity to form a government. The attack had two separate spearheads: Beaverbrook once more, and now Churchill. Rothermere provided aggressive newspaper support for both. But although Churchill exposed a real cleavage over the Indian issue, the effectiveness of these critics was not due primarily to specific policy differences. It was more the result of a general lack of confidence in Baldwin's leadership which continued to infect all levels of the party despite the Caxton Hall meeting, and which was deepened by recurring instances of his limpness and clumsiness.

After Caxton Hall the dissentients had remained unconvinced, despite obligatory public acquiescence in the outcome. Page Croft thought Baldwin had won a 'doubtful victory', Gretton that in reality his leadership had been 'smashed' and was preserved only temporarily through the party's fear 'of giving the press lords a triumph'. After 'the horrible spectacle of the last seven years of chop and change' and weakness in diehard and 'whole-hog' directions, Conservative diehards remained convinced that another Baldwin government would 'destroy [the party] as the alternative to socialism'.[56] However, the criticism of such irreconcilables mattered less than a broader rank-and-file opinion which remained puzzled by and resentful about what it considered to be such un-Conservative decisions as concession of the flapper vote, failure to extend safeguarding before the 1929 election, and support for the Irwin Declaration. It was disheartened by Baldwin's attachment to the 'old gang' of elderly ex-Cabinet ministers and his apparent reluctance to be nasty towards socialists. It doubted whether Baldwin had any real desire or capacity to implement party policy.[57] The view that Baldwin was soft and ineffectual was reflected in

---

[55] N. Chamberlain to Simon, 2 Feb. 1931, Simon papers; to I. and H. Chamberlain, 8 Feb., 1 March 1931, NC 18/1/725, 728, and to Grigg, 25 Feb. 1931, Altrincham papers. Dawson diary, 12 Feb. 1931, for Baldwin and Grigg. Horne to Simon, and to Grigg, both 4 March 1931, respectively Simon and Altrincham papers.

[56] Page Croft to Beaverbrook, 5 Nov. 1930, Beaverbrook papers C/101, and to N. Chamberlain, 8 Nov. 1930, Croft papers 1/7/9–10; Gretton in Headlam diary, 16 Nov. 1930, and to Tyrrell, 1 Nov. 1930, Gwynne papers 24.

[57] E.g., party opinion reported in Smithers to Fry, 1 and 12 Jan. 1931, SB 166/275–8, 47/233–5; and in Lane-Fox to Irwin, 28 Jan. 1931, Halifax papers 19/221.

scepticism about the leadership's commitment to retrenchment. It seemed to be confirmed by a 'futile' Baldwin speech in a censure debate on 27 November and further weak performances during January.[58] It had a personal edge in such statements as *The Daily Mail*'s reference to rumours about Baldwin's family finances – 'It is difficult to see how the leader of a party who has lost his own fortune can hope to restore that...of his country' – and a Scottish Conservative's allusion to his socialist son – 'How can a man who cannot rule his own family expect to rule a nation?'.[59] It was played upon during the winter by Beaverbrook's, Rothermere's, and Lloyd George's revived criticism of Baldwin's 1923 American debt settlement, which once more obliged Conservative leaders to undertake an extensive defence of his decision.[60] It also became a central theme in Beaverbrook's revival of the Empire Crusade.

Beaverbrook was angry at the Caxton Hall defeat, anxious to recover face, and still combative, but uncertain how to proceed. In resuming negotiations with Chamberlain on 5 November he was probably unsure himself whether he wished to make peace, to score a point, or to turn Chamberlain against Baldwin. Certainly Beaverbrook managed to string Chamberlain along for three weeks, convincing him that the Crusade was beaten and that Chamberlain was about to gain a 'great achievement' in halting Beaverbrook–Rothermere disruption of the party.[61] Meanwhile Beaverbrook decided to shift the focus of his campaign from imperial trade to domestic agricultural protection, basing its continuation upon lack of confidence in Baldwin's commitment to an outright tariff policy including food taxes. Baldwin's 'defensive' attitude in the 27 November censure debate became a pretext for letting negotiations lapse.[62]

Chamberlain saw in Beaverbrook's action as much a device to remain in the limelight as a genuine policy conviction. But he was

[58] A. to I. Chamberlain, 28 Nov. 1930, AC 5/1/522; Amery diary, 27 Nov. 1930, 20, 21, and 22 Jan. 1931 (first in *LSA* II, 137).

[59] Baldwin quoting *Daily Mail* in speech, *The Times*, 18 March 1931; Provand to Gilmour, 18 March 1931, Gilmour papers 383/34.

[60] See material in SB 109; also MacDonald diary, 27 Jan. 1931 for Baldwin asking to consult the relevant Cabinet papers.

[61] N. to I. Chamberlain, 8 and 22 Nov. 1930, NC 18/1/716, 718, and to Bridgeman, 18 Nov. 1930, Bridgeman papers. Compare Beaverbrook to Melchett, 11 Nov. 1930, Beaverbrook papers C/243.

[62] Beaverbrook to Melchett, 11 Nov., 1 Dec. 1930, and to Wargrave, 29 Nov. 1930, Beaverbrook papers C/243, C/320; Beaverbrook to N. Chamberlain, 28 Nov. 1930, NC 8/11/8.

not initially alarmed by the possible party consequences, because he himself now believed that the future of agriculture lay in tariff-protected livestock farming, and so welcomed pressure which might help persuade Baldwin to accept definite food taxes.[63] This complacency was shaken from mid December as Beaverbrook first attacked the appointment of an official Conservative candidate in the Empire Crusade seat of South Paddington, and then announced that Crusade candidates would again contest by-elections against Conservatives.

In resuming the Empire Crusade, Beaverbrook intended to justify his previous efforts and avenge earlier setbacks. He had sensed that Baldwin could still be pushed, and now meant to 'go out more violently than ever' against the Conservative party, forcing Baldwin to 'give in or give up'. Increasingly he meant the latter, as he discerned the presence of 'masses who want to wipe out the present Conservative hierarchy'.[64] But renewed flattery of leading Conservative protectionists brought support only from Hannon (who was on Beaverbrook's payroll). Despite their own doubts about Baldwin's leadership Page Croft, Amery, Lloyd, Horne, and the others had had enough of newspaper intervention. For the sake of increased newspaper support, Beaverbrook again conducted an uncomfortable alliance with Rothermere. Although he avoided Rothermere's proposal of fusing the Crusade with the United Empire party, he had to concede prominence to economy and India. Beaverbrook also had support from the Norfolk NFU, which formed itself in January into an 'Agricultural party'. But despite the policy emphasis on agricultural protectionism, his main attention remained upon London and the Home Counties. These were the heartlands of his and Rothermere's newspaper readership where, partly for that reason, substantial sections of conservative opinion appeared to be disillusioned with the Conservative party.

During the East Islington by-election of February Beaverbrook's principal theme was that, while Baldwin constantly changed policy and was not really serious about the Empire, he himself so much wanted a proper Conservative policy that in order to get it he was not afraid of breaking up the Conservative party.[65] Although the

[63] N. Chamberlain diary, 5 Dec. 1930; N. to I. Chamberlain, 5 Dec. 1930, NC 18/1/719.
[64] Beaverbrook to Hannon, 29 Dec. 1930, Hannon papers 18, and to Borden, 7 Jan. 1931, Beaverbrook papers C/12; Beaverbrook to Page Croft, 28 Jan. 1931, Croft papers 1/4/17.
[65] Beaverbrook speeches, *The Times*, 4 and 6 Feb. 1931.

Crusade fielded a poor candidate,[66] he obtained a thousand votes more than the Conservative. Conservative managers sought consolation in the hope that the overall result – Labour retention of the seat on a divided Conservative vote – would rally the party and electors against Beaverbrook and Rothermere. But no obvious backlash developed, which seemed to confirm that the party was demoralised. Beaverbrook and Rothermere felt confident enough to challenge Baldwin's leadership directly in the St George's, Westminster seat made vacant by the death of Worthington-Evans. In this they were encouraged by the impact of Churchill and the Indian issue.

Churchill had remained within the Conservative Business Committee in October because on the issue of opposition to food taxes there was nowhere attractive for him to go. His weakness was humiliatingly obvious in the lack of enthusiasm with which Baldwin and other members asked him to remain. Yet in staying his prospects were scarcely better. Churchill's convictions and reputation as an anti-protectionist, the resentment created among colleagues by tortuous attempts to reconcile his past with current party policy, and the evident fact that he was a chief target of hostility against the 'old gang', all told against his occupying a leading position in the next – protectionist – Conservative government.[67] It therefore took little for Churchill to 'have no desire to join such an administration' and to feel he would be 'better able to help the country from outside'.[68]

In these circumstances, the development of Churchill's opinions about India had a powerful functional aspect. They gave him purpose, restored him to prominence, and reattached him to important sections of Conservative and anti-socialist opinion. On the same day that he refrained from leaving the Business Committee he joined the Indian Empire Society.[69] During a series of speeches to safeguard his position in his own constituency he skirted around the trade question and proclaimed that the pre-eminent political issue was resisting 'defeatism' in India.[70] After it became apparent in mid

[66] The first Crusade candidate was suborned by Conservative Central Office, while the second was a bad speaker: see Beaverbrook to Rothermere, 3 Feb. 1931, Beaverbrook papers C/285; N. to H. Chamberlain, 14 Feb. 1931, NC 18/1/726.
[67] For resentment, N. Chamberlain diary, 6 Nov. 1930; for old gang, Churchill in Amery diary, 6 Nov. 1931 (LSA II, 88).
[68] Churchill to R. Churchill, 8 Jan. 1931, in WSC v (2), 243.
[69] Gilbert, Churchill v, 372.
[70] Speeches in The Times, 29 Oct., 4, 6, and 7 Nov. 1930.

November that the Round Table Conference was moving towards federation, he accepted an Indian Empire Society invitation to address a City meeting so that he could lead a 'stand about India'.[71]

There, on 11 December, Churchill mounted a wide-ranging challenge to prevailing orthodoxies about India. He declared that the Indian political classes were a tiny minority, whose gloss of Western ideas had no relation 'whatever' to the real life of India, and among whom the extremists were, and would remain, the dominant force. The Indian delegates at the Conference 'in no way' represented the effective forces in India: the moderates and the Princes favoured large changes only because 'weak-minded' British policies were compelling them to prepare for a 'Gandhi Raj'. With an illiterate population and many mutually antagonistic races, religions, and sects, withdrawal of British control would mean either 'ferocious internal wars' or 'Hindu despotism', with 'measureless suffering' to the people. The turmoil could still be ended by a 'plain assertion of the resolve of Parliament to govern'. Parliament could not be bound by any Conference decision, and although the 1920 Government of India Act had contained a pledge to extend Indian constitutional development, if that 'experiment' failed – as it had – Parliament had an 'unchallengeable' right to restrict or reverse it. Such action was now necessary because of Britain's 'mission...and duty to the Indian masses', and because the loss of India would result in 'the downfall of the British Empire'.[72]

This speech secured Churchill strong support from Rothermere's newspapers. Rothermere took the view that 'if India [were] not held there [was] nothing for England but bankruptcy and revolution', and flattered Churchill with suggestions that he could 'quite soon' capture the premiership. Thereafter he gave equal publicity to Beaverbrook and Churchill in the belief that their dual assault would bring down the Conservative organisation and the 'duds that surround their dud...leader'.[73] Beaverbrook, however, kept his distance from Churchill because of his difference with him over protection and his belief, at least initially, that Churchill had been through 'too many shifting phases' to carry conviction.[74] Nevertheless, with Beaverbrook attacking Conservative subservience to the

[71] Churchill to Jacob, 23 Nov. 1930, in *WSC* v (2), 225.
[72] *The Times*, 12 Dec. 1930.
[73] Rothermere to Churchill, 13 Dec. 1930, 29 and 31 Jan., 3 Feb. 1931, in *WSC* v (2), 231, 253–4, 257; Rothermere to Beaverbrook, 31 Jan. 1931, Beaverbrook papers C/285.
[74] Beaverbrook to Borden, and to Brisbane, 7 and 13 Jan. 1931, Beaverbrook papers C/52, C/64.

'socialists' over India in order to please Rothermere and further
damage Baldwin, Churchill felt that they were 'converging'.[75]
Churchill's speech had the Indian Empire Society 'feed[ing] out of
[his] hand', and together with Rothermere's agents it planned a
Churchill-led demonstration in Lancashire to exploit opposition to
Indian tariffs.[76]

The speech also brought alliance with Gretton's and Page Croft's
diehard group and with a wider group of strong imperialists.
Together these came close in early 1931 to converting the
parliamentary party's India Committee into their own 'policy
Soviet'.[77] The most important individual was Lloyd, not just as an
EIA and EEU leader but as a former Governor of Bombay who had
been a diehard hero since his dismissal by the Labour Cabinet from
the High Commissionership of Egypt, and who now vigorously
articulated the assumptions, prejudices, and contempt of the
Conservative right. Though once a close associate of Irwin, he
considered the Irwin Declaration a 'great betrayal' and the Round
Table Conference 'disastrous', representing an 'abdication' to a
'Brahmin autocracy' controlled by 'Russian money and influence'.[78] The Conservative leadership's acquiescence in the abandonment of the Simon Report was for him just a further instance of
the 'hold which crypto Socialists or sentimentalists have on the party
these days'. Far from accepting Baldwin's concern to win the
electoral middle ground, he thought 'no election [was] worth
winning on any other platform' than that of inflexible Conservatism.[79]

These various connections meant that while the Indian issue
provided Churchill with the 'great comfort' of a question he cared
about 'far more than office or party or friendships', it also gave him
a sense of being politically 'a great deal stronger'.[80] Although
Reading's acceptance of federation wrecked his strategy of Con-

---

[75] Beaverbrook speech, *The Times*, 6 Feb. 1931. Churchill to R. Churchill, 7 Feb. 1931, in
  WSC v (2), 264.

[76] Churchill to R. Churchill, 8 Jan. 1931, in *WSC* v (2), 243. For arrangements see letters to
  Hunter, ibid., 234–5, 239–40, 245–6.

[77] Amery diary, 16 March 1931 (*LSA* II, 156).

[78] G. Schuster, and Dawson, to Irwin, 7 and 25 Nov. 1930, Halifax papers 19/161, 172; Lloyd
  to Wacha, 26 Jan. 1931, Lloyd papers 11/1; Lloyd to Amery, 10 Feb. 1931, Amery papers.
  See G. Lloyd and E. Wood [i.e., Irwin], *The Conservative Opportunity* (1918).

[79] Lloyd to Lady Milner, 21 Jan. 1931, Lady Milner papers c420/3; Lloyd memo of talk with
  Baldwin, 4 March 1931, Lloyd papers 19/5. For Lloyd possibly having party leadership
  ambitions, see Lady Houston to Pulvermacher, late 1930, in Day, *Lady Houston*, 91–3.

[80] Churchill to R. Churchill, 8 Jan. 1931, in *WSC* v (2), 243.

servative–Liberal alliance and ended his 'last despairing hope that we should see again the great Lloyd George come to the aid of our country', he now intended to 'fight... to the end' on India in the belief that the Conservative party alone could be captured for a platform of imperialist, anti-socialist resistance.[81]

Churchill's activities disturbed the rest of the Conservative leadership, but became dangerous only after Baldwin misjudged his response to them. Dismissing Churchill as having regressed to the 'subaltern of Hussars of '96' and, after the 11 December speech, as 'gone quite mad',[82] Baldwin trusted Hoare and the Conservative Round Table Conference delegation to produce a widely acceptable Indian policy within the tripartite approach. He had 'no doubt' that he could control the party on the issue.[83] By satisfying reformers and reassuring doubters, Hoare's policy did indeed command assent from all Business Committee members except Churchill. Until the end of Hoare's speech in the Commons debate on the Conference resolutions on 26 January the India Committee also seemed amenable.[84] Later in the debate, however, Baldwin not only sharply repudiated a Churchill attack on the Conference agreement but also lectured Conservative backbenchers on the party's duty to 'implement' a federal constitution. This upset many Conservative MPs who thought Churchill's speech 'inopportune rather than wrong in itself', and for whom the word 'implement' suggested departure from Hoare's 'non-commitment' towards acceptance of a still undefined constitutional project.[85]

As a result Churchill was conscious of having 'at a stroke become quite popular in the party', and quickly proceeded to capitalise upon it.[86] He distanced himself from Baldwin by resigning publicly from what was meant to be the secret Business Committee. He joined Lloyd at the India Committee in trying to 'make trouble' over Irwin's release of Gandhi and, at the Indian Empire Society demonstration in Manchester on 30 January, he accused the

[81] Churchill to Sinclair, 8 Jan. 1931, Thurso papers II/85/3.
[82] Baldwin to Davidson, 13 Nov., 15 Dec. 1930, in Davidson, *Memoirs of a Conservative*, 355–6.
[83] Baldwin (and Salisbury) in Hailey to Irwin, 9 Dec. 1930, Halifax papers 19/184.
[84] Lane-Fox and Amery diaries, 20 Jan. 1931, and for reception of Hoare's speech, Amery diary, 26 Jan. 1931 (*LSA* II, 145).
[85] *HC Deb*, 247, col. 746, 26 Jan. 1931. A. Chamberlain to his wife, 2 Feb. 1931, AC 6/1/785; Amery and Lane-Fox diaries, 26 Jan. 1931.
[86] Churchill to R. Churchill, 7 Feb. 1931, in *WSC* v (2), 264.

Conservative leadership of failing in its essential function as a 'stabilising force'.[87]

Baldwin attempted to steady party opinion on 9 February by affirming to the India Committee his 'entire agreement' with Hoare's policy.[88] But the damage had now been done. The Committee was only 'partially satisfied'. Doubts had been raised about that policy as too advanced, and confidence in Baldwin's judgement slumped.[89] News of the Irwin–Gandhi talks further threatened his position, while an anxious India Committee resolved against Conservative participation in any British delegation to continue round-table talks in India. Lloyd, whose views were particularly violent – it was 'far better to wreck the Conservative party' than acquiesce in Baldwin's attitude, and the Conference policy was 'the greatest crime in the history of our people' – now evoked 'great enthusiasm' among most India Committee members.[90] On 24 February Churchill was received with 'acclamation' at the party's Central Council meeting, helping to precipitate a unanimous appeal for firm government in India. Within six weeks there had been an 'astonishing' change in Churchill's position.[91] It looked as if he might not just overturn the leadership's Indian policy, but 'split the Conservative party...more seriously...than Beaverbrook'.[92]

The cumulative effect of the Beaverbrook and Churchill assaults, party nervousness about India, sustained criticism from the Rothermere and Beaverbrook newspapers, the East Islington by-election and Baldwin's fumbling was a renewed party crisis. This was not so deep-rooted in the local and provincial Conservative associations as that of the previous October.[93] Nevertheless it was much more serious for Baldwin, because this time the party managers turned against him and – crucially – the collective leadership cracked.

From late January the Central Office, the whips, Business Committee members, and especially Neville Chamberlain as party chairman received from agents, provincial leaders, candidates, MPs, and friendly observers reports of widespread feeling that Baldwin

---

[87] Churchill to Baldwin, 27 Jan. 1931, in *The Times*, 30 Jan., and see Amery diary, 24 Feb. 1931 (*LSA* II, 149); Lane-Fox to Irwin, 28 Jan. 1931, Halifax papers 19/221.
[88] *The Times*, 10 Feb. 1931.   [89] Amery diary, 9 Feb. 1931 (*LSA* II, 147).
[90] Amery diary, 9 Feb. 1931 (*LSA* II, 147); Lloyd speech, *The Times*, 12 Feb. 1931.
[91] Central Council minutes, 24 Feb. 1931; Churchill to his wife, 26 Feb. 1931, in *WSC* v (2), 280–2.   [92] Astor to Garvin, 25 Feb. 1931, Astor papers.
[93] Ball, *Baldwin*, 125–6, 141–3.

CONVERSATION FOR TWO.

MR. WINSTON CHURCHILL. "I HOPE I INTRUDE."

4 'Conversation for Two': Winston Churchill and the Irwin–Gandhi talks
(*Punch*, 4 March 1931)

could not be trusted with party policy and had become an electoral liability.[94] These reports found a receptive audience in men weary of recurrent party crises. Central Office officials were 'bordering on despair'.[95] Neville and Austen Chamberlain, Hoare, Cunliffe-Lister, Hailsham, and Amery, who felt they had done their best for Baldwin by publicly renouncing any automatic claim to office in order to deflate the 'old gang' charge,[96] by providing him with policies and encouraging him to show fight, were exasperated by his apparent complacency and inability to present their work effectively.[97]

By late February these party leaders thought the party criticism so great that Baldwin should resign, and would be obliged to do so. In conditions where a hostile 'explosion' seemed imminent,[98] such thinking was quickened by anxiety to retain control over succession to the leadership. They could not allow anyone to be forced, or seem to be forced, upon the party by 'Press Lords'. For protectionist and Indian reasons all wanted to exclude Churchill,[99] and they preferred one of their own to an outsider like Horne. The succession mattered to Amery, who thought he had a chance of it, and was now promoted by Baldwin to the Business Committee in an attempt to disarm him.[100] It mattered also to Hailsham, who knew he had growing support as a candidate of the Conservative right. It also mattered to Austen Chamberlain, Hoare, and Cunliffe-Lister, who wanted Neville Chamberlain, and to Neville Chamberlain himself, who assumed that he was the favourite.[101]

There was, however, a serious difficulty. The individual most responsible for reporting party feeling to Baldwin and so most likely to secure his retirement was Neville Chamberlain, as party chairman. But Chamberlain continued to have scruples about action which

[94] E.g., N. to H. and I. Chamberlain, 31 Jan., 14 and 21 Feb. 1931, NC 18/1/724, 726, 727; Derby to N. Chamberlain, 25 Feb. 1931, NC 8/10/21; Amery diary, 26 Feb. 1931 (LSA II, 150); and A. to I. Chamberlain, 28 Feb. 1931, AC 5/11/532. There was also, it seems, a serious fall in party subscriptions.

[95] Bowyer reported in Hannon to Beaverbrook, 4 Feb. 1931, Beaverbrook papers C/155.

[96] E.g., Salisbury to Bridgeman, 6 and 7 Nov. 1930, Bridgeman papers; Amery diary, 6 Nov. 1930 (LSA II, 87); Baldwin speech, The Times, 26 Nov. 1930.

[97] E.g., Amery diary, 12 and (for Hoare) 22 Feb. 1931 (LSA II, 148, 149); A. to M. Chamberlain, 6 Feb. 1931, AC 4/1/1306.

[98] N. Chamberlain diary, 23 Feb. 1931; A. to I. Chamberlain, 28 Feb. 1931, AC 5/1/532. N. to H. Chamberlain, 14 Feb. 1931, NC 18/1/726.

[99] For anti-Churchill sentiments, see A. Chamberlain to his wife, 27 Jan. 1931, AC 6/1/783; N. to H. Chamberlain, 31 Jan. and (for Hailsham) 1 March 1931, NC 18/1/724, 728.

[100] Amery to Beaverbrook, 31 Dec. 1930, Beaverbrook papers C/5; Amery diary, 26 Feb. 1931 (LSA II, 150).

[101] A. to I. Chamberlain, 28 Feb. 1931, AC 5/1/532. N. Chamberlain diary, 23 Feb. 1931; Amery diary, 24 Feb. 1931 (LSA II, 149).

might operate to his own benefit, and also knew that any suspicion of disloyalty might damage his own position. At first he could not 'see any way out', and sought advice – and exemption from any blame for whatever might happen – from political friends.[102] Escape was provided by Topping, the chief party agent, who with Chamberlain's encouragement submitted a memorandum which gave an ostensibly objective report of the strength of party disillusionment with Baldwin.[103] Discussion with Austen Chamberlain, Hailsham, Hoare, Cunliffe-Lister, the chief whip Eyres-Monsell, and Bridgeman, confirmed Neville Chamberlain's own view that the memorandum should be shown to Baldwin. With the exception of Bridgeman, all thought it must cause his immediate resignation. Austen Chamberlain savoured the prospect of avenging Baldwin's victories over him during the party crises of 1922–3.[104]

A hesitation over when Baldwin should be informed was ended when announcement of the Empire Crusade candidature in the St George's by-election induced the Conservative candidate, Moore-Brabazon, to withdraw rather than fight in defence of Baldwin's leadership. Chamberlain sent Topping's memorandum to Baldwin on 1 March with a covering letter mentioning whom he had consulted and stressing the 'extreme difficulty' of the party situation.[105] An awkward interview between them later that day produced some misunderstanding. But whether Baldwin volunteered to resign immediately (as Chamberlain understood) or whether Chamberlain said he and his colleagues wanted him to go (as Baldwin understood), there is no doubt that Baldwin correctly interpreted the spirit of Chamberlain's actions and words, and that, feeling a gun at his head, he concluded he had no choice but to retire.[106]

What saved Baldwin was the Beaverbrook–Rothermere intervention at St George's. Bridgeman and Davidson argued strenuously against immediate resignation in the face of this attack from the

---

[102] N. Chamberlain diary, 23 Feb. 1931; Lady Hilton Young and Amery diaries, 24 Feb. 1931 (latter in *LSA* II, 149).

[103] N. Chamberlain diary, 23 Feb., 1 March 1931. Topping memo, 25 Feb. 1931, SB 166/50–3 (printed in Macleod, *Chamberlain*, 139–41).

[104] Bridgeman diary, 28 Feb. 1931 (Williamson, 243–4); N. Chamberlain diary, 1 March 1931; A. to I. Chamberlain, 28 Feb. 1931, AC 5/1/532.

[105] N. Chamberlain diary, 1 March 1931; N. Chamberlain to Baldwin, 1 March 1931, SB 166/47–9.

[106] N. Chamberlain diary, 1 March 1931, and to H. Chamberlain, 1 March 1931, NC 18/1/728. For Baldwin's version, see Jones memo, 11 March 1931, SB 166/54–6 (partly in Jones, *Diary with Letters*, 4) and N. Chamberlain diary, 25 March 1931.

'vile Press', proposing instead that Baldwin should confront his critics by contesting the seat himself.[107] Their appeals aroused Baldwin's fighting instincts and his moral outrage. Business Committee members, whips, and Central Office officials, confronted with the proposal on 2 March, argued that the party leadership must not be submitted to the decision of a single constituency. But they now accepted that Baldwin could not retire in conditions which would seem like a triumph for the 'Press Lords'.[108]

This did not mean that they thought Baldwin could or should remain long. They considered his position ultimately irretrievable. During the following week Hoare and Amery tried to organise a movement to make this clear to Baldwin.[109] The succession remained a live issue. On 5 March Neville Chamberlain and Hailsham agreed that Hailsham's membership of the Lords did not necessarily exclude him from the party leadership and premiership, and settled between themselves that either would serve under the other, with leadership in the Commons or Lords as compensation. This arrangement seemed to be strengthened when Horne showed readiness to support Baldwin against 'press dictation' in return for high office in a Conservative government.[110] Austen Chamberlain, who had long feared that his half-brother's prospects of the succession were hampered by occupancy of the party chairmanship, pointedly asked Baldwin on the 11th to release Neville Chamberlain from the post.[111] Among leading Conservatives, including Horne as well as Business Committee members, support for the new Conservative candidate at St George's, Duff Cooper, was all the stronger because it was assumed that if he won Baldwin's departure would be eased.

However, once Baldwin had decided to fight he had every intention of staying. His resolve was strengthened by his colleagues' and the party managers' apparent change of mind on the 2nd, which suggested that their judgement was untrustworthy; by some letters

---

[107] Bridgeman diary, 1 March 1931 (Williamson, 244); Davidson to Irwin, 6 March 1931, Halifax papers 19/254; Baldwin in Jones memo, 11 March 1931, SB 166/54–6.

[108] N. Chamberlain diary, 3 and 25 March 1931; Baldwin in Jones memo, 11 March 1931, SB 166/54–6; Davidson to Irwin, 6 March 1931, Halifax papers 19/254.

[109] Amery diary, 2, 5 (for N. Chamberlain), 6 (for Hoare and Hailsham), 7 (for A. Chamberlain), and 10 March 1931 (*LSA* II, 151–3, 155); A. to H. and I. Chamberlain, 7 and 13 March 1931, AC 5/1/533, 534; N. to I. Chamberlain, 7 March (misdated Feb.) 1931, NC 18/1/729.

[110] N. to I. Chamberlain, 7 March 1931, NC 18/1/729; N. Chamberlain diary, 8 March 1931.

[111] Amery and N. Chamberlain diaries, 11 March 1931 (former in *LSA* II, 155); A. to I. Chamberlain, 13 March 1931, AC 5/1/534.

of support, and by his own conviction that there was 'no one' to replace him 'who would not be in an even more difficult position than himself'. His determination was further reinforced by an interview with Lloyd who said he should resign for policy reasons which Baldwin considered strategically disastrous, and by Davidson arguing that Topping's memorandum was motivated by personal hostility, which suggested that Neville Chamberlain did not understand the true mood of Central Office and the party.[112] As suspicion grew that his colleagues were guilty of wishful thinking (in the case of Neville Chamberlain) or outright disloyalty (in the cases of Austen Chamberlain, Hoare, and Hailsham),[113] Baldwin became very angry, not only with them but with all those who had precipitated the trouble or yielded before it. He had a 'Party of fools'; diehards who had loathed Churchill for years were now absurdly supporting him. Distrusting his official advisers, he heeded alternative advice – that of Davidson, Dawson, Jones, and Mrs Baldwin.[114] As his colleagues detected his resentment towards and lack of confidence in them, they in turn became resentful and annoyed. Neville Chamberlain on the 13th took Austen's advice and resigned the party chairmanship. On the 24th he accused Baldwin of committing if not intentional snubs then of displaying 'inexcusable' negligence towards his colleagues.[115]

The recovery of Baldwin's position was therefore undertaken in the face of considerable ill-feeling in the highest reaches of the party. It was greatly assisted on 5 March by news of the Irwin–Gandhi pact, which restored confidence in Irwin and by association Baldwin, produced a 'tremendous revulsion of feeling' in the party against Churchill and Lloyd, and evoked reflections on Baldwin's dealings with Providence.[116] Otherwise it relied largely upon Baldwin's own exertions, beginning with a speech on the 6th emphasising the

---

[112] Baldwin in N. Chamberlain diary, 25 March 1931, in Jones memo, 11 March 1931, SB 166/54–6, and in Lloyd memo, 4 March 1931, Lloyd papers 19/5.

[113] Baldwin in Jones memo, 11 March 1931, SB 166/54–6, and reported by Davidson *via* Ball in N. Chamberlain diary, 11 March 1931.

[114] N. Chamberlain diary, 11 March 1931; Baldwin in Jones memo, 11 March 1931, SB 166/54–6; Davidson to Irwin, 6 March 1931, Halifax papers 19/254; Dawson diary, 3 March 1931.

[115] N. Chamberlain diary, 11, 14, 21, and 25 March 1931; N. Chamberlain to Baldwin, 13 and 24 March 1931, SB 166/58–60 and NC 8/10/30.

[116] Amery and Lane-Fox diaries, 5 March 1931 (first in *LSA* II, 143); Davidson, Dawson and Spender-Clay (repeating Buchan's dictum that 'God Almighty was so busy looking after Baldwin that he had no time to look after the rest of the world'), all 5 March 1931, Halifax papers 19/248, 250, 251.

preservative facets of Hoare's Indian formula. There was a setback on the 9th when he blundered into a Churchill–diehard trap of authorising publication of an India Committee resolution reiterating the party's refusal to send a delegation to India, which received hostile presentation as a rejection of all further participation in the Round Table process. As Baldwin had earlier inflamed the diehards, so now this dismayed the 'progressives', and revived the view that he should resign in the very near future.[117] But in a Commons' debate on the 12th he swept Churchill, Lloyd, and the diehards aside and reassured the rest of the party with a highly impressive declaration of faith in Irwin's strategy. This enabled the loyalists to impose a humiliating defeat upon Churchill at the India Committee on the 16th.[118] Speaking in St George's on the following day he dealt even more decisively with Rothermere and Beaverbrook in a withering attack upon 'power without responsibility'.

On 19 March St George's was won by Duff Cooper, and on the 24th and 25th the air was cleared first with Neville Chamberlain and then with the whole Business Committee as Baldwin submitted himself to a frank – in Austen Chamberlain's case brutal – expression of their grievances against his manner of leadership, though making it plain that he still proposed to continue.[119] His recovery was such that, with Beaverbrook smarting personally under the double sores of Baldwin's vitriol and the St George's defeat, Neville Chamberlain was able on the 29th to obtain his and the Agricultural party's public submission to the Conservative party's trade policy in the 'Stornoway Pact'.[120]

Baldwin had survived and made peace with his closest colleagues. The impact of the Indian issue had nonetheless been considerable. It weakened the Conservative opposition and strengthened the Labour government during an awkward period, and it had important consequences for the future effectiveness and composition of the collective Conservative leadership. True, during the winter the Conservative party became the party of retrenchment as well as

[117] Amery diary, 9 and 10 March 1931 (*LSA* II, 154); Lane-Fox diary, 10 March 1931; Lane-Fox to Irwin, 12 March 1931, Halifax papers 19/266; Astor and Baldwin (admitting the blunder) in Jones memo, 11 March 1931, SB 166/54–6.

[118] Amery diary, 16 March 1931 (*LSA* II, 156); *The Times*, 17 March 1931.

[119] N. Chamberlain diary, 25 March 1931, and to H. Chamberlain, 28 March 1931, NC 18/1/732; Amery diary, 25 and 26 March 1931 (*LSA* II, 157–8); Bridgeman diary, 28 March 1931 (Williamson, 245).

[120] N. Chamberlain diary, 28 March 1931; Beaverbrook–N. Chamberlain letters in *The Times*, 30 March 1931.

imperial protectionism, which placed it more firmly at the head of prevailing economic and financial opinion. But Reading's acceptance of federation reinforced the undeclared Liberal–Labour pact and made Indian policy into a political asset for the Cabinet, while Churchill's rebellion renewed the impression that 'there [could] be no united drive amongst the Tories under Baldwin'.[121] Baldwin's survival perpetuated Churchill's self-exclusion from the Conservative inner leadership and preserved the principle of tripartite co-operation on Indian policy, but only for the time being. Only in retrospect do the events of March seem decisive for Baldwin and for Indian policy. Difficulties during the spring in persuading Simon and other dissident Liberals to form themselves into an effective group[122] indicated that the Labour government's defeat would be further delayed, prolonging the period in which Baldwin's shortcomings as opposition leader might cause problems. There was every likelihood of further trouble from Churchill, the Indian Empire Society, Rothermere, and the parliamentary diehards and imperialists when the second Round Table Conference met in the autumn to discuss the details of federation. Baldwin, having received a nasty shock about the state of feeling towards himself in the party and among his senior colleagues, was likely to be even more cautious than usual in taking responsibility for big decisions affecting the party's future. On the other hand, the failure of Neville Chamberlain's attempted coup against Baldwin had weakened neither his position within the party hierarchy, nor his self-confidence and readiness to act as the real power behind Baldwin. It became a matter of great significance that the public announcement in early April of Chamberlain's retirement from the party chairmanship also reported his appointment to lead opposition to the Finance Bill, replacing Churchill as the Conservative 'shadow' Chancellor of the Exchequer.

[121] MacDonald diary, 26 Jan. 1931; Benn to Irwin, 18 Feb. 1931, Halifax papers 6/56.
[122] N. to I. Chamberlain, 5 April 1931, NC 18/1/733, and see below, p. 211.

CHAPTER 6

Retrenchment and containment

The state of confidence... is a matter to which practical men
always pay the closest and most anxious attention.

J. M. Keynes, *The General Theory of Employment, Interest and
Money* (1936)

[We are] supporting a Government which, in spite of the fact
that it [is] undesirable to say so publicly, [is] undoubtedly
incompetent.

Lloyd George at Conference on Liberal Organisation,
18 March 1931

The Govt. is acting as if it were going to remain in for 2 years,
and apparently LG and his friends are to support them.

Passfield to B. Webb, 29 April 1931[1]

'ECONOMY'

During the winter of 1930–1 economic conditions continued to
deteriorate, without sign of relief. Statistics published during early
1931 revealed the extent of the downturn over the previous year, and
continuing falls in prices, export earnings, industrial production,
profits, and employment. By February unemployment had risen to
almost 2·7m. Despite falling prices and living costs, there were still no
significant reductions in money incomes. Imports had also held up,
with the iron and steel industry and cereal farming especially
suffering increased import competition. The balance of payments
was deteriorating seriously, the current account surplus having
fallen from £138m. in 1929 to an estimated £39m. in 1930, with a
deficit likely for the coming year.

To all this were added during January and February anxieties
about the budget and sterling, combined in a manner which
foreshadowed the financial crisis of the following summer. From

---

[1] Respectively *JMK* VII, 148; memo in LG G/84/10; Passfield papers II:3:(i):27:31.

published revenue and expenditure returns it seemed evident that an appreciable budget deficit was 'unavoidable'.[2] Sterling, which had been weak against the French franc since May 1930, fell in November to a level where gold withdrawals became profitable. By late January the Bank of England's gold reserves had declined from £160m. to the disturbingly low figure of £139m. Fears that these movements reflected not merely Continental banking problems but foreign doubts about the stability of sterling seemed to be confirmed in January by falls against the American dollar, and in February by a slump in forward exchange prices.[3] The gold standard was threatened, and in the City there appeared 'on every hand...a growing manifestation of anxiety [about] the financial plight of the country'. Significantly, the market in British government stocks became highly sensitive to political developments, beginning on 5 February when rumours that under Liberal pressure the Cabinet had agreed to a 'development loan' caused a sharp fall.[4]

These conditions sharply increased pressures for protection and especially, now, for retrenchment. The NFU attacked the government for 'indifference' to agricultural decline, rejecting the view that farmers must adjust their methods and opposing the Land Utilisation and Marketing Bills as first steps to nationalisation. Yet it also threatened to end co-operation with Conservative leaders if they supported marketing. Its position remained that the only solution was protection, by food taxes – not the Conservative quota proposals.[5] Most industrialists now insisted that protection was not just necessary in itself, but the essential condition for further rationalisation. In return for a tariff on iron and steel, Balfour was prepared even to accept state supervision over rationalisation.[6] Business criticism of government finance became increasingly sharp: Lewis spoke of 'the industries of this country...being crucified on a cross of national extravagance', the FBI of a 'prime and urgent necessity that there should be a drastic reduction in national

[2] 'City Notes', *The Times*, 1 Jan. 1931.
[3] 'The Money Market', *Economist*, 7 Feb. 1931; Keynes to Case, 21 Feb. 1931, in *JMK* xx, 485–6.
[4] 'The Week in the Markets', *Economist*, 7 Feb. 1931; 'The Stock Exchange', *The Times*, 6 and 7 Feb. 1931.
[5] NFU statement, *The Times*, 7 Jan. 1931; E. T. Morris to Baldwin, 31 Dec. 1930, SB 31/294–5; *NFU Yearbook for 1931*, 444, 452.
[6] FBI statement, *The Times*, 3 Feb. 1931; Balfour at EAC 10th meeting, 11 Dec. 1930, and see National Federation of Iron and Steel Manufacturers statement, *The Times*, 16 Jan. 1931.

expenditure'.[7] Unemployment insurance was a special target, as moral or social assumptions fused with arguments about cost. The system was 'sapping the independence and enterprise of the people'; eradication of 'abuses' would 'improve [their] morale'.[8] Balfour so doubted that 'any party politician' had the 'courage' to tackle the issue that he now spoke publicly of a need for a 'national agreement'. Morris talked about industry giving politicians 'the sack'.[9]

Some industrialists also became openly critical of wage levels. A NCEO document sent in February to party leaders, MPs, and newspapers, not only ascribed Britain's economic problems largely to high living standards relative to its international competitors. It also placed the blame squarely upon government, arguing that these standards were determined mostly through 'high rates' of unemployment benefit, statutory wage-fixing machinery, and central and local government wages. It wanted a Committee on National Economy to reduce social service expenditure 'considerably' below the 1929 total; reduction of unemployment benefits to 1921 levels (a 33 per cent cut) and transference of transitional claimants to a means-tested system; repeal of wage-fixing legislation, and reduction of all government wage-levels to those prevailing in the export industries.[10]

City financiers too were on the offensive, especially as they began receiving reports of foreign lack of confidence in British financial stability.[11] In January most clearing bank chairmen demanded 'a drastic reconsideration of all...expenditures'.[12] Even those bankers who thought gold maldistribution a contributory cause of depression now despaired of the chances of international co-operation, and believed that domestic adjustments could no longer be avoided.[13] On 27 January the Friends of Economy, supported by many leading financiers, inaugurated their campaign in the City with a crowded public meeting. They called upon the government and local

[7] Lewis speech, and FBI statement, *The Times*, 16 Jan., 3 Feb. 1931.

[8] NCEO statement, 'The Industrial Situation', *The Times*, 13 Feb. 1931.

[9] Balfour speech and Morris statement, *The Times*, 15 Jan., 19 Feb. 1931.

[10] NCEO, 'The Industrial Situation', *The Times*, 13 Feb. 1931. See Rodgers, 'Employers' Organizations', 330: 'probably the most abrasive report produced by any group of employers between the wars'.

[11] E.g., Granet reported in Norman diary, 26 Jan. 1931, and in Norman to Fergusson, 27 Jan. 1931, BoE G3/198/45.

[12] Goodenough and also Paton, Beckett, Goschen, Beaumont Pease speeches in *Economist*, 24 and 31 Jan., 7 Feb. 1931.

[13] E.g., Brand to Hawtrey, and to Keynes, 24 Feb., 2 March 1931, Brand papers 28, 198.

authorities 'to cease from all expenditure which is not absolutely essential'.[14]

Although this meeting was addressed by Grey and Horne, the decline in financial confidence was exacerbated by fears that politicians generally would ultimately baulk at the unpopularity of retrenchment. The collapse of the Commons debate on retrenchment in mid December seemed indicative, as did the reluctance of many MPs to become associated with the Friends of Economy.[15] The extreme nervousness of responsible financial opinion is exemplified by Brand, whose politics were Liberal:

> I am beginning to regard the situation as a dangerous one ... and it doesn't seem to me that our political leaders have any idea of it ... The trouble is that democracies seem unable constitutionally to make Budgets balance. It is impossible to get candidates for Parliament not to promise to spend money. In one country after another drastic economies can only be made by suspending the constitution, and I am not at all sure that our time is not coming.[16]

Such opinions and the pressure of economic and financial deterioration resulted in the advocates of expansionist policies or improved living standards becoming increasingly isolated or defensive. Although the TUC pressed for extension of unemployment insurance to agricultural workers, its greater concern was to preserve the existing system against the threat posed by the Royal Commission on Unemployment Insurance.[17] In March it issued a statement proposing international economic co-operation and nationalisation of industries to enforce rationalisation: yet its principal purpose was to defend existing wage-levels against the NCEO criticism.[18]

The gravity of the situation certainly pushed a few towards monetary heterodoxy. Bevin hardened in his view that 'the deterioration of the conditions of millions of workers was too high a price to pay for the maintenance of ... international banking in London'. Some replacement should be found for the gold standard,

---

[14] *The Times*, 28 Jan. 1931. City supporters included Goodenough, Beaumont Pease, F. Schuster, Brand, D'Abernon, and five Bank of England directors.

[15] 'City Notes', *The Times*, 12 Dec. 1930; The Friends of Economy, *First Annual Report*, 1.

[16] Brand to Keynes, 30 Jan. 1931, Brand papers 30.

[17] Bondfield to MacDonald, 29 Dec. 1930, and Citrine to MacDonald, 30 Jan., 26 Feb. 1931, JRM 441; LPNEC, 24 Feb. 1931; TUCGC, 17 Dec. 1930, 28 Jan., 24 Feb. 1931; Skidelsky, *Politicians*, 263–7.

[18] 'Short Statement on Economic Policy', 16 March 1931, *TUCAR 1931*, 259–61.

from which 'only the *rentier* classes stood to gain'.[19] Hawtrey moved
from criticism of the Bank of England's 'extreme conservatism' to
public advocacy of credit expansion even at the risk of gold losses,
and (apparently) to private belief in the desirability of devaluation.[20]
According to Keynes, there were now 'quite a number' of people,
some of a 'surpris[ing]' sort, favouring abandonment of the gold
standard.[21]

These, however, remained highly untypical, and they included
neither Keynes himself, nor McKenna. Paradoxically, Keynes's and
McKenna's desire for reflation now brought them to positions very
similar to those of the financial authorities. McKenna alone of the
bank chairmen continued to look largely to monetary remedies for
the depression: cheap and easy money, renewed American and
French overseas lending, central bank co-operation. But these
objectives required a high degree of financial confidence, which was
now plainly in short supply. His reaction consisted of rare expressions
of optimism: there was '[no] danger of devaluation', and 'those who
advocated a devaluation before we returned to the Gold Standard...no longer...favour...such action'.[22]

Keynes similarly recognised that expansionist policies now
required serious attention to matters of confidence, for both financial
and political reasons. This evoked some of his most sinuous reasoning.
In case events forced abandonment of the gold standard he did not
want to be 'too much committed' to it, yet he was 'ready to support
[it] for the time being and give it every chance in [his] power'.[23] In
fact he thought the City's pessimism 'complete moonshine' and
considered that a real crisis – '*if there is going to be one*' – was 'some
appreciable way off' and still avoidable, because the 'fundamental
position remain[ed] extraordinarily strong'.[24] Nevertheless Keynes
accepted – belatedly, given six months of Bank of England and

[19] EAC 13th meeting, 16 April 1931.

[20] Hawtrey in Streat diary, 15 Jan. 1931, in Dupree I, 12, and (retrospectively) in Moggridge, *British Monetary Policy*, 228 n4. For Bellerby expressing similar doubts, see Skidelsky, *Politicians*, 293.

[21] Keynes to Case, 21 Feb. 1931, *JMK* xx, 485. This may have been over-drawn: except for the evidence in the previous note, nothing survives to identify these people.

[22] Speech, *Economist*, 24 Jan. 1931; McKenna to Steel-Maitland, 5 Jan. 1931, Steel-Maitland papers 254.

[23] Keynes to Lubbock, 7 March 1931, extract in Lubbock to Brand, 9 March 1931, Brand papers 30. See also Keynes at EAC 13th meeting, 16 April 1931, and to Martin, 21 April 1931, *JMK* xxviii, 12–13.

[24] Keynes to Case, 21 Feb. 1931, and memo to National Mutual Board, 18 Feb. 1931, *JMK* xx, 485–6, xii, 17–19 (my italics).

Treasury statements – that in current conditions it was 'absolutely hopeless' to expect an early international financial conference, and futile to continue giving priority to loan-financed public works. For the Bank and Treasury successfully to initiate international cooperation and for the Labour government to survive and introduce an expansionist 'policy of the left',[25] it had become necessary to re-establish suitable conditions. His solution was a 'confidence package' of firm measures to reassure foreign financial opinion, obtain a budget surplus, and strengthen the trade balance. The exchange position should be 'relentlessly defended' and the Bank of England's gold reserve increased. 'Grave abuses' of the dole should be 'reform[ed]' and further social service expenditure postponed. Above all, for budget as well as for 'macroeconomic' reasons, Keynes now wanted a revenue tariff. He campaigned vigorously for this from early March with private appeals to ministers and a much-discussed public pronouncement of his apostasy from free trade.[26] So vital did a tariff seem to Keynes, that in trying to frighten MacDonald into pressing for it he contradicted his own private view in asserting that 'a crisis of financial confidence … [was] … *very near*'.[27]

Although Keynes's ultimate objectives remained avoidance of wage cuts and defeat of 'the spirit of contractionism and fear',[28] to slower minds he must have seemed a convert not merely to protection but to orthodox financial prescriptions. His March statement made public the previous autumn's clash between leading economists, and triggered the pre-concerted counter-attack of his critics. Robbins, Beveridge, and Gregory (the other professional economist on the Macmillan Committee) argued on conventional free-trade lines that the greatest need was for that 'readjustment of wages' which Keynes most wanted to avoid.[29] But this tariff controversy obscured the fact that most economists now agreed upon the urgency of restoring budget equilibrium and 'reforming' unemployment insurance. H.

[25] Keynes to Martin, 19 April 1931, in *JMK* xxvii, 11, and to MacDonald, 5 March 1931, JRM 677; Clarke, *Keynesian Revolution*, 201, 209–11.

[26] 'Proposals for a Revenue Tariff', *New Statesman*, 7 March 1931, and 'Put the Budget on a Sound Basis', *Daily Mail*, 13 March 1931, in *JMK* ix, 231–8, xx, 489–92; EAC 12th meeting, 12 March 1931.

[27] Keynes to MacDonald, 5 March 1931 (original emphasis), JRM 677.

[28] 'Proposals for a Revenue Tariff', in *JMK* ix, 238.

[29] See above, p. 68. Robbins article, Beveridge and Gregory letters in *New Statesman*, 14 March 1931, and see 'A Committee of Economists under the Chairmanship of … Beveridge', *Tariffs: the Case Examined* (Aug. 1931).

D. Henderson had probably prompted Keynes's new initiative, appealing in February for a 'responsible approach to the whole financial situation'. Gregory thought the Royal Commission on Unemployment Insurance had a 'clear duty' to denounce 'the stupidities of the present system', and 'had a chance of doing good far more important than anything the [Macmillan Committee] could do'.[30]

The predominant movement in economic and financial opinion therefore supported the advice of the financial authorities. But this gave those authorities little confidence that the politicians would accept the advice. During the winter several pressures pushed the Bank of England towards a more overt political role. Its sponsorship of industrial rationalisation was questioned by ministers unhappy at the slow progress. This raised the spectre of nationalisation and led Norman to warn (or threaten) Snowden that government intervention would have dire consequences in the financial markets.[31] As the Macmillan Committee inquiry neared completion, all kinds of 'unfriendly recommendations' were feared. To protect the Bank's constitution, pre-emptive reforms, including an advisory council of commercial, industrial, and financial representatives, were seriously considered.[32] Keynes's early drafts for the Committee report, presenting what the Bank considered to be a 'defeatist' attitude towards cost adjustments and a 'half-hearted' defence of the gold standard, caused dismay and produced considerable efforts to obstruct him. Other Committee members and the Treasury were warned of the 'undesirability' of his drafts, and Lubbock, the Bank's representative on the Committee, tried to shift the report towards the Bank's evidence.[33]

There were further pressures as gold losses stimulated political interest in gold maldistribution, and American proposals for a conference on stabilisation of silver prices attracted ministerial interest as a means to improve trade with Asia. Norman persuaded Snowden that efforts to summon a gold conference would probably meet American and French resistance, and was cool towards the silver question as diverting attention from more fundamental

[30] H. D. Henderson to Keynes, 14 Feb. 1931, in *JMK* xx, 483–4; Gregory in Streat diary, 24 March 1931, in Dupree I, 48.

[31] BoE Cte, 17 Dec. 1930, 14 and 28 Jan. 1931; Clay, *Norman*, 336. For the effect, see Graham in Streat diary, 18 Feb. 1931, in Dupree I, 30.

[32] BoE Cte, 3 Dec. 1930, 7 Jan. 1931. Norman's proposals were rejected by the Committee.

[33] Lubbock to Brand, 1 and 12 Jan. 1931, and to Ismay, 9 March 1931, Brand papers 28, 30; Harvey to Leith-Ross, 20 March 1931, T188/274.

problems. But he could not prevent the Cabinet pursuing the idea of some international economic conference.[34] This was despite the Bank's own international initiative, the 'Kindersley Plan', which aimed to 'correct' excessive American and French gold accumulation and to 'start the wheels' of foreign lending 'going round again' by inducing them to invest in an international credit corporation. In early 1931 this plan was submitted to other central banks and the BIS. But, as half-feared, the BIS was too weak to impose it, while French and American bankers rejected the implied criticism of themselves and declined to shoulder the risks of international responsibility. From March the scheme withered.[35]

Anglo-French treasury discussions on bilateral monetary relations complicated matters further.[36] The Bank disliked these partly as an intrusion into its own responsibilities, but mostly because of the greatest pressure of all: a mounting sterling crisis. The weakness of the sterling–franc exchange was initially blamed upon distortions within the French financial system, and when gold losses began the Bank had followed earlier practice towards 'abnormal' pressures and applied various exchange expedients.[37] But subsequent French offers of assistance (a long-term loan and central bank discussions) were rejected, for several reasons. Norman wanted to preserve London's prestige, and to avoid further dependence on French markets and exposure to French diplomatic pressure for the perpetuation of reparations.[38] But above all French assistance was refused because the Bank's perception of the causes of exchange difficulties changed. From November 1930 American and French financial authorities advised that sterling's weakness resulted from Britain's deteriorating balance of payments, and foreign worries about the 'unbalanced budget and high wage level coupled with the "dole" payments'. In January reports of foreign expectations that sterling might be devalued made it plain that the problem was no longer external distortions but internal maladjustments.[39] For such

[34] BoE Cte, 3 Dec. 1930; Addis diary, 12, 18, and 19 Feb. 1931; Norman in Leith-Ross to Hopkins and Snowden, 6 Feb. 1931, T175/53; Clay, *Norman*, 369–70; Williamson, 'Financiers', 117–18.

[35] BoE Cte, 7 Jan., 4 and 25 Feb., 4 March 1931; Norman to Kindersley and to McGarrah, both 2 Feb. 1931, and to Harrison, 3 March 1931, G3/198/56, 58, 113; Clarke, *Central Bank Cooperation*, 178–9. Skidelsky, *Politicians*, 286, describes the plan as 'astonishingly imaginative'. [36] See below, p. 201.

[37] Williamson, 'Financiers', 121; Clay, *Norman*, 369; Clarke, *Central Bank Cooperation*, 175–7.

[38] Clay, *Norman*, 370; Clarke, *Central Bank Cooperation*, 178, 180–1; Leith-Ross notes of interviews with Pouyanne, 5 and 16 Dec. 1930, T160/430/F12317/1.

[39] BoE Cte, 19 Nov., 3 Dec. 1930; Williamson, 'Financiers', 121; Clay, *Norman*, 369; Clarke, *Central Bank Cooperation*, 175–7.

conditions (given the gold standard), exchange devices were no real help and might easily be counter-productive in postponing the solution – measures to balance the budget and reduce costs. To the Bank it seemed clear that defence of sterling had become a matter for the Treasury and the politicians.

In the face of these various pressures, especially the last, the Bank began a campaign of political education. Norman started 'labouring unceasingly with the Chancellor, [Baldwin] and others... to bring home the danger, and induce them to face the facts and... put the nation's financial house in order'.[40] Treasury officials were told that their Paris negotiations were an evasion of the real problem.[41] The Bank directors Grenfell, Peacock, Addis, Kindersley, and Kitson appeared on the platform of the first Friends of Economy meeting. Norman privately encouraged business agitation for all-round income cuts, and attempted to influence the City editor of the *Daily Herald*.[42] Clay suggested that the King might be persuaded to set an example of voluntary sacrifice, while Sprague, another Bank Advisor, became a leading publicist for retrenchment and deflation.[43]

More directly, in mid January Norman told Snowden that if 'loss of gold, Budget prospects, socialist legislation or any other cause' threatened a flight from sterling, he would feel obliged to raise the bank rate in order to focus public attention upon the 'unsatisfactory position'.[44] Perhaps because Snowden assured him that the budget problem would be tackled, an actual rate increase was postponed and instead open-market intervention was used to attract foreign funds back to London.[45] This device helped stop the gold losses but for several weeks the exchange improvement was difficult to sustain, and Norman remained worried that the gold standard and the London capital market were at risk. An immediate crisis had been

---

[40] Peacock to Oliver, 1 Aug. 1931, Oliver papers.

[41] Waley note of a conversation between Leith-Ross, Sprague and Siepmann, 30 Jan., 1931; and Leith-Ross note of a talk with Norman and Hopkins, 17 Feb. 1931, T160/430/ F12317/2.

[42] For Chambers of Commerce, see BoE Cte, 25 Feb. 1931, and Streat diary, 24 Feb., 2, 17, and 31 March 1931, in Dupree I, 33–5, 45, 52–3. For *Daily Herald*, Williams, *Nothing So Strange*, 96–101.

[43] For Clay, Streat diary, 11 Feb. 1931, in Dupree I, 24–5; for Sprague, Macmillan Committee, *Evidence*, qq. 9230–67, 9285–98, 18 and 19 Feb. 1931, and speech, *The Times*, 18 Feb. 1931.

[44] BoE Cte, 14 Jan., 4 March 1931; Norman to Fergusson, 27 Jan. 1931, G3/198/45 (evidently the incident described in Lockhart diary, 13 Sept. 1931, in Young I, 185).

[45] BoE Cte, 21 and 28 Jan., 4 Feb. 1931; Clay, *Norman*, 371; *Economist*, 31 Jan., 7 Feb. 1931.

averted, but the Bank was now convinced that 'the future...depend[ed] more on politics than on finance'.[46] Discerning a close connection between sterling and the budget, the Bank of England had firmly added its authority to the pressures for retrenchment.

The Treasury differed from the Bank of England in only one important respect: it was less pessimistic about the chances of early international co-operation. Snowden's concern was sharpened by parliamentary interest in the gold question,[47] and by a need to appear serious about international action in order to rebut one argument against domestic retrenchment. The problem was finding the means of promoting such co-operation. As well as supporting the Kindersley Plan, the Treasury had hopes of the League of Nations Gold Delegation and proposed converting the American initiative on silver into a general economic and financial conference.[48] More immediately promising were bilateral talks proposed by French finance officials, which Leith-Ross seized upon as an opportunity to ease pressures on London and persuade the French to increase their international lending. His talks in Paris during early 1931 produced an agreed public statement which though vague seemed reassuring to the financial markets, and obtained assurances of serious attention to the Gold Delegation's report and some minor alterations in French financial practices.[49]

Yet the talks also produced French and Bank of England warnings that the gold movements now had a more fundamental cause. These warnings reinforced the evidence of nervousness in the financial markets, including the sudden depreciation of gilts on 5 February. Snowden countered the last by a parliamentary statement denying any Cabinet intention of raising a 'spectacular development loan', while his officials treated the incident as proof of the financial danger of such 'Keynesian' loan proposals.[50] Nevertheless Snowden and Treasury officials understood that the root cause of the market dislocation was doubt about the existing budget position. Not that they needed convincing of the need for retrenchment. The

---

[46] Norman quoted in Moggridge, '1931 Financial Crisis', 837. For worries, BoE Cte, 11 March 1931; Clay, *Norman*, 371; Sayers, *Bank of England*, 233–4.

[47] See BoE Cte, 3 Dec. 1930; Leith-Ross to Smith, 8 and 14 Jan. 1931, T160/430/F12317/1.

[48] Leith-Ross to Hawtrey, and to Strakosch, 2 and 11 Dec. 1930, T188/15B, and to Hopkins and Snowden, 6 Feb. 1931, T175/53; Cabinet 16(31), 4 March 1931.

[49] See Leith-Ross memos, May 1930–Feb. 1931, in T160/430/F12317/1–2; public statement, *The Times*, 25 Feb. 1931; Moggridge, *British Monetary Policy*, 240–1.

[50] *HC Deb*, 247, cols. 2255–8, 5 Feb. 1931; P. J. Grigg, *Prejudice and Judgment*, 244.

significance of the bankers' warnings and market movements was
that these confirmed their expectations of the results of current
policy, and supplied further 'ammunition'[51] for Snowden's months-
old battle with the Cabinet and Labour party. Snowden also
'welcomed' the Friends of Economy agitation, believing 'drastic
reduction' in expenditure required pressure from a 'strong public
opinion'.[52] After preparing the way in December with a 'depressing
speech' to Labour MPs and an alarming report to MacDonald,[53] on
7 January he produced a Cabinet paper describing not just an
immediate but a long-term crisis in government finance.

Snowden described the budget prospect as 'grim', with estimated
deficits of £40m. from 1930, and £50m. or possibly 'upwards of £70
millions' for 1931. Moreover, as the Unemployment Insurance Fund
had become hopelessly insolvent and obviously incapable of repaying
its debt, the point was approaching where its annual £40m.
borrowing had to be added to budget charges. The problem could
not be solved by any early trade recovery because of lags in revenue
and expenditure, and because, although prices had fallen, most
expenditure consisted of fixed money charges. Yet Britain 'cannot
afford a Budget with any sort of deficit'. With falling receipts and
rising expenditure already producing a 'dangerous level' of floating
debt, the 'necessary consequences of unsound State finance' would
be increased interest rates and difficulty meeting further vital
borrowing requirements. As suggested by 'disquieting' indications
of foreign opinion, there might also be a flight from sterling 'fraught
with the most disastrous consequences – not merely to the money
market but to the whole economic organisation of the country'. The
deficit could not be removed by suspending Sinking Fund payments,
a breach of statutory obligations which would damage government
credit, depreciate gilts, and delay plans for substantial retrenchment
through war loan conversion. It would in any case be inadequate to
meet the budget deficit. Snowden implicitly excluded a revenue
tariff, while increases in direct taxation were ruled out as 'certain'
to dampen hopes of revived business confidence. The message was
clear. There would have to be 'substantial reductions in existing
expenditure'. Yet large cuts were not immediately possible from
defence estimates nor from most areas of civil estimates. The main

---

[51] Lockhart diary, 13 Sept. 1931 (referring to Jan.) in Young I, 185.
[52] Snowden, *Autobiography* II, 891–2.
[53] Political Notes, *The Times*, 11 Dec. 1930; MacDonald to Snowden, 22 Dec. 1930, JRM
1305.

cause of 'Budget chaos' – threatening 'grave danger to the economic and financial stability of the country' – was the 'vast cost' of transitional benefit. It was to this item that the Cabinet should give its 'immediate and earnest consideration'.[54]

Snowden reinforced the message in a lengthy address to the Cabinet on 14 January,[55] and shortly afterwards sought support from public opinion and broadened the issue to the whole unemployment insurance system. Treasury evidence to the Royal Commission on Unemployment Insurance on 29 January stated that, since transitional benefit payments had 'entirely upset' budget equilibrium, reduction of this liability was 'among the most pressing financial needs of the State'. Continued borrowing for unemployment insurance 'on the present vast scale...would quickly call in question the stability of the British financial system'.[56]

Snowden claimed not to be 'scare-mongering', and the problems were indeed genuine enough. Nevertheless these were 'remorseless and highly political statement[s]',[57] designed to put pressure on the Cabinet, shape the Royal Commission's inquiry, secure wider parliamentary support, and restrict the range of available options. A link between the budget and unemployment insurance on the one hand and the sterling exchange and financial markets on the other, was officially sanctioned. Attention was directed not just upon the conventional budget, but upon the idea that it ought properly to include the unemployment insurance deficit. It became more difficult for the Cabinet to seek parliamentary approval for further Insurance Fund borrowing without proposing to 'rehabilitate' the whole system.[58] In all this, Snowden and the Treasury not only had the support of most economic and financial opinion, but also of most political opinion – Liberal as well as Conservative.

LIBERALS TO THE RESCUE

From November 1930 the issues of India, retrenchment, and unemployment; the Conservative agreement on trade policy and readiness to take office; the incipient ILP and Mosleyite rebellions against the government, and TUC insistence upon repeal of the

[54] 'The Financial Situation', CP 3(31), 7 Jan. 1931.
[55] Cabinet 6(31), 14 Jan. 1931.
[56] Hopkins in Royal Commission on Unemployment Insurance, *Evidence* I, 381–3, and qq. 3264–351. For Snowden's approval, see minute on Hopkins to Snowden, 19 Jan. 1931, T161/491/S 35711/01, and public admission in *HC Deb*, 247, col. 1626, 3 Feb. 1931.
[57] McKibbin, 'Second Labour Government', 113 (*Ideologies*, 216) referring to Hopkins' evidence.   [58] This point was made in Cabinet 12(31), 5 Feb. 1931.

Trade Disputes Act – all these increased the importance of the Liberal parliamentary party as the balancing group in the Commons. Paradoxically, its importance was increased still further as Liberal differences widened. Labour ministers became more concerned with retaining adequate Liberal support to preserve their parliamentary majority, while Conservatives became more hopeful of obtaining sufficient Liberal assistance to defeat the government.

Lloyd George's and Samuel's attempt to exploit this renewed Liberal potential consisted of a five-month effort to convince Liberal MPs that the existing *ad hoc* (and mostly secret) understandings with the Cabinet should be converted into a definite alliance. This, they argued, was the only sure means to prevent an early Conservative and protectionist victory, persuade the government to adopt more effective economic policies, and extract electoral reform. Lloyd George's shift, crucial in parliamentary terms, from opposition to the Irwin Declaration twelve months previously to acceptance of Indian federation – preferring Reading's advice to the alternative Liberal position of Simon and, by extension, throwing over Churchill – was integral to this strategy. The party-management problem was less the minority of Liberal MPs who wanted the Labour government defeated, than a majority who wished to avoid a Conservative government yet considered the Labour Cabinet 'incompetent', were hostile towards Trade Disputes Act repeal, and wanted the Liberal party to retain freedom of action.[59] These MPs confronted Lloyd George with a dilemma. To help persuade them to keep the government in office, he had publicly to criticise and threaten it. Yet those attacks jeopardised private negotiations aimed at shifting the Cabinet towards attitudes and measures agreeable to Liberal views and interests. However grudgingly acknowledged by ministers, Lloyd George's attempts to solve this problem greatly assisted the Cabinet's efforts to contain the intense pressures upon itself.

After the rebellions of 4 November the Liberal leaders' first step was to attempt to re-impose party discipline. Liberal MPs unanimously elected Sinclair to succeed Hutchison as chief whip, but with Lloyd George's support Sinclair accepted only on condition that parliamentary party decisions were obeyed, and that another rebellion would automatically mean his resignation.[60] Then, after

---

[59] See Simon notes on Liberal leaders' meetings, 20 and 27 Nov. 1930, and report on Liberal Candidates' meeting, 4 Dec. 1930, Simon papers.

[60] Morris-Jones diary, 12 Nov. 1930; Hutchison notice to Liberal MPs, 13 Nov. 1930, Runciman papers 221.

further negotiations with MacDonald and Henderson, Lloyd George and Samuel proposed to meetings of leading Liberal MPs and peers on 19 and 20 November a two-year written and published Liberal–Labour pact. Its terms involved agreement upon unemployment, agricultural, town planning, and unemployment insurance policies, and upon the alternative vote and a trade union bill. Crewe supported a pact, but Foot wanted a much looser arrangement. Maclean was undecided, while Simon, Lambert, Brown, Tudor Walters, and Hamilton were in various degrees opposed. Lloyd George and Samuel then attempted a compromise, suggesting a pact for just one parliamentary session.[61] But at a further meeting a week later Maclean, Tudor Walters, and Hamilton wanted Liberal support to be made conditional on the merits of individual government policies rather than tied to a time span, while Simon and Reading (fresh from their conversation that morning about 'national government'), with Brown and Macpherson, were against any binding arrangements. Lloyd George's only line of retreat was to fudge the issue with reflections on the distinction between an 'agreement' and an 'understanding', and to abandon the attempt to force a decision.[62] Consequently his speech to the Liberal Candidates' Association on 5 December, intended to announce the pact, had to be a 'skilful performance on the tightrope'.[63] He pandered to the audience by attacking the government's record, yet proposed to give it 'another chance'; he denied the existence of any 'pact or deal', while expounding 'the course we ought to pursue'.[64]

By then, however, Liberal dissidents had already determined upon independent courses. In late November Phillipps and Johnstone persuaded Grey and Runciman (who had not attended the leaders' meetings) to lead a Liberal Council campaign 'to revive the fortunes of the Liberal Party through a programme of reasoned and rigid economy'. They believed such a programme would win 'neutral support',[65] and hoped to exploit the Friends of Economy

[61] Simon notes, 20 Nov. 1930, Simon papers; and see MacDonald diary, 18 Nov. 1930 for Lloyd George's and Samuel's prior negotiations with ministers.
[62] Simon notes, 27 Nov. 1930, Simon papers.
[63] Comment on published report in N. Chamberlain diary, 6 Dec. 1930. For Lloyd George's intentions, see Rowland-Evans note of conversation with Liberal Candidates' secretary, 20 Nov. 1930, Simon papers.
[64] *Manchester Guardian*, 6 Dec. 1930. See also Morris-Jones diary, 11 Dec. 1930, for similar Lloyd George statements to parliamentary party.
[65] Phillipps and Johnstone, and Phillipps, to Simon, both 1 Dec. 1930, Simon papers.

campaign, whose launch was preceded on 24 January by joint appeals from Grey and Runciman for 'drastic and determined reduction of existing charges'.[66] Phillipps and Johnstone also attempted to unify the dissident movements by asking Simon to join the Liberal Council and the economy campaign, and – like Conservatives – by flattering his criticisms of Lloyd George.[67]

Simon spoke at provincial meetings of the Friends of Economy from March, but declined identification with the Liberal Council. This was partly because he regarded Grey and Runciman as political has-beens,[68] but mostly because of Neville Chamberlain's much more attractive suggestions on 1 December. Simon embraced Chamberlain's idea of co-operation with the Conservative leadership to defeat the Labour government, with the prospect of entering a Conservative-dominated government in a senior position – which for Simon came to mean the Foreign Secretaryship. He was prepared to move towards acceptance of tariffs, and would have liked some pledge of electoral reform. Failing that he wanted Conservative guarantees for the seats of those Liberals prepared to follow him. That condition was necessary because though claiming a 'considerable following in the country', he so far had few followers in the Commons.[69]

During the winter, while remaining within the Liberal Advisory Committee (shadow cabinet), Simon sought wider support for revolt against the Lloyd George–Samuel strategy. He denied that the alternative vote could really help the Liberal party, and concentrated attacks upon the weakest point in Liberal–Labour relations, the Trade Disputes Bill.[70] Assisted by the Conservative offer on seats, he tried to consolidate into an effective opposition group such critics of the government as Hutchison, Lambert, Brown, Shakespeare, Hore-Belisha, and Rothschild. He also established relations with

[66] Grey–Runciman letter in *The Times*, 26 Jan. 1931, and similar letter in Liberal newspapers, reprinted as Liberal Council pamphlet, *National Economy*, in Runciman papers 244. See also Johnstone and Phillipps letter in *The Times*, 28 Jan. 1931, claiming the Friends of Economy as a Liberal Council initiative.

[67] Phillipps to Simon, and to Rowland-Evans, 1 and 15 Dec. 1930, and Johnstone to Simon [Jan. 1931], Simon papers.

[68] Simon to Phillipps, 16 Dec. 1930, Simon papers. For Simon and the Friends, see Manchester and Edinburgh meetings, in *The Times*, 4 March, 10 April 1931.

[69] Simon note, 1 Dec. 1930, Simon papers; N. Chamberlain diary, 5 Dec. 1930, N. to I. Chamberlain, 5 Dec. 1930, NC 18/1/719. For Simon's ambition, see Amery diary, 26 March 1931 (*LSA* II, 158).

[70] Simon to Sinclair, 11 Dec. 930, Simon papers; Simon speech and letter, *The Times*, 15 and 23 Dec. 1930.

Grigg, who in February broke with Lloyd George for 'going left ... with a vengeance' and who was himself attempting to organise a 'Liberal–Unionist party'.[71]

Nevertheless, despite these fifth columnists and the November rebuffs, Lloyd George, Samuel, and Sinclair managed by considerable finesse both to enter into closer relations with ministers and to retain control over most Liberal MPs. The existence of a pact between themselves and the Cabinet was still denied,[72] but the denial remained true only in that there were no formal, binding terms of alliance. Relations were under constant, occasionally acrimonious re-negotiation as new issues arose. But there was now consultation and co-operation on all important parliamentary business as well as continuing talks about unemployment policy. This did not mean that criticism of the government ceased. Lloyd George still complained of ministerial lack of energy and 'ineptitudes on unemployment', and saw his role as 'trying to bring this cowardly government up to the mark' – a task he sometimes considered 'hopeless'.[73] But such views about Cabinet economic policies continued to be subordinated to the objective of Liberal party survival.

The chief basis of Liberal–Labour convergence was now reciprocal support of a trade union bill against an electoral reform bill. Shortly after the 27 November Liberal leaders' meeting, Lloyd George and Samuel persuaded Henderson and MacDonald to announce the early introduction of an electoral reform bill.[74] Lloyd George then used Liberal candidates' criticism of the government on 5 December, Liberal MPs' dislike of trade disputes repeal, rumoured Conservative promises of support for dissident Liberals, and publication of the Mosley manifesto to suggest that the government faced imminent defeat in the Commons and to demand immediate introduction of the electoral bill, clear concessions towards Liberal employment

---

[71] Grigg to Lloyd George, 16 Feb. 1931, Lloyd George papers G/8/11/9, and reported in Amery diary, 10 Jan. 1931. For dissentient Liberal backbenchers, see Shakespeare, *Let Candles Be Brought In*, 133.

[72] E.g., Sinclair speech, *The Times*, 11 Dec. 1930: 'there is no sort or kind of a pact, written or verbal'.

[73] Lloyd George message for Henderson in Noel Baker memo [Dec. 1930], Noel-Baker papers 2/3; Lloyd George to Hartshorn, in *The Times*, 27 Dec. 1930, and to F. Stevenson, 4 Feb. 1931, in Taylor, 141.

[74] The announcement was made on 4 December: Henderson to MacDonald, 5 Dec. 1930, JRM 330, indicates prior arrangement with Lloyd George.

proposals, and acceptance of a firmer 'basis' for continued parliamentary co-operation.[75]

In detail these demands were only imperfectly achieved, but they secured their broader purpose. Ministers still resisted specific Liberal employment plans, and the electoral reform bill was postponed into the New Year. But Lloyd George, Samuel, and Sinclair obtained consultation in the drafting of both that and the Trade Disputes Bill,[76] and in early January met Henderson, Clynes, and Snowden to arrange business for the next parliamentary session.[77] Fulfilling their own side of the deal, they first persuaded most Liberal MPs to abstain on the second reading of the Trade Disputes Bill – though only after Sinclair had threatened resignation, Muir had pronounced the party organisation incapable of fighting an election, and Lloyd George, 'fighting in a corner – tooth & nail', had declared that if they really wished to commit 'suicide' they should at least find a better reason.[78] Then, after Conservatives threatened a censure motion on unemployment, Liberal leaders forestalled it with a motion which, though calling for increased national development works, was acceptable to the Cabinet. When Conservatives substituted a censure motion on expenditure, they countered it with a milder amendment proposing appointment of an economy committee.[79]

Lloyd George's reward for getting the Cabinet off these potentially fatal hooks was a secret meeting with MacDonald and Sankey on 2 February which he considered might mark a new 'epoch'. Sankey agreed to chair a joint ministerial–Liberal committee to consider Liberal amendments to the Trades Disputes Bill. MacDonald accepted Liberal advice in preparing his speech on the Liberal unemployment motion.[80] A further meeting attended by their

[75] For a series of Lloyd George messages for MacDonald, Henderson, or the government chief whip, see Lloyd George to Sinclair, 7 Dec. 1930, and two Sylvester memos for Sinclair, both 8 Dec. 1930, Thurso papers; Noel Baker memo [Dec. 1930], Noel-Baker papers 2/3; Kennedy to MacDonald, 24 and 30 Dec. 1930, JRM 330; MacDonald diary, 4 Jan. 1931, and Lothian to Lloyd George, 4 Jan. 1931, LG G/12/5/36.

[76] Clynes to Samuel, and Samuel to Clynes, both 19 Dec. 1930, and Kennedy to MacDonald, 24 Dec. 1930, JRM 330; F. Stevenson to Lloyd George, 6 Jan. 1931, in Taylor, 135–6. For Trade Disputes Bill, Cabinet 73(30), 17 Dec. 1930.

[77] MacDonald diary, 4 Jan. 1931; Lothian to Lloyd George, 4 Jan. 1931, LG G/12/5/26; Sinclair message in F. Stevenson to Lloyd George, 7 Jan. 1931, in Taylor, 137: these all concern arrangements for a meeting on 9 January, for which no record survives.

[78] Morris-Jones diary, 21 Jan. 1931: the vote was 32 to 10 for abstention.

[79] Morris-Jones diary, 27 Jan. 1931; MacDonald in Nicolson diary, 28 Jan. 1931 (Nicolson I, 68); Parliamentary Correspondent, The Times, 27 and 30 Jan., 2 Feb. 1931.

[80] MacDonald and Sankey diaries, 2 Feb. 1931, and Lloyd George to F. Stevenson, 3 Feb. 1931, in Taylor, 141. For joint committee, see Cabinet committee minutes, 4 Feb. 1931,

advisers resulted in co-ordination of ministerial and Liberal contributions to the unemployment debate, and arrangement of a further series of talks on specific unemployment and agricultural policies.[81] A Cabinet request on the 11th for Liberal acquiescence in further Unemployment Insurance Fund borrowing provided another opportunity to force Cabinet attention to Liberal proposals during the successive debates on retrenchment and unemployment on 11 and 12 February.[82]

Yet although Lloyd George, Samuel, and Sinclair had tightened the Liberal grip over the Cabinet, they were constrained by their concern to prevent a Conservative victory and secure electoral reform. Too much could not be demanded from MacDonald and Henderson, in case this precipitated a Cabinet or Labour party rebellion and government defeat. It was as much because of the Cabinet's own internal differences as of Liberal pressure that it accepted the Liberal economy committee motion on the 11th.[83] Even more significant was Lloyd George's and Samuel's acknowledgement during the unemployment debate on 12 February that Liberal policy was 'substantially the same programme' as that of *Labour and the Nation.*[84]

The Liberal–Labour debate over unemployment policy at the 1929 election was thus resolved. It has been seen that Keynes had been converted to a 'confidence package'; now the Liberal leadership capitulated to the Labour position and buried *We Can Conquer Unemployment.* Despite Keynes's theoretical contribution, at the party leadership level the Liberal–Labour differences had always been largely synthetic, as the June–September 1930 policy conferences had revealed. Lloyd George's submission now had something to do with the economic conditions, obviously less favourable than those of early 1929 for a massive public-works programme. But the more important reason was the deterioration in the Liberal party's political position relative to that of Labour.

Lloyd George's new tactic for putting pressure upon the Cabinet was to mobilise the Labour party against it. He tried to outbid

CAB 27/446, and Sankey diary, 4, 9, and 16 Feb., 2 March 1931; for Liberal experts' advice, MacDonald diary, 4 Feb. 1931, and Lloyd George to F. Stevenson, 4 Feb. 1931, in Taylor, 141–2.
[81] Parliamentary Correspondent, *The Times*, 11 Feb. 1931; MacDonald to Bondfield, Greenwood, Lees-Smith, and Morrison, 19 Feb. 1931, JRM 1176.
[82] Note of interview between Bondfield and Sinclair, 11 Feb. 1931, JRM 1311.
[83] See below, pp. 221–2.
[84] Lloyd George in *HC Deb*, 248, cols. 728–9, 12 Feb. 1931, and see Samuel, ibid., cols. 631–46.

ministers by calling for more vigorous implementation of Labour employment policies, and by mounting an extended attack upon the City. Since the war the 'money barons' had, he said, been 'invariably wrong' – over deflation, the American debt, and 'the precipitate establishment of the gold standard' – and they were also partly responsible for the world depression, so the Cabinet should not allow them to establish a 'veto' over national development.[85] Lloyd George's speech was considered irresponsible by financially orthodox Liberals and Labour ministers.[86] But it did him considerable good with the Labour left, symbolised by an invitation from Lansbury to join the Labour party. This allowed Lloyd George to present himself as an 'Independent' champion of 'the class from which [he] sprang', and to present Lansbury's colleagues as the real obstacles to a 'progressive' alliance.[87] In late February, however, much of the effect was lost when he was unable to prevent his party voting in committee against a crucial clause in the Trades Disputes Bill, forcing the Cabinet to abandon the whole bill. But by now the Cabinet was dependent upon Liberal parliamentary support for much more than one particular bill; its loss jeopardised neither co-operation nor electoral reform. Upon Lloyd George the effect was to instill a determination to confront and isolate Simon and other Liberal critics.

On 16 March a majority of Liberal MPs ignored a parliamentary party decision to support abolition of university seats under the Representation of the People Bill. This contributed to a government defeat and triggered Sinclair's threatened resignation as chief whip.[88] On the following day a 'defiant, resolute' Lloyd George told the Liberal parliamentary party he 'had no use for a disorganised rabble', and that 'those who could not agree to [his proposals] could go their own way'.[89] On the 18th Lloyd George, Samuel, and Sinclair once more negotiated with MacDonald, Henderson, and Thomas the terms for a definite Liberal–Labour alliance.[90] These terms – the 12 February unemployment policy motion, retrench-

---

[85] *HC Deb*, 248, cols. 728–34, 12 Feb. 1931.

[86] E.g., Reading in Dawson diary, 15 Feb. 1931; 'Lloyd George and the City', *Economist*, 21 Feb. 1931; MacDonald diary, 15 Feb. 1931; Snowden at PLP meeting, in Parliamentary Correspondent, *The Times*, 18 Feb. 1931.

[87] Lansbury to Lloyd George, and Lloyd George to Lansbury, 13 and 16 Feb. 1931, LG G/11/4/1, 2. For another, anonymous, invitation, see 'A Labour Member' to Lloyd George, 13 Feb. 1931, LG G/20/2/41.

[88] Sinclair to Lloyd George, 17 March 1931, Samuel papers A/155/VIII/10; Parliamentary Correspondent, *The Times*, 18 March 1931.

[89] Morris-Jones diary, [17] March 1931.   [90] MacDonald diary, 18 March 1931.

ment, disarmament, the Round Table Conference recommendations, free trade, electoral reform, agricultural development, and land taxes[91] – were then presented forcefully by Lloyd George and Samuel to meetings of the Advisory Committee, parliamentary party, and candidates' association as a reaffirmation of Liberal principles agreed before the 1929 election. As in November they met considerable resistance. But by the wholly disingenuous means of denying the existence of a pact and presenting the terms as an assertion of Liberal independence, they persuaded a majority of MPs – thirty-four in number – to accept co-operation with the government, and Sinclair withdrew his resignation.[92]

The success seemed more secure than the verbal sleight of hand and the parliamentary party's vote suggested. For of those seventeen MPs who voted against the leadership, most did not support Simon. Despite impressive speeches against the Trade Disputes Bill, Simon had persuaded only five other Liberal MPs to vote against its second reading. He failed to obtain the support of that key figure, Reading, and lacked 'sufficient hold even over his immediate following to unite them into a body of dissidents'.[93] Despite Conservative encouragement, this weak support made him reluctant to make a clean break from the rest of the party.[94] Simon's problem was partly that, while he and other Liberal dissidents wanted Conservative assistance in constituencies, tariffs – which he publicly if tentatively accepted for revenue purposes in early March[95] – remained a price unacceptable to most Liberal opponents of the government. In addition, his 'silky', 'suave', equivocal, personal manner repelled some of the dissidents.[96] Grigg, who was now actively seeking Conservative support for a Liberal–Unionist organisation (and his own parliamentary candidature), was exasperated by Simon's hesitations and had virtually abandoned the idea that he could

[91] See Sinclair to Fisher, 20 March 1930, Fisher papers 10, and Lloyd George statement, *The Times*, 27 March 1931.

[92] Advisory Committee, parliamentary party and candidates' meetings summarised or reported in *The Times*, 24, 25 and 27 March 1931. For Lloyd George's persuasiveness, see Morris-Jones diary, 25 March 1931; Morris-Jones, *Doctor in the Whips' Room*, 83; Shakespeare, *Let Candles Be Brought In*, 133.

[93] N. to I. Chamberlain, 8 Feb. 1931, NC 18/1/725. For Simon's efforts with Reading, see Lloyd George in Clarke *Diary*, 112, 9 March 1931.

[94] N. to I. Chamberlain, 8 Feb. 1931, NC 18/1/725, 733.

[95] Simon to Reading, 2 March 1931, Reading papers F118/101, and speech, *The Times*, 4 March 1931. For Lambert asking about seats, see N. to I. Chamberlain, 21 March 1931, NC 18/1/731.

[96] Morris-Jones diary, 29 Nov. 1930, 27 Jan., 10 Feb. 1931; Pybus in Grigg to N. Chamberlain, 28 March 1931, Altrincham papers.

provide a lead.[97] Much more representative of Lloyd George's critics was Brown, who was in touch with Simon but differed from him in preferring a course of true Liberal independence.[98]

Other critics were even less of a threat. Runciman announced in February that because of his business commitments he would resign his seat at the next election. Grey, despite his support for retrenchment, declared in March that the government deserved to be kept in office for its foreign and Indian policies. He was promptly claimed as a supporter of the party leadership's strategy.[99] Mander and Edge had now become so keen upon that strategy that they anticipated the leadership, the former publicly advocating formation of 'a joint progressive government', the latter obtaining a 'courtesy whip' from government managers.[100]

Consequently Liberal leaders and managers did not regard the open division between Liberal MPs as a setback. On the contrary, it had been deliberately engineered, because 'it was far better to have 45 [sic] who would act together...than 58 who would not'.[101] It was an act of clarification designed to restore party discipline. Another indication of this new determination was that Lloyd George began to plan a fresh campaign to resuscitate popular Liberalism and regain the electoral ground lost since the general election.[102] Such confidence had several sources. Liberal representatives had been the 'arbiters' of the Round Table Conference, and Reading's authority was expected to secure Liberal domination over the final settlement.[103] The embarrassment of the Trade Disputes Bill had been removed, an electoral reform bill was passing through the Commons, and enough Liberal MPs now accepted the leadership's position to guarantee the government a parliamentary majority. A firm hold seemed to have been acquired over the Cabinet which, however

---

[97] Grigg to Baldwin, and to N. Chamberlain, 27 Feb. and 28 March 1931, Altrincham papers.

[98] Brown at Liberal candidates meeting, *The Times*, 27 March 1931; and Brown to Simon, 27 March 1931, Simon papers.

[99] Runciman statement, and Grey speech picked up in Samuel speech, *The Times*, 20 Feb., 18 and 27 March 1931.

[100] Mander letter, *The Times*, 1 April 1931; Edge to MacDonald, 19 March 1931, JRM 1176.

[101] Lloyd George at Conference on Liberal Organisation, 18 March 1931, LG G/84/10.

[102] 'A.H.M.S.' to Sylvester, 5 March 1931, Sylvester to G. Owen, 10 March 1931, and Conference on Liberal Organisation, 18 March 1931, LG G/20/2/42, G/15/16/1, G/84/10.

[103] Lloyd George to Lothian and Reading, 4 Feb. 1931, Lothian papers 251/508–10; Lloyd George reported in MacDonald to Benn, 10 Feb. 1931, JRM 1176, and in Sinclair to Reading, 28 Feb. 1931, Reading papers F118/81.

'incompetent', might now be forced to yield to Liberal advice and accept effective measures, the credit for which would fall to Liberals. Expectations were increased when MacDonald proposed weekly conferences on Cabinet and parliamentary business.[104] It was possible to think of a general election postponed until 1932, when trade recovery and the alternative vote might produce a Liberal revival.[105]

THE LABOUR GOVERNMENT SURVIVES

Labour ministers had expected a difficult winter, but had been too divided, overwhelmed, artless, or exhausted to prepare themselves with new policies, tactics, or excuses. By the end of 1930 there was throughout the Labour movement an 'awful' sense of 'gloom, ... futility, & exasperation': the situation was 'all tragically ... different from what [they] had hoped & dreamed a Labour Government would be like'. The 'black cloud' of rising unemployment overshadowed the few areas of creditable work, such as India.[106] Hartshorn refused to speak in a Commons unemployment debate in December because there was nothing new for him to say.[107] Trevelyan could neither extract agreement on voluntary schools from Church and chapel leaders, nor explain his policy intelligibly in Cabinet.[108] There were troubled consciences and party difficulties about suspension of social reform, and mounting apprehension about the pressures for retrenchment. Coal disputes in December and a stoppage in South Wales in January over implementation of the government's Mines Act, and a prolonged cotton dispute delaying reorganisation of that industry, added to the misery.

In all directions there were indications of disaffection. The slump of the Labour by-election vote was now the worst suffered by any post-war government, with seats saved only by special efforts (Whitechapel and East Bristol) or Empire Crusade intervention (East Islington). Failure to introduce a cereals policy and agricultural unemployment insurance threatened electoral collapse in

---

[104] MacDonald to Lloyd George, 20 March 1931, JRM 1176.
[105] Lloyd George in Clarke *Diary*, 112, 9 March 1931; Sinclair to Fisher, 20 March 1931, Fisher papers 10.   [106] Dalton diary, 29 Dec. 1930 (Pimlott, 135).
[107] MacDonald diary, 15 Dec. 1930; MacDonald to Hartshorn, 20 Dec. 1930, JRM 1308.
[108] Cabinets 72, 73(30), 10 and 17 Dec. 1930, and Cabinets 7, 7A, 8(31), 16, 19, and 20 Jan. 1931; Dalton diary, 17 Dec. 1930 (Pimlott, 135).

rural constituencies.[109] Cole's organisation of two new groups, the Society for Socialist Inquiry and Propaganda and the New Fabian Research Bureau, to generate and publicise new socialist ideas manifested the disillusionment of Labour intellectuals with the Labour government, despite denials of hostility towards the Cabinet and efforts to obtain blessings from Henderson, who obliged, and from MacDonald, who did not.[110] That the intellectuals were able to recruit younger ministers (Attlee, Dalton, and Cripps) and trade union leaders (Bevin and Pugh) was hardly flattering to those pioneering propagandists who now constituted the party leadership. The TUC leaders' 'perplexity and uneasiness' at being 'consistently cold-shoulder[ed]' by ministers became outrage when they were not consulted about the appointment of the Royal Commission on Unemployment Insurance, which they suspected of being intended to force benefit cuts.[111] The ILP MPs persisted with votes against the government and criticism of the PLP standing orders, and in early 1931 pressed within the PLP for an election programme on 'strong Socialist lines'. In ILP branches disaffiliation from the Labour party had become a serious issue.[112] During January the Mosleyite MPs agitated inside the NEC and PLP for a national party conference on unemployment.[113] Trade union, ILP, and Mosleyite MPs remained separate centres of discontent; the ILP could be dismissed as a 'group of insignificants', the Mosleyites as '10th rate', and their manifesto as 'a very damp squib'.[114] Henderson and other party managers contained the number of active rebels to under fifteen.[115] Nevertheless these malcontents threatened the government's fragile parliamentary majority and set a dangerous precedent for other backbench MPs, themselves much preoccupied with the 'misdoings of the Cabinet'.[116] When the government did suffer a serious Commons defeat – on Scurr's amendment on 21 January to safeguard Catholic education under the School Attendance Bill – it

[109] Addison and Bondfield to MacDonald, 3 Feb. 1931, JRM 441.

[110] Cole to B. Webb, 9 Dec. 1930, Passfield papers II:4:(i):70, to MacDonald, 9 Dec. 1930, JRM 1175, and to M. MacDonald, 14 Feb. 1931, M. MacDonald papers 2/3/27; M. Cole, Cole, 175–80.

[111] Citrine reported in Bondfield to MacDonald, 21 Nov. 1930, PREM 5/74; Citrine (for General Council) to MacDonald, 18 Dec. 1930, in TUCGC; Skidelsky, Politicians, 262–9.

[112] Memorandum on Labour party–ILP relations [Feb. 1931], in LPNEC; PLP, 27 Jan., 10 Feb. 1931; Scottish ILP conference, The Times, 12 Jan. 1931.

[113] PLP, 21 and 27 Jan. 1931; LPNEC, 28 Jan. 1931.

[114] MacDonald diary, 7 Dec. 1930, 4 March 1931; Passfield to B. Webb, 8 Dec. 1930, Passfield papers II:3:(i):103 (Webb Letters III, 340).

[115] PLP, 27 Jan., 10 Feb. 1931.   [116] B. Webb diary, 25 Nov. 1930.

was at the hands of round fifty of its own backbenchers. Although the Cabinet shrugged off the defeat, it was a serious blow to party morale and discipline.[117]

Continued economic deterioration, deepening financial problems, ineffective economic policies, pressures for retrenchment, a fragile parliamentary position, party demoralisation: these still signified that the only practicable alternative to government defeat, and probably a Labour electoral rout, was riding out the economic recession through yet closer alliance with the Liberal leadership. This course was made more urgent by fears, fostered by Lloyd George, that Conservative guarantees for the seats of Liberal rebels would otherwise erode the prop of Liberal parliamentary support.[118] After twelve months of negotiation and Cabinet evasion, the Labour minister most responsible for forcing a definite alliance was Henderson.[119] As principal party manager, he was particularly concerned in late 1930 to propitiate an angry TUC by securing trade disputes repeal – an imperative which meant he brooked no further nonsense about stalling on the chief Liberal demand. He manoeuvred a reluctant MacDonald into announcing introduction of an electoral reform bill.[120] Then on 17 and 18 December Henderson persuaded the National Executive Committee and parliamentary party to accept the alternative vote. This triumph of party management, reversing the decision of May, was achieved by creating an impression of toughness towards the Liberals over rejection of proportional representation, and by denying any 'definite arrangement or pact'.[121]

The continued denial of a pact by both the Labour and Liberal leaders was a pious fraud to mollify their respective parties. But for MacDonald and Snowden it was also a satisfactory pretence, a psychological trick to licence their continued enmity towards Lloyd George. MacDonald greatly resented his criticisms and efforts to control the Cabinet: 'to try & work with him was useless'; it was better to be independent and let Liberals vote against the

---

[117] MacDonald diary, 21 Jan. 1931; Dalton diary, 21 and 22 Jan. 1931 (Pimlott, 136). Thirty-six Roman Catholic Labour MPs voted against the government, and some 20 other MPs abstained.

[118] MacDonald diary, 4 Jan. 1931; Clynes in Dalton diary, 20 Jan. 1931 (Pimlott, 136).

[119] E.g., Henderson to MacDonald, 5 Dec. 1930, JRM 330, and reported by Sinclair in F. Stevenson to Lloyd George, 6 Jan. 1931, in Taylor, 136.

[120] MacDonald to Henderson, and MacDonald to Henderson, both 5 Dec. 1930, JRM 330.

[121] LPNEC, and Dalton diary, both 17 and 18 Dec. 1930 (latter partly in Pimlott, 134–5).

government '& be done with it'.[122] Snowden, the chief target of Lloyd George's criticism, was even more bitter: Lloyd George was 'determined to humiliate…and discredit' the government, he was 'playing a double game…with the Tories', and 'neither the Trade Union Bill nor the Electoral Reform Bill [were] worth being in shackles to him'.[123] These attitudes were futile: the political conditions were inexorable. A meeting of MacDonald, Snowden, Henderson, Clynes, and Thomas on 2 January accepted the need for closer co-operation with Liberal leaders.[124] After Lloyd George had delivered enough Liberal votes to get the government over the 'high hurdle'[125] of the Trade Disputes Bill second reading, and then dished the Conservatives over their censure motions, MacDonald on his own initiative flattered him with a secret meeting where he made an elaborate performance of desperately needing assistance.[126]

Closer relations did not mean that leading ministers were any nearer to believing or accepting Liberal unemployment policies. True, Graham was sufficiently worried by trade prospects and the Labour party's 'terribly anxious' condition to propose in December a 'determined effort to take the Liberals at their word in the unemployment schemes'.[127] But this obtained no support, not even from Henderson. On 21 January the Cabinet again agreed that 'it would be a mistake…to pretend that it was possible, by means of relief works, and so forth, to make much impression on the unemployment figures'.[128] MacDonald thought it to the government's credit that it had resisted 'flashy stuff, e.g. Liberal programmes' which, where not 'mere propaganda', would have 'ruin[ed] the country'.[129] This position seemed amply justified when Liberal leaders conceded virtual agreement with the principles of government policy before the 12 February unemployment debate. While the Cabinet accepted that implementation of existing public works schemes within existing criteria could be accelerated, even here confidence was absent. In agreeing to listen further to Liberal advice, MacDonald had no expectation of learning anything useful: they had 'nothing', or 'very very little', to offer, but it was necessary

---

[122] MacDonald diary, 29 Dec. 1930, 4 Jan. 1931; MacDonald to Snowden, 22 Dec. 1930, JRM 1175.   [123] Snowden to MacDonald, 30 Dec. 1930, JRM 1175, 1176.

[124] MacDonald reported in Lothian to Lloyd George, 4 Jan. 1931, LG G/12/5/26.

[125] Dalton diary, 28 Jan. 1931 (Pimlott, 137).

[126] MacDonald to Lloyd George, 28 Jan. 1931, JRM 1309; Lloyd George to F. Stevenson, 3 Feb. 1931, in Taylor, 141.

[127] Graham to MacDonald, 30 Dec. 1930, JRM 676.   [128] Cabinet 9(31).

[129] MacDonald diary, 2 Feb., 13 April 1931; MacDonald interview, Daily Herald, 1 Jan. 1931.

'to humour them'.[130] Acceptance of the Liberal unemployment motion on the 12th amounted to no more than 'making some more fuss' about the government's existing policies.[131] As for Lloyd George's attack on the City, that was merely 'a pure rushing gush of demagogy' which evaded his own part in burdening the nation with war debt.[132] Lansbury's enthusiasm was untypical: if other Cabinet members had known of his invitation to Lloyd George, they would have ascribed it to simple-mindedness.

The Cabinet's intention remained to obtain Liberal parliamentary votes without forfeiting the Labour government's separate identity. The chief problem was still that of finding independent economic initiatives which seemed practicable. Some ministers sustained themselves with radical suggestions. Lansbury gained a sympathetic hearing with an old Labour plan to unify the coal industry under a corporation. Graham persistently, and MacDonald briefly, spoke of state compulsion for cotton and other industrial reorganisation.[133] Hartshorn tried to raise the issue of iron and steel protection, and MacDonald to revive that of a cereals quota.[134] MacDonald, recognising the regional dimension of the unemployment problem – of old industrial areas becoming derelict while new industries developed elsewhere – proposed national industrial planning. Prompted by the Gold Delegation, the American silver proposal, and increased cross-party interest in monetary questions, Mac-Donald, Graham, and Thomas invested much hope in international action.[135]

None of this came to anything. Compulsory industrial rationalisation and national planning would have involved confrontations with Conservatives, employers, the City, and local authorities, which the government had neither the will-power to attempt nor the authority to win. Moreover, in the difficult budget situation and

---

[130] Cabinet 9(31), 21 Jan. 1931; MacDonald diary, 8 Feb. 1931; MacDonald to Johnston, 4 April 1931, JRM 1309.

[131] MacDonald to Hartshorn, and to Greenwood, 16 and 20 Feb. 1931, JRM 5, 677.

[132] MacDonald diary, 15 Feb. 1931; and Snowden at PLP meeting, in *The Times*, 18 Feb. 1931.

[133] Hankey to MacDonald, 7 Jan. 1931, JRM 248; Cabinet 9(31), 21 Jan. 1931; Postgate, *Lansbury*, 264. For rationalisation, MacDonald at EAC 10th meeting, 11 Dec. 1930; Graham in MacDonald diary, 12 Jan. 1931, and in *HC Deb*, 248, col. 540, 11 Feb. 1931; BoE Cte, 17 Dec. 1930, 14 Jan. 1931.

[134] Janeway thesis, 'Economic Policy of Second Labour Government', 120; MacDonald in Cabinets 71, 72(30), 3 and 10 Dec. 1930; MacDonald to Snowden, 26 Jan. 1931, JRM 677.

[135] MacDonald at EAC 10th meeting, 11 Dec. 1930; Cabinet 16(31), 4 March 1931; Graham in Streat diary, 18 Feb. 1931, in Dupree I, 31.

delicate state of financial markets in early 1931, Bank of England warnings that such proposals for increased expenditure might 'precipitate a general catastrophe' had conclusive persuasive force.[136] Proposals for protection would cause obvious difficulties with both Labour and Liberal parties, and continued to be smothered by Snowden and Graham. By April ministers understood that the American, French, and British authorities had such divergent views on monetary issues that even if a conference could be arranged, it would be unlikely to succeed.[137]

What ministers had left to say still sounded too obviously like evasion, wishful thinking, or weak excuses. The government had difficulty 'simply because it [had] to face insoluble things'; when the world economic system was 'faulty' no government could secure any 'marked alleviation' of depression 'within 12 or 18 months'. There were however 'a good many signs' that the bottom had been reached, and recovery was beginning.[138] The unemployment figures were inflated by insurance 'abuses', including short-time work organised by employers to economise on wages.[139] Although the effect of public works, by their 'very nature', must be 'disappointingly small', a 'permanent reduction of unemployment' was being prepared through industrial rationalisation and agricultural settlement. Meanwhile unemployment insurance had been maintained, so there was comfort in the fact that 'our people... [had] been able to have a glimmering of fire in their grates [at] Christmas'.[140]

Yet even that provision was threatened, as Snowden made retrenchment the dominant issue in Cabinet. At the 14 January meeting no minister questioned his presentation of the budget problem and its possible effects upon national credit. Nor were his rejections of Sinking Fund suspension and substantial increase in existing taxes challenged. It was accepted that 'the financial situation was very serious and urgent', and conceded that some retrenchment was required.[141]

---

[136] MacDonald diary, 12 Jan. 1931; Clay, *Norman*, 336; Graham in Streat diary, 18 Feb. 1931, in Dupree 1, 30.   [137] MacDonald at EAC 13th meeting, 16 April 1931.

[138] MacDonald diary, 6 Jan. 1931; MacDonald interview ('Britain is on the Upgrade') *Daily Herald*, 1 Jan. 1931; Cabinet 9(31), 21 Jan. 1931; Thomas and Graham speeches, *The Times*, 3 and 5 Jan. 1931.

[139] MacDonald at EAC 10th meeting, 11 Dec. 1930; MacDonald [two] and Clynes speeches, *The Times*, 13 Dec. 1930, 8 and 23 Jan. 1931.

[140] Thomas speech, *The Times*, 3 Jan. 1931; Cabinet 9(30), 21 Jan. 1931; MacDonald interview, *Daily Herald*, 1 Jan. 1931.   [141] Cabinet 6(31), 14 Jan. 1931.

This, however, raised differences over the highly sensitive issue of social justice – over the incidence of expenditure cuts and the possibilities for limiting these by new taxes or other expedients, over how the burden of balancing the budget was to be distributed between the social classes. Graham, Alexander, and Thomas, appointed to confer with Snowden, each proposed an 'all round cut' in expenditure. Alexander and Thomas linked this to special taxation of *rentiers*, those receiving fixed interest on government securities. These interest payments were both a budget charge and an unearned income that had increased in real terms as prices had fallen, and so was a growing target for those in the Labour party concerned with just sacrifices. Alexander also suggested debt conversion and sequestration of estates in Chancery, and Graham changes in tax schedules and increases in excise duties. Thomas proposed a tariff, which Graham, in order to minimise unpleasant economies, now accepted for revenue purposes alone.[142] MacDonald had in December pledged to support Snowden 'in any proposal... to reduce expenditure', but he had also perceived that the budget deficit might provide the lever to obtain some kind of tariff.[143] For the time being, however, MacDonald refrained from pressing this, because it would antagonise Snowden and complicate financial discussions when, like Snowden, he wanted the Cabinet to face the chief budget problem – unemployment insurance.

MacDonald and Snowden had hoped that 'the exposures' of the Royal Commission on Unemployment Insurance would 'so crystallise public opinion' that the Cabinet would be persuaded to accept benefit cuts.[144] The Commission had been requested to submit an early interim report, but its chairman and some of its members were so unfamiliar with the insurance scheme that this was repeatedly delayed.[145] In early February, however, a need for parliamentary authorisation of further increase in the Unemployment Insurance Fund's borrowing powers and extension of transitional benefit gave MacDonald, Snowden, and Bondfield an opportunity at Cabinets on the 5th and 11th to press ministers for

---

[142] Undated notes of Cabinet committee discussions in T171/287.

[143] MacDonald diary, 22 Dec. 1930, 12 and 14 Jan. 1931.

[144] MacDonald reported in Greig to Gwynne, 12 Jan. 1931, Gwynne papers 19, and (probably also by Greig) in Smithers to Fry, 12 Jan. 1931, SB 47/233-4.

[145] Cabinets 12, 13(31), 5 and 11 Feb. 1931. For calibre of Commission members, see Clay to Beveridge, 7 Jan. 1931, BoE SMT/5/1/28; Streat diary, 17 Feb. 1931, in Dupree I, 44-5.

'emergency action...on their own initiative'. Their arguments were
the 'general financial situation', widespread 'abuse', parliamentary
criticism, and, a new justification, the fall in the cost of living. Their
proposals were reductions in benefit rates (by less than the fall in
living costs), abolition of 'abuses' by married women and seasonal
workers and through systems of short-time employment, and, more
tentatively, non-renewal of transitional benefit.[146]

These proposals provoked a row. Greenwood had already publicly
declared that 'he would die in the last ditch' against social service
cuts. Henderson was in MacDonald's view 'bullying', and some
others felt as strongly.[147] If the proposals were adopted 'without
corresponding financial sacrifices elsewhere', the burden of restoring
solvency 'would fall exclusively on the unemployed,...the poorest
element in the population'. This was 'hardly consistent with
the...general policy of the Government...of "work or maintenance"'. This Cabinet opposition forced MacDonald, Snowden, and
Bondfield to withdraw their proposals, and accept both a six-month
extension of transitional benefit and an increase in borrowing powers
of £20m. rather than the usual £10m., to a new total of £90m. Yet
cuts were not rejected altogether. Only Lansbury proposed a
complete alternative, an emergency income tax. Shaken by the
financial situation, alarmed by Treasury and Bank of England
warnings, softened by reports of 'abuses', Henderson and most other
Cabinet members had been driven from outright opposition to
retrenchment towards concern for preserving some conception of
social justice and justifying cuts to the Labour movement. They only
postponed decision and established a principle. It was agreed that
after the Royal Commission reported and before the summer recess
there would be legislation dealing with unemployment benefits 'on
a more permanent basis', and that, if substantial cuts were to be
imposed, these would be only part of a 'comprehensive...policy for
spreading the burden of the existing financial difficulties throughout
all classes of the community'.[148]

What all this might mean in practice was unclear. Internally
divided, the Cabinet had again shelved responsibility – producing

[146] Floud to Bondfield, 5 Feb. 1931, PREM 5/74; Bondfield, 'Unemployment Insurance.
Emergency Financial Proposals', CP 31(31), 5 Feb. 1931, CAB 23/90B; Cabinet 12(31),
5 Feb. 1931.
[147] Greenwood speech, The Times, 13 Jan. 1931; MacDonald diary, 11 Feb. 1931. This is the
incident described in Skidelsky, Politicians, 239, but there misdated as summer 1930.
[148] Cabinets 12, 13(31), 5 and 11 Feb. 1931. For Lansbury, see memo, 6 Feb. 1931, in Garside,
British Unemployment, 53–4, and Postgate, Lansbury, 264.

formulae without deciding whether or how they were to be implemented. Snowden, however, had uses for both the postponement and the principle. Although he considered retrenchment in unemployment insurance a major objective, this was far from being his only one. The principle of shared sacrifices might also allow solutions to wider problems of budget balance, financial confidence, and industrial cost-competitiveness, and thereby reduce pressure for protection. Postponement would give time to plan that other great retrenchment project, war loan conversion, provided that financial confidence could be restored, not least by avoiding any reduction in the Sinking Fund.[149] It might also make some kind of 'national treaty' possible. Treasury and Inland Revenue officials were not opposed in principle to increased taxation of *rentiers*, though they advised that a new, separate, *rentier* tax was impracticable and proposed instead an adjustment within income tax. What they disliked was the idea that this might be the principal form of imposition. In effect, they too saw the point of spreading the burden, even if their aim was to minimise tax increases while that of many Cabinet members was to minimise social service cuts. The officials' advice was that the Alexander–Thomas proposal of all-round cuts in government-funded incomes coupled with *rentier* taxation would have a 'stupendous[ly]' good effect upon 'the morale of the country and its reputation abroad'. But the political difficulties of obtaining such all-round sacrifice were also 'stupendous'. They seemed surmountable only 'by agreement between Parties and by the House of Commons acting in accordance with the Prime Minister's idea of a Council of State'.[150] Although Snowden showed no interest in MacDonald's other idea – national government – he accepted this reasoning. The postponement allowed time to prepare political opinion, but he needed both an opportunity to begin this work and a device to force serious attention to comprehensive financial measures.

'The House of Commons came to [Snowden's] assistance', in the form of the retrenchment motions for 11 February.[151] Liberal support would frustrate the Conservative censure. But in order to ensure Liberal acquiescence in renewed financing of unemployment insurance, the Cabinet authorised Snowden to accept the Liberal

149 For conversion plans revived in January but postponed during the February market uneasiness, see Sayers, *Bank of England*, 433–4.

150 Fergusson (reporting Fisher, Hopkins, P. J. Grigg) to Snowden, 'Very Secret', 6 Feb. 1931, T171/287; and see P. J. Grigg to Snowden, 2 April 1931, IR 63/10.

151 Snowden, *Autobiography* II, 892.

motion for an economy committee while enunciating the principle of all-round sacrifice.[152] Snowden's speech, constrained by pressures both to reassure the financial markets and avoid a Labour party crisis, resorted to calculated equivocation – but its tenor was plain. Though the financial position was 'fundamentally sound', currently it was serious. While the 'temporary crisis' could be surmounted 'without any very great efforts', restored budget equilibrium and industrial progress made it necessary to consider 'drastic and disagreeable measures'. Though these measures would 'involve some temporary sacrifices from all and those best able to bear them [would] have to make the largest sacrifices', nevertheless unemployment insurance finance could not continue in its existing form.[153]

Snowden repeatedly asserted that no effective retrenchment was possible without a 'united House of Commons'. This was not simply intended to advance the idea of shared sacrifices. It was a recognition of the likelihood that some Labour and perhaps Liberal MPs would rebel against unemployment insurance cuts, in which case the Cabinet would need Conservative assistance. A 'united House' was obtained at least so far as the Conservatives (after defeat of their own censure motion) joined the Liberals and the government in voting for an economy committee. The three party leaderships also concurred on the committee's character. Snowden and the Treasury ensured it would be rigorous by re-using the terms of reference of the Geddes 'axe' committee of 1921–2, by excluding MPs in order to reduce internal party-political disputes, and by appointing as chairman Sir George May, a leading actuary and secretary of Prudential Assurance. The Labour party nominees included an obligatory trade union leader, Pugh, but the Conservatives and Liberals nominated accountants and businessmen.[154]

Snowden's speech and acceptance of a committee relieved immediate pressures upon government financial policy. There was a bad start when Geddes repudiated his putative offspring as an evasion of immediate action – 'fiddling while Rome is burning'.[155] Snowden's hints of new taxation precipitated falls in gilts and sterling, which were aggravated into a 'minor crisis of confidence' by Lloyd George's attack the following day on the City and by

---

[152] Cabinet 13(31), 11 Feb. 1931. Cf. Marquand, 589, which incorrectly implies that this decision resulted from a Bondfield–Sinclair discussion on the borrowing bill.
[153] HC Deb, 248, cols. 440–9, 11 Feb. 1931.
[154] See papers in T160/398/F12414, esp. Fisher to Snowden, 16 Feb. 1931.
[155] Geddes statement, The Times, 12 Feb. 1931.

announcement of the unusually large increase in unemployment insurance borrowing powers. By late February, however, recognition of Snowden's 'courage' and commitment to retrenchment, together with the successful outcomes of the Anglo-French treasury talks and Bank of England market operations, had restored confidence in the financial markets.[156] Having created an expectation of stern action once the economy committee reported, the government had no difficulty passing its unemployment insurance finance bill, while Snowden felt none about considering temporary expedients for balancing the budget.

Initially ministers were worried that the movement towards retrenchment and all-round sacrifice might be jeopardised by an employers' wage-cutting campaign, a prospect sharpened by distribution of the NCEO manifesto. The danger was that such a campaign might provoke so much trade union resistance that a Labour government would be unable to act in a manner which appeared to follow the employers' lead. It was quite apparent to ministers that the difficulties of introducing retrenchment 'against [trade union] wishes' were 'almost insurmountable'.[157] Accordingly on 19 February MacDonald and leading ministers met NCEO leaders to appeal for restraint, and then the TUC General Council to offer reassurance. Their message to both was that the two sides of industry should maintain consultation on national economic problems, and that any agreement between them 'would weigh very powerfully with the government'. The extremely optimistic implication was that 'industry' might produce a 'national treaty' of its own.[158] If there had ever been a possibility of that, the chance had long since passed. The NCEO was perhaps restrained by the indications that the Cabinet intended to do something. But the TUC General Council was not reassured: the events of February had further increased its suspicions of 'a Cabinet of which only a very very small number can be regarded as Socialists [and]...a Chancellor under the domination of Bankers and Financiers'.[159]

[156] Keynes to Case, 21 Feb., 9 March 1931, in *JMK* xx, 485–7; City Notes, *The Times*, 13, 14, and 17 Feb. 1931; *Economist*, 14, 21, and 28 Feb. 1931.
[157] Ministers reported in Weir notes, 'Impressions formed from the Conference' [19 Feb. 1931], Weir papers 12/6; MacDonald reported in Lloyd George to F. Stevenson, 3 Feb. 1931, in Taylor, 141.
[158] Transcript 'Meeting between the NCEO...and members of the Government', 19 Feb. 1931, and 'Impressions formed from the Conference', Weir papers 12/1, 12/6.
[159] Bromley to Trevelyan, 3 March 1931, Trevelyan papers 142.

Despite initial concern, there was also no immediate difficulty
with the Labour parliamentary party. The ILP group divided
against the economy committee motion, and a substantial number of
other Labour MPs abstained; two put their names to the Liberal
unemployment motion for the following day, and some cheered
Lloyd George's attack on the City.[160] But at a special parliamentary
party meeting on 17 February Snowden soothed fears by implying
that 'disagreeable measures' meant only further taxation and
temporary suspension of new social reform, and in March an ILP
motion to *increase* pensions and benefits was easily defeated.[161] Even
so an unofficial meeting of the more worried backbenchers appointed
a committee to send the Cabinet their own suggestions for resolving
the financial problem without 'reduction in working class standards'. These MPs, including members of a party Currency Group
formed in December, combined hostility to finance capitalism with
crude Keynesianism. They argued that the 'policy of deflation has
gone too far, and...too much importance is attached to...rigid
adherence to the gold standard': 'even a fall in the Exchange would
be preferable to a continuance of the slump'. Specific proposals
included a moratorium on war debts and reparations, restriction
and taxation of foreign investments, Sinking Fund suspension,
taxation of *rentiers* and land values, and reduced arms expenditure.[162]
However, most Labour MPs were uninterested in, because mystified
by or alarmed at the possible implications of, monetary unorthodoxy,
and had been reassured by Snowden's statement.[163] In early March
Snowden fell ill, and needed a prostate gland operation. By the time
he had recovered and seen the proposals a month later, there was
obviously no pressure behind them. His instruction was simply 'Do
nothing'.[164]

While the government was successfully containing the retrenchment issue, it suffered another bad period of parliamentary, party,
ministerial, and policy difficulties. The School Attendance Bill
(raising the school leaving age to fifteen) was defeated in the Lords

---

[160] There were 545 MPs from all parties participating in the division on the Conservative
censure motion, but only 489 in the economy committee division immediately afterwards.
For Brown and Cocks supporting the Liberal motion, PLP, 10 Feb. 1931; for cheers,
MacDonald diary, 15 Feb. 1931.
[161] PLP, 17 Feb., 3 and 10 March 1931; *The Times*, 18 Feb. 1931.
[162] Lindsay to Snowden, 3 March 1931, enclosing Taylor, Kenworthy, Chuter Ede, Wise,
Winterton, Marley, Philips Price, West note and 'Memo. for consideration of Cabinet', 26
Feb. 1931, T171/287; Kenworthy, *Sailors, Statesmen*, 302.
[163] Philips Price, *Three Revolutions*, 266.
[164] Snowden minute on Hopkins to Fergusson, 9 April 1931, T171/287.

on 18 February. Although the Cabinet decided to pass it under the Parliament Act, Trevelyan – harassed and disillusioned – chose the occasion to resign. In doing so he announced that he had for 'some time' been 'very much out of sympathy' with general policy, and that not retrenchment but 'big socialist measures' were required.[165] The Commons majority came under serious threat: the New party MPs were lost and there were persistent small rebellions, with the majority falling to five on 13 March over a coal industry matter. Labour abstentions and a Liberal rebellion brought a government defeat on the 16th over abolition of university seats. After the Cabinet row over unemployment insurance, Bondfield tested MacDonald's confidence in herself by offering resignation.[166] Hartshorn died in mid March, and the Chief Whip was close to a breakdown.[167] With the death of Russell and resignation of Arnold (ostensibly for health reasons, but actually because he felt neglected), with Parmoor persistently ill, and Passfield talking about retirement, ministerial representation in the Lords was close to collapse.[168] There were further serious problems within the coal industry during March over implementation of the Coal Mines Act. An apparent success in naval disarmament negotiations with the French and Italians – which restored some party morale in early March[169] – collapsed three weeks later. Renewed efforts by MacDonald, Addison, and Thomas to produce a cereals policy, and – now with Graham's support – to obtain a revenue tariff, were again frustrated. A Cabinet committee failed to reach agreement over a quota.[170] With Snowden absent ill but with his wife and Treasury officials vigilant on his behalf, other ministers dared not force decision on cereals, and were prevented even from discussing the inclusion of a revenue tariff in the budget.[171]

Under the pressures of early 1931, MacDonald was again depressed and exasperated. He continued to resent the way other

---

[165] Trevelyan to MacDonald, 19 Feb. 1931, Trevelyan papers 142.

[166] Bondfield to MacDonald, 6 Feb. [Jan. written] 1931, JRM 1176; date confirmed by MacDonald diary, 9 Feb. 1931.

[167] For Kennedy, Duff to MacDonald, 14 March 1931, JRM 1176.

[168] Arnold to MacDonald, 5 March 1931, JRM 1312, and to Amulree, 9 March 1931; MacDonald diary, 6 March 1931; Williamson, 'Labour Party and the House of Lords', 328–9.

[169] Dalton diary, 6 March 1931 (Pimlott, 138–9); B. Webb diary, 8 March 1931 (Cole, 268).

[170] Graham at EAC 12th meeting, 12 March 1931; Cabinet 16(31), 4 March 1931.

[171] Mrs Snowden to Keynes, 7 March 1931, in *JMK* xx, 489, and to MacDonald, 27 March 1931, JRM 1176; Fergusson to Forber, and Forber to Fergusson, 4 and 26 March 1931, T175/52. For the effect of Snowden's absence, Cabinets 16, 17, 18, 21(31), 4, 11, 18, and 31 March 1931; MacDonald diary, 9, 10, and 11 March 1931.

parties sought 'partisan victories' instead of trying to 'help the country'.[172] He was infuriated by 'treacher[ous]' Labour rebellions and by what he considered to be the party managers' 'shilly-shallying' over party discipline.[173] He still considered himself ill-served by inadequate colleagues: the near success in naval disarmament was due to his own intervention, the breakdown to Henderson's mistakes. Having to run 'half a dozen departments', he was so overwhelmed with detail that he could not 'plan policy'.[174] He wanted to reconstruct the government, but thought there were not enough competent Labour politicians available. The Cabinet had 'too many stiff and inflexible minds', and was 'hopelessly divided' and 'paralysed' on economic policy. On unemployment insurance, it remained 'weak', failing in its 'duty'.[175] Snowden was 'impossible' over trade issues, and Henderson 'visionless' over retrenchment.[176] Yet he felt unable to impose his own views, because this might well precipitate Cabinet and party crises and, probably, a government collapse with devastating electoral consequences for the Labour party.

MacDonald's thoughts about the future varied according to his mood. Sometimes he spoke of retirement.[177] On other occasions he thought the financial position so serious that he reverted to the idea of 'national government'. Although parliamentary co-operation seemed impossible because of party feeling, 'private conversations' supplied 'signals and sign posts [that could] not be overlooked'.[178] After Henderson's 'bullying' against cuts on 11 February, his thoughts were that 'we must not break at the moment... but I shall not go much further'. On 1 March they were of leaving or splitting the party, since national government was an 'attractive' idea but not one acceptable to the Labour party. Yet he could also declare that 'some of us get increasingly convinced' that the economic system 'should be revised... in a socialist direction'.[179]

None of these statements expressed anything so substantial as an intention. They were largely a form of escapist political fantasy,

---

[172] MacDonald to Peacock, 15 April 1931, JRM 677.
[173] MacDonald diary, 22 Jan. 1931; MacDonald to Kennedy, 17 March 1931, JRM 1176.
[174] MacDonald diary, 22 and 29 Jan., 16 Feb., 1 and 30 March 1931; MacDonald in Citrine note, 29 Jan. 1931, Citrine papers 7/8.
[175] MacDonald diary, 9, 11, 16 Feb., 1, 4, 8, and 15 March, 16 April 1931.
[176] MacDonald in Lloyd George to F. Stevenson, 3 Feb. 1931, in Taylor, 141; MacDonald diary, 11 Feb. 1931.   [177] Citrine note, 29 Jan. 1931, Citrine papers 7/8.
[178] MacDonald to Greig, 6 Feb. 1931, Greig papers (JRM 1440).
[179] MacDonald diary, 11 Feb., 1 and 4 March 1931.

though in part also mental preparation for developments which might follow a government collapse. Despite self-pity and frustration, MacDonald's efforts to maintain the Labour government in no way slackened. Increasingly there were reasons, additional to the educational value expected from the Unemployment Insurance Commission and the May Committee, for thinking that matters would not deteriorate and might improve. MacDonald's 'gorgeous success' at the Round Table Conference had been crowned by the Irwin–Gandhi pact and only slightly dented by Indian cotton duties.[180] The second conference might well yield similar successes. The Conservative opposition was again hampered by internal divisions. In late March unemployment returned to the usual seasonal trend and started to fall. Abandonment of the Trade Disputes Bill, to which the TUC General Council reluctantly agreed, directed its wrath against the Liberals and removed a parliamentary embarrassment. The New party's creation evoked not sympathy but anger among Labour MPs, and a ministerial speaking campaign in Mosleyite constituencies removed fears that they had substantial local Labour support.[181] Many of Trevelyan's colleagues considered him a failure and were undisturbed by his departure, while most other Labour MPs – except the ILP – regarded his apparently sudden conversion to 'socialism' and attacks upon the Cabinet as absurd and misplaced.[182] The shock of government defeats made more MPs amenable to pressure for tightened party discipline.[183] Scrutiny of the parliamentary list in mid March showed that there was still a reasonable working majority if Lloyd George could deliver the Liberal support he claimed to retain.[184] Lloyd George was no longer causing embarrassment over unemployment, and MacDonald hoped for his support against Snowden on agricultural quotas. Two new Cabinet members, Morrison and Johnston (Hartshorn's replacement), were an immediate success, finding something new to say about existing employment policy.[185] Although the government was no nearer

---

[180] B. Webb diary, 22 Jan. 1931 (Cole, 263); Cabinets 10, 11(31), 28 Jan., 4 Feb. 1931.

[181] E.g., Dalton diary, 6 March 1931 (Pimlott, 139).

[182] MacDonald diary, 18 Feb., 3 March 1931; Sankey diary, 18 Feb. 1931; Philips Price to Trevelyan, 4 March 1931, Trevelyan papers 142.

[183] See Joint sub-committee on party discipline, 10 and 17 Feb., 30 March 1931, in LPNEC.

[184] MacDonald to Kennedy, and Kennedy to MacDonald, 17 and 18 March 1931, JRM 1176.

[185] MacDonald to Lloyd George, and to Addison, 20 March and 14 April 1931, JRM 1176, 1312; MacDonald and Dalton diaries, 16 March 1931.

dominating the economic problem or resolving its divisions over retrenchment and trade, by mid April it seemed to be in a stronger position, helped by the unexpected weakness of the Liberal dissentients. On the 16th a Conservative censure motion was defeated by a Labour–Liberal majority of fifty-four.

Moreover, however hopeless things had seemed during the winter, however serious the internal differences on policy, MacDonald's leadership had not been challenged. There were the usual complaints about his manner, but also much admiration for his efforts in desperate conditions. In January Cabinet members were to be found saying 'it would be disastrous if anything happened' to MacDonald, and Henderson that 'no man could hold the party together, and do what [he] had done'. Despite the proposed unemployment insurance cut, Lansbury – that embodiment of socialist rectitude – had in March 'more respect for MacDonald now than [he] ever had'.[186]

---

[186] Citrine note, 29 Jan. 1931, Citrine papers 7/8; Lansbury to Trevelyan, 17 March 1931, Trevelyan papers 142.

CHAPTER 7

Towards a two-party system

The ideal would be to banish party divisions and to unite in a
national Government for say five years to deal with India, the
Dole, Finance, Tariffs and Empire but alas I fear this is
Utopian and I see no prospect of it.

Reading to Willingdon, 29 May 1931[1]

'NATIONAL GOVERNMENT' IN ECLIPSE

During the spring and summer of 1931 the relative positions of the
three leading parties were clearly heading for major readjustment.
The nature of that change is less clear, and has generally been
misunderstood or overstated. Few historians nowadays would argue
that the movement was towards a 'national government'. Instead,
most interpret it as a movement towards total Liberal disintegration,
imminent Labour government collapse, and an autumn general
election in which the Conservatives would inevitably obtain a
landslide victory.[2] Given certain circumstances, this was indeed a
possible outcome. But the politics of these months cannot properly be
understood in such terms. The Conservative position was strong but
not invulnerable, while Liberal and Labour leaders were making
arrangements which, in the absence of any new dislocation, might
well have postponed their defeat and conceivably helped them to
decent electoral performances.

During these months expressions of dissatisfaction with the existing
party system continued, both in 'non-party' agitations on specific
issues and by those attached to the idea of 'national government'.

---

[1] Reading papers F118/106.
[2] E.g., Wilson, *Downfall of the Liberal Party*, 366; Wrench, 'Cashing In', 136, 139; Fair,
'Politics of Electoral Reform', 299–301; Ball, 'Failure of an Opposition', 94, and Ball,
Baldwin, 169; Thorpe, *British General Election*, esp. 29–30, 46, 62. A notable exception is
Skidelsky, *Politicians*, 330–3.

Yet in contrast to the previous autumn these appeals evoked little or no attention from the established political leaders. In all three parties – among Labour ministers and Liberal leaders almost as much as within the Conservative leadership – the deep gloom and fear of major disruption receded as the party and parliamentary situations became clearer and the political future began to seem less uncertain.

The extra-parliamentary criticism continued because none of the substantive problems had been resolved: party politics still seemed to obstruct action. From March to July the Friends of Economy in co-operation with local chambers of commerce, ratepayers' associations, the National Citizens' Union, and the Economic League held meetings in fifty provincial towns, and on 22 April held a well-attended cross-party meeting at the House of Commons.[3] In July the NFU organised a non-party memorial from backbench MPs to the Cabinet, calling for disclosure of 'emergency' cereals measures before the parliamentary recess. The FBI in March appealed to all those placing 'country before party' to support retrenchment and protection, and the NCIC circularised every MP with a similar appeal. The NCEO proposed to the Royal Commission on Unemployment Insurance in May a Board of Trustees to administer the system independently of 'political considerations'.[4]

The principal effort to restructure the party system remained that of Mosley, already committed through the formation of the New party. But the project had to live on hope rather than achievement. Its launch misfired badly, because Mosley fell ill and W. J. Brown withdrew at the last moment.[5] The next attempt to make an early splash was an intensive and expensive by-election campaign during April for Mosley's secretary, Young, in the Labour seat of Ashton-under-Lyne. This yielded useful publicity but attracted only 16 per cent of the voters, aroused unexpectedly strong and sometimes violent local Labour resistance, and handed the seat to the Conservatives. Thereafter Mosley decided against fighting further by-elections for the time being and to concentrate upon organisation, propaganda, and fund-raising, aiming to create a national base and

---

[3] Friends of Economy, *First Annual Report*, 1, 3–4; Abel, *Benn*, 68–9, 157–61. For Commons meeting, convened by a Privy Councillor from each party (Herbert, Jones, Wedgwood), see *The Times*, 18 and 23 April 1931.

[4] *The Times*, 25 and 30 July (NFU), 12 March (FBI), and 22 April, 21 May 1931 (NCIC); Royal Commission on Unemployment Insurance, *Evidence*, 1005–11.

[5] Details in Skidelsky, *Mosley*, 243–4, 247–8.

re-launch the party with fifty candidates in the autumn.[6] He avoided the House of Commons until early July, and then led New party MPs onto the opposition benches and condemned Labour and Conservative alike for failure to solve the unemployment insurance problem by creating employment.[7] But while the party's leaders agreed that opposition to the old parties and reform of parliamentary procedure were their most promising popular appeal, differences emerged over the character of the 'revivalism', the 'new national psychology', and the 'New Britain' that all wished to offer.[8] Mosley's expectation of support from the young Conservatives (whom he now described as 'fascist in character'), insistence upon a highly disciplined and centralised movement, rumoured dispatch of aides to study Hitler's methods, and creation of a Youth Movement to resist disruption of meetings, all aroused unease in Strachey and Young whose allegiance remained with 'socialism'.[9]

Nevertheless high optimism prevailed. Great significance was attached to the sympathy – and little to the ambiguity, qualifications, or criticism – expressed by Keynes, Garvin, Churchill, Macmillan, Moore-Brabazon, Hore-Belisha, Cook, and the Prince of Wales.[10] Mosley's claims of strategically placed support reflected some wishful thinking and a desire to impress his lieutenants. Yet with prominent sections of extra-parliamentary opinion still critical of existing party politics, there remained good reasons for thinking that if the New party could win seats or if the established parties became further discredited, it could rally the disillusioned and the rebellious and become an effective centre force. It did not seem absurd for Nicolson to resign from Beaverbrook newspapers and become editor of Mosley's newspaper on the chance that within five years he might become Foreign Secretary in a Mosley coalition.[11]

The alternative of coalition between the established parties continued to exercise *The Observer* and various busybodies. Astor thought in March that the diehard threat to the tripartite Indian process 'forc[ed] our National Government to the front as a

[6] Nicolson diary, 28 May, 2, 5, 7, 11, and 12 June 1931; Strachey, 'The Progress of the New Party', *Week-end Review*, 20 June 1931.

[7] *HC Deb*, 254, cols. 2140–7, 8 July 1931.

[8] Nicolson diary, 7 and 16 June 1931; Strachey, 'The Progress of the New Party'; Mosley speech, *The Times*, 1 July 1931.

[9] Nicolson diary, 28 May, 6, 10, 16, and 25 June, 3 and 17 July 1931 (partly in Nicolson I, 75, 80). For aides to Germany, *Daily Herald*, 6 and 8 June 1931.

[10] Nicolson diary, 6 and 30 May, 8 and 22 June, 20 and 22 July 1931 (partly in Nicolson I, 74, 76, 77). [11] Nicolson diary, 18 June 1931 (Nicolson I, 79).

reality'.[12] Just as Garvin had applauded Mosley, so now he encouraged the Simon–Grigg attempt to force party realignment, while still hoping that Lloyd George would provide the lead for a national government.[13] Seely possibly persisted through the spring with coalition arguments to the King, MacDonald, Reading, and other political leaders.[14] Greig certainly continued to interpret and communicate MacDonald's musings about a national government as a definite and continuing desire to form or join one. He was perhaps the unnamed person who in early July approached Stonehaven, the new Conservative party chairman, with an apparent sounding from MacDonald.[15] There were also new contributions. Meston, a former senior Indian civil servant, member of the Indian Empire Society, and Liberal peer appealed on economic grounds in May for 'the formation of a great national party from the best men in the three existing parties'.[16] Sir Abe Bailey, a South African millionaire with long-established interests in promoting political projects, held a dinner on 23 June for prominent politicians, financiers, newspaper proprietors, and editors to promote the idea of a MacDonald-led 'national government'. His guests included MacDonald himself, Garvin, Astor, Camrose, Churchill, Amery, Lloyd, Derby, Stonehaven, Samuel, Crewe, McKenna, Brand, D'Abernon, Strakosch, and Wigram, Stamfordham's successor as the King's private secretary.[17]

Yet although the 'national government' idea was kept alive, its proponents made no new impression upon leading politicians. During the second quarter of 1931 none considered all-party coalition a serious proposition within usefully foreseeable circumstances. In May Reading wrote of 'talk amongst some of us of the

[12] Astor to Garvin, 12 March 1931, and see Astor to Macmillan, 19 June 1931, Astor papers.
[13] Garvin to Grigg, 6 May 1931, Altrincham papers; to Simon, 16 and 26 June 1931, Simon papers, and to Keynes, 5 April 1931, in Skidelsky, *Politicians*, 295.
[14] See Seely in Amery diary, 4 Aug. 1931 (*LSA* II, 190); also Lloyd George in Stevenson diary, 18 Feb. 1934, in Taylor, 254, who may or may not be misdating incidents: see above, p. 154.
[15] Greig reported by Elibank on 15 July in N. Chamberlain diary, 24 July 1931, and in N. to H. Chamberlain, 18 July 1931, NC 18/1/748. For unnamed person, N. Chamberlain diary, 6 July 1931, and N. to I. Chamberlain, 11 July 1931, NC 18/1/747. Fair, 'Conservative Basis', 146–7, believes overtures really came from MacDonald.
[16] Speech, *The Times*, 14 May 1931. For Meston as a possible Labour minister in 1924, see Cowling, *Impact of Labour*, 369.
[17] MacDonald diary, 23 June 1931; and for guest list, Bailey to MacDonald, 22 June 1931, JRM 1753. Bailey had been an intermediary between Beaverbrook and N. Chamberlain the previous November, and Grigg asked him to fund the Liberal–Unionist movement in June 1931. For earlier activity, see Cowling, *Impact of Labour*, 215.

urgent need for unity', but he saw 'no prospect' of 'national government'.[18] The response of Baldwin, Neville Chamberlain, and Stonehaven to the apparent MacDonald overture was that the idea was 'clearly impossible'. Their party 'would not stand it for a moment', and it was probably just 'an expression of weariness'.[19] It is indeed unlikely that MacDonald would have entrusted a political nonentity with any sort of overture, and whatever substance the statement might have had appears to reflect MacDonald's earlier mood rather than his current one. After March he expressed no interest in 'national government'. His reaction to Bailey's effort was more one of surprise than of anything else.

This did not mean that leading politicians had ceased to believe in the existence of 'national crisis'. Reading, Baldwin, and Neville Chamberlain treated the 'national government' idea as impracticable or undesirable rather than incommensurate with the scale of problems facing government. The idea remained available in the event of a major political breakdown. What had changed was that breakdown no longer seemed so likely. The Round Table Conference, the Irwin–Gandhi pact, and Baldwin's victory over Churchill and the diehards, suggested that a tripartite, moderate, and successful treatment of Indian policy could be maintained. Appointment of the May Committee had postponed the retrenchment issue, while creating the possibility that its resolution might be shifted on to some 'impartial' basis less dangerous to each party. Those who wanted full-blown imperial protectionism and strong government of the right were reassured by the Conservative party's new firmness, apparent solution of its leadership difficulties, and a belief that it was now capable of obtaining an outright majority at the next general election. Those who wished to maintain free trade and preserve 'progressive' government could look to the Labour government's remarkable capacity for survival, and hope for trade recovery. Those desiring to salvage some form of Liberalism could look to alliance either with Baldwin's brand of Conservatism (rather than a party captured for 'reaction'), or with a Labour government which increasingly looked less committed to socialism than converted to radical Liberalism. Despite the party difficulties of the winter the tendency had been towards a new stability, with alignment into

---

[18] Reading to Willingdon, 29 May 1931, Reading papers F118/106, and see epigraph for this chapter. The 'us' were unspecified, but they certainly included Seely.

[19] N. Chamberlain diary, 6 July 1931, and N. to I. Chamberlain, 11 July 1931, NC 18/1/747.

Labour–Lloyd George Liberal and Conservative–Simon Liberal blocs between the poles of free trade and protection. Without the retrenchment issue to impose a different polarisation, this tendency strengthened from March.

TOWARDS A PROGRESSIVE BLOC

Although Labour ministers found the size of their Commons majority on 16 April 'surprising', they were encouraged to think the government could last for the rest of the year and perhaps longer.[20] Admittedly, events during spring and early summer offered little hope that the burdens of government would soon lighten. For a few weeks unemployment figures were steady at just over 2·5m., but began to rise again in June. Considerable time had to be spent in coal negotiations as owners threatened wage-reductions once the Coal Mines Act restored the seven-hour day, and the union in self-defence demanded new minimum wage legislation. When by late June no settlement seemed likely, the Cabinet faced the embarrassing prospect of having to revive the emergency strike organisation.[21] As it became clear in April that employers' tariff demands and shortage of finance would delay iron and steel rationalisation, the Cabinet accepted Graham's scheme to impose it through a public utility corporation. Further delays then arose as the Bank of England resisted this 'experiment...in socialis[m]' by threatening to withdraw co-operation and claiming it would endanger financial confidence.[22] Additional trouble was laid up as the Cabinet pledge to make cereal farming profitable was privately abandoned. Addison's wheat quota proposal was dropped in June because of continued opposition from half the Cabinet, and MacDonald's acknowledgement that acute embarrassment would arise from introduction of a measure having more Conservative than Labour and Liberal support.[23] Addison, angry and rebellious, was instructed to accept Snowden's view that policy should be redirected towards

[20] MacDonald diary, 17 April 1931; Dalton diary, 16 April 1931 (Pimlott, 142); Henderson in B. Webb diary, 18 April 1931 (Cole, 270); Passfield to B. Webb, 29 April 1931, Passfield papers II:3:(i):27:31.   [21] Cabinets 32, 34, 35(31), 10, 17, and 24 June 1931.
[22] Cabinets 24, 27(31), 22 April, 6 May 1931; BoE Cte, 29 April, 1, and 13 May 1931; memo of Snowden, Graham, and Norman meeting, 11 May 1931, and Snowden to MacDonald, 12 May 1931, JRM 412, 677. See Cabinets throughout June–July 1931 for iron and steel kept on the agenda while awaiting further discussion with Norman.
[23] Cabinets 22, 23(31), both 15 April, and Cabinets 27, 31(31), 6 May, 4 June 1931; Passfield to B. Webb, 4 June 1931, Passfield papers II:3:(i):27:44; Morgan, Portrait, 197.

helping cereal farmers to adopt more remunerative forms of farming. There was a sharp reminder in March of the problems for Indian policy, with savage Hindu–Muslim riots in Cawnpore. A flight from the rupee in June, precipitated by uncertainty about the character of the new constitution, threatened a major Indian devaluation crisis which might fatally complicate a political settlement. Yet Snowden and the Treasury preferred rupee devaluation to any rescue operation which might transfer Indian financial burdens to the British Exchequer. With much difficulty MacDonald in consultation with Conservative and Liberal leaders stitched together a statement which, in seeking to reassure the financial markets while avoiding government commitments, left the problem in a dangerous limbo.[24]

Nor had management become much easier. Snowden's illness exacerbated congestion of parliamentary business by delaying introduction of the Finance Bill. There was further trouble in the House of Lords as Conservative peers under Hailsham threatened to follow their mutilation of the Land Utilisation Bill with similar treatment of the Representation of the People Bill, and plainly intended to harass the government as much as possible. In late April and May ministers gave serious thought to the parliamentary and electoral possibilities of a challenge to the Lords' powers.[25] The government position in the Lords also delayed the long overdue ministerial reconstruction, since MacDonald felt particular difficulty about replacing Parmoor and Passfield, who offered his resignation in May.[26] That MacDonald's two most senior colleagues wanted peerages only complicated matters. Snowden's early elevation, allowing the appointment of a less rigid Chancellor, would have been welcomed by the Cabinet. But when Thomas laid claim to the post Snowden determined to remain until it could be secured for Graham, who unlike Thomas was neither a protectionist nor rumoured to be a stock-exchange speculator.[27] Henderson per-

---

[24] Sankey diary, 11 and 12 June 1931; MacDonald diary, 25 June 1931; MacDonald statement, *HC Deb*, 254, col. 769, 26 June 1931. For details, Tomlinson, 'Britain and the Indian Currency Crisis', 94–5; Drummond, *Floating Pound*, 33–8.

[25] MacDonald diary, 23 and 28 April 1931; note of Parmoor, Ponsonby, Lees-Smith meeting, 12 May 1931, and Lees-Smith to MacDonald, 19 May 1931, JRM 1300, 695: Williamson, 'Labour Party and the House of Lords', 337, 339–40.

[26] MacDonald diary, 16 April, 4 June 1931; Henderson in B. Webb diary, 18 April 1931 (Cole, 270); Passfield to MacDonald, 17 May 1931, JRM 1176, and MacDonald to Passfield, 18 May 1931, Passfield papers II:4:(i):86.

[27] Snowden, *Autobiography* II, 924; B. Webb diary, 13 July 1931; Graham reported in Dalton diary, 29 Sept. 1931 (Pimlott, 156).

sistently demanded a peerage so that he could lighten his parliamentary work and concentrate on the Foreign Secretaryship and party management, which MacDonald much resented as leaving him with a seriously weakened Commons Front Bench.[28] Even Henderson's appointment as president for the 1932 Geneva Disarmament Conference was disliked by the Cabinet, because it would require long absences.[29] Such pressures and irritations induced the usual bouts of despondency in MacDonald.[30]

On the other hand, evasion and wishful thinking had become habitual. Ministers and all the Labour party except the ILP – now plainly isolated – had learnt to live with high unemployment, consoled by expectations of trade recovery and the provision of unemployment benefits. Postponement of the Imperial Economic Conference enabled consideration of Dominion quotas for agricultural produce to be shelved.[31] It was assumed that all serious peace opinion would prefer negotiations at the Disarmament Conference to be conducted by a Labour government with a proven record of disarmament. There was little interest in the forthcoming Macmillan Committee report. Insofar as ministers other than Snowden thought about monetary matters, they continued despite earlier advice to hope that something might come of proposals for international financial co-operation.[32] MacDonald was worried that Sprague's advocacy of all-round deflation of costs might represent official Bank of England objectives, but was reassured by an ambiguously worded Norman letter.[33] A Continental crisis from March – over the Austro-German Customs Union, Austrian bank collapses, and possible German default in reparation payments – at first seemed less a direct threat to British finance than material on which MacDonald and Henderson could again display their diplomatic expertise.

[28] MacDonald diary, 16 April, 11 June, 14 July 1931. See also Dalton diary, 16 April 1931 (Pimlott, 141) and Snowden, *Autobiography* II, 925. The account in Hamilton, *Henderson*, 355–6, of the initiative coming from MacDonald, is the exact reverse of the truth.

[29] Cabinet 29(31), 20 May 1931; MacDonald and Dalton diaries, 20 May 1931 (latter in Pimlott, 146).

[30] MacDonald diary, 19, 20, and 30 April, 20 May 1931; MacDonald to Middleton, 25 May 1931, Middleton papers 27/27 (Marquand, 597).

[31] Cabinet 31(31), 4 June 1931.

[32] H. D. Henderson, and Thomas, to MacDonald, 25 May, 25 June 1931, and Duff (for MacDonald) to Fergusson, 13 July 1931, PREM 1/94; Thomas in Amery diary, 1 July 1931 (*LSA* II, 164).

[33] MacDonald to Norman, 18 and 29 June 1931, and Norman to MacDonald, 25 June 1931, JRM 677; Marquand, 603.

The sense of comparative security was encouraged especially by the existence of the May Committee. This produced two opposed reactions. Most ministers and Labour MPs welcomed the relief from immediate financial scares, and avoided the unpleasantness of thinking about the difficulties the Committee report might cause. But Snowden conducted financial policy in the expectation that the report would force drastic retrenchment. In order to reassure financial opinion and keep his April 1930 pledge to avoid increased taxes on industry, and in contrast to his rigorous Cabinet statement of January, he framed the 1931 budget on optimistic calculations and lenient principles. The realised deficit for 1930 was £23m., but the prospective deficit for 1931 was now given as £37m. rather than the January estimate of £50m. plus.[34] Treasury officials gave their usual warnings of 'grave danger' to financial confidence if strict budget balance was not restored. Snowden nevertheless resorted to the Churchillian device of meeting the deficit largely by raiding a capital fund (the Exchange Account) and by other non-recurrent expedients. His budget speech presented Sinking Fund provision as a guarantee of the 'soundness of our national financial position', and excused the expedients with the argument that a 'temporary emergency' justified 'temporary measures'.

While most ministers admired the budget as a 'clever get-out', to Snowden it was largely a 'make-shift'.[35] Its rationale was only half-hidden, since he repeatedly returned to the theme that Parliament would have to give serious attention to recommendations of the May Committee and Royal Commission on Unemployment Insurance. Not only did Snowden assume expenditure cuts; he may also have expected that these might create conditions in which taxes could be raised in a second budget.[36] In the meantime, for him the principal feature of the budget was provision for the future taxation of land values, fulfilling a long-standing radical commitment. As such it represented his personal device for refurbishing the government's progressive credentials, though in truth it also displayed how

---

[34] For manipulation of deficit estimate, see Fergusson to Fisher, 19 March 1931, T171/287, and Janeway thesis, 'Economic Policy', 91–2.

[35] Dalton diary, 27 April 1931; Snowden broadcast, *The Times*, 28 April 1931.

[36] *HC Deb*, 251, cols. 1391–411, esp. 1396, 1399, 1404, 1408–9, 27 April 1931. Short thesis, 'Politics of Personal Taxation', 276–85, is critical of the budget as irrelevant to existing conditions, but does not appreciate Snowden's medium-term strategy. The reference in Snowden, *Autobiography* II, 904, to an intended second budget may or may not be pure hindsight.

attached he remained to pre-war ideas. Other Cabinet members
regarded it with little enthusiasm, or as another burdensome
complication of government policy.[37]

Existence of the May Committee also influenced Cabinet
treatment of the Royal Commission on Unemployment Insurance's
interim Report, published in early June. A majority report
recommended reductions in benefit payments (justified by the fall in
living costs), a shorter period of benefit entitlement, increased
contributions, a means test on certain transitional benefit claimants,
and measures to control 'abuses' – re-described as 'anomalies' – in
payments to married women and casual, intermittent, and seasonal
workers. The intention was to reduce the Insurance Fund annual
deficit to manageable proportions, from £31.8m. to £7.6m. The
Labour nominees, in a minority report, recommended no major
changes until the Commission had completed its inquiry, and
endorsed only certain proposals concerning 'anomalies'.[38]

These reports did not create the embarrassment which might have
been expected from earlier experience. Unsurprisingly, the ILP
declared outright opposition to the majority report. The TUC
General Council, whose evidence to the Commission had proposed
the maintenance of existing benefits through a special, graduated,
unemployment levy on all incomes, accepted only the restrictions on
married women's and seasonal workers' claims. It organised
demonstrations to 'support...the Government in resisting...pro-
posals for lowering the standard of living of the unemployed'.[39] As
it seems unlikely that the General Council had much confidence in
the Cabinet resisting the majority report, this agitation was really
directed as much against the Cabinet as in its support. In fact a
Cabinet committee under Henderson's chairmanship proposed to
follow the minority report and postpone decision about reduced
benefits and increased contributions, and to adopt only those
majority recommendations concerning anomalies.[40] Snowden raised
no serious objection. He did not resist because he believed the May
Committee would shortly compel more drastic cuts, and was
meanwhile content that the 'abuses' issue was at last being faced.

[37] MacDonald diary, 5 May 1931; Greenwood to Snowden, 18 May 1931, JRM 677.
[38] Royal Commission on Unemployment Insurance, *First Report*: see p. 56 for note by Clay,
the Bank of England adviser, that the majority recommendations 'might reasonably' have
been carried further.
[39] *TUCAR, 1931*, 157–73; TUC statement, *The Times*, 8 June 1931; Social Insurance
Advisory Committee report, 9 June, in TUCGC, 12 June 1931.
[40] Committee on Unemployment Insurance, Report, CP 149(31), 9 June 1931.

Nor did Snowden protest when the Cabinet decided to use the good impression expected from an anomalies bill to request a further six-month extension of transitional benefit and the largest-ever increase in Insurance Fund borrowing, of £25m. to a new total of £115m.[41] MacDonald – who had considered the TUC's evidence 'irresponsible'[42] – was pleased that at least something was to be done to appease parliamentary opposition.

The rest of the Cabinet, most Labour MPs, and the TUC swallowed the Anomalies Bill out of relief that nothing worse was proposed. The ILP were virtually alone in their parliamentary demonstrations against the Bill. It defied the new PLP standing orders, and during the night of 15–16 July forced thirty-two divisions against the government. The only notable politician to support them was Trevelyan. His concern, however, was less objection to the Bill itself than desire to restore his own socialist credentials and prevent ILP expulsion from the Labour party.[43]

Paradoxically, then, the short-term effect of the May Committee's existence was to soothe Labour politics. But the principal reason for optimism was the increasingly close relationship with the Lloyd George Liberals. This became easier to tolerate as it became more apparent that the Liberal party was splitting. However troublesome Lloyd George and his followers might be, they were no longer feared as rival leaders of the forces of progress but could be regarded as adjuncts of the Labour party. From late April MacDonald, Snowden, Henderson, and Thomas discussed government business in weekly meetings with Lloyd George, Samuel, Sinclair, and Lothian. Their first decision was not to precipitate a general election over House of Lords treatment of the Land Utilisation Bill.[44] In contrast to persistent rejection of TUC requests to see confidential government papers, the Cabinet now allowed selected documents to be communicated under Privy Council oath to Samuel and Lloyd George.[45] After Conservative managers declined to help ease the parliamentary timetable, it was at Lloyd George's urging that the guillotine was for the first time applied to the Finance Bill.[46] Graham briefed the Liberal leaders in detail on his plans for the iron and steel

[41] Cabinet 32(31), 10 June 1931.
[42] MacDonald to Bondfield, 6 May 1931, JRM 677.
[43] Trevelyan to his wife, 15 July 1931, Trevelyan papers, Ex 125(2). For ILP defiance, PLP, 7 July 1931.
[44] MacDonald diary, 28 April 1931; Lothian to Stevenson, 29 April 1931, Lothian papers 260/595–7. [45] Cabinets 26, 27(31), 29 April, 6 May 1931.
[46] MacDonald diary, 5 and 19 May 1931.

industry, and a bill on rural housing was agreed after Snowden, again with the May Committee in mind, allowed his objections on cost to be overruled.[47] There may also have been some arrangement about by-elections. In contrast to the general election there was no Labour candidate at Scarborough and Whitby where Liberals had been the second party, and no Liberals at Ashton-under-Lyne, Ogmore, Rutherglen, Gateshead, and Wavertree where Labour candidates had come first or second.

The Lloyd George Liberal leaders refused to be frightened by a falling Liberal poll in by-elections, the sniping of the Simon group, defections of candidates to other parties, and the resignation of the National Liberal Federation chairman, Colonel Kerr. Rather, they counter-attacked. What Lloyd George, Samuel and Sinclair claimed as the chief by-election features were increased abstention and consequent Conservative failure to obtain a clear popular majority. These, they said, demonstrated that no public demand existed for a general election and that Conservatives were trying to snatch a parliamentary majority from a minority popular vote – a 'travesty of democracy'.[48] On free trade, electoral reform, the Lords, land, disarmament, and national reconstruction, it was 'impossible for any Liberalism worthy of the name to align itself with the Conservative party'. On the other hand 'over a large field... the two progressive parties had common purposes'.[49] The Labour government proposed 'no great issue of Socialistic legislation'; rather, 'Liberal legislation [was] going through'. Largely because of Liberal pressure, there was 'an unmistakable improvement' in the government, with the joint rural housing scheme providing an example of effective co-operation.[50] Liberalism's prevailing influence was also manifested in the May Committee's appointment and in taxation of land values, the re-introduction of which 'rejoice[d Lloyd George's] heart'.[51] Against further demands for an 'absolute[ly]' independent and straight Liberal course mounted at the NLF conference in May by Hore-Belisha, Rothschild, Shakespeare, and Brown, Lloyd George could claim practical results against the perils of 'Titanic

[47] Cabinets 24, 26, 34(31), 22 and 29 April, 17 June 1931; Lansbury memo, 'Cabinet Crisis of 1931' [early Sept. 1931], Lansbury papers 25.III.n.1–17.
[48] Samuel, Sinclair, and Lloyd George speeches, *Manchester Guardian*, 23 and 25 April, 16 May 1931.
[49] Samuel speeches, *Manchester Guardian*, 15 May, 8 June 1931.
[50] Lloyd George and Samuel speeches, *Manchester Guardian*, 16 May, 8 June 1931.
[51] *HC Deb*, 251, col. 1413, 27 April 1931.

seamanship in politics' and secured an overwhelming victory.[52] With this NLF success, all the leading Liberal institutions had endorsed Lloyd George's strategy.

As the Liberal unemployment initiatives of 1928–30 had been abandoned, the subject chosen for the new 'great campaign' of Liberal revivalism was free trade. Since the Conservative reversion to protection, this had been Samuel's chief preoccupation and main justification for supporting the Labour government. For Lloyd George its value was not just as a safe issue on which to display radical solidarity, but as a central Liberal tenet which could be used to embarrass anti-Labour dissidents and rally the more atavistic Liberals to the party. Maclean, for instance, swallowed earlier enmities and attached himself to the Lloyd George group, leading for them in the budget debates with the argument that 'an emergency budget' was preferable to 'an emergency tariff'.[53] Despite a last minute hitch when Beauchamp, the campaign chairman, fled the country to escape prosecution for homosexuality,[54] the campaign was launched with a Free Trade Convention on 29–30 May. Lloyd George now emerged as a full-blown, born-again Cobdenite. Free trade was presented as the foundation of economic strength, giving Britain sounder finances, higher wages and standards of living, and lower unemployment, than protectionist countries. Protection would cause 'irreparable damage' to British industries. Worse, it was 'the handmaiden of war'. Liberalism would 'advance...fearlessly against the chariots of selfishness, greed, and ignorance, against the legions of international and racial suspicion'.[55]

The Lloyd George Liberals appear genuinely to have believed that free trade was an issue which would preserve and in some degree restore the party's strength. They regarded protectionism – and consequently much of the Conservative advance – as a bubble inflated by economic depression, which would be punctured by a trade recovery. Despite being the defeated candidate at Scarborough and Whitby, Muir, the new NLF chairman, considered 'Free

---

[52] Shakespeare, *Let Candles Be Brought In*, 134–5; *Manchester Guardian*, 16 May 1931; Sylvester diary, 15 May 1931, in Cross, 28.

[53] *HC Deb*, 251, cols. 1479–85, esp. 1481, 28 April 1931.

[54] See, e.g., Lockhart diary, 7 April 1931, 2 Aug. 1932, in Young, 1, 161, 223, and Dalton diary, 16–17 July 1931 (Pimlott, 148–9). Also Christopher Sykes, *Evelyn Waugh* (Harmondsworth, 1977), 164–6.

[55] Speeches, *The Times*, 1, 10, and 26 June 1931.

Trade… still a winning cause when… vigorously presented'.[56] With
Crewe, he began plans to bring together all free-trade Liberals,
Asquithian Liberal Council members as well as the Lloyd Georgians,
in a new effort to restore and finance the party organisation.[57] Yet
while it was still routinely said in public that 'independence' and
'co-operation' were compatible, the Lloyd George Liberal leaders
saw the party's future in some kind of coalition with Labour – in
supplying responsible and effective radical drive to a muddled but
enviably powerful movement. Already signals were being given.
They expressed 'every desire' to help in the proposed establishment
of public utility companies for iron and steel.[58] In an interview for a
leading Labour newspaper in June, Lloyd George spoke of Liberals
having 'a tremendous amount of common ground' with 'that very
able document "Labour and the Nation"'', of having an open mind
on railway nationalisation, and of a need to confront 'the reactionary
money interests in the City'.[59] To Lothian, who attended the weekly
conferences with Labour ministers, it seemed that his long-cherished
hope was nearing achievement – with a 'gradual coalition… between the two parties of the Left' into a 'semi-Socialist progressive
party'.[60]

TOWARDS A CONSERVATIVE BLOC

Conservative politics during the spring and early summer of 1931
were conducted under the conviction that the party would shortly
win a substantial majority at a general election. There was still
criticism of policy and leadership, but for the time being it was in
eclipse. Gretton and other diehard MPs, now concerned that the
party leaders would allow as much to be conceded in disarmament
as they feared was still likely over India, prepared to repeat what
some of them had done in 1922 to stiffen the party. In early July they
formed a group with their own whips to act independently of the
front bench 'if necessary'.[61] But its membership was impressive

---

[56] Muir to Murray, 20 May 1931, Murray papers; Lothian to Stevenson, 29 April 1931,
Lothian papers 260/595-7.
[57] Crewe to Muir, 28 July 1931, Crewe papers C/34.
[58] Cabinet 26(31), 29 April 1931.   [59] Forward, 13 June 1931.
[60] Lothian to Muir, 18 May, 17 June 1931, and to Stevenson, 29 April 1931, Lothian papers
259/433, 258/390-1, 260/595-7.
[61] Gretton to Beamish, 29 May, 3 June 1931, Beamish papers, 4/1; Remer, and Hannon, to
Beaverbrook, July (no day given) and 16 July 1931, Beaverbrook papers B/203, C/155. For
1922 see Cowling, Impact of Labour, 86-7.

neither in numbers nor influence. Churchill was not asked to join, for as calmer thoughts followed the winter's excitements the 'real Tories' remembered his support for Dyer's dismissal in 1920 and judged him unreliable.[62] Churchill tried to use the Cawnpore riots as the basis for renewed agitation,[63] published his recent Indian speeches, and added some new ones, but mostly used the interval before the second Round Table Conference to concentrate upon journalism and authorship. Rothermere pledged support for the Indian Empire Society in the hope of destroying the Irwin–Gandhi pact, but Beaverbrook was so bored by the success of protectionism within the Conservative party that he talked about returning permanently to Canada.[64] Amery complained about retrenchment being given priority over tariffs in party policy, considered that protection was still not being pushed hard enough, and thought there might be renewed attacks upon Baldwin in the autumn. His contribution was a proposal that Beaverbrook, Lloyd, Page Croft, and himself should mount a new campaign of fiscal 'gospel meetings'.[65] But other Conservative leaders, accustomed to Amery being a tariff bore, took no notice, while Page Croft, also worried about lack of a 'crusading spirit', found a more practical device to prevent the leadership backsliding: he obtained the signatures of all but six Conservative MPs for a 'whole-hog' Commons motion.[66] The triumph of protectionism finally exhausted Cecilian dexterity, Salisbury resigning as Conservative leader in the Lords with a private rebuke to Baldwin that they did 'not belong to the same school of Conservatism'.[67] But, recognising a lost cause, he went quietly on the public ground of ill-health. The Chamberlains continued to complain of Baldwin's inability to present policy with real force.[68] Hailsham, perhaps expecting further opportunities to

---

[62] Knox to Sydenham, 24 June 1931, Stuart papers c620/59; Remer to Beaverbrook, July (no day given) 1931, Beaverbrook papers B/203.

[63] Churchill to Reading, 24 April 1931, Reading papers F118/108/3.

[64] Rothermere to Sydenham, 13 May 1931, Stuart papers, c620/52–3. Lockhart diary, 24 June 1931, in Young, I, 176; Beaverbrook to Page Croft, 1 July 1931, Croft papers 1/4/21.

[65] Amery diary, 16 April, 12, 28, and 30 May, 19 and 24 June 1931 (partly in *LSA* II, 161, 164); Amery to N. Chamberlain, 16 April 1931, NC 7/2/52, to Baldwin, 17 April 1931, Amery papers, and to Beaverbrook 9 and 13 May, 19 June 1931, Beaverbrook papers C/5.

[66] Page Croft to Beaverbrook, 24 June 1931, Beaverbrook papers B/192; Croft, *My Life of Strife*, 183.

[67] Salisbury to Baldwin, June 1931, in Middlemas and Barnes, *Baldwin*, 612.

[68] A. to H. and I. Chamberlain, 12 and 21 June 1931, AC 5/1/542, 543; N. to H. and ?I. Chamberlain, 20 and ? June 1931, NC 18/1/744, 745 (first page of latter missing).

succeed Baldwin, cultivated Beaverbrook with flattering requests for
advice and even a spurious offer of the Lords leadership, before
taking it himself.[69]

What mattered more and kept these tensions in check was that the
party now felt like an effective and successful opposition. A Baldwin
speaking campaign had more bite and was received with more
enthusiasm than his similar effort twelve months previously. The
theme now was that in the face of the Conservative party's 'national
policy' there were no longer any 'Socialist strongholds'; there 'was
not a seat in England that could not be won'. Land taxation was an
easy target, attacked as an 'extra tax on... production', a deterrent
to house-building, and a burden as much upon the investments of
trade unions, friendly societies, building societies, and sports clubs as
upon great landowners.[70] Neville Chamberlain gave the party a
fighting lead against the budget, condemning Snowden's 'hasty
descent from... financial righteousness' and his 'sham optimism...
evasions... [and] makeshift expedients... [as] an overwhelming
confession of the total inadequacy of Free Trade to meet modern
requirements'.[71] In the Lords Hailsham threatened, obstructed, and
mutilated on the ground that Conservative peers were now more
representative of the electorate than the government.

Nevertheless, despite rising confidence Conservative leaders from
both party and electoral perspectives felt a need to tread warily and
avoid pitfalls. When MacDonald seemed in a suspicious hurry to
reassemble the Indian Federal Structure Committee, Baldwin had to
protest and insist upon Hailsham becoming an additional Conservative representative in order 'to keep his own party in line'.[72]
Considerable thought was required in responding to League of
Nations Union preparations for the Disarmament Conference, so as
to avoid alienating either peace opinion or Conservative critics of
further disarmament. The solution, at an all-party disarmament
demonstration on 11 July, was for Baldwin to support the Conference
on the argument that British 'one-sided disarmament' had gone far
enough.[73] There were fears that Hailsham's assaults might provoke

[69] Lockhart diary, 10 June 1931, in Young I, 171; Hailsham to Beaverbrook, 16 June, 11 and
14 July 1931, Beaverbrook papers C/150.
[70] Baldwin speeches, *The Times*, 15 and 27 June 1931.
[71] *HC Deb*, 251, cols. 1469–79, 28 April 1931.
[72] Baldwin to MacDonald, 24 May 1931, SB 105/34–7; Dawson diary, 6 June 1931.
[73] Speech, *The Times*, 13 July 1931; and see material for April–July 1931 in SB 129, 133.

a Cabinet and Lloyd George attack upon the Lords' powers, giving them an opportunity to confront Conservatives with a 'peers versus the people' election.[74] Hoare and Chamberlain, believing the alternative vote would not seriously damage the party, wanted Conservative peers to reduce this risk by allowing the Representation of the People Bill to pass. Chamberlain established a Conservative Research Department committee to prepare counter-proposals if the Lords issue erupted.[75]

The most delicate matter was the party's response to the Royal Commission on Unemployment Insurance's report. As early as May Neville Chamberlain recognised that the issue of unemployment payments might have an 'important influence upon the future of the Party'.[76] On both substantive grounds and as a means to embarrass the government and harness retrenchment agitation, Conservative leaders wanted to give it great prominence. They understood that unemployment insurance was now central not merely to budget stability but to national credit. Chamberlain concentrated upon it because if expenditure were not reduced 'the whole Budget crumples up and its falsity is exposed', and because 'foreign observers' had fastened upon the fund as 'the Achilles heel of [the] country'.[77] Baldwin spoke of 'over-borrowing', when linked to an 'unsettled currency' and 'out of gear' exchange system, as a danger to the livelihoods of 'the poor' and the 'workman'. He was also 'perfectly certain that if sacrifices were needed right through the country ... to get a solvent Budget, the country would not be behindhand in making them'.[78]

The problem remained of what to say about the sacrifices expected from the unemployed. Conservative leaders would have agreed that this was 'the most ticklish politico-social issue that has arisen since the war', one full of dangers.[79] Substantial cuts in benefits and entitlement seemed an urgent necessity, but even before the Royal Commission had reported the Labour cry of 'the Tories

---

[74] Astor to Garvin, 23 and 24 April, 8 May 1931, Astor papers; Bayford diary, 7 May 1931, in Ramsden, 246; N. to H. Chamberlain, 25 May 1931, NC 18/1/739.

[75] Hoare memo, 'The House of Commons and the Electoral Reform Bill' [May 1931], Templewood papers VI:2; N. Chamberlain to Gilmour, 11 May 1931, Gilmour papers, GD 383/35; Conservative Research Department papers 1/35/2; Williamson, 'Labour Party and the House of Lords', 338–9.

[76] N. Chamberlain to Hilton Young, 8 May 1931, Kennet papers 16/7.

[77] N. to H. Chamberlain, 6 June 1931, NC 18/1/74, and in *HC Deb*, 251, col. 1475, 28 April 1931. [78] *HC Deb*, 254, cols. 126–32, 22 June 1931.

[79] Editorial, *Manchester Guardian*, 15 June 1931, in Skidelsky, *Politicians*, 316.

will cut the dole' and suggestion of an identity between Conservative intentions and the NCEO's drastic recommendations were thought to be checking the party's advance in by-elections. Party managers, agents, and candidates warned that a detailed response to these attacks would jeopardise general election prospects.[80] Baldwin wished to avoid commitment and to 'wait and see'. Amery thought nothing effective could be done until the economic situation had been improved by a tariff, and other Business Committee members similarly preferred evasion.[81] Neville Chamberlain, however, wanted firm commitment to a transfer of transitional benefit claimants to means-tested public assistance. In forcing this through the Business Committee his attitude was that he 'would rather run the risk of losing the election than give way on what seem[ed] to [him] a really vital matter'.[82] But on testing his idea on a group of MPs and candidates on 1 July, Chamberlain was told 'very strongly' that if made public it would indeed 'lose... the election'. Consequently he accepted that 'it would be fatal' publicly to propose transfer to public assistance, though he thought it unnecessary 'to say that in so many words'.[83]

This conclusion confirmed the Conservative position. It was implied that the government should adopt all the Royal Commission's majority recommendations, the Anomalies Bill was supported, and further extension of borrowing powers was opposed. But while it was stated that Conservatives had a well-prepared policy, the details were withheld. Although Chamberlain developed proposals for constructive unemployment insurance reform in order to shift the emphasis from the dangerous ground of cuts, the Business Committee determined upon circumlocution and evasion. They '[did] not pledge [them]selves not to reduce benefits', while transfer to public assistance would be demanded only when they considered 'the proper time to say it ha[d] arrived'.[84] Plainly the time would be either after the Labour Cabinet had accepted the responsibility and

---

[80] Hudson to N. Chamberlain, 7 May 1931, and Gower to Ball, 6 June 1931, Conservative Research Department papers 1/14/6; Ramsden, *Making of Conservative Party Policy*, 49–50. Cf. Ball, 'Failure of an Opposition', 92–4, and Ball, *Baldwin*, 156–9, which underestimate the potential perils of the retrenchment issue.

[81] A. to I. and H. Chamberlain, early June (no day given) and 12 June 1931, AC 5/1/541, 542; Amery diary, 11 May 1931 (*LSA* II, 160–1).

[82] N. to I. Chamberlain, 9 May 1931, NC 18/1/737.

[83] Headlam diary, 1 July 1931; N. to H. Chamberlain, 4 July 1931, NC 18/1/746; and to Hilton Young, 2 July 1931, Kennet papers 16/8.

[84] N. to H. Chamberlain, 20 June 1931, NC 18/1/744.

unpopularity of initiating drastic cuts, or after Conservatives had reached the safety of a general election victory.

Conservative leaders wanted to win the general election on protection, and to avoid any danger of losing it over unemployment insurance cuts. Much would depend upon the timing of the election, which in turn appeared more than ever to depend upon the attitude of Liberals. For by May it seemed that the Lloyd George Liberals had 'ceased to be an opposition' and might even be given office, and that the Labour government had therefore 'become a majority Government'. This cast some gloom over the party.[85] It provided further reasons for Hoare and Chamberlain wanting Conservative peers to allow passage of the electoral reform bill. This would remove the principal reason for continued Liberal support of the government, while precedent required compilation of a new electoral register to be followed by an early election.[86] The primary objective, however, was still the erosion of Lloyd George's position through creation of an effective Liberal opposition group.

Grigg remained the most active in promoting such a group. In numerous public statements he presented a skilful case for the establishment and central importance of anti-socialist, 'right centre' Liberalism. To reassure residually free-trade Liberals he emphasised the Conservative tariff committee's proposal, announced by Baldwin in July, of a statutory Tariff Commission to determine tariff levels free from illegitimate political and sectional pressures. To Conservatives he argued that by-election abstentions indicated that they could not obtain an independent electoral majority to impose the drastic protection and retrenchment necessary for national recovery. Since a national government was impracticable, it was only through a new Conservative–Liberal Unionist alliance that a truly national majority could be obtained.[87] He spoke for the Conservative candidate at the Gateshead by-election, and claimed his increased poll as proof for Liberal Unionism.[88] He conferred with Simon, Hutchison, Lambert, and Pybus about forming a distinct parliamentary group, and had hopes of Brown and Hore-Belisha. He recruited Kerr to create a party organisation, tried to raise party

[85] N. to H. Chamberlain, 25 May 1931, NC 18/1/739; Amery diary, 8 May 1931.
[86] Hoare in Bayford diary, 15 May 1931, in Ramsden, 246; N. to H. Chamberlain, 6 June 1931, NC 18/1/741.
[87] Pamphlet, 'Three Parties or Two?', abstracted in *The Times*, 8 May 1931.
[88] Grigg to Dawson, and to Maxse, 10 and 11 June 1931, Altrincham papers, and letter in *The Times*, 11 June 1931.

funds, and began negotiations with Conservative party managers about seats for Liberal Unionist candidates.[89] All this was undertaken in close consultation with Chamberlain, through whom he received prominence from Dawson in *The Times*. In early June he prepared proposals for a joint programme, which Chamberlain submitted to the Conservative Business Committee.[90]

Despite this intense activity, progress was slow. This was partly because Grigg's pretensions plainly exceeded the real strength of 'Liberal Unionism'. The Business Committee was 'not very encouraging' towards a programme they thought 'too ambitious', while Stonehaven thought him too demanding in wanting public support before an organisation actually existed.[91] But the main difficulty remained with the dissident Liberal MPs, especially Simon as the only one Conservatives considered eminent enough to lead the movement. Although Simon, Hutchison, Lambert, Kedward, England, Pybus, Murdoch MacDonald, Evans, Brown, and to a lesser extent Hore-Belisha, Rothschild, and Shakespeare now regularly voted independently of the Lloyd George Liberals, they remained hesitant about forming a separate party. Simon discussed organisation with Kerr. But to Grigg's and Chamberlain's exasperation he would 'not lead himself, and yet block[ed] the way to any effective lead' by anyone else.[92]

The reason for the hesitation of Simon and the other dissident MPs was still the issue of tariffs. Apart from their own scruples, they feared that if this was the main feature of their break with official Liberalism their following might be negligible. Simon would go no further than expressing an 'open mind' on the subject.[93] What he wanted was an opportunity to make the break over a 'very definite' issue of anti-socialism.[94] The issue he chose – on which in a 9 June speech Conservatives thought he at last came up to their expectations[95] – was opposition to the government's provisions for

[89] Grigg to N. Chamberlain, and to Bailey, 4 and 12 June 1931, Altrincham papers. See Davidson, *Memoirs of a Conservative*, 372–3 for some Conservatives thinking there were 74 seats where anti-Lloyd George Liberals should be allowed a free run against Labour.

[90] N. Chamberlain to Grigg, 23 April, 10 June 1931, and correspondence May–June 1931, Altrincham papers; Amery diary, 10 June 1931.

[91] N. Chamberlain to Grigg, 10 and 18 June 1931, and Stonehaven to Grigg, 17 and 20 June 1931, Altrincham papers.

[92] N. Chamberlain to Grigg, 8 May, 8 June 1931, and Grigg to Baldwin, to Dawson, and to Rosebery, 9, 10, and 29 June 1931, Altrincham papers.

[93] Grigg to Bailey, and to Rosebery, 12 and 29 June 1931, Altrincham papers.

[94] Simon to Reading, 2 June 1931, Reading papers F118/101.

[95] N. Chamberlain to Grigg, 10 June 1931, Altrincham papers; Hannon to Beaverbrook, 10 June 1931, Beaverbrook papers C/155.

land taxation. Simon's intervention became part of a dispute between and within the Labour and Liberal leaderships. This dispute had major consequences: it pushed the old Liberal party to its penultimate split, and so brought the new polarisation of the party system very close to a conclusion.

THE LIBERAL SPLIT

Initially, the Lloyd George Liberals had been delighted with land taxation, treating it as essentially a Liberal measure. But Snowden's insistence on presenting it as a 'first step towards the nationalization of land' caused unease, and in early June Liberals discovered that it involved an objectionable 'double taxation' – the imposition of land tax in addition to income tax. Lloyd George and Maclean separately warned MacDonald that 'the whole party' was 'in revolt' against this,[96] which was exactly what made the issue so attractive to Simon. He promptly broadened the dispute by arguing that far from being an imitation of Liberal policy, the measure was an instance of socialist muddle-headedness and injustice.[97] Whether in order to retain control of his own party and outflank Simon, or to tighten his grip over the Cabinet or, as he claimed publicly, out of a 'conscientious scruple',[98] Lloyd George himself made exemption of income-taxed land from land taxation a central issue. The Cabinet for their part resented being brow-beaten, and agreed to resist Liberal amendments.

Both the Lloyd George Liberals and Labour ministers expected the other to concede the point, but it soon became apparent that neither would do so. They were stumbling towards a government defeat on an issue with no electoral advantage to either. Consequently frantic efforts were made to manufacture a face-saving compromise. As often before, Snowden responded to pressure with unyielding obstinacy. With MacDonald again feeling that the Cabinet could not survive repudiation of the Chancellor, it was only after desperate appeals to Snowden that the compromise was accepted and a farcical government collapse avoided.[99]

For MacDonald and other leading ministers, this incident was

---

[96] MacDonald diary, 4 and 8 June 1931.
[97] *HC Deb*, 253, cols. 880–92, 9 June 1931.   [98] *The Times*, 12 June 1931.
[99] MacDonald diary, 9–16 June 1931, and MacDonald to Snowden, JRM 1311 (partly in Marquand, 598–601); Sankey note, 'Cabinet June 15, 1931. Snowden's mad obstinacy', Sankey papers c508/78; Samuel note, 1 July 1931, Samuel papers A/76/1.

final proof that Snowden was intolerable in a post from which he could tyrannise the Cabinet. Government reconstruction had become imperative. For Lloyd George the episode had been 'very frighten[ing]'.[100] The damage inflicted by his bluff being called was magnified when on 24 June Snowden revenged his own climb-down by taunting Liberals for inconstancy to Liberal principles.[101] All Liberals found this humiliation hard to swallow. The Lloyd George Liberal leaders told MacDonald that they could no longer attend consultations with Snowden present.[102] Their failure to take stronger action to preserve Liberal 'self-respect' – demonstrating their 'servility to Socialism' – was given by Simon, Brown, and Hutchison as the chief reason why they now resigned the Liberal party whip.[103] Other Liberals followed in declaring 'independence', including Collins, Rosebery, and Allendale, the party treasurer.[104] With the formal departure of Simon and these others from official Liberalism the way seemed clear for establishment of a Liberal Unionist group allied to the Conservatives.

Lloyd George himself made an overture to Conservative leaders in late June, suggesting that if they conceded the alternative vote he was 'quite prepared to consider' defeating the Labour government 'at once'. Neville Chamberlain, who already thought electoral reform a price worth paying for an early general election, treated this seriously and, after consulting Hoare, Austen Chamberlain, and Hailsham, encouraged further negotiations.[105] However, contrary to appearances Lloyd George was not reacting to the land taxation fiasco by seeking a Conservative alliance. His intention was simply tactical, to bamboozle Conservative leaders into persuading the House of Lords to allow passage of an unaltered electoral reform bill.[106] But Hailsham and the Conservative peers refused to fall into

---

[100] MacDonald diary, 14 June 1931. See also Amery diary, 16 June 1931, for Lloyd George 'looking less self-assured than I have ever seen him'.

[101] HC Deb, 254, cols. 535–41, 24 June 1931.

[102] Snowden, Autobiography II, 911–12; MacDonald diary, 1 July (31 June written) 1931.

[103] Brown, and Simon to Sinclair, 25 and 26 June 1931, and Hutchison to chairman of his constituency party, 26 June 1931, all printed in The Times, 29 June 1931.

[104] The Times, 26 and 30 June, 2, 3, and 20 July 1931 for Collins, Allendale, Rosebery, Charnwood, and Joicey; Nicolson diary, 22 July 1931, for Hore-Belisha interest in the New party.

[105] N. to H. Chamberlain, 4 July 1931, NC 18/1/746, and N. Chamberlain diary, 6 July 1931.

[106] When pressed, Lloyd George's suggested time for defeating the government receded from 'at once' to 'by April': N. Chamberlain diary, 6 July 1931. Cf. Fair, 'Politics of Electoral

this trap, and went ahead with their restrictive amendments to the bill.

Much more indicative of Lloyd George's real intentions were his vicious attack on Simon on 3 July – about leaving 'the slime of hypocrisy in passing from one side to another' – and his warm appreciation for Liberals who expressed support for his position during the land taxation incident.[107] Consultations between Lloyd George Liberal leaders and Labour ministers, including Snowden, were soon resumed. At Lloyd George's suggestion it was agreed that there should be joint propaganda on free trade. He also proposed that MacDonald and himself should launch this campaign by appearing together at a public demonstration in the autumn.[108]

Lloyd George and probably Samuel almost certainly began negotiations with MacDonald and Henderson for even closer relations. In early July Henderson spoke of a possibility that 'L. G. & 20 Liberals or so may soon come clear over', in which case 'L. G. might have to come into the Govt. at once'.[109] Firm support from that number of Liberals would have given the government a secure majority. In addition, for Henderson – the chief architect of the Liberal alliance – coalition seemed the logical device for preventing such embarrassments as the land tax dispute, while Lloyd George recommended himself because 'his vitality [was] amazing & his recent speeches ha[d] made a tremendous appeal' to Labour MPs.[110] For MacDonald, coalition with a Liberal remnant might have seemed an acceptable means of obtaining competent ministers in a government reconstruction whose other major feature would be Snowden's removal from the Treasury. For Lloyd George, with the loss of the Liberal right occurring in any event, it might now have seemed possible to persuade his followers to accept the chance of greater influence over the government, while the Liberal party's future was secured by forcing through electoral reform, if necessary invoking the Parliament Act. Tentative proposals on such terms seem to have been the substance behind two notoriously problematic

Reform', 299–300, and Fair, 'Conservative Basis' 144, which treat the overture as seriously intended.

[107] *HC Deb*, 254, cols. 1657–68, esp. 1667, 3 July 1931; Lloyd George to Fisher, and to Murray, both 3 July 1931, Fisher and Murray papers.

[108] Snowden, *Autobiography* II, 915, 922–3. See also *The Times*, 15 July 1931, for Addison attending a meeting of the Liberal parliamentary party, and Lothian to Reading, 17 July 1931, Lothian papers 259/465, for Lloyd George intending 'to back the Government' against Conservative peers.

[109] Dalton diary, 3–5 July 1931 (Pimlott, 147).   [110] Ibid.

items of evidence: a MacDonald remark to Passfield that the solution to the problem of Cabinet reconstruction 'will have to come ... by moves which will surprise all of you',[111] and a Lloyd George claim that he had been offered a senior Cabinet post.[112]

In early July, then, the leading politicians were on the point of replacing the three-party system with two new coalitions, a Labour–Lloyd George Liberal bloc and a Conservative–Simon Liberal bloc. With these they hoped to withstand or take advantage of the conditions expected in the medium-term future – the trouble likely in the autumn from the May Committee report, and either deeper economic depression or else a trade recovery. From 15 July, however, the future again became highly uncertain and other possibilities had to be taken into account as the continental banking crisis reached London.

---

[111] MacDonald to Passfield, 14 July 1931, Passfield papers II:4:1:88a. The interpretation of this statement in B. Webb diary, 20 July 1931 (Cole, 275–6) followed in Bassett, *Nineteen Thirty-One*, 51, 410 – that MacDonald intended going to the Lords – is disproved by MacDonald diary, esp. 11 June 1931. See Skidelsky, *Politicians*, 328–9, and for a further possibility, Williamson, 'Labour Party and the House of Lords', 340.

[112] Lloyd George memo dictated to Frances Stevenson, now lost but printed in Frank Owen, *Tempestuous Journey. Lloyd George, His Life and Times* (1954), 717. There are two difficulties about this document, aside from its disappearance: (i) Owen dated it to 'the last days of July', which has caused confusion (e.g., Campbell, *Lloyd George*, 294–5). The date is certainly incorrect. The memo refers to MacDonald considering a parliamentary adjournment 'early in August', but this was accurate only until a MacDonald announcement of 9 July (*HC Deb*, 254, col. 2276) that the adjournment would be at the end of July. The memo must therefore date from early July. (ii) Lloyd George spoke of becoming Leader of the House of Commons and either Foreign Secretary or Chancellor of the Exchequer. This seems unlikely. Labour MPs would hardly have accepted parliamentary leadership from a Liberal, MacDonald would hardly have trusted Lloyd George with such crucial departmental posts, and Henderson would certainly not have relinquished the Foreign Office. Lloyd George may simply have been boasting to his mistress. If actual posts had been discussed, the proposal was most likely for some non- or lesser departmental post, suitably dressed up to appear more impressive.

PART III

The crisis

CHAPTER 8

The financial crisis: July 1931

[W]ithin a few hours we may have to declare a moratorium,
& ... make big changes in the Govt!
> Thomas reported in Dalton diary, 16–17 July 1931[1]

THE MACMILLAN REPORT

The most significant statement of economic and financial thinking in summer 1931 was the Report of the Macmillan Committee on Finance and Industry, completed in May and published on 13 July. The result of an eighteen-month inquiry conducted against the background of a world depression which transformed the conditions in which the Committee had been appointed, this Report drew upon the accumulated wisdom of its own expert members and fifty-seven witnesses from many schools of thought. On a drafting sub-committee which included Macmillan, Gregory, Brand, and Lubbock, the 'leading spirit' was Keynes.[2] His analysis shaped much of the Report. Even so, he was hardly more successful here than with the EAC or Committee of Economists in securing agreement upon his own prescriptions.

In accordance with a mounting body of opinion, now including so wide a range as FBI and TUC leaders, Hawtrey, Leith-Ross, Strakosch, Blackett, Stamp, and Addis, most Committee members favoured more positive monetary management. They did not, however, recommend devaluation. The gold standard was supported on Keynes's argument of expediency – preserving financial confidence, and ensuring that Britain retained the prestige to supply international leadership. But as a long-term domestic reform a larger, more flexible fiduciary note issue was proposed, to allow greater fluctuation of the gold reserves and increased insulation from

---

[1] Pimlott, 148.   [2] *JMK* xx, 270–1; Macmillan, *A Man of Law's Tale*, 196–7.

world pressures.[3] As a principle of international action, central banks should co-operate in regulating credit in such a fashion as to stabilise world prices, investment, and enterprise. For 'the present emergency' there should be concerted British, American and French provision of cheap credit and loan-guarantees, in order to re-start large-scale international lending and borrowing.[4]

Monetary management and reflation were not, however, unanimous recommendations. The Macmillan Report, even more than that of the Committee of Economists, was based upon an agreement to differ. Instead of Robbins there was now the more considerable figure of Bradbury, a former Treasury Permanent Secretary and major influence on the 1918–25 policy of gold standard restoration. In a dissenting memorandum Bradbury criticised existing policy as already excessively managed, opposed the fiduciary issue proposal as a 'dangerous innovation', and wanted reversion to a fully 'automatic' gold standard. On similar premises Lubbock, the Bank of England's watch-dog on the Committee, expressed doubt that 'positive action' by bankers could relieve the depression. Rather, it was in non-monetary directions that 'the conditions of... revival must principally be sought'.[5]

The chief differences were over emergency domestic proposals. Like almost everyone else, Keynes had moved a good deal since early 1929. He still wanted public works, but if he had won the theoretical argument for loan finance he now conceded the practical obstacles to rapid implementation. He treated public works as a long-term programme of 'capital development' and gave priority instead to a tariffs plus export bounties scheme.[6] McKenna, Bevin, the businessman Frater Taylor, the financier Tulloch, and Co-operative Society executive Allen joined him in proposing tariffs and bounties, capital development, and, as a last resort, a 'national treaty' to obtain equitable reductions of all money incomes.[7] Bevin and Allen differed from Keynes and the rest of the Committee in proposing more radical solutions and a different priority. If international action proved unobtainable, they wanted serious consideration given to

[3] Macmillan Committee, *Report*, paras, 251–8, 322–9.
[4] Ibid., paras. 306, 314–19.
[5] Ibid., pp. 263–81 (Memorandum of Dissent) and 241 (Reservation).
[6] Ibid., Addendum I, paras. 34, 39–52 esp. 48 (*JMK* xx, 296–307). Against the more positive statement on 'development' made to a Liberal party organiser, Keynes to Herbert, 29 May 1931, in *JMK* xx, 527–8, must be set the detached view in Keynes to Martin, 21 April 1931, in *JMK* xxviii, 12–13, as well as that of the Addendum.
[7] Macmillan Committee, *Report*, Addendum I (*JMK* xx, 283–309).

devaluation. Their next preference, before tariffs were tried and certainly before any 'national treaty', was state planning and nationalisation of basic industries, services, and the Bank of England.[8] The cotton-master Lee believed much remained possible by state-assisted industrial rationalisation. The coal-owner Raine wanted outright imperial protectionism.[9] Gregory and Brand reversed Keynes's preferences, like Bradbury rejecting capital development, deprecating tariffs, and arguing for reduction of domestic costs, including wages and salaries.[10]

For the Cabinet, the Macmillan Report repeated the frustration already endured from the EAC. Even if the large areas of disagreement were set aside, it was not clear that those of most agreement provided acceptable or practicable guides for economic recovery. Further capital expenditure had already been rejected as impractical and ineffective, while tariffs divided the Cabinet and would have wrecked the undeclared pact with Liberal leaders which kept it in office. International reflation remained an attractive idea which the Bank of England continued to pursue, but nobody yet knew how to secure American and French co-operation.[11] From the Report's emphasis on action by banks Snowden also concluded that its recommendations were 'in large measure outside the sphere of action by the Government'.[12] Moreover, as sterling had recently been threatened and most City bankers thought international reflation impractical,[13] any attempt by the Bank of England alone to expand credit was likely to encounter problems of confidence quite apart from the question of effectiveness. This would be especially so during an international financial panic, which already existed on the Continent and which almost immediately diverted Treasury and Cabinet attention from the Report.[14] Even in conditions prevailing

---

[8] Macmillan Committee *Report*, 209–10, 239–41 (Reservation to Addendum I, and Reservation to Report).

[9] Ibid., 237–8, 257–62 (Addendum IV, and Raine Reservation).

[10] Ibid., 210–37, 263–4, 279–81 (Addenda II and III, and Memorandum of Dissent).

[11] Snowden to MacDonald, 2 June 1931, JRM 285. For the Bank supporting a BIS committee to encourage long-term lending, and proposed action on medium-term debts, see Norman to Francqui, 27 April 1931, BoE G3/198/173, and BoE Cte, 1 May 1931.

[12] Snowden, *HC Deb*, 225, col. 461, 15 July 1931. Generally, see McKibbin, 'Economic Policy of the Second Labour Government', 108–9 (*Ideologies*, 211–12), and cf. Skidelsky, *Politicians*, 296, and Marquand, 603.

[13] E.g., 'Banking Half-year', *The Times*, 23 July 1931.

[14] At Cabinet 36(31), 1 July 1931, the Report was referred to the Treasury for comment. MacDonald at Cabinet 38(31), 15 July 1931, proposed a sub-committee on the Report, but this was postponed until the Treasury commentary became available: it never did, being overtaken by events.

during the drafting of the Report, the logic of the recommendation shared by most Committee members – acceptance of existing sterling parity – pointed less towards the prescriptions of Keynes than towards those of Gregory, Brand, Lubbock, and Bradbury.

Despite Blackett, Stamp, and Addis, this was the dominant Bank of England attitude. From March the sterling exchanges were firmer, gold losses were recouped, and financial commentators wrote optimistically of re-established 'world confidence in sterling'.[15] But the Bank had no such illusions. It knew that this recovery resulted not from genuine improvements in confidence or in the balance of payments, but from attraction of volatile foreign short funds which might just as quickly be withdrawn. A bank rate reduction in May, to $2\frac{1}{2}$ per cent, reflected despair at the general economic conditions, not hope.[16] Government finance therefore remained a matter of intense concern, and there was a growing sense that, failing international action, national and international recovery required fundamental adjustments. Grenfell, a key figure as Bank director, senior partner of Morgan Grenfell & Co, and Conservative MP for the City of London, stated publicly that any businessman responsible for such accounts as those of the Unemployment Insurance Fund or such a 'faked statement' as the budget would have been gaoled.[17] Norman feared that his appeals to political leaders had 'utterly failed to arouse more than a superficial interest'.[18] Considering Snowden to be 'all right and not at all socialistic' but constrained by socialist MPs,[19] Norman and Sprague tried to help him by privately addressing the Labour party's Currency Group three times during May and June. Their message was the need to reduce British costs to foreign levels.[20] The implication was clear enough. Sprague also delivered well-publicised talks suggesting something similar to Keynes's 'national treaty', including *rentier* taxation, but emphasising wage and salary cuts. Norman spoke privately of a 'deflation of labour'.[21]

[15] *Economist*, 2 May 1931: but see ibid. 25 April, 16 and 23 May 1931.
[16] Howson, *Domestic Monetary Management*, 67–8.
[17] Speeches, *The Times*, and *HC Deb*, 251, cols. 1719–23, both 29 April 1931.
[18] Peacock to Oliver, 1 Aug. 1931, Oliver papers.
[19] Stimson diary, 8 April 1931.
[20] Norman diary, 6 May, 8 and 15 June 1931; Angell, 'Notes on visit to Norman', 8 June [misdated May] 1931, Angell papers M37–3; Kenworthy, *Sailors, Statesmen*, 303–4; Philips Price, *Three Revolutions*, 267.
[21] For Sprague, *The Times*, 13 May 1931; *Journal of the Royal Statistical Society*, 44 (1931) 541–9; and reported in H. D. Henderson to Vincent, 6 June 1931, PREM 1/93. For Norman, Stimson diary, 1 and 7 April 1931.

THE EUROPEAN BANKING CRISIS

Yet although the Bank of England wanted firm domestic 'adjustments', it was still prepared to await future political decision rather than press for immediate action. This remained true even after the onset of banking crises in Austria in mid May and Germany in early June, and of an international crisis of financial confidence in early July – despite long-standing Bank, Treasury, and ministerial fears that a German crisis might have 'awful consequences' for British finance.[22] The dangers were obvious: to City banks lending to Germany, to sterling if similarly embarrassed foreign banks recalled assets from London, and to the budget through loss of reparations receipts. But while it was thought that a German crisis could precipitate a British crisis, it did not seem inevitable that it would do so.[23] Once an international crisis had begun, it was not obvious that it would become a crisis of confidence in British credit. Even when this did become plain, its magnitude was not immediately clear. In understanding the financial crisis and its immense political impact, it is necessary to examine the shifting perceptions of its causes, extent, and possible remedies, which over three months created distinct phases and dramatic changes of pace.[24]

Initial confidence in the British position was sustained for several reasons. Since capital fleeing from Central Europe passed through London, sterling was initially strengthened. By early July total international reserves (gold and foreign currency) were the highest since 1928. As the financial panic was an international phenomenon, the solutions seemed to lie in international, not domestic, measures. Above all, it was hoped that the crisis would force an all-round cancellation of reparations and war debts. This was a longstanding objective of all British policy-makers and commentators, including Keynes. It was regarded as essential for international pacification, economic recovery, financial stability, and smooth operation of the gold standard, and it could be considered a more fundamental contribution to international economic recovery than the Macmillan

---

[22] E.g., Hopkins, Norman, Addis, Grenfell in Hopkins to P. J. Grigg, 19 Aug. 1929, T176/13; Snowden, and Thomas, to MacDonald, 16 and 18 Aug. 1930, JRM 676, 577.

[23] Cf. Moggridge, *British Monetary Policy*, 195, for criticism of 'ineptness'. The account given below is highly selective: for diplomatic context and detail, see Bennett, *Germany and the Diplomacy of the Financial Crisis 1931*; Carlton, *MacDonald versus Henderson*, chs. 10–11; Clarke, *Central Bank Co-operation*, 182–201; Boyce, *British Capitalism*, 313–43.

[24] This account of the British financial crisis from July to mid-August is based upon Williamson, 'Bankers Ramp?' (see also Burk, *Morgan Grenfell*, 146–54). It differs largely in being reinforced by Bank of England evidence.

Committee's majority recommendations.[25] Revision of the peace treaties and of inter-governmental payments was an area where MacDonald, Snowden, Henderson, Norman, and Treasury officials all had well-deserved reputations from negotiation of the Dawes and Young Plans, and could reasonably expect to achieve further successes.

The chief difficulties were French determination to maintain reparations, in order to prevent Germany regaining its pre-war strength, and the expectation of the United States, the chief recipient of inter-governmental payments, of full repayment of war debts. During early June, MacDonald, Henderson, and Norman helped convince the American government that European financial and political stability depended upon all-round suspension of inter-governmental claims. The Hoover moratorium of 20 June, though only for one year and involving a British budget loss of about £11m., was enthusiastically welcomed in London both as immediate assistance to Germany and to international confidence, and as the first step towards cancellation. 'Suspension ought to mean that we shall not make the mistake of resuming.'[26] When French pro-crastination re-started the German crisis and imposed guarantees for resumed reparation payments on the expiry of the moratorium, British policy-makers sought to 'keep the Hoover plan "alive"'[27] and restore the possibility of cancellation. The Cabinet proposed a London conference of all interested governments, asserting that a 'political' initiative was needed to save Germany. More decisively, Norman on 9 July blocked international bank assistance to the Reichsbank. Among his reasons was a belief that the German crisis would be best solved by allowing it to become so desperate that the French and other creditor governments would be compelled to accept cancellation of reparations.[28]

The German crisis did become desperate, on 13 July, when the Darmstadter und Nationalbank suspended payments and the German government ordered temporary closure of all other banks. Foreign credits in Germany were frozen – some £65m.-worth owed

---

[25] E.g., Brand in Macmillan Committee, *Report*, 216–17.
[26] MacDonald diary, 21 June 1931; and see Vansittart notes, 23 June 1931, in *DBFP* 2/ii, 94–6.
[27] Harrison-Norman telephone conversation, 8 am, 9 July 1931, FRBNY Harrison papers.
[28] Harrison–Norman telephone conversations, 8 am, 9 July, and 13 July 1931, FRBNY Harrison papers; Vansittart to MacDonald, 15 July 1931, PREM 1/95; Bennett, *Germany*, 225–6; Clarke, *Central Bank Co-operation*, 196. Other reasons included a belief that the flight from the mark was largely internal, and that German authorities should impose more rigorous controls and deflation.

to City banks – affecting many financial institutions throughout Europe, precipitating a scramble for liquidity and accelerating international capital flights. How far Norman's decision contributed to this panic is uncertain, but given the existing severity of the German crisis the answer is probably very little.[29] Nevertheless for the purposes of achieving cancellation and a major breakthrough for international financial recovery, Norman had accepted some risk to sterling.[30] But he had not appreciated the scale of the risk. The Bank had already given substantial emergency credits to Austria, Hungary, and the Reichsbank, and it had no doubts about its ability to make further temporary loans.[31] Though a Joint Committee of City Bankers was formed to arrange mutual aid, there were no immediate worries about the solvency of City banks.[32] Despite the Bank's fears about Britain's medium-term financial position, confidence in the City's ultimate international strength remained.

So, although the German collapse produced a European financial crisis likened to that of August 1914, the sharp fall in sterling and heavy gold losses marking the start of the British crisis on 15 July were unexpected.[33] Many City analysts could not understand the 'panicky attitude' of continental sterling holders, and interpreted it as a nervous overreaction to the German crisis.[34] The Bank of England, however, immediately understood that if the panic continued the consequences for Britain might be devastating: persistent gold losses jeopardising the gold standard and banks so threatened that bankruptcies could be prevented only by a moratorium,[35] inflicting perhaps irreparable damage to the City's reputation and the nation's foreign earnings.

The violent exposure of the City's vulnerability also had,

---

[29] See, however, German ambassador's aide-memoir and memo, both 13 July 1931, in *DBFP* 2/ii, 181, 184–5.

[30] I owe this point to conversation with Roberta Dayer. See Dayer, *Finance and Empire*, 223–7; also Clarke, *Central Bank Co-operation*, 196–7.

[31] Only the previous day he had been prepared to extend large credits to the Reichsbank: see Harrison–Norman telephone conversation, 2 pm, 8 July 1931, FRBNY Harrison papers. Assertions that the Bank was over-extended (e.g., Norman–Luther conversation, 9 July 1931, in Bennett, *Germany*, 225) were designed to block requests for further credits.

[32] BoE Cte, 9 July 1931; Sayers, *Bank of England*, 503–5; Clay, *Norman*, 381.

[33] *Economist*, 18 July 1931; telegrams, Harrison–Norman, 15–16 July 1931, in Clay, *Norman*, 384; Williamson, 'Bankers Ramp?', 778–9.

[34] *The Times*, 16 July 1931; *Economist*, 18 July 1931. I.e., it was not at first ascribed to those causes identified by historians – continental liquidity problems, fears for the solvency of British banks with German commitments, the revelation in the Macmillan Committee Report of London's short-term indebtedness.

[35] For possible moratorium, see Norman in MacDonald diary, 15 July 1931; Addis in Dalton diary, 15 July 1931 (Dalton, 255).

potentially, large implications for government and politics. Almost everyone – bankers, businessmen, economists, and political leaders – feared that forced devaluation and bank failures might cause general economic disruption, quickly followed by social hardships and political instability: conditions of such unpredictability that no sensible person could expect advantage from them. The chaos inflicted upon Central Europe by the immediate post-war currency derangements was a recent, dreaded, precedent. The much less severe strains in Britain itself during the successive inflation and deflation of 1919–21 had seemed bad enough. Given such fears, it was almost automatically assumed that drastic government action might be justified to defend the banking system and sound money, as represented by the gold standard.

A 'distraught' Norman immediately alerted MacDonald and Snowden of the threat. These warned the Cabinet and then Baldwin and Lloyd George, in case all-party co-operation was required to rush through emergency legislation imposing a moratorium and exchange controls.[36] Yet in this first phase of the sterling crisis the problem was plainly external, so the Bank looked to external solutions. Warning that otherwise a moratorium might be necessary within three days,[37] Norman advised immediate Cabinet action to relieve the German crisis. Late on 15 July MacDonald therefore brought the London Conference forward to the 20th. In the hope that this Conference would place Central Europe on 'a more satisfactory and permanent basis', the Bank then deferred a defensive increase in bank rate.[38]

The Conference announcement steadied the financial markets. But it also reopened differences between the creditor powers, which in turn produced a sharp division among British policy-makers, with important repercussions. MacDonald, Snowden, and Norman had long considered France the principal threat to European stability and believed that successful international action, whether on reparations or disarmament, required resistance to French claims. In

---

[36] MacDonald and Dalton diaries, and Cabinet 38(31), all 15 July 1931; N. Chamberlain diary, 24 July 1931.

[37] Dalton diary, 15 July 1931 (Dalton, 255). In N. Chamberlain diary, 24 July 1931, MacDonald is reported as claiming that Norman asked for a moratorium but that he had replied, 'I won't give it you – you must get through this without a moratorium'. This might be accurate, but was more likely a MacDonald elaboration.

[38] MacDonald diary, and Cabinet 38(31), both 15 July 1931; Norman to Harrison, tm 16 July 1931, in Clay, *Norman*, 384; Harrison-Norman telephone conversation, 3.50 pm, 16 July 1931, FRBNY, Harrison papers.

order to deny the French opportunity to impose new conditions upon German ministers, MacDonald arranged the London Conference to follow immediately after a scheduled visit by Henderson and himself to Berlin.[39]

Henderson in contrast believed the problem of France required conciliation of French opinion, if necessary achieved by pressure upon Germany, and differed further in giving disarmament priority over the reparations issue. When the financial panic broke upon London on 15 July he was in Paris for disarmament talks. Wanting French co-operation over disarmament and indifferent to the terms for quick settlement of the German crisis, yet conscious of differing from MacDonald and Snowden, Henderson without consultation supported French efforts to compel German renunciation of reparations revision and acceptance instead of an international loan tied to political conditions. In order that German ministers could come to Paris to negotiate with the French, he also postponed the British ministerial visit to Berlin.[40]

There were, then, two conflicting British policies – pro-French by the Foreign Secretary; pro-German by the Prime Minister, Chancellor of the Exchequer, and Bank of England. As Henderson's activities became known, there was a furious reaction from London. MacDonald, Snowden, and Norman together sabotaged the loan plan, the first two by refusing Treasury assistance, the last by informing the Germans and Americans that Henderson had no authority in such matters.[41] Henderson's arrangements nevertheless ensured French attendance at the London Conference, because German ministers did concede that the reparations issue should be excluded from its agenda.

The episode was significant firstly for its effect upon the Labour leaders. Neither side interpreted the other's actions simply in terms of different policy assessments. MacDonald attributed Henderson's initiative to 'vanity'; Henderson complained of 'suspicion and jealousy'.[42] Though yet another incidence of long-standing personal

[39] MacDonald diary, 16 July 1931; MacDonald to Henderson, 16 July 1931, JRM 677.
[40] Carlton, *MacDonald versus Henderson*, 200–2, 204–8. For the contrasting attitudes, see MacDonald diary, 5 and 11 July 1931 (French behaviour 'inconceivably atrocious'), and Henderson in Dalton diary, 1 July 1931 ('the Germans are intolerable': Dalton, 254).
[41] Harrison–Norman telephone conversation, 3.50 pm, 16 July 1931, FRBNY, Harrison papers (*FRUS 1931* I, 268–9); Henderson memo, 20 July 1931, Vansittart to Tyrrell, 16 and 17 July 1931, in DBFP 2/ii, 192–3, 204–5, 209, 210–11; Dalton diary, 16 July 1931 (Dalton, 255–6).
[42] MacDonald diary, 16 July 1931; Dalton diary, 20 July 1931 (Dalton, 256–7).

tension, it was one which left little respect and mutual confidence remaining to sustain much further disagreement.

By exposing French rigidity the episode also showed there was little prospect of the seven-power London Conference of 20–3 July achieving reparations revision, especially as the Americans soon proved equally adamant in resisting a review of inter-governmental payments. The British bargaining position had weakened further, as the City's loss of funds since the 15th left the Bank of England without adequate financial resources to assist Germany alone or to provide effective leverage against the French and Americans.[43] Norman was so alarmed – 'frightened to death' according to MacDonald[44] – by daily gold reserve losses of around £2m. that he persuaded Snowden to make one last effort to achieve a radical international solution to the German, and now British, crises. In open conference on the 22nd Snowden attacked every proposal which did not address the 'fundamental cause' of Germany's problems.[45] But MacDonald, though privately sympathetic, as Conference president had to repudiate him in order to preserve French and American co-operation in more limited measures – a standstill agreement to stabilise existing short-term loans in Germany, and a BIS inquiry into German long-term credit requirements.[46]

Over the next few weeks the German banking system was saved by the standstill and financial controls. But the Conference had done nothing to ease the general liquidity panic. Other European financial institutions with funds locked within Germany recalled assets from elsewhere. American banks began to doubt the security of European banks. The entire international financial system was shaken, and London, as the financial centre holding the largest quantity of foreign deposits and bills, now became the principal victim of capital flights. The British crisis remained. Several City financial houses were in difficulties, but most coped by readjusting their assets or borrowing from their clearing banks, and a British moratorium became unnecessary. Only Lazards had to be saved from collapse,

[43] Stimson–MacDonald telephone conversation, 17 July 1931, in *FRUS 1931* I, 271–2; Norman and Leith-Ross on the 19th in MacDonald diary, 22 July 1931; Norman in note of discussion with German ministers, 21 July 1931, T188/30.
[44] MacDonald reported in Stimson diary, 22 July 1931.
[45] Snowden in Conference minutes, 22 July 1931, in *DBFP* 2/ii, 458–61.
[46] MacDonald to Stimson, undated but 22 July 1931, Stimson papers reel 81; MacDonald diary, 22 July 1931.

secretly, by the Bank of England.[47] Pressure was now concentrated on the Bank itself, as the sterling exchanges fell again on 22 July, gold losses increased to £5m. a day and, with the City short of funds, it became difficult to place Treasury bills.[48] On the 23rd the Bank therefore began defensive measures: bank rate was raised to $3\frac{1}{2}$ per cent, foreign currency reserves were used to support the exchanges, and further exchange assistance was obtained from the Bank of France and Federal Reserve Bank of New York.

The Bank of England did not suppose that these measures were adequate. With the failure of the London Conference to provide an international political solution, the British crisis had entered a second phase. It was obvious that a crisis of confidence in sterling itself threatened, as foreign financiers began to doubt the Bank's ability to sustain continued gold losses. Two sets of options were considered for more substantial defensive action. One was to borrow from other financial centres, accumulating sufficient funds to reassure those with demands upon London. French ministers, realising that continued financial panic might ultimately damage French banks, now responded to suggestions made by MacDonald and Snowden during the London Conference and expressed readiness to help by arranging to have credits made available for the Bank of England.[49] The situation had now become so critical that the Bank's earlier objections towards French assistance subsided, and on 25 July Kindersley was sent to Paris for consultations at the Bank of France. With Snowden's permission Norman also arranged to consult J. P. Morgan, senior partner of the British government's financial agents in the USA, about the possibility of a government loan in New York.[50]

Bank credits could supply short-term assistance, and a government loan longer-term defence. But both Norman and Treasury officials thought it unlikely that the government could borrow abroad

[47] Norman and Addis diaries, both 17 and 18 July 1931; BoE Cte, 22 July 1931; Sayers, *Bank of England*, 530–1. For Kleinworts also being in difficulty, see Norman diary, 24 July 1931, and Diaper, 'Merchant Banking in the Inter-War Period', 69.

[48] 'Very Secret' memo to Snowden, unsigned and undated but evidently Hopkins, 24 July 1931 [hereafter described as such], T175/51; *Economist*, 25 July 1931.

[49] Snowden reported in Stimson–Hoover conversation, 21 July, Stimson papers reel 164; MacDonald in Conference minutes, 22 July 1931, in *DBFP* 2/ii, 468; Laval in Stimson diary, 24 July 1931.

[50] Phillips memo, 23 July 1931, T160/435/F12568/1; Hopkins 'Very Secret' memo to Snowden, 24 July 1931, T175/51. For the significance of J. P. Morgan & Co for the Bank and Treasury, see Burk, *Morgan Grenfell*, 126–45.

without first removing all doubts about the soundness of government finances. It also seemed obvious that as distrust of sterling developed, 'the first thing at which foreigners [would] look [was] the budgetary position'. Aware of Britain's deteriorating trade balance, 'excessive production costs', and the City's short-term vulnerability, foreign holders of sterling assets would consider the budget deficit a liability competing with their own claims.[51] That is to say, the international liquidity panic now connected with that linkage between sterling, the budget, and domestic costs which the Bank, City, and Treasury had been nervously observing since the winter. This analysis pointed towards application of the Bank's second set of options, already foreshadowed in Norman's warnings to Snowden during January: an increase in the fiduciary note issue and further sharp rises in bank rate. These measures might restore foreign confidence directly by making more of the gold reserves available for export and imposing deflationary pressures upon the domestic economy, and indirectly by persuading the government to tackle the budget and balance of payments deficits.[52]

The second phase of the crisis was therefore one where the balance of judgement lay between wholly banking expedients to obtain external exchange support, and measures partly intended to force political decisions on internal adjustments. What seemed obvious was the severity of the situation and its likely consequences. As Norman and Treasury officials warned Snowden and MacDonald on 23 and 24 July, there was now 'real danger of our being forced off the gold standard'. If this occurred it was expected that 'the pound would depreciate to an unknown extent', prices of food and imports would increase 'involving all sorts of social and industrial difficulties', and 'commerce and banking would be completely dislocated'.[53] With confidence now the crucial issue, the Macmillan Report offered no help at all. Instead MacDonald instructed Graham to examine immediate trade prospects, and Snowden 'to study [the] Budget situation'.[54]

[51] Hopkins 'Very Secret' memo to Snowden, 24 July 1931, T175/51; and see Norman–Morgan conversation 26 July 1931, in Morgan to J. P. Morgan & Co, tm 31/4894, 29 July 1931, MGC file 'German Crisis 1931'.

[52] Williamson, 'Bankers Ramp?', 780–1. For 'two schools of thought', Norman to Harrison, tm 247/31, 28 July 1931, FRBNY papers. Sayers, Bank of England, 393, is confused over the fiduciary issue increase: for clarification see Williamson, 'Bankers Ramp?', 784, esp. n1.

[53] Hopkins 'Very Secret' memo and 'Supplementary note' to Snowden, both 24 July 1931, T175/51; and see Norman diary and BoE Cte, both 27 July 1931 for possible 'collapse'.

[54] MacDonald diary, 23 July 1931.

THE MAY REPORT

At this point the conclusions of the May Committee on National Expenditure became known. The Committee majority – May, the Liberal nominees Jenkinson and Plender, and the Conservatives Royden and Cooper – were actuaries, accountants, and bankers whose careers and fortunes had been built upon the soundest financial practice.[55] Treating their task as analogous to a company rescue, they relentlessly expressed views now widely held in the financial and business communities. Government accounts were strictly calculated, to include not just conventional budget charges but borrowing for the Unemployment Insurance Fund and Road Fund, and full maintenance of the Sinking Fund.[56] On these criteria the budget deficit for 1932–3 was estimated as £120m., which, given contemporary expectation of budgets balancing at around £750m., was a frightening figure.

The Committee majority thought existing taxation already appropriated 'an unduly large proportion of the national income'. The deficit was ascribed wholly to expenditure growth, treated as a 'mistake' which had added to national 'burdens' and become 'definitely restrictive of industrial enterprise and employment'.[57] The problem was political irresponsibility. Facing an electorate ignorant of national economic problems and demanding '"reforms"' – in reality 'mostly...privileges or benefits for particular classes at the cost of the general taxpayer' – 'all parties' had bought support with 'lavish promises'. Successive governments had undertaken 'expensive schemes' without 'a careful balancing of national interests'. Blame was attached partly to the 1924–9 Conservative government, but mostly to the 1924 and 1929 Labour governments.[58] As between 'politics' and 'finance' there was no question which had

---

[55] Jenkinson, Plender and Cooper had been prominent in reconstruction of financially unstable businesses; Jenkinson especially was a 'zealot about purity and accuracy of accounts'. See details in *Dictionary of Business Biography* and *Who was Who*.

[56] Committee on National Expenditure, *Report* [hereafter May Committee *Report*], paras. 3, 27–30, 564. No minutes of evidence or even a list of witnesses were published: see MacDonald in *HC Deb*, 256, cols. 511–13, 14 Sept. 1931, refusing information. No private committee papers have survived.

[57] May Committee *Report*, paras. 23, 31–2, 25.

[58] Ibid., paras. 22, 573–4, 2–7. See McKibbin, 'Economic Policy of the Second Labour Government', 114 (*Ideologies*, 217), for 'spurious even-handedness'. Jenkinson, in a Reservation (May Committee *Report*, 225–6) blamed poor analysis and accounting procedures rather than political misappropriation.

to give way: 'a solution has to be found if democracy is not to suffer shipwreck on the hard rock of finance'.[59]

The budget problem was not, therefore, 'a transient feature to be bridged by temporary expedients'. Removing the deficit wholly or largely by taxation would aggravate current economic difficulties; only strict economy could restore trade and employment.[60] The Committee majority would have preferred retrenchment alone, as part of a reduction of incomes throughout the community. But failing that it left some £25m. to be met by taxation, preferably not involving 'further burden[s] on productive industry'.[61] Their proposed economies totalled £96·5m. The criteria for selecting these included falls in living costs; an even narrower interpretation of 'economic benefit' for public works than the Treasury's; and a view that whereas long-established expenditures had stood the test of time and created rights and vested interests, there was 'a powerful argument' that if 'the nation did without [a service] a few years ago...it cannot be essential'.[62] The recommendations included some administrative savings, and pay reductions for police and pre-1925 entrants to the fighting services. But the proposed cuts were mostly concentrated in employment schemes and social services: less road-building, land drainage, afforestation, and house-building; reduced doctors' fees and educational grants; a 20 per cent cut in teachers' salaries. The largest saving, £66·5m., was on unemployment insurance. The Royal Commission's interim recommendations were adopted on cessation of borrowing and limitation of benefit to twenty-six weeks, but exceeded with new proposals to raise contributions to 10d., apply a means test for all transitional benefit – and, on the cost of living criterion – to reduce standard benefit by 20 per cent.

These proposals constituted an attempt to reverse much of the post-war social and unemployment policies. The budget had been unbalanced and the economy burdened by what was assumed to be largely unnecessary, wasteful, and counter-productive expenditure upon improving working-class living conditions.[63] On such reasoning, it seemed perfectly in order for the working classes to sacrifice most.

The majority Report raised starkly the fundamental issue of 'sound finance' as against 'social justice' and, indeed, 'democracy'.

---

[59] May Committee *Report*, para. 574.   [60] Ibid., paras. 31, 29, 565, 567.
[61] Ibid., paras. 569–70.   [62] Ibid., paras. 32, 272, 274–8, 358, 565.
[63] For specific examples, see ibid., paras. 277, 471, 501–2.

Here it was contradicted in a minority Report by the Labour nominees, Pugh, a TUC General Council member, and Latham of the Automobile Trades Association. Following TUC thinking, they treated the budget and economic difficulties as resulting less from public expenditure than 'the policy of deflation...and return to the gold standard', aggravated by the world price fall.[64] They accepted some administrative savings, the cut in police and fighting service incomes, and a reduction in teachers' salaries, though by $12\frac{1}{2}$ per cent only. But for them policies accepted by Parliament and the electorate were irreversible: social service and development expenditure could not be 'irresponsible'. It was 'a matter for gratification' that all parties had undertaken expenditure 'consistent with the right and proper course of democratic government and progress', and reducing 'the past inequitable distribution of the national income'. Such expenditure was of 'the highest social and economic value'. By improving the economic structure and the population's health and efficiency this was 'essential' to modern industry, and so represented true economy.[65] It would also be 'unfair' to impose sacrifices upon the principal victims of economic depression without comparable sacrifices from 'others more favourably situated'. Sacrifices should be 'common to all and in proportion to...ability to bear the burden'. This was especially appropriate because the real waste was 'luxury' spending by private individuals; because the greatest proportionate increase in expenditure was actually payments on the National Debt; and because holders of such fixed-interest securities had received the most 'effortless benefits' from the price fall, and should accordingly be the first subjected to any cost of living test. For Pugh and Latham, the 'equitable' solution was taxation of British holders of National Debt and other fixed-interest-bearing investments.[66]

The two reports, then, placed the burden of restoring budget equilibrium upon two different social classes. The minority had, however, accepted the majority's calculation of the budget deficit. This total of £120m. was what most impressed, and alarmed, financial and political opinion. In terms of most current thinking and discussion, the majority recommendations seemed by far the more pertinent. During a crisis of financial confidence, giving priority to taxation of investments seemed not merely irrelevant but

[64] May Committee, Minority Report, 270. [65] Ibid., 227–29, 232, 260–3.
[66] Ibid., 228, 230, 235–9, 270.

dangerous. The minority Report was ignored – except by the TUC General Council.

The Committee majority ensured that the Report was completed before the Parliamentary summer recess, believing that preparations for implementing retrenchment should begin 'immediately', ready for legislation in the autumn. Its main conclusions were known to Snowden, Hopkins, and Norman on 23 July.[67] None thought the sterling crisis a reason to postpone the Report's publication. Though realising the exposure of a huge budget deficit would have a 'devilish' effect upon financial confidence,[68] they assumed the Bank of England could ride out the immediate strain. For them the risks of publication were exceeded by the Report's importance as a contribution to the solution of the crisis.

Despite Norman's knowledge of Snowden's views, he remained 'much disturbed because the Government pa[id] no attention to his repeated warnings and seem[ed] to be looking forward to an indefinite period of unbalanced budgets'. As expected, Morgan's reaction on 26 July to the proposed British government loan was that 'before they could wisely borrow in USA the Government would have to show at least some plan of restoration of financial stability and should at least have expressed the intention to reduce expenditures to come within their means'. Norman thought this market assessment 'quite right', because 'you cannot make a loan unless your house is in order'.[69]

In these circumstances the May Report served the Bank's purposes precisely, placing the Cabinet under political pressure to respond immediately with statements of intent and in the near future with definite measures. It contributed to the Bank's decision on 28 July to put its first option of foreign borrowing into 'abeyance'. Kindersley reported that French credits were available, and London clearing banks agreed to co-operate in borrowing arrangements.[70] But the German panic now seemed to be subsiding, the Bank's exchange support operations had stopped the gold drain to France, and a Joint Committee of City bankers gave assurances that their institutions

---

[67] May Committee *Report*, paras. 39–40. Hopkins 'Very Secret' memo to Snowden, 24 July 1931, T175/51, and Norman reported by Baldwin in N. Chamberlain diary, 24 July 1931.

[68] Harrison–Norman conversation, 29 July 1931, in Moggridge, *British Monetary Policy*, 195.

[69] Norman on 26 July, reported in Morgan to J. P. Morgan & Co., tm 31/4894, 29 July 1931, MGC file 'German Crisis 1931'; Peacock to Oliver, 1 Aug. 1931, Oliver papers; Harrison–Norman conversation, 29 July 1931, in Clarke, *Central Bank Co-operation*, 205.

[70] Harvey in Hopkins memo, 'French discussions', 28 July 1931, T175/56; Hopkins to Snowden, 'Secret', 27 July 1931, T175/51; BoE Cte, 27 July 1931.

could, without serious risk, comply with the London Conference standstill recommendations. Sterling remained weak, but it appeared that the crisis was being contained. With strong support from leading City bankers, the Bank of England therefore decided to deal with residual gold losses to Holland, Belgium, and Switzerland and with the expected impact of the May Report by measures intended both to strengthen market confidence and to sustain pressure upon the Cabinet – the Bank's second option of 'self-help with action at home'. On 29 July preparations began for a three-month increase of the fiduciary issue from £260m. to £275m., and on the 30th bank rate was raised to 4½ per cent.[71]

At the Treasury Hopkins thought the May Committee majority's budget calculations 'show[ed] no mercy', and 'exaggerated' the problem. On conventional criteria – excluding the Unemployment Fund and Road Fund deficits – his own estimate of the prospective budget deficit for 1932–3 was £70m. Nevertheless the principle of the majority Report was in line with Treasury thinking, and Hopkins knew 'the figure of £120m. will be flashed around the world'. Henceforth that would be the operative figure, the one to which foreign financiers would look. Consequently something very like the majority's recommendations would become necessary to restore foreign confidence in British credit. The Report was decisive: either it would 'mark a long step in our downward career' or it 'must be the beginning of our recovery'. Hopkins therefore advised Snowden that the Report's publication had to be accompanied by a clear indication that it would be acted upon. An announcement should be made of a Cabinet committee to prepare budget proposals during the summer recess for immediate presentation when Parliament reassembled.[72]

For Snowden, the majority May Report and the Bank of England and Treasury warnings of a sterling crisis were confirmation of his own advice since January. In accordance with his strategy for securing retrenchment while defusing its potentially explosive political effects, he now aimed to manoeuvre the Cabinet, Labour MPs, and the Liberal and Conservative parties together into serious treatment of the May Committee majority Report. This required preparation and time, making it desirable to avoid parliamentary

---

[71] Norman to Harrison, tm 247/31, 28 July 1931, FRBNY papers; Harvey in Hopkins memo, 'French discussions', 28 July 1931, T175/56; Goodenough to Norman, 27 July 1931, BoE G1/468/4271/3; BoE Cte, 27 and 29 July 1931.
[72] Hopkins 'Very Secret' memo to Snowden, 24 July 1931, T175/51.

5 Sir Richard Hopkins (Controller of Finance, The Treasury)

debate before the recess and imperative to avoid renewed financial
panic. The Bank was instructed to avoid any foreign borrowing
arrangement which might need parliamentary approval, and was
encouraged to prefer making more gold available with the assistance

of the fiduciary issue increase.[73] Publication of the May Report
appears to have been deliberately delayed until the last day of the
session. Yet on the principle that the Committee was an all-party
matter advance copies of the Report were given in confidence not
just to Cabinet ministers but to the Liberal and Conservative
leaders. On Snowden's further principle that 'no Government could
carry out drastic economies without the support of the whole House
of Commons', these were asked to consult their colleagues and then
meet ministers during the recess for 'joint consideration' of the
Report.[74]

'NATIONAL GOVERNMENT' REVIVED

Just as during July the financial crisis fell into two phases, so there
were two successive effects for government and party politics. Both
had a large potential to disrupt the existing relationships between
parties, injecting new uncertainty into what had seemed since the
start of the year to be an increasingly settled pattern for the future.
The first, on the 15th, was the prospect of a moratorium within a
matter of days, requiring immediate exchange controls and then
organisation of an early resumption of payments. The second, from
the 24th, was the prospect of reassuring foreign financial opinion
over the succeeding weeks or months, by tackling the budget
problem as revealed by the May Report. While the first concerned
matters of high banking and monetary policies, the second involved
central issues of party conflict. Most ministers and leading politicians
treated the two as politically distinct; but some carried over ideas
stimulated by the first into their thinking about the second.

Unless very carefully presented, a moratorium might easily
precipitate the result it was intended to prevent: a sudden collapse
of confidence in British financial institutions and sterling, with
massive damage to trade, industry, and employment. A minority
Labour government alone, itself responsible for allowing the budget
deficit to accumulate, patently had little chance of sustaining foreign
confidence during a moratorium and providing satisfactory assurance of resumption. It might have succeeded with public support
from the Liberal and Conservative parties, which on such an issue
would undoubtedly have been given. Nevertheless the 'national

---

[73] Hopkins 'Secret' note, 27 July 1930, T188/30; BoE Cte, 27 July 1931.
[74] Snowden to Samuel, 5 Aug. 1931, and Samuel memo, 13 Aug. 1931, Samuel papers
A/78/1, 3; and see MacDonald in *HC Deb*, 256, col. 290–1, 10 Sept. 1931.

government' idea instantly re-emerged. Soon more political leaders had become interested in it than at any previous time. This had been anticipated as early as 11 July by Wigram, the royal secretary, who expressed both the quality of the Palace's financial and political intelligence and its wishful thinking in advising the King that a German crash and British moratorium could make it 'quite possible that Your Majesty might be asked to approve of a National Government'.[75] The sudden revival of the idea testifies to the extent to which private discussion, public advocacy, and rumour during late 1930 had created an expectation that if an emergency were to occur a coalition might be desirable or else difficult to avoid.

Cabinet ministers were shaken by the reported threat to the banking system on 15 July. Since few pretended to understand international finance they were bewildered and frightened, and glad to leave to MacDonald and Snowden 'decision on all matters arising out of the... crisis'.[76] They entrusted the matter to these two even though MacDonald said that 'if a moratorium became necessary [the] Government would have to go out of office and a national government be formed in its place'. The suggestion was not considered sinister. According to Lansbury, '[n]o one raised any objection':

it was felt... that if such a financial crisis as necessitated a moratorium did arise, it would be better that all parties should be responsible... [W]e ourselves were only a minority and could not, even if we wished, get emergency powers to take over the banks and control credit.[77]

Henderson was in Paris, but MacDonald informed him by telephone and the matter was raised on his return. His principal concern was to secure party acquiescence: to ensure that a national government was 'seriously considered and approached in the proper way' by reference to 'a specially convened Labour conference'.[78]

For not just MacDonald but for all Cabinet members, the notion of a 'national government' was a reflex to a horrifying financial and

---

[75] Wigram to the King, 11 July 1931, RA GV M2329/2 (Nicolson, *George V*, 449). See Amery diary, 4 Aug. 1931 (*LSA* II, 190) for Seely as one possible influence.

[76] Cabinet 38(31), 15 July 1931.

[77] Lansbury memo, 'Cabinet Crisis of 1931', early Sept. 1931, Lansbury papers 25.III.n.

[78] Henderson speeches in *TUCAR 1931*, 400, 10 Sept., and *HC Deb*, 256, col. 28, 8 Sept. 1931. See Dalton diary, 28 Aug. 1931 (Dalton, 280) for Henderson in Paris, also 16–17 July (Pimlott, 148: epigraph to this chapter) for Thomas. Although the Lansbury and Henderson evidence is retrospective, in both cases the fact that it dates from after the August events positively strengthens its reliability.

economic prospect. It related to a genuine 'national' issue with little consequence for party principle, though control of banks had 'socialist' connotations. As an arrangement to face an emergency, it implied no permanent alteration of the party system. As it depended upon a contingency, it was not a settled objective. So, in contrast, five days later MacDonald asked departmental ministers to search for some 'big and desirable piece of legislation' to strengthen the Labour government's position during the autumn parliamentary session.[79] Rumours that MacDonald and other ministers had spoken of 'national government' soon reached Labour MPs and Labour newspapers, arousing the obvious misunderstandings and suspicion of treachery.[80] Yet knowledge of the circumstances and of united Cabinet support (especially that of Henderson and Lansbury) would almost certainly have smothered serious party criticism.

MacDonald perhaps mentioned 'national government' when informing Baldwin and Lloyd George of the possible moratorium. But in any case both had enough experience of the idea to anticipate its revival. Lloyd George immediately understood that existing alignments, including the Lloyd George Liberal–Labour government alliance, might be overturned either very soon or whenever the financial crisis got out of hand. He claimed to have 'every reason to believe that Baldwin and Ramsay at the slightest drop in the pound will come together in a Coalition'.[81] The prospect appeared to present him with an attractive possibility, but also with a large danger. So, preparing for every eventuality, he responded in three ways. The possibility was the admission of himself and other Lloyd George Liberals into a 'national' Cabinet. His first response, shortly after 15 July, was to make it plain to Conservative leaders that he would expect this: he had 'come to the conclusion that matters [were] working up to a crisis', and that 'by the autumn the situation of the country [might] be so serious that only a National Government [would] be able to deal with it'.[82] The danger was that, with the

[79] MacDonald to heads of departments, 20 July 1931, JRM 385.

[80] Dalton diary, 16–17 and 22 July 1931 (Pimlott, 148; Dalton, 257, 287); *Daily Herald*, 20 July 1931; *New Leader*, 24 July 1931. Brockway, *Inside the Left*, 216, seems based upon a misdating. The episode became the source for many later suggestions of a MacDonald plot: see, e.g., Cripps in Dalton diary, 5 Sept. 1931 (Dalton, 281), and Lansbury contradicting his own memo in B. Webb diary, 27 Aug. 1931 (Cole, 285).

[81] Nicolson diary, 21 July 1931 (Nicolson I, 81).

[82] Lloyd George reported by Kingsley Wood in N. to H. Chamberlain, 18 July 1931, NC 18/1/748; N. Chamberlain diary, 24 July 1931.

Simon group available as alternative Liberal candidates for office, Conservative leaders might want to exclude the Lloyd George Liberals, and that MacDonald and Snowden might seize the opportunity to escape from dependence upon them. So Lloyd George's second response, on 21 July, was to guard against becoming altogether marginalised by gathering Churchill, as principal Conservative dissident, and Mosley, as New party leader, with their respective lieutenants, Sinclair, Bracken, and Nicolson, to propose formation of a 'National Opposition' to any MacDonald/Baldwin-led national government.[83]

For Mosley, the Lloyd George proposal promised achievement of his objectives since the autumn: a national union of activists, restoring himself to the political centre, against 'old gang' leaders and party machines. In this context a New party crisis on 23 July, when Strachey and Young resigned, accusing Mosley of 'fascism', could be presented as a timely purge of its left wing which would facilitate alliance with Churchill and Lloyd George.[84] Churchill, however, treated Lloyd George's proposal as merely an amusing speculative game. Now intent upon retaining contact with the main body of Conservatives over the Indian issue, his contributions were not 'constructive'.[85] It was, in truth, difficult to see on what shared policy basis a Lloyd George–Churchill–Mosley opposition might operate, or to imagine where it might recruit substantial par-liamentary and electoral support. Nor did it seem likely that many of Lloyd George's Liberal followers would join it. Lloyd George's third response, apparent on the 22nd, was therefore to steel himself to possible disappointment: 'he would certainly not oppose...He would sit quiet, otherwise it would be said that he was crabbing a national government'.[86]

Lloyd George did not know how prophetic his statement was to be. Four days later he fell seriously ill and a prostate gland operation was arranged for 29 July. Consequently it was his deputy, Samuel, whom Snowden approached to make arrangements about the May Report. This probably made little difference to the Lloyd George Liberal response, given their responsibility for the May Committee's appointment and public commitment to retrenchment, yet at the

---

[83] Nicolson diary, 21 July 1931 (Nicolson I, 81–2). For Lloyd George's sense that MacDonald and Baldwin might want him 'out of it', see Sylvester diary, 22 July 1931, in Cross, 31.
[84] Nicolson diary, 23 July 1931 (Nicolson I, 82–3).
[85] Nicolson diary, 21 July 1931 (Nicolson I, 82).
[86] Sylvester diary, 22 July 1931, in Cross, 31.

same time their alliance with the Cabinet and desire to secure the Representation of the People Bill, which remained on the parliamentary timetable for the autumn.[87] They had every reason to help the Cabinet turn the 'awkward corner' so patently facing it in the Report. Samuel consulted the Advisory Committee of Liberal leaders, who after discussion left Reading, now Beauchamp's replacement as Liberal leader in the Lords, and Maclean, mover of the original Commons resolution for an Expenditure Committee, to confer with him over the reply to Snowden. They offered support 'in every way in any practicable measures of economy...based on the Report' and, sharing Snowden's concern to disperse political responsibility as widely as possible, declared themselves 'very ready to co-operate' in any three-party action.[88] By this Reading, who feared the Cabinet would 'only go a little way' towards retrenchment,[89] would certainly have included the possibility of 'national government'. But Samuel and Maclean had not previously shown interest in that idea, and despite the seriousness of the political prospects probably expected simply an arrangement to attach temporary Conservative parliamentary support to the Labour–Lloyd George Liberal alliance. Maclean on 30 July spoke publicly of the situation being 'beyond the power of the Government to handle adequately alone', and possibly requiring 'that a majority of the House of Commons should resolve itself into a Committee of Public National Financial Safety'[90] – a version of the 'Council of State' notion.

Contrary to Lloyd George's suspicions, Baldwin remained hostile to 'national government'. From frequent meetings with Norman and, in late July, conversations with Grenfell and Morgan, he was well-informed about the financial crisis and 'very worried' by it.[91] Yet in a speech two days after the 15 July moratorium scare he rejected 'national government' as neither 'possible or necessary', again raising disagreement over imperial protectionism as the insuperable obstacle. After early intimation of the May Committee

[87] For timetable, Snowden in *HC Deb*, 255, col. 2294, 29 July 1931.
[88] Samuel to Snowden, 29 July 1931, T172/1741; Samuel memo, 13 Aug. 1931, Samuel papers A/78/3; Hobhouse to Sinclair, 30 July 1931, and Sinclair to Hobhouse, 1 Aug. 1931, Thurso papers III/3/5; Foot quoted by Ede in *HC Deb* 256, col. 61, 8 Sept. 1931.
[89] Reading to Samuel, 30 July 1931, Samuel papers A/155/VIII/24.
[90] *The Times*, 31 July 1931.
[91] Norman diary, 9 June, 2 and 22 July 1931; Grenfell to Morgan, 21 July 1931, MGC file 'German Crisis 1931'; Amery diary, 28 July 1931 (*LSA* II, 166).

recommendations from Norman, he remained determined that all talk of 'national government' should be 'stamped out'. When asked by Neville Chamberlain he denied that MacDonald had 'ever' approached him on the subject, notwithstanding MacDonald's 1 December sounding.[92] When Snowden consulted him about the May Report, Baldwin agreed to send him the Conservative leadership's impressions within two or three weeks. Yet although the Business Committee discussed the financial situation on 29 July, he made no arrangements for replying to Snowden during the recess.[93]

Baldwin was prepared to support the government in emergency exchange measures obviously 'necessary for the national interest', but was clear that these and the treatment of the May Report were its responsibility alone. The Labour government should govern: if it could not, it should resign. The Conservative party's position as alternative government was not to be compromised. Above all the Labour government's effort to nationalise its own impending crisis over the budget had to be resisted. If MacDonald proposed a 'national government', Baldwin would 'refuse unhesitatingly'. Labour and its supporters must 'learn its lesson'. Its 'entirely false ideas on Finance and Economics' which were undermining the country's 'economic foundations' had to be exposed, and this would best be achieved by the Labour government imposing cuts and demonstrating that 'even a Socialist government must have sound finance'. If it refused and left office, it would have admitted its own irresponsibility, failure, and unfitness, and Conservatives would be certain to win the next election.[94]

Even so, it seemed possible that if the sterling crisis became desperate public pressure for a 'national government' might become irresistible. Baldwin was not only concerned to prevent such pressure developing; his instinct was to suppress even private speculation about what the party might do in those circumstances, in case such thinking became self-fulfilling. The attitude of other

---

[92] *The Times*, 18 July 1931; N. Chamberlain diary, 24 July 1931. For 1 December see above, p. 160.

[93] Snowden to Samuel, 5 Aug. 1931, Samuel papers A/78/1; Amery diary, 29 July 1931 (*LSA* II, 167). No Conservative source mentions Baldwin's communication with Snowden, or advance copies of the May Report. Though Treasury files contain Samuel's reply to Snowden, there is none from Baldwin.

[94] Steel-Maitland to Baldwin, 28 July 1931, Steel-Maitland papers 94/2, arising from discussion with Baldwin, and plainly reflecting his views: see Baldwin in N. Chamberlain diary, 24 July 1931.

Conservative leaders was, however, less negative. As in December, Amery persuaded himself that a 'national government' might advance the cause of imperial protectionism, and now promoted the idea that any emergency government should be on 'war cabinet lines'.[95]

Much more significant was a rapid development in Neville Chamberlain's thinking. 'National government' had not previously interested him, and he had emphatically dismissed the idea as recently as 6 July. Yet after the 15th he 'began to take the idea very seriously'. The initial reason was not simply the financial crisis, but the effect of Lloyd George's expression of interest in 'national government', inflaming Chamberlain's deep-rooted fear and hatred towards him. Chamberlain immediately assumed that Lloyd George would work hard to achieve 'national government', and might be able to manoeuvre the Conservative party into a dangerous position. If the financial situation became really serious and there was a 'very powerful movement' for 'national government', perhaps supported by the Rothermere and Beaverbrook press, and if Conservative leaders then refused to join a MacDonald emergency cabinet but Lloyd George agreed, the result might be a Labour–Liberal 'national' coalition much stronger than the existing government. Lloyd George could then play the patriot, and would be poised to regain dominance over a Cabinet. Faced with such a prospect of a patriotic non-Conservative alliance, leaving Conservatives exposed to public criticism and electoral defeat, Chamberlain thought that Conservative leaders might instead prefer to enter a 'national government'.[96]

Neville Chamberlain no more wanted a 'national government' than did Baldwin, but there were real and important differences between them. Unlike Baldwin, Chamberlain accepted that there might just be conditions where, if only defensively, it could be to the party's advantage to join such a government. He also thought Conservative leaders had to be mentally prepared for such a contingency. Early information about the May Report's contents intensified his concern, which by the end of July had become independent of fears about Lloyd George. After Baldwin had

[95] Amery diary, 19 and 23 July 1931, also 3 and 4 Aug. 1931 (partly in *LSA* II, 165, 166, 190).
[96] N. to H. Chamberlain, 18 July 1931, NC 18/1/748; N. Chamberlain diary, 24 July 1931. For Chamberlain speaking 'with great hatred about LlG', see Lady Hilton Young diary, 22 July 1931. For 6 July, see above p. 233.

repeatedly declined to discuss the matter seriously with him, Chamberlain undertook the preparation himself. Following the Business Committee meeting on the 29th, he 'exchanged ideas' with his closest collaborators – Hoare, Cunliffe-Lister, Hailsham, and Austen Chamberlain. Like Neville Chamberlain none wanted a 'national government' or thought it a '*very* probable' prospect; but they 'agreed that it might become unavoidable'. Whereas Baldwin thought tariffs would and should be an obstacle to coalition, they considered that in an emergency tariffs could be made the condition for a coalition.[97]

CRISIS POSTPONED?

By the end of July, then, 'national government' had been restored to a high place on the political agenda. Stimulated by considerable press comment,[98] it was now regarded more seriously than during the previous October to December. Its status remained unchanged – a last resort, not an objective – but with sterling in a fragile state, uncertainty had become more intense: the political system seemed more susceptible to some breakdown which might disrupt 'normal' expectations. None desired the financial conditions which might make 'national government' an immediate issue. With the threat of a moratorium lifted, everyone hoped that the Labour Cabinet would be able to act upon the May Report in more stable conditions in the autumn. In their separate ways, Snowden, Neville Chamberlain, and the Bank of England directors between them tried to make this certain. As a result the political season ended in what would, just ten days previously, have seemed a surprisingly calm atmosphere.

At the last Cabinet before the recess, on 30 July, MacDonald and Henderson had just returned from their postponed two-day visit to Berlin. This had been a success, and the meeting was 'very "cordial and jovial"'.[99] In connection with the European financial crisis MacDonald warned that 'there might be emergencies' during the recess, and that ministers should therefore be prepared to return 'in case of urgent necessity'. After reports on various other matters, in

[97] N. Chamberlain diary, 24 July 1931; N. to H. Chamberlain, 2 Aug. 1931, NC 18/1/750; A. to I. Chamberlain, 2 Aug. 1931, AC 5/1/550. Ball, 'Conservative Party and Formation of the National Government', 161, and Ball, *Baldwin* 173–4, mistakenly assumes an identity of thinking between Baldwin and other Conservative leaders.

[98] E.g., Editorials in *The Times*, 18 and 31 July 1931; *Morning Post*, 29 July 1931, and see references in note 80 above.

[99] B. Webb diary, 4 Aug. 1931 (Cole, 277).

accordance with Snowden's desire for time and preparation the May Report received only 'preliminary discussion'[100] – even though it plainly placed the Cabinet 'in a very tight place'.[101] No minister raised any question about its publication or its consequences for financial confidence. Following Hopkins's advice to Snowden, a Cabinet economy committee of MacDonald, Snowden, Henderson, Thomas, and Graham was appointed to meet on 25 August, to receive departmental observations and prepare recommendations.[102]

Chamberlain, learning of City fears that a parliamentary row about financial policy might further disturb financial confidence, with Business Committee agreement offered to pull his punches in a debate later on 30 July, in return for an assurance of Cabinet preparation of retrenchment measures during the recess. Snowden 'at once jumped at the offer', agreeing with Chamberlain on the seriousness of the situation and the need for 'the country ... to face up to ... realities'.[103] Accordingly, though Chamberlain reiterated criticism of the April budget, he expressed confidence in the stability of the financial system. Snowden again warned of the dangers of an unbalanced budget and declared retrenchment a responsibility of the whole House of Commons, but promised that the government would 'take every possible step' to ensure that the soundness of British credit would 'in no way be impaired'. As further reassurance to financial opinion, on the 31st MacDonald, in an unusual public disclosure of Cabinet business, announced the appointment of the Cabinet economy committee.[104]

Advance notice of Chamberlain's intention[105] and the ministerial statements probably contributed to a shift in the Bank's policy on 30 July. Certain now that Snowden was 'thoroughly alarmed', that MacDonald 'in his woolly-headed way' realised there was 'something wrong',[106] and that the Conservative opposition would insist upon retrenchment, the Bank was less worried that the politicians would exploit foreign borrowing as an opportunity for further delay. That Norman, suffering from nervous stress, became too ill on 29

---

[100] Cabinet 40(31), 30 July 1931; Lansbury memo, 'Cabinet Crisis of 1931', Lansbury papers 25.III.n.   [101] B. Webb diary, 4 Aug. 1931 (Cole, 277).

[102] Cabinet 40(31), 30 July 1931.

[103] N. to H. Chamberlain, 2 Aug. 1931, NC 18/1/750; Snowden, *Autobiography* II, 929 (though dates and some details are inaccurate).

[104] *HC Deb*, 255, cols. 2497–514, 30 July, and 2623–4, 31 July 1931.

[105] For Chamberlain informing Peacock, see N. to H. Chamberlain, 2 Aug. 1931, NC 18/1/750.   [106] Peacock to Oliver, 1 Aug. 1931, Oliver papers.

July to remain at the Bank, may also have altered the balance of opinion there. In addition, the Bank remained vulnerable. After the 'most dangerous' three weeks 'from the point of view of British credit, that any man...has passed through',[107] some £30m. in gold and £20m. in foreign exchange had been lost – almost halving the international reserves. Small gold losses continued, and the impact of both the May Report and increased internal demand for currency in advance of the August Bank holiday had to be sustained. For some or all of these reasons, it was now decided that 'self help' should be reinforced by the earlier proposal of foreign credits. The Federal Reserve Bank of New York and the Bank of France, both anxious to halt the international liquidity panic before it jeopardised their own banking systems, each provided £25m. for three months. These credits, it was believed, would be such a striking demonstration of central bank co-operation that their simple announcement would reassure the financial markets.[108] To prevent political misunderstanding, the Deputy Governor, Harvey, told MacDonald that the credits had been obtained 'in order to allow the Government time in which to facilitate plans for balancing the Budget', but would be 'of no permanent avail' without definite government action.[109] Probably by arrangement, the Joint Committee of City bankers reinforced the warning by an appeal to ministers that 'every effort should immediately be made to restore confidence' by cutting expenditure, balancing the budget, and improving the trade balance.[110] Following the rise in bank rate on 30 July, the foreign credits and increased fiduciary issue were announced on 1 August.

These defensive measures were considered perfectly adequate to uphold confidence in sterling, even allowing for the May Report's publication on 31 July. MacDonald had been sufficiently apprehensive to arrange for Parliament, like the Cabinet, to be adjourned in such a way that it could be recalled at short notice.[111] But on 1 August Treasury officials assured him that Snowden's and his own announcements of Cabinet preparations for balancing the budget had had an 'excellent effect' upon financial opinion, and neither they nor the Bank of England thought any further statement

[107] Ibid.
[108] Harvey to Cullen, 1 Aug. 1931, BoE G3/210/213; Williamson, 'Bankers Ramp?', 785.
[109] BoE Cte, 29 and 30 July 1931.
[110] Joint Committee of the British Bankers' Association and the Accepting Houses Committee to MacDonald and Snowden, 30 July 1931, JRM 260.
[111] HC Deb, 255, col. 2638, 31 July 1931.

6 Stanley Baldwin and Mrs Baldwin leaving London for Aix-les-Bains, 8 August 1931

on the May Report was necessary.[112] The Bank thought the acute demand upon its reserves was over, and that its own action had provided a 'respite'. It even reopened enquiries about a government loan in the USA.[113] Snowden told the Conservative and Liberal leaders there was 'no great urgency' about reporting their opinions on the May Report, as the Cabinet expected to have 'tentative conclusions' ready only in September.[114]

It is ironic that, after ten months of a pervading sense of 'national crisis', and after recurrent speculation about a Labour government collapse, party realignments and 'national government', the situation now seemed reasonably stable. Believing any real crisis to be postponed until the autumn, the political world dispersed from London for the summer vacation. The King and Wigram travelled

---

[112] N. Butler memo to MacDonald, 1 Aug. 1931, PREM 1/96.
[113] Kindersley in Dawes, *Journal as Ambassador*, 373, 29 July 1931; Peacock to Oliver, 1 Aug. 1931, Oliver papers; Harvey to Cullen, 1 Aug. 1931, BoE G3/210/213. For loan, Harvey–Harrison telephone conversation, 30 July 1931, FRBNY Harrison papers; J. P. Morgan & Co to Morgan Grenfell, tm 31/2371, 8 Aug. 1931, MGC.
[114] Snowden to Samuel, 5 Aug. 1931, Samuel papers A/78/1.

to Sandringham, the Cabinet Secretary to Dauphine, the editor of *The Times* to Yorkshire. Mosley, after a speech on the need for a government with 'guts',[115] left for Cap d'Antibes; Churchill went to Biarritz. Although Lloyd George would plainly be incapacitated for weeks, Samuel went to Sheringham and Sinclair to Caithness. Maclean was already in Cornwall. Reading at the age of seventy had just married his secretary, and left to honeymoon on the Continent. Baldwin went to Aix-les-Bains, after further repudiations of the 'national government' idea.[116] Neville Chamberlain was in Perthshire, from where he observed with relief that Conservative newspapers were damping down coalition rumours.[117] Amery, though considering the May Report 'a political bombshell', left for Austria.[118] Hoare went to play tennis at Cromer. MacDonald departed for Lossiemouth, from where he wrote asking for Keynes's views on the May Report; but he was chiefly preoccupied with a visit to Stimson, the US Secretary of State who was on vacation nearby, to discuss disarmament and reparations revision. Henderson and Sankey were at Llandrindod Wells, Thomas and Clynes at Brighton, Graham at Filey. The only Cabinet minister remaining on duty was Snowden, alternating his workdays between the Treasury and his Surrey home. At the latter, on 7 August, he received a Bank of England letter announcing a new phase of the financial crisis, which precipitated just such a political crisis as had been half-expected for so long.

[115] *The Times*, 3 Aug. 1931.
[116] Baldwin reported in Amery diary, 31 July 1931 (*LSA* II, 167) and Hankey diary, 6 Sept. 1931 (Roskill, *Hankey* II, 548); speech, *The Times*, 3 Aug. 1931.
[117] N. to I. Chamberlain, 9 Aug. 1931, NC 18/1/751, and see, e.g., *Morning Post* editorial, 5 Aug. 1931.
[118] Amery diary, 1 Aug. 1931.

CHAPTER 9

The political crisis: August 1931

So soon as a Parliamentary Party subordinates itself to the edicts of any non-Parliamentary body, it ceases to be responsible...its decisions must be taken on broader grounds than those held by any outside body. Its duty is not to take orders but to consider advice. The political organ in society... must ever be the supreme organ & its responsibility belongs to itself.

> MacDonald diary, 4 July 1926 (referring to trade unions)

'United we stand, divided we fall' is one of the first things I learned in the Trade Union Movement 48 years ago when I became a member of it.

> Arthur Henderson at TUC Conference, 10 September 1931

From the party point of view the chance of getting 'economy' out of the way before a General Election and of destroying the enemy's most dangerous weapon by identifying the present Govt. with 'Economy' is so important that it would be worth much to obtain it.

> Neville Chamberlain to Gwynne, 17 August 1931

Some day the historian who would tell the story of these days,...would say that never did any political party in this country so sacrifice party interests to national need as did the [Conservative] party in August 1931.

> Neville Chamberlain speech, 11 September 1931[1]

THE CRISIS OF CONFIDENCE

The onset of the third phase of the British sterling crisis dramatically accelerated the pace of political action. As envisaged by Cabinet and party leaders in late July, the timetable for dealing with the May

---

[1] Henderson speech in *TUCAR 1931*, 405; Chamberlain letter in Gwynne papers 17 (the written date appears to be 13 Aug. but internal evidence is conclusive for the 17th); Chamberlain speech in *The Scotsman*, 12 Sept. 1931.

Report was that the Cabinet economy committee would meet towards the end of August, the Cabinet would present a scheme to Lloyd George Liberal and Conservative leaders in September, and final decisions would be reached before Parliament reassembled on 20 October. Instead these arrangements had to be compressed into a period of twelve days. Proposals, consultations, and bargains on issues of the first importance for national policy, living standards, class relationships, and party interests were made under great pressure within days or hours rather than with deliberation over months and weeks. The action was not just rapid: it became immensely complicated as the positions of those chiefly concerned altered suddenly and repeatedly.

The pace was set by the international financial markets and the Bank of England. The Bank had been confident that its own measures and ministerial statements would hold the exchanges until the budget was balanced and faith in sterling placed beyond doubt in the autumn. As expected, sterling made some recovery when the foreign exchanges reopened after the British Bank holiday weekend of 1–3 August. But it then began to slide, followed on the 5th by a serious break, originating in Paris but spreading immediately to other financial centres.

The immediate reasons for the renewed crisis were that the Bank of England miscalculated the mood of the markets, and the markets misunderstood the Bank's actions.[2] The Bank had made no arrangements for actually using its central bank credits in exchange support operations, and once pressure upon sterling resumed it decided to control rather than prevent gold losses. It thought the mere announcement of the credits should have re-established confidence, and it remained determined that their existence should not give a 'misleading impression' to the politicians by concealing the underlying causes of sterling's vulnerability.[3] It was therefore prepared to allow limited gold losses and in time raise bank rate again 'in order to make the... Government understand the seriousness of their position'.[4] But temporary withdrawal of support for

---

[2] This chapter makes substantial use of Williamson, 'Bankers Ramp?', and also of Thompson-McCausland memo, 'The Crisis of July–September 1931', BoE 14/316 [hereafter cited as Thompson-McCausland, 'Crisis']. Boyce, *British Capitalism*, 345–7, in arguing that the Bank deliberately forced an immediate political crisis, conflates its longer-term objectives with its immediate expectations.

[3] Thompson-McCausland, 'Crisis', 20; Harvey to Cullen, 1 Aug. 1931, BoE G3/210/213.

[4] Siepmann reported in Lacour Gayet–Harrison telephone conversation, 7 Aug. 1931, FRBNY Harrison papers; and see Sayers, *Bank of England*, 394–6.

sterling on the Paris market damaged confidence by creating rumours of disagreement between the Bank of England and the Bank of France. Then, when the Bank treated this as a transitory misunderstanding and did not use the credits to prevent gold losses, its inaction was 'misinterpreted all over the world as a fundamental weakness in the London position'.[5] Caustic Bank of France and Federal Reserve Bank advice persuaded the Bank of England to reverse its policy, and from 7 August the credits were used to keep the exchanges above the gold export price. But the flight from sterling was now so intense and persistent that support operations soon threatened to consume the credits,[6] imposing a very short timetable if confidence was to be restored in time to prevent an unstoppable process of their expiry, sudden exchange collapse, massive gold loss, and forced abandonment of the gold standard.

The Bank had certainly blundered, its concern with domestic political results blunting its sensitivity towards financial opinion. But in trying to keep the government exposed to unmistakable indications of exchange pressure, the Bank was simply continuing its strategy of late July. It had intended to maintain the momentum behind the existing political process for tackling the May Report from late August onwards, not to precipitate a crisis. The exchange trouble of 5 August was altogether unexpected. Nevertheless the markets' reactions – not just to the Bank's decisions that day but to its various announcements from 30 July to 1 August – were so perverse and violent that they were swiftly understood to be a renewal of the earlier, deep-seated foreign distrust of sterling in a form which could well be decisive.

Realising this, the Bank expected immediate political action and was relentless about obtaining it. The fundamental problems seemed to be the May Report's exposure of the large budget deficit and, more particularly, fear that the government would be unwilling or unable to impose retrenchment. '[T]he cause of the trouble was not financial but political & lay in the complete want of confidence in H.M.G[overnment] existing among foreigners'.[7] In these circumstances, another increase in bank rate would appear an evasion, and

---

[5] Lacour Gayet–Harrison telephone conversation, 7 Aug. 1931, FRBNY Harrison papers. For Paris see BoE Cte, 5 Aug. 1931, and Leith-Ross to MacDonald, 5 Aug. 1931, JRM 260.

[6] The cost of support operations and depletion of the credits can be followed in Bank of England memo, '£ Sterling' [27 Aug. 1931], PREM 1/97 (printed in Cairncross and Eichengreen, *Sterling in Decline*, 66, 68).

[7] Harvey and Peacock reported in N. Chamberlain to Cunliffe-Lister, 15 Aug. 1931, Swinton papers 274/2/1/11–12 (Feiling, *Chamberlain*, 191), and see BoE Cte, 6 Aug. 1931.

7 Montagu Norman (Governor, Bank of England) leaving Britain to convalesce
in Canada, 15 August 1931

so aggravate foreign distrust. The Bank had already in late July done
everything it could unaided, so 'the remedy was in the hands of the
Govt. alone'.[8] Yet it still doubted that the markets' message of 5–6
August would be understood or heeded. Moreover, use of the credits
would now remove public symptoms of a sterling crisis until it was
too late.[9] With Norman, after attending at the Bank on the 5th,
again falling ill – and leaving Britain on the 15th to convalesce in
Canada – none of the responsible directors had much acquaintance
with ministers' views. Harvey even imagined that Snowden might
seriously consider devaluation.[10] The Bank therefore thought
ministers needed to be 'frightened', and everything possible done to
persuade them to act appropriately and quickly.[11] This exercise in
political management was undertaken in three ways: sharp warnings

---

[8] Harvey to Snowden, 6 Aug. 1931, JRM 260; MacDonald diary, 11 Aug. 1931 (Marquand,
      614).   [9] Thompson-McCausland, 'Crisis', 20–1.
[10] BoE Cte, 11 Aug. 1931. For Norman see Norman diary, 5 to 15 Aug. 1931.
[11] Norman, early Aug., reported in Jones, *Diary with Letters*, 11, 14 Sept. 1931, and see BoE
      Cte, 6 Aug. 1931.

8 Sir Ernest Harvey (Deputy Governor, Bank of England)

to ministers, communication with Liberal and Conservative leaders, and a proposed recall of Parliament.

Writing to Snowden and MacDonald on 6 August, and at meetings after MacDonald's return to London on the 11th, Harvey and Peacock reported an 'extremely grave' situation, where sterling could be saved only by immediate steps to produce 'the sign which foreigners expect': ministers had 'a few days – a fortnight at most' to 'prove' that the budget was to be balanced.[12] Thereafter, while the Bank conducted its own 'desperate struggle' to support the exchanges in anticipation of government action, it quite deliberately maintained 'strong pressure' upon MacDonald and Snowden.[13] Harvey repeatedly 'rubbed in' that promises were no longer sufficient and, very unusually, supplied them with details of the Bank's daily losses and estimates for expiry of the credits.[14]

In obtaining ministerial permission to report its 'apprehensions' to Conservative and Liberal leaders, the Bank's ostensible concern was to prepare them for the possibility of emergency legislation. But it had a further motive: to mobilise party-political pressure upon the Cabinet. Although on 11 August MacDonald and Snowden seemed suitably alarmed, Harvey and Peacock remained 'in serious doubt as to whether any action would be taken'.[15] Though reassured about Snowden's attitude they thought MacDonald 'so conceited and fluffy headed that it [would] be difficult to keep him up to scratch', and they had even less confidence in the rest of the Cabinet.[16] Maclean, who happened to be back in London, was seen immediately, and messages were sent to Samuel, who returned on 12 August, and to Baldwin and Neville Chamberlain, who both returned on the 13th. When Hoare later became involved, he received similar briefings. As all their interviews with the political leaders suggested that urgent measures would be forthcoming, the Bank directors did not for the time being persist with the proposal of immediate recall of Parliament. But once political negotiations began in earnest Harvey, Peacock, Grenfell, and Shaw between them kept the Conservative and Liberal leaders well informed of the exchange position and the Bank's views.

Yet for all this intense political intervention, impatience with politicians, and manifest attempts to determine the pace and parameters of government action, imputations of Bank of England

---

[12] Harvey to Snowden, copy to MacDonald, 6 Aug. 1931, JRM 260; MacDonald diary, 11 Aug. 1931 (Marquand, 614–15).

[13] Harvey to Bradbury, 17 Aug. 1931, BoE G3/210/247, and see BoE Cte, 12, 13, and 18 Aug. 1931.

[14] Harvey to MacDonald, 12 Aug. 1931, JRM 260; Harvey to Snowden, 18 Aug. 1931, in Thompson-McCausland, 'Crisis', 28–9.

[15] Harvey and Peacock in N. Chamberlain to Cunliffe-Lister, 15 Aug. 1931, Swinton papers 174/2/1/11–12 (Feiling, *Chamberlain*, 191).

[16] Grenfell to Morgan, 12 Aug. 1931, MGC, and see BoE Cte, 12 Aug. 1931.

9 Edward Peacock (Director, Bank of England)

'dictation' require much qualification. Both convention and prudence demanded that the Bank distance itself from overt political partisanship, and Harvey was sensitive to the risks of criticism if he were 'to step beyond [his] province' of monetary advice.[17] There was no thought of forcing a change of government, if only because such a political crisis could only delay policy decisions. Rather, since the May Committee had been established with all-party support, since Conservative and Liberal leaders had expressed readiness to support Snowden if he 'squarely face[d] the issues', and since Snowden plainly wanted such support, the Bank's concern was to push ministers and party leaders further along the path they themselves had already chosen, in the expectation that they would together 'fix up a joint plan'.[18] Certainly the Bank had contributed over many years to a political culture which, by prescribing certain conceptions of 'sound finance', imposed constraints upon what governments thought they could do. But then so had civil servants, businessmen and many politicians, Labour as well as Conservative and Liberal. Moreover, the issue had now become satisfaction of an opinion over which the Bank had little influence, that of nervous foreign financial markets. In August 1931 the Bank's general advice, however insistently given, was conventional. It was also, as will be seen, readily accepted by all politicians directly concerned. Devaluation was presented as 'a major disaster' to be avoided, not as an alternative policy.[19] A balanced budget had to be secured, in conformity with the stated intentions of all leading politicians since at least January, but as soon as possible rather than in the autumn. Naturally Bank directors had their own ideas on how that balance should be obtained, with unemployment insurance cuts prominent. But their official advice consisted of broad outlines, which were submitted not as demands but as suggestions: 'savings, though not exactly on May lines' and an emergency tariff – a new proposal from the free-trade Bank, now wanted in order to minimise direct tax increases and help the balance of payments.[20] Naturally, they knew perfectly well that the May Report and public commitments by Conservatives, Liberals, and Snowden made it superfluous to

[17] Harvey to Snowden, copy to MacDonald, 6 Aug. 1931, JRM 260.

[18] Grenfell to Morgan, 12 Aug. 1931, MGC.

[19] Peacock to Oliver, 1 Aug. 1931, Oliver papers; see also BoE Cte, 11 Aug. 1931, and MacDonald diary, 11 Aug. 1931 (Marquand, 614).

[20] MacDonald diary, 11 Aug. 1931 (slightly misprinted in Marquand, 615). For tariff advice, see also Baldwin to N. Chamberlain, 15 Aug. 1931, NC 7/11/24/1; Maclean to his wife, 18 (actually 19) Aug. 1931, Maclean papers c468/116.

press their own views on retrenchment. But that was precisely the point: specific budget measures were left to the politicians. In the event these measures were to fall short of even the Bank's broad advice.

Virtually all other financial, business, and economic advice to ministers, whether solicited or unsolicited, whether private or published, supported the Bank of England. McKenna accepted that in a confidence crisis only the most orthodox responses were likely to be effective. He therefore joined other leading clearing bank chairmen in 'most earnestly' reinforcing the 30 July appeal by the Joint Committee of City Bankers.[21] Business opinion regarded the May Report as ending all possible excuse for postponing retrenchment.[22] H. D. Henderson, like Hopkins, thought the Report exaggerated the budget problem, but that it now defined the terms for avoiding what he considered to be the very much worse consequences of a sterling collapse.[23] Keynes was only a partial exception. Although he thought the international financial crisis had made the gold standard less easy to sustain, and considered the May Report majority recommendations – if 'taken in isolation' – a socially unjust and futile attempt 'to make deflation effective', his advice shifted once he became aware that the confidence crisis had resumed. On 5 August, before this was apparent and when no decisions were expected until the autumn, he argued that over the coming months loss of the gold standard was 'nearly *certain*', and that the best course was to 'convert disaster into success' by deliberate devaluation and creation of an imperial currency union. But by the 12th he had direct information from the City of the immediate crisis and realised that it might force far-reaching measures, with the May recommendations perhaps becoming part of a comprehensive, more equitable 'national treaty'. In these circumstances he advised that it was 'still possible... to keep on the gold standard if we deliberately decide to do so', and would 'support

[21] Beaumont Pease, Goschen, Lawrence, Paton, McKenna, Meers, Goodenough, Beckett, and Holland-Martin to MacDonald, 6 Aug. 1931, JRM 260. For chairmen of the 'big five' clearing banks (i.e., including McKenna) 'co-operating most loyally' with the Bank, see Grenfell to Morgan, 14 Aug. 1931, MGC.

[22] See Balfour memo, 31 July 1931, circulated by MacDonald to EAC members, 7 Aug., in Howson and Winch, *Economic Advisory Council*, 88. For other indications, see Association of British Chambers of Commerce, London Chamber of Commerce, Ernest Benn, Weir, NCIC, National Chamber of Trade, letters and statements in *The Times*, 14, 18, 20, and 22 Aug. 1931.

[23] H. D. Henderson memo, 'The Economy Report', to MacDonald, 7 Aug. 1931, JRM 260 (see H. D. Henderson, *The Inter-War Years*, 71–7).

for the time being whichever policy was made' provided action was sufficiently drastic to be effective.[24] This slide from pressing for a preferred ideal to addressing the practical issue was consistent in Keynes's own terms, but such equivocation was hopeless as policy advice in an emergency. Ultimately he appeared to reinforce the Bank's advice; certainly MacDonald thought he did.[25] The Bank itself interpreted a Keynes article which attacked the May Report yet accepted some retrenchment and again recommended a revenue tariff to mean that he 'might be able to render useful service if he were acquainted with the real facts'.[26]

Snowden and Treasury officials did not doubt the 'imminent peril'. Snowden accepted that going off the gold standard would have 'disastrous consequences', producing 'utter chaos'.[27] Such prospects made it seem self-evident that 'socialism' now required temporary working-class sacrifices. The crisis was the great reckoning – not just for sterling and monetary stability, but for that public expenditure problem on which Snowden and the Treasury had wanted decision since the previous autumn and had expected the May Committee to supply the means. For those reasons, but also because like the Bank of England they thought the Cabinet would still be reluctant to face the issues, they added their own quota of pressure in the shape of three additional financial problems.

These problems were genuine enough, but the emphasis now given them was intended to raise the stakes in anticipation of tough ministerial bargaining. A Snowden–Hopkins memorandum for the Cabinet economy committee presented, firstly, a new budget

[24] Keynes to MacDonald, 5 and 12 Aug. 1931, JRM 260 (*JMK* xx, 590–4). Here I agree more with McKibbin, 'Economic Policy of the Second Labour Government', 111n (*Ideologies*, 214n) than with Clarke, *Keynesian Revolution*, 223–4. Keynes's further proposal on the 5th of a committee of ex-Chancellors of the Exchequer seems as bizarre on *ad hominem* as on practical grounds. Whatever their earlier attitudes towards him, in summer 1931 Baldwin, Horne, and Austen as well as Neville Chamberlain were hardly amenable to Keynes's views on the gold standard and retrenchment. Lloyd George was leader of the party responsible for the May Committee. As just described, McKenna plumped for the gold standard once a real confidence crisis began.

[25] See MacDonald to D'Abernon, 10 Sept. 1931, JRM 1314, for Keynes hesitating but then seeming 'to recognise that...something very hurried...which could not in principle be defended but which was imposed upon us by immediate necessity, had to be done'. Cf. Marquand, 610–11, 613–14.

[26] BoE Cte, 18 Aug. 1931. See Keynes, 'Some Consequences of the Economy Report', *New Statesman*, 15 Aug. 1931 (*JMK* ix, 141–5); also Keynes to MacDonald, 12 Aug. 1931, JRM 260 (*JMK* xx, 594), which admits the article had 'little...bearing on the immediate situation'.

[27] Hopkins and Snowden in Snowden to MacDonald, 7 Aug. 1931, JRM 260; Cabinet 44(31), 22 Aug. 1931.

forecast. The assumption in the April budget of trade revival was replaced by one of deterioration into 1932, with unemployment rising to three million soon and perhaps four million later. The consequent budget outlook was 'very appalling', worse than that suggested by the May Report. Adding losses under the Hoover moratorium and the effects of economic deterioration in reducing revenue and increasing unemployment insurance expenditure, the estimated 1932–3 deficit was raised from £120m. to £173–178m. – later rounded down to £170m. – and the current year's was calculated at £47m. These estimates followed the May Report's criteria by including the Sinking Fund, and accepting as 'irrefutable' the argument that borrowing for the Unemployment Insurance Fund must cease.[28]

Secondly, Hopkins revealed that there was a 'nasty' technical problem about financing that Fund's deficit. The existing 'un-obtrusive' method – selling government stock which represented Savings Bank deposits, and replacing it with unsaleable Treasury IOUs – now threatened the security of the Savings Bank, and would have to end 'within a few months'. One alternative, of the Fund borrowing directly in the financial markets, would generate obvious 'Dole Bonds' which investors were unlikely to find attractive, and whose failure would be 'an admission of national bankruptcy'. The purpose of this (undoubtedly overdrawn) statement of the problem was to suggest that if borrowing was not ended by political decision it would in any case become financially impossible.[29]

Thirdly, Snowden and Hopkins asserted that the limits of direct taxation of higher incomes had been reached. To increase tax levels here would produce serious problems of evasion and, by eating into capital and eroding enterprise, diminishing returns. It was therefore proposed to spread the tax burden to 'the mass of citizens' whose existing contribution was 'comparatively light', through increased excise duties and especially by reduction of income tax allowances (Snowden, of course, excluding all thought of a revenue tariff). But

---

[28] Snowden (i.e., Treasury) memo, 'Forecast of the Budget Position', NE(31)2, undated but about 10 Aug. 1931, T171/288.

[29] Ibid. The problem had worried the National Debt Office, Bank of England, and Treasury since February, but was revealed to Snowden only in August: see Norman to M. Headlam, 5 March 1931, Hopkins to Harvey, 18 May, 6 Aug. 1931, and Hopkins memo for Snowden, 10 Aug. 1931, BoE G3/198/118, G1/154/1292/1. The association with the notorious 'Post Office Savings Bank scare' in the subsequent October is obvious, but that was a garbled distortion of the problem, not countenanced by the Treasury: see Hopkins to Fergusson, 11 Nov. 1931, T172/1752.

these proposed changes would raise only £48m.[30] Despite their argument against further direct taxation, Snowden and Hopkins cannot have supposed that the remaining part of the budget deficit – £130m. – could be met solely by retrenchment, or that further taxation would not become necessary. Like the rest of their advice, these initial proposals were pitched to manoeuvre the Cabinet into accepting retrenchment measures close to the May Committee majority's total of £96m.

MACDONALD'S INITIATIVE

Initially MacDonald and Henderson both thought the resumed sterling crisis might be distinct from the budget problem. They suspected a French-inspired attack upon the pound aimed at strengthening French reparations diplomacy.[31] But all doubts about the reality of a confidence crisis were dispelled after their return to London, MacDonald receiving reports from Snowden, Harvey, and Peacock on 11 August, and Henderson from MacDonald and Snowden on the 12th. MacDonald obtained additional advice from McKenna and some EAC members, but none dissented from Bank of England and Treasury assessment of the situation.[32] Thereafter MacDonald feared a 'disaster': the run on sterling spreading to Government securities and Savings Bank deposits, compelling 'an Act of Moratorium for both the Bank and the State' with 'perfectly appalling' consequences, including a price collapse and five million unemployed.[33] Far from supposing the Bank to be trying to dictate, MacDonald and Snowden asked for daily reports from Harvey.[34]

Together MacDonald and Snowden took decisions which further determined the terms and pace of political discussion. They publicly reiterated the Cabinet's determination to balance the budget. This produced a small improvement on the exchanges which seemed to confirm the Bank's advice, and ministerial ability to control the

---

[30] Hopkins memo, 'Economy or Taxation', undated, and Thompson to Hopkins, 10 Aug. 1931, IR 63/132; Snowden memo, 'Forecast of the Budget Position', undated, T171/288.

[31] MacDonald to Stimson, 9 Aug. 1931, Stimson papers reel 81, and see Johnston, *Memoirs*, 108–9, for Henderson sending a Cabinet colleague to investigate in Paris, where French ministers gave satisfactory assurances.

[32] MacDonald diary, 11 Aug. 1931, for meeting with McKenna. For him, and for H. D. Henderson and Keynes, see above. H. D. Henderson to MacDonald, 11 Aug. 1931, JRM 260, records a proposed EAC meeting (in the event impossible at such short notice).

[33] MacDonald reported in Citrine, *Men and Work*, 281; in TUCGC, 20 Aug. 1931, and in Dalton diary, 24 Aug. 1931 (Dalton, 272); MacDonald to D'Abernon, 10 Sept. 1931, JRM 1314. [34] Thompson-McCausland, 'Crisis', 23.

situation.[35] The Cabinet economy committee's meeting was brought forward to the 12th. Since the Bank was recalling the Liberal and Conservative leaders, interviews were arranged with them too. These arrangements simply 'telescoped' the procedure prepared in late July for securing all-party support in Cabinet action upon the May Report.[36]

There was, however, an important difference between Mac-Donald and Snowden about how to proceed. MacDonald was more sensitive to the political resonances of budget measures. Both wanted to push the Cabinet towards substantial retrenchment, but, while Snowden originally sought to do this by withholding proposals for really large tax increases, MacDonald considered it better to bring these forward. He did not at this stage pursue the Bank's suggestion of a revenue tariff which, as a second issue dividing the Cabinet, might divert attention from retrenchment. Rather, MacDonald thought that just as the sterling crisis brought pressure upon the Cabinet to impose what Conservatives, Liberals, bankers, and businessmen wanted, so it could equally be used to persuade all these to accept measures which would make retrenchment more palatable to the Cabinet, Labour movement, and working classes. Essentially, MacDonald proposed a compromise between the May Committee's majority and minority reports, to spread the burden over the classes, achieve a financial and social balance, and meet one view of 'social justice'. Half of the budget deficit would be met by expenditure cuts, including unemployment insurance cuts, the other half by increased taxation, including taxation of higher and *rentier* incomes. Specific impositions would be determined on the uniform measure of '1924 Standards' of real income. Upon this principle of 'equal sacrifice',[37] MacDonald hoped to manufacture a political consensus. Snowden recognised the potential of these tactics, and adjusted his proposals accordingly. But securing the principle would also mean obtaining Conservative and Liberal assent to tax increases. The budget problem therefore became a matter not of satisfying bankers' conditions, but of striking a bargain with leaders of the other parties.

MacDonald's initiative was a clever improvisation. It met

---

[35] *The Times*, 12 Aug. 1931; Harvey to MacDonald, 12 Aug. 1931, JRM 260; MacDonald diary, 13 Aug. 1931.

[36] MacDonald diary, 11 Aug. 1931; MacDonald reported in N. to A. Chamberlain, 14 Aug. 1931, AC 39/3/26.

[37] MacDonald diary, 13 Aug. 1931 (Marquand, 615); MacDonald note of Cabinet committee decisions, undated but 13 Aug. 1931, JRM 1316.

Snowden's objective of retrenchment, and it seemed to have real prospects of securing all-party co-operation and delivering the Cabinet from political disaster. At Cabinet economy committee meetings on 12 and 13 August Henderson, Graham, and Thomas raised no doubts about defending the gold standard. Nor did they question the Treasury's revised budget forecast and the proposed cessation of Unemployment Insurance Fund borrowing. By appearing to defeat Snowden's original harsh conception of the appropriate remedies, MacDonald's proposal of 'equal sacrifice' for the time being stilled Henderson's and Graham's unease over expenditure cuts. Suggestions for obtaining shared sacrifices were referred to the Treasury for comment. Government departments, most of which had rejected those May Report's majority recommendations relating to themselves, were instructed to present their own proposals for cuts of equivalent amounts when the committee re-convened after the weekend.[38] As in mid July, Henderson's first concern was to ensure that the Cabinet received Labour party support. Against MacDonald's and Snowden's reluctance to risk further political complications, he insisted upon arranging meetings with the national executive committee, parliamentary party executive, and TUC General Council for the 20th.[39] On the other hand Henderson and Graham endorsed the consultations with Conservative and Liberal leaders. Remarkably, the plan was to submit definite proposals to these on the 18th, before the Cabinet met on the 19th.[40] To all appearances, the Cabinet committee hoped to produce a budget scheme so delicately poised upon the principle of 'equal sacrifice' as to command Conservative and Liberal support and then be adopted by the full Cabinet and the Labour executives.

At preliminary meetings with Samuel and later Baldwin and Neville Chamberlain on 13 August, MacDonald and Snowden gave robust impressions of the committee's intentions. The free-trader,

[38] Because of the delicate party-political issues involved, the committee met in strict secrecy, without secretaries to take minutes. For ministers not confiding in their officials, see Duff to Wigram, 19 Aug. 1931, RA GV K2330(1)/3. There is some fragmentary evidence of its proceedings, and one sustained (but self-serving) description: 'Memorandum' [Sept. 1931], copies in Addison, Lansbury, and Passfield papers, hereafter cited as 'Graham memo' from attribution in Passfield papers IV:26/34.

[39] Citrine, in *TUCAR 1931*, 79, 7 Sept. 1931, and Henderson in *HC Deb*, 256, col. 37, 8 Sept. 1931, correct McKibbin, 'Economic Policy of the Second Labour Government', 117 (*Ideologies*, 221) on origin of meeting.

[40] MacDonald note of Cabinet committee decisions [13 Aug. 1931], JRM 1316; Snowden, *Autobiography* II, 940–1; Graham memo, para 11; Henderson in *HC Deb*, 256, cols. 28–31, 8 Sept. 1931.

Samuel, was told that pressure for a revenue tariff was being resisted. Baldwin and Chamberlain were told that retrenchment would reach the May majority's total, and that *rentier* taxation was under consideration. The Cabinet would 'sympathetically' consider Liberal and Conservative views and ask them to demonstrate a 'benevolent' attitude. But it would retain final responsibility for the budget scheme. With Liberal and Conservative leaders prepared to offer general support on those terms, MacDonald proposed to recall Parliament on 1 September in order to pass a supplementary budget and economy bill.[41]

If MacDonald was to stitch together a deal between the party leaderships, he needed as much time as possible for negotiations. Before returning to Lossiemouth for the weekend he asked the Treasury and Bank to enquire if an American loan to the government would be possible, to help support sterling until Parliament met. For form's sake the Bank put this to their New York advisors, but as expected received the same reply as in late July: it would be impossible to persuade American banks to subscribe to a loan without clear proof that 'a strong budget program' was to be implemented.[42] The political timetable was to remain at the mercy of the panic in the financial markets.

LIBERAL AND CONSERVATIVE CALCULATIONS

Samuel, Baldwin, and Chamberlain fully accepted that the exchange position was dangerous, and that drastic retrenchment and tax increases were needed urgently. Even so, they thought the implications for their own parties were straightforward. Like MacDonald they dispersed to their holiday resorts late on 13 August, in a concerted attempt to reduce the crisis atmosphere.[43] Although they had accounts of their interviews with Bank directors and ministers sent to senior colleagues, none considered it necessary to summon their 'shadow cabinets'.

Samuel sent his account to Lloyd George, Reading, Crewe, Maclean, and Sinclair, and chose Maclean, as the leadership's

---

[41] Samuel memo, 13 Aug. 1931, Samuel papers A/78/3; N. to A. Chamberlain, 14 Aug. 1931, AC 39/3/26; G. Lloyd (Baldwin's secretary), and N. Chamberlain, to Cunliffe-Lister, 14 and 15 Aug. 1931, Swinton papers, 174/2/1/26–8, 11–12.

[42] C. P. Duff memo, 'The Financial Crisis', 28 Aug. 1931, JRM 1316 [hereafter Duff, 'Financial Crisis']; Grenfell to Morgan, 14 Aug. 1931, MGC; Williamson, 'Bankers Ramp?', 790. [43] G. Lloyd to Cunliffe-Lister, Swinton papers 174/2/1/26–8.

'economy' expert, to accompany him at the three-party conference. To both Samuel and Maclean the Liberal role appeared simple. They were allies of the government, not leaders of an opposition party, and they had no reason to suppose that the crisis offered them new opportunities. In party-political terms, their objective was to preserve the *status quo*. The Cabinet was to be encouraged to adopt substantial retrenchment, and on that issue Conservative co-operation was to be welcomed as part of a united national effort, like that of 1914.[44] But the Liberal line had to remain independent of that of the Conservatives who, it was suspected, would try to force a general election, kill off electoral reform, and impose protection. Samuel claimed to 'feel more anti-Tory now than...ever'.[45] The principal Liberal problem was to prevent Conservatives, now backed by Bank advice, from exploiting the situation to establish 'a Protectionist Tariff...under the name of an Emergency Tariff for revenue'.[46]

Unlike Samuel and Maclean, Baldwin and Chamberlain as opposition leaders had every reason to see immediate connections between the national crisis and their party's prospects. Baldwin thought the position so straightforward that he was furious at being recalled. Well briefed on the sterling crisis before he left and having stated Conservative readiness to support the Cabinet in appropriate measures, he thought there was little further to be learnt or said, and that the Cabinet must have no opportunity to shuffle off its responsibilities. He therefore intended to resume his holiday as soon as possible.[47] He was impatient at the successive meetings with MacDonald and Snowden, and Harvey and Peacock, and rather than disturb his holiday again asked Chamberlain to take his place at the three-party conference. Chamberlain was unaware of Baldwin's earlier meetings with bankers and did not grasp the value of physical distance in avoiding unwanted entanglements. He assumed that Baldwin had 'given no thought to the situation', and

---

[44] Samuel memo, 13 Aug. 1931, Samuel papers A/78/3 (distribution list attached); Maclean speech, *Manchester Guardian*, 13 Aug. 1931 – delivered in response to Bank advice: see Maclean to Sinclair, 16 Aug. 1931, Thurso papers III/3/5.

[45] Samuel to Trevelyan, 14 Aug. 1931, Trevelyan papers 144.

[46] Sinclair to Samuel, and Samuel to Sinclair, 14 and 18 Aug. 1931, Thurso papers III/3/5; and see Maclean to his wife, 18 [i.e., 19] Aug. 1931, Maclean papers c468/116.

[47] Grenfell to Morgan, 14 Aug. 1931, MGC. Grenfell had met Baldwin immediately upon his arrival in London, so Baldwin had the latest Bank information even before his interviews with ministers and Harvey and Peacock. Horne also turned up, superfluously, to offer advice.

was shocked by his attitude but glad to be left in charge.[48] Yet Chamberlain himself thought the position 'fairly simple',[49] and at this stage his views were similar to those of Baldwin. Nevertheless there were some differences, which later became highly important. Consequently, this temporary transfer of effective party leadership had large effects.

Chamberlain and Baldwin were 'agreeably surprised' at how far 'the Bankers had succeeded in frightening' MacDonald,[50] and concluded that the Cabinet really would impose substantial expenditure cuts. This being so, the Conservative position was straightforward because national interest and party advantage would coincide. Disingenuously, Chamberlain told MacDonald and Snowden that the nature of the cuts was of 'minor importance' provided total retrenchment was close to the May Report majority figure. In fact he knew full well that such a total was impossible without 'thorough reform of unemployment insurance'.[51] If that could be secured, the Conservatives would have 'done the trick': the sterling crisis would be overcome by the restoration of foreign confidence, the budget crisis would be resolved by a Labour Cabinet reversing its 'extravagant' policies, and the Labour party would bear the political and electoral costs of unpopular cuts.

From the national point of view the reduction of expenditure is the vital thing. Nothing else will convince the world that we have the courage to save ourselves. From the Party point of view could any conceivable thing be more valuable... than to get this terrible question of economy out of our way and tightly strapped on the back of a Socialist Govt.?[52]

Baldwin, similarly, thought it would be a 'wonderful lesson' to have the consequences of socialist finance exposed. His perception of the party-political opportunity went further even than Chamberlain's: the Lloyd George Liberals were to be presented as being 'just as responsible as the govt. for the crisis', because they had kept it in

---

[48] N. to A. Chamberlain, 14 Aug. 1931, AC 39/3/26, and to H. Chamberlain, 16 Aug. 1931, NC 18/1/752. This is a good instance of Chamberlain's frequent incomprehension of Baldwin.   [49] N. Chamberlain to Bridgeman, 19 Aug. 1931, Bridgeman papers.

[50] G. Lloyd to Cunliffe-Lister, 14 Aug. 1931, Swinton papers 174/2/1/26–8.

[51] N. Chamberlain to A. Chamberlain, 14 Aug. 1931, AC 39/3/26; to Cunliffe-Lister, 15 Aug. 1931, Swinton papers 174/2/1/11–12, and to Bridgeman, 19 Aug. 1931; N. Chamberlain diary, 22 Aug. 1931.

[52] N. Chamberlain to Bridgeman, 19 Aug. 1931, Bridgeman papers, and see also the first Chamberlain epigraph to this chapter.

office.[53] On 'both national and party grounds' it seemed so important to obtain retrenchment from the Labour government that Chamberlain was prepared to accept MacDonald's notion of 'equal sacrifice'. Taxation of *rentiers* was a 'danger' – possibly upsetting investors and Conservative supporters – but if it was the 'necessary price [for retrenchment by Labour] the object is worth the money'.[54]

Other leading Conservatives were less certain. Baldwin, Bridgeman, Amery, and Horne advised Chamberlain to press for a revenue tariff, as the Bank also recommended. A tariff would reduce the amount required from direct taxation, help sterling by improving the trade balance, and fatally compromise a free-trade government.[55] Here Chamberlain differed. Despite his own protectionism, he ignored the advice of his leader and the Bank of England. He thought insistence upon a revenue tariff now would be a 'dangerous game'. The Cabinet might use it not in place of direct taxation but to run away from the 'crux' of retrenchment – dropping its part of an 'equal sacrifice' bargain, and possibly placing a Conservative party still insistent upon cuts in a risky electoral position. With the agreement of Hoare, the colleague Chamberlain chose for the three-party conference, he therefore decided not to raise tariffs or any other tax issue but to concentrate wholly upon retrenchment.[56] This decision to postpone the tariff question was crucial: its effect was to nail the Labour Cabinet inescapably to the rack of retrenchment.

There was another difference between Baldwin and Chamberlain: that of late July, over what should be done if during a crisis the Labour Cabinet could not continue alone. The obvious danger now was that the retrenchment issue might be turned back against the Conservative party. If the Cabinet were to reject cuts and resign, a Conservative government imposing social service cuts could face a united Labour opposition which might successfully brand it as a rich man's government and place it in 'a bad electioneering position'.[57]

[53] Baldwin to N. Chamberlain, 15 Aug. 1931, NC 7/11/24/1 (partly in Middlemas and Barnes, *Baldwin*, 621).

[54] N. Chamberlain to Gwynne, 17 [13 written] Aug. 1931, Gwynne papers 17, and to Bridgeman, 19 Aug. 1931, Bridgeman papers, and reported in G. Lloyd to Cunliffe-Lister, 14 Aug. 1931, Swinton papers 174/2/1/26–8.

[55] Baldwin to N. Chamberlain, 15 Aug. 1931, NC 7/11/24/1; Horne to Baldwin and to N. Chamberlain, 15 and 18 Aug. 1931, Bridgeman to Baldwin, 16 Aug. 1931, SB 44/22–34, 39–47, 35–8; note to Amery diary, 15 Aug. 1931 (*LSA* II, 191).

[56] N. Chamberlain to Bridgeman, 19 Aug. 1931, Bridgeman papers; N. Chamberlain diary, 22 Aug. 1931, referring to 20th.

[57] Bridgeman to Baldwin, 16 Aug. 1931, SB 44/35–8. For earlier expression of this fear, see A. to I. Chamberlain, 2 Aug. 1931, AC 5/1/550.

Baldwin was ready to face that prospect and thought that, sooner or later, the inevitable outcome was a Conservative government. Otherwise, he would not have returned to his holiday abroad. Chamberlain, however, still entertained a different possibility. His attitude was that 'there is – *at present anyway* – no suggestion of a National Government'.[58] Yet as matters stood, he thought the most likely political result of the crisis was an election 'in conditions offering us the utmost advantage, seeing that we would no longer be saddled with the unpopularity of economy, but could concentrate on tariffs & Imp[erial] Preference as the restorers of prosperity'.[59]

In mid August, then, MacDonald, Snowden, Baldwin, Chamberlain, Samuel, and Maclean all expected the linked sterling and budget crises to be solved through all-party agreement to a Labour Cabinet programme of 'equal sacrifices'. All were intent upon the 'national interest'. Yet the drastic nature of the proposed remedies – certain to affect and offend large social groups – also demanded attention to party consequences. Though speaking of Cabinet responsibility, MacDonald and Snowden intended to implicate Conservatives and Liberals in Cabinet policy, thereby spreading responsibility for retrenchment and extracting consent to direct taxation. This might cushion the government from Labour party and electoral revulsion against social service cuts. Baldwin, Chamberlain, Samuel, and Maclean, however, took them at their word about the Cabinet's responsibility. The Lloyd George Liberals wanted their Labour allies to remain in office in order to preserve free trade, pass electoral reform, and assist Liberal revival. The Conservatives wanted the Labour Cabinet to remain in office for the duration of the crisis, suffering the odium both for allowing it to occur and for imposing the remedies. This would be permanent warning against socialist illusions, and place the expected Conservative election victory beyond all doubt.

HENDERSON'S INTERVENTIONS

All these expectations crumbled between 17 and 20 August. Early agreement upon an all-party package was upset, first, because Treasury preparation of tax proposals took longer than expected, forcing the three-party conference to be postponed until the 20th,

[58] N. Chamberlain to Gwynne, 17 [13 written] Aug. 1931, Gwynne papers 17.
[59] N. to H. Chamberlain, 16 Aug. 1931, NC 18/1/752.

after the Cabinet meeting. By then the prospect of obtaining Liberal and Conservative assistance had been weakened by differences between ministers.

When the Cabinet economy committee resumed on 17 August, departmental replies revealed no new suggestions for cuts. But a Snowden–MacDonald paper proposed the adoption of many May Committee majority recommendations. With Bondfield's support they lowered the proposed unemployment benefit cut from 20 per cent to 10 per cent, the figure they had together suggested in February and which now seemed a key element in an 'equal sacrifice' package. Transitional benefit was to be transferred from the Exchequer to public assistance authorities – the means-tested 'poor law'.[60]

At this point the years of tension between Henderson and the other two leading ministers began to tell, as Henderson started a running criticism of the MacDonald–Snowden approach. Mutual sympathy, understanding, and trust were conspicuously absent. Suspecting that MacDonald and Snowden would allow sacrifices to fall mostly on social services, Henderson 'at once showed his hand'. He objected to cuts being discussed first, spoke of the 'inadequacy' of existing unemployment benefits, and asked to see 'the whole scheme', meaning tax increases.[61]

Now and later, however, Henderson proceeded from a shallow basis in financial analysis. He neither questioned the Bank and Treasury assessment of the problem, nor offered a fundamentally alternative solution. Snowden's and MacDonald's response to his initial objection – that a crisis demanded emergency measures – disarmed him: 'he could not reply but lapsed into sulky silence'.[62] In any case, over the next two days a 'whole scheme' was produced for achieving MacDonald's conception of 'equal sacrifice'. The Cabinet committee approved Snowden's new taxation proposals, totalling £37m. for the current year and £88·5m. for 1932–3, to cover half the £170m. deficit. These included the earlier excise increases, and a one-third reduction in income tax allowances: together with reduced rates of relief, this would reverse fiscal policy

[60] Henderson in HC Deb, 256, col. 27, 8 Sept 1931; Bondfield memo on Report of Committee on National Expenditure, 11 Aug. 1931, CAB 27/454.

[61] MacDonald diary, 17 Aug. 1931 (Marquand, 615–16), confirming Graham memo, para. 6, and Henderson in HC Deb, 256, cols. 27, 29, 8 Sept. 1931. Some alternative advice was available: see Pethick-Lawrence to Henderson [19 Aug. 1931], Pethick-Lawrence papers 5/39–42, for mobilization of overseas assets, and Dalton, 266, for suspension of Sinking Fund.   [62] MacDonald diary, 17 Aug. 1931 (Marquand, 616).

since 1925 by bringing the 'lower middle classes' back into the direct tax net. In addition standard income tax was raised 6d. to 5/- (the 1922–3 level) and surtax received a 10 per cent surcharge. On Inland Revenue advice, a separate *rentier* tax was rejected as administratively impractical: instead, *rentiers* were to contribute through greater differentiation against unearned income.[63] Overall the proposed increases in direct taxation were higher than any since 1920. Some were so large that Treasury and revenue officials warned that much tax evasion would occur unless expenditure cuts were so substantial that the Cabinet programme appeared to be 'a fair and just plan demanding equal sacrifices from all sections of the community'. This was perhaps an unusually overt instance of pressure from officials, but it agreed exactly with Snowden's and MacDonald's views.[64]

Henderson's particular concerns were the inter-connected matters of the Labour movement's unity and the concept of 'social justice'. As chief party manager he was acutely sensitive to party opinion, expressions of which had by 17 August become distinctly hostile. Labour newspapers declared that no Labour government could implement the majority May Report. A 'rather difficult' Henderson interview with Citrine gave a foretaste of TUC criticism, and junior ministers were beginning to threaten resignation.[65] It was plain enough that social service cuts were likely to cause serious party divisions, even with compensating taxation of the wealthy. Henderson therefore began trying to shift MacDonald's notion of 'equal sacrifice' towards something less objectionable to the party and TUC. Whereas MacDonald and Snowden, preoccupied with financial confidence and Liberal and Conservative acquiescence, looked to sacrifices divided equally in total between retrenchment and taxation, Henderson looked to the minority May Report idea of sacrifices proportionate to ability to bear the burden. As an experienced politician with orthodox financial views, he did not

---

[63] P. J. Grigg to Snowden, 17 Aug. 1931, and Fisher, Hopkins, P. J. Grigg, Dyke memo, 18 Aug. 1931, T171/288; Cabinet economy committee report, CP 203(31), 19 Aug. 1931. See also Graham memo, para. 10, where the details make nonsense of Henderson's and Graham's later claims not to have received 'the complete picture' of budget proposals. The argument in Malament, 'Snowden', 31–2, that *rentier* taxation was silently dropped, arises from a misunderstanding.

[64] Fisher, Hopkins, P. J. Grigg, Dyke memo, 18 Aug. 1931, T171/288; and see Middleton, *Towards the Managed Economy*, 61.

[65] For the Labour press, Skidelsky, *Politicians*, 350–1, 364; for Citrine, Henderson to Middleton, 14 Aug. 1931, Labour party papers LP/PRO/31/2; for resignation threats, Lawrence in Hamilton, *Henderson*, 378, also Pethick-Lawrence, *Fate Has Been Kind*, 165.

suppose that this principle could be rigorously applied. He joined in compiling retrenchment proposals, but with Graham he tried to have these mitigated by other expedients. In each case there was obstruction from Snowden. War-debt conversion was rejected as impossible in existing financial conditions, though remaining a Treasury objective. Henderson now reluctantly accepted a revenue tariff, despite its offensiveness to Labour free-trade attitudes, because it was preferable to unemployment insurance cuts. But in the face of Snowden's determined opposition the question was referred to the full Cabinet.[66]

   In practice, Henderson's notion of 'social justice' narrowed to defending a symbol of that central Labour principle of 'work or maintenance' – the existing rates of unemployment insurance benefits. On his insistence the committee rejected the proposed 10 per cent benefit cut, overturning MacDonald's and Snowden's hopes and the Conservative leaders' expectations. Yet Henderson was drawing very fine distinctions. He accepted that the Exchequer had to be relieved of the £20m. for transitional benefits, and proposed to finance these by a 1s. deduction from unemployment benefits, a 'premium'. Like all Cabinet ministers he must have been conscious that as prices had fallen the real value of benefit payments had risen, making some reduction less onerous in fact than in appearance. Given this, the notion of a 'premium' seemed attractive because it had long been standard practice with trade union benefits. Yet however small and disguised, the effect would still be a cut in benefit rates. Henderson and Graham also accepted most other majority May recommendations, including income cuts for teachers and other public employees, cessation of borrowing, increased insurance contributions, and restrictions on entitlement to unemployment benefits. However, the removal of the 10 per cent benefit cut reduced the cuts in unemployment insurance to £13m. and the overall total of proposed retrenchment to £78·5m. – less than the May majority figure, lower than the proposed tax increases, and insufficient to remove the budget deficit.[67]

   No Cabinet committee member was satisfied with this pro-

---

[66] Graham memo, para. 9; Henderson in Sankey diary, 19 Aug. 1931, and in Dalton diary, 20 Aug. 1931 (Dalton, 267).

[67] CP 203 (31), and Cabinet 41(31), 19 Aug. 1931; Morrison to Greenwood, 10 Sept. 1931, Morrison papers. Henderson's support for the 'premium' and acceptance of other unemployment insurance savings explains Sankey's recollection that he had 'agreed to...cut in the dole': see Sankey diary, 24 Aug. 1931, and McKibbin, 'Economic Policy of the Second Labour Government', 120 (*Ideologies*, 224).

gramme; none considered it definitive. Henderson and Graham insisted throughout that the committee's work was provisional, in order to keep escape routes open if Cabinet and party reactions were hostile. They also hoped to replace some proposed cuts by a revenue tariff. MacDonald, Snowden, and Thomas hoped to have the cuts increased, in order to make certain of Liberal and Conservative support and of restoring financial confidence. MacDonald was 'disappointed & disheartened', unsure whether he could persuade the Cabinet 'to do the right thing'.[68]

An all-day Cabinet meeting on Wednesday 19 August satisfied no one. Fear of collapses in sterling and unemployment insurance finance, fear of parliamentary defeat, lack of any 'clear idea' of their own on 'the way out', and Henderson's qualified approval did however break most other ministers' resistance to the large cuts proposed by the Cabinet committee.[69] Only Lansbury, and perhaps Greenwood and Johnston, opposed all the social service cuts.[70] The notion of 'equal sacrifice', with its promises of direct tax increases and Liberal and Conservative co-operation, was gratefully adopted. Some ministers underscored the point by making their acceptance of cuts dependent upon the other parties' accepting the tax proposals. The new taxation seemed so satisfactorily large that it was not examined in detail. Henderson's and Graham's rejection of the 10 per cent unemployment benefit cut was confirmed. Most ministers accepted that transitional benefit could not remain a budget charge, but they refused to subject claimants to the hated public assistance means test. The problem was therefore referred to a new Cabinet committee.[71]

At Henderson's insistence the chief Cabinet issue, occupying much of the day's discussion, was a revenue tariff. Its importance was that

[68] MacDonald diary, 18 Aug. 1931; MacDonald to Wigram, 19 Aug. 1931, RA GV K2330(1)/2.
[69] Passfield to Pease, 1 Sept. 1931, in MacKenzie, *Webb Letters* III, 361; B. Webb diary, 21 [22 written] Aug. 1931 (Cole, 280; MacKenzie IV, 251).

   Apart from Cabinet minutes there are four useful extended, if retrospective and tendentious, accounts of Cabinet meetings: (i) 'Notes on the Cabinet and the Crisis' [Sept. 1931], copies in Addison, Morrison, Lansbury, and Passfield papers, hereafter cited as Greenwood notes from attribution in latter IV:26/34; (ii) Lansbury memo, 'The Cabinet Crisis of 1931' [Sept. 1931], Lansbury papers 25.III.n, hereafter Lansbury, 'Cabinet Crisis'; (iii) Thomas memo [March 1932], and (iv) Thomas notes, 14 March 1932, both M. MacDonald papers 6/3, hereafter cited without date and location.
[70] Lansbury, 'Cabinet Crisis'; Sankey diary, 1 Jan. 1932; Dalton diary, 27 Aug. 1931 (Pimlott, 152); and see Postgate, *Lansbury*, 269.
[71] Cabinet 41(31), 19 Aug. 1931; B. Webb diary, 21 [22 written] Aug. 1931 (Cole, 280; MacKenzie IV, 251); Greenwood notes.

it appeared to offer badly needed flexibility in bargaining with the
Conservative leaders and, given Bank of England support, even with
the Liberals. In the previous day's committee meeting, MacDonald
and Thomas had joined Henderson and Graham in pressing it, but
for the opposite reason. For them it offered a substitute not for
further cuts but for some direct taxation if, as seemed probable,
Liberal and Conservative leaders thought this too heavy. It also
seemed a possible sweetener to industrial opinion. Between them
MacDonald and Henderson were now able to create a Cabinet tariff
majority. But to the annoyance of both, Snowden's resistance to the
slightest hint of protection remained the one absolutely immovable
rock of his radicalism, and Alexander, Benn, Passfield, Parmoor, and
Lees-Smith supported him. As these six free-trade purists threatened
resignation, decision was postponed until after the following day's
consultations with outside groups.[72]

These consultations with Liberal and Conservative leaders,
Labour executives, and the TUC General Council, would clearly be
crucial. Senior ministers did not consider the Cabinet decisions
'hard and fast', but as proposals to help edge matters towards all-
round agreement. Henderson expected the Labour and TUC bodies
to criticise the cuts, and Conservatives to insist on a tariff – pressures
which together might persuade the six Cabinet free traders to yield.
MacDonald and Snowden still thought the £78·5m. retrenchment
total, now made still more provisional by the differences over the
£20m. of transitional benefit, insufficient in comparison with direct
taxation, but thought Liberal and Conservative criticism might
persuade the Cabinet to accept further cuts and (in MacDonald's
case) a revenue tariff.[73] All three were to be disappointed.

THE LABOUR CRISIS

When MacDonald and Snowden met Chamberlain, Hoare, Samuel,
and Maclean on Thursday morning, 20 August, everyone present
had their own reason for avoiding all mention of a revenue tariff.
After Snowden had detailed the proposed £78·5m. expenditure cuts,
Samuel's and Maclean's reactions were that these were 'courageous

[72] Cabinet 41(31), 19 Aug. 1931; B. Webb diary, 21 [22 written] Aug. 1931 (Cole, 280);
Henderson in Dalton diary, 20 Aug. 1931 (Dalton, 267–8); MacDonald diary, 19 Aug.
1931; MacDonald in S. MacDonald notes, 22 Aug. 1931.
[73] For doubts about budget programme, MacDonald diary, 19 and 20 Aug. 1931; for
bargaining flexibility, MacDonald reported in Duff–Hardinge telephone conversation, 20
Aug. 1931, RA GV K2330(1)/4.

and not unsatisfactory', Chamberlain's that they were 'not bad'. But the 'shock' of hearing for the first time that the prospective budget deficit was now £170m. transformed their attitude.[74] Chamberlain declared that this revised estimate made it 'wrong' to propose retrenchment lower than the May majority's total. His chief concerns were the retrenchment expectations of Conservatives and financiers, and resistance to very large increases in direct taxation. But he found a more attractive 'social justice' argument to make the point: that public employees might be resentful and resist the proposed salary and wage cuts if unemployment benefit rates remained unchanged.[75]

MacDonald and Snowden made no attempt to disguise their agreement. They themselves thought such a benefit cut necessary, and they had expected Chamberlain's verdict. As this specific cut would clearly become the chief condition for three-party agreement, they also intended using the Conservative reaction to increase pressure upon the Cabinet, thereby enabling negotiations to continue. They claimed to have used similar arguments themselves. Snowden even volunteered the further justification that because of increased benefits and falling prices the unemployed were 36 per cent better off than in 1924. MacDonald and Snowden implied that Cabinet consideration of unemployment insurance was continuing, and on the understanding that further decisions would be forthcoming a further three-party consultation was arranged to follow the next Cabinet meeting.[76]

With ministerial bargaining room rapidly shrinking, an obvious move was to play one set of party leaders off against another. Later that day MacDonald summoned Chamberlain, but he again declined to discuss a tariff. Samuel had tried to help the Cabinet by suggesting temporary suspension of the Sinking Fund. That, however, remained unacceptable to Snowden, and when Mac-Donald and Graham saw Samuel separately he categorically refused to consider a revenue tariff. Like Chamberlain, he now pressed for an unemployment benefit cut.[77]

---

[74] Samuel to Lothian, 21 Aug. 1931, Lothian papers 143/12; and see Samuel memo, 'Course of Events August 20th–23rd 1931', Samuel papers A/78/7 [hereafter, Samuel, 'Course of Events']; N. Chamberlain diary, 22 Aug. 1931. For reactions, MacDonald diary, 20 Aug. 1931; Snowden, *Autobiography* II, 939.

[75] N. Chamberlain diary, 22 Aug. 1931.

[76] N. Chamberlain to his wife, 21 Aug. 1931, NC 1/26/446; N. Chamberlain diary, 22 Aug. 1931.

[77] Cabinet 42(31), 20 Aug. 1931; N. Chamberlain to his wife, 21 Aug. 1931, NC 1/26/446; Samuel, 'Course of Events'.

This was a fateful moment, for two reasons. First, it marked a shift in the relationships between parties. As concerned as the Conservatives to mitigate direct taxation, unwilling to be outdone by them on retrenchment, and encouraged by MacDonald's and Snowden's statements that they hoped for further cuts, Samuel and Maclean had decided to follow Chamberlain's lead. Although this became apparent only on the next day, by doing so they had abandoned the Lloyd George–Liberal alliance with the Labour Cabinet and set the party upon a quite different course. Second, the specific question of reduction in the rates of unemployment benefit now became the central issue of the sterling, budget, and political crises. The sum involved was small: on a 10 per cent cut, around £12m. But the question had far greater significance than the mere money saving. Just as Henderson made resistance to this cut the symbol of continued commitment to the maintenance of working-class living standards and Labour party principles, so MacDonald, Snowden, Neville Chamberlain, Hoare, Samuel, and Maclean together made its imposition the touchstone for 'equal sacrifice', all-party co-operation, and sound finance.

Even while MacDonald and Snowden prepared for a further Cabinet effort, however, their prospects of success were undermined by the meetings that same day (20 August) with Labour party executives and TUC leaders. Here the key figure was Henderson. The party management task was to hold together a Cabinet looking to the broad, national, responsibilities of government, and a wider Labour movement looking to a specific, Labour, interpretation of working-class interests and certain to dislike the Cabinet's proposals. Henderson's tactic was to seek acquiescence in the Cabinet's current proposals by presenting himself as successfully conducting a 'tremendously hard fight' against even worse cuts.[78] Faced first by parliamentary party consultative committee members who felt that 'any attempt to implement [the May majority] recommendations must provoke the most serious crisis the party has yet faced',[79] Henderson converted them to offering the Cabinet help 'in every possible way'. Then, after a joint National Executive–TUC General Council meeting, Henderson persuaded the National Executive to leave matters to the Cabinet by a 'quite moving' appeal for trust. Both the parliamentary and national executives declared strong

[78] Henderson in Dalton diary, 20 Aug. 1931 (Dalton, 269).
[79] Ede in *HC Deb*, 256, cols. 62–3, 8 Sept. 1931.

opposition to benefit cuts, but Henderson reassured them by more or less explicit undertakings that benefit rates would be unchanged and that some proposed cuts would be replaced by a revenue tariff.[80]

Thus far, Henderson had staved off immediate trouble from the Labour party. Yet he had done so by committing the Cabinet precisely in that area where MacDonald and Snowden had told Liberal and Conservative leaders that the Cabinet remained undecided. This contradiction was crucial for future Cabinet discussion: in itself it would have produced confrontation between Henderson and the other two ministers. However, what would make Henderson absolutely refuse to depart from his commitments to the party executives was the TUC General Council's reaction, which became apparent only late in the evening.

A Cabinet was held meanwhile to receive reports of the day's various ministerial meetings. Here MacDonald's and Snowden's hopes of edging the Cabinet towards further retrenchment faced an immediate difficulty. The Cabinet committee on transitional benefit found Henderson's proposed 'premium' inadequate and impractical, and could agree upon devices to save only a small part of the £20m. This jeopardised even the Cabinet's existing £78·5m. retrenchment scheme, already criticised by the Liberal and Conservative leaders. Snowden thereupon reopened the question of deeper unemployment insurance cuts – arguing for 'equal sacrifice' in comparison to other cuts and to tax increases, and for a cost-of-living reduction by comparison with lower benefits tolerated by the 1924 Labour Cabinet.[81] But before any of this could be discussed, the meeting had to break up until the next day so that senior ministers could receive a TUC General Council deputation. The critical Cabinet discussion of further cuts would therefore proceed under the shadow of the TUC's response to the Cabinet's existing proposals.

The TUC leaders had entered that afternoon's joint meeting with the national executive in an angry mood, and left even angrier. Already suspicious about Cabinet intentions, they were outraged by MacDonald's and Snowden's attitude. These two ministers plainly expected trouble, and tried to evade serious consultation. MacDonald spoke in the most general terms about the financial and

[80] Lindsay to MacDonald, 20 Aug. 1931, JRM 260; S. Hirst in *TUCAR 1931*, 84, 7 Sept. 1931. See LPNEC, 20 Aug. 1931, for Henderson even persuading it to settle down to routine business.

[81] Cabinet 42(31), 8.30 pm, 20 Aug. 1931; Thomas notes. The Cabinet committee consisted of Bondfield (chairman), Graham, Greenwood, and Johnston.

political position and 'equal sacrifice', offering no details of Cabinet proposals. Only when Citrine protested that the General Council could express no opinion on such information did Snowden describe the Cabinet's current retrenchment (but not taxation) proposals. His statement that these did not include an unemployment benefit cut – strictly accurate, but disingenuous given his own objectives – contributed to later difficulties, especially as Henderson had then presented it to the National Executive as a definite pledge.[82] But more important still was the General Council's attitude towards those cuts already mostly accepted by Cabinet members, including Henderson.

For TUC leaders, MacDonald's and Snowden's statements confirmed their worst fears about the Cabinet, fears which dated from 1924 but which had grown rapidly since the previous autumn. It seemed that, having gradually submitted to financial orthodoxy, ministers had now been so naive as to be frightened by bankers. To Bevin and Citrine the sterling crisis was unconnected with the budget or unemployment insurance. Rather, its causes lay partly in the City's mistaken investment decisions and partly in a fabricated 'capitalist' anti-labour scare. The 'City must not be saved at the expense of the working class'; the TUC could no longer tolerate an apparently limitless 'continuance of…deflation'. Here was the fruit of the General Council's independent economic policy developed since 1926, and here, at least, the Macmillan Committee had produced immediate results. Bevin had become sufficiently confident about monetary questions to doubt that the crisis would result in financial 'disaster', and consequently was willing to risk devaluation. The greatest danger seemed to come not from the sterling crisis but from the politicians who, irrespective of what the TUC might say, were plainly intent upon immediately balancing the budget by social service cuts, and who, ignoring the trade unions' essential function, assumed that public service wage-negotiation procedures could be set aside arbitrarily. The General Council's response, delivered by a deputation to the Cabinet economy committee, was that any sacrifices must fall as declared by the May minority Report – according to 'capacity to pay'. Unlike Henderson they applied the principle rigorously to exclude all cuts in unemployment insurance and in public service incomes except, maliciously, those of ministers. Their alternative proposal for unemployment insurance was that it

[82] LPNEC-TUCGC joint meeting, 3 pm, 20 Aug. 1931; Snowden, *Autobiography* II, 941; Dalton diary, 20 Aug. 1931 (Dalton, 269). For savage criticism of MacDonald statement, see Citrine in *TUCAR 1931*, 79, 7 Sept.

10 Ernest Bevin and Walter Citrine

should be financed by a graduated levy on the whole community. There should be war-debt conversion and Sinking Fund suspension. Ignorant of Snowden's taxation proposals, they suggested a *rentier* tax. They also mentioned a revenue tariff, but on this they were themselves deeply divided and could give no definite view until the full TUC had been consulted.[83]

The General Council did not expect adoption of these proposals, so contrary to what bankers, the Treasury, Conservatives, and Liberals were known to want. Thoroughly disillusioned with the

[83] Bevin statement, 17 Aug. 1931, in Bullock, *Bevin* I, 480; TUCGC, 4.20 pm, 20 Aug. 1931; Bevin and Citrine at TUC General Council subcommittee-Cabinet economy committee meeting, 9.30 pm, 20 Aug. 1931, in TUCGC; Citrine in *TUCAR 1931*, 82, 7 Sept.

Cabinet for stumbling into a conflict of policies, outraged as much by Henderson's as by MacDonald's and Snowden's acceptance that working-class living standards must suffer, regarding itself as now the only firm defender of labour interests, it had abandoned the Labour government as a lost cause. Expecting the financial and party-political pressures to force the government's collapse in any event – if not in the imminent future then by a later parliamentary or party crisis – the General Council preferred to precipitate that collapse rather than compromise itself. Its chief concerns now were to establish the terms of TUC support for whatever bits of the Labour party emerged from the wreck, and to give the clearest possible signal that efforts by private employers to imitate government in a general wage-cutting campaign would be resisted.[84]

For Henderson, the General Council's attitude promised a party management nightmare. His immediate reaction was to shift his own ground, proposing not just a revenue tariff but Sinking Fund suspension and abandonment of most of the unemployment insurance cuts.[85] Yet, torn by a 'double loyalty' to the Cabinet and the wider Labour movement, he did not cave in completely to the General Council. For him, the political wing of the movement retained some autonomy from the industrial wing. He did not join Lansbury in outright opposition to all the proposed social service cuts. Rather, Henderson sought a new compromise which would still balance the budget yet be acceptable to the party, even in the teeth of TUC criticism; a package pitched more towards holding the Labour party together than winning Liberal and Conservative co-operation. He hoped this package would save sterling, but knew it would mean parliamentary defeat by a combined Conservative–Liberal opposition. Labour unity took priority over government survival.[86]

MacDonald accurately judged the General Council's statement to be 'practically a declaration of war'.[87] His initial reaction was that this alone must mean 'the end' of the Cabinet and of his leadership. The government could not continue in the face of such opposition from so powerful a body within the Labour movement, and 'a leader

[84] For fear of general wage-cutting, see ibid. For indication of expected Cabinet collapse, see Bevin statement, 17 Aug. 1931, in Bullock, *Bevin* I, 480.

[85] MacDonald diary, 20 Aug. 1931 (Marquand, 620–1).

[86] For 'double loyalty', Dalton diary, 20 Aug. 1931 (Dalton, 269). For a good description of Henderson's position at this stage, see Thorpe, 'Henderson', 121–3.

[87] MacDonald diary, 20 Aug. 1931 (Marquand, 620), and see MacDonald in M. MacDonald diary, 21 Aug. 1931, for TUC 'ultimatum'.

who gets too far ahead of his following is simply a voice crying in the wilderness'.[88] Yet MacDonald's morale very soon recovered. The effect of the General Council's opposition upon him was to be the reverse of that upon Henderson: it stiffened his determination to press for further retrenchment.

Press speculation that the Cabinet would evade substantial expenditure cuts had further damaged financial confidence, and depletion of the central bank credits had become so rapid that it seemed sterling might collapse before Parliament could meet. Still hoping that sterling might be rescued by government borrowing in New York,[89] MacDonald thought matters had now come to a choice between the Labour Cabinet itself taking the decisions needed to secure three-party co-operation and restore financial confidence, or resigning to allow another government to take them. To remain in office with a programme which would not prevent a financial crash – which is how MacDonald saw Henderson's position – would be politically disastrous for the Labour party. Yet equally, for the Cabinet to evade responsibility by resignation would involve 'great humiliation'.[90] To run away from a national crisis would destroy the work, including MacDonald's own lifework, of establishing Labour as a party fit to govern and possessing real power to advance progressive causes. This would certainly be so if instead of taking a 'national', non-class position, the Cabinet was seen to submit to TUC views. Resignation would be 'the end of Labour Government for 25 years'.[91] For MacDonald the issue had now also become that of defending the constitutional role of a parliamentary party. 'If we yield now to the TUC we shall never be able to call our bodies or souls or intelligences our own.' It would 'never be said of [him] that [he] allowed the Labour party to be ruled by narrow self-interested sections rather than the well-being of the country'.[92]

MacDonald considered the General Council narrow and selfish even though he supposed it 'voice[d] the feeling of the mass of workers'. It looked only to 'superficial appearances': by defending nominal incomes it was in fact endangering the real standards of

---

[88] MacDonald reported in Duff to Wigram, 21 Aug. 1931, RA GV K2330(1)/5.
[89] Harvey and Hopkins in Vincent to MacDonald, 20 Aug. 1931, PREM 1/96; MacDonald in Grenfell to Morgan, 19 Aug. 1931, MGC.
[90] MacDonald diary, 20 Aug. 1931 (Marquand, 621).
[91] MacDonald in Duff to Wigram, 21 Aug. 1931, RA GV K2330(1)/5.
[92] MacDonald diary, 21 Aug. 1931 (Marquand, 625); MacDonald in S. MacDonald notes, 22–3 Aug. 1931, and in M. MacDonald diary, 21 Aug. 1931. See also Nicolson, *George V*, 458, and Marquand, 624–5.

living.[93] To Snowden, Thomas, and himself it seemed self-evident that in high finance the Bank and Treasury were experts while the TUC was ignorant, its proposals irrelevant to the 'actual problems that faced the Government'.[94] No less than Henderson, they believed they were preserving the best long-term interests of the working classes and the Labour party. Henderson's shift appalled them: he had simply 'surrendered' to the TUC.[95] Nevertheless, though depressed at the prospects late on the 20th, MacDonald awoke on Friday, 21 August 'in a fighting mood', determined to save sterling, the Labour government and Labour party; to 'tak[e] up the [General Council's] challenge' and obtain cuts in un-employment benefit rates.[96]

MacDonald's and Snowden's first step was to counteract the likely effect of the TUC attitude within the Cabinet by obtaining the Bank of England's opinion on what would now be needed to save sterling. Harvey was notably more candid than previously, ex-pressing a definite view on 'political' matters, for three reasons. First, some £30m. of the £50m. bank credits had been consumed in exchange support without the flight from sterling abating, and the Bank now considered a government loan or credit a matter of extreme urgency.[97] Yet the New York Federal Reserve Bank could not lend to foreign governments, while Morgans again advised that American private banks would not subscribe to a loan unless definitely assured of 'real reform' in British government finance and, implicitly, assured also of receiving their interest payments and being repaid.[98] Second, Harvey had heard from Chamberlain on the 20th that the Conservative and Liberal leaders were pressing for further expenditure cuts.[99] So in replying to MacDonald and Snowden, he knew he was simply repeating existing political 'advice'. Third, he was asked to be explicit. His advice – that to balance the budget without 'very substantial economies', including

[93] MacDonald diary, 20 Aug. 1931 (Marquand, 621).
[94] MacDonald to Citrine, 21 Aug. 1931, JRM 260; Snowden at Cabinet 43(31), 21 Aug. 1931.
[95] MacDonald diary, 20 Aug. 1931 (Marquand, 620–1); and see Sankey diary, 21 Aug. 1931 for MacDonald–Henderson 'personal quarrel'.
[96] MacDonald diary, 21 Aug. 1931 (Marquand, 625); MacDonald in M. MacDonald diary, 21 Aug. 1931.
[97] Bank of England memo, '£ sterling', 27 Aug. 1931, PREM 1/97; Peacock to Steel-Maitland, 16 Aug. 1931, Steel-Maitland papers 120/3; Harvey in Vincent to MacDonald, 20 Aug. 1931, PREM 1/96.
[98] Grenfell to Morgan, 19 and 21 Aug. 1931, MGC. Williamson, 'Bankers Ramp?', 790.
[99] N. Chamberlain to his wife, 21 Aug. 1931, NC 1/26/446.

unemployment insurance cuts, would have a 'most detrimental effect', and that further delay threatened 'great dangers' – was not dictation, but precisely what MacDonald and Snowden expected and wanted to hear.[100]

When the Cabinet met at 10 am, Snowden reported the TUC's statement, and MacDonald reported Harvey's. MacDonald then argued that pending the reassembly of Parliament it was 'imperative' that there should be a government capable of decisive action in the event of an emergency, and that the best course was for the existing one to produce an appropriate programme. This succeeded in persuading the Cabinet to defy the General Council and renew its consideration of cuts.[101] Passfield was not alone in thinking that MacDonald was still acting in 'all good faith', and that the TUC General Council, in its insensitivity to their dilemma, were 'pigs'.[102] On the other hand Henderson's stand was effective, reinforcing the resistance of the doubters. MacDonald was unable to persuade the Cabinet to accept further cuts, or even prevent reduction in its existing proposals. Of twenty-one Cabinet members, only eleven supported a 10 per cent cut in unemployment benefits. Smaller percentage cuts were considered and Henderson, still trying to create a compromise of his own, again pressed the 'premium'. But other ministers rejected these suggestions as either too little or too much. Increased employees' contributions and a means test for transitional benefit were accepted, but no other transitional benefit savings were adopted and a proposed twenty-six week limitation on insurance payments was dropped. The effective savings on unemployment insurance were reduced to just £8m. The teachers' salary cut was reduced from 20 per cent to 15 per cent. Overall, the Cabinet's final retrenchment scheme totalled £56·375m., some £22m. less than that provisionally accepted on the 19th.[103]

In the afternoon expedients to cover the remaining part of the budget deficit were considered. Lees-Smith revived the proposal to suspend the Sinking Fund,[104] which had both TUC and Liberal

[100] MacDonald in Cabinet 43(31), 21 Aug. 1931. See Williamson, 'Bankers Ramp?', 797.
[101] Cabinet 43(31), 21 Aug. 1931.
[102] B. Webb diary, 22 Aug. 1931 (Cole, 281; MacKenzie IV, 252); also Thomas notes.
[103] Cabinet 43(31), 21 Aug. 1931, including CP 203(31) Revise; MacDonald diary, 22 Aug. 1931; Lansbury, 'Cabinet Crisis'; Greenwood notes; Sankey diary, 20 (actually 21) Aug. 1931. Sankey ran together events of different days, probably because he wrote retrospectively: this causes confusion in McKibbin, 'Economic Policy of the Second Labour Government', 117–18 (*Ideologies*, 221).
[104] Duff to Wigram, 21 Aug. 1931, RA GV K2330(1)/5.

support. Hopkins and the Bank had advised that a temporary suspension would not be thought 'improper' by financial opinion, provided it was accompanied by substantial retrenchment.[105] Yet the Cabinet had now reduced its retrenchment programme. Snowden accordingly attempted to close off that escape and to force further cuts by declaring suspension to be 'utter[ly] impractica[l]'. Nevertheless he was overborne by a Cabinet majority. Sinking Fund suspension was then held to make a revenue tariff unnecessary. MacDonald and Snowden were to report the programme immediately to Bank directors and the Conservative and Liberal leaders, inform junior ministers of their salary cuts, and arrange the recall of Parliament.[106]

Most ministers, considering their work done, dispersed to their homes for the weekend. The budget was to be balanced, but by means which Snowden and the Bank of England said were inadequate to halt the flight from sterling. Henderson and other ministers had neither contested this, nor accepted Bevin's scepticism about the possibility of some disaster. They simply closed their minds to the financial consequences of their decisions. Although one political consequence was clear – government defeat once Parliament met – what mattered more was that their programme seemed defensible to their party and electoral supporters. In contrast MacDonald and Snowden, as soon as benefit cuts had been rejected, had told the Cabinet that its programme was 'impossible'. They participated in examining other proposals only so that the Cabinet's full decisions could be reported to the Bank of England and the other party leaders. They were angry, exasperated, distraught – displaying at these next two meetings a 'reckless attitude'.[107]

During the Cabinet meeting the Bank of England had concluded that the situation was now desperate. At the current pace of exchange support operations, its existing resources appeared sufficient to last just four more days. One way or another, some decision would have to be made over the weekend. The position had become so serious that senior directors considered suspension of the gold standard imminent, and discussed at length the possible

[105] Bank directors in Samuel, 'Course of Events'; Hopkins to Snowden, 20 Aug. 1931, T171/288.
[106] Cabinet 43(31), 21 Aug. 1931; Passfield in B. Webb diary, 22 Aug. 1931 (Cole, 281; MacKenzie IV, 252).
[107] Cabinet 43(31), 21 Aug. 1931; MacDonald diary, 22 Aug. 1931 (Marquand, 626); N. Chamberlain to his wife, 23 Aug. 1931, NC 1/26/447.

expedients for containing an expected financial panic.[108] A life-line
had, however, appeared. Although a long-term American loan still
depended upon parliamentary action, the Federal Reserve Bank and
Morgans now advised that private bankers in the USA and France
might contribute to short-term credits – if the government announced proposals likely to satisfy 'public sentiment'.[109]

The anticipated four-day deadline and this prospect of deliverance
had been reported to Conservative and Liberal leaders while the
Cabinet was sitting.[110] Once it had ended, MacDonald and Snowden
were informed. But on hearing the revised Cabinet programme
Harvey and Peacock confirmed MacDonald's and Snowden's fears:
they advised that it was not only inadequate but likely to worsen the
situation. To potential American and French lenders who already
believed unemployment insurance expenditure to be a heavy burden
on British industry, the new taxation, the insurance contributions,
and the Sinking Fund suspension would be regarded as 'impairing
the security for their loans'.[111] Nevertheless – contrary again to
simple notions of 'bankers' dictation' – MacDonald instructed
Harvey to make a formal request for government credits. From sheer
desperation, he also proposed that the American and French
bankers need not be informed of the increased budget deficit and
proposed Sinking Fund suspension, ignoring Harvey's protest that
this would constitute a 'fraudulent prospectus'.[112]

At a three-party conference immediately afterwards Chamberlain,
Hoare, Samuel, and Maclean – again as MacDonald and Snowden
had expected – dismissed the Cabinet's reduced retrenchment
proposals as 'derisory', and complained of the 'injustice' of so small
a proportion falling on unemployment insurance.[113] The ministers
said they 'entirely agreed',[114] but could obtain no more. If the
programme failed to elicit financial assistance Snowden expected
'the deluge', MacDonald that Parliament would have to impose a

---

[108] BoE Cte, 21 Aug. 1931. The prospect had first been mentioned on the 18th, when Bank
officials were instructed to prepare contingency plans.
[109] J. P. Morgan & Co. to Grenfell, tm 31/2380, 10 am, 21 Aug. 1931, MGC; Harrison to
Harvey, tm 301/31, 21 Aug. 1931, FRBNY papers; Thompson-McCausland, 'Crisis', 32.
[110] N. Chamberlain diary, 22 Aug. 1931.
[111] Cabinet 44(31), 22 Aug. 1931; MacDonald diary, 22 Aug. 1931.
[112] MacDonald and Harvey in N. Chamberlain diary, 22 Aug. 1931; Williamson, 'Bankers
Ramp?', 798–9.
[113] Maclean to Grey, 22–4 Aug. 1931, Runciman papers 245; MacDonald diary, 22 Aug.
1931.
[114] Samuel, 'Course of Events'.

moratorium.[115] When Hoare protested against such fatalism, MacDonald asked whether the Conservative and Liberal leaders were 'prepared to join the Board of Directors'. Though expressed 'in a semi-jocular way', the Conservative and Liberal leaders understood that this was a genuine suggestion. Hoare replied 'that if seriously made [it] was a proposition which would demand serious consideration'. Samuel proposed that the Conservative and Liberal leaders should withdraw to confer together.[116] From this meeting an agreed strategy emerged. How seriously the proposition should be treated was less clear to MacDonald himself.

A 'NATIONAL' SOLUTION

The 'national government' idea was so familiar as a possible emergency arrangement that once the political crisis began, discussion about it became 'amazing[ly] widespread'.[117] Conservative newspapers, all clamorous for incisive retrenchment, aired much (largely inaccurate) speculation about it, some with favour but *The Times* notably critical. One or two Conservative and Liberal backbench MPs, including Morris-Jones, a proponent of the previous autumn, took up the call. Some on the political fringes assumed 'national government' was all but inevitable.[118] Whatever their own views, as the crisis deepened political leaders expected the idea to be proposed from one quarter or other.

Snowden, believing that Conservatives would demand a tariff, had publicly declared on 17 August that 'national government' was 'out of the question'. On the 22nd, assuming an imminent Labour Cabinet collapse, he anticipated his ministerial retirement by announcing that he would not stand at the next election.[119] MacDonald and Thomas, however, certainly considered 'national government' one of several possible means of containing the political

[115] N. Chamberlain diary, 22 Aug. 1931, and N. Chamberlain to his wife, 23 Aug. 1931, NC 1/26/447.
[116] N. Chamberlain diary, 22 Aug. 1931, confirmed by Maclean to Grey, 22–4 Aug. 1931, Runciman papers 245. For a different interpretation of the evening's events, see Ball, 'Conservative Party and the Formation of the National Government', 165–6; Ball, *Baldwin*, 177.   [117] Dawson to Grigg, 9 Aug. 1931, Altrincham papers.
[118] E.g., *Daily Mail*, 10 Aug. 1931; *Evening Standard* and *Daily Express*, 11 Aug. 1931; *Observer*, 16 Aug. 1931; G. Kindersley letter, *The Times*, 11 Aug. 1931; Morris-Jones speech, *Liverpool Post*, 11 Aug. 1931; Nicolson to Mosley, 14 Aug. 1931, in N. Mosley, *Rules of the Game*, 196; Bevin statement, 17 Aug. 1931, in Bullock, *Bevin* I, 480.
[119] Interview, *Daily Herald*, 17 Aug. 1931; Snowden to Heywood, 22 Aug. 1931, in Snowden, *Autobiography* II, 959. Of course Snowden had for months intended retiring to the Lords: the significance lies in the date of his announcement.

crisis. Faced with Cabinet resistance to further cuts on the 19th, Thomas had said that if ministers could not impose these themselves they would have to support another Cabinet which would. MacDonald had then 'adumbrated the possibility of a National Government'.[120] At this point, MacDonald and Thomas appear to have meant an arrangement similar to the wartime coalitions: the Labour party leaders should tolerate honest differences, and in the national interest agree that some Labour ministers might continue in an emergency Cabinet headed by Baldwin, as leader of what now seemed to be the largest united party.[121] Yet MacDonald's obvious preference, on which he expended enormous effort, was still to keep the Labour Cabinet in office and so far as possible maintain Labour party unity. He had no other settled intention, because none was possible. The current crisis raised matters of deep party-political differences, making 'national government' seem less possible than in mid July.[122] It would now be extremely difficult to persuade even substantial sections of the Cabinet to accept such an arrangement, let alone Labour MPs and the party organisation. That MacDonald nevertheless raised the idea in Cabinet and later with Liberal and Conservative leaders represented desperate attempts, at moments of extreme difficulty, to find for the sake of the Labour party's reputation some respectable alternative to wholesale Cabinet resignation.

The chief effect of the three-party conference on 21 August was that Liberal and Conservative rejection of ministerial proposals steeled MacDonald to make another attempt with the Cabinet. While Chamberlain, Hoare, Samuel, and Maclean were conferring together, he recalled those ministers still available to report the Bank's and party leaders' views, and then summoned the full Cabinet back for another meeting the following morning.[123] MacDonald's main objective was to use the Bank's warning to obtain further cuts, sufficient to satisfy the Conservative and Liberal leaders and make it possible to borrow abroad. In the likely event of failure, however, a secondary intention was to discover whether, in

---

[120] Greenwood notes, and see Alexander in B. Webb diary, 1 Jan. 1932. These sources and their retrospective character may appear suspect. But there is no other reason to doubt their accuracy, nor to draw the sinister implications intended. MacDonald gave characteristically vague hints in MacDonald to Bailey, 11 Aug. 1931, JRM 673, and to Wigram, 19 Aug. 1931, RA GV K2330(1)/2.

[121] See 'some ministers' reported in Duff to Wigram, 19 Aug. 1931, RA GV K2330(1)/3.

[122] A point well made in Bassett, *Nineteen Thirty-One*, 64–5.

[123] MacDonald diary, 22 Aug. 1931; Duff, 'Financial Crisis'.

the light of the intensified sterling crisis, a substantial number of ministers might even now accept a 'national government'. Failing all this, a Cabinet meeting would still be necessary if the Labour government was to resign in time to enable a Conservative-led government to prevent a financial crash.

Like MacDonald, the Conservative and Liberal leaders still wanted the Labour Cabinet to remain in office and solve the budget and sterling crises. But they now had to decide how to persuade it to do so and, more pressingly, what to do if it would not. At this critical moment, with MacDonald necessarily tentative over what might replace the Labour Cabinet, Neville Chamberlain as acting leader of the parliamentary opposition and prospective alternative government became the leading force, the one with most power to initiate. He had made certain of a united Conservative and Liberal stand for further retrenchment in meetings with Hailsham, Cunliffe-Lister, Eyres-Monsell, and Kingsley Wood on 20 August, and with Samuel and Maclean on the following morning. Then, suspecting during the 21st that the Cabinet had serious divisions, he reverted to his calculations of late July. He expected MacDonald either to submit to Cabinet opposition, propose inadequate cuts, and precipitate a financial collapse; or to persist, accept a Cabinet split, and propose a national government. He did not expect MacDonald simply to resign. Nor did he contemplate a Conservative or Conservative–Liberal government. Rather, Chamberlain thought that a Mac-Donald 'national government' proposal 'could not be refused'. Hoare and Cunliffe-Lister, consulted during the 21st, agreed.[124] Three-party participation in budget decisions would greatly assist the restoration of financial confidence. But this would now also be, defensively, to Conservative advantage. If the Labour Cabinet would not impose unpopular expenditure cuts, responsibility for them would be better shared by representatives of all three parties than borne by Conservatives and Liberals against united Labour opposition – which would carry considerable political, electoral, financial, and social risks of polarisation between classes, between rich and poor. As during the previous week, but with a different conclusion, national and Conservative party interests appeared to coincide. These interests were now so pressing that contrary to the

---

[124] N. Chamberlain to his wife, 3 pm, 21 Aug. 1931, NC 1/26/446; N. Chamberlain diary, 22 Aug. 1931. See also Cunliffe-Lister to his wife, 'Friday' [21 Aug. 1931], Swinton papers, 270/3/22, written after lunch with Chamberlain (see latter's pocket diary, NC 2/29/28), but before the 4.45 pm three-party conference.

terms proposed in late July, it seemed acceptable that MacDonald rather than Baldwin should head any 'national government'. Hence Hoare's encouraging reply to MacDonald's question at the three-party meeting; hence also at the subsequent Conservative–Liberal consultation Chamberlain's evident 'willing[ness] to join' a 'national government'.[125]

Samuel has usually been regarded as chiefly responsible for the 'national' solution, because of advice he later gave the King. Yet he was one of the very last leading politicians seriously to consider the idea, and as acting leader of a small, split, party he had no reason to think it was practical or desirable until Chamberlain showed him that it could be so. His first reaction to MacDonald's question had been that MacDonald should resign.[126] For Samuel and Maclean the situation was highly delicate. On the one hand, concern to restore financial confidence and impose retrenchment was breaking the Lloyd George Liberal–Labour Cabinet alliance. On the other, co-operation with the Conservative party alone was unattractive, because it would impair Lloyd George Liberal 'radical' credentials and might well involve embarrassment over tariffs. Yet to stand aside altogether would render them ineffective and discredited. It would also create an opportunity for the Simon group to take office as 'patriotic' Liberals. Reading, who had returned on the 13th and been consulted regularly by Samuel and Maclean, was certainly an influence. He had now publicly expressed his preference for a 'national government'.[127] The attraction of the idea to party leaders who had been excluded from office for over a decade is patent, with Maclean anticipating that he might for the first time receive a Cabinet post.[128]

The Conservative and Liberal leaders' consultation resulted in agreement that by a threat of combined Conservative–Liberal opposition in Parliament MacDonald should be compelled to avert the financial 'catastrophe'. He should do this preferably with the existing Cabinet, alternatively with a 'reconstruct[ed]' Cabinet, and only in the last resort through resignation to allow action by some other government. But they also agreed that a threat of such importance required endorsement from their respective colleagues.

[125] Maclean to Grey, 22–4 Aug. 1931, Runciman papers 245 (which reports it as a direct statement). [126] N. Chamberlain diary, 22 Aug. 1931.
[127] Reading statement, *The Times*, 15 Aug. 1931. Reading had wanted to attend the three-party talks, but Samuel preferred Maclean. For close consultation, see Reading notes in Reading papers F118/131.
[128] Maclean to his wife, 21 Aug. 1931, Maclean papers, c468/119.

In informing MacDonald that further consultations were needed, however, they ensured that the retrenchment issue was reopened by persuading him that his instructions to Harvey concerning foreign credits should be postponed.[129]

Chamberlain and Hoare again consulted Hailsham, Cunliffe-Lister, Eyres-Monsell, and Kingsley Wood, who all 'concurred entirely'.[130] Chamberlain also decided to recall Baldwin from France. Samuel obtained Reading's agreement by telephone and consulted Lloyd George in his sick bed. Lloyd George appears to have told his intimates that he was opposed to the May Report and to Samuel's attitude, yet Samuel claimed that Lloyd George considered the Cabinet proposals 'totally inadequate'. Moreover Lloyd George proposed that if the Labour Cabinet remained divided the King should, as during the December 1916 crisis, summon a Buckingham Palace conference of party leaders. Use of that precedent clearly implied a readiness to have Lloyd George Liberals represented in a 'national' coalition, in accordance with his hopes of mid July.[131]

Returning to Downing Street in the evening, Chamberlain, Hoare, Samuel, and Maclean concerted their tactics before meeting MacDonald alone. MacDonald was informed that as their parties considered the Cabinet retrenchment proposals inadequate, the Labour government would be defeated as soon as Parliament met. In the meantime, however, MacDonald's 'bounden duty' would be to prevent a financial crash, and for that purpose each party would 'give him any support in [their] power' – either 'with his present or in a reconstructed Govt.'. If necessary, he should see the King at once. The phraseology was elliptical but the meaning transparent. According to Chamberlain, 'National or All Party Government was not mentioned but...it was obvious to everyone that it was not excluded'. According to MacDonald, Chamberlain said plainly that if he 'wished to form a govt. with their cooperation they were willing to serve under me'.[132]

The Conservative and Liberal leaders had delivered an ul-

[129] N. Chamberlain diary, 22 Aug. 1931; Samuel, 'Course of Events'; MacDonald diary, 22 Aug. 1931.   [130] N. Chamberlain diary, 22 Aug. 1931.

[131] F. Stevenson in Sylvester diary, 23 Aug. 1931, in Cross, 37; Samuel in N. Chamberlain and MacDonald diaries, 22 Aug. 1931. For 1916 conference, see Nicolson, *George V*, 289–91.

[132] N. Chamberlain to his wife and to I. Chamberlain, both 23 Aug. 1931, NC 1/26/447, 18/1/753; N. Chamberlain and MacDonald diaries, 22 Aug. 1931 (last in Marquand, 627).

timatum, but one intended to help MacDonald and offering him a means of escape. As such it had the desired effect. MacDonald was 'deeply grateful', because the ultimatum served his own immediate intention of getting the Cabinet to reconsider, but also presented him with a new prospect. At the previous three-party conference he had felt cornered and desperate, even speaking of leaving the Cabinet and joining Conservatives and Liberals in opposition. Now he had an alternative to 'great humiliation': not merely the possibility of a national government, but one he himself might lead. Nevertheless he still did not positively want 'national government'. That prospect was only slightly less depressing than resignation, because with retrenchment as its purpose a national government would probably be repudiated by much of the Labour party. Leaving the party he had 'founded, nursed, cherished, built up' would be like 'killing his own child'. Rather, the possibility of 'national government' remained a reserve position. Armed with the Conservative–Liberal threat, MacDonald's first intention was to save the Cabinet and party. Again in a 'heroical mood', he spoke of asking ministers to support new proposals and telling those who rejected them to go 'where they liked'.[133] Despite the Conservative and Liberal offers of support, he still sought to enlarge the Labour Cabinet's bargaining space by trying again to divide those two parties. At the end of the three-party meeting he asked Samuel and Maclean to remain, but was unable to persuade them to accept cuts lower than the Conservative demands.[134]

MACDONALD'S PERSEVERANCE

MacDonald co-ordinated his renewed effort with Snowden at the Cabinet on Saturday morning, 22 August. He first reported the Bank's and Conservative and Liberal leaders' views, and Snowden increased pressure by implying, with no evident foundation, that the Conservatives and the Bank had altogether rejected suspension of the Sinking Fund. Warning again of the 'appalling consequences' of leaving the gold standard, Snowden declared that his primary duty and that of 'every responsible' Labour leader was to prevent what might be a 50 per cent reduction in workmen's living standards, rather than to preserve the Labour Movement 'in its present form'.

[133] N. Chamberlain to his wife and to I. Chamberlain, both 23 Aug. 1931, NC 1/26/447, 18/1/753; N. Chamberlain and MacDonald diaries, 22 Aug. 1931.
[134] MacDonald in Cabinet 44(31), 22 Aug. 1931; Maclean to Grey, 22–4 Aug. 1931, Runciman papers 245.

Confronting ministers with the alternative of a 'practical certainty of
a moratorium by Wednesday', MacDonald made a new proposal.
Significantly he suggested submitting this to the Conservative and
Liberal leaders first, then to Bank directors. MacDonald, at least,
understood that the effective condition for government borrowing
was not any bankers' terms but three-party agreement. His proposal
would add another £20m. to the existing retrenchment programme
in place of taxation, partly by various minor savings but mostly by
a 10 per cent cut in unemployment benefit yielding £12·25m. This
would establish a new total of £76m. in expenditure cuts.[135] A large
minority opposed the 10 per cent cut, with Henderson now joining
Lansbury, Alexander, Johnston, Greenwood and, less certainly,
Graham and Passfield, in threatening resignation. The proposal was
therefore rejected, with Snowden and Thomas recording their
dissent.[136]

Cabinet members had not previously doubted Bank of England
advice. All had agreed to urgent balancing of the budget. But with
the issue now narrowed to unemployment insurance, the status of
the Bank's advice began to be questioned. Hints in *The Daily Herald*
of a 'bankers' ramp' encouraged this; so too did MacDonald's
emphasis upon the Bank's advice, which created an impression that
it more than Conservative and Liberal leaders had demanded the
cut in benefit rates. Some ministers probably really believed that
bankers were exploiting the crisis to attack unemployment insurance.
Others, knowing that it was the Conservative and Liberal leaders
who specified this cut, were perhaps seeking further justification for
resistance. Probably most were uncertain what to think, but simply
hit out blindly against influences which were unfamiliar and easily
considered sinister. MacDonald declared 'in the most emphatic
terms that there was no ground whatever' for supposing there was
a bankers' 'conspiracy'. Henderson, however, wanted 'an enquiry
into the constitution of the banks', while Graham declared that 'the
City [was] bluffing the Government'.[137] Yet no minister felt

[135] Harvey at BoE Cte, 22 Aug. 1931 for MacDonald–Snowden preliminary meeting;
Cabinet 44(31), 9.30 pm, 22 Aug. 1931; Greenwood notes. Malament, 'Snowden', 32–3,
does not grasp that Sinking Fund suspension remained part of the Cabinet's final
proposals.

[136] Cabinet 44(31), 22 Aug. 1931; Greenwood notes; Lansbury, 'Cabinet Crisis'. The names
can be compiled from MacDonald and M. MacDonald diaries, and S. MacDonald notes,
all 23 Aug. 1931, in Marquand, 630–2, and from B. Webb diary, 23 Aug. 1931.

[137] Cabinet 44(31), 22 Aug. 1931; Henderson reported by MacDonald in M. MacDonald
diary, 23 Aug. 1931 (Marquand, 632); Graham by Passfield in B. Webb diary, 23 Aug.
1931 (Cole, 282; MacKenzie IV, 253).

confident that a financial crash was not imminent, or thought that
the Cabinet should now continue regardless with its programme of
the previous day. Henderson and the other dissentients declared that
if Conservatives, Liberals, and bankers persisted in considering the
Cabinet proposals inadequate, the Cabinet should resign and allow
another government to be formed. The whole Cabinet therefore
agreed that, as the Conservative and Liberal leaders had suggested,
MacDonald should inform the King of its difficulties and advise that
he consult the other party leaders.[138]

Faced with a deeply divided Cabinet, MacDonald now turned to
the alternatives proposed by the Conservative and Liberal leaders.
As the ministers threatening resignation were both numerous and
influential within the Labour party, and as he thought no
comparable replacements existed among the junior ministers, he did
not consider reconstructing the existing Cabinet. Instead he
proposed to the Cabinet a 'national government', containing a
'nucleus' of Labour ministers, to last for six weeks or until the
emergency was over. This would be preferable to a government in
which Conservatives would have 'all [the] initiative' and it was, he
claimed, 'what the King desired and might propose'. He had no
illusions about the political consequences. The 'nucleus' helping to
impose cuts 'wd. be slaughtered' by the rest of the Labour
movement. Nevertheless he hoped for support from a significant
number of ministers. Thomas seemed favourable, but Henderson
and others in 'hotly reject[ing]' the idea clearly expressed the
general feeling, so Snowden – concluding it was impractical –
declared the Cabinet 'unanimous[ly]' opposed.[139]

MacDonald had always envisaged 'national government' as an
arrangement between whole parties, or at least substantial parts of
them: only this would secure roughly equal shares of power,
consideration, office, and odium or honour for each government
partner. Faced with such hostility among Labour leaders, he knew
he could obtain very little other Labour support. He would be, or

---

[138] Cabinet 44(31), 22 Aug. 1931; MacDonald notes, undated but 22 Aug. 1931, JRM 1316;
Passfield in B. Webb diary, 23 Aug. 1931 (Cole, 282; MacKenzie IV, 253); Duff,
'Financial Crisis', for telephone discussion with Wigram at 11.30 am, to alert the King.

[139] MacDonald notes [22 Aug. 1931], JRM 1316; Passfield in B. Webb diary, 23 Aug. 1931
(Cole, 282; MacKenzie IV, 253); Greenwood notes. MacDonald's source for the King's
view might have been Seely or Greig some weeks or months previously, or else Wigram,
who had spoken with MacDonald on the 11th: see Duff, 'Financial Crisis'. Obviously the
evidence here controverts subsequent claims embedded in Labour polemics and
historiography that MacDonald did not consult the Cabinet about the 'national
government' possibility.

would seem to be, a prisoner of Conservatives and Liberals. With an insignificant Labour following, they might not allow him a leading place or even want him in a coalition at all. MacDonald therefore reverted to thinking that if the existing Cabinet collapsed his least humiliating, and perhaps only possible, course would be to leave office altogether. This remained his attitude for the next thirty-six hours.

Yet MacDonald's persistence and inventiveness were still not exhausted. He made another, despairing, effort to manoeuvre the Cabinet into saving itself. He suggested asking the Conservative and Liberal leaders' opinions on his proposal for an extra £20m. expenditure cuts, again hoping to make retrenchment more palatable by spreading responsibility for it. On the 'distinct' understanding that the Cabinet was 'in no way committed to the proposal' and was 'merely seeking information', Henderson and the other dissentient ministers reluctantly acquiesced.[140]

A further three-party consultation was therefore held shortly after midday. On MacDonald and Snowden explaining the new proposal, Chamberlain, Hoare, Samuel, and Maclean said that, if the Bank of England considered it sufficient to restore financial confidence and obtain foreign credits, they would accept it – but only for those specific purposes. Their answer was conditional upon a definition extracted from MacDonald by Chamberlain and Samuel of what their 'agreement' would mean in parliamentary terms. Desperately needing their support for the chance of saving the Labour Cabinet, MacDonald's reply had been that Conservatives and Liberals should allow a Labour government Economy Bill at least a second reading, but would then be free if they so wished to press for further cuts by amendments in committee.[141]

Chamberlain's reactions to both the proposal and the procedure spoke volumes about his politics throughout the whole crisis. On 20 August Conservative and Liberal leaders had refused support for expenditure cuts totalling £78·5m. The Conservatives asked for a total around the May majority figure of £96·5m., while the Liberals were prepared to accept a lower figure, about £85m. Since then Bank directors had advised that this last total – half the estimated budget deficit – probably represented the minimum required if

---

[140] Cabinet 44(31), 22 Aug. 1931; MacDonald diary, 23 Aug. 1931; Greenwood notes.
[141] N. Chamberlain diary, 22 Aug. 1931; N. Chamberlain to his wife and to I. Chamberlain, both 23 Aug. 1931, NC 1/26/447, 18/1/753; Samuel, 'Course of Events'.

further borrowing was to be possible.[142] But Chamberlain's calculation of the tactical possibilities had now raced ahead. He had wanted a high retrenchment total partly in order to reduce the taxation total. His prior objective, however, had been to obtain the unemployment insurance cut, as the crucial signal to foreign financial opinion, as the essential break with budget extravagance, and for party and electoral purposes. His interest in MacDonald's new proposal was accordingly much more in the 10 per cent benefit cut than the £20m. total. Indeed, since Snowden expressed scepticism about the other proposed cuts, the Conservative and Liberal leaders ignored those and assumed the proposal involved just the additional £12·25m. from unemployment insurance. The new total was therefore about £68m.,[143] considerably less than the sum they had previously demanded and lower than that advised by the Bank. Chamberlain, however, was not an echo of the bankers even on banking matters, and not so pessimistic about the prospects for foreign borrowing. This allowed him more tactical freedom than that available to the other party leaders. Given 'any sort of encouragement' he believed the Americans would lend from fear that a British crash might spread throughout Europe, and the French from hope that it might give them influence over British foreign policy. The Bank was simply 'wrong' in thinking that American and French bankers would consider MacDonald's proposal inadequate.[144] The key was not the retrenchment total but the benefit cut, for both national credit and party interest. Once MacDonald had conceded the limited definition of 'agree', Chamberlain 'saw at once that [he] had played straight into [their] hands'. The 'national government' idea now seemed redundant, and Chamberlain's expectations of the previous week revived. Conservatives would be free to press for further cuts and less taxation. Yet with the Labour Cabinet cutting unemployment insurance, the Labour party would be 'irrevocably split', 'shaken to its foundations', 'its sting drawn' – even, perhaps, unable to 'last long'.[145]

For MacDonald and Snowden, what mattered was that the

---

[142] N. Chamberlain diary, 22 Aug. 1931; Reading in Dawson memo, 22 Aug. 1931, Dawson papers; Cabinet 43(31), 21 Aug. 1931.

[143] N. Chamberlain diary, 22 Aug. 1931; Samuel, 'Course of Events'.

[144] N. Chamberlain diary, 22 Aug. 1931; N. Chamberlain to his wife, 23 Aug. 1931, NC 1/26/447. Cf. Ball, 'Conservative Party and the Formation of the National Government', 170, 173, and Ball, *Baldwin*, 181, 184, for Conservatives close to being an 'echo' of the City.

[145] N. Chamberlain to his wife and to I. Chamberlain, both 23 Aug. 1931, NC 1/26/447, 18/1/753.

Conservative and Liberal leaders had not rejected the proposal. Reporting to the Cabinet, they proposed submitting it to the Bank of England with permission to ask Harrison of the New York Federal Reserve Bank for advice on whether it would be sufficient to allow the government to borrow from American banks. Although this was resisted by the six dissentients the Cabinet again acquiesced, though again emphasised that it remained uncommitted to the proposal. On Harvey and Peacock accepting this procedure, the Cabinet adjourned until Sunday evening when the New York reply was expected and when it would reach a final decision.[146]

The Bank directors themselves were 'shocked' to learn that the Cabinet's proposed retrenchment remained as low as £68m., and doubted that it would be adequate to satisfy potential lenders. But they were reassured by Liberal and Conservative confirmation that the budget programme would have all-party support.[147] Once again it was the politicians, not Bank directors, who determined the budget proposals. Moreover, the Bank had now become just the intermediary between the Cabinet and potential lenders in New York and Paris. A Bank official was sent to Paris, where he was unable to contact week-ending Bank of France governors. But after a sceptical first reaction Harrison reported that Morgans would consider a formal request, which the Treasury sent on Sunday morning.[148] This formal proposal was for short credits and/or long loans of £50m. each in New York and Paris, explicitly not for budget purposes but to defend sterling, to be obtained on the following basis: the 10 per cent in unemployment payments and other economies totalling £68m., additional taxation of around £60m., an emergency Sinking Fund suspension, with undertakings that Unemployment Insurance Fund borrowing would cease and future budgets be balanced out of current income.[149]

Learning from MacDonald on Saturday evening of Morgans' encouraging response, Conservative and Liberal leaders thought the Labour Cabinet would probably accept MacDonald's proposal and

[146] Cabinet 45(31), 2.30 pm, 22 Aug. 1931.
[147] Reading notes [22 Aug. 1931], Reading papers F118/131; Morgan Grenfell, 'Memorandum' [record of 22 Aug.–23 Sept. 1931], MGC file 'Gold Standard 1931' [hereafter cited as Morgan Grenfell 'Memorandum']; N. Chamberlain to his wife, 23 Aug. 1931, NC 1/26/447; BoE Cte, 22 Aug. 1931.
[148] Harvey–MacDonald telephone conversations, 7.20 pm and 10.20 pm, 22 Aug. 1931, PREM 1/96; Morgan Grenfell, 'Memorandum'; MacDonald diary, 23 Aug. 1931; BoE Cte, 22 Aug. 1931.
[149] Harvey to Morgan Grenfell, for transmission to J. P. Morgan & Co., 23 Aug. 1931, MGC.

remain in office. Their attitude was reflected concisely by the Bank of England when commending the Cabinet programme to Harrison and Morgans: 'Great importance attached here to psychological effect of a cut in cost of social services being inaugurated by a socialist Government'.[150] News on Sunday morning that Mac-Donald had been in audience with the King was at first regarded as simply another effort by him to put pressure on the Cabinet. Chamberlain was almost jubilant, feeling he himself had 'every reason to be satisfied' at having 'got the government into a most difficult position'.[151]

The more inexperienced Cabinet members shared these expectations – of the 'Labour Cabinet carrying economy as Peel did free trade',[152] acting in the national interest yet against the wishes of, and with disastrously divisive effects upon, the Labour party. But those ministers who mattered had little or no confidence in the government's continuance. To Henderson, Lansbury, Greenwood, Johnston, and other dissentients it was 'perfectly evident' that the Cabinet would break up whatever the reply from New York, for the simple reason that after the Saturday sessions they had held a separate meeting to prepare a collective resignation.[153] They were not prepared to accept one specific proposal – the cut in un-employment benefit rates – which they thought would fatally compromise the collective party leadership in the eyes not just of the TUC but of the rest of the party. It was better to end the Labour government and allow others to impose the cut, facing the inevitable charges of 'running away' as best they could.

On learning of the dissentients' meeting, MacDonald, Snowden, and Thomas immediately interpreted it as a Henderson-led 'intrigue' against themselves. MacDonald, in his now habitual disparagement of Henderson's motives, assumed that he wanted to seize the Labour party leadership for himself. MacDonald considered his own chance of prevailing against the dissentients to be slight. Exhausted, despondent, and disillusioned, he was now barely

[150] Harvey to Harrison, tm 343/31, 22 Aug. 1931, FRBNY papers.
[151] N. Chamberlain to his wife, 23 Aug. 1931, NC 1/26/447.
[152] Lees-Smith in Beveridge diary, 22 Aug. 1931; and see Sankey diary, 22 Aug. 1931, for utter incomprehension of the meaning of what he was witnessing.
[153] Lansbury, 'Cabinet Crisis'; Johnston in Dalton diary, 27 Aug. 1931 (Dalton, 275–6); Thomas memo; MacDonald diary, 23 Aug. 1931 (Marquand 630); Postgate, *Lansbury*, 269.

11 Arthur Henderson, Arthur Greenwood, and George Lansbury leaving
Downing Street, August 1931

inclined to try. He thought the Cabinet had shown itself incompetent
'to face an emergency'. The dissentients 'disgusted' him. They
lacked the 'guts' to face the situation and wanted to 'shirk
responsibility'; rather than face the realities, they mouthed
sentimental 'trash' about the virtues of the unemployed. Their

policy ideas were 'claptrap'.[154] They, not he, had betrayed party principle, capitulating to those pedlars of 'a Poor Law frame of mind' who were bringing 'rack and ruin' to the socialist movement.[155] He also wished 'to have no further dealings with the Trade Unions'.[156] Yet by insisting upon the unemployment benefit cut, MacDonald knew he was committing 'political suicide'. Whether he persuaded the Cabinet to accept the cut or whether he supported it from outside office, he would be castigated by much of the Labour party. A 'national government', now it was obvious that this would be supported by very few other Labour Cabinet members, remained unattractive: he would seem a 'ridiculous figure', clinging to office and salary. As success in Cabinet seemed unlikely he reconciled himself to leaving office with the other ministers, but then giving independent support to a Conservative or Conservative–Liberal government. So too did Thomas and Snowden, and the three apparently decided to make a public statement to that effect.[157] At 10.30 am on Sunday, 23 August, MacDonald advised the King that if the Cabinet split he would have 'no other course but to resign'.[158]

THE KING'S CONTRIBUTION

Although the King and his secretaries had been away from London, they were well-informed of the Cabinet's difficulties. They had received daily telephoned reports from MacDonald's secretaries, as well as the usual distribution of Cabinet papers. In order to avoid harmful press speculation, they had on MacDonald's advice travelled as announced from Sandringham to Balmoral on 21 August, but on being told during the 22nd that they might be asked to return to London, the King in exasperation at such 'shilly-shallying' decided to do so even before the request was made.[159] Reaching London early on the 23rd, Wigram immediately began to sound out opinion in anticipation of the King's audience with MacDonald. He failed to reach Baldwin, but contacted Dawson and

---

[154] MacDonald diary, 23 Aug. 1931, and MacDonald in M. MacDonald diary, 22 and 23 Aug. 1931, and in S. MacDonald note, 23 Aug. 1931 (Marquand 630–2); Thomas notes.
[155] MacDonald to Bennett, 8 Aug. 1931, JRM 1176 (Marquand, 609).
[156] MacDonald in Wigram memo, 23 Aug. 1931, RA GV K2330(2)/1.
[157] See MacDonald diary, 23 Aug. 1931, and MacDonald in M. MacDonald diary and S. MacDonald notes, 23 Aug. 1931 (Marquand, 630–2), and in N. Chamberlain diary, 23 Aug. 1931.   [158] Wigram memo, 23 Aug. 1931, RA GV K2330(2)/1.
[159] Duff, 'Financial Crisis'; Wigram memo, 22 Aug. 1931, RA GV K2330(2)/1 (Nicolson, *George V*, 460).

was himself contacted by Peacock who, as the King's personal financial adviser, was the Bank of England's obvious contact with the Palace. Peacock impressed the need for very urgent decisions, as Bank resources were now 'measured in *hours* rather than days' and foreign financial opinion required 'a very striking message from the politicians *quickly*'.[160] Dawson, as *The Times* editor considered a reliable barometer of non-Labour opinion, had since returning to London on 19 August spoken with Kindersley of the Bank, Maclean, Reading, and Chamberlain, and attended Conservative leaders' meetings. His own view remained that 'national government' was impractical and undesirable. '[E]verything' should be done to persuade MacDonald to carry cuts through a Labour Cabinet, as the only means of permanently 'reversing a policy of extravagance.'[161]

In an emergency, keeping the existing Cabinet in office was the obvious course. Wigram and the King first attempted this when MacDonald arrived at the Palace, offering him words of confidence, encouragement, and flattery: 'he was the only person who could settle the crisis'. They were, however, well-prepared in case the Labour Cabinet could not continue. They had been so since the previous October, and were now presented with an opportunity to make their views effective. Although during most interviews that day they observed the constitutional form of seeking advice, their real objective was to obtain agreement with the King's own view. For Wigram the main obstacles to 'a National Emergency Government' seemed to be the difficulty each party leader would feel in serving under another, and the problem of finding a suitable 'neutral head'.[162] The King now cut through this difficulty. From MacDonald's report it was evident not merely that the Cabinet would probably disintegrate, but that if MacDonald's position depended only upon Labour support he might become politically negligible, unable to exercise any influence or to enter a 'national government' run by Conservatives and Liberals. If there were to be serious all-party representation in a 'national cabinet', the solution was plain: to have MacDonald in a post beyond reliance on a party. On MacDonald advising that the Conservative and Liberal leaders

---

[160] Peacock to Wigram, 23 Aug. 1931, and Wigram memo of lunchtime conversation with Peacock and another Bank director, Anderson, 23 Aug. 1931, RA GV K2330(1)/6, (2)/1.

[161] Memo of Dawson–Wigram conversation, 23 Aug. 1931, Dawson papers. See also Dawson diary, 19–23 Aug. 1931, and Dawson to Bridgeman, 22 Aug. 1931, Bridgeman papers.

[162] Wigram to Rumbold, 3 Aug. 1931, RA GV M2329/10.

should be consulted, the King said he would 'advise them strongly' to serve under MacDonald as Prime Minister. He ignored MacDonald's objection that if the Labour leadership divided he would have a 'hopeless [Parliamentary] position'.[163]

The King assumed that he could have a decisive influence, and MacDonald undoubtedly obtained encouragement from him. On the same reasoning as that of the King, the only post which MacDonald could now seriously contemplate in any 'national government' was that of Prime Minister: a position sufficiently powerful to compensate for lack of a substantial Labour following, and to counteract the inevitable accusations that he had become a 'Tory slave'. Yet to conclude that the King was chiefly responsible for the outcome is to misconceive the true relationship between the Crown and party politics. The King could not command. Whatever he said to party leaders, and whatever he himself supposed, he was powerless if those leaders concerned did not themselves regard a course of action as politically both possible and desirable. Mac-Donald understood this. The King's personal support helped, but the most important consideration continued to be the attitudes of the Liberal and Conservative leaders. The intimations he had received from Samuel and Chamberlain late on 22 August had been based on the assumption that he would have substantial Labour support. As such they had become redundant. There also remained an area of total uncertainty: the attitude of Baldwin. He would be vital, as official leader of the party which might now have to provide the principal Commons voting strength for a 'national government'.

Samuel happened to be the first party leader that Wigram was able to contact. Since receiving MacDonald's proposal of further cuts, Samuel had consulted Maclean, Crewe, Reading, and Lloyd George.[164] His advice to the King had been agreed in advance as the course which eminently suited both national and Liberal party interests. Yet it was also a course which the small, free-trade Liberal party could not have contemplated until Chamberlain had shown it to be possible. As the cuts would be 'unpalatable' to the 'masses', the 'best government' to impose them would be a Labour one. But as this now seemed impossible, Samuel recommended a 'national

---

[163] MacDonald diary, 23 Aug. 1931 (Marquand, 630), and note the King's relief that MacDonald did not advise him to send for Henderson.

[164] Maclean to his wife, [23] Aug. 1931, Maclean papers c468/121–2, and to Grey, 22–4 Aug. 1931, Runciman papers 245.

government' under MacDonald. This would be preferable to a Conservative government because, he said, it would be 'more likely to carry the working classes with [it]'.[165] What he did not say was that Lloyd George Liberals could not support a Conservative government likely to introduce a revenue tariff. That the King reported MacDonald as now saying he would have little Labour support mattered little to Samuel. The major point was to spread responsibility for retrenchment and avoid a protectionist government. This advice was considered important at the Palace not because Samuel was the first to propose 'national government', but because he was the first party leader to agree with the King's own purpose.[166] For the rest of that day, he would be the only one actively to do so.

The Conservative summoned to the Palace was Baldwin, who had been fully briefed on the three-party negotiations by Chamberlain on his arrival back in London on the previous evening. Baldwin approved of Chamberlain's actions so far as the Labour Cabinet had apparently been manoeuvred into imposing retrenchment. But to Chamberlain's 'impatien[ce]', he 'hoped and prayed that he might not have to join a National Government'.[167] Baldwin remained as reluctant as in December and again in late July to become entangled in a coalition. As well as being personally suspicious of coalition, after the March rebellion against his leadership he had greater reason than Chamberlain to be sensitive to how his party might react. He feared that entry into another coalition might cause a similar split to that of 1922, the more so if he allowed himself to become formally subordinate to a socialist Prime Minister. To Baldwin the preferable course, because safer in terms of party management, would be to form a Conservative government and obtain Liberal assistance in passing emergency legislation through the existing Parliament. The party would then have to deal as best it could with Chamberlain's principal concern, the electoral dangers of retrenchment.

If Baldwin had stuck to this position, 'national government' would have been impossible or, conceivably, possible only at the cost

---

[165] Wigram memo, 23 Aug. 1931, RA GV K2330(2)/1; Samuel, 'Course of Events'. Maclean to Grey, 22–4 Aug. 1931, Runciman papers 245, reports Samuel saying the King himself declared that he wanted a 'national government'.

[166] For Samuel's advice presented as decisive, see Wigram memo, Sept. 1931, in Nicolson, *George V*, 461. Given the subsequent controversy over the King's role, it is not surprising that both his secretary and biographer should have been at pains to emphasise Samuel's role.   [167] N. Chamberlain to his wife, 23 Aug. 1931, NC 1/26/447.

of serious disagreement between Baldwin and Chamberlain. Yet Baldwin had no reason to force the issue, as the situation remained 'kaleidoscopic'. With Chamberlain's report as his only guide it seemed unlikely that MacDonald intended, or would feel he had sufficient Labour support, to join a 'national government'. His own views were confirmed on Sunday morning by discussion with Dawson, whose advice he then sought about appointments for a largely Conservative government.[168] For the next twenty-four hours Baldwin took no other initiative, but listened, sounded the opinion of other leading Conservatives, and allowed the situation to be shaped around him by Chamberlain, MacDonald, Samuel, and the King.

When Baldwin saw the King on the Sunday afternoon they talked past each other, each drawing a different understanding of what had been said. To the King's straight question of whether if the Cabinet resigned Baldwin would serve under MacDonald in a 'national government', Baldwin replied that he was 'prepared to do anything to save the country'. He then added that, if MacDonald resigned he would be ready to form a government himself, with Liberal support for retrenchment. The King understood this to be a clear affirmative to his question,[169] a misinterpretation with important consequences. Baldwin had in fact turned the direct question towards what he considered desirable and also probable, especially as the King reported MacDonald as expecting little Labour support. Speaking later with Chamberlain and Hoare, Baldwin gave no hint that the King had even mentioned 'national government', but implied that he had been asked to form a government if the Labour Cabinet collapsed. On Chamberlain strongly advising him to persuade MacDonald, Snowden, and other Labour ministers as well as Liberals to join his government, Baldwin 'agreed' in the sense that he was beginning to see Chamberlain's point in principle. But he saw no reason to treat it as a serious possibility.[170]

Everything now depended upon the New York bankers' reply. As Chamberlain had anticipated, Harrison and Morgans were ready to assist. Apart from genuine friendliness towards Britain, the restoration of confidence in sterling appeared crucial to international monetary stability, and, it followed, to their own banks' interests.

---

[168] Baldwin to his wife, 23 Aug. 1931, in Middlemas and Barnes, *Baldwin*, 626; Dawson memo, 23 Aug. 1931, Dawson papers.

[169] Wigram memo, 23 Aug. 1931, RA GV K2330(2)/1, and see Nicolson, *George V*, 461–2.

[170] N. Chamberlain diary, 23 Aug. 1931, and N. Chamberlain to his wife and to I. Chamberlain, both 23 Aug. 1931, NC 1/26/447, 18/1/753.

Their ability to help was, however, constrained by the expectations of lenders over whom they had only limited influence, the American investing public and private banks. Their assessment remained that a public loan would require definite parliamentary action to re-establish a balanced budget. But a private bankers' credit might be more quickly obtained, provided there were an announcement of a budget programme capable of restoring confidence in sterling and British government finance, and so offering surety for repayment. Contrary to notions of American banking dictation, Harrison and Morgans did not determine the composition of this programme. The details had in fact been proposed tentatively – without promise of their implementation – by MacDonald, seeking to satisfy conditions for political support from Conservative and Liberal party leaders. Meeting on Long Island on a Sunday, the Morgans' partners felt themselves to be in an invidious position, unable to assess the likely response of the financial markets to MacDonald's proposals. Anxious to help nevertheless, they offered to organise a private bankers' credit, but referred back to London the assessment of whether the programme could restore confidence – asking for assurance that it had the 'sincere approval and support' of the Bank of England and the City.[171]

The Cabinet had reassembled (with Parmoor absent) at 7 pm, but had to adjourn as Morgans' reply had not yet been received. When Harvey delivered it around 9.10 pm, MacDonald informed the reassembled Cabinet that, given Conservative and Liberal con-currence with his proposal, the Bank of England and leading City bankers were also prepared to support it. The assurance required by Morgans could therefore be given.[172] Nevertheless after MacDonald had read out their telegram there was an outcry.[173] Although the telegram was correctly recognised by some Cabinet members to be 'rather inconclusive',[174] and although the specific retrenchment proposals were actually MacDonald's, the cry was of 'bankers'

---

[171] J. P. Morgan & Co to Morgan Grenfell, tm 31/2382, 22 Aug. 1931, and to Grenfell, tm 31/2383, 23 Aug. 1931, MGC, copies in JRM 260, and Cabinet 46(31), 23 Aug. 1931. See also Williamson, 'Bankers Ramp?', esp. 774–6, 790, 800–2. In order to avoid unnecessary and perhaps disputatious explanation, MacDonald and Snowden had not explained that negotiations were now being conducted with Morgans, so the Cabinet assumed the reply came from Harrison. This was enshrined in its minutes, and caused confusion during the 'bankers' ramp' controversy.   [172] Cabinet 46(31), 23 Aug. 1931.

[173] Harvey (who was waiting outside the Cabinet room) reported in Morgan Grenfell 'Memorandum', and in Nicolson, *George V*, 464.

[174] Passfield to B. Webb, 24 Aug. 1931, Passfield papers III:3:(i):27:69, and in B. Webb diary, 25 Aug. 1931 (Cole, 284).

dictation'. This outcry had almost certainly been concerted by the dissentient ministers, in order to arouse enough opposition to MacDonald's proposal to force the whole Cabinet's resignation. It appears to have been so effective that some of the more confused ministers were persuaded that bankers really had imposed specific conditions.[175] Any efforts at last-minute conciliation collapsed. After an 'impassioned appeal' by MacDonald for acceptance of his proposal, each Cabinet member was asked to express his or her view.[176]

Eleven ministers supported the unemployment benefit cut: MacDonald, Snowden, Sankey, Benn, Amulree, Morrison, Passfield, Lees-Smith, and three trade unionists, Thomas, Bondfield, and Shaw. Nine were opposed: Henderson, Graham, Lansbury, Greenwood, Johnston, Alexander, Addison, and two trade unionists, Adamson and Clynes, the last less definitely than the others.[177] With such a large split, the Cabinet agreed unanimously upon resignation. It was also agreed that the King should be immediately informed, and advised to summon a Baldwin–Samuel–MacDonald conference on the following morning.[178]

Peacock had dined with the King at the latter's request, in order to inform him about the financial negotiations. After telephoning to Harvey at Downing Street, Peacock was able to forewarn the King both of Morgans' reply and MacDonald's intention to resign.[179] On MacDonald arriving at 10.15 pm looking (Wigram thought) 'scared and unbalanced', the King urged him to make no hasty personal decision but to consider the 'national' alternative. MacDonald 'was the only man to lead the country through this crisis', and the King

---

[175] For ministers believing in US bankers' 'dictation', see Sankey diary, 22 [i.e., 23] Aug. 1931, and Lees-Smith in Lamont to Grenfell, 13 Jan. 1932, MGC; both were nevertheless in the Cabinet majority supporting cuts. See Williamson, 'Bankers' Ramp?', 804–5.

[176] For attempted Shaw and Thomas conciliation, Thomas memo; and see Sankey memo, 'Last Months of Lord Chancellorship', 7 June 1935, Sankey papers c512/186–97, for a less plausible account implicating Henderson. For MacDonald appeal, Cabinet 46(31), 23 Aug. 1931 (Marquand, 634).

[177] Note [? by Howorth], 'Division of Cabinet on 10%', in PREM 1/96 and JRM 1316, and note 'Cabinet disgruntles', also JRM 1316. There was confusion over the exact division, apparently because Clynes was equivocal: there is a question mark against his name in the first note, it is omitted from the second note ('Cabinet disgruntles'), and Thomas notes record that Clynes 'hesitated for a moment'. MacDonald mistakenly reported to the King that the minority numbered eight. Some secondary sources are unaware that Parmoor was absent.   [178] For Cabinet decision, see Cabinet 46(31), 23 Aug. 1931.

[179] Thompson-McCausland, 'Crisis', 35, 37. Again, subsequent controversy (here over both the Bank's and the King's role) resulted in public reticence: in Nicolson, *George V*, 464 (followed by Rose, *George V*, 375) it is implied that Peacock's and the King's conversation was confined to wheat and barley prices!

'hoped he would reconsider the situation'. The King also stated that the Conservatives and Liberals would support him. MacDonald then telephoned from the Palace to arrange a meeting 'as soon as possible' that evening with Baldwin and Samuel, before returning with Peacock to Downing Street and informing the Cabinet that the King had agreed to convene the party leaders' conference.[180]

What Cabinet members considered the purpose of the Palace conference to be is unclear. On seeing the King, MacDonald gave every appearance of intending to resign with the rest of the Cabinet.[181] Some ministers perhaps thought that 'the situation might be saved by concessions from the other leaders'.[182] With financial collapse threatened within three days some, including Henderson – who apparently strongly favoured the Palace conference[183] – possibly thought Labour leaders still had a responsibility to help support sterling, and that some all-party statement should be made to steady matters during the formation of a largely Conservative government. It seems clear, however, that MacDonald and several other ministers anticipated that the conference might result in a 'national government'. Although ex-ministers later found it convenient to accuse MacDonald of deceiving them, after the Cabinet discussion of 22 August they had no cause for surprise. Henderson certainly predicted the outcome.[184]

As for MacDonald, his visit to the Palace had elicited important information. This was not the King's support for 'national government', which he had already heard that morning. Rather it was the King's statement – apparently the fruit of his audiences during the afternoon – that, despite MacDonald's inability to promise much Labour support, Samuel and Baldwin would accept him as 'national' Prime Minister. The description of Baldwin's attitude, though inaccurate, was especially significant. In reality the King's effective role had been as a confidential – and, crucially, an unreliable – messenger between the party leaders. For MacDonald, this message made 'national government' once again seem possible.

[180] Wigram memo, 23 Aug. 1931, RA GV K2330(2)/1 (partly in Nicolson, *George V*, 464); MacDonald in M. MacDonald diary, 24 Aug. 1931; Cabinet 46(31), 23 Aug. 1931. For versions of the King's own, blunter, account circulated in royal circles, see W. R. Inge, *Diary of a Dean* (1949), 161, and Lockhart diary, 30 June 1932, in Young I, 222.

[181] Harvey in Morgan Grenfell, 'Memorandum', and Wigram memo, 23 Aug. 1931, RA GV K2330(2)/1.   [182] Greenwood notes.   [183] See Thomas memo.

[184] Dalton diary, 24 Aug. 1931 (Dalton, 271), and see below, p. 375.

Conservatives and Liberals had apparently accepted the condition vital to his prospects for Cabinet influence, public reputation, and self-respect – that he remain Prime Minister.

MacDonald's purpose in immediately summoning Baldwin and Samuel to a meeting so late in the evening may have been, as he told the Cabinet, to inform them of the New York bankers' reply. It may also have been to tell them of the Cabinet's resignation and arrangements for the Palace conference. But a further purpose was to seek confirmation or otherwise of the King's statement. This statement plainly remained prominent in MacDonald's mind during his next two meetings. With Snowden present on both occasions and offering no criticism, he was the first to mention 'national government' – negatively, yet in a manner inviting rebuttal. After discussing the exchange prospects with Harvey and Peacock, MacDonald declared that with so few followers he 'could not expect to lead a National Government as he could now bring no assets to contribute'. Harvey and Peacock, knowing the views of Chamberlain, Samuel, and the King, both expressed disagreement.[185] A very similar conversation took place with the Conservative and Liberal leaders when they arrived around 11 pm.

Baldwin had brought Chamberlain, who worked hard to convince MacDonald that he should remain in a 'national government'. Although MacDonald might have few parliamentary followers, he could 'command much support in the country'. He would be criticised if he supported the new government without joining it; he also had considerable influence with foreign opinion. Samuel 'strongly' supported Chamberlain. Baldwin said nothing. Only when later pressed by Chamberlain did he express approval, though adding that he had remained silent because the appeal to MacDonald seemed hopeless. MacDonald said his mind 'was not finally made up', but seemed impressed by the argument that he had influence with American opinion. Nevertheless he appeared so despondent that Chamberlain, Baldwin, and Samuel all departed believing that MacDonald would leave office. Samuel, expecting Baldwin to form a Conservative–Liberal emergency government, immediately attempted to guarantee and advance Liberal party

---

[185] Harvey in Morgan Grenfell, 'Memorandum'; Thompson-McCausland, 'Crisis', 37. That Snowden was present makes nonsense of the claim in Snowden, *Autobiography* II, 952 (which implies he was not present), that he had no inkling of MacDonald's thinking.

interests, enquiring about offices, obtaining a promise that the tariff
question would be postponed, and trying unsuccessfully to extract a
commitment to electoral reform.[186] In fact MacDonald had very
nearly been persuaded.[187] For obvious reasons he later placed most
emphasis for his decision upon the King's influence. The decisive
elements, however, were Chamberlain's and Samuel's appeals and
perhaps most of all Baldwin's silence, because it appeared to indicate
concurrence.

Ultimately the King probably had the most effect upon Baldwin.
Yet even here his influence would have been limited if Baldwin had
not felt stronger pressures: that Chamberlain especially, then
Samuel, and eventually MacDonald had created a situation where
to disagree would seem 'unpatriotic', with damaging consequences
for the Conservative party and his leadership. At the Buckingham
Palace Conference from 10 am on Monday, 24 August, the King
pressed strongly for the formation of a 'national government'. He
'trusted there was no question of the Prime Minister's resignation:
the leaders of the three Parties must get together and come to some
arrangement'.[188] Samuel had been prepared for this for three days.
MacDonald now thought it preferable and possible for him to put
'national duty' before his own retirement. No government could be
formed without Baldwin's positive assistance. Chamberlain, Samuel,
MacDonald, the sterling crisis, and now the King: 'in the[se]
circumstances...there was nothing for anyone in [Baldwin's]
position to do but promise full co-operation'.[189]

The details agreed by MacDonald, Baldwin, and Samuel
contained 'safeguards' for each. The National government would be
an emergency arrangement – not a party coalition but 'a co-
operation of individuals', and restricted to MacDonald's budget
programme. These conditions helped to justify and dignify Mac-
Donald's position, and for Samuel ensured no embarrassment over
tariffs. Statements that the government would last only for the
duration of the emergency and that the next election would be

---

[186] N. Chamberlain diary, 23 Aug. 1931; N. Chamberlain to his wife, 24 Aug. 1931, NC
1/26/448; Baldwin to his wife, 24 Aug. 1931, in Middlemas and Barnes, *Baldwin*, 628;
Samuel in Maclean to Grey, 22–4 Aug. 1931, Runciman papers 245.
[187] See MacDonald in M. MacDonald diary, early 24 Aug. 1931 (Marquand, 636).
[188] Wigram memo, 24 Aug. 1931, RA GV K2330(2)/1 (Nicolson, *George V*, 465–6).
[189] Baldwin speech, in Middlemas and Barnes, *Baldwin*, 629.

fought by the parties separately suited Baldwin's own preferences, suggested that protection was only temporarily postponed, and reduced the danger of Conservative criticism.[190] None imagined that the National government had much future.

[190] 'Memorandum written at the Conference at Buckingham Palace, August 24 1931...', Samuel papers A/78/11.

CHAPTER 10

First effects

It is a tremendous thing that economies including a cut in the dole shd. be prepared by a Govt. headed by MacDonald & with Snowden & other Socialists in it.

Cunliffe-Lister to his wife, 24 August 1931[1]

The next election will be fought, not by a Labour Government on an admittedly difficult defensive, but by a Labour movement united and eager ... At one stroke, without an election, and with ample time to prepare for an election on unusually favourable ground, [Labour party members] have been relieved of their anxieties. Yesterday they dreaded a contest: to-day they are almost within sight of their clear majority in the House of Commons.

Graham article, *Daily Express*, 31 August 1931

THE EMERGENCY GOVERNMENT

The announcement of the National government shattered the pattern of politics. It not only split the Labour leadership; it transformed the position and prospects of all parties and every politician. Amnesia became endemic, as the only means to accommodate sudden, extreme transpositions. Conservatives and Liberals forgot MacDonald's, Snowden's, and Thomas's share of responsibility for the crisis; the Lloyd George Liberal leaders forgot their alliance with the Labour Cabinet; resigning Labour Cabinet ministers tried to forget most of their decisions during the previous two weeks. When almost the whole Labour party joined the TUC in out-and-out opposition, a deep national division along class lines threatened. The government's declared objective of restoring 'sound finance' had fundamental implications for public expenditure and social policy. Almost as plainly, its very existence might have large consequences for the questions of protection, imperial trade, and

[1] Swinton papers III/313/1/5.

India. National policy and party politics as these had developed
since 1918 seemed to be at issue, and analogies with the crisis of war
again became common.[2] The intense activity confined during the
previous week to small groups of leading figures now burst upon the
whole political system. The pressure was the more intense because
sterling remained under threat and because the specific distribution
of financial sacrifices became matters of public debate. Defence of
financial stability on the one hand and working-class incomes on the
other – each conceived as protecting a vital 'national interest' –
produced an extraordinary atmosphere of occasion and purpose.
Yet, as the government had declared itself to be a temporary
arrangement, this was accompanied by a sense of great pre-
cariousness – of large risks or wide opportunities.

The National government received an enthusiastic welcome from
all non-Labour newspapers and journals, and from those bankers
and businessmen who had long wanted retrenchment and 'a
complete change in the outlook of our political leaders'.[3] However
distantly, its formation was an outcome of that atmosphere of
'national crisis' which some had helped create during the previous
autumn. Of those who had then taken up the idea of 'national
government', the King felt the greatest satisfaction. In his innocent
manner he had enjoyed being 'able to play the Sovereign for once,
& give a lead to his rattled Ministers',[4] and considered the new
government as peculiarly his own achievement. Whereas the new
Labour opposition were cowards and 'party men... thinking of
themselves', MacDonald had shown 'strength of character &
devotion to duty' in 'putting aside all personal & party interest in
order to stand by the country'.[5] Henceforth he had the King's strong
personal support. Greig, Gwynne, Schuster, Buchan, Chilcott, and
Lady Londonderry, whose emphasis had been anti-Labour, congratulated themselves upon their prescience and initiative.[6] Others,
however, were less content. Lloyd George, Churchill, Mosley,

---

[2] E.g., editorial, *Manchester Guardian*, 25 Aug. 1931; Hankey diary, 6 Sept. 1931 (Roskill, *Hankey* II, 544–5).

[3] Morris statement, *The Times*, 1 Sept. 1931. See extracts from other newspapers in *The Times*, 26 Aug. 1931.

[4] Members of the King's entourage reported in J. Pope-Hennessy, *Queen Mary* (1959), 548.

[5] Wigram memo (plainly reflecting the King's views), 24 Aug. 1931, RA GV K2330(2)/1/18–20; the King to MacDonald, 27 Aug. 1931, in Nicolson, *George V*, 489.

[6] See Gwynne to Greig, 7 Sept. 1931, Greig papers; F. Schuster to Baldwin, 1 Sept. 1931, SB 44/74–75, and letter, *The Times*, 3 Oct. 1931; Buchan to MacDonald, 25 Aug. 1931, JRM 1314; Chilcott, 'National Government at Last', Sept. – Oct. 1931, in *Political Salvation*, 69–77.

Amery, Horne, and Simon were omitted from office – the first physically, the others politically, powerless at the critical moment. It was not the 'national government' they would have wanted. For some, the Labour party's opposition detracted from the achievement. For Garvin and Seely the new government was a 'God-send' in the circumstances, but they would have preferred a more 'broadly & solidly national' arrangement. Both appealed privately to Henderson to partake in the spirit of 'unity'.[7] Reading, though personally a chief beneficiary of the new arrangements, similarly declared that 'National Government [was not] quite the correct term' and hoped that if further difficulties arose it still would 'not be impossible for a really national Government to be formed'.[8]

Nor was the National government that which MacDonald had occasionally envisaged. He had never imagined a 'national government' to be possible without all or much of the Labour party as a major partner. Yet now he remained Prime Minister in defiance of the party secretary and the TUC, and without expectation of support from the party's institutions. In these circumstances his attitude towards his party was awkward and ambivalent. Notoriously, he did not attend its decisive national executive and parliamentary party meetings from 26 to 28 August. But this did not mean (as often assumed) that he was indifferent to Labour opinion. Quite the reverse: he remained preoccupied with it, and made intense efforts to influence it. He did so because he wished to defend the national credit, his own conception of party and working-class interests, and his personal honour, but also because he had no intention of permanently separating from the Labour party. This was manifest both in the terms he agreed at the Buckingham Palace Conference, and in the way he announced those terms immediately afterwards to the concluding Labour Cabinet meeting. He placed the blame for an accelerated run on sterling that morning squarely upon those dissentient ministers who had prevented the Cabinet from reaching agreement the previous evening. 'Saving the country from financial collapse' and the King's request left him 'no other course' but to help in a national government. In emphasising that this would be an arrangement not of parties but of 'individuals', that after the 'emergency period' the parties 'would resume their respective

[7] Garvin to Lothian, 25 and 26 Aug. 1931, Lothian papers 257/259, 263, to Reading, 26 Aug. 1931, Reading papers F118/24/23–4, and editorial, *Observer*, 30 Aug. 1931; Seely to Reading, 18 Sept. 1931, Reading papers F118/131; Wigram to Seely, 28 Sept. 1931, Mottistone papers 4/31–2.   [8] Speech, *HL Deb*, 82, cols. 8–9, 8 Sept. 1931.

positions', and that the general election would be fought without party pacts, he implied that outright Labour opposition was inappropriate because he had safeguarded the party's position and because the differences were narrow and transitory. In declaring that the new government would make 'no serious departure' from the retrenchment programme which the Labour Cabinet had authorised him to submit (however tentatively) to bankers and Conservative and Liberal leaders on 22 August, he meant to drive the point home.[9]

These were parting shots intended to disarm the Cabinet dissentients. This might also have been MacDonald's purpose in now offering Henderson the peerage he had desired for months. Yet as the new circumstances patently made it difficult for Henderson to accept, a stronger motive was probably simple malice.[10] MacDonald had now lost all desire to conciliate those dissentient ministers who had shown 'weak human nature' and had 'run away' from their 'duty' at the 'orders of the TUC', choosing 'the easy path of irresponsibility' and leaving 'others to bear the odium'.[11] Mac-Donald's real efforts were directed over the heads of the dissentients and TUC leaders towards the rest of the party. Two hours after the Cabinet meeting he recounted his version of events to the junior ministers, originally summoned to be informed of their salary cuts. He followed this with a letter to each of them that evening, another next day to every Labour backbench MP, and further extensive correspondence with many party members. A BBC broadcast on 25 August contained a special appeal to Labour supporters. He tried hard to neutralise the *Daily Herald*.[12] He supplied Garvin with intimations of how the 'real' story of the crisis 'would blow [his] late colleagues out of the water', and recruited Donald, an old friend and former newspaper editor, to direct 'propaganda' on his behalf and arrange meetings with other newspaper proprietors and editors.[13]

MacDonald asked party members to 'suspend judgement' until the facts could be 'dispassionately considered', and attempted a

---

[9] Cabinet 47 (31), 12 am, 24 Aug. 1931; Passfield to B. Webb, 24 Aug. 1931, Passfield papers II:3:(i):27:69 (*Webb Letters* III, 359).

[10] Offer recorded in Duff memo, 25 Aug. 1931, JRM 1316. See Marquand, 644, for the former interpretation.

[11] MacDonald diary, 24 Aug., 1 Sept. 1931; MacDonald to Lindsay, 24 Aug., and to Elias and Bondfield, 25 Aug. 1931, all JRM 1314 (the last also in Marquand, 644-5).

[12] MacDonald to Elias, 25 and 27 Aug. 1931, JRM 1314, and Dalton to Noel Baker, 4 Sept. 1931, Noel-Baker papers 3/62.

[13] MacDonald to Garvin, 25 Aug. 1931, JRM 1314; MacDonald diary, 26 Aug. 1931, and Rosenberg memos, 28 Aug. 1931, JRM 1316 for Donald (editor of *Daily Chronicle* 1902-18).

strong defence of his decision as concerned with the best interests of labour. He had 'changed none of [his] beliefs', and aimed – despite an unavoidable but temporary interruption – to maintain 'everything we stand for'. His action might 'embarrass the party' for a time, but the financial crisis had threatened 'the most dire results to the mass of the working classes'. He justified the 10 per cent unemployment benefit cut by arguing that it left recipients $1\frac{1}{2}$ per cent better off than in 1929, that it was preferable to a much larger reduction through forced devaluation, that to leave benefits untouched while everybody else suffered sacrifices was 'unjust in equity', and that from self-respect the unemployed themselves would want to make their contribution. He tried to subvert the dissentients by telling junior ministers that the Cabinet had accepted 'fairly drastic economies' but then reneged, inviting a financial collapse which would have resulted in the party being 'swept away in ignominy... by popular clamour'. By remaining in office he had salvaged something of the party's reputation for fitness to govern, while leaving it 'untrammelled' to prepare a return to its general policy, protected against any 'coupon election'.[14] Later, reacting to Labour criticism, his claim was even more explicitly to have 'saved the party'.[15]

Yet in seeking Labour support MacDonald suffered several handicaps, some self-inflicted. Knowing that *prima facie* his action would probably outrage many party members and that the dissentients and TUC leaders would control the party machine, his temperamental self-pity got the better of him. His personal appeals to junior ministers were ingenuous and counter-productive. He admitted that he expected to be 'denounced and ostracized', and declared that young men with promising careers should think twice before putting their 'heads into the [same] noose' as himself.[16] The need to make offices available for Conservatives and Liberals, and uncertainty about how many and which posts would remain in his own gift, delayed approaches to individuals. Over-defensiveness and the convention of budget secrecy produced an unfortunate emphasis in his BBC broadcast upon the benefit cut rather than taxation of the

[14] MacDonald at undersecretaries' meeting, in Dalton diary, 24 Aug. 1931 (Dalton, 272–3); MacDonald to junior ministers and to Labour MPs, 24 and 25 Aug. 1931, JRM 1314; MacDonald broadcast, *The Times*, 26 Aug. 1931.
[15] E.g., MacDonald to Morrison, Parmoor, Cripps, and M. Hamilton, 27, 29, and 30 Aug., 1 Sept. 1931, JRM 1314 (last in Marquand, 650–1).
[16] MacDonald in Cabinet, in Passfield to B. Webb, 24 Aug. 1931 (*Webb Letters*, III, 359), and at junior ministers meeting, Dalton diary, 24 Aug. 1931 (Dalton, 273).

rich.[17] Further unintended offence was caused as pride, fear of rebuff, anger, and exhaustion stopped him attending party meetings where the dissentients and TUC leaders would dominate.

MacDonald's specific recruitment efforts were patchy and the response poor. Immediately after the 24 August Cabinet he asked Snowden, Thomas, and Sankey to remain in their offices. The first two chose themselves because of their stand on retrenchment, and evident readiness to defy party opinion. Sankey had been similarly helpful, and had special importance as co-ordinator of preparations for the imminent second Round Table Conference. Besides, although Sankey attended the parliamentary party meeting to offer the conciliatory formula that while 'J. R. M. had saved the country, ... Henderson had saved the soul of the Labour party', privately he though Henderson had shown 'most distressing ... weakness' and self-interest in submitting to the TUC, and that the party had 'gone mad'.[18] Amulree was added later. Like Sankey, he was not a party politician but a lawyer with a MacDonald peerage. Shaw dithered before declining an offer. Morrison took MacDonald's comments about young men more literally than they were intended. Bondfield, though an early supporter of unemployment benefit cuts, was sacrificed because her presentation of policy had been poor. Other members of the Cabinet majority were dropped because they occupied offices needed for Conservatives or Liberals. Junior posts were retained by two more lawyers and MacDonaldite dependents, Aitchison and Jowitt (the latter making his second shift of allegiance in two years), and accepted by Malcolm MacDonald and Gillett (who was a banker). Further, unsuccessful, offers were made on no obvious principle: to Pethick-Lawrence and Snell, who were older men whose careers perhaps seemed almost over, but also to Shinwell, Cripps, Kennedy, De La Warr, Malone, McNeill Weir, Manning, and Isaacs, who all had careers before them.[19]

The odds were obviously high against MacDonald obtaining substantial Labour parliamentary support. Nevertheless he had perhaps hoped for a third of Labour MPs,[20] and remained

[17] See, e.g., Compton in Dalton diary, 25 Aug. 1931.
[18] Dalton diary, 28 Aug. 1931 (Dalton, 278); Sankey diary, 24, 28, and 29 Aug. 1931.
[19] Pethick-Lawrence, *Fate*, 165; Snell, *Men*, 253; Shinwell, *Conflict*, 110; Estorick, *Cripps*, 88; Kenworthy, *Sailors, Statesmen*, 265–6; De La Warr in *HL Deb*, 82, col. 35, 8 Sept. 1931; Dalton diary, 27 Aug. 1931 (Pimlott, 153) and MacDonald undated draft ministerial list, JRM 1316; Weir, *Tragedy*, 389, 395; Donoughue and Jones, *Morrison*, 163, 586.
[20] Thomas in Donoughue and Jones, *Morrison*, 586; Henderson in B. Webb diary, 20 Sept. 1931 (Cole, 288; MacKenzie IV, 258); Kenworthy, *Sailors, Statesmen*, 307.

unconscious of having himself mismanaged matters. After setting junior ministers a stiff test of determination to follow him, he was still bitterly disappointed when so few rose to the challenge. They were, he thought, 'deserters'.[21] Apart from those taking office, only five MPs declared for him, forming a total Commons 'MacDonaldite' group of just twelve. Five unbeneficed Labour peers completed the tally. MacDonald consoled himself by claiming support from old pioneer 'real socialists' as against 'the trade union section', and detecting signs of a large following in the constituency parties.[22] In reality, however, few Labour voices balanced the deluge of non-Labour praise for his 'patriotism', 'courage', and 'heroism'.

After MacDonald's apparent doubts late on 23 August, his decision at the Palace Conference surprised Samuel, Baldwin, and Chamberlain. This only sharpened their satisfaction at the outcome. The Liberal Advisory Committee and Conservative Business Committee unhesitatingly and unanimously approved the terms negotiated by Samuel and Baldwin. Their members were all certain that something very important had been achieved, irrespective of how large or small MacDonald's parliamentary following might be. Maclean, who as an Asquithian had suffered a thwarted political career, was glad to have at last done some 'real good' for the country.[23] Even Baldwin, the most reluctant entrant into the National government, was soon 'in happier spirits than he [had] been for a long time'. His spirits rose as he embraced Chamberlain's view that once the Labour Cabinet had split, a Labour-led government to impose retrenchment was 'the best thing that could have happened', and that the Conservative party could be made to understand this – that 'politically [Conservatives were] in velvet'.[24]

MacDonald, Baldwin, and Samuel together took basic decisions about appointments late on 24 August. The Cabinet's size was limited to ten as an obvious device to speed decision-making and emphasise the government's emergency and temporary character. The allocation of Cabinet seats would be four Labour, four Conservatives, and two Liberal. MacDonald had already chosen his

---

21 See Picton-Turberville, *Life*, 259; MacDonald diary, 24, 26, and 27 Aug., 1 Sept. 1931; MacDonald to Bondfield, 25 Aug. 1931 (Marquand, 645: a good example of MacDonald's tangled state of mind).

22 For old socialists, MacDonald to Middleton, 29 Aug. 1931, Middleton papers 27/29, and statement, *The Times*, 31 Aug. 1931. His claim had some substance – see Tillett and Turner, below p. 373. For rank-and-file, MacDonald diary, 2 Sept. 1931.

23 Maclean to his wife, 24 Aug. 1931, Maclean papers c468/127.

24 N. Chamberlain to his wife, 24 and 25 Aug. 1931, NC 1/26/448, 449; Baldwin to Page Croft, 26 Aug. 1931, Croft papers 1/3/16.

12 The National government Cabinet, August 1931: (standing) Sir Philip
Cunliffe-Lister, J. H. Thomas, Lord Reading, Neville Chamberlain, Sir Samuel
Hoare; (sitting) Philip Snowden, Stanley Baldwin, Ramsay MacDonald, Sir
Herbert Samuel, Lord Sankey

three colleagues. Samuel chose Reading, as the most eminent active
Liberal politician, leader in the Lords, and prominent 'national
government' advocate. Baldwin chose Neville Chamberlain, and
after consulting him added Hoare and Cunliffe-Lister. Baldwin
himself took a managerial position as Lord President. Otherwise,
since the government would be short-lived, ministers were wherever
possible to remain in or return to their previous, familiar, posts. For
balance their juniors would wherever possible be from other parties.

Despite unusual restraint engendered by the atmosphere of
emergency and sacrifice, the Conservative and Liberal invasion of
office – 'so vast a crowd & so few loaves'[25] – still involved significant
party and personal complications. The major appointments were
not settled for some days, and a list of lesser offices was unusually
delayed and never completed.[26] Just how far MacDonald exerted
prime ministerial power over appointments is unclear. Nevertheless

[25] A. Chamberlain to his wife, 6.30 pm, 24 Aug. 1931, AC 6/1/801.
[26] The last appointment was made as late as 22 September. Eventually five posts remained
unfilled, perhaps not all for reasons of economy.

it is plain that Conservative leaders were accommodating towards Labour ministers at some risk of difficulties for themselves, while raising objections to certain Lloyd George Liberals. Most notably, MacDonald successfully refused a Cabinet place for Hailsham, whose bruising diehard style made him 'particularly obnoxious to the Labour party'. Although Baldwin and Chamberlain persuaded MacDonald that Hailsham might be Lord Chancellor outside the Cabinet, this fell when Sankey declined to move to the India Office.[27] MacDonald's choice of Reading for the India Office[28] was changed, probably because Baldwin feared this might annoy Conservative diehards. Reading received ample compensation in the Foreign Secretaryship. The Conservative Inskip rather than the Liberal Birkett became Solicitor-General, while Hoare rejected one proposed Liberal undersecretary and Chamberlain three, including Lloyd George's son.[29]

For the Liberal party the National government offered escape from earlier tensions and the promise of great new opportunities. It is testimony to the party's ultimate allegiance to property and the taxpayer, its tenuous commitment to 'radical economics' in 1927–9 and 'progressive politics' in 1930–1, and its desperate reliance upon short-term tactical chances, that virtually all Liberals had no hesitation in accepting that the acting party leaders had done the 'perfectly plain and simple' thing in supporting 'sound finance', retrenchment, and a National government. A special meeting of Liberal peers, MPs, and candidates on 28 August required only a few words of 'Liberal' reassurance; dismissal of the bankers' ramp accusation, promises that the rich would share in the sacrifices, commitment to the best interests of 'the poorer classes'. Just one candidate expressed Keynesian scepticism.[30] The alliance with the Labour government had been wrecked, but that had been a cause of Liberal division and demoralisation. The Representation of the

[27] N. Chamberlain diary, 24 Aug. 1931; Sankey diary, 25 Aug. 1931. MacDonald personally detested Hailsham: see, e.g., MacDonald to Beauchamp, 15 May. 1931, JRM 1176. For Snowden refusing to have Hilton Young as Financial Secretary because of his 'superior airs', see N. Chamberlain to his wife, 25 Aug. 1931, NC 1/26/449.

[28] MacDonald undated draft ministerial list, JRM 1316; Reading reported in Catto to Reading, 25 Aug. 1931, Reading papers F228/70–1.

[29] Hyde, *Birkett*, 325; Hoare, 'The First National Government', Templewood papers VII:1; N. Chamberlain to his wife, 1 Sept. 1931, NC 1/26/454, and telephone message for Baldwin, 7 Sept. 1931, SB 44/19.

[30] Report of party meeting, 28 Aug. 1931, LG G/20/2/43. For some private doubts from 'radicals', see F. Owen in Dalton diary, 26 Aug. 1931 (Pimlott, 152), and Owen, Griffiths, Mander in Tweed to F. Stevenson, 31 Aug. 1931, LG G/28/2/3. On the other hand the Liberal Summer School radical, E. D. Simon, became Chamberlain's junior minister.

People Bill which had seemed the only chance for the party's survival was lost under a Palace Conference agreement to suspend controversial non-financial legislation. But the prospect of future electoral reform paled before immediate access to power, patronage, and influence, and the possibilities for party reunification and a reconditioned electoral appeal. Liberals exulted in what most had virtually ceased to expect – 'Liberalism... once again... occupy[ing] in [government] counsels and in Parliament its rightful position',[31] and Liberal politicians taking office. Brooks's Club was 'full of gleeful Liberal ghosts from the past'.[32] There was much 'office hunger'.[33] Samuel returned to the Home Secretaryship from which he had been ejected in 1916, Tudor Walters to the Paymaster-Generalship he had lost in 1922. For Maclean (Board of Education), Sinclair (Scotland), Lothian (Duchy of Lancaster), Pybus (Transport), Foot (Mines), five other Liberal junior ministers and two whips, this would be their first experience of government office. Given the Liberal party's limited parliamentary strength, its allocation of both Home and Foreign Secretaryships in Cabinet, almost half the other Cabinet-rank offices, and a large sprinkling of lesser posts, was generous. Samuel seized whatever he could. When the War Office unexpectedly became available he even pressed into service the seventy-three-year-old Whig relic, Lord Crewe.[34] Samuel wanted offices not just to exhibit Liberal importance, but to spread them across the party and bind it back together. Samuel, Maclean, Reading, and Sinclair together made a concerted attempt to 'bury the hatchet' and reunify the Liberal party. One remarkable, previously unimaginable, instance was Maclean publicly expressing 'deep and sincere' regret at Lloyd George's absence.[35]

These efforts were largely supererogatory, as the crisis highlighted the shared ground of retrenchment, subordinated all other differences, and evoked spontaneous plaudits for Samuel and Maclean. By 'a miracle' the crisis had produced the rare sight of Liberals disporting themselves as if they were a united party.[36] Nevertheless the pattern of appointments was important, because it induced a

---

[31] Maclean in report of Liberal party meeting, 28 Aug. 1931, LG G/20/2/43.
[32] Hilton Young to his wife, 24 Aug. 1931, Kennet papers 107/3.
[33] Tweed to F. Stevenson, 31 Aug. 1931, LG G/28/2/3.
[34] Samuel to Runciman, 29 Aug. 1931, Runciman papers 215. See Crewe to Samuel, 25 Aug. 1931, Samuel papers A/78/14, for earlier declining office.
[35] Reading in Reading memo, 11 Sept. 1931, Reading papers F118/131; Maclean in Report of party meeting, 28 Aug. 1931, LG G/20/2/43.
[36] Grigg to N. Chamberlain, 15 Sept. 1931, Altrincham papers. See also Bernays, *Special Correspondent*, 23.

permanent rearrangement of Liberal groupings. While Crewe and
Reading supplied reassuring symbols from earlier phases of
governing Liberalism, Maclean provided a crucial link with the
anti-Lloyd Georgian Liberal Council. His entry into the government
received benediction from Asquith's daughter, and Grey attended a
special Liberal party meeting on 28 August to pronounce his 'entire
agreement' with the Liberal ministers.[37] By the fortuitous combination of the crisis and Lloyd George's illness, the Liberal Council
now moved back into the centre of Liberal party politics – with one
important exception. Although Runciman had announced his
intended political retirement, like other leading Liberals he
immediately understood that the National government offered an
opportunity to re-establish his career, and felt deeply offended when
Samuel failed to offer him a Cabinet post.[38] Consequently, although
Runciman became an active supporter of the government, it would
be from a position ostentatiously independent of the Liberal ministers.
As for that other dissentient group, the Simon Liberals, a gesture was
made towards these with Pybus's appointment. But Simon himself
was ignored, because he had been too unpleasant too recently, and
probably because Samuel thought the crisis removed the ground for
Simonite revolt and made him harmless to the rest of the party. This
seemed to be confirmed when Simon sent the party meeting a
message of congratulations and support for his 'Liberal friends',
when Kedward and Hore-Belisha moved resolutions of confidence in
the leadership, and when Brown expressed readiness to 'come back
to the Party'.[39]

Even so Samuel would have offered more in 'Simonite' directions
had he not been Lloyd George's deputy. Too ill to be considered for
office but expecting a full recovery, Lloyd George had more reason
than other Liberal leaders to focus upon the future. Consequently,

[37] V. Bonham Carter to Maclean, 25 Aug. 1931, Maclean papers c468/130–3; Report of
party meeting, 28 Aug. 1931, LG G/20/2/43. For Maclean informing other Liberal
Council leaders of the previous week's negotiations, see Maclean to Grey, 22–4 Aug. 1931,
Runciman papers 245.

[38] The explanation for Runciman's non-appointment is a little complicated. Samuel initially
assumed he would not want office, but when alerted by Maclean tried to offer him the War
Office outside the Cabinet. But Runciman was on a sea cruise off Scotland and could not
be contacted in time, so Crewe had to be appointed instead. All this was explained to
Runciman, but he still felt aggrieved towards Samuel: see Maclean and Samuel tms to
Runciman, 24–7 Aug., Samuel to Runciman, 29 Aug., 3 Sept., and Runciman to Samuel
and to Collins, both 1 Sept. 1931, all Runciman papers 215.

[39] Report of party meeting, and Sylvester memo, both 28 Aug. 1931, LG G/20/2/43. For
Brown, Reading memo, 11 Sept. 1931, Reading papers, F118/131.

he had a more ambivalent attitude towards the new government. With previous party alignments thrown into confusion and the Cabinet committed to a short existence, he saw possibilities for an uncommitted 'man of emergency' to collect various disorientated parties and groups – possibly including Labour elements – into some new coalition. His first thoughts were therefore to emphasise his detachment, and to face in as many directions as possible. In a message to Samuel he supported the unemployment benefit cut but objected to cuts in agricultural development, took up Labour accusations of bankers' 'dictat[ion]', and called for further sacrifices from *rentiers*.[40] He sent no message to the party meeting, but primed his daughter Megan to express reservations about the government. Samuel and Reading, however, pre-empted her and expurgated Lloyd George's private statements, claiming his 'complete accord with what was being done'.[41] The party's evident support for Samuel and the ministerial appointments of such close followers as Lothian and Sinclair, eventually persuaded Lloyd George to be more positive towards the government – a position still compatible with being a leader 'in reserve'.[42] He allowed his son to take junior office, while another dependant, Goronwy Owen, became chief Liberal whip on Sinclair becoming a minister.

Nevertheless Lloyd George did not enter into the mood of reconciliation. With the Liberal party apparently in a strong position, he felt able to settle some scores. When consulted by Samuel on junior appointments he certainly vetoed Brown, and probably Collins and other 'Simonites'. These exclusions added new personal grievances to earlier differences, with far-reaching consequences.[43] If the Liberal party now had a basis for reunification, the Simon Liberals as well as Runciman remained semi-detached. Though it had office and influence, every leading Liberal understood that the emergency government offered probably the last decent

---

[40] Lloyd George memo, 25 Aug. 1931, Samuel papers A/78/12. Lloyd George's comments in Sylvester diary, 24 Aug. 1931, in Cross, 37, about 'keeping outside' merely acknowledged the inevitable, and do not indicate what his attitude would have been if he had been fit.
[41] Report of party meeting, and Sylvester memo, both 28 Aug. 1931, LG G/20/2/43.
[42] For this conception of Lloyd George's role, see Lothian to Garvin, 26 Aug. 1931, Lothian papers 257/261–2; Sinclair (after visiting Lloyd George) to Fisher, 30 Aug. 1931, Fisher papers 10/128, and Lloyd George to MacDonald, 30 Aug. 1931, JRM 1314.
[43] Samuel, *Memoirs*, 205; Morris-Jones, *Doctor in the Whips' Room*, 86; Bernays, *Special Correspondent*, 78–9. For Brown, N. Chamberlain message for Baldwin, 7 Sept, 1931, SB 44/19, and Reading memo, 11 Sept, 1931, Reading papers F118/131. For Collins, Crewe to Samuel, 27 Aug. 1931, Samuel papers A/78/15.

chance to secure their political futures, and that they had very little
time in which to turn the situation to party, electoral, or personal
advantage.

For the Conservative party the formation of the National
government was a complication, upsetting expectations that the next
government would be Conservative, 'imperial', and protectionist –
one in which many individual Conservatives would have had
reasonable claims to office, and from which all had anticipated
measures thought vital for national and party interests. The new cry
of 'national unity' neither altogether replaced assumptions that
Conservatives were the exclusive guardians of 'national policy', nor
suppressed fears that events might have 'jockeyed them out of a
successful appeal to the nation'.[44] Nor did it prevent personal
grievances. Even among Conservatives, 'patriotism' was a debat-
able matter. If Conservative leaders themselves recognized the
immediate advantages of a National government, they understood
the need to check doubts, suspicions, and disappointment. A
Baldwin statement on 24 August was designed not just to reassure
financial opinion by presenting the government as 'a guarantee'
that national finances would be 'put...in order', but also to soothe
Conservative opinion with assurances that it was formed for a
'limited period' and required 'no party...to sacrifice any of [its]
principles'.[45] With disappointed aspirants to office, Baldwin's
technique was to say that their prospects in a future Conservative
government were unprejudiced.[46] Given that the Conservative party
formed around two-thirds of the National government's likely
parliamentary support yet received only half the offices, a
disproportionate number of aspirants were disappointed. But once
Baldwin was reconciled to a National government, he had grasped
that prominent Labour and Lloyd George Liberal representation
would emphasise the government's 'national' character and spread
the electoral risks of any unpopularity resulting from retrenchment
and tax increases. His failure to fight harder for Conservative
appointments or to bother about the Simon Liberals, represented
not weak leadership (as even Chamberlain thought[47]) but a

[44] Conservative MPs reported in Collins to Runciman, 28 Aug. 1931, Runciman papers 215.
See also Ormsby-Gore to Baldwin, 24 Aug. 1931, SB 44/50, and Hilton Young to his wife,
24 and 26[?25] Aug. 1931, Kennet papers 107/3.   [45] The Times, 25 Aug. 1931.
[46] Speech at party meeting, The Times, 29 Aug. 1931; and specific promises in Hilton Young
to his wife, 26[?25] Aug. 1931, Kennet papers 107/3, and A. Chamberlain to his wife,
6.30 pm, 24 Aug. 1931, AC 6/1/801.   [47] N. Chamberlain diary, 25 Aug. 1931.

realisation both that the party had gained a strong tactical position and that this would fully restore his own authority as party leader.

Baldwin's confidence was also reflected in the distribution of Conservative appointments. Insofar as any general plan existed, it was to complete the reconstruction of the collective leadership begun while in opposition and to advance younger talent, ending earlier discontent about the 'old gang' and blockages to promotion. Chamberlain returned to the Health ministry, Cunliffe-Lister to the Board of Trade, and Hoare obtained the promotion to the India Office for which he had angled so hard, though only as third choice. Betterton, the party's expert on unemployment insurance, received promotion to the difficult but crucial Ministry of Labour. Of the 'young Conservatives', Elliot obtained promotion to Financial Secretary, and Stanley his first office. Baldwin acknowledged few obligations to former Cabinet colleagues, and despite the two years of challenges to his leadership felt little need to appease existing or potential critics. Austen Chamberlain received unusual attention, but in order to ease him towards semi-retirement *via* demotion to the Admiralty,[48] not because Baldwin feared the sort of damage he had almost caused in March. Horne had ceased to be a threat, and as India was not the current issue Churchill could not be one. Both could safely be ignored.

If trouble were to develop within the Conservative party, its likely sources would be the protectionists and the diehards. From these perspectives two front-bench Conservatives – Amery and Hailsham – each intended to pose a threat to Baldwin. Amery's basic complaint was simple; the crisis had not been used to impose tariffs. But this formed just part of an alternative analysis with similarities to that of TUC and Labour critics. To him it seemed that the sterling crisis had been exaggerated, and bankers had 'dictated'. Retrenchment was an 'essentially secondary' issue, the 'real' issues of trade depression had been 'shirked', and a 'great opportunity' to exploit TUC interest in tariffs – even to create 'a real national coalition, including the Trade Unions' – had been missed.[49] All this was connected with a sharp sense that, with most Conservative leaders entering the government, a role of alternative 'Unionist' leader had

---

[48] N. Chamberlain diary, 24 and 25 Aug. 1931; A. Chamberlain to his wife, 6.30 pm, 24 Aug. and 25 Aug. 1931, AC 6/1/801–2.

[49] Amery diary, 25 and 29 Aug. 1931, and to his wife, 25 Aug. 1931, in *LSA* II, 192–3, 195; Amery to Beaverbrook, 26 Aug. 1931, Beaverbrook papers C/5, and to Garvin, 27 Aug. 1931, Amery papers.

become available. Disappointed that Baldwin had even denied him the satisfaction of refusing to join a Cabinet containing free-traders, Amery nevertheless felt 'rather elated' at his own prospects – supposing that he was 'sure' to 'gain' as an ex-minister free to campaign for tariffs and the government's earliest possible dissolution.[50] He therefore cranked up the familiar instruments of agitation, got Page Croft to summon an EIA meeting, and urged Beaverbrook to resume the Empire Crusade.[51]

At almost any other time during the previous two years the cry of 'protection in danger' would have produced a party crisis. But now, though many Conservatives felt misgivings about postponement of tariffs and alliance with free-traders, Amery's attitude seemed extreme and absurd. Chamberlain was not alone in finding him 'as tiresome as could be' in his doctrinaire refusal to accept the leadership's version of events and prospects.[52] Any anxiety Baldwin might have felt about Amery evaporated when Page Croft congratulated him on a 'wise' course, and promised full support if assured that party policy on imperial protectionism would not be compromised in the longer run.[53] Approval from the leader of the protectionist backbenchers meant that for the time being Amery mattered very little, and demonstrated that most Conservative MPs would readily accept a 'patriotic' interpretation of the crisis and allow retrenchment priority over protection. Although Amery made a 'poisonous speech' at the EIA meeting, his only significant supporter was Lloyd, relishing a notion that Baldwin could be 'eliminate[d]' by Conservative revulsion at coalition and unsuccessfully trying to excite fear of concessions on India as well as on tariffs. Page Croft, armed with a Baldwin assurance, had no difficulty in averting hostile gestures against the Conservative ministers.[54]

---

[50] Amery diary, 25 Aug., 7 Sept. 1931, and to his wife, 25 Aug., 4 Sept. 1931, in *LSA* II, 192–3, 197–8.

[51] Amery diary, 25 and 26 Aug. 1931 (*LSA* II, 192–3); Amery to Beaverbrook, 26 Aug. 1931, Beaverbrook papers C/5. For other efforts, see letter, *The Times*, 27 Aug. 1931, and Amery to Garvin, 27 Aug. 1931, Amery papers.

[52] N. Chamberlain to his wife, 26 Aug. 1931, NC 1/26/450; Steel-Maitland 'Diary of events during crisis of 1931' (entry for 25 Aug.), Steel-Maitland papers 120/3/3.

[53] Page Croft to Baldwin, 25 Aug. 1931, Croft papers 1/3/15. This letter possibly led Baldwin to postpone an arranged interview with Amery: see Amery diary, 25 Aug. 1931 (*LSA* II, 192).

[54] Kingsley Wood in N. Chamberlain to his wife, 1 Sept. 1931, NC 1/26/454; Amery diary, 26 Aug. 1931 (*LSA* II, 193–4); Bowyer report of EIA meeting, 27 Aug. 1931, SB 105/63–7; Croft, *Life*, 191.

Hailsham was important not just as Conservative leader in the Lords but as a 'standard bearer' of the Conservative right.[55] Unlike Amery, he had attended the leaders' meetings which had endorsed the original decision for National government. Believing 'they could not have acted otherwise',[56] he accepted Baldwin's request to move the official resolution at a special party meeting on 28 August. Since Gretton also promised 'all the support in [his] power', the diehards were reassured and Baldwin received – unusually in his recent experience of party meetings – a standing ovation and unanimous vote of confidence,[57] later mirrored by Conservative activists throughout the country. Yet Hailsham embodied a genuine ambivalence felt by many Conservatives towards the government, which he had personal reasons for wanting to emphasise. He was furious that Baldwin had not pressed his claims to a Cabinet place and the Lord Chancellorship, and offers of lesser posts only reinforced his view that Baldwin was 'jealous and afraid' of him as a possible alternative leader.[58] Resentment soon nourished a view that the government was in part a Liberal trap sprung by Samuel to obtain office and frustrate a Conservative election victory.[59] Like Amery he concluded that the government must be ended quickly and that he should take a leading part in ending it. He distanced himself from it by taking a holiday instead of attending to his duties in the Lords and at the Round Table Conference. He lent himself to Amery's ideas for a campaign to make certain that the Conservative leaders were 'pull[ed] ... out of the cabinet'.[60] He also encouraged Beaverbrook, who had hurried back from Canada convinced of a fresh opportunity to display his power, taking the view that Baldwin had thrown away a 'great chance' to get tariffs. Beaverbrook opened his newspapers to government critics, fed Amery's ambitions, and aimed 'to spike Baldwin's guns through the agency of Hailsham'.[61] So while the discipline of a national crisis and the

[55] N. Chamberlain to his wife, 26 Aug. 1931, NC 1/26/450.

[56] Amery diary, 30 Aug. 1931 (*LSA* II, 195).   [57] *The Times*, 29 Aug. 1931.

[58] N. Chamberlain to his wife, 26 Aug. 1931, NC 1/26/450; Amery diary, 30 Aug. 1931 (*LSA* II, 195).

[59] Hailsham to Lady Milner, 29 Aug. 1931, Lady Milner papers C361/2; Lady Milner diary, 2 Sept. 1931.

[60] Amery diary, 30 and 31 Aug. 1931, and Amery to his wife, 1 Sept. 1931, in *LSA* II, 195–6; Hailsham to Amery, 2 Sept. [1931], Amery papers; and for his absence, Dawson to Hailey, 16 Sept. 1931, Hailey papers E220/22/21–3.

[61] Lockhart diary, 31 Aug., 1 Sept. 1931, in Young I, 182; Beaverbrook to Terrell, 1 Sept., and to Gwynne and Amery, 2 Sept. 1931, Beaverbrook papers, B/205, C/149, C/5; Amery diary, 31 Aug. 1931 (*LSA* II, 196).

opportunity to achieve retrenchment meant there were no immediate party management problems for Baldwin, the possibility of a Hailsham – Amery – Beaverbrook alliance emphasised the need for extreme care.

THE 'NATIONAL' POLICY

As a political arrangement the National government answered the problem of requiring financial sacrifices from a workforce and electorate whose reactions might easily be resentment and, worse, class bitterness. It was an attempt to dissipate these feelings by designating cuts and taxes as necessary, shared, 'national' sacrifices. This task had also to be reconciled with party principles, policies, and expectations. Such were the preoccupations of National government leaders as politicians. But as ministers they had another concern. As an executive arrangement the National government was formed to defend sterling, obtain foreign credits, and restore British credit. The Cabinet had to mediate between on the one hand an international banking community which had 'no conception of the appalling difficulties of handling large bodies of men with votes',[62] and on the other the British electorate and the parties composing the government.

It seemed obvious that formation of a 'strong Government' pledged to retrenchment would impress British and foreign financial opinion.[63] But the initial effect was ruined by a misjudged *Times* editorial on the morning of the Palace Conference, which in appealing for urgent political decisions revealed that the central bank credits were 'approaching exhaustion'.[64] This news had a 'disastrous effect' upon confidence, causing the Bank's heaviest daily loss so far (almost £12m.), and leaving only sufficient foreign exchange reserves for two or three more days.[65] The Bank obtained emergency assistance from the Treasury and the Federal Reserve Bank, but this could only help a little.[66]

---

[62] Dawson to Oliver, 25 Aug. 1931, Oliver papers, reporting views of his City friends.

[63] Grenfell to Morgan & Co, tm 31/4934, 24 Aug. 1931, MGC; Harrison to Harvey, tm 307/31, 24 Aug. 1931, FRBNY.

[64] See Sayers, *Bank of England*, 399–400. The editorial was written by Coote, but presumably used information from Dawson, who may have obtained this indirectly from Chamberlain or Baldwin, or directly from Peacock: see Dawson diary, 22–4 Aug. 1931.

[65] Grenfell to Morgan & Co, tm 31/4934, 24 Aug. 1931, and to Lamont, 27 Aug. 1931, MGC; BoE Cte, 24 Aug. 1931; Addis diary, 24 Aug. 1931.

[66] Harrison to Harvey, tm 307/31, 24 Aug. 1931, FRBNY; BoE Cte, 25 Aug. 1931. For transfer of dollar securities from the Treasury, see material in T160/F2655/02. Kunz, *Battle*, 113, by misreading $28m. as £28m. inflates the assistance available.

So, even while the National government was being formed, its leaders came under Bank of England pressure as intense as that previously felt by the Labour Cabinet. The change of ministers did not alter the Bank of England's analysis, objectives, or methods. The sterling crisis was about confidence in the *British* government, whether Labour or National. The 24 August exchange panic made it 'absolutely necessary' to obtain the short-term credits 'at the earliest possible moment'.[67] Harvey, Peacock, and other Bank directors remained as active as they had been during the previous two weeks in pressing political leaders for rapid decisions and reassuring public statements,[68] especially once TUC and Labour opposition became clear. Bank directors themselves tried to counteract this opposition. Peacock explained the Bank's views to Citrine on the 24th and other General Council members on the 25th; denials of *Daily Herald* accusations of Federal Reserve Bank 'dictation' were inserted in other newspapers.[69]

Ministers hoping that the government's formation would practically end the crisis were left without any doubt that there was still 'a terrible job' before them.[70] Statements of the Cabinet's intention to take 'whatever steps' were necessary to restore confidence helped check the panic and limit exchange losses by the 26th. But then negotiations in Paris raised technical difficulties, while the $4\frac{1}{2}$ per cent interest required by Morgans was considered 'excessive' by the Bank and as dangerous ammunition for the Labour opposition by MacDonald. When appeals elicited the alarming reply that 'not a single' American bank really wanted to lend money to the British government – that confidence in British credit had sunk so low – Snowden concluded that there was simply no choice but to accept Morgans' terms.[71] With exchange losses increasing yet again, 'several weeks'' work involving over a hundred American and

---

[67] BoE Cte, 24 and 25 Aug. 1931. Hopkins note of interview Harvey, Peacock with MacDonald and Baldwin, and Hopkins to Bank, both 25 Aug. 1931, T160/435/F12568/1.

[68] See Peacock advice to the King in Wigram memo, 24 Aug. 1931, RA GV K2330(2)/1/18–20; Harvey, Peacock, MacDonald, Baldwin interview, 25 Aug. 1931, T160/435/F12568/1; Harvey to Samuel, 29 Aug. 1931, BoE G3/210/268.

[69] Steel-Maitland 'Diary of events during crisis of 1931', 24–5 Aug. entries, and Steel-Maitland to Peacock, 25 Aug. 1931, Steel-Maitland papers 120/3/3; Harvey to Peacock 25 Aug. 1931, BoE G3/210/264. For the press, Harvey to Harrison, tm 359/31, 26 Aug. 1931, FRBNY papers.

[70] N. Chamberlain to his wife, 25 Aug. 1931, and to H. Chamberlain 27 Aug. 1931, NC 1/26/449, 18/1/754.

[71] Morgan Grenfell 'Memorandum', 25 and 27 Aug. 1931 entries; MacDonald and Morgan in Stimson memo, 27 Aug. 1931, Stimson papers (partly in *FRUS 1931* I, 563–4); BoE Cte, 26 Aug. 1931.

French banks were 'compressed into two or three days' to secure the new credits of £40m. each before the reopening of business on Monday 31 August.[72]

Like the central bank credits of late July, these government credits of late August provided ample foreign currency to support sterling. But there was no complacency now about British credit. Despite the new government's statements large sterling sales continued, and the previous month's experience showed that even massive exchange intervention was useless in the absence of confidence. The Bank now sought a public announcement of specific budget proposals from ministers, together with a propaganda campaign to counteract Labour opposition statements.[73] Awaiting the government's programme preyed as much upon the City's nerves as upon those of the foreign markets, with a new twist of fears about items other than retrenchment. From 29 August gilts fell so sharply that on 2 September the Bank on its own initiative felt obliged to anticipate the budget. From its private knowledge of the Cabinet proposals, it assured the Stock Exchange unofficially that there would be no special *rentier* tax nor a forced war loan conversion.[74]

Given the government's purpose, the Bank of England was naturally the Cabinet's principal advisor. While MacDonald had kept Harvey and Peacock at a distance from the Labour Cabinet for fear of embarrassing confrontations, the two were summoned before the new Cabinet to report the Bank's advice. But the National government was not in any direct sense a 'bankers' government'. When requested the Bank gave its opinion on certain tax proposals, but it did not take advantage of the new government to press for further retrenchment, even though it had considered MacDonald's 22 August programme inadequate. As under the Labour Cabinet, its efforts were chiefly directed towards obtaining rapid decisions. Here its patience was again stretched, as Cabinet discussions of budget measures took longer than the Bank considered prudent. This delay arose not because of negotiations with bankers, but because the new ministers were not content simply to adopt the Labour Cabinet—

[72] Duff note, 28 Aug. 1931, PREM 1/97; Hopkins to Fisher and Snowden, 31 Aug. 1931, T160/557/F12570/1. Details of negotiations are in Kunz, *Battle*, 114–17.

[73] Harvey to Samuel, 29 Aug. 1931, BoE G3/210/268; Grenfell and Peacock seeing N. Chamberlain, 31 Aug. 1931, in Morgan Grenfell, 'Memorandum'; Harvey and Peacock in Cabinet 53(31) app., 3 Sept. 1931.

[74] BoE Cte, 2 Sept. 1931; Harvey in Cabinet 53(31) app., 3 Sept. 1931; Sayers, *Bank of England*, 463–4.

MacDonald scheme of 21–2 August. They subjected it to a scrutiny which produced new ideas and exposed unexpected difficulties.

Each Cabinet partner felt the 'strangeness' of their new company, and there were some tensions. Nevertheless, driven by consciousness that they 'had staked everything, and nothing could justify their attitude except success', they initially found each other 'more helpful than [they] had expected'.[75] The crucial tasks were referred to three-party Cabinet committees on Finance (Snowden, Neville Chamberlain, Samuel, and later Reading), Economy (MacDonald, Baldwin, Cunliffe-Lister, Maclean) and Procedure (MacDonald, Cunliffe-Lister, Sinclair).[76] The outlines had been set at the Palace Conference: cessation of unemployment insurance borrowing, 'equitable' sacrifices, retrenchment amounting approximately to the Labour Cabinet's proposed total of £70m., suspension of the non-contractual Sinking Fund, no tariffs.[77] Snowden, in contrast to his fierce defence of chancellorian prerogatives in the Labour Cabinet, accepted the new political realities not just by allowing his budget statement to be scrutinised in committee but by permitting Samuel and Chamberlain to consult officials and Bank directors themselves. As it was proposed that borrowing should cease immediately, the Treasury revised the current year's estimated deficit upwards to £74m.: that for 1932 remained £170m. After cuts and partial Sinking Fund suspension, taxation totalling £39m. would be needed in a supplementary budget for the current tax year, and £80m. for 1932–3.

The Cabinet reassessment revolved around the political implications of the 22 August package: whether the change of government might seriously alter those effects and, for Conservative and Liberal ministers, specifically whether what had seemed desirable from a Labour government would be as desirable or as safe when it came from a government containing themselves. The chief initiative came from Lothian. He saw the fundamental political issue in its rawest terms, fearing that the crisis had made 'socialism à la Karl Marx...inevitable'.[78] If a government now mostly representing the Conservative and Liberal 'prosperous classes' simply adopted existing proposals for impositions upon the unemployed and small taxpayers without making some very large contribution of their own,

[75] A. Chamberlain at meeting of ministers, app. to Cabinet 48(31), 26 Aug. 1931; N. Chamberlain in Amery diary, 2 Sept. 1931 (*LSA* II, 196); MacDonald diary, 2 Sept. 1931.
[76] Cabinets 48, 51(31), 26 Aug., 2 Sept. 1931.
[77] Samuel memo, 24 Aug. 1931, Samuel papers A/78/11.
[78] Lothian in Headlam diary, 29 Aug. 1931.

this might 'align party politics on lines of class warfare for 20 years' and probably 'destroy the Liberal party'. His conclusion was as radical as his analysis, surpassing anything proposed by the Labour opposition. There should be a capital levy to cancel £2,000m. of war debt, relieve the budget annually of £100m. in debt charges, strengthen the gold standard and, by these means, maintain national unity.[79]

It is indicative of how tense and fundamental the political issues – as well as substantive policy problems – had now become that Chamberlain and Samuel gave time to such a scheme, one involving not just further direct taxation but connotations of conscription of wealth. Themselves sensitive to the danger highlighted by Lothian, they were re-examining the idea of a separate *rentier* tax. But like their Labour predecessors they found from the Inland Revenue that it was impractical.[80] Since Lothian's scheme was financially so radical they consulted the Bank of England. Though claiming to be 'much attracted to the political advantages', Harvey and other Bank directors warned that it might 'immediately induce a flight from the £ & also be taken by the Socialists as a precedent to be repeated *ad lib.*'.[81] The first part was a reasonable assessment of how the financial markets might react; but the second, overtly political, opinion was equally decisive in steadying Samuel's and Chamberlain's judgement. Instead they adopted the Bank's own answer to the debt problem. The long-prepared plans for voluntary war loan conversion were resuscitated, by taking powers in the Finance Bill to permit action once financial conditions improved.[82]

Further proposals for re-adjusting the tax burden were considered, but examination only revealed the limited administrative, financial, and political room for manoeuvre. Conservatives reserved the right to make modifications if they formed the next government,[83] in other words to substitute tariff income for some direct taxation. In existing conditions, however, Chamberlain no less than Samuel acknowledged the political rationale for increased and extended direct

[79] Lothian to Samuel 25 Aug. 1931, and to Garvin, 26 Aug. 1931, Lothian papers 143/13–17, 257/261–2.
[80] Fergusson to Samuel and Chamberlain, 27 Aug. 1931, T171/288, enclosing P. J. Grigg memo of 17 Aug.
[81] N. Chamberlain diary, 27 Aug., 3 Sept 1931; BoE Cte, 27 Aug. 1931; Lothian to Samuel, 31 Aug. 1931, Lothian papers 143/26–8.
[82] Harvey to Samuel, 29 Aug. 1931, BoE G3/210/268; BoE Cte, 1 Sept. 1931; Snowden, Financial Statement, *HC Deb*, 256, cols. 310–11, 10 Sept. 1931.
[83] Cabinet 52(31), 2 Sept. 1931.

taxation – as essential counterparts to effective retrenchment in an 'equitable sacrifice' package. The final tax proposals were substantially those proposed by Snowden within the Labour Cabinet: increased beer, tobacco, petrol, and entertainments duties, with £57m. in direct taxation, including the 10 per cent on surtax, 6d. on income tax, and one-third reduction in allowances. In real terms these increases were heavier than those in any previous budget, and almost doubled the number of income tax payers. The fears Lothian had expressed were met by emphasis upon the differentiation against *rentier* incomes, as the 'only method' by which the 'principle of ability to pay' could be 'justly' applied in those directions.[84]

Proposals for retrenchment caused greater Cabinet differences. The Economy Committee agreed on various minor adjustments to the Labour Cabinet's proposals, but Conservative ministers especially wanted to use the opportunity of a National government to obtain more radical changes in expenditure policies. Chamberlain proposed reductions in housing subsidies, and he and Betterton reopened the unemployment insurance issue. A further attack upon 'anomalies' was suggested, until it was realised that 'very controversial and difficult' legislation would be needed. They proposed to increase the unemployment benefit cut to 11 per cent and, in accordance with the Conservative Research Department's plans, to transfer transitional benefit recipients to Public Assistance.[85]

These proposals threatened serious embarrassment to Labour members of the Cabinet, particularly to MacDonald. He disliked the Conservative pressure in principle, with its prospect of 'economy becoming a mania'. He had made explicit commitments about retrenchment to the last Labour Cabinet meeting, and wanted to avoid giving further substance to Labour opposition taunts of his betrayal to Conservatives and Liberals. He also wanted to subvert those attacks, by exposing the virtuous pretensions of his former colleagues.[86] Keeping not just to the total sum of retrenchment considered by the Labour Cabinet but also to most of its specific

[84] Snowden statement, *HC Deb*, 256, col. 306, 10 Sept. 1931. It should be added that the estimated 1931 surplus still depended on raids upon capital funds (the April use of the Exchange Account, and now the Sinking Fund). Even now budgetary policy fell short of the professed 'sound finance'.

[85] Economy Committee Report, CP 208(31), and N. Chamberlain and Betterton, 'Unemployment Insurance', CP 211(31), both 28 Aug. 1931.

[86] MacDonald diary, 1 Sept. 1931; also Sankey to MacDonald, 1 Sept. 1931, Sankey papers c508/112.

proposals would strengthen MacDonald's strategy for neutralising the opposition leaders. Put in these political terms, Conservative and Liberal ministers fully appreciated MacDonald's point. Chamberlain dropped the housing subsidy proposal, and the unemployment benefit cut was kept at 10 per cent. The Cabinet also adopted a MacDonald compromise for keeping transitional benefit nominally outside the 'poor law', with the Public Assistance Authorities conducting means tests only as agents of the Ministry of Labour.[87]

So like the tax proposals, the retrenchment scheme was very similar to that which the Labour Cabinet had agreed on 21 August, with the addition of MacDonald's proposals of the 22nd. It included £25·8m. from unemployment insurance, obtained by increased contributions and limitation of entitlement as well as benefit cuts, with a further £10m. saved by means tests upon transitional benefits. Employment creation expenditure would virtually cease. There were cuts in income of 15 per cent for teachers, and around 10 per cent for police, the armed forces, civil servants and panel doctors, and other salary cuts varying from 20 per cent for senior, to 10 per cent for junior, ministers and judges.

It was well understood that the taxation and retrenchment measures would cause hardship for many people, and might have severe political consequences. The unemployed, now numbering 2·8m., would not be the only ones to suffer. They would also include lower-paid public servants, the 1·5m. to 2m. new direct taxpayers created by the reduction in allowances and – proportionately the most heavily burdened – those on moderate incomes who would have to bear both cuts in income and new income tax demands.[88] Even with appeal to 'national unity' and 'equitable sacrifices', and with increased taxation of the wealthy, the Cabinet feared public protests, an electoral backlash, perhaps non-cooperation or even strikes. The day before details of cuts were published, it arranged to 'up-date' the emergency Transport and Supply Committee.[89] Much seemed to depend upon how the impositions were presented. The expenditure White Paper was altered in draft to emphasise the sacrifices of senior public servants: the salary cuts of ministers, MPs,

[87] Economy Committee Report, CP 208(31), and N. Chamberlain and Betterton, 'Unemployment Insurance', CP 211(31), both 28 Aug. 1931; Cabinets 50 and 52(31), 1 and 2 Sept. 1931. See Lowe, *Adjusting to Democracy*, 156, for this as an 'ingenious improvisation' which was 'on balance, advantageous to all', including claimants.

[88] For the effect of tax changes, see Mallet and George, *British Budgets*, 392–3, and Short thesis, 'Politics of Personal Taxation', 290–3.   [89] Cabinet 55(31), 9 Sept. 1931.

judges, civil servants, and servicemen were moved to the top of the list, and the unemployment insurance cuts placed almost at the bottom.[90] The King was prevailed upon to surrender £50,000 and the Prince of Wales £10,000 per annum from the Civil List in order to strengthen the public example of 'patriotic sacrifice'. Conservative MPs resolved that 'they could not face the electorate unless their salaries were cut at least as much as the teacher's'.[91] In the hope that a strong sense of 'common sacrifice' might make recipients of cuts less resentful, it was decided to take advantage of the current atmosphere of crisis and to implement all cuts together on 1 October – even though this meant disregarding contractual negotiating processes. In order to achieve this, the Procedure Committee recommended compression of parliamentary debate through a one-clause Economy Bill, giving the government powers for one month to implement cuts by Orders in Council.[92] This device had normally only been used in wartime emergencies, and it aroused almost as much Labour opposition as the cuts themselves. But it embodied the ministerial view that with so much at stake 'it would be necessary to overwhelm all opposition. That could only be accomplished by boldness in execution'.[93]

There was to be considerable protest, some of which seriously embarrassed the government. But assisted by the unshaken constitutionalism of the Labour opposition and TUC leaderships, most of this protest remained within the law. Despite the acute polarisation over policy and the upheaval in party alignments, conflict was contained within the familiar territory of political argument and rhetoric. Once Parliament met, this political battle became everything the Conservative and Liberal leaders could have wished. It became less a conflict of their own parties representing the 'prosperous classes' against a Labour party representing the 'working classes', than one between an alliance claiming to be 'national' and an 'irresponsible' opposition. Most advantageously of all, it became a dispute between two sets of Labour tribunes over what best constituted working-class interests. In the presentation of potentially unpopular taxes and cuts, Conservatives and Liberals were able to take second place to the MacDonaldites. Baldwin,

[90] Compare Hankey, 'Economy: Draft White Paper', CP223(31), 8 Sept. 1931, with earlier version, CP221(31), 4 Sept. 1931.   [91] Amery diary, 9 Sept. 1931 (*LSA* II, 199).

[92] Committee on Parliamentary Procedure. Conclusions, CP 209(31), 28 Aug. 1931. For problems over implementation, see Cabinet 49(31), 31 Aug. 1931.

[93] A. Chamberlain at ministerial meeting, app to Cabinet 48(31), 26 Aug. 1931.

benignly treating the Labour–MacDonaldite differences as il-
lustrating 'the many-sidedness of truth', effortlessly resumed his
moral authority over the whole House of Commons.[94]

On the first day, 8 September, MacDonald opened a confidence
debate. Snowden introduced the budget on the 10th, and on the
11th MacDonald proposed and Thomas supported the second
reading of the Economy Bill. Their main arguments turned on
financial realities, national interests, and sacrifices 'spread as fairly
and as evenly as human ingenuity can devise'.[95] But almost as
prominent was a bitter counter-attack against the Labour opposition
leaders. Although the MacDonaldites had expected to be denounced,
they were still surprised, hurt, and outraged by the character of the
criticism – personal as well as 'unpatriotic' attacks, with brazen
repudiation of cuts accepted in Cabinet.[96] They reacted by
converting what had been conceived as a strategy for disarming the
opposition leaders into a means to demolish them. First MacDonald
implied and then Snowden said outright that 'nine-tenths' of the
cuts had been 'adopted and approved by the late Government'.[97]
The difficulty was that if this line of attack was to penetrate, it
required the sort of detail which would breach conventions of
Cabinet secrecy. Cabinet secretaries compiled statements of the
Labour dissentients' 'commitments' in order to provide ministers
with debating 'ammunition', but on their advice this use of Cabinet
minutes was disguised by reference to details revealed in the
negotiations with Conservative and Liberal leaders.[98] Thomas – the
principal victim of Labour criticism, losing his trade union post and
pension – used this tactic to devastating effect on the 11th, supported
on the 14th by Samuel and Chamberlain.

With Conservative and Liberal voting strengths combined – let
alone the dozen MacDonaldites – there was little doubt that the
government would have a parliamentary majority. On 8 September
the division was 309 to 249. It seemed clear that the Economy and
Finance Bills would pass without difficulty. But this would just be
the first stage of the political process. At some point after the cuts and

---

[94] *HC Deb*, 256, col. 67, 8 Sept, 1931. For the effect, see Alexander, ibid.; Amery diary, 8 Sept.
      1931 (*LSA* II, 199); Nathan to Lloyd George, 13 Sept. 1931, LG G15/7/21.
[95] Snowden, *HC Deb*, 256, col. 312, 10 Sept. 1931.
[96] E.g., MacDonald diary, 8 Sept, 1931; Snowden, *Autobiography* II, 957.
[97] *HC Deb*, 256. cols. 18–19, 302, 315.
[98] Howorth memos, 25 Aug., 3 and 10. Sept 1931, Howorth to Hankey, and Hankey to
      MacDonald, 3 Sept. 1931, all JRM 260; Hankey diary, 13 Sept. 1931 (Roskill, *Hankey* II,
      552–3).

taxes had been imposed – when voters would be of unusually uncertain temper – the electorate would have to be faced. The problem for each National government partner was how to convert the collective parliamentary triumph into electoral success or survival for themselves.

THE OPPOSITION

The Labour party and the TUC together provided much the most formidable opposition, but it was not the only one. There were also Mosley's New party and Keynes. Mosley remained significant because he represented an alternative position to that of the established parties, one which had gained increased relevance as their positions were disrupted. As the August crisis developed he identified it as the shakedown he had long foreseen, and as his vindication and opportunity. The old parties seemed to be wrecking themselves and clearing the ground for himself: 'everything is moving towards us – few movements have been so speedily or so dramatically justified'.[99]

The formation of the National government did not initially disprove this, because it was a temporary arrangement. It appeared to promise chaotic party conditions across the political right and centre, which would enable the New party to be 'buil[t] up' and to become an important element within the 'national' area vacated by its dissolution. So Mosley did not contemplate rejoining Labour. But neither did he attach himself to the government. More openly than before, he aimed to carry sections of working-class and progressive opinion into a radical movement of frightened propertied voters and discontented 'activists' on the right. Here his July discussion with Lloyd George and Churchill offered one model. He competed with National government members in trying to administer the *coup de grace* to the Labour party, while treating the government with calculated ambivalence. He voted against it on 8 September, yet offered broad support for more decisive measures and especially a General Powers Bill, seeking to capture parts of its following by outbidding its leaders on the 'national emergency' cry. This seemed possible because the Conservative leadership had postponed tariffs, enabling Mosley to expound what much conservative and progressive opinion believed: that the real problem was not the budget but the industrial crisis. Against the willingness of the Labour

[99] Mosley to Nicolson, 16 Aug. 1931, Nicolson papers.

dissentients as well as the National Cabinet to reduce living standards, he presented the New party as alone possessing a constructive programme. This still included 'Keynesian' loan-financed national development, but the emphasis had now shifted squarely to 'scientific protection'.[100]

As a successful prophet expressing some of the doubts and hopes of National government followers, Mosley re-established himself as a leading figure and his party as a serious proposition. He attracted new or renewed interest from Churchill, Amery, Percy, Hore-Belisha, Melchett, various 'young Conservatives', and at least two ministers, Elliot and Jowitt.[101] New party recruitment increased, further financial assistance seemed obtainable, Nicolson prepared a national newspaper, *Action*, and fifty candidates were planned. In mid September 'all' still seemed to be 'going splendidly' and Mosley was 'full of hope' as the government completed its legislative purposes and a new phase of uncertainty and possible disruption opened.[102]

Keynes once again offered a radical policy alternative, but he was now more adrift than ever from the concerns of political leaders. Well before August he had become disillusioned with the existing party system as obstructive to constructive planning, and with Labour and Liberal specifically for what he considered to be their antediluvian preoccupation with free trade and land taxation.[103] By May he would 'without question' vote for the New party, and in early August was impressed that Mosley's predictions of political crisis had been proved right.[104] Yet after 24 August he did not suppose that Mosley could influence events, and his own policy preoccupations cut across Mosley's tactics for appealing to the 'national' forces. Towards the National government Keynes's initial reaction was as equivocal as his advice to MacDonald two weeks previously. Instinctively he felt 'very unhappy about the whole course of events', disliking the Conservative entry into office and the concentration upon retrenchment at the expense of capital de-

---

[100] Nicolson diary, 26 and 31 Aug. 1931 (partly in Nicolson 1, 88); Lockhart diary, 27 Aug. 1931, and Nicolson to Lockhart, 11 Sept. 1931, in Young 1, 182, 185; Mosley statement, *Manchester Guardian*, 28 Aug, 1931; *HC Deb*, 256, cols. 72–82, 158–60, 8 and 9 Sept. 1931.

[101] Nicolson diary, 31 Aug., 9, 10, and 11 Sept. 1931; Conway diary, 8 Sept. 1931; and see Amery diary, 8 Sept. 1931 (*LSA* 11, 199).

[102] Nicolson diary, 31 Aug., 1, 9, and 10 Sept. 1931.

[103] 'Sir Oswald Mosley's Manifesto', 13 Dec., 1930, 'Mr Snowden's Budget', 28 April 1931, Keynes to Herbert, 21 and 29 May 1931, in *JMK* xx, 473–6, 520–3, 527–8.

[104] Nicolson diary, 29 April, 6 May 1931 (Nicolson 1, 71–2); Nicolson to Mosley, 14 Aug. 1931, in N. Mosley, *Rules of the Game*, 196.

velopment and tariffs. Yet he also thought that some retrenchment, including unemployment benefit cuts, was 'justifiable', and that with opinion still unprepared for devaluation drastic budget measures were inevitable. He believed a strong government might just possibly achieve an effective deflation.[105]

After a week, however, his views clarified, as he understood that the government intended what he had consistently worked against – a partial deflation. Once its measures had been announced he was outraged. By his analysis the fundamental problem for sterling was the balance of payments, for which there were four possible remedies: tariffs, all-round reduction of money incomes, exchange and capital controls with pressure upon France and the USA to enforce sensible international credit policies, and devaluation. He came to 'loathe this ridiculous Govt'[106] which chose none of these options, but instead produced a programme which he estimated would increase unemployment by 400,000 and, worse, which was, he thought, by penalising public employees, grossly offensive to social justice. Keynes grasped what even Labour dissentients initially overlooked, that for all the emphasis on 'equal sacrifices' the income cuts were in reality much more onerous than the nominally similar percentage increases in direct taxation. It was 'a most foul iniquity' that teachers' salaries were cut by 15 per cent while the 'well-to-do' suffered by only 3 per cent or 4 per cent. To an all-party meeting of MPs on 16 September he described the programme as not just 'wrong' but 'perfectly mad'. Believing the government too 'deluded' to adopt any sensible alternatives, Keynes now came out openly for devaluation as both desirable and inevitable. Ministerial fears of catastrophic depreciation he dismissed as 'quite [barmy]'.[107]

The strong language, the evident effort to shock, reflected Keynes's sense of powerlessness. His views were contradicted by other economists as well as the financial authorities, and they provoked equally strong reactions from Conservative and Liberal MPs: 'great nonsense', 'unmitigated twaddle', 'taken leave of his wits'.[108] A few individual Labour MPs were impressed, and it was to

[105] Keynes to Stamp, 27 Aug. 1931, and 'Notes on the Situation', in *JMK* xx, 595–8. See Howson and Winch, *Economic Advisory Council*, 92, for the article as 'peculiarly temporising'.
[106] Keynes to B. Webb, 1 Sept. 1931, Passfield papers II:4:1:90.
[107] Keynes articles, 'We Must Restrict Our Imports', 10 Sept. 1931, and 'A Gold Conference', 12 Sept. 1931; Keynes to Case, 14 Sept. 1931, and speech notes, 16 Sept. 1931, in *JMK* ix, 238–42, xx, 598–611.
[108] Lane-Fox diary, 16 Sept. 1931; Buchan to his wife, 17 Sept. 1931, Tweedsmuir (Queens) papers; Simon in Dalton diary, 16 Sept. 1931 (Dalton, 290). For economists' defences of

these and to Citrine and Bevin that Keynes now looked for sensible contributions to public debate. But he had little expectation from the Labour party as a whole, which despite a major policy shift seemed from his perspective to be almost as disastrously muddled as the government.[109]

Within the Labour party MacDonald's, Snowden's, and Thomas's decision to join the parties of the propertied classes in cutting working-class incomes came as a enormous shock. Nevertheless first reactions were commonly mixed. Confused, anxious party members looked to parliamentary leaders who were themselves much less clear than they and their historians later claimed. Revulsion against an attack upon social services and wages, transgressing an elemental Labour principle, was an instinctive reaction. Defence of the unemployed; disbelief in an 'equality of sacrifice' which involved real hardship for the poor but only a 'contribution' from the rich; loyalty to or sympathy with the working classes[110] – these were commitments felt by all, and in that sense there was soon 'evidence of practical unanimity'.[111] Yet there were contrary pressures: the cry of national emergency, and the respect still commanded by MacDonald and Snowden as socialist apostles and party founders. No pattern is discernible. Those with sympathy for the MacDonald-ites included both party veterans and rising newcomers, from working-class and from comfortable origins. Had MacDonald's appeals for support been less muddled and made sooner – before the party executives had declared themselves – more would certainly have joined him. These included members of the Cabinet majority: perhaps Benn and Shaw, definitely Bondfield and Morrison – whose 'esteem for MacDonald...had been increased 100 per cent' by the crisis.[112] Among junior ministers Cripps 'admire[d] immensely' the

the gold standard, Clay broadcast, The Times, 8 Sept. 1931, and Beveridge in Dalton diary, 17 Sept. 1931 (Dalton, 284).

[109] See Keynes to Pethick-Lawrence, 28 Aug., 13 Sept. 1931, Pethick-Lawrence papers 2/208 (expressing sympathy, and readiness to read proofs of book on crisis); Keynes in B. Webb diary, 23 Sept. 1931, for Citrine as a 'key man', but 'hearty contempt' for the party; Keynes to Case, 14 Sept. 1931, in JMK xx, 605.

[110] E.g., Phillips, and Milner, to MacDonald, 27 Aug., 1 Sept. 1931, JRM 1314, 1315.

[111] Dalton diary, 25 Aug. 1931 (Dalton, 274).

[112] Morrison in Strauss diary, 25 Aug. 1931, and see Donoughue and Jones, Morrison, 162–8. See also Benn speech, The Times, 31 Aug. 1931, for warm references to MacDonald even after party executive statements; Samuel to Runciman, 29 Aug. 1931, Runciman papers 215, for Shaw nearly remaining in office; Bondfield to MacDonald, 24 Aug. 1931, JRM 1314, for 'deep sympathy and admiration '.

MacDonaldites' 'courage and conviction', and took advice before declining office with 'very deep personal regret'.[113] Other ministers and MPs were 'mystified' by the action of men they 'loved and revered', and felt 'infinite sorrow'.[114] Feelings were often ambivalent – dislike of MacDonald's decision, but respect for his motives. Many expressed desire to avoid personal recriminations. Tillett spoke to the parliamentary party about 'class war', but privately offered MacDonald 'every good wish'.[115] Turner, who joined in nominating Henderson as new party leader, was 'sure no one [could] utter a word of blame or condemnation' against MacDonald and Snowden. Like Cripps, Morrison, and others, he hoped the separation would be short.[116] Certainly some were angry and hostile, but of these Attlee, Pethick-Lawrence, and others acknowledged MacDonald's 'sincerity', and many felt impelled to justify themselves to him.[117] Dalton's outright contempt was untypical of initial party reactions, while the sense of 'breathing cleaner air' which he (and the Webbs) felt at the MacDonaldite departures was achieved by forgetting how fully the 'dear old man' Henderson (and Passfield) had been part of the MacDonald regime.[118]

Instinctive defence of the unemployed and low paid did not answer MacDonald's arguments of necessity and prevention of worse hardships. The most obvious alternate policy – shifting the whole burden of budget impositions on to taxation of the rich – might precipitate financial collapse. Many party members probably felt nothing more sophisticated than an attitude that if cuts were

113 Cripps to MacDonald, 28 Aug. 1931, JRM 1314 (Estorick, *Cripps*, 88–9). His decision might well have been different had he not been abroad until after party executive statements were published. For a similar attitude, see Snell to MacDonald, 26 Aug. 1931, JRM 1315.

114 Ammon, Middleton, and Lunn, to MacDonald, 26, 27, and 30 Aug. 1931, JRM 1314, 1315. For a wide selection of other examples, see Marquand, 649–50.

115 Dalton diary, 28 Aug. 1931 (Dalton, 279); Tillett to MacDonald, 25 and 31 Aug. 1931, JRM 1315. For Tillett later asking for and receiving help from MacDonald over personal financial difficulties, see MacDonald to Grant, 7 April 1932, MacDonald (NLS) papers.

116 Turner to MacDonald, 29 Aug. 1931, JRM 1315 (published in *Daily Herald*, 1 Sept. 1931); Riley, Cripps, and Dunnico, to MacDonald, 26 and 29 Aug., 1 Sept. 1931, JRM 1315, 1314, 383; Morrison, c. 26 Aug. 1931, in M. MacDonald diary, 15 Jan. 1932.

117 Compare Attlee to MacDonald, undated, JRM 1315, with Attlee in Dalton diary, 24 Aug. 1931 (Dalton, 272); and Pethick-Lawrence to his constituents, 26 Aug. 1931, Noel-Baker papers 3/62, with Pethick-Lawrence in Passfield to B. Webb, 24 Aug. 1931 (*Webb Letters* III, 359). For justifications, see, e.g., Phillips, Manning, Milner, Kenworthy, Wilkinson letters in JRM 1314, 1315.

118 Dalton diary, 24 and 27 Aug. 1931 (partly in Dalton, 274, 276); B. Webb diary, 24 and 25 Aug. 1931 (Cole, 283–4; MacKenzie IV, 254–6).

necessary these were the business of the 'capitalist' parties, while Labour's role was simply to protest.[119] Most of the dissentient ex-Cabinet ministers began with little else. For them the change of government posed awkward problems. Although about to form an opposition and confident of substantial party support, it was not evident what degree and kind of opposition they should or could mount. They had accepted the prevailing characterisation of the financial crisis, and been warned at their last Cabinet that sterling had become still more precarious. Though baulking at the unemployment benefit cut, they had gone a long way with MacDonald and Snowden – further than the rest of the party would easily understand – and had been told that the National government would inherit the retrenchment programme they themselves had largely helped to compile. They were to oppose a government proposing just a six-weeks' existence, and to differ publicly from a pre-eminent Labour leader who had left it unclear whether he intended to leave, split, fight, or rejoin the party. If some felt a 'certain relief' at the break with the MacDonaldites, Graham was deeply distressed at separation from his mentor, Snowden, and others felt similar unease.[120]

Such dilemmas and sentiments threatened to paralyse action. At the last Labour Cabinet other ministers on Henderson's advice 'accepted silently the accomplished fact' of MacDonald's decision, and on Sankey's motion unanimously thanked him for his chairmanship. Immediately afterwards the dissentients met to consider the position over lunch in Lansbury's room at the Office of Works. Though expecting 'bitter attack and controversy', they decided to issue no immediate statement and make no policy pronouncement until Parliament and the parliamentary party met.[121] For the time being, 'opposition' would be dormant.

This decision to wait and see was chiefly the work of Henderson, almost universally regarded as the 'only possible leader' of the opposition.[122] MacDonald's assessment of Henderson's attitude had been wide of the mark. He was agitated and anxious about the

[119] E.g., Shinwell in Dalton diary, 24 Aug. 1931 (Dalton, 273).

[120] Passfield in B. Webb diary, 25 Aug. 1931 (Cole, 284; MacKenzie IV, 256). For Graham, see Dalton diary, 9 Jan. 1932 (Dalton, 299), and Graham, *Graham*, 187, 192–3, 195.

[121] Passfield to B. Webb, 24 Aug. 1931, Passfield papers II:3:(i):27:69 (*Webb Letters* III, 359), and in B. Webb diary, 25 Aug. 1931 (Cole, 284; MacKenzie IV, 256); Cabinet 47(31), 24 Aug. 1931. Cf. Morrison's self-serving invention in Nicolson, *George V*, 467.

[122] Dalton diary, 24 and 28 Aug. 1931 (Dalton, 274, 279). For this para. see also Thorpe, 'Henderson', 123–6.

Cabinet split, and sensitive to possible embarrassment over his own participation in proposing expenditure cuts. He remained fearful about the sterling crisis, and still thought some measure of party co-operation might help in its solution.[123] He probably believed that MacDonald's retrenchment programme, however unacceptable to the Labour movement, was now the only means of preventing a financial collapse. He might well have agreed with Sankey that MacDonald and himself were between them saving the nation and saving the party. Yet like MacDonald, Henderson thought that to surrender office during a national crisis was to risk political obliteration.[124] The idea of defining the issue as one of 'class war' never occurred to him. Rather, for both national and party reasons the sensible course seemed to be 'responsible', selective, opposition, including retention of some connection with MacDonald. Despite their latest differences, Henderson even now considered MacDonald an invaluable asset to the Labour party and so fastened upon his comments about the transience of the new government. He urged MacDonald's familiars and his own followers not to treat the split 'too seriously': it was 'only an interlude in the life of the Party, like the war', and as then the party 'mustn't drive J.R.M. and others out'.[125] Now that a National government had been formed Henderson in effect wanted what MacDonald had suggested the previous week – a Labour agreement to differ like that which had held the party leadership together during the differences of 1914 to 1918.[126] But Henderson foresaw great difficulties within the party. Escape beckoned, just as it had for MacDonald. He was half-tempted by the peerage offer, consulting his family and then declining it only 'for the present'.[127] 'Very reluctant' to become party leader, he tried to press the job upon Clynes. Though he eventually accepted out of duty, the insistence of colleagues, and pride, he conceived his task to be 'responsible guidance' – 'to exercise a restraining influence' upon Labour opposition.[128]

[123] Dalton diary, 24 and 28 Aug. 1931 (Dalton, 271, 279); Henderson in Garvin to Lothian, 26 Aug. 1931, Lothian papers 257/263.
[124] Dalton diary, 24 Aug. 1931 (Dalton, 271).
[125] Dalton diary, 24 Aug. 1931 (Dalton, 274); Duff memos, 25 and 26 Aug. 1931, JRM 1316 (Marquand, 644); Stimson diary, 27 Aug. 1931. For MacDonald still being treated as a full party member and invited to meetings, see Middleton and Lindsay letters, 24, 25, and 27 Aug. 1931, JRM 1314, 383.
[126] For the 1914 division, see Marquand, 168–80.
[127] Duff memos, 25 and 26 Aug. 1931, JRM 1316 (Marquand, 644).
[128] Dalton diary, 24 and 28 Aug. 1931 (Dalton, 274, 279); and see Henderson statement, *Manchester Guardian*, 29 Aug. 1931.

Yet Henderson's first concern, for which he had forced the Cabinet's resignation, was to secure the Labour movement's unity. His two aims – restraint and unity – very quickly proved incompatible. On 26 August, just two days after the parliamentary leadership's decision to make no statement, the three Labour executives on Henderson's suggestion declared 'vigorous' opposition to the government and appointed a joint committee to draft a policy manifesto.[129]

There were several reasons for Henderson's abrupt turnabout. Though seeking some tolerance towards the MacDonaldites he did not want an extensive party split, and with allegiances initially uncertain MacDonald's appeals to junior ministers and MPs were a threat requiring some rejoinder. A firm statement would also give direction to the Labour press, an important consideration because even the *Daily Herald* momentarily wobbled.[130] It also became obvious that a few ex-ministers were so determined to damn the new government that something had to be said if disciplined collective leadership was to be re-established. These ex-ministers included Cabinet dissentients who unlike Henderson immediately shed the cares of office, and aimed to construct a definite, unambiguous, opposition stance. As much from calculation as conviction, they sought to cut through immediate embarrassments by shifting responsibility for the crisis wholly away from the Labour Cabinet, and by recasting the issues in more starkly labour and socialist terms. What they proposed had less to do with describing events in the recent past than prescribing the character of future political debate, regardless of any effect on financial confidence. Addison was the first. He had arrived at the lunchtime meeting on 24 August with a draft press statement declaring that the Cabinet had resigned in the face of Bank of England dictation, and that the Labour opposition's aim was to defend parliamentary control.[131] Another Cabinet dissentient – perhaps Lansbury – gave the *Daily Herald* a story about Federal Reserve Bank 'dictation', and some second rank figures were equally insensitive to Henderson's concerns.[132]

[129] LPNEC, 26 Aug. 1931.   [130] Dalton diary, 24 Aug. 1931 (Dalton, 271, 274).
[131] Addison, 'Draft statement…for discussion with dissenting colleagues, lunch…24 Aug. 1931', Addison papers box 5; see Addison speech, *The Times*, 27 Aug. 1931. He said nothing about American 'dictation': cf. Morgan, *Portrait*, 203.
[132] *Daily Herald*, 25 Aug. 1931. Lansbury became a convinced proponent of the 'bankers' ramp' explanation; for early contact with the *Daily Herald* controllers, see Dalton diary,

Above all, however, there was pressure from the TUC General Council. On the afternoon of 24 August Citrine and Bevin pressed Henderson 'most strongly' for an immediate conference of the party executives to define the Labour movement's attitude towards the National government.[133] They were 'full of fight', Bevin making comparisons with the General Strike and promising to 'put everything' into the struggle.[134] This was melodrama, but it had a definite purpose. The TUC's actions were significant precisely because it did not react as it had in 1926. Its defeat then, subsequent falls in trade union membership, and increased unemployment since 1929, made it unwilling to risk industrial action even against sweeping wage and benefit cuts. There would be no general strike, no 'direct action'. Still less was encouragement given to other forms of working-class agitation, which were treated as impugning TUC competence. The General Council summarily rejected proposals by the National Unemployed Workers' Movement for a march and other gestures.[135] Rather, the TUC leaders did a reverse of 1926 and concentrated upon mobilising the Labour party, with the object of winning the next general election. Yet they were even less happy now than in 1926 with the party's parliamentary leaders. Their stance was not aimed solely against the MacDonaldites; they were also 'very irritable & full of suspicion' towards the Cabinet dissentients.[136] Although publicly TUC leaders helped shield these from Labour criticism, they had not forgotten that for two years all ministers had failed to show 'proper consideration' towards them, nor that the cuts proposed to them on 20 August had come from the whole Cabinet. All Labour parliamentary leaders had to some extent been compromised, so they considered themselves the only solid defenders of working-class interests and the Labour movement's integrity. They remained unrepentant about their resistance to the Labour Cabinet proposals, meeting ministerialist accusations of TUC 'dictation' by arguing that responsibility for the condition of millions of workers gave them every right to intervene.[137] They now had every intention of imposing their own views upon the party.

24 Aug. 1931 (Dalton, 273–4). For a memorandum attacking MacDonald's concern with the budget, see Pethick-Lawrence to his constituents, 26 Aug. 1931, Noel-Baker papers, 3/62 (copies circulated to colleagues); for Dalton, see Dalton diary, 24–7 Aug. 1931.
[133] Citrine in *TUCAR 1931*, 83.   [134] Dalton diary, 24 Aug. 1931 (Dalton, 274).
[135] TUCGC, 3 and 4 Sept. 1931.
[136] Dalton diary, 26 Aug. 1931; and see Citrine in B. Webb diary, 23 Sept. 1931.
[137] Citrine in *TUCAR 1931*, 85–7, 7 Sept.; Hayday in *LPACR 1931*, 201–2, 6 Oct.

MacDonald was at least right in this: that Henderson would make no effective stand against the TUC. Having tied himself to the stake of the Labour movement's unity, Henderson could not now jeopardise it by a second confrontation between the political and industrial leaderships. Moreover, trade union cash would be essential for what would be 'the most vital General Election in which the Movement had ever been compelled to take part'.[138] Short of another party crisis, Henderson had no choice but to acquiesce. At the 26 August joint meeting of the General Council, National Executive, and parliamentary executive, he tried unsuccessfully to retain some sort of control by taking the lead in what he could not resist. On the 27th he signed the joint manifesto, which endorsed some criticisms and suggestions which he and other dissentients had made the previous week, but repudiated much more of what they had believed and accepted. Further, as reassurance to the TUC Henderson publicly acknowledged its power. To 'mark unity' he invited the General Council to attend the parliamentary party meeting, promised close consultation with it, and stressed that the Labour party had been a TUC creation.[139] Within days of the 20 August confrontation between Cabinet and TUC, Henderson had conceded what he, every bit as much as MacDonald and Snowden, had always resisted – the view that the party was essentially an adjunct of the trade union movement.

Henderson's defeat and the assertion of TUC power had profound effects not just for the Labour party but for the whole political system. The 27 August manifesto immediately raised the pitch of debate. It defined the issues less as restoration of financial confidence and defence of sterling than as resistance to finance capitalism and defence of the working class. Blame for the sterling crisis lay upon the policy of 'private banking interests' and 'deliberately alarmist' newspaper reports. Neither national solvency nor budget stability were really at stake: the problem was more the hostility of 'international and national financial interests' towards Britain's 'bad example of taxing the rich to provide for the necessities of the poor', and having wage-levels underpinned by unemployment insurance. The National government, far from being 'national', had emerged as the panic-stricken agent of cosmopolitan reaction and class war. 'Without authority from the people', it intended 'a

---

[138] Henderson in LPNEC, 27 Aug. 1931.
[139] LPNEC, 27 Aug. 1931; Dalton diary, 28 Aug. 1931 (Dalton, 277); Henderson statement, *Manchester Guardian*, 29 Aug. 1931, and speech in *TUCAR 1931*, 403, 405, 10 Sept.

complete change in national policy'. Its 'equality of sacrifice' was merely a 'phrase', as little would be demanded of the wealthy while 'the slender means of the poor' were 'further depleted'. As economically unsound as it was unjust, this would increase unemployment and reduce purchasing power, deepening the 'underlying crisis'. It was also socially dangerous: private enterprises would follow the example of public service wage cuts, producing 'embittered conflict and industrial chaos'. To all cuts in incomes, social services and public works, 'determined opposition' was promised. For the immediate crisis the proper remedies were mobilisation of overseas assets, Sinking Fund suspension, *rentier* taxation, and debt conversion. More generally, Labour policies of national reconstruction and international co-operation, including reparation and war debt revision, offered the 'only basis' for economic recovery. The 'masses' and 'all men and women of good will' were asked to rally to the defence of 'true national interests' and 'constructive efforts towards the new social order'.[140] The imprint of the General Council is clear. Within a fortnight, notwithstanding interviews with Bank of England directors, it further amplified the crisis into 'a financiers' revolution more ruthless and complete than a military dictatorship could accomplish'.[141]

The manifesto eased matters for 'bewildered and distressed' MPs at the parliamentary party meeting on 28 August.[142] It offered a plausible answer to MacDonald, justified their instinctive dislike of the cuts yet explained away the financial emergency, and evoked both familiar demons and soothing socialist images. It turned attention from the obscure mysteries of the monetary economy to what they knew and understood, the 'real' economy of incomes and distribution. Sympathy for MacDonald, already weakened by his broadcast emphasis on benefit cuts, suffered further from a 'querulous letter' excusing his non-attendance at the party meeting, and from the General Council's presence. Just seven MPs voted against adoption of the manifesto.[143] The TUC intervention had propelled the Labour party into outright opposition to the National

---

[140] LPNEC, 27 Aug. 1931.
[141] Hayday presidential address in *TUCAR 1931*, 66, 7 Sept. For meetings with Peacock and Harvey, see Steel-Maitland, 'Diary of Events during the crisis of 1931', Steel-Maitland papers 120/3; Citrine, *Men*, 280–1; Thompson-McCausland, 'Crisis', 40.
[142] Pethick-Lawrence, *Fate*, 167.
[143] Dalton diary, 28 Aug. 1931 (Dalton, 277); Sankey diary, 28 Aug. 1931; Denman to Amulree, 28 Aug. 1931, Amulree papers c386/146.

government on a class interpretation of the financial and political crises, shown that politically the best solution to the problem of financial confidence was to ignore that problem's existence, and focused policy upon the conscription of wealth.

The parliamentary party also elected Henderson party leader, with Clynes and Graham as his deputies. Henderson's position was now doubly extraordinary. In reaction to the MacDonaldite apostates the party was thrusting apotheosis upon faithful 'Uncle Arthur'. Yet Henderson's own opinions barely counted. He disliked what was happening to the party – the result, he thought, of 'mob psychology'[144] – and his attitude was closer to that of the seven dissentient MPs than that of the General Council and of the manifesto published over his name. He thought the shift towards doctrinaire socialism dangerous to both financial confidence and the party's electoral prospects, and expected it to provoke awkward questions about his conduct in Cabinet. Even now he sought 'restraint'. His first speeches as party leader, in the Commons on 8 September and to the TUC on the 10th, were concerned as much to pull the party back from damaging positions as to answer MacDonaldite imputations. All former Cabinet ministers knew defence of their role in Cabinet might be difficult. They had made a special point of retaining relevant Cabinet papers, and soon decided to compile agreed accounts of the August Cabinet committee and Cabinet meetings.[145] But for Henderson defence of past positions, of consistency with earlier assumptions and commitments, was the only sort of opposition to the government which he considered both prudent and attractive. He ignored the 27 August manifesto and implicitly rejected both its financial premises and political thrust. He expressed 'embarrassment' at opposing the MacDonaldites – 'a direct loss to the labour movement' whose 'withdrawal' he did not treat as necessarily permanent. No licence was given to party self-criticism; no faults of omission or commission by the Labour government were confessed. It had not been responsible for the financial crisis, which had resulted from hostile 'propaganda'. But he accepted that a genuine crisis existed, and said he 'would not dream' of making 'any complaint against the bankers'. Not only

---

[144] Henderson in Stimson diary, 5 pm, 27 Aug. 1931 (i.e., after three executives' endorsement of manifesto).

[145] Cabinet 47 (31), 24 Aug. 1931. For origin of Graham and Greenwood memoranda, see Greenwood to Morrison, 3 and 25 Sept. 1931; notes in Addison papers, box 5 file 55/11, and in Passfield papers, IV:26.

had 'all' ministers agreed to consultation with Conservative and Liberal leaders, but he himself did not oppose 'national government' in principle – only the manner in which the present one had been formed. The Cabinet had been in 'absolute agreement' on balancing the budget. Henderson's complaint was that the problem had been approached from the 'wrong end'. He claimed to have opposed 'any interference with the efficiency of the social services', and to have led resistance to unemployment benefit cuts. His principal alternative remained a revenue tariff. While conceding that the party must now recast its 'immediate objects to some extent', the manifesto to which he appealed continued to be *Labour and the Nation*.[146]

That Henderson's speeches were well received by the party and TUC shows only that he had become an icon. His admission that the Cabinet had 'provisionally accepted' expenditure cuts of £56m. worried backbench MPs who had expected even firmer resistance. Although other ex-Cabinet members used and built upon Henderson's line of defence, the ambiguities of the Cabinet discussions soon exposed them to vigorous ministerial counter-attack. They ignored Henderson's other points as completely as he had ignored the 27 August manifesto. *Labour and the Nation* and the Labour Cabinet's policy assumptions were well removed from what many party members and the TUC now wanted: acknowledgement of shortcomings and mistakes, a fresh start in policy. Far from Henderson securing a retreat from the 27 August manifesto, there were soon advances upon it. He was unable even to restrain. Insofar as his leadership had any substance it was 'little more than administrative and formal'.[147] Moreover, policy advances took different forms in different parts of the movement: even Labour unity remained shallow and uneasy.

Although the General Council had imposed its will at critical moments, it did not arrogate a right of regular supervision of the parliamentary party. But equally, it did not relinquish its own right to opinions on national economic and financial policies, and it now felt no inhibitions in following through its own interpretation of the crisis. From attacking monetary deflation, it followed that 'the Labour Movement was quite prepared to face' going off the gold standard. From the assertion of 'bankers' dictation' the conclusion was plain: 'until we govern the banks, the banks will govern us'. So

---

[146] *HC Deb* 256, cols. 25–40; *TUCAR 1931*, 398–405.
[147] McKibbin, 'Henderson', 101 (*Ideologies*, 65).

banks joined coal, iron and steel, and transport as targets for early nationalisation. More broadly, the crisis was presented as 'the parting of the ways'. The failure of capitalist organisation and its persistent assault upon working-class incomes had again been exposed, and the 'lesson' was that 'economic and financial interests...can no longer be left uncontrolled and unregulated'. In early September the General Council obtained Congress sanction for a large undefined extension of its policy-making powers, in order to develop 'an economic policy based on planning'.[148] Yet within its own industrial field it privately maintained its pre-crisis assumptions that practical advances could best be achieved by 'collaborations of Capital and Labour'.[149] This characteristic General Council desire for the best of all worlds – excluding political accommodation with the National government, preserving an independent voice in national policy, yet seeking industrial accommodation – meant that it remained an awkward partner for the party leadership.

Henderson's writ was no more effective within the parliamentary party. With the end of the Labour government and re-affirmation of 'socialist' positions, Arnold, Trevelyan, and the ILP MPs Jowett and Wise fell back into line behind the Labour party leadership. But the other ILP leaders, though accepting the 27 August manifesto, rejected Henderson-inspired appeals to 'merge their little group in the larger unity' and voted against him in the leadership election.[150] They refused to join in the Labour and TUC whitewash of Henderson and the other Cabinet dissentients, whom they considered to be as responsible as MacDonald for 'the policy which resulted in the present situation'. Worse, they had still not repudiated the 'gradualist evolutionary view'.[151] For the ILP too, there was a parting of the ways. Capitalism was collapsing, the crisis consisted of a desperate but futile bankers' plot to save it, and their 'miserable hireling' the National government had declared 'war on the workers', with 'indecent, inhumane' cuts and 'Fascist methods'. A 'revolutionary situation' was 'rapidly approaching', requiring

---

[148] Citrine statement, *The Times*, 29 Aug. 1931; Hayday Presidential Address, Pugh and Bevin speeches, and 'Report on the Financial Situation of August, 1931', in *TUCAR 1931*, 66, 406–8, 518–19, 7–10 Sept.

[149] Citrine in B. Webb diary, 23 Sept. 1931. For General Council defence of continuing talks with NCEO and FBI, see *TUCAR 1931*, 361–4, 8 Sept.

[150] Henderson, Dalton, Jowett in LPNEC, 27 Aug. 1931, and Dalton at PLP in Dalton diary, 28 Aug. 1931 (Dalton, 279); PLP, 28 Aug. 1931.

[151] Maxton statement, and article in *New Leader*, reported in *The Times*, 24 Aug. and 3 Sept. 1931. See also Dowse, *Left in the Centre*, 175–6.

adoption of 'a new revolutionary outlook' and 'tactic'. Parliamentary opposition could not be the Labour movement's only resource: the working class should be organised not just to resist cuts but to win control of the economic and financial system for the community. Accordingly, in contrast to the TUC the ILP established contact with the National Unemployed Workers' Movement.[152]

ILP rhetoric was intended to provoke 'revolution' through the ballot box, not by violence.[153] Nevertheless it was unwelcome to both Labour party and TUC leaders, who had no wish for spontaneous militancy by their own activists or among the working classes themselves, which might lead to violence or help the Communists. Continued ILP disregard for the parliamentary party's standing orders might subvert party discipline, while ILP comments on the ex-Cabinet ministers' record were uncomfortably close to the truth.

Minimising embarrassment from the left was perhaps a significant motivation for a rapid shift among Henderson's colleagues.[154] But there were other, stronger, imperatives. The 27 August manifesto licenced such attitudes as those of Addison and Lansbury, while for other ex-ministers it became the starting point for brainstorms of political creativity. At the very least, the easiest course in internal Labour politics would be to swim with the TUC tide. In addition, if parliamentary opposition was to be in earnest, it made elementary tactical sense to widen the difference beyond details of Cabinet discussions which 'the country' might consider trivial.[155] The new freedom to enunciate simple socialist 'truths' offered not merely an emotional temptation. The difficulties and fate of the Labour government could be interpreted as showing that there was nothing to be lost and everything to be gained from having the courage of one's faith. Also, contrary to Henderson's pessimism, other ex-ministers were excited by the electoral possibilities. They believed that the crisis could be used to bury the Labour government's record, that opposition to cuts would restore and extend Labour support among the working classes and other recipients of state payments, and that the exposure of capitalism's unregenerate character would demolish non-socialist progressive positions. Dalton supposed the new min-

---

[152] ILP statement in *The Times*, 26 Aug. 1931; *New Leader*, 28 Aug. 1931; Maxton and Brockway speeches *HC Deb*, 256, cols. 49–54, 458–67, 8 and 11 Sept. 1931; Middlemas, *The Clydesiders*, 261.

[153] Brockway in *HC Deb*, 256, cols. 255–6, 467, 9 and 11 Sept. 1931, for assuming lawful methods.

[154] Cripps to Graham, 1 Sept, 1931, in Estorick, *Cripps*, 92.　　　[155] Ibid.

isters could be given such a 'hell of a time' in the Commons that it would be a 'mistake to defeat them too soon'.[156] Graham publicly prophesied the imminent disappearance of the Liberals, defeat of Conservatives by the vengeful masses, and achievement of a clear Labour parliamentary majority.[157] In contrast to the accommodations of the past, there now seemed clear advantages in an election on 'a direct fight between Socialism and Capitalism'. It suddenly appeared as if transition to 'socialism' could and should be accelerated. Cripps, just four days after offering MacDonald help in reuniting the party, reasoned that it was 'absolutely necessary to throw off at once and for all the attitude of compromise – and to come out boldly with a slap-up Socialistic policy'.[158] Even Morrison, temporarily marginalised by his MacDonaldite sympathies, declared that the 'moral' of the crisis was 'clear': 'Labour must move to the Left – the real Socialist Left'.[159] Some also understood that the MacDonaldite departures created opportunities for personal advancement, which helped ripen the rhetoric. Dalton – during a twenty-four hour descent upon his constituency – proclaimed that he 'would sooner go to Hell with the Durham miners and their heroic wives than share an Earthly Paradise with our three Lost Leaders'.[160]

After 27 August, then, parliamentary party leaders started their own stampede towards 'real' socialism. Despite the exhilaration, they understood that 'for the future, slogans were not enough' – neither to answer the National government, nor convince electors, nor form the programme for the next Labour government, perhaps as imminently as Christmas. It would be necessary to 'hammer out a firm detailed policy of Socialist reconstruction'.[161] The result was a Finance and Trade Committee established in early September. Chaired by Graham, it included Addison, Alexander, Greenwood, Johnston, Dalton, Cripps, Attlee, Pethick-Lawrence, Wise, Lees-

---

[156] Dalton diary, 27 Aug. 1931 (Pimlott, 153).

[157] Graham in *Daily Express*, 31 August 1931 (See Bassett, 202–3).

[158] Cripps to Graham, 1 Sept. 1931, and for agreement, Graham to Cripps, 2 Sept. 1931, in Estorick, *Cripps*, 91–3.

[159] Morrison speech, *The Times*, 8 Sept. 1931. Morrison's shift may have been assisted by a visit to Cripps, for which see Dalton diary, 5 Sept. 1931 (Dalton, 281).

[160] Dalton diary, 1 Sept. 1931 (Dalton, 280); and for expectation of office, entries of 26 and 27 Aug. 1931 (ibid., 276; Pimlott, 152).

[161] Dalton diary, 28 Aug. 1931 (Dalton, 279), and (for Christmas), Dalton to Noel-Baker, 4 Sept. 1931, Noel-Baker papers, 3/62; Cripps to Graham, and Graham to Cripps, 1 and 2 Sept. 1931, in Estorick, *Cripps*, 91–2; Morrison speech, *The Times*, 8 Sept. 1931.

Smith, and Arnold.[162] This group, largely overlapping with a new parliamentary executive, quickly took control of the parliamentary party from Henderson's hands. What they produced represented a major break with previous party policy.

Opposition to the National government's Finance and Economy Bills was based squarely upon the principle of ability to pay, going well beyond the positions taken in Cabinet. Only now was it grasped that a 10 per cent increase in taxation was not equivalent to a 10 per cent cut in income: in real terms MacDonald's 'equality of sacrifice' was not equality at all.[163] All cuts in benefits, wages, salaries, social services, and public works would be reversed. The alternatives now offered were war loan conversion, Sinking Fund suspension, withdrawal of derating relief to prosperous businesses ('a sheer dole'), and steeper taxation of personal wealth. Despite Henderson's preference, the revenue tariff was dropped because it threatened serious party differences.[164] Nevertheless the Labour party would still 'abide by every sound principle in public finance':[165] there would be increased redistribution, but no fundamental reassessment of fiscal policy. Monetary issues became much more prominent, for obvious reasons. Cancellation of reparations, the League of Nations Gold Delegation report, and the Macmillan Committee recommendations were presented as the chief solutions to the sterling problem. Also, Wise and then other Finance and Trade Committee members, perhaps influenced by Keynes as well as the TUC, began to indicate scepticism about the gold standard.[166] But the main shift was towards ideas of physical state control. As the fundamental causes of the economic and financial crises seemed to be industrial failure and 'colossal monetary mismanagement', public direction of

---

[162] Graham to Cripps, 2 Sept. 1931, in Estorick, *Cripps*, 93; Dalton diary, 3 and 7 Sept. 1931 (Pimlott, 154); PLP, 8 Sept. 1931; Finance and Trade Policy Committee minutes, 9 Sept. 1931, Angell papers BB1–6.

[163] The point appears to have been made first by Pethick-Lawrence: *HC Deb*, 256, cols. 400–2, 10 Sept. 1931. It was subsequently taken up by Clynes, Greenwood, Graham, and Dalton.

[164] Graham and Dalton, *HC Deb*, 256, cols. 692–4, 791–5, 15 Sept. 1931. Henderson thought one purpose of the Finance and Trade Committee was to prepare tariff proposals (see PLP, 8 Sept. 1931, and speech in *TUCAR 1931*, 399–400, 10 Sept.) and Clynes also remained favourable: Amery diary, 14 Sept. 1931 (*LSA* II, 200). For complications and rejection, Cripps to Parmoor, 12 Sept. 1931, in Estorick, *Cripps*, 96; Graham, *HC Deb*, 256, cols. 695–9, 15 Sept. 1931.

[165] Graham, ibid., col. 317, 10 Sept. 1931. None took up Pethick-Lawrence's idea that budget balance should be measured over a period of years: ibid., col. 406.

[166] Wise, Graham, Dalton in ibid., 332–41, 688, 694, 795, 10 and 15 Sept. 1931; Dalton diary, 17 Sept. 1931 (Dalton, 284); Finance and Trade Policy Committee, and Greenwood memo, both 18 Sept. 1931, Angell papers BB1–8.

industries, banking, and credit became an immediate priority.[167] This was associated with increased sensitivity towards the problems facing socialist government in a capitalist world. The rhetorical temptations of the 'bankers' ramp' accusation – 'the First Labour Government had been destroyed by a Red Letter, and the Second by a Banker's Order' – had proved irresistible, even to Cabinet members who should have known better.[168] More important, it seemed likely enough that the election of a Labour government committed to reversing the cuts and imposing nationalisation would precipitate another financial crisis. Consequently the Committee considered its 'most immediate task' was to prepare an 'Extension of the Emergency Powers Act'.[169] Those preparations remained secret. Nevertheless the parliamentary leadership's intentions were plain enough from its strong reactions to the Cabinet's implementation of retrenchment by Orders in Council. The usually mild Clynes described this procedure as a device 'to suppress the Opposition', 'a mockery of Parliamentary government', a 'revolutionary measure'; yet on the other hand he declared that it could 'be taken as fully justifying the drastic manoeuvres which a Socialist majority in a future Parliament will take to give effect to its will'.[170]

Here was the most far-reaching effect of the August crisis: with the MacDonaldite split and in defiance of Henderson, the Labour party abandoned its previous strategy of political accommodation. From an explicit position of working-class defence, it became committed to repudiate the prescriptions and to control the institutions of capitalism as matters of immediate policy. It also appeared to threaten procedures which might alter the constitutional basis of British parliamentarism. This change in the character of the Labour party was the fundamental feature around which politics revolved during September and October.

[167] Graham to Cripps, 2 Sept. 1931, in Estorick, *Cripps*, 92; Finance and Trade Policy Committee minutes, 9 Sept. 1931, Angell papers BB1–6; Clynes, Johnston, and Graham *HC Deb*, 256, cols. 436, 478, 700, 11 and 15 Sept. 1931; and see Bevin observations in *LPACR 1931*, 191, 6 Oct.

[168] Dalton diary, 28 Aug. 1931 (Dalton, 278), and speech, *The Times*, 2 Sept. 1931; Clynes and Johnston, *HC Deb*, 256, cols. 437, 481, 11 Sept. 1931.

[169] Finance and Trade Policy Committee minutes, 9 Sept. 1931, Angell papers BB1–6.

[170] *HC Deb*. 256, col. 436, 11 Sept. 1931; *The Times*, 21 Sept. 1931.

CHAPTER 11

The emergency government's crisis: September 1931

Let us realize that the crisis with which we are faced may destroy the very foundations of Great Britain and India.

Hoare to Willingdon, telegram, 18 September 1931

Never before in the history of our country has a new Government had to make so conspicuous an admission of failure in so short a time.

Addison speech, House of Commons, 21 September 1931[1]

A 'NATIONAL' FUTURE?

The National government had declared that its sole purpose was to overcome the immediate financial emergency. Once that task had been completed – which was expected to be after six weeks – Parliament would be dissolved, with the succeeding general election fought not by the government partners together but by each party separately. Given such a short timetable, termination of the government became a major issue within days of its formation. MacDonald himself raised it with Baldwin on 5 September. Once the budget and retrenchment measures had been announced, debate within the government parties and in the press became intense. By mid September the issue had become not complete termination but a choice between two alternatives, each contravening the spirit if not the letter of the government's original terms. There would either be an early general election fought by a reconstituted National government, or the existing National government would continue without an election into the following year. Both alternatives implied that the party system would undergo some permanent rearrangement.

The reason for this shift was simple: fear of the Labour party. As

---

[1] Respectively Templewood Indian papers 13/6–11, and *HC Deb*, 256, col. 1345.

the character of its opposition became apparent, the National
government partners concluded that the Labour party had changed
into something much more dangerous than it had shown itself to be
in the 1920s. It had become an overtly class party, sectional,
irresponsible, confiscatory, 'revolutionary'. Those like Reading
who had wanted Labour included in a wider 'national' co-operation
were disillusioned, and agreed that this transformed Labour party
had to be defeated, and defeated decisively. Yet all assumed that
Labour promises to restore benefits, wages, salaries, and services and
to soak the rich would make it a formidable electoral opponent. If
each partner fought an early election separately, the Labour party
might well deny the National government's successor a sufficient
majority to maintain financial confidence and deal effectively with
the outstanding economic problems. Worse, Labour might win the
election, and if this did not itself immediately precipitate renewed
financial crisis, a sterling collapse, and economic chaos, it might
through punitive taxation and attacks upon capitalist institutions
produce similar results. Not just financial and economic stability,
but also political and social stability seemed to be at stake. Fear of
Labour became so strong that it obscured immediate fears for
sterling. Within the Conservative party especially, it contributed to
a political stance which undermined the financial advice of the Bank
of England, and complicated responses to new exchange and budget
crises in mid September.

The other common ground between the National government
partners remained anxiety about general economic conditions,
concern itself replete with political implications. Unemployment
rose to 2·8m. in September and the government's own published
estimates for unemployment insurance expenditure predicted an
average of 3m. for 1932. This would cast more families (and voters)
into the range of the reduced unemployment benefits and means test,
probably strengthening Labour's appeal. Agricultural prices, industrial production, and exports had continued to fall sharply. Trade
figures published in early September revealed a deficit as large as the
previous year, and with invisible earnings also shrinking there would
plainly be a large balance of payments deficit.

Everyone accepted that once the budget deficit had been
overcome, the trade deficit would have to be tackled. This continued
to be seen as a major cause of difficulties in the 'real' economy,
whether falling profits or rising unemployment. The movement of

opinion towards protection gathered pace. Alongside statements from industrialists, agriculturalists, and chambers of commerce which ladened newspapers and politicians' postbags with support for the government's retrenchment measures, there were as many in support of tariffs. Several former free-trade business organisations announced their conversions, most prominently the Manchester Chamber of Commerce.[2] Churchill, Simon, and Runciman each took the opportunity to escape from free-trade commitments which had become embarrassments to their personal political positions. A new, often decisive, argument for protection was that it could compensate producers and merchants for the increased tax burden. Against this, staunch free-traders argued that government re-trenchment set an example for cost reduction across the economy, which if achieved would make protection even less defensible. Either way, correction of the trade balance was increasingly seen as fundamental to making sterling truly secure. The political question therefore became not simply that between free trade or protection, but whether decision on the trade balance should be part of the existing government's task of dealing with the financial emergency.

The attitude of the Conservative party, as the largest government partner, would obviously be crucial. In pledging the party leaders to an early election, Baldwin had not been influenced simply by his own nervousness about party feeling. An early election appeared to be the means to obtain tariffs, which all Conservatives now regarded as vital to save and restore the national economic and financial structure. Equally, an early election remained integral to the strategy which Neville Chamberlain had contrived for the Con-servative leadership during the August crisis: a National government to split the Labour leadership and implicate other parties in imposing unpopular cuts and tax increases, leaving the Conservative party free to win the next election on its positive remedy of imperial protectionism.[3] That manoeuvre had been recognised to involve some risk of an electoral backfire. The Labour opposition's repudiation of retrenchment now sharpened this apprehension, while making it seem more urgent to see the strategy through and seize the maximum advantage from the situation. As Hoare wrote, the cuts and tax increases would be 'very unpopular' but

---

[2] Manchester Chamber statement, *The Times*, 15 Sept. 1931, and see Streat diary, 17 Sept. 1931 in Dupree I, 90–1, for its marked impression upon MPs.

[3] For a restatement, see N. Chamberlain diary, 3 Sept. 1931.

I am sure that the longer the Government goes on the more unpopular it will become. If we can fight the election in an atmosphere of great emergency, I feel sure we can win. If, however, we drag on and have fathered on us all the iniquities of our predecessor, we shall come to as big a smash as the Coalition reached in 1922.[4]

Such calculations became almost universal among Conservatives of all shades of opinion; it was vital to strike before 'Henderson & Co...consolidate[d] their counter-attack and...cause[d] their own failure to be forgotten'.[5]

Amery's agitation for an early election and for continued commitment to the full protectionist policy therefore pushed against wide open Conservative doors.[6] His contempt for the budget – 'the very worst type of Cobdenite Snowdenish finance, aggravating all our troubles'[7] – was idiosyncratic, but other Conservatives even while applauding the budget thought 'it was merely giving the patient medicine when recovery without an operation is impossible'.[8] Yet it seemed impossible for a government containing Lloyd George Liberals and Snowden to introduce tariffs. For this reason Baldwin at the 28 August party meeting had expressly divided treatment of the economic problem into two separate political stages, the budget and the trade balance. After the National government had completed the first, 'agreement ends and we part company'.[9]

After Parliament reassembled, however, the assumption that the Conservative party should fight the election alone quickly receded. Two problems became apparent. One arose from the very success of Conservative strategy in August. As the chorus of approval of the National government showed, the great mass of anti-socialist, average, non-party, liberal, and even conservative opinion – which since 1929 had become frightened by economic and imperial troubles, exasperated with party politics, and impatient for 'strong government' – had been relieved and impressed. For Conservative

[4] Hoare to Willingdon, 2 Sept. 1931, Templewood Indian papers 1/1–6.
[5] Amery to Gwynne, 8 Sept. 1931, Gwynne papers 14. Further examples are Steel-Maitland to Garvin, 29 Aug. 1931, Garvin papers; Hilton Young to Amery, 7 Sept. 1931, Amery papers; Churchill speech, HC Deb, 256, col. 45, 8 Sept. 1931; Stanley to Headlam, 14 Sept. 1931, Headlam papers 47/243.
[6] For agreement with Amery, see Amery diary, 28 Aug., 2, 4, and 7 Sept., and Amery to his wife, 4 Sept. 1931, in LSA II, 195–8.
[7] Amery diary, 14 Sept. 1931 (LSA II, 200).
[8] L. Scott to Amery, 9 Sept. 1931, Amery papers. See also Steel-Maitland to Garvin, 29 Aug. 1931, Garvin papers; Page Croft, HC Deb, 256, col. 34, 10 Sept. 1931.
[9] The Times, 29 Aug. 1931.

leaders to insist upon the government's disintegration without seeming to put 'undue party advantage' before the 'national interest' would be a delicate matter.[10] A decision on the 9th to allow MacDonald the full prime-ministerial right to determine the actual time for the dissolution of Parliament helped to shift formal responsibility,[11] yet it also handed MacDonald the power to delay the election. The second and more serious problem was connected with the reasoning for an early election. If the Labour party had now become a formidable electoral threat, how could Conservatives alone be certain of obtaining a decisive anti-socialist majority?

Conservative opinion on these problems was diverse. In early September Rothermere and the *Daily Mail*, Dawson in *The Times*, and Mann, editor of *Yorkshire Post* and a spokesman for northern Conservatism, all appealed publicly or privately for the National government to stay together and postpone the election.[12] Garvin and the *Observer* wanted an early tariff election, but as defeat by Labour 'class-campaigners' and 'pound-smashers' might be 'as dangerous as defeat in war', he also wanted electoral deals between the National government partners.[13] Churchill, despite his own exclusion from the government, welcomed it as embodying his long-standing objective of a revived anti-socialist coalition. On 8 September he called for all Liberals to discard free-trade 'pedantry' and join in an early election to smash the Labour challenge to 'the fundamental interests of the state'.[14] Beaverbrook went still further, proposing that, in order to capture support from floating and Liberal voters for tariffs, Conservatives should fight the election under MacDonald as Prime Minister. Protectionist Simon Liberals could replace the free-trade Lloyd George Liberals, and Snowden would take retirement.[15] When his plan was first revealed publicly in the *Sunday Express* on 6 September, it won an immediate convert in Amery, who on the 8th echoed Beaverbrook's appeal to MacDonald to adopt tariffs and lead a National government election campaign. Neither Beaverbrook nor Amery suffered criticism from other

---

[10] E.g., N. Chamberlain to his wife, 1 Sept. 1931, NC 1/26/454.
[11] Amery diary, 9 Sept. 1931 (*LSA* II, 199).
[12] *Daily Mail*, from 7 Sept. 1931; Dawson diary, 7 Sept. 1931 (including conversation with Mann); editorial, *The Times*, 8 Sept. 1931; Mann to Baldwin, and to Davidson, 7 and 11 Sept. 1931, Baldwin papers, 44/93–5.
[13] Editorials and Garvin articles, *The Observer*, 30 Aug., 6 Sept. 1931.
[14] *HC Deb*, 256, cols. 40–9.
[15] N. Chamberlain diary, 3 Sept. 1931; Lockhart diary, 5 Sept. 1931 in Young I, 184.

Conservative protectionists, which suggested that in the face of the new Labour threat these would not insist upon imperial protectionism being a purely Conservative achievement.[16]

For all the differences of emphasis, cumulatively these various statements indicated that there was substantial Conservative party and newspaper support for an anti-socialist electoral alliance, provided that it were protectionist. A 'National' appeal would camouflage the Conservative partisan desire for an early election. By attracting elements of Liberal, non-party, and even Labour support, it would strengthen the popular vote for protection and the Conservative party. MacDonald was regarded as the key, not just as the necessary symbol of 'National' effort but for his supposed electoral appeal. 'Ramsay Mac's political corpse [was] worth a lot of seats.'[17]

These indications of Conservative opinion confirmed the independent conclusions of Conservative leaders. The party calculations which had originally led them into the National government had now become compelling arguments for an election held by a reconstituted National government. It is ironic but significant that those easing the Conservative leadership's path were mostly critics or enemies of Baldwin. Amery, angry that Baldwin had disregarded his own claims to office, now considered him to lack 'even the minor qualifications of a leader'.[18] Beaverbrook was honestly malicious. In his scheme 'to remove [Baldwin] from public life', MacDonald would be made in effect 'Leader of the Conservative Party'.[19] But Baldwin felt himself sufficiently secure to take the risk that most Conservatives would accept postponement of a Conservative prime ministership. After MacDonald sounded out his intentions on 5 September, he had moved carefully, testing the water. He was impressed when Dawson shifted to a version of the Beaverbrook–Amery line: MacDonald to lead a protectionist alliance to the polls, then either taking office in a Baldwin government or undertaking some official commission in the Empire. On the 10th he encouraged Dawson to take these ideas to MacDonald.[20] Chamberlain, Hoare, and Cunliffe-Lister were in broad agreement. By 16 September

---

[16] Amery diary, 6 and 8 Sept. 1931 (*LSA* II, 197–8, 199), and *HC Deb*, 256, col. 112. For private indications of agreement, see EIA executive, 9 Sept. 1931, in Croft, *My Life*, 193; Lloyd, and Remer, to Beaverbrook, 15 and 18 Sept. 1931, Beaverbrook papers B/200, B/203.   [17] Linlithgow to Dawson, 20 Sept. 1931, Dawson papers.

[18] Amery to his wife, 4 Sept. 1931, and Amery diary, 6 Sept. 1931 in *LSA* II, 197, 198.

[19] Beaverbrook to Derby, 14 Sept. 1931, and to F. Harrison, 19 Sept. 1931, Beaverbrook papers C/114, B/198.   [20] Dawson diary, 10 and 14 Sept. 1931.

Baldwin himself had spoken with MacDonald, and wanted the existing government broken up and reconstituted as a National protectionist government for an early election.[21] Favourable Conservative (and non-party conservative) reactions to Dawson's call in that morning's *Times* for 'A National Appeal' reinforced Baldwin's instincts. The chief uncertainty surrounded MacDonald's attitude, including his willingness to dispense with the free-trade Liberals.

The main Conservative objective was an anti-socialist coup. But as Conservative leaders moved towards a National election appeal, they became conscious of the opportunity to achieve another great ambition. On 3 September Chamberlain repudiated Beaverbrook's proposals for ejecting the Lloyd George Liberals as a 'cynical' and 'discreditable intrigue against...colleagues'. Yet on the 11th he spoke publicly of the Liberal party deserving electoral extinction for having kept the Labour government in office, while praising the Simon Liberals for their 'courage' in opposing that course. By the 19th Chamberlain had made Beaverbrook's idea his own.[22] Just as the formation of the National government had been used to split the Labour leadership, so its perpetuation might be used to complete the dissolution of the Liberal party. Once the trade balance began to replace retrenchment as the pressing issue, protectionist hatred of free-trade Liberalism had re-surfaced. Close proximity made it still more virulent. In hoping to see 'the end' of the Lloyd George Liberals,[23] Chamberlain and other Conservative leaders especially relished the prospect of seeing the end of Lloyd George himself. But in his absence Samuel provided nearly as good a target. Conservative backbenchers obliged to submit to his ministerial lead 'all loath[ed]' him. His Conservative colleagues soon grew to detest his casuistical manner and minute defence of Liberal principles and interests.[24] Baldwin, normally a tolerant man, could 'hardly be civil' towards him.[25] For immediate anti-socialist purposes Conservative leaders would consider arrangements with Lloyd George Liberals about seats, but for protectionist reasons they wanted no prolonged alliance in government. For that, Conservatives looked to the Simon Liberals.

---

[21] Baldwin in MacDonald diary, 14 Sept. 1931, in Hilton Young to his wife, 16 Sept. 1931, Kennet papers 107/3, and in Amery diary, 16 Sept. 1931 (*LSA* II, 201).

[22] N. Chamberlain diary, 3 and 19 Sept. 1931; speech, *The Times*, 12 Sept. 1931.

[23] N. to I. Chamberlain, 19 Sept. 1931, NC 18/1/755.

[24] Lane-Fox diary, 9 Sept. 1931; Cunliffe-Lister to his wife, 1 Sept. 1931, Swinton papers 270/3/22; Hankey diary, 26 Sept. 1931 (Roskill, *Hankey* II, 563).

[25] Hilton Young to his wife, 15 Sept. 1931, Kennet papers 107/3.

The Liberal party unity which followed the government's formation lasted about three weeks. Simon, Hutchison, Brown, and their followers who had opposed Lloyd George's support for the Labour government felt themselves vindicated by the crisis. Yet that 'dangerous, unscrupulous opportunist' had now denied them recognition or reward.[26] As 'patriotic Liberals' and strong anti-socialists, they too wanted a joint Conservative–Liberal appeal in an early election to rout the Labour party[27] and 'prove that John Bull still has grit'.[28] But they soon anticipated that the free-trade Liberals might obstruct such an appeal. In exasperation Grigg gave up and became a Conservative candidate. Simon and the others, however, recognised that another opportunity for an alternative Liberalism had arisen, and began signalling their availability. Simon ingratiated himself with MacDonald, in almost embarrassing offers of personal support.[29] When Parliament met, he sat on Conservative benches. Then on 15 September he ended ten months' hesitation and took the plunge, declaring the financial emergency as reason to 'abandon... the system of free imports'. Despite assistance from Page Croft in composing the speech, as a case for protection it was jejune. From a Liberal, it nonetheless created a sensation.[30] With Hore-Belisha, Shakespeare, Brown, and several other Liberal MPs also announcing that 'Free Trade had ceased to count',[31] it was plain that the Simon Liberal group was again in business.

Runciman had similar ambitions to revive his career, but he thought Simon's recantation 'smug' and 'sly'.[32] He attempted something much more subtle. As a self-confessed 'bigoted Free Trader', but also as a wartime President of the Board of Trade, on 10 September he called for the trade balance to be redressed by prohibiting imports of luxuries.[33] As a device used during the war, this had a good patriotic pedigree; in curbing conspicuous expenditure, it suggested sacrifice and social justice; in limiting imports, it had protectionist features – yet it could be considered

---

[26] Morris-Jones diary, 7–11 Sept. 1931. Brown had particular cause for resentment, as he was in financial difficulties and needed a ministerial salary: see Mrs E. Brown to Simon, 8 Sept. 1931, Simon papers.

[27] Morris-Jones diary, 7–11 Sept. 1931; Hutchison in Nathan to Lloyd George, 13 Sept. 1931, LG G/15/7/21.   [28] Lambert letter, *The Times*, 1 Sept. 1931.

[29] For offers to move the Commons vote of confidence, and to make his own parliamentary seat available for MacDonald, see Simon to MacDonald, 1 Sept. 1931, JRM 1315.

[30] *HC Deb*, 256, cols. 719–31; Croft, *My Life*, 194; Amery diary, 15 Sept. 1931.

[31] Tweed to Sinclair, 15 Sept. 1931, Thurso papers III/3/5; Morris-Jones speech, *The Times*, 16 Sept. 1931.   [32] Runciman to his wife, 15 Sept. 1931, Runciman papers 303.

[33] *HC Deb*, 256, col. 331.

compatible with free-trade principles. It commanded wide support among government supporters, both protectionists and free-traders, and at a stroke re-established Runciman as a major figure.

In its party aspect Runciman's proposal was intended as a departure from free trade to form a *via media* between the Liberal and Conservative parties, which could then fight the election in alliance.[34] However, what made him the 'darling of the [Liberal] parliamentary party'[35] was that most free-trade Liberals saw his plan as a device both to defend free trade and to postpone the election. From the beginning Liberal ministers and their backbench followers wanted the National government to remain in office until at the very least the April 1932 budget. Policy arguments and party interests converged. A delayed election would see the government's task of solving the financial emergency 'well on its way to completion' by carrying through implementation of the cuts.[36] It would enable action on the trade balance which, they said, was integral to that task and not, as Conservatives asserted, a distinct second stage. An early election would damage financial confidence, and – reversing the argument of the Conservatives – the Labour party could be beaten only after voters had been educated in the beneficial effect of cuts. In addition Liberal ministers enjoyed the exercise of power, and considered this the best and probably the only means to rehabilitate their party's reputation. Given the poor condition of the Liberal party organisation, time and the opportunity to exploit the prestige of office would also be needed to revive local associations and to find funds and candidates for a respectable electoral effort.[37] Liberals would simply 'not [have] much chance' in an early election against Conservative as well as Labour opposition.[38] In this reasoning, Lloyd George now concurred with Samuel, Reading, and Maclean.[39]

Their chief problem was that, linked to retrenchment, free trade

[34] Conversation with Baldwin in Runciman to his wife, 17 Sept. 1931, Runciman papers 303. See also Runciman note on Muir to Runciman, 10 Sept. 1931, for refusing presidency of a free trade defence committee.

[35] Tweed to Sinclair, 15 Sept. 1931, Thurso papers III/3/5.

[36] Maclean memo, 14–19 Sept. 1931, Runciman papers 245; Sinclair and Maclean in Tweed to Stevenson, 31 Aug. 1931, and Samuel in Report of party meeting, 28 Aug. 1931, LG G/28/2/3 and G/20/2/43.

[37] For unpreparedness for an election, see Thorpe thesis, 'General Election of 1931', 223–4.

[38] Collins to Runciman, 28 Aug. 1931, Runciman papers 215; Sinclair and Maclean in Tweed to Lloyd George, 31 Aug. 1931, LG G/28/2/3.

[39] Lloyd George to MacDonald, 30 Aug. 1931, JRM 1314, and reported in Reading memo, 11 Sept. 1931, Reading papers F118/131.

had become equally the symbol of separate Liberal identity and a constraint upon party strategy. On strict free-trade arguments the trade balance should be rectified not by reducing imports but by increasing exports through further cuts in expenditure and costs: by more of the same medicine, with still greater risk of unpleasant reactions from the patients. Unlike Conservatives, free-trade Liberals had almost nothing new to offer, no striking alternative to further sacrifices by large parts of the electorate. Keynes's influence had by now been virtually erased. A Lloyd George-style expert 'inquiry' organised by Lothian could suggest only private sector wage and salary cuts and further public retrenchment, albeit not in public works for 'national development' purposes.[40] Other Liberals, far from trying to think of anything new, reverted consciously to the remedies of the past. Hirst, an old Gladstonian pregnant with a book on the master's finance, returned to public prominence with an appeal for further retrenchment to allow reductions of taxation.[41] He then helped turn a new party committee intended to provide Liberal propaganda for the National government into a Free Trade Defence Committee. As a body of 'Free Trade Die-Hards' this committee sent all Liberal MPs a Hirst memorandum attacking Runciman's proposal, and mobilised the National Liberal Federation executive against it.[42]

This development had important consequences. It began a divergence between the Liberal party organisation and parliamentary leaders who were more sensitive to strategic problems, and so less dogmatic. Maclean agreed that 'pure Gladstonianism' was the answer to the financial and economic crises, and imagined there to be great significance in 'Tories...cheering a radical free trade budget'. Nevertheless, if it would postpone the election he was prepared to include Runciman's proposal within Gladstonian prescriptions.[43] Reading, similarly anxious for postponement, almost rivalled Runciman in inventiveness, proposing imperial barter

[40] Liberal Economic Group memo, 'Liberalism and the Crisis of the £', sent to senior Liberal ministers 18 Sept. 1931, Lothian papers, 143/55–72; see also [Layton], 'The First Lap' and 'Restoring the Balance', *Economist*, 12 and 19 Sept. 1931.

[41] Hirst diary, 5 Sept. 1931, in Hirst, 5; and letter in *The Times*, 5 Sept. 1931. The Preface to F. W. Hirst, *Gladstone as Financier and Economist* is dated October 1931.

[42] Tweed to Sinclair, 15 Sept. 1931, Thurso papers III/3/5; Hirst diary, 14, 15, 16 Sept. 1931, in Hirst, 6.

[43] Maclean to Murray, 4 Sept. 1931, Murray papers; Maclean memo, 14–19 Sept. 1931, Runciman papers, 245.

arrangements, import prohibitions, and prohibition of capital exports.[44] More important, in mid September Samuel began a different kind of shift. Recognising that Conservative pressure might make an early election inevitable, he aimed to ensure that Liberals would fight it as members of the existing National government. This seemed vital for the preservation of the Liberal party. An election pact with Conservatives would secure the seats of Liberal MPs, and might prevent the Simon Liberals tearing the party to pieces. The principal obstacle – a trade policy capable of linking free-trade Liberals with Conservatives (and Simon Liberals) – seemed to have been overcome by Runciman. The resistance of most Liberals to an election was another problem, but here Samuel thought he had a trump card in the moral authority of Grey. Frightened by the nature of the Labour opposition, Grey had his own distinctive attitude – that the emergency government was vulnerable to the charge of lacking a mandate for its 'extraordinary steps', that trade unions might therefore start a strike movement, and that consequently an election was desirable as soon as possible.[45] Confident of Grey's public support, Samuel followed Baldwin in urging MacDonald to lead the government through an election campaign.[46]

The timing and character of an election now depended mostly upon MacDonald. His attitude was determined very largely by what he thought had happened to his own party. In present conditions the Labour party was 'not fit to govern' and constituted a danger to the nation; it had acquired 'rather detestable but nevertheless electorally effective cries'.[47] For two weeks after the National government's formation, he spoke firmly of himself as a Labour party politician. He had 'not left [his] Party' and had 'no intention of doing so'. When the emergency government ended, he would resume 'Socialist propaganda' in order to get the party straight again.[48] But already that tension which had always existed between the Labour party of his imagination and the Labour party in reality had virtually forced

[44] Reading to MacDonald, 10 and 11 Sept. 1931, PREM 1/97, and to Snowden, 11 Sept. 1931, T172/1746.
[45] Grey in Lady Hilton Young diary, 13 Sept. 1931 (Kennet, 283), and in Murray to Cecil, 16 Sept. 1931, Cecil papers 51172.
[46] See Samuel in Runciman to his wife, 17 Sept. 1931, Runciman papers 303; Hankey diary, 20 Sept. 1931 (Roskill, *Hankey* II, 560); MacDonald diary, 15 Sept. 1931.
[47] MacDonald diary, 1 Sept. 1931; MacDonald to Baldwin, 5 Sept. 1931, SB 44/90–1 (Marquand, 655).
[48] Ibid.; MacDonald to Middleton, 29 Aug. 1931, Middleton papers 27/29; MacDonald to Benn, 1 Sept. 1931, JRM 1315.

a break. In MacDonald logic 'saving the Labour party' now meant
saving it from itself by excluding it from government. If the Labour
opposition won the next election there would be a financial crisis
which would 'ruin' the party as well as the country.[49] Exposure in
the Commons to the new Labour party stance pushed MacDonald
still further. Once free from that 'ill-assorted body', 'how could one
ever...join it again[?]'.[50]

While increasingly certain that the Labour party had to be denied
office, MacDonald was uncertain about how this could be best
achieved and about his own role in it. The suggestion that he might
lead a National government into the election was first made to him
privately by Beaverbrook on 3 September.[51] Two days later he
raised the issue of the government's future with Baldwin. In one
respect he saw little difficulty: restoring the trade balance seemed
'the only real cure for our present ills', and on the principle of import
controls (if not on detailed devices) he now felt 'not...far removed'
from Conservatives. But in all other respects his situation compelled
ambiguity. If he were to retain authority, credibility, and self-respect
as 'National' prime minister, he needed the support of both
Conservatives and Liberals, including the free-traders. Though
conscious that his value as a Labour answer to the Labour
opposition gave him some power of initiative, he was even more
conscious that he had to await Conservative and Liberal views and
try to establish some balance between them. He therefore hinted at
his own readiness either to lead an early election campaign, or to
stay on if the election were postponed, or to retire.[52]

Retirement was not a serious proposal. Consciousness of his own
ability and influence, pride, and a sense of duty all impelled him to
believe that he still had much to contribute as statesman and
politician, on India, disarmament, and international economic
policy, as much as on domestic questions. He did not deceive himself
about the differences between the National government partners,
but continued to believe that with a modicum of goodwill men of
diverse views could co-operate and support 'progressive' causes. He
also thought he had a valuable asset: despite losing the Labour
parliamentary party, he 'could count upon detaching at least a

[49] MacDonald to Baldwin, 5 Sept. 1931, SB 44/90-1 (Marquand, 655).
[50] MacDonald diary, 8 Sept. 1931, and see Marquand, 658.
[51] Beaverbrook reported in N. Chamberlain diary, 3 Sept. 1931, and Lockhart diary, 5 Sept.
1931, in Young I, 184. There is no evidence on this meeting in MacDonald's own papers.
[52] MacDonald to Baldwin, 5 Sept. 1931, SB 44/90-1 (Marquand, 655).

quarter of the Party in the country'.[53] His approach to Baldwin was a tentative but unmistakable plea for Conservatives to help sustain his political career. Once Parliament met he tried systematically to establish a 'MacDonaldite' position. He attempted to capture four Labour MPs who abstained in the 8 September vote.[54] He also fed lobby correspondents with daily political briefings, and met controllers of a broad spread of national and provincial newspapers.[55]

It was important to MacDonald that his chief Labour colleagues wanted an early election. Snowden, combative instincts aflame, wished to take his financial policy to a decisive electoral test against his former colleagues. Though unable to contemplate permanent coalition with protectionists, he saw Runciman's proposal as an expedient to keep the government together for the election.[56] Thomas had long favoured protection, had found in the government's cross-party atmosphere his 'spiritual home', and now responded to the movement of Conservative opinion. By 16 September he had told MacDonald and indicated to Conservative leaders that he wanted a MacDonald-led protectionist coalition to fight an October election and 'smash' the Labour party.[57]

MacDonald himself could see the advantages of an early election, but still had considerable doubts. It might jeopardise financial confidence, and he had staked his reputation and career upon saving sterling. By exposing differences over trade policy and very likely forcing Liberal resignations, it might weaken the government's 'national' credentials. It was also unclear what would happen to himself and his supporters after an election. Snowden was largely unconcerned, intending to retire with a peerage. Thomas wanted MacDonald to lead a permanent coalition, but MacDonald could

[53] MacDonald reported in Lady Lee diary, 11 Sept. 1931, in Lee III, 1326.
[54] For emotional MacDonald meeting with abstainers, see Angell notes, 8–9 Sept. 1931, Angell papers 032-26; Strauss diary, early Sept. 1931; Picton-Turbervill, *Life*, 257–60. Denman was the only convert: see Denman, *Political Sketches*, 3–8.
[55] For briefings channelled through his son, see memos from 9 Sept. 1931 in M. MacDonald papers 6/2. For newspaper controllers, Donald to MacDonald, 14 Sept. 1931, JRM 1314.
[56] Samuel in Runciman to his wife, 17 Sept. 1931, Runciman papers 303; Hankey diary, 20 Sept. 1931 (Roskill, *Hankey* II, 560). See also Snowden's notorious taunt to his 'old associates' in *HC Deb*, 256, col. 801, 15 Sept. 1931: 'only a few weeks, possibly, remains before the place that knows them now will know them no more'.
[57] Cazalet diary, Sept. 1931, in James, *Cazalet*, 137. Thomas in Dawes, *Journal*, 389, 15 Sept. 1931, and in Davidson memo, 15 Sept. 1931, Davidson papers (Davidson, *Memoirs of a Conservative*, 376).

not count on this. When Baldwin and Samuel urged him in mid September to lead the election fight, neither suggested he could remain Prime Minister thereafter. Yet, as in August, to him it seemed impossible to remain except as Prime Minister. To lead an election campaign only to install not merely a Conservative-dominated but a Conservative-led government would be an intolerable indignity.[58]

MacDonald's first preference was therefore for the National government to save the country from the Labour party by remaining in office into 1932, settling the trade and other outstanding questions itself, and postponing awkward electoral problems until financial and political conditions had eased. Like Liberal ministers, he thought completion of the government's task required more time: it was impossible to draw 'any line between this time of crisis and a normal condition'.[59]

In mid September MacDonald tried to take the policy initiative, in order to show other Cabinet members that there remained important work to do. He reopened with the United States government the issue of reparations and war debts, hoping for negotiations on cancellation but also reviving the idea of a world economic conference.[60] Very optimistically, he circulated the report of the Committee of Economists which the Labour Cabinet had ignored ten months previously.[61] Most significant of all, on the 10th he appointed a Cabinet committee on trade, consisting of Snowden, Chamberlain, and Reading. This soon became preoccupied with immediate issues of sterling defence, and was reconstituted under his own chairmanship as a Financial Situation Committee.[62] But for MacDonald its original purpose was to spotlight the trade deficit as a source of continuing 'emergency', and to produce a policy which would enable the existing Cabinet to deal with it. Himself reluctant to swallow the whole Conservative tariff package, he hoped it could manufacture some compromise acceptable to ministerial free traders.[63] As a political instrument, however, the committee proved

[58] MacDonald diary, 15, 16 and 17 Sept. 1931.
[59] MacDonald to Baldwin, 5 Sept. 1931, SB 44/90–1 (Marquand, 656).
[60] MacDonald to Stimson, 15 Sept. 1931, Stimson papers.
[61] Hankey note, covering report, CP234(31), 14 Sept. 1931.
[62] MacDonald to committee and Cabinet members, 10 Sept. 1931, SB 44/107–9, NC 7/11/24/16; MacDonald diary, 11 Sept. 1931. The committee's appointment was leaked to the press, perhaps by design: see Parliamentary correspondent, The Times, 14 Sept. 1931.
[63] MacDonald to Baldwin, 5 Sept. 1931, SB 44/90–1 (Marquand, 656). See MacDonald diary, 13 Sept. 1931, for re-examining Oct. 1930 plans 'mishandled' by the 'incompetent' Graham.

a disappointment. It stimulated a Cunliffe–Lister attack upon Runciman's proposal as infringing treaty obligations and inadequate to rectify the deficit, and a Snowden–Chamberlain onslaught upon Reading's idea of prohibiting capital exports, as dangerous to financial confidence.[64] It also failed to restrain pressure for an early election.

On 16 September the Cabinet discussed the government's future. Against MacDonald's, Samuel's and Reading's resistance, the Conservative ministers with Thomas's and Snowden's support obtained something close to a decision that an election should be held at the earliest possible date.[65] The Conservatives agreed in principle to anti-socialist arrangements over seats, and the Conservative and Liberal party organisers were instructed to negotiate.[66] But it remained an open question whether the Cabinet could stay together, or whether a major reconstruction would become necessary.

NEW PROBLEMS

These Cabinet preliminaries for an election, with the attendant prospect of a sharp increase in political uncertainty, began in the most extraordinary circumstances – amid plain evidence that the Cabinet's policies were now at severe risk. Over a period of eight days, beginning on 14 September, three crises broke. Collectively these were more serious in their policy implications than those of August, and as potentially devastating in their political consequences. Two, over expenditure cuts and sterling, became embarrassingly public, but the other, concerning Indian finance, was no less dangerous for being kept from Parliament and the press. That Conservative leaders nevertheless continued to press for an early election, even defying advice that this would jeopardise sterling, reveals much about their fundamental concerns and priorities.

Some of the prospective recipients of income cuts had begun protests as soon as these became known. There were marches and demonstrations by unemployed men, but the government was able

---

[64] Cunliffe-Lister memo, 14 Sept. 1931, NC 8/12/4; Cunliffe-Lister to his wife, 15 Sept. 1931, Swinton papers; Financial Situation Committee, 14 and 17 Sept. 1931, CAB 27/462.
[65] MacDonald diary, 16 Sept. 1931 (for substance unminuted in Cabinet 57(31), same date); Baldwin and Samuel in Runciman to his wife, 17 Sept. 1931, Runciman papers 303; Hoare to Willingdon, 17 Sept. 1931, Templewood Indian papers 1/12–15.
[66] MacDonald diary, 16 Sept. 1931; Baldwin in Runciman to his wife, 17 Sept. 1931, Runciman papers 303; Tweed in Sylvester diary, 17 Sept. 1931, in Cross, 30.

to isolate these as a law and order problem. Objections by judges were more troublesome because of their argumentative power, appeal to the principle of judicial independence, and threat to the example of official self-sacrifice.[67] Their resistance persisted for two years. Teachers, regarding their 15 per cent cut as 'unjust and inequitable' as compared to the 10 per cent norm, were the most active, bombarding ministers, MPs, and newspapers with deputations, letters, and petitions.[68] But the most serious protest was by men of the Atlantic Fleet gathered for naval exercises at Invergordon. On 14 September there were indications of unrest, on the 15th crews on many of the battleships and cruisers declined to obey orders to set sail, and on the 16th control of most of the fleet was lost.

Admiralty officials as much as senior officers were at fault for failing to provide the naval ratings with proper information on the proposed cuts, and to anticipate that some would have a genuine grievance. The departmental head, Austen Chamberlain, smarting under the humiliation, the 'mental hell', of his own ministerial demotion, had considered himself a mere 'caretaker' and instigated no enquiries of his own, nor warned the Cabinet of possible difficulties.[69] Realising their mistake and fearing that an attempt to impose discipline would escalate resistance, the commanding officers and Admiralty advised cancellation of the fleet exercises, dispersal of the ships to their home ports, and postponement of the cuts to allow re-examination, with an implied promise of redress.

Although the newspapers called the men's action 'mutiny', it was really passive disobedience. Even so, resistance in the premier armed service was of the utmost seriousness. The Cabinet, meeting with Chamberlain and the Admirals present on the morning of 16 September, was appalled at the Admiralty's mismanagement[70] and stunned by the blow to national prestige, service discipline, and its retrenchment programme. But most ministers were equally alarmed at the possibility of violence, and ready to swallow Admiralty advice. According to MacDonald, the Labour ministers – whose reputations were wholly committed to successful imposition of cuts – were

---

[67] See, e.g., Lord Merrivale (President, Admiralty division, and former Conservative Cabinet minister) to Baldwin, 12 Sept. 1931, SB 44/114–15, and protests recorded in Sankey, CP246(31), 25 Sept. 1931.

[68] See, e.g., H. C. Boll (secretary, Manchester NUT) to Reading, 10 Sept. 1931, Reading papers F118/131; Lane-Fox diary, 10 Sept. 1931.

[69] A. Chamberlain to his wife, 26 Aug.–9 Sept. 1931, AC 6/1/803–10.

[70] MacDonald diary, 16 Sept. 1931; Hoare memo, 'First National Government', Templewood papers VII:1.

responsible for steadying the meeting and insisting upon face-saving measures. To make concessions in one case – worst of all, to appear to surrender to force – might be a precedent for other recipients of cuts, encouraging a spread of resistance with 'incalculable consequences'. The Cabinet eventually agreed that public statements should emphasise that the Fleet dispersed under Admiralty orders, implying that obedience represented an end to the protest. It rejected the advice to postpone the cuts. Instead, Austen Chamberlain would promise Admiralty re-consideration and redress of genuine grievances, but only after MacDonald had made a general statement about the incidence of the cuts. This statement would assert that the Cabinet had already accepted that 'particular classes of persons' (not specifying naval ratings) might be 'unfairly affected', and that these anomalies could be removed 'without materially affecting the Budget Estimates'.[71]

MacDonald and Austen Chamberlain were given a rough time in the Commons by Labour MPs pressing for revision of other cuts. But they managed to postpone a debate while Admiralty orders were issued, and until it was seen that they had been obeyed. When the debate was held on the evening of the 17th, the Cabinet concession and the restraint of front bench Labour spokesmen themselves fearing a further breakdown of naval discipline resulted in withdrawal of an opposition motion. But how the naval crews would behave once they reached their home ports remained a matter of acute anxiety.

The Indian crisis began on the same day as the naval troubles. Since July the Government of India's financial problems had developed into linked exchange and budget crises similar to those in Britain. Although real and intractable matters of financial substance were involved, the critical issue revolved around the political question of 'safeguards' for British financial interests in any new Indian constitution.[72] For the Government of India, the 'root difficulty' was 'political policy', which no 'mere financial measure' could solve: the uncertainty whether 'safeguards' would be adequate to guarantee the rupee exchange rate and Indian financial stability, against nationalist pressure for devaluation and tax remissions. The

---

[71] Cabinet 56(31), MacDonald diary, and MacDonald and A. Chamberlain statements, *HC Deb*, 256, cols. 820, 823, all 16 Sept. 1931. See also press briefing, 17 Sept. 1931, in M. MacDonald papers 6/2/46–7, for MacDonald instruction: 'Give the idea that the Admiralty were quite firm'.

[72] For the various financial aspects, see Moore, *Crisis of Indian Unity*, 211–14; Tomlinson, 'Britain and the Indian Currency Crisis', 95–6; Drummond, *Floating Pound*, 38–43.

British government's June promise of financial support, intended as temporary political underpinning to the Indian government, helped for only a few weeks. By August operations to defend the rupee exchange had again begun to deplete Indian sterling reserves. In early September the drain came within sight of forcing either devaluation or default in the government's external payments. On the 7th – the day the second Round Table Conference opened – Willingdon asked for immediate fulfilment of the British government promise in the form of a sterling credit.[73]

The Government of India's own contribution towards restoration of financial confidence would be emergency measures to balance its budget. As in Britain, the government had borrowed to meet current expenditure, and budget estimates had proved optimistic. Sir George Schuster, the Finance Member (equivalent to Chancellor of the Exchequer), had appointed a Retrenchment Committee, and insisted that cuts must precede taxes. Like Snowden he argued that the limits of taxation were being reached and, faced with the enormous risks of inflaming nationalist opinion, like MacDonald he looked to the principle of equality of sacrifice. The problem was his belief that an emergency budget might meet 'irresistible popular hostility' unless it included reductions in Indian Civil Service salaries.[74] The India Office strongly objected, because these service salaries were guaranteed by statute and to alter them now would raise the key issue of financial 'safeguards'. Conservatives and Liberals would probably oppose the necessary legislation on the grounds that cuts would demoralise the service, curtail recruitment, and paralyse administration. Worse, the proposal might destroy Conservative and Liberal confidence in the strength of 'safeguards', and so 'be fatal to the chances of an agreed Reform Act for India'.[75] Benn had resisted Schuster's pressure during the August crisis in Britain. In early September the issue came to Hoare.

In London it was believed that a flight from the rupee would be 'an economic catastrophe of the first magnitude', while default would be 'disastrous for India' and 'a shattering blow to British credit'. A 'really formidable crisis' now existed, in which Britain and

[73] Note by Financial Department, India Office, 2 Sept., circulated as CP226(31), 10 Sept. 1931; Willingdon to Hoare, tms 739, 757, 1 and 7 Sept. 1931, in CP232(31) [15 Sept. 1931].

[74] Finance Department, Government of India, to Benn, tms 1754, 1989, 14–15 July and 9 Aug. 1931, and airmail letter, 11 Aug. 1931, IOR L/F/7/2438.

[75] F. Stewart (India Office) to Benn, 22 Aug. 1931, IOR L/F/7/2438.

India would 'sink or swim together'.[76] Nevertheless, given Britain's own exchange crisis, the Treasury rejected the Government of India's request for a sterling credit. More remarkably, the problem now revealed that the Cabinet would adopt a quite different attitude when the object of political anxiety was the Conservative party rather than the Labour party. In the British crisis, the National government decided to use Orders in Council in order to break contracts, change statutory payments, and impose income cuts against Labour opposition. Yet faced with an Indian crisis, against prospective Conservative opposition the same government felt unable to introduce legislation to override service contracts. Hoare, with unanimous Cabinet support, was even firmer than Benn. 'The British public would at once...conclu[de] that Parliamentary safeguards were merely paper safeguards and could be easily removed.' The Conservative party's reaction would be 'simply disastrous': its MPs 'would vote against it to a man'. It would have 'the worst possible effect' upon the Round Table process. It was 'simply...not practical politics'.[77]

This 'complete *impasse*'[78] led to a war of nerves. Schuster had anticipated resistance from London, and now resorted to desperate tactics. His budget proposals sent for India Office approval on 9 September included not just service cuts but increased cotton duties, which were bound to revive Cabinet concern about the effect on Lancashire industry. As a means to emphasise his problem, they also failed to cover the whole deficit. Even more startling, on the previous day Schuster had recommended that, in the absence of a sterling credit, there should be voluntary devaluation of the rupee. This, he admitted, involved great risks to Indian credit and external obligations. But it would preserve India's currency reserves, make service cuts unnecessary, end the 'practically universal' Indian condemnation of monetary policy, and remove a major nationalist grievance.[79]

In London there was shock and anger. Schuster's proposed

---

[76] Note by Financial Department, India Office, 2 Sept., circulated as CP226(31), 10 Sept. 1931; Hoare to Willingdon, 11 Sept. 1931, Templewood Indian papers 1/7–11.

[77] Hoare to Willingdon, 2 and 11 Sept., and tm 8-U, 14 Sept. 1931, Templewood Indian papers 1/1–6, 7–11 and 13/2–5; Hoare to Government of India, tm 2626, 8 Sept. 1931, IOR L/F/7/2438; Cabinet 55(31), 9 Sept. 1931.

[78] Schuster to Kershaw, tm 2283, 10 Sept. 1931, IOR L/F/7/2438.

[79] Finance Department, Government of India, to Hoare, tm 2280, 9–10 Sept., app. to Cabinet 58(31), 17 Sept. 1931; Schuster memo in Willingdon to Hoare, 8 Sept., in CP232(31) [15 Sept. 1931].

devaluation seemed another 'lamentable' instance of 'defeatism', an
attempt to 'appease Indian agitation'. Hoare had now 'taken
Schuster's measure – as a born funk and sneak'.[80] India Office and
Treasury officials, Reading, MacDonald, and Hoare agreed both to
reject devaluation and to reaffirm refusal of a credit. The
Government of India should 'play for time', continue using its
reserves to support the rupee, and 'pray for the dawn' of such a
recovery in sterling as would enable the Treasury to authorise a
credit.[81] Against service cuts Hoare mobilised Simon who, Willingdon was told, was so 'bitterly opposed' that he would lead
Conservative backbenchers in a Commons vote of censure.[82]

In Delhi there was equal shock and annoyance that the London
government so blatantly put British political concerns before India's
vital financial interests. Choosing service cuts as the test of strength,
on 14 September Schuster and most of the Viceroy's Council
threatened resignation. At another time this would have been
confidently treated in London for what it was: further pressure
aimed at carrying the issue. But the Cabinet and especially the
Conservative leadership were now in too vulnerable a position to
take a risk over the threat being a bluff. Resignations of senior
Government of India officials would publicise the crisis with severe
consequences for the rupee and perhaps sterling. Conservative party
confidence in the Cabinet's – and its own leaders' – Indian policy
would certainly be damaged. Indian nationalism might well be
strengthened, and the Round Table Conference might disintegrate.

Now Hoare and MacDonald themselves played for time. They
offered some concessions: public reaffirmation of the June undertaking,[83] and the proposal of a campaign for voluntary cuts led by
the Viceroy, Governors, and senior officials on the model set in
Britain by the King. If that campaign failed, they would accept
inquiry into salary rates which might then make legislation
politically possible. But in London financial confidence and
Conservative opinion still seemed to impose tight constraints, so
firmness was maintained in other directions. Hoare and MacDonald
warned that any resignations would be regarded as 'political'[84] – for

[80] Hilton Young to his wife, 9 and 10 Sept. 1931, Kennet papers 107/3: this from a minister
favouring a credit to India, who was present at the crucial meeting.
[81] Hoare to Willingdon, tm 7-U, 10 Sept., in CP232(31) [15 Sept. 1931].
[82] Hoare to Willingdon, 11 Sept., and tm 8-U, 14 Sept. 1931, Templewood Indian papers
1/7–11, 13/2–5.   [83] MacDonald in *HC Deb*, 256, col. 672, 15 Sept. 1931.
[84] Hoare to Willingdon, tm 8-U, 14 Sept. 1931, Templewood Indian papers 13/2–5.

officials, constitutionally improper. As an 'extreme measure' justified by the 'national emergency', Hoare also infringed the fiscal autonomy convention and tried to impose an alternative budget upon the Government of India. On 17 September the Cabinet rejected Schuster's budget as 'wholly inadequate' and accepted the India Office's counter-proposals. In order to strengthen financial confidence in India there should be immediate announcement of an emergency budget, which within two years would secure strict balance through voluntary salary cuts, other retrenchment, and sharp increases in taxation. British domestic concerns also had to receive consideration. Since increased cotton duties might 'knock the final nail in the Lancashire coffin' and have 'the worst political reactions', there should be an equivalent excise on Indian cotton[85] – irrespective of the likelihood of severe Indian opposition.

The Cabinet approved such strong instructions because a flight from the rupee now appeared to have begun, but also because on 17 September there were special reasons for avoiding both further shocks to confidence in sterling and any upset to Conservative party opinion. Announcement of the British budget programme had not halted withdrawals of funds from London and sales of sterling, and exchange support operations had used up about half the government credits. Events were rapidly coming to resemble those of August, with MacDonald facing a divided cabinet (on the election issue) and struggling to hold it together in the face of a sterling crisis. On the 16th he had elicited a firm statement of the King's support for his efforts to postpone an election,[86] but this support had no more effect upon the 'National' Cabinet than on its Labour predecessor. MacDonald then tried once again, as on 21 August, to discipline a divided Cabinet by calling in the Bank of England, asking Harvey for its considered opinion on how an election would affect defence of sterling.[87]

Cabinet ministers were conscious of a connection between the election issue and the state of financial confidence, even if they disagreed on what it was. In these respects, it seemed that 'the future

---

[85] Cabinet 58(31), 17 Sept. 1931, with app., Hoare to Government of India, tm 2733, 18 Sept. 1931; Hoare to Willingdon, tm 9-U, 18 Sept. 1931, Templewood Indian papers 13/6–11.
[86] MacDonald to the King, 14 Sept. 1931, and Wigram (for the King) to MacDonald, 16 Sept. 1931, JRM 1314.
[87] MacDonald diary, 16 Sept. 1931; BoE Cte, 16 Sept. 1931; Harrison-Harvey conversation, 16 Sept. 1931, FRBNY Harrison papers.

of the government depends on the future of sterling'.[88] The Bank of
England, however, thought the reverse – that the future of sterling
depended on the future of the government. It believed the
withdrawals had several causes. The 'whole... world had [become]
very sick': American, Swiss, Dutch, and Scandinavian fears about
their own banks' liquidity had been added to continuing Central
European problems. The British balance of payments deficit,
estimated by the Bank at £60–100m., was causing natural outflows.
But to the Bank, its City informants, and its advisers abroad, the
obvious distrust of sterling itself again seemed to have largely
political causes. The announcement that the National government
was only a temporary arrangement had disturbed international
opinion.[89] The Labour manifesto, showing that the 'Socialists' had
'not changed their doctrines' and that the National government was
'not a national government at all', had then caused real nervousness.[90] As early as 3 September, Harvey warned the Cabinet
that exchange prospects 'depend[ed] largely on political developments'.[91] When it became known that an early election was
proposed, 'the financial world [was] a good deal upset'. 'For the
indecision of the previous political crisis... was now substituted the
open fear of a profound national cleavage' and of an election victory
by a Labour party explicitly repudiating sound finance.[92] Though
the Bank directors did not express it in these terms, their meaning
was plain: if Labour opposition was the principal cause of continued
foreign distrust of sterling, Conservatives were nearly as culpable in
demanding an election which might result in a Labour government.

As earlier, the Bank believed that against exchange losses caused
by political uncertainty, banking weapons alone were ineffective.
Gold shipments, bank rate increases, or credit restriction might only
fuel the loss of confidence.[93] The Bank, Treasury officials, and the
Financial Situation Committee agreed that mobilisation of British
overseas assets should now be considered, but such a complex
operation would take time. As the trade deficit had taken the place

[88] Hoare to Willingdon, 11 Sept. 1931, Templewood Indian papers 1/7–11.
[89] Peacock in app. to Cabinet 53(31), 3 Sept. 1931.
[90] Rodd (at BIS) to Harvey, 5 Sept. 1931, in Thompson-McCausland, 'Crisis', 42; and see
    Lamont to Grenfell, 29 Aug. 1931, MGC.
[91] App to Cabinet 53(31), 3 Sept. 1931. See also Peacock–Grenfell–Chamberlain conversation
    in Grenfell to Lamont, 1 Sept. 1931, MGC.
[92] Peacock at Financial Situation Committee, 17 Sept. 1931, CAB 27/462, and reported in
    Cabinet 59(31), 17 Sept. 1931; Thompson-McCausland, 'Crisis', 41.
[93] Harvey in app. to Cabinet 53(31), 3 Sept. 1931, and at BoE Cte, 16 Sept.1931; Thompson-
    McCausland, 'Crisis', 44–5.

occupied in August by the budget deficit, the Bank and much of the City now strongly favoured a tariff.[94] Yet this only brought matters back to politics and the decision on an election. Some City financiers wanted a quick election to obtain a Conservative government and end the uncertainty.[95] But the Bank of England, sensitive to foreign opinion, thought an election could only damage sterling. It thought this true of any kind of election, but especially so of an election fought by the parties separately, where Labour's chances of success would be increased. Any Labour government would now, it seemed, mean nationalisation of the Bank. Defence of sterling, of national credit and sound finance, and of the Bank's own institutional independence converged and reinforced personal political attachments. All these produced a strong preference at the Bank for the National government to remain in office as a barrier to the Labour party.[96]

On the day MacDonald asked the Bank's opinion about an election a crisis had been reached, as daily exchange losses rose to £4m. and made it likely that the government credits would be exhausted in another ten days. As in early August, the issue had become 'whether further efforts should be made to maintain the £ or whether they should acknowledge defeat'. The Bank itself wanted to continue the defence and began enquiries to Paris and New York about yet further credits. But it knew such credits would be difficult to raise, and that the difficulty would be much increased if an election were announced.[97] Accordingly the Bank decided that its answer to MacDonald's question should be that 'it would be impossible with existing resources to maintain the Gold Standard during the period necessary to conduct a General Election'. Its preferred advice was that the National government should immediately announce that an election was not contemplated, and that it intended to tackle the trade deficit and undertake voluntary war loan conversion. It should also provide diplomatic support for the Bank's requests for new credits.[98] Yet Harvey and Peacock knew the

[94] BoE Cte, 17 Sept. 1931; Peacock at Financial Situation Committee, 17 Sept. 1931, CAB 27/462; Sayers, *Bank of England*, 410–11.
[95] See de Trafford in Lockhart diary, 13 Sept. 1931, in Young I, 185; and Cunliffe-Lister to his wife, 15 Sept. 1931, Swinton papers.
[96] See Peacock–Grenfell–Chamberlain conversation in Grenfell to Lamont, 1 Sept. 1931, MGC; Harvey and Peacock (implicitly) at Financial Situation Committee, 3 Sept. 1931, CAB 27/462: Sprague reporting 'with one exception, all his colleagues' in Church to MacDonald, 6 Sept. 1931, JRM 1314.
[97] Harvey and Peacock at Financial Situation Committee, 17 Sept. 1931, CAB 27/462.
[98] BoE Cte, 17 Sept. 1931.

Cabinet might not accept this advice. Aware of the contrary political pressures, they supplied themselves with a secondary line of advice based around the Conservatives' attitude.

At this point in the struggle for the gold standard, the parts which Henderson and the TUC General Council had taken in August were played by Neville Chamberlain and the Conservative party. Anti-socialism, commitment to protection, fear of Labour prospects, and determination not to lose the chance of election victory were together so fundamental to Conservative interests that they preferred their own counsel to that of the Bank of England. On 9 September the Conservative leadership's reaction to City fears about an election had been that an early election must be held even at the risk of 'another scare and a flight from the pound'.[99] As the sterling crisis returned on the 16th the Bank found to its dismay that most Conservative backbench MPs shared this attitude, and that their leaders could not be shaken out of it.[100] It was no use to them that, ironically, on the 15th both Churchill and Amery had responded to the exchange crisis by accepting the case for postponement of the election, Amery even appealing to the Labour opposition to accept protection and join 'a real National Government'.[101] Neither had any support or influence on this matter. From the Bank's perspective no effective political appeal existed beyond the official Conservative leaders.

Their position had some basis in economic analysis, but in such terms it was not much more coherent than that of Henderson. Conservative leaders certainly placed great emphasis upon protection for industrial and agricultural purposes. Since their period in office from 1924 to 1929, they had obviously shifted more towards a producers' than a financiers' policy, and more towards economic nationalism than internationalism. It seems likely that all this contributed to their willingness to run risks with sterling, but if so it operated unconsciously. None articulated a view that protection and the gold standard were alternative positions. None indicated any desire for devaluation. For Conservative leaders as for the Bank of

---

[99] Conservative Business Committee decision reported in Hilton Young to his wife, 9 Sept. 1931, Kennet papers 107/3. See also Amery diary, 9 Sept. 1931 (*LSA* II, 199).

[100] For Chamberlain, and a meeting of Conservative MPs, 16 Sept. 1931, see Morgan Grenfell 'Memorandum', 14–15, and for the Bank's anger, Crump to Lothian, 18 Sept. 1931, Lothian papers 143/15. Cf. Ball, *Baldwin*, 192, which has Conservative leaders 'still bound by the views of the bankers'.

[101] Churchill and Amery, *HC Deb*, cols. 711–12, 744–5, 15 Sept. 1931; Amery diary, 3, 14, and 15 Sept. 1931 (partly in *LSA* II, 200).

England, defence of sound money remained a major objective: indeed this had now become a further argument for tariffs. Amery's turnabout on the election issue demonstrates how the two policies could seem to be connected. The main difference between the Conservative leaders and the Bank (and Amery) was more a matter of political assessment. Electoral imperatives made Conservative leaders impervious to even the most authoritative financial advice.

The Bank's answer to MacDonald's enquiry about the likely effect of an election was delivered by Harvey and Peacock at the Cabinet's Financial Situation Committee on 17 September. They stated that, for the purpose of defending sterling, 'the ideal course' would be postponement of an election, and they expressed 'grave doubts' that in existing conditions the exchanges could be held for the period of an election campaign. Chamberlain was unmoved. He declared that the Cabinet still wanted to maintain the gold standard, but there were 'great objections' to the National government remaining in office. It 'might become unpopular', and doubts about its stability and ultimate success at the polls might destroy confidence. Discussion therefore proceeded on the assumption that an early election would be held, and that the Bank would help arrange the financial conditions to make this possible. Ministers well understood that during this election campaign there could be a 'disastrous' crash of sterling, and some attention was given to financial and economic 'precautions' which might then become necessary. In the face of Chamberlain's determination, however, Harvey and Peacock changed tack and declared that the French and Americans had such considerable sterling investments and such strong interests in restoring international stability that their governments 'would not dare allow [Britain] to go off the Gold Standard'. If requested by the British government, these governments might help persuade their bankers to provide further credits so that the election period 'could be tided over'. But it would be vital to offer American and French lenders 'sufficient certainty for the establishment of a stable Government'. So against their own better judgement, Harvey and Peacock ultimately gave advice which supported the Conservative leadership's view: 'from the point of view of raising further credits abroad it would be fatal for the three Parties to enter an Election independently'.[102]

---

[102] Financial Situation Committee, 17 Sept. 1931, CAB 27/462, and report by MacDonald in Cabinet 59(31), 17 Sept. 1931.

Under Conservative pressure, then, the Cabinet from 16 September was on the brink of a general election, despite the outbreak of three policy crises. The Financial Situation Committee of the 17th met while the ships of the Atlantic Fleet were still sailing to their home ports, and before it was certain that their crews had been fully pacified. An hour or so later, the Cabinet met to hear Austen Chamberlain's proposals for the Commons naval debate, and then to consider Hoare's response to the rupee crisis. Yet, in spite of an evident danger of 'a gigantic financial smash in India', the Cabinet found it 'impossible' to discuss this matter fully because 'an even more urgent and critical question' had arisen – the sterling crisis. At a second meeting, MacDonald reported Harvey's and Peacock's advice, including their opinion that 'the risk of a General Election' had contributed to the exchange difficulties.[103]

'The world [was] completely out of joint',[104] and seemed likely to remain so for weeks to come. During August all political leaders had agreed that the sterling crisis made it impossible to call an election. Yet now, despite the naval unrest, the rupee crisis, and the renewed sterling crisis – despite the situation appearing to be 'one of the gravest that has ever faced the country', with 'inflammable material' on 'every side'[105] – the Cabinet did not decide against an early election. Rather, it agreed that MacDonald, Baldwin, and Samuel should continue discussing election arrangements on the following day.[106] This Cabinet had been formed to overcome the national emergency and save the country from what it believed and publicly declared to be the terrible financial, commercial, industrial, and social consequences of being forced off the gold standard. Yet Baldwin, Neville Chamberlain, Hoare, and Cunliffe-Lister, supported by Thomas and Snowden, with MacDonald and Samuel acquiescent, now ignored plain warnings and knowingly faced a high risk of precipitating the disaster they were supposed to be preventing. Here was an outstanding instance of 'politics' prevailing against 'policy'. To this extent had the National government leaders been carried by fear of the new Labour opposition, and Conservatives also by the prospect of a protectionist triumph, Samuel by anxiety to safeguard Liberal seats, and Snowden, Thomas, and MacDonald by anger and contempt towards former colleagues.

---

[103] Cabinets 58, 59(31), 17 Sept. 1931. See also N. Chamberlain diary, 19 Sept. 1931.
[104] N. Chamberlain diary, 19 Sept. 1931.
[105] Hoare to Willingdon, tm 9-U, 18 Sept. 1931, Templewood Indian papers 13/6–11.
[106] Cabinet 59(31), 17 Sept. 1931; MacDonald diary, 18 Sept. 1931.

All had not yet been finally settled. Before the election could be called, the details – the platform and the seats – had to be arranged. Differences over manifesto statements about trade were certain: there might still be ministerial resignations. Difficulties were already emerging for each government partner. Senior Conservative organisers claimed that the party in the country would 'bitterly resent' an election appeal led by MacDonald rather than Baldwin.[107] Despite Samuel's use of the Grey card and attempt to obtain Runciman's help in finding an election policy formula, on the 17th Lloyd George Liberal MPs rejected his proposed arrangements about seats and reaffirmed opposition to an election. On the following day the Liberal Advisory Committee confirmed these decisions, which were strongly supported by Maclean and Lloyd George himself.[108] At this, MacDonald's doubts revived. On the 18th he told Baldwin and Samuel that he could not remain Prime Minister during the election if the outcome would be the establishment of a Conservative government.[109] Yet the momentum was becoming unstoppable. Neville Chamberlain thought the advice of the Conservative organisers 'idiotic'.[110] On hints from Mac-Donald's secretaries, Hore-Belisha began a Simon Liberal petition promising MacDonald Liberal replacements in the event of resignations by Lloyd George Liberal ministers. Greig joined Hore-Belisha in seeking funds to run MacDonaldite candidates.[111] There would be much hard bargaining to come. Nevertheless, as Cabinet ministers dispersed on Friday 18 September to their various weekend retreats, they thought an election imminent.

NEAR DISASTER

As ministers left London, decisions were being taken which brought the issues of sterling, the rupee, and expenditure cuts to a climax. The Bank of England, in a last exercise of its traditional independence, unilaterally decided that the gold standard should no longer be defended. With hindsight it has appeared inevitable that the combination of an international liquidity crisis and British

---

[107] Stonehaven to Baldwin, 18 Sept. 1931, enclosing Topping, Maxse, Gower memo, SB 44/148, 150–2; and see Eyres-Monsell and Stonehaven in Runciman to his wife, 17 Sept. 1931, Runciman papers 303.

[108] Samuel in Runciman to his wife, 17 Sept. 1931, and Maclean memo, 14–19 Sept. 1931, Runciman papers 303, 245; Sylvester diary, 17 and 18 Sept. 1931 in Cross, 38–9.

[109] MacDonald diary, 18 Sept. 1931.

[110] N. to I. Chamberlain, 19 Sept. 1931, NC 18/1/755.

[111] Rosenberg memos, 18 and 19 Sept. 1931, JRM 1314.

balance of payments deficit would force abandonment of the gold standard some time in autumn 1931.[112] But these general conditions do not explain the specific time and motive of the Bank of England's final decision. On the afternoon of 17 September Bank directors still advised that the gold standard could and should be defended. Yet on the following morning they decided that further defence was futile and that preparations for suspending gold payments should begin.[113]

The most obvious explanation for this reversal is deterioration in the exchange position. Withdrawals had continued to escalate, and the Bank's daily loss on exchange support increased to over £10m. on the 17th. One cause appeared to be the Invergordon incident, striking a further blow to foreign confidence by suggesting that government authority had been subverted. However, Harvey mentioned Invergordon at that afternoon's Financial Situation Committee meeting without indicating that it might be fatal to sterling. A further problem was a renewed European liquidity panic associated with an acute banking crisis in Amsterdam. Cabinet ministers received notification of this just before their meeting dispersed around midnight on the 17th, in a Harvey message asking that diplomatic requests for French and American assistance should be postponed until its effects 'could be weighed'.[114]

The addition of this Dutch crisis to the effects of Invergordon may have been sufficient in itself to convince the Bank that the position had become hopeless. However, it probably had a further reason: Harvey's and Peacock's revised assessment of the political situation. The new exchange pressures reduced the already uncertain chances of maintaining sterling, yet senior ministers had been undeterred by warnings of the financial dangers of an election. To Bank directors it must have seemed that the Cabinet had placed desire for an election before defence of the gold standard, and regarded new credits chiefly as a political convenience, to prop up sterling for long enough to complete an election campaign. Neville Chamberlain was indicative. Bank directors had become accustomed to regarding him as the most 'reliable' minister,[115] but he now appeared the most resistant to Bank advice. To Peacock's suggestion that the National government should continue in order to restore the trade balance,

---

[112] See, e.g., Moggridge, 'The 1931 Financial Crisis'; Cairncross and Eichengreen, *Sterling in Decline*, 72–83.   [113] BoE Cte, 18 Sept. 1931.
[114] Financial Situation Committee, 17 Sept. 1931, CAB 27/462; Cabinet 59(31), 17 Sept. 1931; MacDonald diary, 17 Sept. 1931.
[115] Morgan Grenfell, 'Memorandum', 14–15.

Chamberlain had replied – notwithstanding Conservative claims made for an 'emergency tariff' – that effective measures 'would take a long time to carry through Parliament'.[116] Even if there were to be a 'National' election appeal, the Bank now thought it unlikely that foreign opinion would be reassured. The Cabinet's concession over naval pay cuts had 'a deplorable effect abroad',[117] worse even than Invergordon itself. It appeared to demonstrate a lack of government firmness which, especially in the run up to an election, might result in further concessions and renewed budget difficulties.

With the cracking of the political underpinning for financial confidence, efforts to withstand the latest exchange onslaught seemed useless. During 18 September the flight from sterling was even greater. Although the Bank still feared the consequences of abandoning the gold standard, it now appeared best not to prolong the agony and suffer further reserve losses but to arrange for the end to come in the least injurious manner. Once Bank directors had made up their own minds, they placed the matter beyond all question and any ministerial intervention. They asked MacDonald and Snowden to proceed with appeals for French and American government help, but did not tell them that the Bank's intention was now simply to warn those governments of the crisis and to imply that every possibility had been explored.[118] In contrast to their statements on the 17th that the French and Americans would feel obliged to help, Harvey and Peacock henceforward decried this possibility.[119] The French government offered a fresh credit, but the Bank declined it as insufficient. Although the United States government felt unable to help, Harrison and Morgans urged the Bank to use bank rate and exchange controls, and to 'fight to the last minute hoping that something might happen'. The Bank told them that there was no way of 'stemming the tide'.[120] The Bank also allowed the exchange rate to fall and gold to be lost, in order to demonstrate the 'inevitability' of its decision.[121]

[116] Financial Situation Committee, 17 Sept. 1931, CAB 27/462.
[117] Rodd (at BIS) to Harvey, 19 Sept. 1931, in Thompson-McCausland, 'Crisis', 42; Sayers, *Bank of England*, 404.
[118] Thompson–McCausland, 'Crisis', 49; Sayers, *Bank of England*, 411 (which, however, assumes this was also the ministerial intention).
[119] E.g., Harvey in 'Note of Meeting', 18 Sept. 1931, PREM 1/97.
[120] Harrison–Harvey conversations, 19 Sept. 1931, FRBNY Harrison papers; Morgan & Co to Morgan Grenfell, tm 31/2461, 20 Sept. 1931, MGC 'Gold Standard 1931'.
[121] BoE Cte, 18 Sept. 1931; Sayers, *Bank of England*, 406. For the gold loss presented as the last straw, see Harvey to Brennan, 20 Sept. 1931, BoE G3/310/318.

Only after the close of business and around £18m. in further exchange losses was MacDonald recalled from Chequers (Snowden being unavailable), to face a *fait accompli*. Harvey informed him that the pound would continue to be supported on Saturday morning, 19 September, in order to allow time over the weekend to prepare financial opinion for the shock. In the meantime the Bank should be authorised to suspend gold payments, with legislation to be passed on Monday.[122] During Saturday, 19 September, Baldwin, Samuel, and Hoare, were informed, the latter to allow the effect upon the rupee to be considered. As parliamentary co-operation would be necessary to rush the bill through all its stages, MacDonald informed Henderson on the 20th. The Bank took all the important decisions, in consultation with the chairmen of the clearing banks and Stock Exchange, and where necessary with Treasury officials and Hankey, as Cabinet and Privy Council secretary. Bank rate would be raised to 6 per cent. The Stock Exchange would be closed. Banks would remain open, though proclamations for a Bank Holiday were prepared in case of any panic. British banks would impose informal restrictions on exchange transactions, and foreign banks in London were asked to co-operate. Bankers and officials drafted the press statement, announcement to foreign governments, and the Gold Standard (Amendment) Bill. The Cabinet was informed late on Sunday afternoon, 20 September – four weeks almost to the hour after its Labour predecessor had disintegrated.

The National government did not suffer a similar fate. Its survival of the loss of the gold standard appears so effortless that in retrospect it can seem as if no problem existed. Of course the government was assisted by its very character as a broad-based coalition, commanding wide political confidence. Despite foreign financiers' anxiety about the effects of an election, it also commanded financial and business support for its reassertion of sound budgetary practice. Nevertheless it had suffered a major reverse with large repercussions, creating many difficulties in policy and presentation, and its survival unscathed required considerable exertions of political will.

One repercussion was a 'battle royal with the Viceroy and his Council'.[123] This renewed crisis in London–Delhi relations again not only had great implications for India but gave important indications of the Cabinet's state of mind. India Office experts met throughout

---

[122] 'Note of Meeting, 9.45 pm', between MacDonald, Harvey, Peacock, and Treasury officials, 18 Sept. 1931, PREM 1/97.
[123] N. to H. Chamberlain, 26 Sept. 1931, NC 18/1/756.

the weekend of 19–20 September to consider the implications of sterling devaluation for Indian monetary policy. They decided that the risk of a 'headlong' flight from the rupee, and consequent massive depreciation, inflation, and default, was too great to allow any other course than maintenance of the existing sterling–rupee ratio.[124] Perhaps from a genuine slip over the time difference between London and Delhi, but more likely in order to ensure that Schuster had no chance to implement his 8 September proposal to unpeg the rupee, Hoare informed the Government of India of the gold standard suspension only minutes before Indian financial markets were due to open on the 21st. Schuster, however, had received the news from a press agency ninety minutes earlier. He had time enough to obtain from Willingdon an Ordinance suspending sterling exchange dealings, in the belief that otherwise the British crisis would precipitate the 'disaster' of panic rupee sales.[125]

The disagreement between the British and Indian governments' prognostications was both genuine and absolute. Hoare reacted abruptly to Schuster's action. He insisted upon immediate cancellation of the Ordinance, instructed Bombay and Calcutta officials to disregard the Viceroy's orders, and informed the Round Table Conference that the exchange rate would be maintained.[126] No financial damage resulted from Hoare's contradiction of Government of India measures, because the Ordinance had also ordered the closure of Indian exchanges and banks for three days. The shock to the Government of India itself was nonetheless immense. Willingdon felt outraged by the subversion of his authority: 'no Viceroy had ever received a communication of that sort from any Secretary of State'.[127] He and his Council were also furious at the India Office's refusal to accept their advice and appreciate the strength of nationalist opposition to further depletion of India's currency reserves. They responded with blackmail: they would cancel the Ordinance only if the British government supported the exchange with an immediate £50m. sterling credit.[128]

[124] Hoare to Finance Department, Government of India, tms 2756, 2787, 2803, 20, 22, and 23 Sept., app. to Cabinet 63 (31), 23 Sept. 1931.
[125] Willingdon to Hoare, tms 789, 791, 21 and 22 Sept. 1931, Templewood Indian papers 11/18, 19; Finance Department, Government of India to Hoare, tm 2364, 22 Sept., app. to Cabinet 63(31), 23 Sept. 1931.
[126] Hoare to Willingdon, tm 2761, 21 Sept. 1931, Templewood Indian papers 11/18.
[127] Willingdon to Hoare, 22 Sept. 1931, Templewood Indian papers 5/7–8.
[128] Finance Department, Government of India to Hoare, tm 2364, 22 Sept. 1931, app. to Cabinet 63(31), 23 Sept. 1931.

Hoare compounded his offence in renewed differences over the Indian budget. Schuster, having failed to shake Hoare by his resignation threat of the 14th, agreed to attempt voluntary salary cuts. But he and the Viceroy's Council rejected the cotton excise as politically provocative. Hoare and the Cabinet, however, remained as anxious about Conservative party opinion as about the Indian financial crisis, while loss of the gold standard had revived anxiety about the electoral prospects in Britain. With uncertainty about the public mood increased, the Cabinet could not 'afford to sacrifice the Lancashire seats'. Instead of an excise, Hoare proposed that the intended cotton duty should give a preference for Lancashire over foreign imports – a measure almost equally provocative to nationalist opinion.[129]

Hoare informed the Government of India that both prongs of his policy had unanimous Cabinet support, and that the Treasury still refused any sterling credit.[130] But Willingdon and his Council were now in no mood to yield easily on either the exchange or the cotton duty. On 23 September they telegraphed their rejection of Hoare's rupee policy: 'we are all united in this, and unless you can meet us it will be impossible for us to carry on as a Government'.[131] This renewed resignation threat, now including the Viceroy himself as well as his Council, constituted an unprecedented act of defiance. In London it was treated with the greatest seriousness. An emergency Cabinet attended by India Office and Treasury officials stood by its previous decision on the exchange and would have liked to force Schuster's dismissal.[132] Nevertheless, alarmed by the prospect of resignations, it despatched a series of extraordinarily tense and suppliant appeals to Delhi. Hoare sent a 'very full explanatory telegram' to justify his policy. Reading, as an ex-Viceroy, asked Willingdon 'not to leave the bridge when the ship is in such dire distress'. MacDonald and Baldwin on the Cabinet's behalf pleaded with him 'to stand by us in the greatest Imperial emergency since the War'. Schuster's policy, a break-up of the Viceroy's Council, public knowledge of conflict between London and Delhi – any of these threatened 'incalculable disaster for India'. Concerted resignations

[129] Hoare to Willingdon, tm 10-U, 22 Sept. 1931, Templewood Indian papers, 13/12–13.
[130] Cabinet 62(31), 22 Sept. 1931; Hoare to Willingdon, tms 2783, 10-U, 22 Sept. 1931, Templewood Indian papers 11/20. See Sankey diary, 22 Sept. 1931, for at least one Cabinet member disliking Hoare's dictatorial manner.
[131] Willingdon to Hoare, tm 794, 23 Sept. 1931, app. to Cabinet 63(31) of same date.
[132] Cunliffe-Lister in Amery diary, 23 Sept. 1931 (*LSA* II, 203); Cabinet 63(31).

13 The Earl of Willingdon and Lady Willingdon, early 1931

'would be comparable to the resignations of a general staff in the face of an enemy'.[133]

Under this barrage, Willingdon and Schuster gave way and

[133] Hoare to Finance Department, Government of India, tm 2803, 23 Sept. 1931, app. to Cabinet 63(31); Reading to Willingdon, and MacDonald and Baldwin to Willingdon, tms 12-U, 13-U, both 24 Sept. 1931, Templewood Indian papers 13/15, 16–18.

withdrew the Ordinance.[134] But the Cabinet remained nervous of renewed differences,[135] and having gained the main point became conciliatory. The 24 September appeals had been accompanied with promises of British government assistance, if necessary, with India's sterling payments. On the 25th the Cabinet anticipated Schuster's rejection of a preference for British cotton imports and agreed that it had 'no alternative but to give way'.[136] Hoare made elaborate apologies to Willingdon for his interventions on 21 September, although when in October it became apparent that the Government of India's fears about the rupee exchange had been misplaced, he hinted at retribution through abolition of the fiscal autonomy convention.[137] Later, however, when voluntary salary cuts proved insufficient, the Cabinet conceded that service contracts would have to be adjusted by legislation during the next Parliament.

Apart from its importance for imperial financial policy, containment of the Indian currency and budget crises helped to preserve not just the Round Table Conference but also the National government itself. The Cabinet's appeals on 23–4 September reflected real anxiety about Indian finance, and about the damaging effects which Government of India resignations would have upon Indian nationalist and Conservative party opinion. Even so, assessed simply as a response to the Indian problem the appeals were an over-reaction. Willingdon and his Council were unlikely actually to have resigned: the consequences for Indian financial and political stability were all too plain. The Cabinet's appeals more accurately expressed its nervous tension arising from British political conditions, a sense of vulnerability in the immediate aftermath of the collapse of its policy *raison d'être*, defence of the gold standard. The potential for political embarrassment and electoral disaster was manifest: the Labour opposition's improved opportunity to present National government policy as misconceived, and to persuade large parts of the electorate that the cuts were unnecessary. The danger of financial panic and economic dislocation seemed as great: a destruction of both foreign and domestic confidence in British banks and the pound, chaos in export dealings, and sharp increases in import prices.

In the event, abandonment of what had for months been an

---

[134] Note added to Cabinet 63(31), 23 Sept. 1931.
[135] N. to H. Chamberlain, 26 Sept. 1931, NC 18/1/756.
[136] Cabinet 64(31), 25 Sept. 1931. See Willingdon to Hoare, tm 9-U, and Hoare to Willingdon, tm 15-U, both 26 Sept., in CP249(31), 28 Sept. 1931.
[137] Hoare to Willingdon, 2 and 9 Oct. 1931, Templewood Indian papers 1/21–27, 28–37.

increasingly artificial exchange rate relieved pressures in the financial markets, and proved to have unexpected economic benefits. In that sense, it may be that the efforts made by bankers, officials, and ministers from 19 to 21 September to preserve financial confidence were largely redundant. But those efforts had a further importance: they rescued the political reputations of the National government and its components. In a tacit collusion to limit the political as much as the financial damage, bankers very largely did the Cabinet's work for it. The Bank of England's preparations for suspension had been concerned to make it appear unavoidable – the result not of any domestic failings but 'of developments abroad for which we are not responsible'.[138] The aim had been to avoid any appearance of 'irresponsible devaluation', which might shatter British credit abroad and set 'a damaging precedent to...other countries'.[139] Hence the preliminary warnings to the French and American governments, the decision to allow last-minute gold losses, an admission that £200m. in gold and foreign exchange had been expended in sterling defence, but also an assurance that the Bank and government credits of July and August would be repaid in their gold values. In subsequent public statements and in communications with foreign bankers, Bank of England directors presented the problem as wholly due to external causes.[140] They gave no hint of their own belief that confidence in sterling had been compromised by Conservative pressure for a general election.[141] Ministers departed from the Bank's presentation only in implying that Labour opposition and the naval unrest bore some of the blame.[142] The Bank also helped prevent a further shock to financial confidence and another political embarrassment by organising a City rescue of a failing merchant bank, after the Treasury had decided that the Cabinet could hardly lend money to a bank while simultaneously imposing cuts in living standards.[143]

[138] MacDonald and Snowden (drafted by Bank directors and Treasury officials) to Stimson and Flandin, 18 Sept. 1931, BoE G1/459.

[139] Thompson–McCausland, 'Crisis', 44.

[140] See, e.g., Harvey to Brennan, and to Vissering, 20 and 25 Sept. 1931, G3/210/318, 335.

[141] For private expressions of this belief, see Harvey on the 19th reported in Samuel memo, 'The Present Situation', CP243(31), 24 Sept. 1931, and Peacock in Wigram memo, 28 Sept. 1931, RA GV K2331(1)/18.

[142] Snowden in *HC Deb*, 256, col. 1203, 21 Sept. 1931, and broadcast in *The Times*, 22 Sept. 1931.

[143] For the Anglo-South American Bank's problems and rescue, see Sayers, *Bank of England*, 263–6. For Hopkins refusing government assistance 'for political reasons', see BoE Cte, 23 and 25 Sept. 1931.

There was also considerable anxiety about the reactions of the general population, especially as MacDonald, Snowden, Runciman, and other ministers had answered Labour opposition criticism with claims that abandonment of the gold standard might cause German-style hyperinflation and destroy personal savings. The Board of Trade asked food wholesalers to co-operate in avoiding immediate price rises, hinting that the alternative would be government control. The clearing banks wanted to remain open, in order to prevent alarm: but they stressed the 'vital importance' of good preparation of the press.[144] MacDonald proposed a committee of experts, especially those 'having influence with labour', to advise the newspapers.[145] But this committee proved unnecessary, since the press readily followed official briefings and Snowden made a highly effective broadcast on 21 September. '[T]he pound', he declared, 'will not go the way of the mark'; 'there is not the slightest cause for the least anxiety about the money you have in the banks'; it would be 'silly...to indulge in panic buying and hoarding of commodities'.[146]

The bankers' greatest service to the Cabinet was in endorsing a neat Treasury formula for the official press notice, which immediately became a key ministerial instrument:

It is one thing to go off the gold standard with an unbalanced budget and uncontrolled inflation; it is quite another thing to take this measure, not because of internal financial difficulties, but because of excessive withdrawals of borrowed capital.[147]

This explained why leaving the gold standard would not now be the 'disaster' which ministers had earlier predicted. The restoration of sound government finance would prevent massive currency depreciation. As a statement about financial psychology or, really, an assessment of how financial markets would respond to the presentation of policy, this proved to be perfectly accurate. But the statement also made a government failure look very much like a government success. Most important of all, it justified pressing on with the Economy Bill.

At the 20 September Cabinet meeting MacDonald suggested that

[144] BoE Cte, 19 Sept. 1931.
[145] Notes of meetings, 18 and 19 Sept. 1931, PREM 1/97.
[146] *The Times*, 22 Sept. 1931.
[147] Cabinet 60(31), 20 Sept. 1931. For Bank directors and clearing bank chairmen helping the Treasury prepare the draft, see BoE Cte, 19 Sept. 1931.

owing to 'the new situation' some cuts in working-class and teachers' incomes might be mitigated. He was genuinely concerned about the hardships which the Economy Bill would inflict, but he was also sensitive to Labour opinion. More than anyone else MacDonald had justified cuts on the argument that prices had fallen, yet like others he had also said that leaving the gold standard would result in prices rising. It 'might therefore be represented in Parliament' that the justification for cuts had ceased, and 'the opposition [to them] would be strengthened'. Conservative and Liberal leaders, however, had wanted retrenchment quite irrespective of concern about the gold standard, in order to balance the budget without confiscatory levels of taxation. Neville Chamberlain – 'hard & dogmatic' in Mac-Donald's view – led the insistence that the Cabinet 'should not falter'. The clinching argument, soothing MacDonald's anxieties, was that of the Treasury's press notice.[148]

Next morning, however, even Chamberlain accepted that the Cabinet had to falter a little. The Admiralty had reports from commanding officers, naval intelligence, and MI5 that the Invergordon protest had gained further support and would be repeated in the home ports on the following morning: 'the Fleet...was completely out of hand'. The protest had originally been spontaneous but now, it was asserted, 'Communist agents' were active. Petty officers had begun to join the protest and, as the authorities could not be certain that army and air force personnel would obey orders to coerce the sailors, there were 'no means...available to enforce discipline at such short notice'. The Admiralty thought it had no alternative to further concession, reducing all naval pay cuts to a standard 10 per cent.[149] The Cabinet also had to consider that a further outbreak of naval protest, again damaging financial confidence, could not be risked at the delicate moment when sterling had just been floated and when a panic might cause its value to plummet. With the public now expecting price rises, it seemed even more likely than on the 16th that a naval protest might be imitated by other recipients of cuts.

The position had become very dangerous, and the Cabinet

---

[148] Cabinet 60(31), 20 Sept. 1931; MacDonald diary, 20 Sept. 1931.

[149] 'Summary of Statement by Sir A. Chamberlain to Cabinet', 21 Sept. 1931, CAB 23/90B; N. Chamberlain diary, 22 Sept. 1931; Hankey diary, 26 Sept. 1931 (Roskill, *Hankey* II, 556–7). See also Stanhope (Admiralty undersecretary) to Bridgeman, 21 Sept. 1931, Bridgeman papers, for prospect of 'Bloodshed tomorrow'.

thought itself 'helpless'.[150] It nevertheless retained enough self-possession to conceal its withdrawal. As before, the concession to the Navy was camouflaged within a wider concession, presented as fulfilling the promise of the 16th to investigate hardship cases. MacDonald announced on 21 September that all pay cuts for lower ranks of the defence forces, for the police and for teachers would be reduced to 10 per cent. The £3·5m. involved would be obtained by administrative cuts elsewhere.[151]

Privately, Cabinet ministers felt 'humiliated'.[152] But the public presentation worked. There was no naval trouble on the 22nd, and the real reason for the concessions was not suspected. MacDonald's announcement on the 21st encouraged Henderson to offer no official Labour opposition to the Gold Standard (Amendment) Bill, which despite unofficial Labour obstruction was successfully rushed through all its stages in an evening.

The Cabinet, then, managed to keep up appearances. The departure from the gold standard could easily have made it look foolish. Instead, after desperate activity behind the scenes to contain the naval trouble and Indian crisis, it retained the impression of firmness. It was helped by the performance of sterling, which fell from par ($4.86) not calamitously but in stages and steadied at around $3.85 at the end of the week, and by that of Government stocks, which followed a similar pattern after the Stock Exchange opened on the 23rd. Nevertheless the events of 18–21 September had transformed the context of policy, and promised to have a large effect upon the political prospects.

[150] N. Chamberlain diary, 22 Sept. 1931.
[151] Cabinet 61(31), and MacDonald in *HC Deb*, 256, col. 1271, both 21 Sept. 1931.
[152] N. to H. Chamberlain, 26 Sept. 1931, NC 18/1/756.

PART IV

Crisis overcome

CHAPTER 12

The political reconstruction

The present situation is a curious vindication of Safety First as a cry.

Bridgeman to Baldwin, 25 October 1931

The election programme of the Labour party...is the most fantastic and impracticable ever put before the electors...This is not Socialism. It is Bolshevism run mad.

Snowden broadcast, 17 October 1931

'The Commander-in-Chief of the progressive forces...and his two leading generals, nauseated by the disorderly, disrespectful, disobedient and generally incompetent crowd behind them, escaped one night into the fortified camp of the defenders of privilege and property, bargained with them for pride of place, turned about face and marched, with bands and flags flying, and massacred their old followers...A comic incident marked this dramatic event. A little old man with his daughter, his son and one follower, watched from a lonely hill-top, this act of treachery. He yelled with all his might against the advancing army; nobody listened to him, nobody cared. For all remembered that thirteen years ago, as a great progressive leader, he had done exactly the same thing himself...'

B. Webb diary, 28 October 1931[1]

A SOCIALIST PLATFORM

The departure from the gold standard removed one of the premises of policy since 1920, and one of the bases for the emergency government alliance of August. By doing so it offered all parties and political groups an opportunity to reassess their position; to reconsider their financial and economic policies, and their political strategies. In the Labour party the first effect was to expose the

---

[1] Respectively Baldwin papers 45/121–2 (slightly misprinted in Williamson, 250); *The Times*, 19 Oct. 1931; Cole, 293–4.

distance between Henderson and most of his colleagues, back-benchers, and the TUC. A leadership crisis was avoided, but only by a second and decisive defeat of Henderson's own preferences. This defeat had large consequences for the Labour party's future.

In mid September Henderson remained 'very depressed & upset' at what the August crisis had done to the Labour party.[2] In his anxieties and aims, he came close to the MacDonald of the period from October 1930 to August 1931. Leading the Labour party was, he found, 'worry and toil'. Disliking his nearest colleagues' attitudes, he encouraged the Webbs to prepare an alternative party pro-gramme, just as MacDonald had cast about ineffectually for ideas.[3] He 'hated the position into which he had been driven against his own wish'. Dreading a sterling collapse, alarmed that the Labour Cabinet's resignation and subsequent Labour manifesto had estranged moderate opinion, and fearful of the electoral conse-quences, he became desperate to demonstrate some commitment to putting 'the country first'. He wanted to restore Labour's credentials as a national party, and so edge it back into the political centre. He clutched at a straw offered by a private appeal from Seely on 18 September for all-party co-operation, expostulating that the Labour Cabinet's differences over cuts had been narrow and could still be 'surmounted by negotiation and agreement'.[4] When during the 20th MacDonald made urgent efforts to contact him, Henderson persuaded himself that MacDonald's intention was to regain Labour party support.[5]

In deliberate contrast to MacDonald's action in August, Hender-son resolved to take no decision on such an overture without approval from the party executives, TUC General Council, and Labour MPs. But personally he had 'an open mind as to what it may be necessary to do'.[6] What he hoped for is unclear. Unless his own reluctance to acknowledge the hardening of Labour and TUC feeling had totally blinded him to political realities, he cannot have supposed that the party would consider supporting (still less entering) the existing National government. Probably he thought Cabinet disagreements over an election, combined with its post-Invergordon concession about hardship cases, might be leading

---

[2] Sankey diary, 12 and 13 Sept. 1931; B. Webb diary, 20 Sept. 1931 (Cole, 287; MacKenzie
     IV, 258).   [3] B. Webb diary, 20 and 21 Sept. 1931 (Cole, 287-9).
[4] Seely to Reading, 18 Sept. 1931, Reading papers, F118/131.
[5] B. Webb diary, 20, 21, and 23 Sept. 1931 (Cole, 288-90).
[6] B. Webb diary, 20 and 21 Sept. 1931 (Cole, 287, 289).

towards a reconstructed government prepared to mitigate the expenditure cuts. Such a change might vindicate Labour opposition to the cuts and enable the party leadership to co-operate with and perhaps even rejoin a MacDonald Cabinet, thereby erasing the damaging impression that it had run away.

Henderson was therefore doubly surprised when, on reaching Downing Street late on the 20th, MacDonald reported that the gold standard would have to be suspended. Sharing MacDonald's fears of the financial consequences but also anxious to display Labour responsibility, Henderson promised Labour assistance in the necessary legislation. Although his Commons speech next day on the Gold Standard (Amendment) Bill declared that the government's budget programme had failed, asked for it to be reconsidered, and sought clarification of the Treasury's new powers, he nevertheless offered Labour party abstention from the division as its contribution to national unity.[7]

The result was revolt in the parliamentary party. For most of Henderson's colleagues and backbench followers, events since 16 September had confirmed the financial and political analyses they had developed since the fall of the Labour government. They regarded abandonment of the gold standard less as a potential financial and economic disaster for the country than as a palpable political disaster for the government. Coming after the Invergordon protest and accompanied by concessions on expenditure cuts, they thought it had set the National government on the run and they intended to chase it to the death. In the 21 September debate Wise of the Finance and Trade Committee, Addison from the front bench, and an assortment of ILP and other Labour MPs all ignored Henderson's advice and attacked the government and the Gold Standard (Amendment) Bill. Any shred of justification for 'a disgraceful Economy Bill and discreditable Budget' had now gone. In order to 'protect the poor people...against exploitation' the cost of living should be controlled. The proposed exchange controls would be useless without comprehensive control over the City.[8] One hundred and forty-eight Labour MPs divided against the Closure, 114 defied Henderson and voted against the Second Reading, and

---

[7] MacDonald diary, 20 Sept. 1931; Henderson, *HC Deb*, 256, cols. 1299–304, 21 Sept. 1931.
[8] *HC Deb*, 256, cols. 1304–11 (Wise), 1345–50 (Addison) and, for a notable assault by Bevan, cols. 1332–9.

193, including five ex-Cabinet ministers, supported a Wise–Addison amendment to extend controls to banks and British-owned funds.

Henderson's speech brought to a head not just dissatisfaction at his attitude but suspicion of his intentions, already fuelled by newspaper speculation that he was disposed to join the National government.[9] At party meetings on 22 September, Henderson was challenged about these newspaper stories. Susan Lawrence – previously a Henderson 'idolater' – condemned his failure to give 'a fighting lead' against the Bill, and harsh words were exchanged between Henderson and Addison.[10] The suspicions lingered. As moved by Lawrence at the party's national executive on 28 September, the purpose of expelling the MacDonaldites from the Labour party – explicitly (and insultingly) on the analogy of the Mosleyite expulsions – was to end any further notions of Labour opposition rapprochement with them.[11]

Henderson was furious at this sabotage of his attempt to re-establish Labour responsibility, at Addison for encouraging 'very definite opposition' to the Gold Standard (Amendment) Bill at 'so serious' a moment for the party no less than the country, and at implications that he harboured thoughts of betraying the party.[12] Rumours spread that he had threatened to resign the leadership.[13] So long as Cabinet intentions about an election remained uncertain, Henderson possibly continued to hope that if it broke up the Labour party might be propelled back into government alongside Mac-Donald. He certainly appears to have resisted the MacDonaldite expulsions. Proposals for restoring Labour unity made to Mac-Donald by two Labour backbench MPs, Malone and Dunnico, suggest that Henderson's attitude did not wholly lack support within the parliamentary party.[14]

Yet Malone and Dunnico themselves had little importance, and in

[9] For *Manchester Guardian*, 18 and 19 Sept. 1931, see Thorpe, 'Henderson', 130.

[10] PLP, 22 Sept. 1931; Malone reported in Rosenberg memo, 22 Sept. 1931, JRM 1314 (which suggests one critic – Thurtle – was inspired by Lansbury, his father-in-law); Henderson to Addison, 23 Sept. 1931, Addison papers 94. For Lawrence, see Usher to MacDonald, 23 Sept. 1931, JRM 1314, and B. Webb diary, 16 Sept. 1931.

[11] LPNEC, 28 Sept. 1931: the proposal had not been on the agenda.

[12] PLP, 22 Sept. 1931; Malone in Rosenberg memos, 22 and 23 Sept. 1931, and Usher to MacDonald, 23 Sept. 1931, all JRM 1314; Henderson to Addison, Addison papers 94 (see Morgan, *Portrait*, 205).

[13] Malone in Rosenberg memo, 23 Sept. 1931, JRM 1314 (Marquand, 661).

[14] For approaches, see Rosenberg memos, 22 and 23 Sept. 1931, JRM 1314, and MacDonald diary, 27 Sept, 1931 (Marquand, 662). For a Malone-Dunnico 'plot', see Thorpe, 'Henderson', 130–3. For other reunion hopefuls, see Arnold to MacDonald, 27 Sept. 1931, JRM 1176; Turner, *HC Deb*, 257, col. 238, 29 Sept. 1931.

the nature of overtures they had reason to inflate the number of Labour MPs who sympathised with them. The harsh realities were that Henderson had gravely misjudged the mood of the parliamentary party, and a majority of MPs had repeatedly defied his leadership. He cannot have mistaken these latest manifestations of outright opposition to the National government. The importance of the 20–8 September incidents lay less in the indications of Henderson's moderation and potential support than in the demonstration that all other Labour leaders and the greater majority of Labour MPs rejected any accommodation with 'capitalist' (and apostate) politicians and policies. Henderson understood. Recoiling from the risks of falling into the same dilemma which MacDonald had faced during August, and into a leadership crisis which could only damage the party further, he quickly reverted to his late August position of leading from behind. Speaking on 25 September he adopted the whole of the parliamentary executive's new programme, with its specific proposals for the 'drastic reconstruction of economic life'.[15] At the next parliamentary party meeting, he completely denied any overtures to ministers.[16] Thereafter his acquiescence in party pressure was eased in two ways. Conversation with Keynes corroborated his colleagues' view that there was life beyond the gold standard.[17] Then, the realisation that the MacDonaldites, Conservatives, and Liberals might remain together in an anti-Labour coalition suggested that a radical platform might have strategic advantages.

MacDonald's decision to lead an emergency government against the Labour party had seemed bad enough; his evident willingness to lead an election campaign against it appeared despicable. For most Labour members it cut the last remaining threads of sympathy or regret. Former admirers like Morrison started to bury their pasts.[18] Together with the Cabinet's decision to persist with the Finance and Economy Bills despite the loss of the gold standard, it greatly reinforced the notion of 'capitalist' conspiracy and sharpened a siege

[15] Burnley speech, *The Times*, 26 Sept. 1931. Henderson's policy statements closely followed the PLP 'Draft Resolutions' for the party conference, 24 Sept. 1931 (copy in Angell papers BB1–7). These were based on the work of the PLP's Finance and Trade Committee, and so in lineal descent from the 27 August manifesto.

[16] PLP, 29 Sept. 1931.   [17] Dalton diary, 1 Oct. 1931 (Dalton, 290–1).

[18] Morrison had tried to remain friendly: see Morrison to MacDonald, 17 Sept. 1931, Morrison papers. For shock at MacDonald's intention, see Morrison and Shinwell speeches, *The Times*, 28 Sept. 1931. Shaw, another near-MacDonaldite, had resigned his parliamentary candidature after the Cabinet's fall, but now withdrew this and stood at the election.

mentality. Although the probability of electoral pacts between the National government partners now made it seem unlikely that the Labour party could win a general election, a fighting spirit was sustained by anger and righteousness, and by a hope to do well by the strength of their case and the setbacks in government policy. As the Labour party conference of 5-8 October showed, the movement also drew closer together and Henderson was restored to his pedestal.[19] Only Maxton and his ILP hardliners stood out, doubting the party's new socialist commitment and still refusing to submit to PLP standing orders. As a result they were denied official Labour party endorsement for the election.[20] But relations between the parliamentary and TUC leaders were now 'much improved', assisted by the removal of earlier differences over monetary policy through suspension of the gold standard – which Bevin celebrated as a personal vindication[21] – and by General Council approval of the parliamentary party's new programme.[22]

This programme had been produced by Graham and the Finance and Trade Committee. After near-unanimous adoption by the party conference, Laski reworked it into an election manifesto.[23] The commitment to physical and 'democratic' controls was unequivocal. Besides disarmament, reparation and war debt cancellation, Indian constitutional reform, and reversal of the unemployment and social service cuts, the programme promised public ownership of the banking and credit system, coal mines, power, transport, iron and steel industry, and land. It also promised National Investment, Import, Export, and Agricultural Marketing and Wages Boards, and participation of workers in the management of socialised enterprises. The conference debate hammered home the point: party leaders intended that no Labour government should ever again be 'the caretaker of the existing order of society'.[24] Capitalism was 'an

---

[19] B. Webb diary, 10 Oct. 1931 (Cole, 291; MacKenzie IV, 261); Trevelyan to his wife, 5 Oct. 1931, Trevelyan papers Ex 125(2). Against the former's observation of party disillusionment can be set the latter's record of a 'very vigorous and hopeful spirit'.

[20] *LPACR 1931*, 174–6, 178–9, 5 Oct.; LPNEC, 7 Oct. 1931.

[21] Speech in *LPACR 1931*, 191–2, 6 Oct.

[22] Dalton diary, 2–8 Oct. 1931. For General Council approval, see LPNEC, 28 Sept. 1931. Cf. Thorpe, 'Henderson', 135: citing Dalton diary, 28 Sept. 1931 (partly in Dalton, 285), this implies Bevin and Citrine hostility. The mss diary, however, shows that their requested 'large alterations' were merely verbal and did not at all concern the fundamentals of socialisation.

[23] LPNEC, 28 Sept. and 5 Oct. 1931; Dalton diary, 2–8 and 7 Oct. 1931. The programme was published as conference resolutions in *The Times*, 30 Sept. 1931.

[24] B. Webb diary, 10 Oct. 1931 (Cole, 292; MacKenzie IV, 262).

accident', and was now 'breaking to pieces before their eyes'.[25]
Morrison declared that the limits to reform within capitalism had
been reached, Cripps that 'the only thing that is not inevitable now
is gradualism'.[26]

A 'NATIONAL' PLATFORM

The National government's failure to preserve the gold standard and
the Labour opposition's determination to persist with 'socialism'
together had an effect common to all the National partners. They
confirmed the beliefs that an immediate return to the old three-party
battle would be far too dangerous, and that the National government
should convert itself into an anti-socialist alliance. The other effect,
however, was to widen the earlier differences over how the National
government should be continued. The policy issue upon which these
differences turned now became definitely free trade against
protection. So while the government's external politics were those of
a newly overt anti-socialism, its internal politics were a reversion to
the conflicts of 1923 or 1903–13. The attempts to resolve these
internal differences involved manoeuvres of much complexity but
also great importance, as they converted the temporary alliance of
August into more lasting, and in some cases permanent, realignments.

Stiffened by the opposition of Liberal meetings on 17 and 18
September to an election, Samuel's and Lloyd George's immediate
reaction to gold standard suspension was to 'jump at the idea' that
it made an early election unjustifiable. To them it seemed obvious
that devaluation, by increasing import prices and cheapening export
prices, made a tariff unnecessary. All cause for internal Cabinet
policy disagreement had been removed.[27] In a memorandum to the
Cabinet, Samuel argued that pressure for an election had precipitated devaluation, and that if the pressure continued the depreciation of sterling might become unstoppable. An election held
when the expected price rises coincided with imposition of the cuts
and means test would inflame the unemployed, possibly leading to
riots and 'loss of life', and might result in a Labour victory. On the
other hand, the existing Cabinet could now stay in office with the

---

[25] Clynes and Pethick-Lawrence in *LPACR 1931*, 177, 188, 5 and 8 Oct.
[26] Ibid., 177, 205.
[27] Samuel in N. to I. Chamberlain, 19 (continued on 20) Sept. 1931, NC 18/1/755; Lloyd
George statement, *The Times*, 21 Sept. 1931.

agreed purpose of stabilising sterling and mitigating the impact of depreciation. Here Samuel, in an attempt to appease the Conservatives, offered an important concession which became the basic position of his Liberal group. While remaining opposed to dogmatic protectionism, if – after extensive inquiry – it could be shown that tariffs were 'indispensable' to restore the trade balance, Liberal ministers would assent to them as a matter of expediency.[28]

Samuel knew that MacDonald, deeply depressed and frightened by the suspension of the gold standard, had come to similar conclusions. But MacDonald was not so frightened that he had any interest in the Dunnico–Malone overture or in conciliating Henderson. On the contrary, his contempt for the Labour opposition hardened still further, because he thought it had shown itself 'hostile to the national interest' by contributing 'to a very considerable extent' to loss of the gold standard.[29] Rather, MacDonald now considered the financial conditions so threatening that the existing government had to continue. As a constructive objective he suggested that suspension offered the 'finest chance ever given' to persuade the American and French governments to agree to a world financial conference, an idea originally inserted for cosmetic purposes in Snowden's speeches on the suspension.[30] MacDonald told Samuel that 'there is not even a theoretical justification for an election now'. He also told Hore-Belisha that his Simonite Liberal petition had become redundant.[31]

The reactions of Conservatives were, however, completely the reverse. For them the release from anxieties about the gold standard removed the financial arguments against an election, while political tactics made it seem still more essential.[32] Depending on circumstances, delay in delivering a full protectionist programme might either cause tensions within the Conservative party and disillusionment among Conservative voters (if the world depression

---

[28] Samuel, 'The Present Situation', CP243(31), 24 Sept. 1931.

[29] MacDonald diary, 20 and 28 Sept. 1931; MacDonald to Wilson, 22 Sept. 1931, JRM 1540.

[30] MacDonald to Baldwin, 23 Sept. 1931, SB 44/166–9. See Snowden in Cabinet 60(31), and *HC Deb*, 256, col. 1296, 20 and 21 Sept. 1931.

[31] MacDonald to Samuel, 20 Sept. 1931, Samuel papers A/81/2 (Samuel, *Memoirs*, 209), and to Hore-Belisha, 21 Sept. 1931, JRM 1314. MacDonald's claim in the first of these that he would have opposed an election irrespective of suspension was designed specifically for Samuel's consumption, and may be disregarded as evidence of his position on 17–18 September.

[32] See Hoare to Willingdon, 25 Sept. 1931, Templewood Indian papers 1/16–20; N. Chamberlain and Amery in Amery diary, 20 Sept. 1931 (*LSA* II, 202); Baldwin and Hoare in Hankey diary, 26 Sept. 1931 (Roskill, *Hankey* II, 562).

deepened, commercial dumping increased, and employment and wages fell), or else weaken the wider political effectiveness of the tariff argument (if devaluation improved the trade balance). Worse, delay might bring continuously rising prices, leading to increasing resentment at the income cuts and higher taxes, and thereby allowing the Labour party to consolidate and extend its electoral support.

At the same time loss of the gold standard greatly strengthened earlier arguments against the Conservatives breaking up the 'national unity' and standing alone. An election fought independently by each National partner immediately after the government had failed in its express purpose would be a considerable risk. But a 'National' appeal under MacDonald, which could exploit the renewed atmosphere of crisis and fasten blame for the trouble upon the Labour opposition, would very likely result in a large electoral victory. These were not the calculations of Baldwin and other party leaders alone. Within days of suspension of the gold standard the party organisers and almost all Conservative backbench MPs, including the EIA protectionists, encouraged by City and business opinion, had arrived at the conclusion reached the previous week by Baldwin, that there should be a joint MacDonald–Baldwin–Simon protectionist appeal.[33] Neville Chamberlain even looked to this alliance crystallising into a 'National Party'. In order to strengthen the alliance against the new uncertainties and expected loss of free-trade support, he also seriously considered electoral arrangements with Mosley and the New party.[34]

Thomas, by now metamorphosed into an anti-Labour protectionist, also made it known that he still wanted a quick election.[35] So too did Simon and his Liberal supporters. Simon himself (this time with Amery's assistance) rebutted the devaluation argument against tariffs in the Commons, and began raising an election fund.[36] Despite MacDonald's rebuff, Hore-Belisha persisted with his petition

[33] For 1922 Committee, Middlemas and Barnes, *Baldwin*, 641: and for EIA members and City and business opinion, Croft, *My Life*, 194, and Amery diary, 23 and 24 Sept. 1931 (partly in *LSA* II, 203–4).

[34] N. to I. Chamberlain and to H. Chamberlain, 19 and 26 Sept. 1931, NC 18/1/755, 756. For Mosley's overture and negotiations, see below p. 446.

[35] Amery to Beaverbrook, 22 Sept. 1931, Beaverbrook papers C/5; Hankey diary, 26 Sept. 1931 (Roskill, *Hankey* II, 563).

[36] Simon in Buchan to his wife, 21 Sept. 1931, Tweedsmuir (NLS) papers; speech in *HC Deb*, 256, cols. 1668–71, 23 Sept. 1931; Amery diary, 24 Sept. 1931 (*LSA* II, 204); Simon to Inchcape, 24 Sept. 1931, Simon papers.

and obtained the signatures of some twenty-five Liberal MPs, including Simon, Hutchison, Brown, Collins, Kedward, Morris-Jones, Shakespeare, and Macpherson, but also Runciman.[37] When this became public knowledge and produced an open row within the Liberal parliamentary party,[38] Conservative leaders knew that their moment to force a Liberal split had come. On 24 September they agreed on 'the great importance of pitching [their] tariff demands high enough to make sure of getting rid of Samuel and, if possible, Reading'.[39]

So far, the events of 19–21 September had simply brought earlier Conservative thinking to a climax. However, they did produce one major shift, with large implications. On the 23rd Baldwin learnt that MacDonald had turned against an early election.[40] This concentrated Baldwin's mind upon the difficulty of MacDonald's own position, but also upon the potential embarrassments for the Conservative party if, in order to get an election, it had to take the blatantly partisan step of removing MacDonald. Baldwin answered this problem by proposing that Conservative leaders should promise to serve under MacDonald as Prime Minister not just until the election but in the next Parliament. Other party leaders accepted this almost by acclamation on 24 September.[41]

Perhaps, as Neville Chamberlain wrote, this displayed the Conservative party as 'a wonderful embodiment of good sense, patriotism and honesty'.[42] But it also represented a hard-headed assessment of its electoral chances in the more brittle conditions following the government setbacks and difficulties since 18 September. A National appeal under MacDonald appeared certain to succeed to a degree which a purely Conservative appeal, or even a Conservative–Simon Liberal appeal, seemed unlikely to do, if it succeeded at all. Even more than previously, MacDonald – and to a lesser extent Snowden and Thomas – seemed the decisive weapon against the Labour party. If the price of assured election success and the defeat of socialism was MacDonald continuing to lead the government, Conservatives thought it well worth paying. As for the

---

[37] Liberal memorial to MacDonald [22 Sept. 1931], JRM 1314. This contains 28 names, but a few Lloyd George Liberals signed under a misapprehension: see, e.g., Birkett to Hore-Belisha, 22 Sept. 1931, in Hyde, *Birkett*, 329.

[38] Parliamentary correspondent, *The Times*, 22 and 23 Sept. 1931.

[39] Conservative Business Committee decision, in Amery diary, 24 Sept. 1931 (*LSA* II, 204).

[40] MacDonald to Baldwin, 23 Sept. 1931, SB 44/166–9.

[41] Amery diary, 24 Sept. 1931 (*LSA* II, 203–4); N. Chamberlain diary, 24 Sept. 1931.

[42] Ibid. (see Feiling, *Chamberlain*, 195).

personal aspects, Baldwin himself had now learnt the attractions of power without ultimate responsibility, and become confident that in emulating Bonar Law's self-sacrifice of 1918 he would not suffer Austen Chamberlain's fate of 1922. Baldwin's prospective successor, Neville Chamberlain, comforted himself with the belief that even within the National government he remained the real power behind the throne, and gave Baldwin emphatic support.[43]

As Baldwin expected, the decision to offer MacDonald the premiership in the next Parliament smoothed matters. MacDonald accepted that continued Conservative insistence upon an early election meant that it could no longer be avoided, and decided that since he could remain Prime Minister he could respectably lead the election fight. However, Baldwin was mistaken in supposing that MacDonald had accepted his own idea of ditching the Lloyd George Liberals to achieve a protectionist platform,[44] just as Samuel was wrong in concluding that MacDonald had 'sold himself completely to the Conservatives'.[45]

One way or another, since June 1929 and especially since July 1931 MacDonald had borne responsibilities, endured workloads, and negotiated crises greater than those faced by any other living politician except Lloyd George. The personal strain had been enormous and had taken its toll. He was living close to nervous exhaustion, making him easily depressed and sometimes physically ill. On 21 September he suffered a collapse, and had to rest until the 25th. Over the next ten days Conservative and Liberal colleagues would complain that he was indecisive and self-contradictory. Yet MacDonald had his own clear objective and a good sense of how to reach it. Despite appearances, he managed the Conservative and Liberal leaders with great skill, and now succeeded in what he had so nearly achieved during August, keeping a split Cabinet together.[46]

MacDonald's resistance to an election collapsed because suspension of the gold standard had been less painful than he had expected, and because if the largest government partner supported by leading newspapers wanted an early election, continued political

---

[43] N. to H. Chamberlain, 26 Sept. 1931, NC 18/1/756; Amery diary, 24 Sept. 1931 (*LSA* II, 204).

[44] For Baldwin's interview with MacDonald, see Amery diary, 25 Sept. 1931 (*LSA* II, 204), and Hankey diary, 26 Sept. 1931 (Roskill, *Hankey* II, 563). For Baldwin's pledge to MacDonald, see Jones, *Dairy with Letters*, 56, 14 Sept. 1932.

[45] Reading memo, 8 pm, 25 Sept. 1931, Reading papers, F118/131.

[46] For contrasts in MacDonald's condition, see Hankey diary, 13 Sept. and 7 Oct. 1931 (Roskill, *Hankey* II, 553).

unsettlement would wreck all efforts at policy-making and financial stabilisation.[47] In a now well-practised manoeuvre, before the next Cabinet meeting he equipped himself with the instrument of Bank of England support. From Harvey he obtained the circumspect, but useful, advice that the 'existing uncertainty' about an election was 'undoubtedly harmful' to financial confidence, and that the government should as soon as possible end the uncertainty one way or another.[48] MacDonald also set fully in motion the organisation of his small group of personal followers into a National Labour electoral machine.[49] But he was perfectly conscious of the potential weaknesses and possible strengths of his own position. He saw the trap laid by Baldwin: his aim became to prevent the National government becoming a Conservative front, and himself a 'Tory slave'.[50] Against this the obvious guarantee would be retention of the Lloyd George Liberals within the government. He also understood that Conservative concession of his continued premiership was an admission that they needed him for electoral purposes, and that this gave him some leverage against them.

Given this insight, MacDonald took a firm and independent line with Baldwin and, on 28 September, with the Cabinet. Although he did not exclude a MacDonald–Baldwin–Simon appeal as a last resort, he kept his private view well hidden. Instead he argued that such a combination fighting on a protectionist platform would be interpreted by the electorate as a partisan device, destroying the advantages of a 'National' appeal and so assisting the Labour opposition. Therefore 'a national appeal must be made by those who have formed the National Government'. Both as a genuine 'national' approach and in order to accommodate the Lloyd George Liberals, this appeal should be for a 'doctor's mandate' – for power to take whatever measures seemed desirable, including tariffs 'should...conditions require it'.[51]

Probably prompted by MacDonald's enquiry, Bank of England

---

[47] Reading memo, 26 Sept. 1931, Reading papers F118/131; MacDonald, 'Notes...on a General Election', CP247(31), 26 Sept. 1931.

[48] BoE Cte, 28 Sept. 1931; Harvey to MacDonald, 28 Sept. 1931, BoE G3/210/336.

[49] Markham (for MacDonald) to Denman, 28 Sept. 1931, and for meeting of MacDonaldite MPs and peers, Denman memo, 30 Sept. 1931, Denman papers, 4, and see Denman, *Political Sketches*, 9–10. For arrangements, Glyn memo, 30 Sept. 1931, JRM 1778.

[50] MacDonald diary, 25 Sept. 1931; and MacDonald in Hankey diary, 26 Sept. 1931 (Roskill, *Hankey* II, 563), and in press briefing, 28 Sept. 1931, M. MacDonald papers, 6/2/44.

[51] MacDonald to Baldwin, 26 Sept. 1931, SB 44/170–1; MacDonald, 'Notes...on a General Election', CP247(31), 26 Sept. 1931; and see Hankey report of Cabinet discussion in Wigram memo, 8 pm, 28 Sept. 1931, RA GV K2331(1)/19.

directors, including Norman (now recovered), became active in informally recommending the same course as best for the sake of sterling.[52] But it was less solicitude for sterling than concern about party prospects which persuaded Conservative leaders to bend. They did not want to lose MacDonald and a 'national' appeal by appearing too intransigent. Accordingly, for the Cabinet on 29 September Neville Chamberlain produced a formula encapsulating MacDonald's idea. The election appeal should be for a mandate 'to carry through whatever plans may appear to us to be best adapted' to restore the economy, including power to control imports 'whether by prohibitions, tariffs or other measures', according to 'the necessities of the case'.[53]

The other half of MacDonald's tactics consisted of pressure upon the Lloyd George Liberals. He now encouraged the Simon group and Runciman,[54] not just because they might be used to replace existing Liberal ministers but because this potential made them an instrument for intimidating those ministers. He sought the co-operation of Grey, who obliged by telling Samuel that, because of 'increasing uncertainty', an election 'cannot be postponed, however great the risk'. For Grey the main objective should be defence of sound finance through a MacDonald-led National government defeating 'the TUC policy'. In order to get that, Liberals could 'hardly exclude all consideration of Tariffs'.[55] In addition Mac-Donald discovered a Liberal ministerial fifth columnist in Reading.

Paradoxically Reading had been persuaded to exert himself by Lloyd George who, distrusting Samuel, asked him to lead resistance to an election, and also to act as Lloyd George's intermediary with MacDonald and representative in the Cabinet. Lloyd George's opposition to an early election was not primarily to do with substantive policy questions – not with retrenchment or banking policy, certainly not with the public works programme of 1928–30, nor even, really, with free trade. He 'did not mind' the cut in road-building, would go further than Samuel towards 'restriction of

[52] Peacock in Wigram memo, 28 Sept. 1931, RA GV 2331(1)/18, and Norman advice to Baldwin in Jones, *Diary with Letters*, 13, 29 Sept. 1931.

[53] N. Chamberlain diary, 29 Sept. 1931; Hankey, 'Note of Events during the week ended October 3 1931' (in effect, this consists of alternative and fuller Cabinet minutes), Hankey papers 1/8.

[54] For meeting at MacDonald invitation, Simon note, 27 Sept. 1931, Simon papers; and for message to Runciman, Runciman to his wife, 28 Sept. 1931, Runciman papers 303. For MacDonald checking their steadfastness, see MacDonald diary, 29 Sept. 1931.

[55] MacDonald to Grey, 28 Sept. 1931, and Grey to MacDonald 29 Sept. 1931, JRM 1320; Grey to Samuel, 29 and 30 Sept. 1931, Samuel papers A/81/8, 9.

imports', and did not exclude 'any proposal, however much [he had] hitherto opposed it'.[56] He 'quite realised that Tariffs should be applied if the situation demanded it'.[57] If, as he later told Samuel, he meant to 'die fighting on the left', in policy terms this amounted just to continued agricultural reform and free imports of some foodstuffs and raw materials.[58] Nor did Lloyd George oppose the National government *per se*. On the contrary, he made desperate efforts to prolong it in its existing form. He appealed beyond Samuel not just to Reading but to MacDonald and the King. He proposed that MacDonald and Baldwin should visit him at Churt. Later he offered to return to London by ambulance in order to meet the government leaders, or attend a Palace conference of ex-Prime Ministers. He made no pre-conditions, but said he 'would do anything to help the country'. He even suggested that 'he was for Tariffs but could not declare his hand at the moment' because Liberal party opinion had not yet been prepared for such a change.[59]

Lloyd George opposed an early election for two reasons. Firstly, since he remained too unfit to lead a Liberal election campaign himself, he did not expect to be treated as Liberal leader afterwards. Secondly, he believed that in existing circumstances an election would wreck his political achievement since 1926 of restoring the Liberal party as a genuine parliamentary force. An early election was a 'trap for Liberals'. It would enable Conservatives to capture the Liberal electorate for their own protectionist purposes, producing such a large Conservative majority that the Liberal party would be smothered. It would expose Liberal MPs as 'plucked boobies'. It would be 'the death-warrant of the Liberal Party as a separate Party'. Therefore, rather than agree to an election the Liberal ministers should threaten to resign. If the threat failed to force MacDonald and the Conservatives to back down, they should obtain the credit of exposing the Conservatives' partisan manoeuvre and fight alone.[60]

---

[56] Reading memos, 11 and 25 Sept. 1931, Reading papers F118/131; Lloyd George to MacDonald, 4 Oct. 1931, JRM 1320.

[57] Lloyd George reported by Geddes in Wigram memo, 2 Oct. 1931, RA GV K2331(1)/26.

[58] Samuel note, 5 Oct. 1931, Samuel papers A/81/25 (Samuel, *Memoirs*, 211); Reading memo, 11 Sept. 1931, Reading papers F118/131.

[59] Lloyd George reported by Geddes in Wigram memo, 2 Oct. 1931, RA GV K2331(1)/26. For Lloyd George's offers of further negotiations, see Geddes in Wigram memo, 5 Oct. 1931, RA GV K2331(1)/30, and Lloyd George, 'Memorandum of a conversation with the Prime Minister', 5 Oct. 1931, LG G/84/9.

[60] Reading memo, 26 Sept. 1931, Reading papers F118/131; Lloyd George memo, 30 Sept. 1931, Samuel papers A/18/11; Sylvester diary, 30 Sept. 1931, in Cross, 39–40.

Reading also had the unique experience of being asked by Asquith's widow to support Lloyd George.[61] Yet Reading was a co-inventor of the national government idea and wanted the Cabinet to keep together somehow. He had now become alarmed at the character of the Labour opposition. Unlike other Liberal ministers he felt no dogmatic attachment to free trade, and he had independently lighted upon the idea of a 'free hand'. These qualities meant that Reading again became a central figure. On reporting Lloyd George's message to MacDonald, he learnt of MacDonald's objectives and instantly re-interpreted his commission from Lloyd George into a promise of assistance to MacDonald. His own view was that with the 'Labour party...at sixes and sevens,...now was the time to strike, before they could re-form ranks', and before economic conditions deteriorated further. Even in an immediate election, only 'a combined national party' could be sure to 'knock out the Socialists'.[62]

Certain of Reading's support, MacDonald at the 28 September Cabinet was not just firm with the Conservative leaders; he also came down hard on Samuel when he raised objections to an election. When at the 29 September Cabinet Samuel contradicted Mac-Donald's description of Chamberlain's formula as a 'very substantial contribution to a solution', he himself faced criticism from Reading. The Cabinet ended with a majority agreeing upon an immediate election, and with Samuel and Reading left to decide – after consultation with other Liberal ministers – whether they could accept Chamberlain's formula and remain in the government.[63] With the passage of the Economy Bill and with the Finance Bill approaching its final stages, decision on the government's future had now become urgent. Parliament would adjourn on 7 October. Before then there were six days of intense negotiation.

The Cabinet had returned to its position of 17 September: on the brink of calling an election, with the position of Liberals as the outstanding question. The major difference was that Samuel now faced much larger difficulties. He had become caught between conflicting pressures. He himself continued to believe that, if an election occurred despite the free-trade Liberals' opposition, it

[61] Lady Oxford to Reading, 2 Oct. 1931, Reading papers F118/131; and see also C. Asquith to Murray, 1 Oct. 1931, Murray papers.
[62] Reading in MacDonald memo, 26 Sept. 1931, JRM 1320, and in Wigram memos, 26 Sept., 1 Oct. 1931, RA GV 2331(1)/17, 23.
[63] MacDonald diary, 28 and 29 Sept. 1931; N. Chamberlain diary, 29 Sept. 1931, and N. to I. Chamberlain, 4 Oct. 1931, NC 18/1/757.

would be electorally fatal for them to stand independently. They would be attacked by Labour for having joined the National government and by Conservatives for having left it. He also feared that if he and other Liberal ministers resigned from the government the Simon Liberals and Runciman would replace them, Grey might criticise their decision, and Reading might remain in office. Together these might exercise such influence over pro-'national' Liberal opinion that the free-trade Liberals could be left as 'a small and isolated faction'.[64]

On the other hand, Samuel had to take account of the contrary attitude of Lloyd George. He remained important as party leader. He was still more important for his possession of a political fund, when the Liberal party organisation remained severely under-financed and faced competition from Simon's and MacDonald's fund-raisers.[65] On 17 September Samuel had optimistically hoped that Lloyd George might remain too ill to be obstructive.[66] But Lloyd George now issued disconcertingly critical press statements. He was visited by Samuel, Maclean, and Sinclair on 30 September, by Reading (again) on 1 October, and by Samuel on the 4th. He nevertheless remained immovable. As in August, however, Samuel and Reading chose to treat him as 'quite out of touch with realities' and – hoping he would still come round and pay up – declared themselves 'unwilling to surrender [their] own judgement'.[67]

Samuel also had difficulties with other Liberal ministers, free-trade Liberal MPs and the party organisation. It required much effort by Samuel to persuade these to accept that Liberal ministers could not afford to resign in protest against an election. But they were still more resistant to accepting any kind of concession over tariffs. Samuel himself was prepared to adjust his previous week's proposal for postponing an election into one for an election manifesto. Though he rejected Chamberlain's original formula, with MacDonald's help he obtained on 1 October a re-wording which in his view guaranteed a genuine 'free hand': that a proper inquiry would determine if import controls were necessary, with the trade

---

[64] All this is spelt out in Samuel memo, 'Action of the Liberal Party Sept.–Oct. 1931', Dec. 1932, Samuel papers A/81/34.

[65] E.g., Inchcape, potentially a large contributor, gave donations to both the Simon and MacDonald funds, but not to the official Liberals.

[66] Samuel in Runciman to his wife, 17 Sept. 1931, Runciman papers 303.

[67] Reading in Wigram memo, 2 Oct. 1931, RA GV K2331(1)/24; Samuel at Cabinet, 1 Oct., in Hankey, 'Notes of Events during the week ended October 3 1931', Hankey papers 1/8.

balance as the sole criterion.[68] Nevertheless Liberal ministers outside the Cabinet rejected this reformulation, refusing to believe that it avoided a prior commitment to protection. Three MPs actually voted against the government, in order to register a view that tariffs would make the dole cut indefensible.[69] On the 4th the NLF executive's reluctant acceptance of an election was coupled with strong free-trade resolutions.[70]

In addition, Samuel faced the hostility of Conservative leaders and most of the rest of the Cabinet. Throughout the negotiations Neville Chamberlain's principle remained that 'MacDonald is the key and...it is essential to get him, and no less essential to keep Samuel out'. Consequently he was always 'searching for the breaking point'.[71] Baldwin, though furious with the Liberal 'yellow bellies', concentrated on soothing the impatience of protectionist MPs.[72] On 1 October the whole Conservative parliamentary party swung between gloom when 'Slippery Sam' accepted the re-worded formula, and joy when Liberal ministers later obliged him to reject it.[73] Thomas's opinion of him was 'unprintable and unwritable'.[74] Snowden, though as much a free-trader as Samuel, still treated defence of his financial policy and defeat of the Labour opposition as the overriding issues, and professed not to understand how Samuel's position differed from Chamberlain's: it was 'Tweedledum and Tweedledee'.[75] But there was a difference, and on 2 October Chamberlain struck: he declared that Conservatives understood the re-worded formula to mean prior commitment to control imports, with a free hand only in the method. This declaration forced Samuel to break off negotiations.[76]

MacDonald tried various devices to get around the Cabinet difference. He encouraged the King to repeat his August performance of bringing the party leaders together. Another Palace

---

[68] Details in ibid.

[69] Mander to MacDonald, 28 Sept. 1931, JRM 1314. See Mander, Harris and Owen, in *HC Deb*, 256, cols. 2024–6, 25 Sept. 1931, and 257, cols. 58–60, 83–7, 28 Sept. 1931.

[70] Parliamentary correspondent, *The Times*, 5 Oct. 1931; *NLF Proceedings 1932*, 105.

[71] Amery diary, 29 Sept. 1931 (*LSA* II, 206); N. Chamberlain diary, 30 Sept. 1931, and N. to I. Chamberlain, 4 Oct. 1931, NC 18/1/757. See the (penetrating) lobby joke in Dalton diary, 30 Sept. 1931 (Pimlott, 156–7).

[72] Baldwin in Buchan to his wife, 30 Sept. 1931, Tweedsmuir (Queens) papers, and in Wigram memo, 1 Oct. 1931, RA GV K2331(1)/23.

[73] See Lady Hilton Young diary, 29 Sept. 1931; Amery diary, 1 Oct. 1931 (*LSA* II, 206), and A. Chamberlain to his wife, 2 Oct. 1931, AC 6/1/820.

[74] A. Chamberlain to his wife, 3 Oct. 1931, AC 6/1/821.

[75] Hankey diary, 3 Oct. 1931 (Roskill, *Hankey* II, 565).

[76] Cabinet 69(31), and N. Chamberlain diary, both 2 Oct. 1931.

Conference was considered, but on second thoughts it seemed constitutionally imprudent for the King openly to assist in creating an anti-Labour electoral alliance.[77] In any case the King had privately lost patience with the niceties of constitutional neutrality and did not want any conference which obliged him, even for form's sake, to deal with Henderson. Believing that if 'a Socialist Government came into power and carried out their extravagant promises to the electorate, this country would be finished', the King applied his personal influence upon Samuel. But in contrast to August, the King now found Samuel 'obstructive' and 'mischievous'.[78] Wigram encouraged an offer by Geddes to mediate between MacDonald and Lloyd George, with whom he claimed to have a special understanding. This initiative resulted in MacDonald making what turned out to be an unsuccessful visit to Lloyd George on 5 October.[79]

As five weeks previously, the King played an important part in sustaining MacDonald's morale: he would 'refuse to accept [the] resignation' of 'the only man who [could] save the country'.[80] MacDonald, as usual when depressed and under great pressure, had murmured things about resignation. Yet later on the 5th he acted with force and considerable skill. In deciding to end 'the cackle', he intended if necessary to accept Samuel's resignation and to fill up with Simon Liberals and Runciman. Confronting the Cabinet with the stark alternatives of no election, a break-up of the government, or an election on some agreed basis, he precipitated a Conservative threat to resign unless there were an election. Then to everyone's surprise Samuel capitulated, accepting a 'National' election appeal by the existing government.[81] Parliament was dissolved on 7 October and the election was called for the 27th.

Samuel had possibly been influenced by a Grey letter in *The Times* on the 3rd. Grey did not offer any considerations new to Samuel, but the publication of his support for an election supplied the sort of

[77] Wigram memo, 29 Sept. 1931, RA GV K2331(1)/20; Wigram to Samuel, 5 Oct. 1931, Samuel papers A/81/28.

[78] Wigram memo, 2 Oct. 1931, RA GV K2331(1)/24, and see Nicolson, *George V*, 492–3. Part of the King's disgust arose from a misunderstanding: that Samuel proposed Labour inclusion in a reconstructed national government, when he had meant only that Henderson could not safely be excluded from a Palace Conference: see Samuel to Wigram, 5 Oct. 1931, Samuel papers A/81/27.

[79] Wigram memos, 2 and 3 Oct. 1931, RA GV K2331(1)/26, 29; Lloyd George 'Memorandum of a conversation with the Prime Minister', 5 Oct. 1931, LG G/84/9.

[80] Wigram memos, 29 Sept., 3 Oct. 1931, RA GV K2331(1)/20, 29.

[81] MacDonald, N. Chamberlain, Sankey, and Hankey diaries, all 5 Oct. 1931 (first in Marquand, 666; last in Roskill, *Hankey* II, 568).

Liberal endorsement which might silence most free-trade critics. The Simon Liberals' decision on 5 October to form an independent Liberal National organisation – in expectation of being asked to join the government very shortly – perhaps made a difference.[82] This threatened Samuel with a similar fate to that of the Labour Cabinet dissentients on 24 August, of simply being replaced by new ministers. Much more important was the Cabinet's agreement to abandon the effort to draft a joint 'national' manifesto. Instead a compromise was reached by which Liberal and Conservative ministers would issue separate election programmes, but be held together by a MacDonald appeal for a 'doctor's mandate'.[83] But in the end Samuel stayed because he thought the free-trade Liberals had no reasonable choice. To have resigned would have appeared absurd when the Cabinet had accepted a 'free hand' (however ambiguous),[84] and it would have exposed them to the full force of Conservative electoral opposition.

THE REALIGNED PARTY SYSTEM

The politics of September and early October had four main effects upon the party system.[85] First, the decision of the National government leaders to fight an election in partnership wrecked Mosley's prospects of forming an alternative 'national' grouping. So well did Mosley think he had done out of the August crisis that he attempted to magnify the renewed crisis of September, in order to highlight his own pose as a 'strong man'. Abandonment of the gold standard was not, for Mosley, a moment for Keynesian relief, but an opportunity to predict 'hopeless, irretrievable disaster' unless government undertook 'drastic measures'.[86] Thereafter, however, Mosley's expectations of exploiting renewed unsettlement shrivelled as it became clear that the National government might become permanent, thereby embodying a more plausible version of political reconstruction than he yet had the resources to offer. With crisis now

---

[82] Simon to MacDonald, 5 Oct. 1931, JRM 1320; Parliamentary correspondent, *The Times*, 6 Oct. 1931. The Simon Liberal and Cabinet meetings began at the same time. It is possible, though not certain, that Simon's message to MacDonald was reported to the Cabinet. But see Foot in Jones, *Diary With Letters*, 15–16, 6 Oct. 1931, 'gloating over the discomfiture' of Simon at being denied office.

[83] N. Chamberlain diary, 5 Oct. 1931; Reading notes [5 Oct. 1931], Reading papers F118/131.

[84] E. g., Lothian to Lloyd George, 7 Oct. 1931, Lothian papers 257/282–4.

[85] This section focuses on crucial high political aspects. For a good detailed account of the election campaign and assessment of the results, see Thorpe, *British General Election*, chs. 7–11.   [86] *HC Deb*, 256, cols. 1319–23, 21 Sept. 1931.

stalking the New party itself, in desperation he sought parliamentary survival by asking Chamberlain for an electoral pact with the Conservative party.[87] But Samuelite acquiescence in the national appeal made the New party altogether superfluous to Conservative electoral strategy, and negotiations lapsed. In these circumstances, Mosley's only chance of continued prominence seemed to lie in shifting back towards the political left. For this purpose he resumed his earlier emphasis upon defence of the working class. He now attacked the National government as strongly as the Labour party, as a 'mere combination of the older politicians' who had failed in the past and whose only agreement now was to disagree. 'Vigour and action' required pressure from a 'virile...ginger group' with 'strong clear' ideas, of which reform of Parliament had now become the most distinctive.[88] Nevertheless the National government appeal swamped the New party. Funds failed to materialise, the launch of its *Action* newspaper was obscured, and Mosley received little media exposure elsewhere.[89] Only 24 candidates could be afforded and the other parties, including previously sympathetic MPs and candidates, simply ignored the New party. At a stroke a movement which for almost a year had seemed to promise much became a 'complete irrelevance'.[90]

Second, the old Liberal party finally disintegrated. Despite the long history of earlier divisions, the last act can be dated precisely to the evening of 5 October 1931. Despite Samuel's acquiescence in the election decision, the Simon Liberals carried through their decision of that evening to form a separate group, issuing their own election manifesto and sponsoring forty Liberal National candidates. This was not a large number, but it included almost half the Liberal MPs (and two ministers, Pybus and Glassey). Moreover most of the 'Simonite Liberal' candidates had a good chance of winning, because they ran in strong Liberal areas and because, as originally promised during the negotiations preceding the August crisis, in most cases – thirty-five in total – Conservative opposition to them was withdrawn. Their further strength was an appeal pitched to

---

[87] N. to H. Chamberlain, 26 Sept. 1931, NC 18/1/756, shows that the approach came from Mosley, not *vice versa* as is implied in Nicolson diary, 1 Oct. 1931 (Nicolson 93).

[88] New party manifesto and Mosley election address, copies in N. Astor papers 1/1/1773; speeches, *The Times*, 18 and 26 Oct. 1931.

[89] For unsuccessful attempt to obtain an election broadcast, see Reith diary, 6 and 16 Oct. 1931, in Stuart, 107, 109.

[90] Skidelsky, *Mosley*, 272 (which otherwise allows Mosley more self-direction than is argued here).

Liberal opinion frightened and disillusioned by two years of the Liberal leadership's support for the Labour government, and by its recent hesitations about the National government. The official Liberals and most of the Liberal Council – now reunited as the 'Samuelite' Liberals – tried to ignore their existence, though Samuel was furious when Simon obtained enhanced status by being allowed a BBC election broadcast.[91]

Still more damaging than Simon to the Samuelite Liberals was Lloyd George's refusal to accept the 5 October Cabinet decision. The Samuelite leaders tried hard to get his co-operation. They sent him their manifesto, re-drafted it in the light of his criticisms, and told him it 'was of great importance to the preservation of the Party' that he sign it.[92] They also gave him one of their allotted BBC broadcasts.[93] But Lloyd George remained unmoved. As his own deputy and all other leading Liberals had publicly defied his leadership, acquiescence would be an humiliation. By detaching himself from them he could lose nothing, but might at least retain prominence. He had possibly hoped to capture the Liberal party machine and candidates.[94] But once these joined in Samuel's 'great betrayal' his withdrawal of support was not a passive affair, even though he remained convalescent and unable to campaign in person. His son and Goronwy Owen resigned their government offices, and Tweed left the party organisation. All prospective disbursements from his political fund were cancelled, except those to his own group of six followers and a few other candidates. In his broadcast and a series of press statements he ignored the 'National'–Labour polarisation, and treated the election issue as resistance to 'a Tory partisan intrigue' at the expense of 'national unity'. He presented himself, extravagantly, as the only untainted champion of free trade, urging Liberals to 'stand by their faith' and advising them, if no other free-trade candidate were available, to vote Labour.[95]

With the failure of Lloyd George's efforts to preserve the first National government, an obvious alternative was to restore the pre-crisis 'progressive alliance'. For this purpose he contacted Henderson

---

[91] Reith diary, 7 and 8 Oct. 1931, in Stuart, 107–8.
[92] Samuel to Lloyd George, 6 and 9 Oct. 1931, Samuel papers A/81/29 and LG G/17/9/17.
[93] Glyn to Churchill, 13 Oct. 1931, in *WSC* v(2), 364–5.
[94] See Parliamentary correspondent, *The Times*, 1 Oct. 1931, for statement from Lloyd George's office.
[95] Broadcast, *The Times*, 16 Oct. 1931; statements in ibid., 9 Oct. 1931, and *News Chronicle*, 26 Oct. 1931; interview, *Daily Herald*, 24 Oct. 1931.

and Addison, and praised the ministerial performances of the Labour dissentients.[96] Yet the sharp polarisation over financial policy made it impossible to manufacture a credible free-trade alliance between nervous Liberal opinion and the Labour party's new-found socialism. Aside from free trade, Lloyd George's stance remained negative or neutral: he neither criticised government measures nor supported Labour policies. In 1918 Lloyd George as Coalition Prime Minister had obtained the largest parliamentary majority so far won at any general election. At the 1929 election he had again largely determined the terms of the debate, and by July 1931 had come close to forcing himself back into Cabinet office. Yet now, at the 1931 election, he was himself at the receiving end of a coalition election coup, and had hardly more relevance to the central issue than Mosley.

The official Liberal organisation had been contracting and candidatures falling for two years. The Liberal parliamentary performance during those two years had cost them electoral support, for which two months in the National government could scarcely compensate. Electoral reform, which might have rescued the party, had been lost. Lloyd George had never definitely committed himself to provide a central election fund, so party organisers did not expect to mount an election effort on the same scale as the last. Nevertheless, being cut off altogether from the principal source of Liberal political finance was a serious blow, leaving Liberal headquarters with 'practically no funds' for itself or for assistance to local associations.[97] Consequently Samuelite Liberals could contest only 111 constituencies, over two hundred fewer than at the previous worst Liberal effort, in 1924. This probably made little difference to their number of successes, but it clearly demonstrated that the Liberals had ceased to be a major electoral force.

Even among the Samuelites there were strains. Samuel was criticised by MPs, candidates, and party organisers for his acquiescence in the Cabinet decision for an election, even though like Samuel and in contrast to Lloyd George they accepted that resistance to socialism and electoral survival left them with no

---

[96] Sylvester diary, 10 Oct. 1931, in Cross, 41; B. Webb diary, 10 Oct. 1931; *News Chronicle*, 12 Oct. 1931, and interview, *Daily Herald*, 24 Oct. 1931. It was also the case that to be certain of holding his own seat against a Conservative–National candidate, Lloyd George needed withdrawal of the Labour candidate and support from Labour voters. In the event he, his son and his daughter had no Labour opponents.

[97] Muir to Liberal associations and candidates, in *The Times*, 10 Oct. 1931.

choice.[98] One major Liberal newspaper – *The Manchester Guardian* – in disgust switched to supporting Lloyd George and the Labour party. The leading Liberal figures hardly helped. Reading at first refused to sign the Samuelite manifesto because he thought it too anti-tariff. Runciman hedged his bets, declining to commit himself either to the Samuelites or the Simonites. Grey also evaded that choice, and invocation of his name was about all that now remained in common between the two main Liberal sections.[99]

The third major outcome of the election decision was a government bloc internally divided on a central policy issue. This meant that its components fought the election campaign almost as much against each other as against the opposition. The Cabinet failure to reach a settlement over the tariff issue resulted in MacDonald's August pledge against a coupon election being fulfilled in an unexpected manner (not in his original sense, of assisting the Labour party). There was no formal arrangement about seats, and little inclination by the two largest government sections to avoid confrontations. The Samuelite Liberals considered their agreement to be with MacDonald alone, and that otherwise they remained an independent party opposed to Conservatives as well as to Labour. Muir instructed party activists to put up as many candidates against Conservatives as finance allowed, except where the effect would be a Labour success.[100] Confident that the Labour party could not now win, Samuel and other Samuelite leaders conducted campaigns – and Liberal headquarters and the Free Trade Defence committee produced propaganda – which were directed more against protection than against socialism. Samuel's election broadcast chiefly argued that the Liberal presence was essential to a genuine National government and a disinterested approach to the trade question.[101]

Conservatives reciprocated, to much greater effect. Conservative leaders had not liked the 5 October Cabinet decision precisely

---

[98] Hirst diary, 6 Oct. 1931, in Hirst, 10; Parliamentary correspondent, *The Times*, 7 Oct. 1931.

[99] Reading memo, 10 Oct. 1931, Reading papers F118/131. For Runciman and Grey not signing the Samuelite manifesto, Samuel to Sinclair, 12 Oct. 1931, Thurso papers III/3/6. For Runciman remaining cordial towards Samuelites, see Maclean to Runciman, 22 Oct. 1931, and for declining the Simonite tag of 'Liberal National', Runciman to Central News, tm, 26 Oct. 1931, both Runciman papers 245.

[100] Samuel, Muir, and other leaders, in Sinclair to Webster, 6 Oct. 1931, Thurso papers II/68/1; Muir to Liberal associations, in *The Times*, 10 Oct. 1931.

[101] *The Times*, 22 Oct. 1931. For free trade as dominant theme, see Samuel's opening election speech, ibid., 9 Oct. 1931.

because it tolerated the Samuelite Liberals.[102] Baldwin took the view
that nomination of Conservative candidates was a decision for local
associations but would receive full Central Office support, and that
the only constraint on the Conservative campaign should be that
Conservative ministers would not speak in Liberal ministers'
constituencies.[103] During the Cabinet search for an election formula,
Amery, Page Croft, Lloyd, and other EIA MPs had not created
trouble because they had occupied themselves with preparations to
oppose free-trade candidates.[104] Together with many Conservative
party organisers, they treated Baldwin's position as giving them
licence 'to wipe out tiresome Liberals'.[105] Only nineteen Conservative candidates withdrew to help Samuelite Liberals. Although
no Conservative ministers suffered Liberal opposition, Samuel,
Maclean, Ernest Simon, and two other Liberal ministers each had
Conservative opponents receiving strong support from leading
protectionists. Even where Conservative opponents to Simonite
Liberals withdrew, Conservative constituency associations often
required written pledges on protection from the candidates.[106] In
some largely agricultural parts of the country, the election contest
'followed the old fashioned lines of 1906'.[107] Conservatives also
created difficulties about National Labour candidates, withdrawing
against MacDonald and Thomas – who were both in danger of
defeat[108] – and a further eleven. But seven, including Jowitt, had
Conservative opponents, and other National Labour candidates
were forced to withdraw. The Conservative party had no intention
of being denied the long-promised Conservative and protectionist
victory, and was prepared to offer only just enough to Liberals and
National Labour to make certain of a complete triumph.

   These tensions produced much ill will between organisers of the
various parties and groups, and considerable irritation between the
government leaders. Baldwin tried to impose some restraint on
Conservatives, publicly rebuking Samuel's Conservative opponent

---

[102] E.g., A. Chamberlain to his wife (2nd letter) 5 Oct. 1931, AC 6/1/824; N. to H.
Chamberlain, 10 Oct. 1931, NC 18/1/758.

[103] Baldwin at party meetings in Amery diary, 6 Oct. 1931 (*LSA* II, 209), and in Croft, *My
Life*, 197–8.

[104] Ibid., 195–7; Amery to Beaverbrook, 5 Oct. 1931, enclosing Page Croft memo, 2 Oct.,
Beaverbrook papers C/5.   [105] Amery diary, 6 Oct. 1931 (*LSA* II, 209).

[106] E.g., Hutchison (Simonite election organiser) to Simon, 'Sunday evening', Simon papers.

[107] Bayford diary, 12 May 1932, in Ramsden, 247.

[108] MacDonald's Seaham seat was under such threat from the Durham miners' union that at
one point he considered finding another constituency: see Wigram memo, 3 Oct. 1931, RA
GV K2331(1)/29. For his difficulties, see Marquand, 651–2, 668–9.

for 'not playing the game'. But even apart from the threats of a Conservative revolt which this provoked,[109] he lacked the inclination to do much more. The character of the National government as established in October 1931, with its free-trade component and Conservative hostility towards the 'twisting eel' Samuel and his Liberal followers,[110] meant that it was still not a stable arrangement, and that the phase of political conflict which had opened in 1926 had still not unravelled itself.

Nevertheless, the fourth and most important outcome of the events of September and October was the maintenance of sufficient co-operation to create a massive anti-socialist electoral force. Despite differences over protection, anti-socialism had been the constant impetus behind the Cabinet negotiations. This was what made the 'organised (or disorganised) Hypocrisy'[111] of the government's unaltered existence tolerable to its components. In contrast to the divisions in the anti-socialist or non-socialist vote at previous elections, Labour candidates were now confronted in very many cases by just a single opponent, largely because of the decreased number of Liberal candidates. Given the prevailing atmosphere of a 'national emergency' and the government's claim to embody 'national unity', opposition to the Labour party and the TUC became very heavily identified with 'patriotism'. Despite the manifest differences between government protectionists and free-traders, their decision to stay together and their presentation of Labour as the really divisive force nevertheless enabled them to exploit that widespread dissatisfaction with party politics evident since the autumn of 1930. The government had support from all important newspapers except the *Daily Herald* and *Manchester Guardian*, and from the Friends of Economy, National Chamber of Trade, National Citizens' Union, and the whole range of business, ratepayers', and taxpayers' organisations. Morris's League of Industry suspended its activities in order to allow its members to concentrate upon supporting 'national' protectionist candidates. The United Empire party dissolved, as Rothermere had now lost interest in it and gave the government vigorous support. The NFU, though stressing its own non-party character, recommended its members to support protectionists.[112] Similarly the Archbishops of

---

[109] Gower, and Amery, to Baldwin, 15 and 17 Oct. 1931, SB 45/44–6, 69–71; and see Croft, *My Life*, 199–200.
[110] A. Chamberlain to his wife, 14 Oct. 1931, AC 6/1/835.
[111] Hirst diary, 2 Oct. 1931, in Hirst, 10.
[112] See League, UEP and NFU statements, *The Times*, 12, 19, and 22 Oct. 1931.

HER PROTECTOR.

14 'Her Protector': *Punch*'s comment on the National government (14 October 1931)

Canterbury and York issued a 'Call to Prayer for the Needs of the Nation', supported by the Federal Council of the Free Churches, which if eschewing party politics appealed for sacrifice during the country's crisis and hour of need. Some bishops and many clergymen abandoned circumlocution and made explicitly pro-government or anti-Labour public statements.[113] Only during wartime had there been anything approaching such a coalition between the creators of opinion.

MacDonald, Thomas, and Snowden played to the full the part expected of them by Conservatives and Liberals, execrating the Labour opposition leaders' desertion of office in August in a manner which highlighted Conservative and Liberal 'patriotism'. In an election campaign attracting intense popular interest, political broadcasts for the first time had a great impact in reaching parts of the electorate which traditional methods could not reach. None was more effective than Snowden's, attacking the Labour manifesto for betraying 'sane and evolutionary Socialism' with a 'revolutionary policy' – 'Bolshevism run mad'.[114] MacDonald joined other government leaders in declaring that Labour would reduce the pound to worthlessness: candidates could buy old vastly depreciated German one million mark notes to wave from their platforms.[115] Simon characterised the issue as being between 'solvency and insolvency', while Runciman, supported by Snowden and MacDonald, claimed that unemployment insurance had been bankrupting the Post Office Savings Bank.[116] All this might have left little for Conservatives to say. Nevertheless Baldwin allowed the veil of his ostensible political generosity to slip. For him 'the great thing this time is to give Socialism a really smashing defeat'.[117] In broadcasts and speeches he not only played his usual tune of constitutional defence but quoted Snowden on 'Bolshevism', and spoke of Labour dishonesty, Gadarene swine, and the threats of open class warfare and of pound notes being worth pennies.[118]

The Labour leaders had expected the election campaign to be

---

[113] For the Archbishops and the Free Churches, *The Times*, 15 Oct. 1931. See also Bishop Bell, Archbishop Lang, and Bishop Winnington Ingram, ibid., 15, 19, and 27 Oct. 1931.

[114] *The Times*, 19 Oct. 1931 (also, Snowden, *Autobiography* II, 1059–64). For the impact of this and other broadcasts see, e.g., Bernays, *Special Correspondent*, 92.

[115] Ibid., 93.   [116] *Manchester Guardian*, 26 and 27 Oct. 1931.

[117] Baldwin in A. Chamberlain to his wife, 8 Oct. 1931, AC 6/1/826; and see Baldwin in Dawson to Bridgeman, 6 Oct. 1931, Bridgeman papers.

[118] *The Times*, 23 and 26 Oct. 1931; *The Daily Despatch*, 27 Oct. 1931. Cf. Middlemas and Barnes, *Baldwin*, 651, which claims he exercised restraint.

savage.[119] Counter-offensive was attempted: the election was said to be unwanted by the country, dangerous to its interests, and a 'mean', 'dishonest', 'discreditable manoeuvre'. MacDonald was 'the captain who brought in pirates and deliberately scuttled the ship', only to become a prisoner of the 'Tory caucus'. Labour alone had a constructive as well as socially just programme. The government was described initially as incapable of agreeing on anything except social reaction, later as a mere vehicle for protectionism. A well-publicised Henderson meeting with Lloyd George and his praise for *Manchester Guardian* editorials showed further sensitivity to the possibility of support from free-trade Liberal voters. Henderson tried to appeal to broad progressive opinion by rooting the Labour election programme in *Labour and the Nation*, and attempted to present Labour as the 'great bulwark between reaction and revolution'. Nevertheless, he stuck essentially to the party line, himself speaking of 'capitalism' as something which could no longer be 'patched up'. Throughout the campaign, however, Labour leaders were forced on to the defensive about their record in office and commitments in the August crisis, and about their inconsistency and 'extremism'. They knew their party was in difficulty, but they had no premonition of how deeply.

[119] Graham in *LPACR 1931*, 196, 6 Oct.; Henderson speech, *Daily Herald*, 8 Oct. 1931. The rest of this paragraph is based on Henderson's election speeches published in the *Daily Herald* or *The Times*.

CHAPTER 13

The defeated

In effect the British nation has done through the ballot box
what Continental countries can only do by revolution. We have
a Dictatorship...

Davidson to William Davidson, 5 November 1931[1]

At the general election on 27 October the National government
partners won the greatest British election victory of modern times,
greatly surpassing even that of 1918 by amassing 554 of the 615 MPs.
The result in part reflected underlying electoral movements,
unchecked by the promised effects of the pre-crisis alliance between
the Labour Cabinet and Lloyd George Liberal leaders – a delayed
election and electoral reform. Many Labour voters had been
disillusioned by the Labour government's inability to contain
unemployment and to deliver further social reform. A large number
of Labour MPs elected in 1929 on a minority vote in three-cornered
contests now suffered defeat as Liberal voters, deprived of the
presence of a Liberal candidate or disenchanted with their party's
parliamentary performance, defected to the Conservative party.
However, the magnitude of the victory obviously resulted from the
impact of the August crisis and the attraction of a National as
against a party government. Very many voters blamed the Labour
government (as now represented by the Labour opposition) for
having made the expenditure cuts and tax increases necessary; as
Conservative and Liberal leaders had hoped when forming the
National government, their parties did not suffer for actually
imposing them. After the suspension of the gold standard had been
explained away and electoral pacts concluded, the appeals to
'national interest', 'national unity', 'equal sacrifices', and 'responsibility' overwhelmed those to 'socialism', 'social justice', and
'class'.

[1] Davidson, *Memoirs of a Conservative*, 376.

455

The Labour party was the most obvious, and the intended, victim. But it was not the only one, nor the most severely damaged. For Lloyd George, Churchill, Amery, Mosley, Keynes, Beaverbrook, and Rothermere – for those who in various ways since 1926 had tried to make major political or policy departures – the election result also meant the loss of influence or prospects. The Labour leaders, remaining in control of a party organisation and an electoral bloc, retained a genuine potential. The others were left with less promising materials for the reconstruction of their positions. How each of the defeated reacted to exclusion reveals much about their fundamental concerns, about the various meanings of the 1931 crisis, and, negatively, about the character of the National government.

LABOUR PERSISTENCE

The Labour party not only failed to win the election; it lost 215 of its 267 seats. This was a disaster made all the more stupefying for being unforeseen at all levels. Plainly the national result was 'overwhelmingly worse'[2] than any Labour party member could have anticipated, but right up to the count many individual Labour MPs had expected to hold their own seats.[3] For some, defeat quite literally meant unemployment and imminent poverty, and the party and several trade unions felt obliged to create work or maintenance schemes for the deserving fallen.[4]

The number of official Labour MPs had been reduced to just forty-six (six other 'Labour' MPs, mostly ILP, were unendorsed). This was even fewer than after the party's first attempt to become a major political force, in 1918. It was 'pathetic to think of the Parliamentary Party...holding their weekly meetings in the little Committee Room that used to serve in 1906'.[5] Worse still, the slaughter included Henderson, thirteen other ex-Cabinet ministers, and twenty-one former junior ministers and whips. Few of these continued to be active or powerful elsewhere within the party.

[2] Dalton diary, 27 Oct. 1931 (Dalton, 295).
[3] See, e.g., Dalton diary, 12, 27, and 28 Oct. 1931 (Dalton, 294–5); Trevelyan to R. Trevelyan, 31 Oct. 1931, Trevelyan papers 232; Strauss diary, 3 Nov. 1931: Pimlott, *Labour and the Left*, 15.
[4] For personal difficulties, see Viant, Shiels, Lawther, Young, Law, and Whiteley letters to Middleton, 5–27 Nov. 1931, Middleton papers 28. LPNEC, Nov. 1931–Jan. 1932 contains details of scheme to employ former MPs (including Shinwell) as lecturers and organisers.
[5] Middleton to Kellogg, 10 Feb. 1932, Middleton papers 29/11.

Although Henderson remained nominally party leader as well as party secretary, he was seriously ill for weeks after the election and then left for six months at Geneva as President of the Disarmament Conference. Adamson, Bondfield, and Clynes returned to their trade union posts, and Alexander to the Co-operative movement. Johnston resumed journalism, and further defeat at the Dunbartonshire by-election in March 1932 left him 'marooned' in Scotland by the expense of visits south. Trevelyan concentrated upon running his Wallington estate; Benn took a rest from politics.[6] Graham died in January, depriving the party of a future Chancellor or Prime Minister.[7] Parmoor took the opportunity of the election defeat to retire from leadership in the Lords, and Passfield from active politics.

Faute de mieux, Lansbury – sole survivor from the 1929–31 Cabinet – at the age of seventy-two became chairman of the parliamentary party,[8] and remained so after Greenwood won the Wakefield by-election in April 1932. Ponsonby became leader in the Lords, while the seatless Addison and Pethick-Lawrence remained important on National Executive sub-committees. Otherwise the defeat completed the removal, begun by the MacDonaldite split, of the strategists, policy-makers, managers, and spokesmen who had led the party into and in office during the 1920s, and replaced them with a younger generation. Attlee by the 'purely accidental'[9] circumstance of being the most senior of eight surviving ex-junior ministers became deputy parliamentary leader, while Cripps as the most accomplished leapt to front bench prominence. Outside Parliament, Morrison and Dalton established powerful positions for themselves on the National Executive and its Committees.

These changes determined the composition of the Labour party's collective leadership for the next twenty years. But neither the shift in personnel nor the election defeat altered the party's policy stance one way or another. The break with the strategy and policies of the 1920s had already been made during late August and September. Labour leaders and their supporters saw no more cause to be

---

[6] Dalton diary, 8 Oct. 1932 (Dalton, *Fateful Years*, 25); Johnston to Lady Warwick, 23 March 1932, Cole papers B/3/5/E/5/5.

[7] See the (uncharacteristically warm) tribute in Dalton diary, 9 Jan. 1932 (Dalton, 299–300).

[8] Wedgwood, a Labour Cabinet minister in 1924, had also survived. But he had detached himself from the party leadership in the late 1920s, and in 1931 was an Independent MP without official Labour party endorsement.

[9] Dalton diary, 8 Oct. 1932 (Pimlott, 169).

frightened off course by an electoral rout than had the Unionist tariff reformers of 1906, though Henderson – like Balfour – continued his attempts to apply a brake.

Steadfastness followed naturally from the ideological rebirth and the bitterness generated by the National government's actions and the election campaign. It was reinforced by Labour explanations for defeat, refracted through these perspectives. Although the party leaders and organisers emphasised the highly unfavourable conditions of the election, most interpreted these not as transitory effects, as they might have done, but as manifestations of something fundamental.[10] The Conservative and Liberal electoral combination had plainly been a major cause: some 400 Labour candidates had faced straight contests, compared with only eighty-two in 1929. In one sense, as a dishonest alliance between free-traders and protectionists, this combination was seen as temporary. But in a larger sense it was regarded as a desperate and all too repeatable contrivance by the propertied classes to prop up a tottering economic system and its vested interests. To some, the election seemed 'an English form of a Fascist coup d'état'.[11]

In this view, the election defeat amply confirmed a socialist political analysis which was more confrontational than gradualist, while the creation of an anti-socialist alliance seemed a tribute to the Labour party's potential. This interpretation received support from Labour answers to the crucial question of why the politicians' manoeuvre had not been overcome through a successful appeal to the electorate. The National government and its powerful supporters had denied the Labour party adequate exposure in the press and pulpit and on the BBC.[12] Above all they had fomented a 'tornado of untruth and vilification' in order to confuse, deceive, and frighten electors – the accusation that ex-ministers had 'run away', the 'inflation stunt', and, most devastatingly, the Post Office savings bank 'scare'.[13] Labour candidates had imagined they were doing

---

[10] Lists of 'causes' can be found in Dalton diary, 28 Oct. 1931 (Dalton, 297), and in Henderson, 'Report on the General Election', in LPNEC, 10 Nov. 1931 (though for Henderson himself drawing different conclusions, see below).

[11] Philips Price to Trevelyan, 2 Nov. 1931, Trevelyan papers 144.

[12] For complaints about allocation of broadcasts, see Henderson's 'Report' and Morrison statement in LPNEC, 10 Nov. 1931.

[13] Lansbury article, *Forward*, 7 Nov. 1931; Henderson, Alexander, and Lansbury statements, *Manchester Guardian*, 29 Oct. 1931; Cripps to Henderson, 29 Oct. 1931, Cripps papers; joint Labour party–TUC press statement, LPNEC, 10 Nov. 1931.

well because the election had been 'a curious case of mass panic, quietly expressed', affecting mostly voters who had not attended meetings, or taking effect only just before the poll.[14] MacDonald's and Snowden's influence was acknowledged to have been considerable, even crucial, but only because of their leading parts in creating a 'terror-stricken' electorate, not because they represented anything positive.[15]

That the 'National' forces had resorted to suppression and misrepresentation fostered the comforting thoughts that the Labour party had been cheated, and that there had been nothing inherently mistaken about its electoral appeal. More deeply, such methods appeared to demonstrate the intellectual bankruptcy of the traditional parties and established economic interests. It was conceded that Conservatives had some positive appeal with tariffs, but also supposed that this had only made a difference to Labour's electoral performance because of disillusionment with the Labour government's poor record in economic and social policies.[16] This record was not always given prominence as a specific explanation for the election defeat. Nevertheless almost everybody who mattered understood the assumptions and policies of the 1929 government to be the root cause of the series of setbacks which had befallen the party.

Yet one undeniable, bright, sustaining fact could be set against all these explanations: the party's popular vote. This had actually been increased in much of South Wales and been largely retained (even where seats were lost) in the other coal and iron areas of Northumberland, Durham, Central Scotland, West Yorkshire, and West Lancashire, in most railway centres and the slums of East London and Glasgow, and in other areas of high unemployment.[17] Labour had received 6·6 million votes, the largest number in any general election apart from 1929, while the party's 30·9 per cent share of the poll compared favourably with that which had made a Labour government possible after the 1923 election. In reality there were problems about the character of this support. Too much

[14] Trevelyan to R. Trevelyan, 31 Oct. 1931, Trevelyan papers 232. See also Dalton diary, 28 Oct. 1931 (Dalton, 298), and Strauss diary, 3 Nov. 1931.

[15] Labour party–TUC press statement, LPNEC, 10 Nov. 1931; Lansbury article, *Forward*, 7 Nov. 1931.

[16] Addison, 'Notes on Questions…' [April 1932], Cole papers B3/5/E/5/3.

[17] See details in Kinnear, *The British Voter*, 50–2; Stevenson and Cook, *The Slump*, 107–9, 288; Thorpe thesis, 'General Election of 1931', 637–8.

remained concentrated in too few constituencies. Some candidates had observed substantial defections of traditional Labour voters,[18] yet it was generally – and probably mistakenly – assumed that gestures towards Liberal voters had been almost wholly unsuccessful.[19] However, such points did not trouble politicians who badly wanted encouragement. To have obtained such popular support against so many adverse pressures seemed in one sense to be 'little short of a miracle'.[20] In a more positive sense it demonstrated great 'bedrock strength':[21] 'you cannot kill the Labour Movement, ... and the bally animal cannot even commit suicide'.[22] Most positively, Labour's popular vote seemed to be a 'solid and determined nucleus' – 'panic-proof, Press-proof, and poison-proof', consisting of 'real Socialists'.[23]

Consolation and confirmation were therefore extracted from every feature of the election result. And although shock and depression remained, adversity also bred a fervour of an almost religious character. The party had no cause for remorse: it had 'kept the faith'.[24] Having suffered a 'drastic purge', it would now be 'purer and stronger'.[25] The defeat would 'ultimately prove [its] salvation': it was what they 'all needed. [They were] back again at things that matter'.[26] These 'days of great difficulty' were 'also days of great hope'.[27] The party felt like 'a small romantic band of brothers again'.[28]

In this mood, with a solid electoral base to build upon and with constructive explanations for defeat, the lessons of 1929 to 1931 seemed plain. There needed to be 'more loyalty to principles and

[18] E.g., Bevin to Wedgwood, and to Cole, 31 Oct. 1931, in Bullock, *Bevin* I, 500, 502. See also Close, 'Realignment', 396–8.   [19] Ibid., 400.
[20] Henderson, 'Report', in LPNEC, 10 Nov. 1931, and see Passfield to Parmoor [Oct. 1931], in Estorick, *Cripps*, 104.
[21] Henderson statement, *Manchester Guardian*, 29 Oct. 1931.
[22] Shaw to Middleton, 5 Nov. 1931, Middleton papers 28/14.
[23] Respectively Cripps to Henderson, 29 Oct. 1931, Cripps papers; Matters to Middleton, 6 Nov. 1931, Middleton papers 28/29; Philips Price to Trevelyan, 2 Nov. 1931, Trevelyan papers 144.
[24] Middleton to defeated Labour MPs, 5 Nov. 1931, taken up in replies by, e.g., Viant and Stamford, 5 Nov., McShane and Matters, 6 Nov., all Middleton papers 28.
[25] Ponsonby to Henderson [Nov. 1931], Ponsonby papers c672/128; Lansbury to Trevelyan, 5 Jan. 1932, Trevelyan papers 145.
[26] Attlee to T. Attlee, 16 Nov. 1931; Muggeridge, and also McShane and T. Smith, to Middleton, all 6 Nov. 1931, Middleton papers 28/23, 26, 27.
[27] Dalton to Lady Warwick, 12 March 1932, Cole papers B3/5/E/5/5.
[28] Williams, *Nothing So Strange*, 106, and for evoking the heroic socialist past, see also Lansbury to Labour MPs, 6 Nov. 1931, Lansbury papers 28/187–8.

programmes and less loyalty to persons'.[29] Political and electoral accommodation towards capitalism were fatal, because they diluted socialism: the 'movement will perish if once again it gets lost in the morass of opportunism'.[30] Accommodation was also futile, and here the behaviour of Liberals had been an object lesson. At the crunch, most had plumped not for progress but for 'reaction'. Although Lansbury made gestures towards Lloyd George and any Liberals who might leave the government, his condition for such free-trade co-operation was their acceptance of socialist policy. Even so, his efforts were deprecated by other Labour leaders.[31] Similarly the old gradualism also seemed futile and fatal, because capitalism had not yielded but had bitten back. Capitalism, although in trouble, could readjust. It would not disappear or collapse of its own accord, but would need to be legislated out of existence.

One thing had not changed. To earlier accusations of un-constitutional action by bankers and National government leaders, Laski now added the charge of a royal coup. But belief that the rules of the game had been perverted or broken did not shake faith in parliamentary democracy itself, even though many Labour leaders and theorists concluded that new safeguards would be needed to ensure that a calm, enlightened, democratic will prevailed. There was not even interest in reviving electoral reform, despite the disparity between Labour's popular support and number of MPs. Labour had suffered from the electoral system this time, but nothing should obstruct achievement of a clear parliamentary majority in the future.[32] The expectation remained that socialism could be secured through the existing political system, if the party went about it in the right way. A great propaganda effort would be needed to give the next Labour government a real socialist mandate. The party had to have effective policies, and know precisely how it meant to implement them once it entered government. Detailed planning

[29] Dalton, 'Answers to Questions...', and Addison, 'Notes on Questions...', both April 1932, Cole papers B3/5/E/5/5, 3.

[30] Lansbury to Cripps [summer 1932], in Postgate, *Lansbury*, 279–80 (mistakenly given as late 1931).

[31] Lansbury speeches and articles, *Daily Herald*, 23 Nov. and 11 Dec. 1931, 14 March 1932; Lansbury resisted by Dalton and Cripps in Dalton diary, 11 Jan. 1932 (Pimlott, 166). But see Morgan, *Portrait*, 215, and Addison to Lloyd George, 18 March 1932, LG papers, for Addison's interest in consultations.

[32] Dalton diary, 28 Oct. 1931 (Dalton, 297), and Lansbury in *HC Deb*, 259, col. 55, 10 Nov. 1931, both calculated the effect of proportional representation, but without interest in it as policy.

seemed to be the answer, and the Russian Five Year Plans now attracted much interest as a model.[33] In order to ensure that future Labour ministers – unlike their predecessors – carried out party policy to the letter, there had to be mechanisms of party accountability and Cabinet reform. There must be 'no more MacDonaldite slush & general phrases': socialism had to be, and be seen to be, practical.[34] 'Our ideas must be clear, our aims must be understood, our plan must be definite.'[35]

These were the conclusions of all sections of the Labour movement. The result was a riot of research, policy-making, and propaganda.[36] The National Executive launched a 'Million New Members and Power' campaign. In December it appointed a Policy Committee, which in turn spawned sub-committees on industrial reorganisation, agriculture, constitutional questions, and finance and trade. The latter, dominated by Dalton, received assistance from a few City experts who had emerged as Labour sympathisers since the August crisis, now formed into the XYZ Club.[37] The TUC General Council's Economic Committee continued to generate policy on unemployment finance, trade, and industrial nationalisation. Cole's New Fabian Research Bureau and Society for Socialist Inquiry and Propaganda (SSIP) were resuscitated after the election, as the SSIP chairman, Bevin, determined to devote more effort to 'educational work'[38] and as socialist intellectuals detected an important role for themselves as pamphleteers and speakers. Aspiring to be policy-makers too, Cole and fellow intellectuals also linked with the parliamentary leaders and individual National Executive members to form a 'House of Commons Group'.[39]

Between these various groups there were organisational jealousies and differences of emphasis, though not as might have been predicted. Immediately after the election the TUC General Council fulfilled a resolution arising from the August crisis of imposing close control over the party, by insisting upon monthly meetings of a

[33] E.g., Attlee in 'Notes on Easton Lodge Week-end', 16–17 April 1932, and House of Commons Group notes, 13 May 1932, Cole papers B/3/5/E/5/7.

[34] Dalton to Cole, 30 May 1932, Dalton, 'Answers to Questions...', and Addison, 'Notes on Questions...', both April 1932, Cole papers B3/5/E/5/6b, 5, 3; Price to Trevelyan, 2 Nov. 1931, Trevelyan papers 144.   [35] NEC Report 1931–2, in *LPACR 1932*, 4.

[36] For a valuable account, see Durbin, *New Jerusalems*, chs. 4–10.

[37] For early contacts, Dalton diary, 11 Sept., 8 Oct. 1931 (Dalton, 284; Pimlott, 157). For XYZ, Williams, *Nothing So Strange*, 111–13, and Davenport, *Memoirs*, 75–8.

[38] Bevin to Wedgwood, and to Cole, 31 Oct. 1931, Bullock, *Bevin* I, 500, 502.

[39] For the formation of this Group (renamed Friday Group in October) see 'Notes on Easton Lodge Week-end', 16–17 April 1932, Cole papers B3/5/E/5/7.

reorganised National Joint Council.[40] It nevertheless reserved its own right to work with other bodies on 'industrial' matters, co-operating with the FBI and the government over the 1932 Imperial Economic Conference. But in the new, harsher political climate such TUC opportunities for consultation with employers' organisations were soon curtailed,[41] while the General Council felt both embarrassed by National Executive objections to such 'collab-oration' yet disarmed by its conciliatory attitude and impressed by its policy initiatives. A compromise was reached which made the Joint Council more of a partnership, tolerating 'expediency' on each side.[42] Dalton and Morrison joined the TUC Economic Committee, and Bevin was consulted by Dalton's finance committee. After the divergence of the past two years, the relationship between the TUC leadership and the national party leaders – though never without some personal clashes – had been largely patched up.[43]

The real differences developed between on the one hand the National Executive and General Council, and on the other the parliamentary leaders, the Cole group of intellectuals, and an ILP rump. The small parliamentary party felt beleaguered not just in the House of Commons, but within the Labour party. It supported the Statute of Westminster and the Indian Round Table process, but otherwise fought a parliamentary guerilla war against the govern-ment, with repeated votes of censure on unemployment, the means test, tariffs, and Ottawa. But with Lansbury as the only MP left on the National Executive, it could no longer control party policy, and it distrusted the National Joint Council as a device to impose control upon itself.[44] Hard-worked and bearing heavy parliamentary responsibilities, the triumvirate leadership of Lansbury, Attlee, and Cripps felt ill-served by the party machine and deprived of appropriate influence upon its policy-making.[45] Cole's House of

[40] TUCGC, 30 Sept. 1931; Hayday in *LPACR 1931*, 202, 6 Oct.; joint GC and NEC meeting, in LPNEC, 10 Nov. 1931.

[41] Dintenfass, 'Politics of Producers' Co-operation', 86–90.

[42] For objections, LPNEC, 26 April 1932; for conciliation, NJC and joint NEC–PLP meetings, ibid. 26 and 27 Jan. 1931; for compromise, NJC in ibid., 26 April 1932.

[43] Bevin's obstruction of the National Executive's transport nationalisation scheme at the 1932 party conference was not a General Council matter but a dispute between his own union and Morrison about workers' representation: see *Bevin* I, 459, 510, 514–15.

[44] Marley to Ponsonby, 27 Jan. 1932, Ponsonby papers c673/18–20. Generally, Pimlott, *Labour and the Left*, 17–18.

[45] Lansbury and Cripps in Dalton diary, 11 Jan. 1932 (Pimlott, 166); Drake to B. Webb, 9 Oct. 1932, Passfield papers II:4:j:8e. Lansbury raised 'the question of general policy and political strategy' to little effect at the Policy Committee: see 17 March 1932 minutes, in LPNEC.

Commons Group offered them alternative research resources, and helped develop their own ideas for a detailed 'plan of action' for a properly socialist government. The parliamentary leaders and the Cole group of intellectuals shared a belief that election of such a government would precipitate a financial and constitutional crisis. They concluded that the next Labour government would require an immediate programme of emergency powers to control the City, together with nationalisation of joint-stock banks, abolition of the House of Lords, reform of parliamentary procedure, and imposition of a comprehensive national plan.

Co-operation between the Labour parliamentary leaders and the Cole group resulted in a 'Programme of Action' presented to the National Executive in June 1932.[46] It was, however, unwelcome. It pre-empted the Executive's own policy documents. Although the Executive also anticipated financial obstruction, most of its members thought the Programme exaggerated the likely scale of resistance to an electoral mandate. It was considered over-ambitious, impractical, and likely to frighten the electorate. Morrison had declined to join the Group, and Dalton refused to sign the Programme. The National Executive shelved it.[47]

At this point the Cole group's activities were complicated by a crisis within the ILP. After the election Henderson and Lansbury had again tried hard to restore relations with it, even offering Maxton Front Bench status.[48] But they refused to re-write the party's standing orders in a manner which would have allowed continued organised dissent; so in July the Maxtonite ILP majority disaffiliated from the Labour party. A SSIP attempt organised by Cole to swallow a substantial affiliationist minority led by Wise resulted instead in a merger, forming a new Socialist League. Wise became chairman, displacing Bevin who thereupon refused to participate, but, as the ex-ILP contingent largely shared the Cole group's policy analysis, Cripps and Attlee remained.[49] Debate about this analysis focused around nationalisation of joint-stock banks, as the symbol of

---

[46] 'Notes on Easton Lodge Week-end, April 16–17th 1932', 'A Labour Programme of Action', 30 May 1932, and Lansbury to Lathan (for NEC), 10 June 1932, all Cole papers, B3/5/E/5/7, and 6a; Attlee, Cole, and Laski at NEC Policy Committee, 16 June 1932 in LPNEC.

[47] Morrison, and Dalton, to Cole, 9 and 30 May 1932, and Dalton in Group minutes, 13 May 1932, Cole papers B3/5/E/5/6a, 6b, 7; Dalton diary, 8 Oct. 1932 (Pimlott, 168); LPNEC, 22 June 1932.

[48] Brockway, Inside the Left, 238; Dowse, Left in the Centre, 177. For the exhaustive negotiations, see LPNEC and PLP, Nov. 1931–July 1932.

[49] Details in Pimlott, Labour and the Left, 44–8.

commitment to an immediate, sweeping 'plan of action' as against the National Executive's preference for a more measured approach and fear of another savings bank scare.[50] The issue was fought at the Labour party conference in October, when Wise and Cripps prevailed against Dalton, Pethick-Lawrence, and Bevin.

The implications of this Socialist League success – the demonstration of the potential for a new socialist left within the Labour party, and Cripps's realisation that he could lead it – would resonate through the rest of the decade. Already National Executive members were suspicious of the League, and distrusted Cripps's judgement.[51] But as yet the differences essentially had to do with the pace at which a Labour government should work. The various components of the party were broadly moving in the same direction, adding strategic and policy detail to the October 1931 conference resolutions for socialism through physical controls, nationalisation, and planning. The August 1931 crisis continued to overshadow thinking during 1932: the key to socialism was thought to be a nationalised Bank of England and a National Investment Board, both supervised directly by a minister of finance. Then came nationalised industries under public corporations, and nationalised land with a National Agricultural Commission and National Commodity Boards.[52] Only from the mid 1930s did the problems of financial policy which had really crippled the 1929–31 government begin to be seriously addressed.

How far the party as a whole had been propelled by the events of 1931 can be measured precisely by the reactions of Henderson – the last member of the old 'big five' leadership to retain authority within the party. Though 'broken-hearted' and embittered by the election defeat, he drew quite different conclusions from those of other Labour leaders. To him, the large popular vote represented the core of 'general support' built up by the strategies of the 1920s. The way to increase it was to 'trim [the party's] sails to catch the wind of disgust' against the National government. He still looked to the old propaganda methods, to *Labour and the Nation*, to 'the old

[50] Dalton in Group minutes, 13 May 1932, and to Cole, 30 May 1932, Cole papers B3/5/E/5/7, 6b; Dalton, and Cole, to Pethick-Lawrence, 15 May, 17 June 1932, Pethick–Lawrence papers 1/181, 160. See Wise in *LPACR 1932*, 189, 4 Oct. for the issue being the 'acid test'.
[51] Dalton diary, 8 Oct. 1932 (Pimlott, 168–9), and Dalton in B. Webb diary, 30 Oct. 1932; LPNEC, 5 Oct. 1932.
[52] See NEC resolutions in *LPACR 1932*. For banking system as the key, see, e.g., 'Notes for Discussion April 16–17 1932', Cole papers B3/5/E/5/7.

policy of "the inevitability of gradualness" and...progressive improvement of [living standards] through social services', and to 'the line of least resistance'. Almost every development within the party since the election appalled him and made him fear for its future.[53]

Henderson finally spoke out at the October 1932 party conference, against a motion instructing the next Labour government – even if in a minority – to 'stand or fall' on immediate promulgation of 'definite Socialist legislation'. Though inspired by the Socialist League, this encapsulated the new stance of most of the party. Henderson barely received a hearing, and the motion was carried unanimously.[54] Within a week he had resigned the party leadership.

Although Henderson remained party secretary, his departure from the leadership marks the end of a long phase in Labour party history. Already the party of Attlee, Dalton, Cripps, Morrison, Bevin, and Citrine which had emerged from the 1931 debacle had laid the groundwork for a socialist government. But at the 1935 election 'socialism' carried the party little nearer to power than it had been after that of 1931. As Henderson had predicted, it would indeed be a 'wind of disgust' with the National government which returned the Labour party to office. More than anything else, it was the impact of Hitler which cleared the road to 1945.

TOWARDS THE EXTREMES

In the 1931 diaspora of the old Labour party, it was not just MacDonald, Thomas, and Snowden who reached unlikely destinations. For some, the crescendo of economic depression, Labour government impotence, and financial and political crisis led to belief in an approaching physical or moral collapse of capitalism, and in the ineffectiveness of the party system and machinery of government. So shocked were they by the events of August to October that they looked to continental autocracies for models of political and economic reconstruction, and envisaged, or did not exclude, extra-constitutional action as a means to emulate them.

---

[53] Henderson, 'Report' in LPNEC, 10 Nov. 1931; Henderson to Cole, 27 April 1932, Cole papers B3/5/E/5/5; Henderson reported in Lansbury to Cripps [summer 1932] in Postgate, *Lansbury*, 280, and in B. Webb diary, 22 Feb., 4 Aug. 1932.

[54] *LPACR 1932*, 204–6. The motion was moved by Trevelyan and supported by Attlee and Cramp, all of the Socialist League.

This underlaid the continued refusal of most of the ILP and its five surviving MPs to acquiesce in Labour party rules. After 1931 Labour strategy became to a large degree what ILP leaders had wanted before 1931. But as Labour leaders accepted 'socialism in our time', Maxton and Brockway abandoned it for a 'revolutionary policy'. The difference was that the ILP now had a more cataclysmic view than even Socialist League members: capitalism was irretrievably breaking down, but its defenders would probably resort to a harsh dictatorship in a last ditch resistance to socialism. In this 'supreme struggle', parliamentary action alone would be useless. The 'mass strength' of the working classes would be needed for the 'capture of power'. The analysis was Marxist and the example explicit. Brockway spoke of the 'explosive effect' which the Russian model could have in bringing British workers to revolutionary consciousness. Maxton likened the ILP–Labour dispute to that between the 'Bolshevists' and 'Menshevists', and dispensed 'lessons from Lenin'.[55] Even so, ILP leaders had no intention of subordinating themselves to the British Communist party, but aimed to steal its clothes as the revolutionary vanguard. So twelve months after the old ILP chairmen MacDonald and Snowden joined with Conservatives and Liberals, the ILP itself left the Labour party in the opposite direction to the strains of 'The Internationale'.[56]

The ILP had been a parent of the Labour party; the Webbs had been its tutors. Yet well before the crisis Beatrice's disillusionment with the Labour government (despite her husband's membership of it) made her doubt the Webbian 'inevitability of gradualness'. By contrast, Russia seemed impressive as a successful 'sudden jump in...evolution'. Critical too of the machinery of government and pondering how to 'combine efficiency with the consciousness of consent', she thought Soviet 'creed autocracy' might be 'deliver[ing] the goods'. Amidst deepening world chaos, she imagined that Russia alone remained unscathed.[57] Though as contemptuous of trade unions and state 'doles' as MacDonald,[58] and although Sidney supported MacDonald's proposed cuts in Cabinet, the 1931

[55] Brockway speech, special ILP conference report, and Maxton lecture, *The Times*, 28 March, 1 and 11 Aug. 1932. See also J. Maxton, *Lenin* (1932).
[56] Special ILP conference report, *The Times*, 1 Aug. 1932. For ILP expectations, Dowse, *Left in the Centre*, 179–86.
[57] B. Webb diary, 30 June, 25 Nov. 1930, 4 and 12 Feb. 1931 (Cole, 245, 260–1, 265; MacKenzie IV, 237, 239).
[58] B. Webb diary, 24 Aug. 1931 (Cole, 283–4; MacKenzie IV, 255).

crisis clarified matters. It exposed the political immaturity and social corruption of the Labour party, its absence of system and public service ethic. Capitalist 'sabotage' and the threat of 'class war' pointed to a need for 'agreed Dictatorship'. American financial 'dictation' (which Sidney, prompted by Beatrice, detected after the event) confirmed a sense that Britain was powerless as between American Capitalism and Soviet Communism.[59] The first was immoral, and was committing suicide; the latter – despite some 'brutality' and 'terror' – was successful, egalitarian, and evoked the workers' 'enthusiasm and devoted service'. On examination the Russian constitution appeared to conform to Webbian principles, and the Russian Communist party to be motivated by the 'spiritual power' of a Comtean 'Religion of Humanity'.[60] The Webbs did not leave the Labour party: they applauded its new commitment to immediate socialisation. But their contribution to its internal debate was to visit the Russian 'Mecca' in 1932 and confirm their preconceptions and delusion[61] that Soviet Communism offered British Labour the blueprint for 'a new civilisation'.

Those Labour MPs who had entered the New party had done so in the expectation of an imminent crisis. When the crisis came, it turned out not to be the one expected, neither so politically nor so economically disruptive. For Strachey, it seemed just the beginning of economic collapse and a Manichean division of the world. Recoiling from Mosley after their July 1931 split, to him the real political threat seemed to be fascism. He took the logical step. Before the election he established contact with British Communist leaders. After his election defeat he consulted the Soviet ambassador and read *Das Kapital*. By April he had drafted the *The Coming Struggle For Power*.[62]

Strachey's assessment of Mosley was only a few months premature. At the election all the New party candidates including Mosley suffered defeat, and its total poll was derisory – under half that of the Communist party. It was also stripped of most of its prospective high political allies. Lloyd George, Churchill, and Beaverbrook lost much of their latent power. Elliot, Stanley, and Hore-Belisha were secure

[59] B. Webb diary, 28 Dec. 1930, 24 Aug., 10 Sept. 1931 (Cole, 260–1, 283–4, 287); B. Webb to Keynes, Robson, and Clay, 3, 11, and 28 Sept. 1931, in *Webb Letters* III, 362, 365–6.

[60] B. Webb diary, 28 Dec. 1930, 4 Feb., 30 June 1931, 4 Jan., 14 and 17 May 1932 (Cole, 260–1, 265, 274, 298–9, 307–9).

[61] For conclusions outlined in advance, see B. Webb diary, 14 and 17 May 1932 (Cole, 307–9).   [62] Thomas, *Strachey*, 110, 113–14, 119.

in government office. Macmillan, back in Parliament, was 'coming down more & more on the left' and employed Young (Mosley's former assistant and Strachey's fellow defector) to help create his own ginger group[63] and promote state planning as the 'middle way' between capitalism and socialism. To all these and to the mass of parliamentary opinion, Mosley ceased to represent a credible force.

From his experiences since August, Mosley drew three conclusions. First, parliamentary extinction showed that 'a new movement cannot be made within the frame of a parliamentary party'.[64] Second, he had been right about the crisis and close to success until cheated by the old party leaders. To return to one of their parties would betray that achievement. Third, much of his analysis remained pertinent. Like Beatrice Webb, since 1930 Mosley had believed that modern problems could not be solved through existing government machinery. Like the ILP and Strachey, he thought it unlikely that a government which combined the forces originally responsible for the 'muddle' could prevent the 1931 crisis from degenerating into a deeper crisis and a revolutionary polarisation of politics. Even if it could, he thought the old parties would simply continue to allow Britain's 'slow decline' into 'a second or third-rate position'.[65]

Though unsure whether his purpose should be to resist communism or prevent national decadence, Mosley was certain that he had no future in 'normal politics'. Following resumed 'communist' disruption of his public meetings during September 1931 he had adopted 'fascism' as a model of party organisation, but during the election campaign had considered it prudent to repudiate the ideology as un-British.[66] Nevertheless 'the vast conception of the Corporate State' involved no large step beyond his autumn 1930 ideas about government. Despite opposition from Nicolson, Forgan, and his wife, he embraced it after the election both as the 'inevitable and historic opponent' of communism and as the active and constructive force of 'political modernism'.[67] After visiting Italy to study Mussolini's achievements, he dissolved the New party and set about capturing the existing tiny British fascist groups. He had no illusions about the quality of these groups. One answer to sceptics

[63] Macmillan to N. Astor, 29 Dec. 1931, N. Astor papers 1/2/86.
[64] Nicolson diary, 24 Nov. 1931 (Nicolson I, 97).
[65] Mosley, 'Old Parties or New?', *Political Quarterly* 3, 27–32, Jan. 1932.
[66] Nicolson diary, 21 and 22 Sept. 1931 (Nicolson I, 91–2); speech, *The Times*, 19 Oct. 1931.
[67] 'Old Parties or New?', *Political Quarterly* 3, 27–32, Jan. 1932.

was that it was 'better... that Fascism be built by me than some worse kind of lunatic'.[68] Another was that however improbable his fascist vanguard appeared, events would force serious politicians to rally to it. Promised newspaper support from Rothermere, who had been thoroughly frightened by the 1931 crisis, who shared the expectation of further crisis, and who looked to Mosley as the necessary 'man of courage', seemed an important precursor.[69] In publishing *The Greater Britain* and forming the British Union of Fascists in October 1932, Mosley was repeating what he had attempted with the New party in early 1931, with the difference that this time he gambled upon the collapse not just of the party system but of the whole national order.

KEYNES AND LLOYD GEORGE

For Keynes, suspension of the gold standard had been a matter for celebration. Personally he felt 'great... inward satisfaction', treating it as vindication of his criticisms of government policy since 1925.[70] Within a fortnight, he decided to publish a selection of these 'Essays in Prophecy' (later 'Persuasion'). In public terms he felt it to be a 'most blessed event', removing the chief deflationary pressure and policy constraint, and opening the possibilities for international and domestic reflation.[71] This, it might have been thought, was a great opportunity for such an inventive and prolific political economist and publicist. Yet for eighteen months Keynes had uncharacteristically little to say on public issues.

This is usually explained as a shift towards theoretical concerns, as Keynes felt compelled by academic criticisms of his *Treatise on Money* to re-think his intellectual premises, a reconstruction which ultimately led to his *General Theory*.[72] There is, however, a further explanation: lack of both political and policy incentives. First, the 1931 crisis destroyed all available political vehicles for his ideas. Despite his dislike of the emergency government he had opposed an early election, fearing it would wreck rational reassessment of

---

[68] Mosley to Beaverbrook, 9 Sept. 1932, Beaverbrook papers C/254; and see Nicolson diary, 19 April 1932 (Nicolson I, 115).

[69] Nicolson diary, 4 and 11 Dec. 1931 (partly in Nicolson I, 97–8).

[70] C. H. Rolph, *Kingsley* (1973), 164; B. Webb diary, 23 Sept. 1931 (MacKenzie IV, 260).

[71] Halley-Stewart lecture, 4 Feb. 1932, in *JMK* XXI, 55–6; *Sunday Express* article, 27 Sept. 1931, in *JMK* IX, 245–9.

[72] For an authoritative account, see Clarke, *Keynesian Revolution*, 229–88.

currency policy and result in the worse evil of Conservative predominance. He encouraged MacDonald's and Lloyd George's efforts at postponement and, in case these failed, even reverted to promoting alliance between Lloyd George Liberals and moderate Labour.[73] The election, therefore, represented a defeat for Keynes. The election campaign was irrelevant to his policy concerns, and with Lloyd George as powerless as Mosley, and with Labour persisting with its 'largely foolish' socialist programme,[74] there were no politicians he cared to support publicly. The result offered little prospect that he might recover a significant role as policy adviser. Believing that 'battered capitalism' must be replaced by an 'organised state', as a long-term prospect he praised some Labour ideas for financial planning.[75] Yet his hope of influencing Labour opinion was subverted by his intellectual contempt for most Labour policy-makers.[76] The government seemed hardly more promising, with Conservative ministers impervious to economists' advice. The full EAC was discontinued and although under MacDonald's patronage Keynes remained on its committees, these seemed unlikely to have much direct effect.

Second and more significantly, contrary to Keynes's expectations he approved of a good many of the National government's policies. Much of what he might have said was simply redundant. He considered a scheme for exchange management to be 'excellent', and the conversion of war loan 'a constructive measure of the very first importance'. The settlement of reparations was another personal vindication, and cause for congratulations to MacDonald.[77] The government shared his objectives of a sterling union and an international economic conference. Nor did Keynes seriously object to its tariff policy. Although he thought devaluation removed much of the economic justification for a general tariff, he did not – as is commonly asserted – withdraw his support for this immediately after

---

[73] Keynes letter, *The Times*, 29 Sept. 1931 (*JMK* IX, 243–4); Keynes to MacDonald, 30 Sept., 1 Oct. 1931, JRM 1320, and to Lloyd George, 1 Oct. 1931, LG G/10/15/6 (*JMK* XX, 617–21). See Dalton diary, 1 Oct. 1931 (Dalton, 290), for Keynes requesting a meeting with Henderson, and *JMK* XX, 617, for meetings with MacDonald and Lloyd George on 4 October.

[74] For criticism of Labour, see Keynes to Case, 2 Nov. 1931, in *JMK* XXI, 9–10.

[75] Nicolson diary, 11 Dec. 1931 (Nicolson I, 98); 'The Monetary Policy of the Labour Party', in *JMK* XXI, 128–37.

[76] See Williams, *Nothing So Strange*, 109, and Davenport, *Memoirs*, 79.

[77] Keynes article, 20 April 1932, and memo, 18 July 1932, in *JMK* XXI, 104–5, 114; Keynes to MacDonald, 12 July 1932, JRM 678 (*JMK* XVIII, 379).

suspension, but argued merely that it had become a less urgent issue.[78] During the election disputes on the matter, he remained silent. During 1932 he was 'not prepared to oppose [general protection] with any heat of conviction'. He publicly approved a revenue tariff and selective protection for iron and steel and agriculture.[79] Keynes even accepted that continued budget 'economy' had 'enormous psychological advantages' for business.[80]

Yet despite the National government's policies being closer to his own ideas for economic expansion than those of any post-war government, as a political 'progressive' Keynes instinctively considered it 'reactionary' and thought there was 'probably no practical good sense in any efforts except those deliberately aimed at ousting [it]'.[81] Instinctively too, he wanted more 'courage' and more positive domestic expansion through increased private and public expenditure.[82] In other words, Keynes was casting about for some solid ground from which to criticise the government. Only in early 1933 did his politics, policy, and theory again unite, as spectacularly as in 1929–30, in *The Means to Prosperity*.

There was, however, to be no Keynes reunion with Lloyd George. His character sketch of that 'syren' in *Essays in Biography* destroyed any such prospect,[83] even in the unlikely event that Lloyd George was then interested in another major campaign. After the election Lloyd George headed only a family group of four Independent MPs and, although he retained a stronghold in Welsh Liberalism, the overall result increased his isolation. One reaction was to call for a reconstructed 'Progressive Party', embracing 'Radicals', Labour, and progressives from other parties. Only now did he attempt to revive the Liberal economic programmes of 1928–30 as a prospective basis for co-operation.[84] But the Labour decision to persist with

[78] Keynes letter, *The Times*, 29 Sept. 1931 (*JMK* IX, 243–4). For the conventional view, see Howson and Winch, *Economic Advisory Council*, 96–7. Acceptance of this interpretation tangles an otherwise accurate account in Clarke, *Keynesian Revolution*, 225, 283–4.

[79] Keynes lecture, 4 Feb. 1932, and article 20 April 1932, in *JMK* XXI, 57, 103–4. See also articles 'Pros and Cons of Tariffs', Nov. 1932, and 'National Self-Sufficiency', July 1933, in ibid., 204–10, 233–46.

[80] Keynes article, 20 April 1932, and Keynes to Macmillan, 6 June 1932, in *JMK* XXI, 107, 110. For his broad verdict on government policies, see article, 1 Jan. 1933, in ibid., 141–5.

[81] Keynes to Macmillan, 7 Sept. 1932, in *JMK* XXI, 127.

[82] Keynes lecture, 4 Feb. 1932, and article, 20 April 1932, in *JMK* XXI, 60–2, 106–7. It is noteworthy that Keynes allowed other economists to initiate public statements here: for Meade-Harrod and Pigou-inspired letters, see ibid., 125–6, 137–40.

[83] For interesting comments on the chronology, see Clarke, *Keynesian Revolution*, 288–9.

[84] Lloyd George to Wallace, 6 Nov. 1931, LG G/33/1/53; interview, *Manchester Guardian*, 2 Nov. 1931; speech, *The Times*, 17 March 1932.

socialism closed off that possibility. Mostly Lloyd George concentrated upon expressing his limitless resentment towards and contempt for Simon, Runciman, and especially the Samuelite leaders. He presented these ministerial Liberals as belonging to a 'reactionary... Tory Government of the Eldon era'.[85] As protection was introduced he presented himself as the one remaining untainted Liberal, whose pre-election warnings had been amply fulfilled. Whereas in his hands the Liberal party had achieved a 'dominant position' before the 1931 crisis, under Samuel's 'fatuous and pusillanimous' leadership it had become 'an insignificant band' which 'did not count'.[86]

These attacks had some effect among disillusioned Liberal organisers, journalists, and activists. In April 1932 Lloyd George and a small group of supporters, using national development as well as free trade, helped push the NLF executive and conference close to repudiation of the Samuelite ministers.[87] Nevertheless in September the NLF finally rallied not to Lloyd George but to the Samuelite leaders. Lloyd George was not really surprised or disappointed. His political efforts had become spasmodic and largely negative. After the election he had taken a long holiday. Thereafter he settled with Frances Stevenson and their two-year old daughter at Churt, rather than returning to a prominent public life in London. It was March before he made a major speech,[88] and June before he spoke in the Commons. There were no new policy 'inquiries', nor any serious representation of the 1928–30 programmes. He repeatedly denied any interest in resuming active political leadership, certainly of the 'annihilated' Liberal party.[89] Instead he spoke of enjoying his independence and the 'new amusement' of writing his memoirs.[90] Politically, Lloyd George just went through the motions, at most imagining himself as a leader in waiting.[91] He had no alternative, understanding that for the foreseeable future the National govern-

[85] Lloyd George to Levi, 24 Aug. 1932, LG G/33/3/58.
[86] Lloyd George to Lewis, 31 Dec. 1931, LG G/12/1/20; Tweed statement and Lloyd George speech, *The Times*, 4 Feb., 17 March 1932.
[87] Lloyd George to Muir, 13 April 1932, LG G/15/6/26; Nathan, and Megan and Gwilym Lloyd George in *NLF Proceedings 1932*, 17–20, 26–7, 27 and 29 April.
[88] For hesitations, see Lloyd George to Tweed, 29 Jan. 1932, LG G/28/2/5; and Tweed in Clarke *Diary*, 141, 29 Feb. 1932.
[89] E.g., Tweed statement and Lloyd George speech, *The Times*, 4 Feb., 11 May 1932; Lloyd George to F. Stevenson, 31 Dec. 1931, 28 Sept. 1932, in Taylor, 171, 192.
[90] Ibid. (28 Sept. 1932); Lockhart diary, 13 April 1932, in Young I, 214.
[91] Clarke *Diary*, 138, 22 Feb. 1932; Lloyd George to F. Stevenson, 23 Sept. 1932, in Taylor, 189.

ment had demolished all effective Liberal or radical positions, and
with it his own power.

Similar damage was suffered by those who had occupied dissentient
positions on the Conservative side: Churchill, Amery, and Beaverbrook. Despite his March 1931 setback, Churchill had remained a
latent force with continuing aspirations to high office, and he was
disconsolate at being outside the National government.[92] Nevertheless he supported the National election appeal as the achievement
of his constant, overriding, aim since 1922 – a revived Conservative–
Liberal alliance capable of 'root[ing] out from Parliament all those
subversive forces which [had] worn down the strength of Britain'.[93]
In another respect, however, a major phase of Churchill's politics
closed, as he accepted that effective anti-socialism no longer required
free trade. In November he finally capitulated to his Conservative
critics of 1926–9, asking Page Croft for admission to the Empire
Industries Association.[94] On the loss of the gold standard he said
very little. He buried his four years as Chancellor of the Exchequer
as a bad memory, and ceased to attend seriously to economic issues.

Exiled on the backbenches for the first time since 1917, Churchill
now intensified his literary work and arranged a long American
lecture tour. Yet he did not relinquish his claim to political
leadership. Maintenance of imperial control remained an area in
which he assumed he still had vital contributions to make, and where
he could regain the prominence he had enjoyed in January 1931.
From the outset he suspected that a government which linked
Baldwin and Hoare with MacDonald and Reading – rather than
tying them down within a Conservative Cabinet – might have
pernicious implications for the Empire. In September he asserted
that an emergency Cabinet had no authority to determine Indian
policy.[95] Once the election had restored Conservative prepon-

---

[92] Lockhart diary, 20 Sept. 1931, in Young I, 186; Hirst diary, 25 Sept. 1931, in Hirst, 8. See
Churchill to Bracken and to Harmsworth, 23 Aug., 4 Sept. 1931, in WSC V(2), 352, 356,
for retaining the right to terminate a contract if he took office.

[93] Speech, The Times, 30 Sept. 1931; and see his rampant anti-socialist articles in Daily Mail,
2, 6, and 22 Oct. 1931. See also Amery diary, 6 Oct. 1931 (LSA II, 209), for Churchill
motion of confidence in Baldwin.

[94] Parliamentary Correspondent, The Times, 13 and 23 Nov. 1931.

[95] HC Deb, 256, col. 46, 8 Sept. 1931.

derance, he aimed to lead a Conservative 'opposition' which would push the Cabinet into repairing past damage and prevent any new backsliding. He publicly reaffirmed his differences with Baldwin, and promised not to 'withhold... [his] advice and counsel'.[96] He resumed common cause with the Indian Empire Society, Lord Lloyd, and the Gretton–Page Croft diehard group, and forged new links with Salisbury and the diehard peers. By setpiece orations and parliamentary skirmishing, he also tried to impress new Conservative MPs as a 'strong man.'[97] His first point of criticism, during November, was the Irish provisions of the Statute of Westminster. Churchill's, Gretton's, and Salisbury's claim that these licenced any future Irish Free State decision to repudiate the Irish Treaty threatened to arouse a Conservative revolt against what appeared to be ministerial gullibility.[98] But his major concern remained India. When in December the Cabinet decided to continue progress towards Indian federation, Churchill, Lloyd, and Salisbury mounted full-scale attacks upon this 'disastrous' blow to imperial power and the peace of India.

In all this, Churchill and the diehards failed utterly. The threatened revolt on the Statute evaporated. In divisions on Indian policy in the Lords and Commons respectively, Lloyd mustered only fifty-eight votes and Churchill just forty-three. They failed not merely because the government had the authority of a recent election victory, but because the Cabinet's composition ensured a policy which offered reassurance in most directions and made Churchill's philippics seem preposterous.[99] Churchill himself briefly felt reassured when the government reimposed repression in India; there was 'nothing to quarrel with them over now'.[100] When he, Lloyd, Salisbury, and the diehards found fresh Irish and Indian matters on which to quarrel in 1932[101] and during the following three years, this pattern would be repeated.

Beaverbrook and Amery also wanted to mount a Conservative 'opposition'. For them as for Churchill, the installation of a National

---

[96] Ibid., 259, cols. 130–1, 11 Nov. 1931. For the impact, see Bernays, *Special Correspondent*, 101–2.

[97] Dawson diary, 12 Nov. 1931; Amery diary, 19 and 25 Nov. 1931 (partly in *LSA* II, 221).

[98] See Amery diary, 19 Nov. 1931, and 1922 Committee minutes, 23 Nov. 1931.

[99] For new MPs being repelled, see A. to H. Chamberlain, 28 Nov. 1931, AC 5/1/566; Cazalet diary, 26 Nov. 1931, in James, *Cazalet*, 139; and Bernays, *Special Correspondent*, 102.

[100] Churchill to R. Churchill, and to Hawkey, 5 Jan., 1 Feb. 1932, in *WSC* v(2), 391, 397.

[101] See, e.g., Churchill to Salisbury, 28 March, 5 and 26 April 1932, and Baldwin to MacDonald, 1 July 1932, in *WSC* v(2), 408, 413–14, 420, 448.

rather than a Conservative government upset expectations about policy and influence, and prompted renewed criticism of the Conservative leadership. Despite the March 'Stornoway pact', Beaverbrook's politics from September were almost as vigorous as they had been after the 1929 election. To him, suspension of the gold standard primarily offered an opportunity to recapture a central political role. In an intended anti-Baldwin move, he offered MacDonald a large election fund if he would lead an immediate tariff election campaign.[102] As the Cabinet debated an election formula he encouraged Conservatives who might help to 'torpedo' Baldwin.[103] During the election he attacked the 'doctor's mandate' and supported those Conservative candidates standing against Samuelite Liberals. After the election, he supposed that the Conservative party could still be mobilised against its leaders, using the claim that Baldwin was incapable of pressing Conservative trade policy in Cabinet.[104] During 1932 he made various gestures towards re-starting the Empire Crusade. He launched a campaign for full agricultural protection, spoke of aiming to 'break up the government', and thought about running independent candidates at by-elections.[105]

As his instrument within the parliamentary party Beaverbrook looked to Amery, whom he encouraged in early 1932 to consider himself the 'next leader of the Party and coming PM'.[106] Amery was vain enough to believe him. Despite his exclusion from the emergency government, during September and October 1931 he still regarded himself as a member of the party leadership, with an unassailable claim to Cabinet office.[107] Contemptuous of the 'doctor's mandate', he largely ignored the existence of the government and treated the election as a Conservative protectionist crusade against free-trade Liberals. That, after this, Amery still expected office in the reconstructed government[108] is a measure of his simplicity. Excluded

---

[102] Beaverbrook to MacDonald, 20 Sept. 1931, JRM 673; MacDonald and Lockhart diaries, 20 Sept. 1931, latter in Young I, 186.

[103] Lockhart diary, 26 Sept. 1931, in Young I, 187. For proposing formation of an alternative Tory Shadow Cabinet, see Beaverbrook to Brentford, tm, 1 Oct. 1931, Beaverbrook papers C/163.

[104] See Amery diary, 29 Oct. 1931 (*LSA* II, 216); Beaverbrook to Bridgeman, 12 Nov. 1931, Bridgeman papers, and to Baumann, 13 Feb. 1932, Beaverbrook papers B/198.

[105] Amery diary, 30 Jan. 1932 (*LSA* II, 228); Beaverbrook to Wargrave, and to Borden, 16 April and 14 Aug. 1932, Beaverbrook papers C/320 and 52.

[106] Amery diary, 26 Jan. 1932 (*LSA* II, 228), and see also entries for 26 Dec. 1931, 4 Feb., 6 July 1932 (ibid. 225, 229, 242).

[107] For efforts to initiate policy, see Amery diary, 22, 23, 24, 25, and 27 Sept. 1931, the last showing the presumption that he would obtain a senior post (partly in *LSA* II, 203, 204–5).   [108] Amery diary, 31 Oct., 3, 5, and 6 Nov. 1931 (*LSA* II, 217–19).

again, he considered the government an 'absurd dishonest Coalition of old gangs'.[109] In the face of the 'moral collapse of Party leadership' and its readiness to continue co-operation with free-trade Liberals, in the new Parliament he worked with Page Croft and the EIA for rapid and full achievement of Conservative trade policy. By harrying Conservative as well as Liberal ministers in the Commons, he felt himself to be 'increasingly looked to as a leader'.[110] Though in 1932 he welcomed the Cabinet's ending of the 'Free Trade superstition', he nevertheless criticised the detail of its measures, especially its reluctance to allow high agricultural protection, and led other strongly protectionist MPs in deputations, amendments, abstentions, or votes against the government. Attending the Ottawa Conference as representative of agricultural and sugar interests, he helped organise 'Soviets' of unofficial advisors and encouraged Dominion ministers in ways which the British ministerial delegates considered downright hostile.[111]

Between them, Amery and Beaverbrook reasserted what had earlier been a powerful position – pressure for comprehensive, 'whole-hog', tariff reform. They addressed what might have been expected to cause Conservative ministers difficulty: that the Cabinet was not exercising a genuine 'free hand', but diluting Conservative policy and jeopardising the cause of imperial economic unity. Yet they aroused little interest among Conservative MPs or activists. Beaverbrook's persistence demonstrated that within a genuine concern for imperial consolidation he was driven by vindictiveness towards Baldwin. Amery's persistence demonstrated what had repeatedly emasculated his effectiveness: a doctrinaire commitment which other leading Conservatives considered impractical and blinkered. But what the contrast between their prominence from July 1929 to March 1931 and their irrelevance after the 1931 election demonstrated above all was the restoration of Conservative party confidence in Baldwin, and its conversion to a 'national' strategy. Like the Labour party, Amery's, Beaverbrook's, and Churchill's time would come again only under the destructive force of Hitler.

[109] Amery diary, 5 and 6 Nov. 1931, 22 Jan. 1932 (*LSA* II, 219, 227).
[110] Amery diary, 31 Dec. 1931 (*LSA* II, 226).
[111] Amery diary, 20 July–24 Aug. 1932 (*LSA* II, 243–57), esp. 17 Aug. for Chamberlain fury. See also Amery to N. Chamberlain, 17 Aug. 1932, NC 7/11/25/1.

THE AFTERMATH OF DEFEAT

Defeat could be fertile. The 1931 crisis created the political respite for Lloyd George to write his *War Memoirs*, and Churchill his life of Marlborough. It produced *Essays in Persuasion* and *The Means to Prosperity*. It also stimulated the major British apologia for Soviet communism, a classic text of British marxism, and the most formal statement of British fascism.

If the seduction of the Webbs, ILP leaders, Strachey, and Mosley by Russian, Italian, and German models is testimony to the disorientating effects of 1931, these were just the exotic instances of a more widespread and far-reaching effect of the crisis: a movement towards ideas of state planning or management, reflecting a loss of confidence whose other characteristic was increased interest in foreign exemplars. After the example of state collectivism during the Great War, varieties of planning or *dirigisme* had become latent in Labour, Liberal, and Conservative versions of radicalism, and these received further impetus from the persistent economic stagnation and unemployment of the late 1920s. But it was the impact of the world recession and then the currency and budgetary crises which really injected ideas about state planning and what would later be called a 'mixed economy' into general political discourse. The market and *laissez-faire*, it could be argued, had finally shown their incapacity to deliver prosperity and to underpin political stability and imperial power. For the purposes either of transforming or of defending the social and political orders, it seemed that the market had to be superseded or complemented by forms of 'rational' economic and social organisation and direction. Mosley's October 1930 memorandum, *The Week-end Review's* 'National Plan' and the formation of PEP had been precursors. So, in another sense, had been the visits to Russia in 1930–1 of Strachey, Bevan, and the Astors, followed in 1932 not just by the Webbs but by Macmillan and Young and by a New Fabian group including Dalton, Pethick-Lawrence, and Margaret Cole. The acceptance of forms of planning by Keynes, Macmillan, and later Percy and the Next Five Years group as well as by Mosley, the Labour leadership, and the TUC laid some of the foundations for a new 'middle opinion' of the 1940s.[112]

---

[112] See, e.g., Arthur Marwick, 'Middle Opinion in the Thirties: Planning, Progress and Political Agreement', *English Historical Review*, 79 (1964), 285–98, and L. P. Carpenter, 'Corporatism in Britain, 1930–45', *Journal of Contemporary History*, 11 (1976), 3–25.

A question which needs to be asked is whether the National government itself contributed to this movement. What can be said so far about the government's complexion is that at the 1931 election it received support from a vast spectrum of popular opinion; that much of its financial policy was approved by Keynes, and that Lloyd George saw no hope of forming a serious Liberal or radical opposition. It also faced opposition movements within the Conservative party, by Churchill and the imperialist diehards, and by Amery and the doctrinaire protectionists.

CHAPTER 14

The National government

I rather like the look of things in India. The late Lord Salisbury said, quoting an American, there were two ways of governing men – 'bamboozle or bamboo'. You seem to be trying both at once.

Churchill to Sinclair, 30 December 1931

I am convinced that this policy [of the Import Duties Bill] and this alone could have saved the Empire. It may not have saved all of it yet. But without it the Empire, as we have known it, was bound to go and to carry with it the greatness of this country.

Neville Chamberlain to Lord Lloyd, 7 February 1932[1]

These gentlemen [the Samuelite ministers]...appear to us as willing and cheerful hostages in a hostile camp...When the opportune moment arrives, however, they will be mercilessly slaughtered by their captors. They have nothing to lose but their chains.

Hubert Phillips et al., Whither Britain. A Radical Answer
(August 1932)

THE 'NATIONAL' TRIUMPH

In late October 1931 the unelected emergency government of August became an elected coalition with support from as many as 67 per cent of voters and a parliamentary majority of around 500. In this, it amply fulfilled the long-standing desire of many financiers, businessmen, industrialists, agriculturalists, publicists, and imperial servants, as well as Conservative and Liberal politicians, for strong, stable, non-socialist government. A 'bloodless [but]...none the less effective...political revolution' had established a 'Parliamentary Dictatorship'[2] committed to, and apparently capable of, saving capitalism and the Empire. Aside from Labour politicians and

---

[1] Respectively Thurso papers II/85/3, and Lloyd papers 19/5.
[2] N. to I. Chamberlain, 29 Nov. 1931, NC 18/1/763, and Jones, Diary With Letters, 20, 28 Oct. 1931.

Mosley, criticism of the machinery of government largely subsided. In contrast to the labours of the 1930–1 Select Committee on parliamentary procedure, that of 1932 was perfunctory and concluded that existing arrangements were adequate.[3] The effect of the election result upon the confidence of the most powerful sections and creators of public opinion in itself did much to disperse that sense of deep national crisis existing since autumn 1930. During the next twelve months the government completed that process. It did not overcome all outstanding domestic problems; nor could it prevent the emergence of new foreign troubles, which later appeared to be as dangerous to national interests as had the economic and imperial troubles of 1930–1. It nevertheless resolved some of the most difficult issues of the previous three years, removed the political sting from others, and otherwise created a reassuring impression of competence.

This is not to say that the government itself was expected to be free from difficulties. The clumsy compromise over the trade issue made that seem unlikely. Consequently even government leaders and their supporters had complex reactions to the election result. On the one hand, they were as much amazed as the Labour party was shocked by 'a greater majority than dreamland ever portrayed'.[4] Although the Cabinet declined one opportunity for thanksgiving in the form of government endorsement for the Archbishops' National Day of Prayer,[5] there was relief and jubilation at the rout of new-style socialism and achievement of a massive mandate. This mandate was especially gratifying because it obviously included support from a high proportion of working-class voters and many recipients of income cuts, and was unencumbered by pledges to anything except whatever the Cabinet might think appropriate.

On the other hand, the extent and character of the victory created an undertow of apprehension. The government's majority was so large that it could easily become unwieldy; lacking pressure from a large opposition, it might tend to fragment. Most worrying was its disproportionate composition, due to a remarkable Conservative party success. Of 518 Conservative candidates, the astonishingly high number of 470 had been returned. Conservatives won in most

---

[3] *Report from the Select Committee on Procedure*, 10 Nov. 1932, esp. para. 5.

[4] Churchill in *HC Deb*, 259, col. 1189, 20 Nov. 1931.

[5] Cabinet 85(31), 7 Dec. 1931, approved MacDonald's rejection of the Archbishop of Canterbury's suggestion as likely to be 'misrepresented ... as a day of partisan thanksgiving'. For the Day of Prayer, see *The Times*, 4 Jan. 1932.

regions and types of seats, obtaining their largest-ever percentage of
the poll (55 per cent). They defeated, sometimes by huge majorities,
not just 182 Labour MPs but also some of their ostensible allies: ten
Liberals (including three junior ministers) and four National Labour
(including the Attorney-General, Jowitt). Every other parliamentary party or group (none numbering more than fifty MPs) was
puny in comparison with this enormous Conservative mass, which
alone constituted a majority of 327 over all the rest. It was 1906 in
reverse, and more: to some Liberals it seemed that 'the "Governing
Class" were once more governing', and that in political complexion
the House of Commons had become another House of Lords.[6] Each
government partner feared difficulties.

MacDonald, Snowden, and Thomas on the whole felt 'triumphant'. Their delight at Henderson and other Labour leaders
paying the price for 'cowardice and folly', and at the 'smash[ing]'
of 'Trade Union tyranny', surpassed their genuine sorrow at the fate
of former followers.[7] Yet MacDonald also thought the election had
'turned out too well': the Conservative preponderance had
'weakened' his own position.[8] As he admitted publicly, the result
was 'embarrassing'. He responded by emphasising its national
character, as a victory as much for the working classes as other
classes. Although just thirteen National Labour MPs had been
elected, MacDonald implied that with Snowden and Thomas he had
secured the votes of a very large number of former Labour
supporters for the National government.[9] With enthusiastic assistance from another former ILP chairman, Allen, during 1932 he
hoped that the National Labour committee could create a
substantial body of non-partisan opinion in support of scientific,
state-directed 'socialist' reconstruction.[10]

For Samuel too, the result had been one for agreed national
purposes. Conservative power was not 'unconditional' and gave no
mandate for protection, because it derived largely from Liberal votes
and withdrawal of Liberal candidates.[11] The number of Liberal

[6] Bernays, *Special Correspondent*, 96; Lothian to Samuel, 28 Oct. 1931, Samuel papers
A/82/10.
[7] MacDonald in Wigram memo, 28 Oct. 1931, RA GV K2331(1)/46, and in Hankey, 28
Oct. 1931; MacDonald diary, 29 Oct. 1931; M. MacDonald to Denman, 29 Oct. 1931,
Denman papers 4. See also Snowden statement, *Manchester Guardian*, 29 Oct. 1931.
[8] MacDonald diary, 29 Oct. 1931.
[9] MacDonald statement, *Manchester Guardian*, 29 Oct. 1931, and see Snowden, ibid.
[10] See material in Gilbert (ed.), *Plough My Own Furrow*, chs. 16–18.
[11] Samuel speech, *The Times*, 29 Oct. 1931.

MPs, of all designations, had increased from fifty-nine at the previous election to seventy-one, of whom sixty-seven were government supporters. Some Liberals, long inured to party divisions, supposed that this represented a Liberal recovery. The NLF listed Simon's Liberal Nationals together with Samuel's official Liberal MPs as if they still formed one party. Samuelites spoke of Liberals as 'now once more the second largest' party.[12] Although the total Liberal vote had more than halved since the 1929 election and now amounted to only a third of the Labour vote, this was attributed to a smaller number of candidates caused by shortage of funds. Such interpretations fed an optimistic verdict on the election. Samuelite Liberals began fund-raising and organisational reconstruction – presenting themselves as finally freed from the incubus of the Lloyd George Fund – in the belief that there now existed 'a real prospect of building up the Party'.[13]

All this was a delusion. Many former Liberal voters had now defected irretrievably either to Conservative or to Labour. The party had been split beyond repair, and few wealthy Liberals would help finance what was in reality only a splinter of the Liberal party, in parliamentary terms not even the largest. The thirty-three Samuelite Liberal MPs were outnumbered by thirty-five Simonite Liberals, who understood perfectly that their value to MacDonald and Baldwin lay in being non-Samuelites. When, immediately after the election, Simon rejected Samuel's claim to control all Liberal ministerial patronage and refused to attend Samuelite meetings, the separate existence of the two main Liberal groups was confirmed.[14] When Lloyd George also declined to attend, Samuel remained with the leadership of just the Liberal rump.

Despite MacDonaldite and Samuelite apprehensions (and, indeed, Labour and Lloyd Georgian criticisms), it would be a mistake to conclude that the general election converted the National government into a 'Conservative' government. Certainly its parliamentary supporters were overwhelmingly Conservative. Cer-

[12] Rea (Liberal whip) to Crook, 13 Nov. 1931, Crook papers d396, and see Lothian to Samuel, 28 Oct. 1931, Samuel papers A/82/10.
[13] Oldham to Samuel, 6 Nov. 1931, Samuel papers A/84/11, and see Hirst and Leif Jones in Hirst diary, 3 Nov. 1931, in Hirst, 13. For finance and organisation, see Sinclair to Samuel, 3 Nov. 1931, and Johnstone to Samuel, 24 and 30 Nov. 1931, Samuel papers A/84/7, 13, 14; Samuelite meeting, 1 Dec. 1931, Thurso papers III/3/5.
[14] Note of Maclean–Simon telephone conversation, 30 Oct. 1931, Samuel papers A/84/3 and (slightly different) Reading papers, F118/131; Samuel to Fisher, 4 Nov. 1931, Fisher papers 10/140; Samuel, *Memoirs*, 214.

tainly many MPs, organisers, and local associations, believing that the party would have won the election even if there had been no crisis, tended to think of the overall result as primarily a Conservative achievement. Page Croft and other strong protectionists treated the result as a 'disastrous defeat' for the Samuelites and free trade.[15] Many MacDonaldite and Liberal MPs were thought to owe their seats to withdrawals of Conservative candidates or to Conservative votes, and there was much reluctance to make concessions towards them at by-elections. Such Conservatives, regarding 'Conservative' as synonymous with 'national', expected the government to use its majority to implement specifically Conservative party policies.

Yet to the Conservative leaders and most other Conservatives it was perfectly plain that the scale of their party's success owed much to the 'National' platform and the alliance with MacDonald, Snowden, Thomas, Simon, Runciman, and their followers – though few would admit to any substantial Samuelite contribution. A large number of Conservative MPs had won seats which they might not otherwise have won, and which they would be unlikely to hold without continued non-Conservative support. The ability of an anti-socialist alliance to capture Liberal, disillusioned Labour, and floating electoral support for broadly 'Conservative' purposes had been profusely demonstrated. The prospect emerged of permanent Conservative domination of government, invulnerable to such an electoral 'swing of the pendulum' as could restore Labour to government in the foreseeable future. Even before the election Neville Chamberlain, an old Unionist, had looked to the de-velopment of 'a National Party...get[ting] rid of that odious title of Conservative which has kept so many from joining us in the past'.[16] Now party organisers who had initially been hostile even to MacDonald leading the election campaign also wanted the coalition amalgamated into a party.[17] So too did Baldwin.[18] He, like all Conservative leaders, had always presented the party as *the* national party, even if, ironically, he had used this claim twelve months previously to reject the 'national government' idea. Now his strategy of the 1920s, of making the Conservative party the magnet for all non-socialist politicians, seemed to have been fulfilled.

[15] Page Croft to Beaverbrook, 29 Oct. 1931, Beaverbrook papers B/192.

[16] N. to I. and H. Chamberlain, 19 Sept., 24 Oct. 1931, NC 18/1/755, 759.

[17] Stonehaven to Baldwin, 15 Nov. 1931, and Central Office memo, 27 Nov. 1931, SB 166/299–300, 46/33–5; National Union Executive Committee, 8 Dec. 1931.

[18] Jones, *Diary with Letters*, 25–6, 28 Jan. 1932.

Establishment of a 'National Party' was to be repeatedly postponed, as the National Labour and Liberal allies believed their value to lie in remaining semi-independent, and as strong Conservative dissident groups appeared from 1933 onwards.[19] Nevertheless the project was not simply a matter of party terminology or organisation. It indicated an important feature of the Conservative leadership's intentions and behaviour. Baldwin, Chamberlain, and other Conservative leaders treated the notion of a 'National' government seriously, and did not make Conservative party policies the precondition for co-operation. In certain areas, including sterling, budget, Indian, and disarmament policies, experience had already shown that a genuinely non-party approach could be compatible with Conservative objectives. Where there was disagreement over fundamentals – over trade policy especially – they proceeded by negotiation, not dictation, and accepted some erosion of party policy as the necessary price for the larger advantages of the National government. In some respects a 'national approach' had positive attractions, because it loosened the constraints of party pressure and enabled issues to be considered more on substantive policy or administrative merits. This was especially true for Baldwin over Indian policy, but also for Chamberlain over tax remission and the details of protection. Given these perspectives, Conservative leaders also expected the election result to produce difficulties, in the shape of managing their own party and preventing backbench MPs forming hostile 'cliques and societies'.[20] In the event, however, the new intake of Conservative MPs positively helped, because diehards and strong protectionists became a smaller proportion of the parliamentary party.

From the beginning the Conservative leaders demonstrated their self-restraint, by allowing the reconstructed government to be much more 'national' in its ministerial composition than in its parliamentary following. Except in a few cases where Baldwin had a particular concern, he allowed MacDonald to reconstruct the government himself,[21] even though MacDonald's obvious aim was to include as many non-Conservatives as possible. With slight changes of personnel, his own National Labour group retained its existing

[19] Cowling, *Impact of Hitler*, 51.
[20] E.g., Baldwin in Wigram memos, 2 and 4 Nov. 1931, RA GV K2331(1)/48, 50, and at National Union Executive Committee, 4 Nov. 1931.
[21] See MacDonald in Dawes, *Journal*, 407, 29 Oct. 1931, for Baldwin 'co-operating to the highest degree'; and Baldwin in Amery diary, 29 Oct. 1931 (*LSA* II, 216).

number of Cabinet and junior posts. Snowden received his peerage but was retained as Lord Privy Seal. Of the Liberals, Maclean and Sinclair entered the Cabinet and Lothian moved to the junior India post, but Reading reluctantly retired to ease the reconstruction.[22] The number of Samuelite ministers was halved, largely because MacDonald and Baldwin insisted on including Simonites, as much to intimidate the free-trade Liberals as because of their larger parliamentary numbers and unqualified support for the government. Samuel objected to Simon receiving a Cabinet seat, while Simon began by asking for Samuel's office and then declined any post inferior to his.[23] This stubbornness won Simon the Foreign Secretaryship.[24] Lesser offices went to others prominent in the Simonite rebellion – Brown, Hore-Belisha, and Shakespeare – while Hutchison received a peerage. Grigg, however, obliged by the presence of a National Labour MP to withdraw his parliamentary candidature, obtained nothing. Runciman's political re-emergence had made such a many-sided impact that almost every government leader wanted him in a senior economic post. He would have become Chancellor of the Exchequer had Conservative party pressure not obliged Baldwin to insist upon Neville Chamberlain; instead, he returned to the Board of Trade.[25] Austen Chamberlain painfully accepted the inevitable and took the dignified course of retirement. Hailsham, again necessary to soothe the Conservative right, had now become sufficiently chastened to accept the War Office with leadership of the Lords. Amery was omitted because MacDonald refused to have such an uncompromising protectionist, but also because in Conservative party terms he had become dispensable and because no Conservative leader now 'ha[d] any belief in his judgement'.[26] Overall Conservative representation was

[22] See Reading to Baldwin, 29 Oct. 1931, SB 45/193, for his hopes of remaining Foreign Secretary.

[23] See Amery diary, 29 Oct., 16 Dec. 1931 (*LSA* II, 217, 225); MacDonald diary, 1 Nov. 1931; Simon to Baldwin, 2 Nov. 1931, SB 45/197–8; N. to H. Chamberlain, 7 Nov. 1931, NC 18/1/760.

[24] So began Simon's remarkable 14-year career as token Liberal, which took him to all major ministerial posts except the highest: Foreign Secretary 1931–5, Home Secretary 1935–7, Chancellor of the Exchequer 1937–40, Lord Chancellor 1940–5.

[25] See MacDonald in Hankey diary, 28 Oct. 1931 (Roskill, *Hankey* II, 571), and Wigram memo, 29 Oct. 1931, RA GV K2331(1)/47, and MacDonald to Baldwin, 3 Nov. 1931, SB 45/199.

[26] N. to H. Chamberlain, 7 Nov. 1931, NC 18/1/760. Cf. Baldwin and Chamberlain in Amery diary, 10 and 11 Nov. 1931, (*LSA* II, 219–20), and Baldwin to Amery, 5 Nov. 1931, Amery papers, for effusive (but hollow) regrets.

increased, but formed only just over half the Cabinet. To that extent, the government had certainly not become simply 'Conservative'.

SAVING THE EMPIRE

The reconstructed government had the considerable advantage that after the frustrations of the previous two years 'the nation want[ed] to feel the hand of the ruler'.[27] Its leaders were ready to apply that hand. The Cabinet was restored to its normal size in anticipation of a heavy workload. MacDonald rose to the opportunities for at last getting things done, setting out an ambitious Cabinet work programme, establishing a committee system to co-ordinate policies, re-circulating papers on which the Labour Cabinet had failed to act, and intervening in many areas of policy and administration.[28] Initially he even proposed a special 'flying squad' of ministers without portfolio to tackle particularly tough problems.[29] For ministers accustomed to Baldwin's or Asquith's relaxed style he appeared to be acting 'as though he were a dictator and not P.M.'.[30] The King's Speech deliberately contained few immediate legislative commitments, in order to free Cabinet ministers for examination of the major areas where action was proposed.[31] However, it did identify those areas: India, Commonwealth constitutional relations, disarmament, international and national finance, the trade balance and imperial trade. The Cabinet was soon attacking all these issues 'at a giddy pace'.[32] In only the second and third, where it faced new, implacable challenges, did problems fail to yield to its touch.

Unexpectedly, India ceased to have serious financial problems and even became a monetary asset. Hoare had no parliamentary difficulties with legislation to reduce official salaries. The parallel sterling–rupee depreciation made it profitable for Indians to sell gold, which unlocked private hoards for export to Britain and

[27] G. Lloyd moving the Address, *HC Deb*, 259, col. 50, 10 Nov. 1931. For the phrase resonating, see Bernays, *Special Correspondent*, 147–8.
[28] For Cabinet size, MacDonald in Cabinet 72(31), 29 Oct. 1931; for committees, MacDonald, 'Cabinet Policy and Work', CP 311(31), 7 Dec. 1931, and Cabinets 87, 88, 89(31), 10, 11, and 14 Dec. 1931. For re-circulated departmental and EAC papers, see, e.g., CP 275, 276, 278, 279, 297(31).
[29] See Wigram memo, 3 Nov. 1931, RA GV K2331(1)/49, and Lothian to Reading, 6 Nov. 1931, Reading papers, F118/131. The idea died with refusals by Simon and Horne to accept non-departmental posts.
[30] N. to I. Chamberlain, 15 Nov. 1931, NC 18/1/761.
[31] Cabinet 72(31), 29 Oct. 1931.
[32] N. to I. Chamberlain, 29 Nov. 1931, NC 18/1/763.

greatly assisted the re-building of the Bank of England's gold reserves.[33] But the constitutional issue remained delicate, and might have become dangerous. Many Conservatives still harboured doubts about the reform process to which MacDonald and Baldwin were committed, and these could have formed an opposition much more formidable than the parliamentary Labour party. With Simon and Hailsham now in the Cabinet, differences between ministers were widened. That Churchill and Lloyd had so few followers in the December 1931 Indian debates was no indication of their potential support had the Cabinet not found a united voice, and its policy and presentation been handled less skilfully. After the huge Conservative successes at the 1931 election, the preservation of the project of All-India Federation – and its eventual embodiment in the 1935 Government of India Act – was in British political terms a major achievement. It was also a good demonstration of a genuinely 'national' approach.

The key lay in an early switch in strategy, initiated as much in Delhi as in London. Experience had taught Willingdon to dislike the Irwin–Gandhi pact. By making Gandhi a 'plenipotentiary in negotiating terms of peace with the Viceroy himself', he thought it had undermined Indian moderates and Princes, hamstrung the administration of law, and demoralised the police and bureaucracy. He aimed to reassert government authority and 'disabuse' Congress of its belief that it formed a 'parallel authority', for which purpose he endeavoured to treat Gandhi as an ordinary Indian politician.[34] Also, in expectation that Congress extremists would eventually break the pact, his officials prepared the most comprehensive and drastic emergency powers ever proposed, to enable them to 'strike at once and strike hard' with a repression more effective than that of 1930.[35] Because Benn had disliked his approach, Willingdon had welcomed the National government as a 'Providential opportunity for settling our Indian problem on non-party lines'.[36]

Hoare, as Benn's 'National' Conservative successor, supported

---

[33] See Tomlinson, 'Britain and the Indian Currency Crisis', 96–7, and Drummond, *Floating Pound*, 43–6. For Indian Pay (Temporary Abatement) Bill, see *HC Deb*, 260, cols. 409–45, 541–51, 25 and 26 Nov. 1931.

[34] Willingdon to Hoare, 28 Aug., 12 Oct. 1931, Templewood Indian papers 5/1–4, 16–17; Willingdon to Bridgeman, 5 Dec. 1931, Bridgeman papers. See Moore, *Crisis of Indian Unity*, 219–66, for detailed background for the following Indian paragraphs.

[35] These plans had been initiated under Irwin's Viceroyalty, in case negotiations for the pact failed, but had been much advanced under Willingdon: see Low, 'Civil Martial Law', 171–3.

[36] Willingdon to Hoare, 28 Aug. 1931, Templewood Indian papers 5/1–4.

Willingdon because he understood that to direct Indian policy successfully it would be necessary to dispel Conservative fears that 'defeatism ha[d] corroded the machinery of government'. He thought the Round Table Conference process fostered a dangerous impression that nationalist leaders were determining British policy, and he wanted it clearly established that the Cabinet was 'dead against anything in the nature of a surrender on the lines of the Irish treaty'.[37] During the second Round Table Conference of September–December 1931 he too refused Gandhi special status, except to tell him 'there was not a dog's earthly of satisfying his demand' for independence. He would have been content to see the Conference collapse, provided responsibility could be laid upon the Indian delegates and did not align 'India' against Britain.[38]

Between what Willingdon wanted to achieve in India and what Hoare wanted to demonstrate in Britain there was a convergence which produced a tougher collective attitude towards Indian nationalism than that of Irwin and Benn in early 1931. Nevertheless Willingdon and Hoare were both clear that reaction would be impossible, and repression alone counter-productive. Earlier promises, however unfortunate, were irreversible,[39] and federation seemed the safest means to fulfil them. But they differed from Irwin and Benn over how to achieve the multiple objectives of safeguarding British interests in India while winning Indian political support, and soothing Conservative opinion without upsetting 'moderate' national opinion in Britain. Their first principle was to regain the initiative and offer concessions only from positions of strength. The second was to marginalise or tame Congress, forcing its acceptance of the new constitutional limits, while simultaneously seeking to conciliate the Hindu moderates, Muslims, and Princes.

Congress largely played into Hoare's and Willingdon's hands. First, at the Round Table Conference Gandhi's opposition to separate electorates for most Indian minorities, and Muslim distrust of Congress, made it impossible for Indian delegates to construct a scheme of communal representation, the precondition of federation. Hoare seized the opportunity to restore Cabinet initiative, by proposing an unquestionably British policy tailored to reassure Conservatives and outmanoeuvre Congress. The Simon Report

---

[37] Hoare to Willingdon, 2 Sept., 2 Oct., 17 Dec. 1931, Templewood Indian papers 1/1–6, 21–7, 100–10.
[38] Hoare to Willingdon, 11 and 25 Sept., 2 Oct., 19 Nov., 3 Dec. 1931, Templewood Indian papers 1/7–11, 16–20, 21–7, 69–75, 84–9; Sankey diary, 9 and 19 Oct. 1931.
[39] See, e.g., Willingdon to Butler, 9 Nov. 1931, 31 May 1932, Butler papers 53/111–12, 54–16.

would become a staging post to federation, in effect squaring the opponents with the proponents of federation.[40] Provincial autonomy would be implemented first, in order to convince British Conservatives that Indian responsibility would be 'safe' and Indian politicians that a strong, British-led, central federal government was indispensable. The federal constitution would then be settled not by another Round Table Conference, but by British commissions and committees. 'Dominion status' would not be mentioned.[41] In early November 1931 Hoare cobbled together an alliance of Muslim and Hindu moderate delegates in support of this approach. Simon and Hailsham wanted the federation pledge withdrawn altogether, but acquiesced when promised that it would be withdrawn if Indian politicians made difficulties over the proposed British 'safeguards'.[42] MacDonald and Sankey were annoyed that Hoare had subverted their own plans to circumvent the minorities problem, but with the Cabinet against them preferred his approach to diehard Conservative readiness to 'rule India with the sword'.[43]

Hoare certainly proposed a 'Conservative' policy. Yet, in retaining the objective of Indian responsibility in central government, it was a policy which would have been more difficult to contemplate within an actual Conservative government. Even so it was soon pushed further in 'National' directions, towards what MacDonald and Sankey wanted. As news of Hoare's proposal to give provincial reform priority over central government reform spread through the Conference, many Indian delegates became distrustful of the Cabinet's commitment to federation. The subsequent outcry turned those who had previously supported his proposal against it.[44]

The effect is revealing, demonstrating that, whatever the opinions of individual Cabinet members towards India, all assumed a

[40] For Hoare cultivating Simon, see Cabinet 51(31), 2 Sept. 1931, and Hoare to Willingdon, 6 Nov. 1931, Templewood Indian papers 1/61–4, 65–8.

[41] For development of Hoare's ideas, Hoare to Willingdon, 25 Sept., 2 and 23 Oct., 6 and 19 Nov. 1931, Templewood Indian papers 1/16–20, 47–56, 65–8, 69–75.

[42] CP273(31), 12 Nov. 1931; Cabinets 77, 80(31), 13 and 20 Nov. 1931; Sankey diary, 13 and 18 Nov. 1931; Maclean to Runciman, 13 Nov. 1931, Runciman papers 245; MacDonald diary, 17 Nov. 1931.

[43] Sankey diary, 9, 14, 15, 19, and 22 Oct, 18, 19, 25, and 27 Nov. 1931; MacDonald diary, 2, 11, 15, 16, and 23 Nov. 1931; MacDonald to Willingdon, 6 Dec. 1931, JRM 698. MacDonald obtained alternative advice from Irwin, and at times would have liked to have been able to dismiss Hoare.

[44] Hoare to Willingdon, 26 Nov. 1931, Templewood Indian papers 1/76–83; Cabinet 82(31), 27 Nov. 1931.

strategy of divide and rule. Faced with loss of moderate and Muslim support, of 'India' uniting against 'Britain', which even Hailsham and Simon recognised as dangerous, the Cabinet immediately reverted to the position that provincial autonomy and central federation should be implemented simultaneously – the policy established by the first Round Table Conference. Nevertheless Hoare, Simon, and Hailsham ensured that the Cabinet retained control over the policy, and preserved the crucial impression of firmness. The system of British commissions of inquiry was retained, and in closing the second Conference on 1 December MacDonald was persuaded to emphasise that federation involved 'reservations' and 'safeguards'.[45] In Parliament MacDonald, Hoare, Simon, Baldwin, Sankey, and Hailsham together mounted an all-round defence on this reform process which smothered most potential criticism to both the left and right.

Second, in India itself Congress played into Willingdon's hands by endorsing resumptions of civil disobedience. When Gandhi declined to disown these outbreaks, the Government of India treated this as breaching the Irwin–Gandhi pact and implemented its long-prepared emergency powers. On 4 January the main Congress bodies were proscribed, and Gandhi and other leaders arrested. Many of the rank and file followed; in a month there were 16,000 prisoners, by May 36,000. Though the repression was drastic and relentless, the government took great care to ensure that its position was not destroyed by another Amritsar massacre. In contrast to 1930, civil disobedience had been all but broken before it had really started. The morale of officials and police was restored, while Hindu and Muslim moderates and the Princes were reassured that Britain was not abandoning India.[46] In London the measures had an 'excellent' effect upon Conservative opinion, and Hoare was cheered in the Commons.[47] MacDonald felt 'nervous' that repression might crowd out conciliation, but he had become disillusioned with Gandhi and was clear about the need to be 'quite firm with political crime'.[48]

What had been achieved was a dual policy: on the one hand repression of Congress, on the other advance to a form of Indian self-

[45] Cabinets 82, 83(31), 27 and 30 Nov. 1931; Sankey diary, 30 Nov. 1931; MacDonald diary, 1 Dec. 1931.   [46] Low, 'Civil Martial Law', 174–7, 188.
[47] Hoare to Willingdon, 8 Jan. 1932, Templewood Indian papers 1/126–32; G. Lloyd to Davidson, 12 Feb. 1932, Davidson Indian papers, c557/27–33.
[48] MacDonald notebook, 1 and 3 Jan. 1932, JRM 1753.

government circumscribed by British controls and checked by 'loyalist' Indians. This course commanded wider support than that pursued by Irwin and Benn, because it more successfully faced in two directions. For 'liberals' in the Cabinet and in Parliament it promised a very large instalment of reform, while repression seemed an unavoidable consequence of Congress recalcitrance. More important, for 'conservatives' and especially the Conservative party it offered assurance that the reforms were as calculated as the repression to preserve British control.

Doubts remained over the Princes' commitment to federation and the moderates' capacity to form an effective electoral force.[49] But after the three commissions of inquiry returned from India in May, the Cabinet was convinced that to proceed with federation would be safe for both India and Britain. Crucially, Baldwin believed the Princes would 'bring stability' to Indian central government, and that the scheme would be acceptable to the Conservative party.[50] After Maclean died in June, MacDonald and Baldwin replaced him with Irwin to provide additional Cabinet support for their shared commitments. In August the India Office decision on the representation of minorities in the proposed new provincial and central assemblies secured Muslim support without upsetting Hindu moderates. Although a third Round Table Conference had to be conceded to please the latter, it was a truncated affair which essentially endorsed Cabinet policy. In the event passage of the Government of India Act would be a long, hard struggle against a Churchill–Salisbury–diehard rearguard action. Nevertheless the crucial decisions which made success possible had been taken within three months of the 1931 election.

Determination to maintain the Empire was as marked in Commonwealth relations as in Indian policy. The expectation that the National government would be more successful than the Labour government in strengthening imperial economic ties helped soothe Conservative and Liberal misgivings about the Statute of Westminster, passed during November.[51] The government nonetheless took a firm stand in relations with the new Dominions, though

[49] For 'white-livered' moderates 'funk[ing] the task of organising a party', Willingdon to Butler, 9 May 1932, Butler papers 54/13–15. For Hoare and Princes, Moore, *Crisis of Indian Unity*, 253–5, 271–3.

[50] Sankey notes of Cabinet India Committee, 26 May 1932, Sankey papers, c509/70–9.

[51] For the point being stressed by ministerial sponsors of the Statute, see Thomas, *HC Deb*, 259, cols. 1182–3, 20 Nov. 1931, and Hailsham, *HL Deb*, 83, cols. 227–8, 26 Nov. 1931.

whereas in India firmness meant avoiding another Irish Treaty, here it meant defence of that Treaty. The Churchill, Salisbury, and Gretton assertions that acceptance of full Dominion autonomy would subvert the Treaty were deflected by a declaration from Cosgrave's Irish government that it could 'only be altered by consent'.[52] But the point of diehard anxiety was the possibility that the anti-Treaty Fianna Fáil party would win the next Irish election, as it did in February 1932. De Valera's notice a month later that he intended to abolish the Royal Oath and subsequent threat to retain land annuities owed to Britain, demonstrated his belief in unilateral treaty revision. In doing so, he challenged the British assumption that the Statue of Westminster would preserve the unity of the Empire. This provoked a sharp Cabinet reaction leading in July to imposition of sanctions – a resort to 'economic war' intended to intimidate and perhaps destabilise de Valera.

It is striking that MacDonald, Sankey, and Thomas, as much as Hailsham and other Cabinet Conservatives, and almost as much as the backbench diehards, believed in the reality of the remaining constitutional ties between Britain and the Dominions, even to the point of using coercion to maintain those links.[53] Despite the Statute of Westminster, Dominion self-government was not regarded as independence. 'Commonwealth' still meant 'British Empire', its constituents lacking the sovereign power of secession. What the Cabinet had not counted upon, and what even dealings with Gandhi had not prepared them for, was an opponent of utter inflexibility – one who seemed impervious to 'reason', an 'impossible fanatic'.[54]

Little needs to be said about disarmament as such, despite the first session of the Disarmament Conference from February to July 1932. This caused no serious domestic complications,[55] and although the issue occupied much Cabinet time it had little expectation of early

[52] *HC Deb*, 260, col. 311, 24 Nov. 1931. For A. Chamberlain and Amery helping the Cabinet here, see A. to I. and H. Chamberlain, 22 and 28 Nov. 1931; AC 5/1/565, 566, and Amery diary, 24 Nov. 1931.

[53] E.g., MacDonald diary, 10 April 1932; MacDonald–Thomas telephone conversation, 11 Aug. 1932, JRM 594.

[54] MacDonald to Archbishop Lang, 13 Sept. 1932, JRM 701; Sankey diary, 15 July 1932; and see N. to H. Chamberlain, 11 June 1932, NC 18/1/786.

[55] But for annoyance at Henderson being the Conference president, see Cabinet 79(31), 18 Nov. 1931, and MacDonald–Simon telephone conversation, 24 July 1932, JRM 702; and for Foreign Office helping Austen Chamberlain to sow dissension within the League of Nations Union, see Simon to A. Chamberlain, and A. Chamberlain to Simon, 24 and 30 May 1932, AC 39/5/35, 36.

success. The difficulty was the incompatibility of each Power's special interests. This made the first session inconclusive and created another problem as new, more nationalist German governments threatened to boycott the Conference unless they obtained recognition of their claims to military equality. More immediately significant was a problem which highlights Cabinet priorities, as well as Britain's foreign policy dilemmas. Service chiefs had long advised that British unilateral disarmament exceeded the point of safety in the event of war. In response the 'ten year rule' – a standing instruction that military plans should assume that no war would occur for ten years – had been introduced in the 1920s to absolve them of responsibility for a condition created by financial and political considerations.[56] The Japanese invasion of Manchuria from September 1931, and especially the attack upon Shanghai in January 1932, exposed the consequences: inability to defend Britain's Far Eastern outposts and interests, let alone deter military aggression.[57] As a result the Cabinet allowed the ten year rule to lapse. Yet it did not order immediate rearmament. This would not just have clashed with the Disarmament Conference; more fundamentally, it clashed with financial policy. The Treasury's verdict prevailed; financial strength was the precondition of effective defence, and as 'financial and economic risks [were] by far the most serious and urgent' now before the country, 'other risks' had to be run until government finances recovered.[58] Similar considerations affected economic policy.

MANAGING THE ECONOMY

Nothing demonstrates how the 1931 crisis transformed political debate about the economy so clearly as the National government's attitude towards unemployment. For the first time since February 1928 the King's Speech did not contain even the words 'unemployment' or 'employment', despite the numbers of unemployed having increased almost threefold in the meantime. MacDonald's scheme of Cabinet committees treated unemployment as a secondary matter. When an employment policy committee was appointed it

[56] For the rationale, Treasury Note, CP105(31), 17 March 1932. For a recent example of its operation, overriding a formal Admiralty warning, see Cabinet 49(31), 31 Aug. 1931.
[57] For an excellent characterisation of the dilemma, see Baldwin in Jones, *Diary with Letters*, 30, 27 Feb. 1932.   [58] Treasury Note, CP105(32), 17 March 1932.

consisted wholly of junior ministers and had instructions to assume 'a very high level' of unemployment 'for some years to come'.[59]

Under Treasury chairmanship this committee produced an epitaph on the employment policies of the previous eleven years. Treasury arguments against the Keynes, Lloyd George, and Mosley public works proposals of 1929–30 now appeared as the lessons of experience from the more limited schemes which had been implemented. At 'unduly burdensome' cost, these had produced 'very limited' employment results. 'Abnormal' schemes crowded out normal trade and employment. The country was poorer for the extra money spent per man on 'uneconomic' relief employment as compared to unemployment insurance. As a recovery policy such schemes were manifestly ineffective, and in their impact upon confidence were counter-productive. Existing schemes should be wound down; new ones should be considered only if clearly remunerative or if needed to stimulate 'individual and public morale'. For the foreseeable future 'by far the most important direct contribution of the State towards assisting the unemployed' would be 'cash allowances'.[60]

In accepting the committee's report the Cabinet chose to have no specific employment policy, other than to maintain the unemployed on unemployment insurance and transitional benefit. In a sense this decision vindicated the 'Treasury view' on public works, but it was achieved less by intellectual conversion – since few politicians had seriously doubted Treasury arguments – than by the change in political and financial conditions. Conservative leaders had always been sceptical about public works; Snowden and Thomas had learnt to become so. Liberal Cabinet ministers had not been directly engaged with Lloyd George's 1929–30 programmes,[61] which anyway had been buried in February 1931. Experience had shown MacDonald that public works were primarily a political rather than an economic exercise, and though wanting to maintain some employment schemes in order to 'keep faith' with working-class

[59] MacDonald, 'Cabinet Policy and Work', CP 311(31), 7 Dec. 1931; Cabinet 89(31), 14 Dec. 1931.

[60] Employment Policy Committee Report, CP36(32), 25 Jan. 1932, accepted at Cabinet 11(32), 3 Feb. 1932: the committee chairman was Elliot, Financial Secretary at the Treasury. See also Treasury memo, 29 Sept. 1932, in Howson, *Domestic Monetary Management*, 92, and Miller, 'Unemployment Policy of the National Government', 453–4, 457, 458.

[61] Lothian, who had been closely involved, was outside the Cabinet and preoccupied with India.

supporters of the government,[62] he was now reconciled to considerably less cosmetic. The financial crisis had shifted the emphases of the economic policy agenda and with the Cabinet possessing a massive electoral mandate, high unemployment had become as politically tolerable as it seemed economically unavoidable. The international economic and financial crises were so deep – and still deepening throughout 1932 – that cyclical recovery seemed certain to be slow, with Britain's particular structural problem remaining for a further period. In a rudimentary forecasting exercise for Neville Chamberlain in March 1932, the Treasury assumed that by 1935 unemployment would have fallen only to 1929 levels.[63]

With 'the sufficiency of the national income to maintain existing standards of life' now 'at stake', employment policy became what Treasury officials had always considered it to be, except when ministers exposed them to political pressure or interrogation by economists – a matter incidental to issues of international competitiveness and the profitability of private enterprise. It was now subsumed in stabilisation of sterling, maintenance of sound finance, and restoration of the trade balance.[64] These began as defensive measures, but it was quickly understood that they could also be recovery policies.

For MacDonald the lesson of the sterling crisis was the need 'to stop the mad follies' of international finance.[65] Developing ideas from early 1931, he wanted a grand international conference on reparations, war debts, gold, silver, credit, and tariffs. The Treasury remained sceptical of French and American willingness to co-operate:[66] both governments reacted negatively to Snowden's 21 September appeal for a conference, and the French still insisted that Britain's problems were of its own making.[67] But MacDonald, Reading, and later Simon persisted. After American hints that war debts might be reconsidered and after German pleas of inability to resume payments at the end of the Hoover moratorium, as a first stage the issue was narrowed to cancellation of reparations. Here the

[62] MacDonald to Betterton, 5 and 21 Nov. 1931, JRM 677.
[63] Hopkins memo, 'Old Moore's Almanack', in Hopkins to N. Chamberlain, 11 March 1932, T171/296. See Baldwin in Bayford diary, 12 May 1932, in Ramsden, 247, for recovery being 'a matter of years'.
[64] Employment Policy Committee Report, CP36(32), 25 Jan. 1932.
[65] MacDonald to Dawes, 20 Sept. 1931, in Dawes, *Journal*, 392.
[66] Hopkins-Fisher memo [to Snowden], 3 Oct. 1931, copy in NC 8/12/1.
[67] Drummond, *Floating Pound*, 122; French ministerial views reported in Leith-Ross to Usher, and Usher to MacDonald, 13 and 16 Nov. 1931, PREM 1/117.

Cabinet had universal domestic support: on this, for instance, the Bank of England, the Treasury, and Keynes wholly agreed.[68] To earlier objectives of removing a leading source of diplomatic friction and economic dislocation, were now added those of releasing British commercial investments frozen in Germany under the Standstill Agreements, and assisting sterling stabilisation. Inducing the French to attend a reparations conference was itself an achievement. The agreement to cancel reparations achieved at the Lausanne Conference of June–July 1932 under MacDonald's presidency was a diplomatic triumph with enormous symbolic importance – for all 'progressive' critics of the Peace, a vindication and promise of 'a new world'.[69]

At Lausanne the British delegation also obtained a further success: French and American agreement to the next stage, a World Economic and Financial Conference with the objectives of restoring international co-operation and arranging concerted action to raise world prices. War debts remained a problem, but the Cabinet was now prepared to take a tough line. If it had not been for Norman's insistence that British credit could not bear an act of repudiation, the Treasury would have immediately ceased payment on the American debt (as it eventually did in 1933).[70] One way or another, the National government had done much to clear the way for international financial reconstruction.

With the gold standard suspended, technically transferring the Bank of England's chief responsibilities to the government, Mac-Donald also expected domestic monetary reconstruction to become Cabinet business. Whether from socialist instincts, two years of frustration in economic policy, the Macmillan Committee recommendations, or sensitivity to recent Labour attacks, he began with radical ambitions. Criticisms of the Bank's directorate 'could not be ignore[d]'. It was widely thought that the country had suffered from obsolescent 'banking conceptions', and that the Bank had inadequate contacts with government and industry.[71] The Cabinet should have 'a controlling hand' in determining the future of sterling.[72] For these purposes he appointed in September 1931 a

---

[68] See, e.g., Shaw, Norman, and Leith-Ross to Keynes, 15 and 18 Jan., 23 May 1932, in *JMK* xviii, 369–70.   [69] MacDonald diary, 9 July 1931, and see Marquand, 723–4.

[70] Clay, *Norman*, 447.

[71] Cabinet 86(31), 9 Dec. 1931; MacDonald, 'Cabinet Policy and Work', CP311(31), 7 Dec. 1931, and see Cabinet 65(31), 28 Sept. 1931.

[72] MacDonald to Baldwin, 23 Sept. 1931, SB 44/166–9.

personal advisory committee of Stamp, Lord Macmillan, McKenna, Brand, H. D. Henderson, and later Keynes, and, after the election, a Cabinet committee on currency questions.[73]

In an obvious sense Norman and the Bank of England should be classed among those defeated in 1931. The loss of the gold standard wrecked the Bank's domestic and international policies, and undermined its independence from government. Yet it adjusted quickly, accepted the new conditions, and suffered no major attacks upon its composition or status. Norman remained Governor for another thirteen years. The Bank was helped by the unexpected absence of panic and disruption, controverting its own predictions: as Norman put it, 'we have fallen over the precipice... but we are alive at the bottom'.[74] It dreaded the prospect of political control,[75] but in the event MacDonald's efforts came to little. Part of the reason was that other Cabinet ministers were sensitive to precedents which might encourage Labour party and TUC demands for nationalisation, and future manipulation of the currency for undesirable political purposes. Norman was asked to consider how criticism of the Bank's directorate might be deflected, but the Cabinet rejected the idea that it might contain representatives of business organisations, probably from concern that the TUC might ask for equivalent representation. With Chamberlain and the former Chancellors Baldwin and Snowden insisting that 'liaison' with Norman 'could hardly be more close', the Cabinet also resolved that 'government control' of Bank policy was 'undesirable'.[76]

In reality this meant only that monetary policy remained too important to be politicised. It remained under government control, but was insulated from the Cabinet. Overall supervision passed to Treasury officials, who determined the large issues with Bank of England advice, while the Bank conducted detailed operations through new committees containing Treasury representatives.[77] This 'non-political' partnership between the Treasury and Bank

[73] Howson and Winch, *Economic Advisory Council*, 100–5 (for PM's, later EAC, Committee on Financial Questions); Cabinet 87(31), 10 Dec. 1931.

[74] Jones, *Diary with Letters*, 31, 27 Feb. 1932.

[75] Norman at BoE Cte, 7 Oct. 1931, and see Clay, *Norman*, 459.

[76] Cabinet 87(31), 10 Dec. 1931, and see N. Chamberlain, in *HC Deb*, 260, col. 2109, 10 Dec. 1931, repudiating currency management by government as likely 'to send the pound after the rouble'.

[77] For new Bank regime of committees, see Sayers, *Bank of England*, 401, 407, 409, 417–19. For Treasury representation, BoE Cte, 9 and 16 Dec. 1931.

was jealously protected. Chamberlain and Norman were apoplectic when they learnt of MacDonald's personal advisory committee on monetary issues. Although assured that the committee was purely advisory, Chamberlain's sharp defence of departmental prerogatives as against committees of outside 'experts' probably contributed to the demise of the full Economic Advisory Council.[78]

However, the chief reason for MacDonald's inaction was not Cabinet obstruction but satisfaction with Treasury–Bank policy, making his committees redundant.[79] After suspension of the gold standard the immediate concern had been simply to 'avoid inflation like the plague'.[80] Nevertheless Treasury officials soon developed a new strategy for sterling, using the Bank of England, Keynes, and other experts as foils, but essentially making up their own minds. As an early return to gold (at any parity) appeared impractical and as the Bank had inadequate reserves to peg the exchanges, sterling was first left to find its own level until an appropriate *de facto* stabilisation could be decided upon. Everyone – Treasury, Bank, the City, economists, and politicians – agreed upon the need for a steady exchange rate, not just to assist British trade but to encourage the Dominions and other countries to base their currencies on sterling. From the wreck of the international gold standards, a British-dominated sterling bloc would be constructed.[81] The exchange rate had to be high enough to retain foreign balances in London, and prevent such rapid price rises as would stimulate wage increases. But the Treasury's main objective now was a rate which secured 'the maximum advantage' for British trade and which, above all, would raise British prices sufficiently to restore profitability without precipitating 'a vicious spiral of inflation'.[82] Experience soon indicated that this rate would be around \$3.50–\$3.70.

So with depreciation making it no longer necessary to force down

[78] N. to I. Chamberlain, and to H. Chamberlain, 29 Nov. and 6 Dec. 1931, NC 18/1/763, 764.

[79] For Treasury preparing memo for the Cabinet committee, but the committee not reporting nor, apparently, even meeting, see Howson, *Domestic Monetary Management*, 82–7.

[80] Hopkins–Fisher memo, 3 Oct. 1931, NC 8/12/2, and see BoE Cte, 28 Sept. 1931. This and the next two paragraphs rely heavily upon Howson, *Domestic Monetary Management*, 79–86, 173–9, and Sayers, *Bank of England*, 416–30.

[81] E.g., Hopkins–Fisher memo, 3 Oct. 1931, NC 8/12/2; Niemeyer memo, 26 Sept. 1931, T175/56; Amery diary, 10 Dec. 1931 (*LSA* II, 224), and see Drummond, *Floating Pound*, 14–19.

[82] N. to H. Chamberlain, 6 Dec. 1931, NC 18/1/764; Hopkins–Fisher memo, 3 Oct. 1931, NC 8/12/2.

costs or to contemplate a sustained attack upon wage levels, the Treasury concentrated instead upon restoring prices to the pre-depression levels of 1929.[83] It was helped by sterling initially performing 'much better than expected'[84] and, after a sharp fall to $3.20 in December, recovering in early 1932 as confidence in other currencies deteriorated. Government stocks were 'booming', the Bank was able to repay the July 1931 central bank credits, while the government, with means provided from the 'astonishing gold mine' of India, repaid its August credits in February 1932.[85] Hopkins felt 'happier than he ha[d] done since 1927'.[86]

The main problem was that the Bank still lacked adequate resources to steady the exchanges. Given the new aim of a competitive rate there was – ironically after the anxieties of 1931 – considerable ministerial unease when sterling strengthened sharply in March 1932.[87] To overcome both this immediate difficulty of 'keep[ing] down the pound'[88] and the long-term problem of stabilising the exchanges, the Treasury invented the Exchange Equalisation Account. Equipped with powers to borrow up to £150m., this supplied the Bank of England with funds to manage the exchange rate.

With confidence in government finance restored and the pound strong at a low exchange rate, it became possible to achieve further Treasury objectives: reduction of debt charges on the budget, and lower interest rates generally to provide 'cheap money and plenty of it to stimulate industry'.[89] Bank rate was brought down in stages from 6 per cent in February 1932 to 3 per cent in April. The Bank had resumed preparations for war loan conversion as early as October, and in early 1932 the Treasury returned to the plans prepared for Snowden a year earlier.[90] After the cuts and tax

---

[83] For objectives, see Hopkins memo, 'Old Moore's Almanack', 11 March 1932, T171/296, and Treasury material in Howson, *Domestic Monetary Management*, 86, 90–1; and see Booth, 'Britain in the 1930s', 503–6.

[84] Peacock at Financial Situation Committee, 6 Oct. 1931, PREM 1/97.

[85] N. to I. and H. Chamberlain, 20 and 27 Feb. 1932, NC 18/1/771, 772. For the importance of Indian gold, see also N. Chamberlain to MacDonald, 5 March 1932, JRM 678, and Phillips, 26 Feb. 1932, in Howson, *Domestic Monetary Management*, 178.

[86] N. to H. Chamberlain, 27 Feb. 1932, NC 18/1/772.

[87] N. Chamberlain to MacDonald, 5 March 1932, JRM 678; MacDonald to N. Chamberlain [9 March 1932], NC 7/11/25/20; Hoare to Willingdon, 11 March 1932, Templewood, Indian papers, 1/210–17.

[88] Hopkins to N. Chamberlain, 6 April 1932, T171/301.

[89] Phillips memo, 5 March 1932, in Howson, *Domestic Monetary Management*, 86.

[90] BoE Cte, 21 and 28 Oct. 1931. For conversion, Howson, *Domestic Monetary Management*, 88–9, and Sayers, *Bank of England*, 430–47.

increases of September 1931, it would now be the turn of the holders of government bonds to make their patriotic sacrifice. Chamberlain's announcement on 30 June of the proposed conversion of £2,000m. war loan from 5 per cent to $3\frac{1}{2}$ per cent was received everywhere with the 'wildest enthusiasm'.[91] With bank rate further reduced to 2 per cent, the subsequent success of the conversion operation marked another major achievement.

An explicitly managed currency, low exchange rate, cheap and plentiful money, lower debt charges, and the objectives of careful domestic and international reflation and creation of a sterling bloc, together gave the Treasury and the Bank of England a coherent set of recovery policies.[92] All substantially met the criticisms they had suffered since 1920. There was a double political effect: MacDonald accepted that the Cabinet had no need to intervene in monetary policy, while all ministers were supplied with constructive policies and positive arguments which could not be mistaken for 'socialism'. If these measures in themselves did not constitute a 'plan' as the radical planners understood it, in comparison with previous practice they nevertheless represented a large dose of deliberate state encouragement to private enterprise.

The Cabinet's own contribution was to stick to sound finance, sustaining a stricter appearance of attachment to conventional canons than the new regime of monetary management warranted. Budgetary rectitude was central to the National government's rationale. It would have been politically necessary even if it had not also seemed essential for the maintenance of the domestic and international financial confidence which made the other policies possible and worthwhile. Nevertheless, although Neville Chamberlain certainly exercised strict budget control, there was no intention of imposing a 'reactionary' policy.

Insofar as the budget had been conceived as having any 'macroeconomic' purpose, this had been removed by devaluation. With deflation no longer an objective, reversal of the 'temporary sacrifices' of 1931 was – given economic recovery, and within the precondition of budgetary balance – a genuine aim, which eventually would be helped by the savings obtained by war loan conversion. But with revenues currently depressed, a predicted slow recovery, and the inexorable 'onward march' of social service expenditure,

---

[91] Hore-Belisha to Runciman, 1 July 1932, Runciman papers 206.
[92] See Booth, 'Britain in the 1930s', 501–6.

Chamberlain did not expect to be able to relax cuts and remit taxation for three or four years, while for 1932 it seemed difficult even to secure a balance.[93] For him, the immediate problem was rather to avoid further direct taxation than to allow the relief from the 1931 tax increases which, given prospective tariff revenues, were expected by many government supporters. In resisting tax remissions he received support from a Cabinet view – held as strongly by Baldwin as by MacDonaldites and Samuelites – that to reduce income tax without reversing the income cuts would upset the notion of 'equal sacrifices' and impair the government's moral authority, causing serious long-term political damage.[94] In these circumstances, an unusual amount of Treasury 'window-dressing' was needed to show balances in the 1931–2 out-turn and 1932–3 forecast. Most notably, in contrast to earlier deliberately pessimistic predictions of unemployment insurance expenditure, a protesting Ministry of Labour was instructed to reduce its forecasted unemployment figures.[95]

Chamberlain's 1932 budget therefore made only minor adjustments to Snowden's scheme of September 1931. Despite an appeal for 'hard work, strict economy, firm courage, unfailing patience' and refusal to seek 'a little popularity by gambling on the future',[96] his statement was widely criticised by government supporters as unimaginative and uninspired, even a 'flop'.[97] More important, there was great business, Conservative party, and to a lesser extent Liberal disappointment at the absence of tax cuts. After their 1931 'sacrifice', businessmen thought early relief from the 'crushing load' of 'unreasonably exorbitant' taxes would be part of the transformation they expected from the National government: a shift from the 'rather sterile task' of protecting consumers, non-producers, and the 'careless and...unfortunate', to the 'far more constructive task of supporting capitalists' who provided work and wages, and whose

[93] Hopkins to N. Chamberlain, 'Speculative Forecast of 1935 on the Basis of "Old Moore's Almanack"', 21 March 1932, and for 1932 forecasts, Phillips and Hopkins memos, 7 and 16 Nov. 1931, 25 March, 4 April 1932, all T171/296.

[94] Baldwin in G. Lloyd to Davidson, 4 March 1932, Davidson Indian papers c557/42–6.

[95] For unemployment figures, Hopkins to Chamberlain, 12 Feb., 19 March 1932, and Floud to Hopkins, and to Fergusson, 12 Feb., 17 March 1932, T171/296. Other documents in this file reveal other expedients, which Hopkins 'clothe[d]...in...a respectable garb'. See also Middleton, *Managed Economy*, 101, 113.

[96] *HC Deb*, 264, cols. 1438–9, 19 April 1932.

[97] G. Lloyd to Davidson, 29 April 1932, Davidson Indian papers, c557/116–22, and see also MacDonald diary and Amery diary (*LSA* II, 240), both 19 April 1932. In contrast, Keynes was quite sympathetic: see *JMK* XXI, 102–7.

'public spirit' would ensure that the consumer 'did not suffer unduly'.[98] Disappointment resulted in renewed pressure for retrenchment from business and taxpayers' organisations, and another Friends of Economy meeting in the City.[99] Conservative backbench MPs fell over themselves to join a 1922 Committee inquiry into further expenditure cuts.[100]

Chamberlain (whose reputation was later fully restored by the conversion operation) encouraged this agitation for retrenchment with Snowden-like remarks about disagreeable measures requiring public support.[101] But this did not mean that Chamberlain or other Conservative leaders intended to submit to party and business pressures and begin another May Committee-style attack on expenditure. Chamberlain gave encouragement just in case he needed further selective cuts for short-term budget purposes.[102] But all Conservative leaders, as believers in limited, 'efficient' state underpinning for social progress, and Chamberlain in particular as an expert in social administration, had no more intention than MacDonald of reversing the whole earlier trend of social provision, and from a 'National' position were ready to defy party pressures. When from late 1932 the Cabinet under Chamberlain's pressure confronted the issue of unemployment benefit payments its purpose was less to reduce expenditure than to rationalise and standardise the system and, especially, to take the whole problem out of party politics and make it a politically less embarrassing and more neutral administrative matter.[103] Moreover, if the retrenchment agitations of 1932 were reminiscent of those of 1930–1, the character of the National government meant they could pose no similar threat. All who called for further cuts expressed the desire to help the government, and the enthusiastic members of the Conservative 1922 Committee merely got themselves into a humiliating tangle.[104] Conservative and business disappointment over income tax was

[98] FBI statements, *The Times*, 15 Jan., 11 Feb. 1932; Lithgow, FBI presidential address, ibid., 14 April 1932. See also Association of British Chambers of Commerce to N. Chamberlain, ibid., 17 March 1932.

[99] Associated Chambers of Commerce and Hirst (for Public Economy League), *The Times*, 22 April 1932; National Chamber of Trade, ibid., 27 April 1932. For Friends, addressed by Grenfell, Geddes, Horne and Ernest Benn, see ibid., 19 and 26 May 1932.

[100] 1922 Committee minutes, 13 and 20 June 1932: 143 MPs asked to participate. See Rentoul, *Sometimes*, 241–3, and Ball, '1922 Committee', 141–2.

[101] N. Chamberlain speech, *The Times*, 10 May and (on 1922 Committee report) 19 Nov. 1932.   [102] N. to H. Chamberlain, 15 and 29 May 1932, NC 18/1/781, 784.

[103] For details of the 1934 reforms, and a favourable verdict, see Lowe, *Adjusting to Democracy*, 154–83.   [104] Rentoul, *Sometimes*, 242–6; Ball, '1922 Committee', 142–4.

more than counterbalanced by satisfaction with Cabinet trade policy.

Given the Conservative party's preponderance in Parliament and the government, there is no difficulty in understanding the introduction of some form of protection and imperial preference. The world recession, the financial crisis, and the movement in business and financial opinion created the opportunity, but the real impetus was political: tariff reform had been an article of faith to many of the most active and powerful Conservatives for almost thirty years. What needs to be explained is how the defeat of free trade was achieved without a complete disintegration of the National government – how the Samuelites and Snowden remained in the Cabinet when import controls were first introduced and why, when those free-trade ministers later departed, MacDonald, Runciman, and other Liberals remained. MacDonald had long been undoctrinaire on the policy question. But for Snowden and for all Liberals as much as for Conservatives, the issues turned upon the beliefs of a lifetime. For Samuelite Liberals in possession of the party machine, they struck at an almost hundred-years' tradition and with it at the very existence of the Liberal party.

By July 1931 the Conservative leadership had adopted a comprehensive and detailed policy prepared by the Conservative Research Department: an emergency tariff to be followed by a 'scientific tariff' settled by a non-political Tariff Commission, a wheat quota, and a 'free hand' to arrange imperial preferences. These were wanted for the reasons that tariff reform had always been wanted: to establish a sheltered domestic market which would restore industrial and agricultural profits, maintain wages, and increase employment; to raise revenue and relieve the direct taxpayer, and – for many, the cardinal point – to create an imperial economic bloc which would also help preserve the Empire as a political unit. The Canadian government's renewed invitation just after the general election to an Imperial Economic Conference at Ottawa strengthened expectations of imperial trade agreements, and was mentioned in the King's Speech. But the October 1931 agreement to perpetuate the National government committed Conservative leaders to Cabinet enquiry and an 'open mind' towards solutions for the economic crisis. Even apart from that, they wished, without sacrificing essential party principles, to consolidate the National coalition into a permanent arrangement. Their own party policy on tariffs would therefore have to be achieved by consensual methods; an essentially 'political' initiative had to be clothed in persuasive 'economic' garb.[105]

The resolution of the trade question – the unscrambling of the National government's internal contradiction – occurred in three stages. First, in November 1931 the Cabinet agreed upon temporary measures to counteract foreign dumping. Like the Economy Act, these Abnormal Importations and Horticultural Products (Emergency Customs) Acts gave ministers extraordinary powers under Orders in Council. Second, in January 1932 a settled domestic policy was established, but only after a Cabinet crisis had been contained by an 'agreement to differ'. This policy was embodied in the Import Duties Act, and later a Wheat Quota Act. Third, at the Ottawa Conference of July and August 1932 trade bargains were struck with Dominion governments. These Ottawa agreements led to ministerial resignations in September.

In Cabinet politics the crucial figure was Runciman, not just because he had departmental responsibility for trade policy, but also because he had been a leading apologist for free trade on Cobdenite lines. Despite a deserved reputation as a 'hard uncompromising radical',[106] he now became highly flexible. Flexibility was indispensable for continued enjoyment of his own political resurrection, but it followed also from a reconstructed economic analysis. For him (as earlier for Keynes), the world recession, the intensification of economic nationalism, and the sterling crisis had temporarily destroyed the conditions which had made free trade valid. It followed that practical free-traders had to adjust and find devices which would provide immediate economic and financial self-defence, yet also compel other nations to help restore international free trade.

Although Chamberlain initiated the Abnormal Importations measure, Runciman quickly made it his own, as a form of his September proposal to prohibit luxury imports, as an anti-forestalling device, and as an instrument which, by correcting the

---

[105] Cf. Eichengreen, *Sterling and the Tariff*, 22–38, which presents an argument for protection offered by Conservative and some non-Conservative ministers as if this was actually the reason for it being pressed in Cabinet.

[106] Hankey diary, 30 Oct. 1931 (Roskill, *Hankey* II, 571).

trade deficit, would help the defence of sterling.[107] As a free-trade case this was so impeccable that Snowden suggested the duties might go so high as 100 per cent.[108] Similarly, on the Cabinet Balance of Trade Committee Runciman accepted the overriding force of monetary objectives. Since there might be excessive depreciation of sterling 'under the free play of economic forces', a favourable trade balance was essential to secure 'a reasonable exchange value of the £' and restore financial confidence.[109] On his suggestion the basis for the Import Duties Act had respectable free-trade antecedents and sweeteners: an all-round 10 per cent revenue tariff, with imperial preferences only if the Dominions offered reciprocal tariff reductions. He then agreed to a further adjustable 'surtax', to be determined by an Import Duties Advisory Committee and used as an instrument to obtain rationalisation of domestic industries and reductions of foreign tariffs.[110]

During 1932 Runciman detached himself from free-trade Liberal institutions, resigning from his former power base, the Liberal Council, despite an offered 'agreement to differ'.[111] Nevertheless he did not simply submit to business and Conservative party pressures. He resisted considerable agitation seeking to force the pace on iron and steel protection,[112] successfully opposed tariffs on basic food-stuffs, and threatened resignation when meat duties were proposed at Ottawa.[113] As he presented it, the Import Duties Act was a Liberal alternative to Conservative party policy, an instrument to help sterling, relieve the direct taxpayer, stimulate industrial efficiency, and bargain for freer trade.[114]

[107] See N. to H. Chamberlain, 15 Nov. 1931, NC 18/1/761; HC Deb, 259, cols. 545–52, 16 Nov. 1931; Chamberlain and Runciman memo, 'Forestalling', CP 274(31), 11 Nov. 1931; Cabinets 76, 77(31), 12 and 13 Nov. 1931.

[108] N. to I. Chamberlain, 15 Nov. 1931, NC 18/1/761.

[109] Committee on the Balance of Trade: Report, CP 25(32), 19 Jan. 1932.

[110] Runciman to MacDonald, 21 Dec. 1931, and N. Chamberlain to Runciman, 26 Dec. 1931, Runciman papers 245; N. Chamberlain narrative ['Notes on proceedings in Cabinet & elsewhere on formulation of Government policy on balance of trade'], 30 Jan. 1931, NC 8/18/1.

[111] Runciman to Phillipps, 4 March 1932, and Phillipps to Runciman, 17 March 1932, Runciman papers 215.

[112] For agitation, see EIA parliamentary committee, and National Union of Manufacturers in The Times, 8 and 9 Dec. 1931; 1922 Committee minutes, 7 Dec. 1931; Amery diary, 1, 7 and 9 Dec. 1931, (LSA II, 222–4). For resistance, Runciman in HC Deb, 259, cols. 1996–2006, 9 Dec. 1931.

[113] N. to I. Chamberlain, 21 Aug. 1932, NC 18/1/795; Baldwin in Jones, Diary With Letters, 50, 29 Aug. 1931.

[114] Runciman to MacDonald, 21 Dec. 1931, and to Professor Simpson, 17 March 1932, Runciman papers 245, 254; HC Deb, 261, cols. 691–708, 9 Feb. 1932.

These developments in Runciman's position had important effects. His arguments had force with other non-Conservative members of the government. They also helped convert protection and imperial preference from a Conservative party policy into a 'National' policy. Chamberlain had been the first Cabinet member to make sterling defence an argument for import controls, using his Chancellorian authority to get Samuel 'alarmed' that the trade deficit threatened depreciation.[115] But thereafter Conservative ministers learnt a great deal from Runciman about the presentation of policy. When Conservative MPs, the NFU, and other agricultural interests protested at omission of foodstuffs from the Abnormal Importations list, Gilmour borrowed Runciman's arguments to obtain the parallel horticultural measure.[116] As chairman of the Balance of Trade Committee, Chamberlain used Runciman as the stalking-horse for protection, expressing his own proposals largely in Runciman's terms, drafting the report through negotiation with him, and then presenting it as 'a brand new National government policy, *quite* different from the old Tory plan'. Such statements were made for tactical purposes. Privately Chamberlain showed little interest in any connection between trade and monetary policies. What he believed he had actually obtained was a 'carefully camouflaged' form of Conservative party policy: 'an Emergency Tariff plus Imperial preference plus a Tariff Commission which will gradually give us a Scientific Tariff'.[117]

The Import Duties Bill represented a major change in national policy, as momentous as suspension of the gold standard. For Chamberlain especially it had enormous political and personal significance. When he introduced the Bill on 4 February 1932, all present were conscious of witnessing an 'immortal' parliamentary occasion.[118] At last 'the nation ha[d] made atonement' to Joseph Chamberlain; '[his] Father's Ghost' could now 'rest in peace'.[119]

---

[115] N. to H. Chamberlain, 15 Nov. 1931, NC 18/1/761; Cabinet 73(31), 10 Nov. 1931.

[116] Gilmour, CP 293(31), 23 Nov. 1931, and *HC Deb*, 259, cols. 787–8, 30 Nov. 1931. For agitation, see, e.g., *NFU Yearbook 1931*, 409–10, and *HC Deb*, 259, for 17 Nov. 1931 debate.

[117] N. Chamberlain to Bridgeman, 26 Dec. 1931, Bridgeman papers, and Chamberlain narrative, 30 Jan. 1931, NC 8/18/1. For example of disingenuous presentation, see N. Chamberlain to Snowden, 15 Jan. 1932, NC 7/11/25/41.

[118] Hore-Belisha to N. Chamberlain [4 Feb. 1932], NC 7/11/25/16, and see other congratulatory letters in the same file.

[119] N. Chamberlain to Lady Milner, 2 March 1932, Lady Milner papers c209/2, and to Lloyd, 7 Feb. 1932, Lloyd papers, 19/5. See also Chamberlain's family pieties in *HC Deb*, 261, col. 296, 4 Feb. 1932.

The tariff delighted the Conservative party, the FBI, and other industrial leaders. Yet it was not the tariff reform of 1903, nor precisely what Page Croft's EIA, Amery's EEU, Beaverbrook's Empire Crusade, and industrial and agricultural interests had wanted. Even allowing for modifications to suit 'National' Cabinet allies, the policy constituted imperial protectionism in a particular sense intended by the Conservative leadership. From their own perspectives Chamberlain and other Conservative leaders had much in common with what Runciman proposed from a Liberal perspective; tariffs were not an end in themselves. In tariff policy as in monetary policy the state would assist private enterprise, helping it to cope with difficulties caused by the chaos in international markets and to assist it towards recovery. But Conservative ministers did not want tariffs simply in order to protect and preserve existing structures. They intended that tariffs should be used to promote greater efficiency. Where appropriate, they would be offered as inducements for the adoption of rationalisation, amalgamation, and marketing arrangements.

This attempt to link tariffs with structural change later ran into difficulties, because the government remained reluctant to coerce recalcitrant industries, opening up awkward political and administrative questions about control, ownership, and the ability of government to direct particular enterprises.[120] However, the genuineness of Conservative ministers' desire for structural improvements was demonstrated in agricultural policy. Here, against the persistent NFU demand for 'fiscal justice' and against criticism from Conservative protectionist MPs, tariffs were withheld from wheat and meat. Instead quotas were used, because these offered a more effective means to facilitate reorganisation. This approach had some success. From 1932 several agricultural marketing boards were established under the Labour government's 1931 legislation.[121]

Conservative leaders also wanted tariffs not simply to increase national self-sufficiency but as levers to restore 'fair' trade, through bilateral trade negotiations with other countries. From November 1932 fifteen such agreements were reached. Tariffs were wanted especially to obtain preferential arrangements with the Dominions, both to 'set [the Empire's] future on a firm foundation' and to widen markets which were believed to offer 'infinitely greater' possibilities

---

[120] See esp. Tolliday, *Business, Banking and Politics*, chs. 13–14.
[121] See Cooper, *British Agricultural Policy*, chs. VIII–IX.

for export growth than foreign ones.[122] The Ottawa Conference, however, proved to be a disillusioning experience. Conservative delegates found what MacDonald had learned at the 1930 Conference: that Dominion ministers – especially Bennett of Canada – put their own Dominion's particular interest first, at the expense of common imperial benefits, let alone British concerns. None would sign a Chamberlain draft of 'principles of imperial trade policy', and South Africa rejected 'anything which suggested that the Empire as such had either principles or policies'.[123]

Yet to Conservative ministers these differences did not suggest any fundamental imperial problem. Rather, they concluded that the Conference had come 'just in time to save [the] unity of [the] Empire'.[124] The bilateral Ottawa treaties did not promise such a short-term increase in British exports as had been hoped. Nevertheless, because they seemed to be only the start of a long-term shift towards greater imperial trade, Conservatives considered them 'excellent'.[125]

For the free-trade ministers – the Samuelites and Snowden – each step towards a tariff reform system raised difficulties. They accepted Runciman's and Chamberlain's trade balance and sterling defence arguments for the emergency duties of late 1931, but only under protest and after distinguishing them from protection.[126] The Import Duties Bill was too much for them. The fiercest opponent was Snowden, already furious because Chamberlain, responding to Conservative and Simonite Liberal parliamentary agitation,[127] had suspended his land valuation scheme.[128] On the Balance of Trade Committee, he denied that sterling and the balance of payments were seriously threatened, pronounced the Chamberlain–Runciman

---

[122] N. Chamberlain to Grigg, 7 Feb. 1932, Altrincham papers; to Lloyd, 7 Feb. 1932, Lloyd papers 19/5; and to H. Chamberlain, 11 June 1932, NC 18/1/786.

[123] N. to H. Chamberlain, 21 Aug. 1931, NC 18/1/795. For detailed examination of the Conference, see Drummond, *Imperial Economic Policy*, chs. 6–8.

[124] N. Chamberlain in Sankey notes of Cabinet, 27 Aug. 1932, Sankey papers c509/99–101, and see Baldwin to Lothian, 4 Sept. 1932, Lothian papers 261/39.

[125] N. to I. Chamberlain, 21 Aug. 1932, NC 18/1/795; Baldwin in Sinclair notes of Cabinet, 28 Sept. 1932, Thurso papers II/85/2.

[126] See Maclean to Runciman, 13 Nov. 1931, Runciman papers 245; Cabinet 77(31), 13 Nov. 1931; Snowden, *Autobiography* II, 1003–7, including Snowden to MacDonald, 2 Dec. 1931.

[127] See *HC Deb*, 259, cols. 499–501, 666–8, 688–9, 846–7, 1004–5, 16–19 Nov. 1931, and ibid., 260, cols. 208–9, 513, 937, 1242, 1693–4, 24 Nov.–8 Dec. 1931.

[128] Chamberlain had originally proposed repeal, but shifted to suspension (on grounds of 'economy') to prevent Snowden's resignation: N. to I. and H. Chamberlain, 29 Nov., 6 Dec. 1931, NC 18/1/763, 764; Cabinet 85(31), 7 Dec. 1931.

tariff to be outright protection, and denounced it on classic free-trade grounds – it would raise living costs, perpetuate domestic inefficiencies, provoke foreign retaliation, and lead to tariff wars. As over land taxation, Conservatives were 'not playing the game' but pursuing partisan aims and ignoring the 'National' mandate.[129]

The Samuelite ministers' position, now and later, was ambiguous. Like Snowden, they thought Conservatives were not playing the game: the Balance of Trade Committee had not undertaken a 'thorough, scientific examination', and its recommendations were protectionist. Yet, unlike Snowden, they had no complaints aside from the trade issue, and were not certain that the payments and sterling issues could be dismissed. They also had ministerial careers before them, parliamentary seats to hold, and the responsibility of leading a national party which faced an uncertain future outside the National coalition. Nevertheless, such was the 'enormity of the political and economic offence' of the Chamberlain–Runciman tariff that they felt honour bound to resign. But they would do so only with 'very great reluctance', and hoped for some 'eleventh-hour occurrence' to 'save' them.[130] As a Committee member, Samuel expressed dissent yet concentrated upon alternative proposals, to correct the trade balance through stimulation of exports.[131]

MacDonald remained the 'key' to the National government's existence.[132] For him the issues of India, disarmament, and financial reconstruction provided ample justifications for its continuation; trade questions were vital in principle, but not decisive in detail. Long before Runciman, he had concluded that as 'the historical foundations of...past economic policy ha[d] gone', import controls were necessary.[133] He did not want simple protection, certainly not food taxes which 'unreasonably lowered' working-class living standards and might produce the 'calamity' of a 'real class movement'. He wanted devices to promote efficient, 'rational', modern production, and to increase world trade by forcing reductions of foreign tariff walls.[134]

Having himself recognised the new economic conditions, Mac-

[129] Snowden, 'Memorandum of Dissent', CP31(32), 18 Jan. 1932; Snowden to N. Chamberlain, 16 Jan. 1932, NC 7/11/25/42; Snowden, *Autobiography* II, 1007–9.

[130] Samuel to Lothian, 21 Jan. 1932, Lothian papers 159/2–3; Sinclair to Fisher, 1 Feb. 1932, Fisher papers, 10/147–9.   [131] Samuel memo, CP32(32), 19 Jan. 1932.

[132] N. Chamberlain narrative, 30 Jan. 1932, NC 8/18/1.

[133] MacDonald to Peach, 20 Feb. 1932, JRM 1442.

[134] MacDonald to Runciman, 28 Dec. 1931, Runciman papers 245; MacDonald note, 'General Considerations Regarding Tariff', 10 Jan. 1932, JRM 587.

Donald was impatient and prepared to be tough towards those he considered to be unreasonably bound by doctrinaire views from the past. Already, during the discussions over the election programme the previous October, he had come close to dispensing with the Samuelites. While reconstructing the government in November, he had anticipated that there might soon be a time when he had to accept Samuel's and Snowden's resignations.[135] On the other hand, he also wanted the government to preserve strong 'National' credentials by retaining as much non-Conservative representation as possible.

Conservative party organisers made matters difficult by persisting in party propaganda and by running Conservatives against other National candidates at by-elections.[136] In Cabinet matters, however, MacDonald found Conservative ministers generally accommodating towards their allies. Chamberlain's and Runciman's proposals for import duties met his own policy concerns, and this compromise between a protectionist and a free-trader seemed to him to fulfil the idea of a 'National', 'open mind' approach. His concern about personnel was met by the readiness of Thomas, Sankey, and other National Labour ministers, and Simon and his Liberal Nationals, to share his own view that the trade issue was subordinate to the other advantages of National government.

Nevertheless MacDonald tried hard to dissuade Snowden and the Samuelites from resigning, even offering them licence to dissent publicly from the Cabinet decision. When they rejected this as 'impracticable and Gilbertian', he thought them 'pettifogging' and 'unaccommodating', and reconciled himself to their departure.[137] However, once it became plain that there would be no other concessions, Samuel, Maclean, and Sinclair seized upon the only available 'eleventh hour occurrence'. At the Cabinet on 23 January they accepted the suggestion, repeated by Hailsham, that the Cabinet should remain intact but 'agree to differ'.[138] Snowden, isolated, preferred acquiescence to resigning alone.

---

[135] See MacDonald in Wigram memo, 3 Nov. 1931, RA GV K2331(1)/49.

[136] For an example of the difficulties, see Stannage, *Baldwin Thwarts the Opposition*, 32–4.

[137] MacDonald diary, 22 Jan. 1932; Samuel memo ['Course of Political Events'] 18–23 Jan. 1932, Samuel papers A/87/7; Snowden, *Autobiography* II, 1010; N. Chamberlain narrative, 30 Jan. 1932, NC 8/18/1.

[138] N. Chamberlain diary, 22 Jan. 1932, and narrative, 30 Jan. 1932, NC 8/18/1; Samuel memo, 18–23 Jan. 1932, Samuel papers A/87/7; MacDonald to the King, 22 Jan. 1932, RA GV K2340/2. It perhaps mattered to the Samuelites that such a breach of constitutional convention was supported by the Cabinet's lawyers, Hailsham, Sankey and Simon (i.e., past, present, and future Lord Chancellors): see Sankey diary, 22 Jan. 1932.

The Cabinet 'agreement to differ' was indeed Gilbertian, and exposed the division not just within the government but between its supporters. Many Conservative MPs, who had hoped the crisis would at last produce a purely protectionist government, were annoyed. They nearly revolted when Samuel and Snowden took full advantage of their licence to make vigorous parliamentary attacks upon the Import Duties Bill.[139] Nevertheless the Conservative leaders had deliberately chosen to exercise tolerance, and had carefully not taken the opportunity to establish a Conservative government. Although they had obtained the policy they wanted, they had sought to demonstrate their attachment to the National principle. Baldwin even hoped that the government would now be consolidated: tariffs might 'drop out of party politics very much like Free Trade did', leaving 'little which really divides [Conservatives] from the bulk of the Liberals'.[140]

This reflected the typical protectionist's incomprehension of the tenacity of free-trade opinion. Yet the Samuelite ministers were not much better attuned to it. They had supposed it would be obvious that by remaining in office they were saving the Liberal party from a hopeless political limbo, caught between the National government and Labour opposition. But most free-trade Liberals were appalled by the 'agreement to differ'. The distance between the Samuelite leadership and their party, already apparent since the previous autumn, became wider. At local, provincial, and national party meetings the Samuelite ministers were attacked for compromising Liberalism. Hirst, already furious at the Abnormal Importations Bill, conducted the party's Free Trade Committee as a new 'Anti-Corn Law League'.[141] A few radical MPs began voting against the government, and reverted to ideas of a progressive alliance with Labour MPs.[142] Similarly a group of Liberal publicists attempted to update *Britain's Industrial Future* as the basis for a 'closer union of progressive and radical forces' against the 'reactionary elements in the state'.[143] In the optimistic belief that the onset of protection offered ideal conditions for an independent Liberal revival, there

[139] See Amery diary, 24, 26, and 28 Jan. 1932 (partly in *LSA* II, 228); EIA deputation to Baldwin [28 Jan. 1932], and Gretton to Margesson, 5 Feb. 1932, SB 32/2-3, 167/47.

[140] Jones, *Diary with Letters*, 25-6, 28 Jan. 1932.

[141] Hirst diary, 21 Nov., 1 Dec. 1931, in Hirst, 13, 14.

[142] Mander and Bernays in G. Lloyd to Davidson, 12 Feb. 1932, Davidson Indian papers c557/27-33.

[143] H. Phillips, A. Holgate, R. Moelwyn Hughes, T. Elder Jones, I. Lloyd, J. Menken, A. Sainsbury, *Whither Britain? A Radical Answer* (August 1932), 9.

were widespread demands for the party to oppose what some now saw as 'a full-blooded Tory government'.[144] At the NLF Conference in April, Muir prevented repudiation of the Liberal ministers only by large concessions to the critics. When Asquith's daughter joined Lloyd George's son in proposing the executive's free-trade resolution, it became plain that something very serious was happening. When the Conference unanimously passed Hirst's amendment anticipating the Ottawa Conference by declaring that commercial treaties must not interfere with parliamentary control of taxation, the Samuelite leaders were placed under warning.[145]

MacDonald's genius for holding split Cabinets together had now landed the free-trade ministers in much the same position as that of the Labour dissentients of August 1931. The Ottawa agreements of August 1932 had a similar Cabinet effect to that of the May Report. The free-trade ministers found the agreements highly objectionable in themselves, and knew that to accept them would provoke a party rebellion. Some imperial tariffs were reduced, but others were raised. Many British tariffs became permanent, weakening their value as bargaining weapons and infringing Hirst's notion of Parliament's fiscal powers. For Snowden they represented 'the final and complete triumph of Tory protectionists'; 'self-respect' and the expectations of free-traders in the country demanded resignation. As strongly as the Labour party, he now thought that MacDonald had sold out to the Conservatives, and wanted to cause maximum damage by an immediate collective free-trade resignation, making MacDonald seem 'not a Prime Minister, but the Chairman of a Tory Cabinet'.[146]

The Samuelite ministers, however, took four weeks over their decision. In general terms, they remained as reluctant to resign and face the harsh political world outside the National alliance as in January. They did not at all share the desire of their party's radicals to seek resumed association with the Labour party, whose new socialist commitment placed it beyond their pale. They again clutched at possible compromises.[147] However, knowing they had little choice, they were concerned mainly to prepare themselves a

---

[144] E.g., *NLF Proceedings 1932*, 33–5, 47–8, 54–67, 27–30 April.
[145] Ibid., 25–32, 36–8, and see Hirst diary, 17 March, 28 April 1932, in Hirst, 21, 22.
[146] Snowden to Samuel, 23 and 29 Aug., 13 Sept. 1932, Samuel papers A/89/1, 7, 32; and to MacDonald 29 Aug., 12 and 15 Sept. 1932, JRM 1325, 678 (see Snowden, *Autobiography* II, 1020–3, 1026–8).
[147] Sinclair to Gilmour, 5 Sept. 1932, Gilmour papers 41; Samuel to MacDonald, 16 Sept. 1932, CP 312(32); Samuel to Grey, and to Hamilton, both 16 Sept., Samuel papers A/89/42, 28a.

decent resignation. They wanted to prevent junior ministers and
MPs from defecting to the Simonites. They wanted the approval of
the Liberal right, of Grey, Reading, Cowdray, Rosebery, Stanmore,
Acland, Hobhouse, and the other elder statesmen, peers, and
plutocrats who provided much of the party's political ballast, social
leadership, and money. They also wanted to make out a good public
case, in order to retain and if possible extend their electoral support.
The result of intense, nervous, consultation was yet another
compromise. In order not to jeopardise the Liberal claim to
responsibility by appearing to associate with Labour, they would
continue to sit on the National government benches and give it
general support.[148]

This subtlety was lost on the rest of the Cabinet, and the free-trade
ministers resigned on 28 September in an acrimonious atmosphere.
Conservative leaders, exasperated by what to them seemed to be
mere hair-splitting, were now glad to 'get rid' of the Samuelites.[149]
The Simonites, faced by total separation from the Liberal party
organisation, were principally concerned to obtain the vacated
offices for themselves and Conservative guarantees for their
parliamentary seats.[150] MacDonald was initially plunged into deep
depression. He felt no difficulties about accepting the Ottawa
agreements, but while in low spirits he feared the government would
no longer appear 'National', making his own position 'degrading'.[151] For a time he again thought about resigning himself.[152] Yet
in the last resort he had long been prepared to face the consequences
of free-trade resignations. Encouraged by the Conservative, Simonite, and other National Labour ministers and by the King's 'entire
support and confidence',[153] he soon decided that the resignations
made him more indispensable as the guarantor of the government's
continuing 'National' character.[154]

---

[148] These consultations were considered so momentous that they generated a vast
correspondence: see esp. Samuel papers A/89.
[149] Hilton Young to his wife, 27 Aug. 1932, Kennet papers 107/4; and see N. Chamberlain
to I. Chamberlain, 12 Sept. 1932, NC 18/1/798. See also Baldwin in Jones, Diary with
Letters, 55, 14 Sept. 1932, for the Samuelites as 'dirty dogs'.
[150] See Runciman to N. Chamberlain, 21 Sept. 1932, NC 7/11/25/35; Shakespeare to
Runciman, and to Simon, 22 and 23 Sept. 1932, Runciman papers, 262, 254; Simon to
MacDonald, and to Baldwin, 27 and 28 Sept. 1932, JRM 1325, SB 46/59–61.
[151] MacDonald to Baldwin, 10 Sept. 1932, SB 167/187–8, and to the King, 11 Sept. 1932, RA
GV K2357/1.   [152] S. MacDonald notes, 23 Sept. 1932.
[153] The King to MacDonald, 12 Sept. 1932, RA GV K2357/2; and see, e.g., Baldwin to
MacDonald, SB 167/189–90; Hoare to MacDonald, 18 Sept. 1932, JRM 698.
[154] Runciman to Wigram, 19 Sept. 1932, RA GV K2357/6; MacDonald diary, 23, 26, and
28 Sept. 1932.

In leaving the government the Samuelites tried to persuade themselves that there would now be another Liberal revival. Their demonstration of independence and self-sacrifice would 'inspire fresh confidence in British Liberalism as a living force'.[155] 'Never since the War or at any rate since the Free Trade election of 1923 have the Liberal party had so much elbow room [in] which to re-form in the centre.'[156] By offering a constitutionalist alternative to Protectionist Conservatism they might even supplant the 'class war-TUC Party'.[157] Such confident assertions were, however, belied by their own hesitations and soul-searchings over the previous twelve months. They knew that in reality they were joining the ranks of the defeated. Yet despite continuing business depression, unemployment almost at 3m., 'hunger marches', repression in India, and 'economic war' with Ireland, the ease with which the National government sustained the departure of the free-traders demonstrated the truth of a Samuelite justification for resignation: that the 'national emergency... ha[d] been overcome'.[158]

[155] Samuel, 'Situation resulting from the Ottawa decisions', 28 Aug. 1932, Samuel papers A/89/5.
[156] Sinclair to Johnstone, 3 Sept. 1932, Thurso papers III/2/1.
[157] Lothian to Jones, 9 Sept. 1932, in Jones, *Diary With Letters*, 53; and see Samuel to Wigram, 16 Sept. 1932, RA GV K2357/4 (Samuel, *Memoirs*, 231–3).
[158] Samuel to MacDonald, 16 Sept. 1932, CP312(32).

Conclusion

> [E]xperiments [were] being made almost daily by this Government, of a scope so new that it might fairly be described as revolutionary, and...the most drastic changes were being made in some of those things which perhaps [it] might have been expected that the Conservative Party would have most doggedly maintained as irremoveable and unchangeable. Any accusation against the National Government that it had no mind, no policy, no spirit of adventure, was totally without foundation.
>
> N. Chamberlain speech, 9 November 1934[1]

The departure of the free-trade ministers not only ended the National government's internal contradiction; it also closed the period of political conflict which had opened with the Liberal revival of 1927–9. Party politics were again stabilised around two blocs, with the areas between government and official opposition and at the extremes to either side occupied only by weak and fragmented forces. The Conservative party had been restored to pre-eminence, but it was now cloaked with 'National' Liberal and Labour partners in a massive anti-socialist alliance. This occupied the whole of the central electoral ground, and released Conservative leaders from dependence upon their more reactionary or dogmatic supporters. Conversely, the Labour party had unquestionably achieved its ambition of becoming the predominant anti-Conservative party of progress. Yet it had been confined to its industrial and urban electoral heartlands and had turned to an introverted preoccupation with socialist doctrine, from which it was rescued only by the Munich crisis and the Second World War.

The irony of the National government was that leading anti-coalitionists of the early 1920s – Baldwin, Neville Chamberlain,

---

[1] *The Times*, 10 Nov. 1934.

MacDonald, Snowden, and Maclean – formed a coalition which did not include the arch-coalitionists, Lloyd George and Churchill (nor, indeed, the aspirant coalitionist, Mosley). In one interpretation of inter-war high politics, seen as motivated largely by fear of Lloyd George and revulsion against the supposed political immorality of his 1918–22 Coalition government, this seems quite deliberate. It is argued that the National government must in some sense have been designed to exclude Lloyd George, Churchill, and other coalitionists.[2] This approach may safely be dismissed. It breaks down in detail,[3] and it trivialises the issues. Fear certainly played a large part in creating the National government, but it was not fear of individuals. The emergency government was formed amid fears of financial collapse, hyper-inflation, a calamitous fall in living standards, and social and political disruption. It was perpetuated as a coalition in the face of additional fears of militant TUC sectionalism, 'revolutionary' socialism, election defeat, and loss of power.

The sterling crisis alone cannot, however, be the whole explanation for the replacement of the Labour government by a National government. The 'national interest' of defending sound money was an objective which all party leaders shared with the City and the Treasury. The political crisis turned, rather, upon the details of balancing the budget. This issue created problems for each party. In attempting to resolve these party issues during August 1931, each set of party leaders to a greater or lesser extent defied Bank of England and Treasury preferences and engaged in tactical manoeuvres right up to the brink of the feared 'deluge'. Each tried to avoid or to disperse responsibility for measures expected to be unpopular with their supporters or with large parts of the electorate.

---

[2] See Kenneth Morgan, *Consensus and Disunity. The Lloyd George Coalition Government 1918–1922* (Oxford, 1979), 1–7, 363–6; Campbell, *Lloyd George*, 3–4, 234, 242, 307–9. Baldwin's critics had earlier taken a similar view: see, e.g., Amery, *Political Life* II, 240, and a Conservative ex-Cabinet minister (probably Amery) in Jones, *Diary with Letters*, xxxii.

[3] To extract from chs. 5–14 above: Churchill had already excluded himself from consideration, by his separation from the Conservative leadership in January 1931, and on financial and economic issues he had simply ceased to matter. Lloyd George had been accepted into alliance by MacDonald before the crisis. The possibility that Lloyd George might enter some 'national government' was what first made Neville Chamberlain think that Conservatives might be well advised to join too. In reality fear of Lloyd George was a reason for involving, not excluding, him from any broad coalition. He continued to be treated as Liberal party leader until he split with Liberal ministers in October. There was no general reaction against the leaders of 1918–22: Austen Chamberlain received office in August but later retired; Horne was offered but declined office in November.

All hoped initially that the May Committee would get them off the hook. Senior Labour ministers wanted all-party co-operation in order to obtain parliamentary support for increased direct taxation and to justify expenditure cuts to their own followers. Conservative and Liberal leaders – the latter even at the cost of their alliance with the Cabinet and at the risk of losing electoral reform – wanted to minimise direct tax increases and to fasten responsibility for expenditure cuts firmly upon Labour ministers. In seeking to confine the political crisis to the Labour party, they succeeded too well. When the Cabinet began to fall apart in the face of an imminent split in the Labour movement, Chamberlain and Samuel feared that without suitable high political management their own parties might become electorally vulnerable to a revulsion not just from large sections of the working classes, but also, perhaps, from parts of the middle classes. 'National' government under MacDonald and Snowden seemed an excellent device not just to impress nervous foreign financial markets and prospective lenders, but also to present unpleasant financial impositions to the British electorate. Baldwin, to the last the chief Conservative opponent of a 'national' solution, accepted this logic. Lloyd George and Churchill, despite certain reservations, also supported this solution and wanted the emergency government to continue. Given their views on 'economy' since 1930, even if Lloyd George had not been physically removed and Churchill politically removed from events, it is unlikely that the outcome would have been much different.

Nor do the events of August 1931 alone explain the National government. Its formation, continuation, and electoral success can no more be understood simply in those terms than can the collapse of the Labour government. Contingency manifestly played a very large part. There was certainly not a deliberate movement by party leaders towards a 'national' government. Until July political effort had been directed towards objectives which, but for the combined sterling and budget crises, would have produced a quite different outcome, based upon a polarisation between a Labour–Lloyd George Liberal alliance and a Conservative–Simon Liberal alliance. Nevertheless, the problems which the National government was intended to address had emerged well before the August crisis. So too had the conditions which would make such a government congenial for its members, welcome to a wide range of interests, and acceptable to much of the electorate.

The economic depression from late 1929 created a large movement of financial, business, *rentier*, direct tax-paying, and rate-paying opinion in favour of public retrenchment. In retrospect it may seem clear that throughout the inter-war period the Conservative party could easily mobilise a large 'coalition of classes and interests' to support 'deflationary' measures. Conventional wisdoms and unfavourable stereotypes of 'labour' united the 'public' – including parts of the non-unionised working classes – in hostility towards organised Labour.[4] After the August 1931 crisis the Conservatives and their allies benefited further from the Labour leadership's adoption of a more definite socialist platform. The 'public' – or as Conservatives themselves would have said, the 'country' – could fairly easily be persuaded to regard this platform as dangerous to the nation and threatening to themselves. Yet, if such social analysis helps explain the outcome of the electoral struggle, it does little to explain the activities of party leaders and governments. In 1931, as in the run-ups to other inter-war general elections, Conservative leaders were not conscious that they occupied so strong an electoral position as appears in hindsight. They were far from certain that substantial retrenchment could be made electorally acceptable, and feared a quite different – and, for Conservatives, disastrous – division, between 'rich' and 'poor': between on the one hand the minority of wealth-holders and high income-earners, and on the other a united working class, with the lower middle classes tilted towards the latter. The Conservative leadership devoted much of their policy and rhetorical effort to the prevention of this kind of class politics. It was their success here which helped to hold together that vital alliance between the various sections constituting the 'public'.

Few politicians operated upon what economists might consider a coherent economic position. This was less because they lacked formal expertise in economics, than because of the various and sometimes conflicting political pressures upon them. They dealt with monetary policy, the budget, social policy, industrial policy, and, in the case of Conservatives, tariffs, as distinct questions. Hence Keynes's complaints from 1925, that despite the return to the gold standard the Conservative government had no strategy for following through the implications in the form of effective 'deflationary' policies. Even on

[4] See the important essay, 'Class and Conventional Wisdom: The Conservative Party and the "Public" in Inter-war Britain', in McKibbin, *Ideologies of Class*, 259–93.

budgetary issues the 1924–9 Conservative government sought the best of all worlds. Despite its huge 1924 election victory and the defeat of the General Strike, its efforts to retrench in areas affecting the working population had been slight. In avoiding increased income tax yet maintaining social services, Churchill simply circumvented budget conventions and obtained fake 'balances' by one-off devices. The problem of an insolvent Unemployment Insurance Fund was also evaded, by the invention of 'transitional benefit'. Labour ministers were therefore justified in declaring that the problems of public finance which confronted them from 1929 had been neglected or exacerbated by their Conservative predecessors. Even during the August 1931 crisis, at least one Liberal leader still thought the Conservatives could not be trusted to face up to retrenchment.[5]

Many of the Conservative party's natural supporters had also long considered the leadership pusillanimous on this question of limiting social service expenditure in order to reduce a supposedly excessive burden of direct taxation. As these groups were unable seriously to contemplate transferring their allegiance to another party, their discontent took the form of impatience with party politics itself for inhibiting their political leaders from doing what seemed necessary. This sense that the party system obstructed sensible measures stimulated a desire for strong, 'non-party' government.

Similar feelings arose around the issues of protection and imperial trade. In the late 1920s many Conservative supporters did not appreciate the Conservative leadership's belief that sensitivity towards 'liberal' opinion was the key to future electoral success, and could not understand its failure to press protection as the party's own positive answer to industrial and agricultural depression, unemployment, high income tax, and socialism. From 1929 the Conservative leadership did move towards a full imperial protectionist programme, and the recession produced a 'landslide' of economic opinion in support of this position. But during 1930 it was by no means certain that a strong Conservative government could soon be formed to implement the programme. Again, party politics seemed to obstruct urgent and vital measures.

Disenchantment with the party system was not only sharpened by the pressures of the economic slump. It arose also from exasperation at a 'hung' Parliament, where Liberal MPs helped sustain a

[5] Sinclair to Maclean, 19 Aug. 1931, Thurso papers III/3/5.

minority Labour government whose policies were widely thought to be aggravating the depression. Party politics, it seemed, had got itself into such a mess that it had ceased to represent or provide effective leadership for the most powerful sections of opinion, and now operated to obstruct the 'national interest'. Discontent was manifested in a proliferation of new political organisations, and in appeals by existing economic interest groups. Those who joined or voted for Beaverbrook's Empire Crusade and Rothermere's United Empire party were not merely dissatisfied with the Conservative party leadership. Morris's National Council of Industry and Commerce and Ernest Benn's Friends of Economy expressed similar frustrations to those of such bodies as the FBI, NCEO, Chambers of Commerce, the NFU and landowners' associations, and the National Citizens' Union. All contributed to the atmosphere of 'national crisis' which became so marked in the autumn of 1930. All would have been content with the election of a Conservative government unequivocally committed to drastic retrenchment and tariffs, but they were even happier with a National government with greater freedom to impose those policies.

The sense of 'national crisis' and exasperation with existing party politics did not just affect elements of the broad political right. It also affected sections of progressive and centre opinion, dismayed at the Labour government's weaknesses or disillusioned by the Liberal party's ineffectiveness. The apparent failure of the non-Conservative parties to rise to the challenges of the economic recession and their consequent electoral vulnerability stimulated interest in new ideas about state intervention and in new political or governmental arrangements. Along this spectrum should be placed not just the ILP, Beatrice Webb, and Cole's Society for Socialist Inquiry and Propaganda but also those who contributed to the *Week-end Review* and formed Political and Economic Planning. This is also the context in which Mosley must be placed. His real importance in 1930–1 did not lie in his policy ideas – his public works proposals or notions of economic 'insulation' – neither of which alone were particularly novel. Rather it lay in his recognition that the fundamental difficulties were those of converting ideas into measures, of achieving effective government action – of power. That he had identified a genuine problem was demonstrated by the outcome of the political struggle. In a diluted form (and without any input of his own) Mosley's objectives of a major realignment, a powerful executive, a small cabinet with special powers, and increased state involvement in economic affairs, were essentially embodied in the National government.

The National government's significance must also be seen in relation to imperial problems. At the very time when the Empire was thought to be increasingly necessary for Britain, it had begun to seem brittle. The Empire had increased importance as a support for Britain's diplomatic position in a world where the United States and Japan had become major powers, and where more states demanded a voice in international affairs through the League of Nations. The idea of the Empire as an economic lifebelt became more salient as post-war efforts to restore the international free-trade economy broke down in 1929–30, leaving a morass of nationalistic policies, shrinking markets, and collapsing prices. The failure of the 1930 Imperial Conference to establish new economic bonds to offset looser constitutional ties, and the civil disobedience, economic boycott, and attacks upon the rupee–sterling parity in India, therefore seemed to strike both at Britain's chances of economic recovery and at the maintenance of its international power. The difficulty over Dominion relations was that it raised precisely those trade questions which divided the parties, and so became another source of impatience with party politics. In contrast, the Indian problem drew the party leaderships together, with Baldwin not merely supporting the Labour Cabinet but calling upon its help in managing his own party.

By October 1930 the financial, economic, imperial, and party-political problems had generated a climate of 'national crisis'. Each raised major difficulties in itself. More important, although not all linked in detail they acquired the appearance of being inter-connected. There seemed to be a general loss of British power and control. This had become especially manifest in the assertiveness of the Dominion governments and in the civil disorder throughout India, but it was equally apparent in economic matters. The depression resulted from breakdowns in international investment, production, and trade about which Britain alone could do little. The United States and France had now become the key creditor powers, and by the time they agreed to co-operate in maintaining the international system it was too late. One way or another, it became increasingly apparent that national policy had to undergo major changes, in order both to adjust to, and to erect defences against, the surrounding chaos. Whether over the Empire, the economy, or public finance, all party leaders were faced with decisions of the greatest political difficulty. Yet the party system had apparently become incapable of producing resolute government.

The idea of 'national government' was a response to these conditions, not simply to the particular political crisis of August 1931. It was an idea which from mid 1930 attracted many of the more vocal sections of opinion. This created a tide of support for the emergency National government which would have made it difficult for Conservative and Liberal leaders to contemplate breaking up the coalition, even if they had not themselves seen good party and electoral reasons for keeping it together. The idea had also become so well established in high politics – not as a positive objective, but as a possible resort in the event of extraordinary difficulties – that in July and August 1931 it already existed as a serious alternative to simple co-operation between two or three parties.

Obviously the crucial figure in all this was MacDonald. His decisions to accept and retain the premiership of a National government need to be understood in several contexts. In the summer and autumn of 1931 he genuinely feared a financial collapse which would result in much worse hardship for the working population than the cuts in benefits and wages. In August he thought the Labour Cabinet had destroyed the Labour party's claims to be a party of government, by declining to do what seemed necessary in the 'national interest'. His socialism, like that of most other Labour party leaders, had always been more concerned with 'community' than with 'class'. It was about service, interdependence, integration, 'rationality', and organisation. It was about securing for poor, badly educated, and otherwise disadvantaged individuals their rightful place of respect and opportunity within the economic, social, political, and moral orders, sharing the benefits – and if need be the burdens – of full membership of the national community. Again like most other Labour party leaders, he always resisted any idea that the party was an agent of the trade union movement. He had also always repudiated the view that socialism was reducible simply to the basic material interests of the working classes: 'it cannot be over-emphasised that public doles, Poplarism, strikes for increased wages, limitation of output, not only are not Socialism, but may mislead the spirit and the policy of the Socialist movement'.[6] In such terms accepting expenditure cuts within a

---

[6] Preface, dated June 1924, to J. R. MacDonald, *Socialism: Critical and Constructive* (1929 edn), xiii.

programme of 'equal sacrifices' seemed consistent with his earlier positions, especially in the face of worse hardships and as the real value of benefits and wages had clearly increased substantially in the previous two years.

Socialism also meant peace, international conciliation, and constitutional advance within the Empire. For MacDonald – again like other Labour leaders – these were as much socialist objectives and vital national interests as were domestic economic and social reform. In 1931 they involved the forthcoming Disarmament Conference and second Indian Round Table Conference. They also involved the Hoover moratorium, and what should follow it. In all three areas MacDonald could rightly claim to have an expertise and record of achievement unmatched by any other political leader. He had certainly done much better in negotiations with the United States than had Conservative ministers from 1926 to 1929, and over India the Conservative party remained divided and uncertain. When, late on the evening of 23 August 1931, MacDonald agreed with Neville Chamberlain that 'his name did carry weight in America',[7] the point had genuine substance. Later he considered that his work on India, disarmament, and cancellation of reparations and war debts, provided good national and 'progressive' reasons for his remaining Prime Minister.

The further context in which MacDonald should be understood is that of the frustrations he had endured as head of the Labour government since 1929. The government did not lack policies; indeed, it had so many that its work repeatedly became congested. Problems arose partly because its intended economic policies proved inadequate to the scale of the economic difficulties, and partly because it lacked the power and internal agreement to adopt alternative policies. The outcome was drift. But this was not through lack of effort on the part of MacDonald and other ministers. The Cabinet began what by previous standards amounted to a large public works programme; but increasing and accelerating this would have meant overriding local authorities, facing resistance from the capital markets, and flouting Treasury and Bank of England advice, for – it appeared at the time – little practical effect. Industrial rationalisation required co-operation or at least acqui-escence from employers and banks; to accelerate the process by legislative coercion – as Graham eventually proposed for iron and

---

[7] N. Chamberlain diary, 23 Aug. 1931.

steel – threatened to end existing co-operation and damage financial and business confidence. Agricultural reorganisation received positive stimulation, but as in industrial schemes this would not progress far without import controls, which faced Labour party opposition. Retrenchment to tackle the deficits in the budget and Unemployment Insurance Fund also ran into Labour resistance. Increased direct taxation would have united many Liberal MPs with the Conservatives and, it was thought, might increase unemployment through deleterious effects upon investment and upon business opinion. Voluntary devaluation was unthinkable, because of fears that it might shatter confidence in financial institutions; it would, in any case, have produced instant parliamentary defeat. Concerted international action was, as the Bank of England found with the Kindersley Plan, obstructed by the French and Americans. In every direction the Labour Cabinet of 1929–31 faced formidable difficulties. Its problems were much greater than those of later Labour governments, which had the advantages of inheriting wartime powers, operating in a more favourable international environment, dealing with more chastened and acquiescent business and financial communities, possessing parliamentary majorities, and facing a Conservative party with a more positive attitude towards state action.

The 'economic radicals' did not offer the second Labour government any obvious means of escape. Mosley's public works programme only highlighted the difficulties already raised by the Cabinet's existing programme and by Lloyd George's plans. These Liberal schemes faced problems of political credibility in view of their specific party purpose, of Lloyd George's record during the onset of mass unemployment in 1920–2, and of his known approaches to Conservative leaders during 1929. They crumbled when exposed to detailed departmental scrutiny from June to September 1930, and as the recession advanced were so modified as to disappear in February 1931. For all Lloyd George's genuine radical intentions before the 1929 election and his gestures thereafter, by the spring of 1931 his section of the Liberal party stood for retrenchment and free trade. It had, in fact, become the most conservative of all the parties.

Keynes not only faced criticism from the financial authorities and fellow economists; his views also seemed fluid, inconsistent, and paradoxical. His intellectual strengths, and his fertile shifting between theoretical and practical concerns, became disabilities when offering advice to politicians. It was not simply that his statements moved between theory and policy, ideal solutions and second-best remedies, rational strategies and his own preferences.[8] As he himself wrote, he had a tendency to 'romance along the lines of [his] own imagination rather than of ascertained fact or existing probability',[9] a trait evident in his letters to MacDonald in August 1931. Aside from this, and more important, Keynes's proposals raised but did not answer the problems of the Labour Cabinet's power. This was true of his ideas both for international co-operation and for capital development. A revenue tariff and selective retrenchment, which Keynes supported in early 1931 (and indeed Mosley's ideas for 'economic insulation') were not only issues which divided the Labour Cabinet. Even had the Cabinet somehow agreed upon tariffs and expenditure cuts, and in the unlikely event of the Labour party being acquiescent, the government would have faced the embarrassment of appearing to concede the case of the Conservative opposition.

None of this is to deny that the Labour government had serious problems in its own assumptions, commitments, and policies. It had innocent notions about 'progress' and of an immanent, emerging consensus on social justice and state regulation. Despite Labour criticism of capitalism, in reality its expectations relied upon the buoyancy and goodwill of private enterprise. Although it believed in the regulation of much economic activity, it remained tied to old radical traditions of free trade. Such slogans as 'work or adequate maintenance' allowed no excuse or escape. Any other government confronted by the economic recession from 1929 would have suffered enormous difficulties and, in terms of its previous programmes and pledges, would almost certainly have 'failed'. But the Labour government suffered more than another might have done because it lacked resourcefulness and flexibility not just in its ideas but in its words. Unlike later Labour governments, including those of 1945–51, it allowed itself insufficiently plausible explanations for major setbacks. It could not absorb policy defeats. Its failure was not simply in policy, but in politics.

MacDonald tried hard in both areas. Although the revelation came to him later than it did to those of the younger generation such as Mosley and Keynes, he grasped during 1930 that the foundations

---

[8] See Clarke, *Keynesian Revolution*, esp. p. 232.
[9] Keynes to Case, 2 Nov. 1931, in *JMK* xxi, 11.

of past policy had been destroyed[10] and that Britain now faced a 'totally different world'.[11] As the world had changed, so he thought the Labour government and the Labour party had no choice but to change too, reassessing commitments and perhaps making some temporary sacrifices of principle. Although he understood that British industry was 'backward in methods' and that 'the financier had played havoc with sound business',[12] given the government's minority parliamentary position and the existing structure of power he did not contemplate an attack upon capitalist institutions. Nor did his Cabinet colleagues until after they had left government. Despite Bank and Treasury scepticism, from early 1931 he looked to an international economic conference. Despite Labour commitments, he also reluctantly turned to import controls and retrenchment in unemployment insurance. MacDonald's occasional interest in all-party co-operation and – if an emergency were to occur – in 'national government' must be seen as ideas to ease the Labour leadership's difficulty in making such departures from party policy and concessions towards its opponents' positions. They did not represent a desire to leave the Labour party. But whether on import controls or retrenchment his immediate problems were inflexible Cabinet colleagues and a potentially rebellious parliamentary party. To him, these seemed to be refusing to accept the national and political imperatives for adjustment.

For eighteen months MacDonald turned from one set of advisors to another, from one policy idea to another, from one political expedient to another, without finding a means to end the government's drift. He certainly became exasperated with his colleagues and party, and wrote or spoke about taking an independent course. But then so at various times did Baldwin and Lloyd George. If other party leaders had kept diaries, it is unlikely that MacDonald's criticisms of his own party in late 1930 would now seem so remarkable. What is unmistakable is that once MacDonald found himself at the head of a National government in circumstances where many policy positions seemed to have become fluid, he saw unexpected opportunities for preserving earlier achievements and securing adjustments in financial and economic policies as well as on imperial and international issues. In this belief he was encouraged

---

[10] See, e.g., MacDonald diary, 9 Feb. 1930, and notebook, 14 Aug. 1930 (Marquand, 537, 555). [11] MacDonald to Peach, 20 Feb. 1932, JRM 1442.
[12] MacDonald diary, 9 Feb. 1930 (Marquand, 537).

by the fairmindedness and emollient manner of Baldwin – whose speeches 'on brotherly love' MacDonald had long admired as representing the 'honest sentiment' of a 'pure Utopian'[13] – and by Neville Chamberlain's apparent receptivity to a good case.

In some senses MacDonald was obviously naive, muddled, and deluded. The activities of the National Labour Committee were hardly likely to convert the National government to a modernised socialism. The Conservative leaders, the real power within the government, remained firmly attached to private enterprise, property, low direct taxation, and social inequality. As self-justification after the Labour party repudiated the National government, MacDonald wanted and needed to believe that he was not a Conservative dupe.

Nevertheless the National government did make serious attempts to address the major social, economic, imperial, and international problems, following through earlier initiatives and making important innovations of its own. Contrary to a common impression, it was not part of some wilderness between the Lloyd George Coalition's reconstruction policies of 1918–20 and those of the Labour governments from 1945 to 1951. As Keynes is often regarded as a touchstone, it should be noted that he was sympathetic towards key areas of government policy during 1932, and retained a respect for MacDonald's judgement even after the 1931 crisis.[14] After the introduction of tariffs he recognised that in 'some important...respects those who are not afraid to use tariffs have a broader conception of the national economic life...[than free-traders]', and that 'national protection ha[d] its idealistic side, too'.[15]

The Lausanne Conference, the World Economic Conference, and the Government of India Act represented central areas of continuity between the Labour and the National governments. Where commitment to a 'sound' budget and maintenance of confidence seemed to allow, Conservative ministers also resumed the development of social services which had been a feature of the 1924–9 Conservative government. The means test was relaxed in late 1932 and, though marred by a debacle over new benefit scales in early 1935, provision of unemployment payments was placed on a more

[13] MacDonald diary, 18 May 1925.
[14] See Keynes to Macmillan, 6 June 1932, in *JMK* XXI, 110. See also B. Webb diary, 23 Sept. 1931, for Keynes having a 'soft spot' for MacDonald in contrast to his contempt for Snowden and the Labour opposition leaders.
[15] Broadcast, 'Pros and Cons of Tariffs', November 1932, in *JMK* XXI, 204–10, at 206–7.

secure basis and then extended to agricultural workers. Slum clearance continued under Greenwood's Act of 1930, assisted by new Housing Acts from 1933. From 1935 plans proceeded to raise the school-leaving age. Employment of women and youths received further regulation, and legislation encouraged the extension of holidays with pay for working men.

More striking were developments in economic intervention, regulation, and management, which were of a quite different order to government activity in the 1920s. Obviously some of these were necessitated by the collapse of the gold standard and by the widespread desire for defence against international dislocations. Exchange management, cheap money, the sterling bloc, and tariffs represented a version of the 'insulation' which Keynes, Mosley, and Bevin had wanted. But these were not the whole story. From the late 1920s leading Conservatives had regarded import controls as a means to restrict not just foreign competition but also competition between domestic producers. Under the National government agricultural policy was transformed, with quotas, levies, subsidies, and commissions of inquiry used to persuade producers to reorganise themselves, regulate output, and improve efficiency. A 1933 Act made Addison's Agricultural Marketing Act work. Morrison's London Passenger Transport Bill was also enacted in 1933, and general Road Traffic Acts followed. Tramp and passenger shipping received subsidies, and Imperial Airways were nationalised. Tariffs and financial inducements became part of the machinery used in 'industrial diplomacy' – substantial informal efforts made to persuade industrialists to rationalise production.[16] Here as in agriculture the government hoped for progress through producers exercising and imposing 'self government' over themselves. But already in the 1930s, where such indirect methods seemed inadequate, for example in cotton and coal mining, ministers accepted the need for further legislative pressure.

From MacDonald's perspective such developments in social and economic policies constituted advances towards a more organised and humane society. For Conservatives they represented a recognition that, in the face of persistent difficulties and now a deep recession, only government initiatives could achieve the economic restructuring and social improvements which would restore the

---

[16] See Richard Roberts, 'The Administrative Origins of Industrial Diplomacy 1929–1935', in John Turner (ed.), *Businessmen and Politics* (1984), 93–104.

profitability and reputation of private enterprise. From 1933 there was clear evidence of economic recovery and, given the fall in the cost of living, the great majority of those in work enjoyed a period of relative prosperity. This enabled the Cabinet to believe that its policies were working. Nevertheless mass unemployment, with all its social hardships, persisted. Conservative leaders would not accept direct government responsibility for the levels of employment. This would have been an admission that private enterprise had failed and could not work, with immense economic, social and political consequences. Even so, Conservative leaders had in their own way adopted a much more positive attitude towards the role of the state. When Neville Chamberlain could speak in 1934 of 'revolutionary' government experiments,[17] and Baldwin declare in 1935 that 'laissez faire' was as dead as the 'slave trade',[18] something important was clearly happening to Conservative politics under the National government.

Despite MacDonald, in 1931 the Labour party rediscovered its radical energies. As important, after the experience of the second Labour government it dedicated itself to confronting the economic and political realities of achieving social justice, redistribution, and equality, in detailed revaluations of what it meant to be 'socialist'. For Keynes too, the period from 1929 to 1932 was seminal, as he shed an old free-trade skin and discovered new notions for a 'General Theory' and for the techniques for fiscal management. Outside the government, Macmillan and other Conservative 'planners' sought a new 'middle way'. Yet there were also 'planners' (and other former admirers of Mosley) who rose within the National government, most notably Elliot and Oliver Stanley, and although the Cabinet attempted to save rather than spend its way out of the depression, in other directions it had begun to adopt new interventionist policy instruments. Despite the rearrangements of the Conservative hierarchy in 1940, the National government of the 1930s also made contributions towards the 'mixed economy' or 'Butskellism' of the 1950s.

[17] See N. Chamberlain epigraph to this chapter, and also Feiling, *Chamberlain*, 229.
[18] Baldwin speech, 25 March 1935, quoted in Cowling, *Impact of Hitler*, 52.

Appendix

THE PERSONNEL

Biographical description is restricted to details relevant for 1926–32. Persons mentioned only once or twice in the text or notes, and whose positions are clear from the context, are in general not listed. Numbers in brackets refer to ages in 1931.

Adamson, William (68). Miner, trade union secretary; Labour MP (W. Fife) 1910–31; chairman, Parliamentary Labour party 1917–21; Secretary of State, Scotland 1924, 1929–31.

Addis, Sir Charles (70). Director, Bank of England 1918–32 (Committee of Treasury 1919–31); vice-chairman, Bank for International Settlements 1929–32.

Addison, Dr Christopher (62). Liberal MP 1910–22, Labour MP (Swindon) 1929–31; Coalition Liberal Cabinet minister 1919–21; Parliamentary Secretary, Agriculture 1929–June 1930, Minister 1930–1.

Alexander, A. V. (46). Secretary, Parliamentary Committee of the Co-operative Congress since 1920; Co-op/Labour MP (Hillsborough) 1922–31; Parliamentary Secretary, Board of Trade 1924; First Lord of the Admiralty 1929–31.

Allen, W. E. D. (30). Belfast businessman; author; Unionist MP (W. Belfast) 1929–31.

Amery, Leo (58). Conservative MP (S. Birmingham) from 1911; First Lord of the Admiralty 1922–4; Secretary of State, Colonies 1924–9 and Dominions 1925–9.

Amulree, 1st Lord (71). Barrister, industrial arbitrator, and government advisor; Baron 1929; Secretary of State, Air 1930–1.

Angell, Sir Norman (57). Journalist, peace campaigner; Labour MP (N. Bradford) 1929–31.

Arnold, 1st Lord (53). Stockbroker; Liberal MP 1912–21; joined Labour 1922; Baron and junior minister 1924; Paymaster-General 1929–March 1931.

Astor, 2nd Viscount (52). Owner of *The Observer*; Conservative MP

1911–19; junior minister 1918–21; succeeded as MP (Sutton, Plymouth) by his wife, Nancy, Viscountess Astor.

Attlee, Clement (48). Labour MP (Limehouse) from 1922; Under-secretary, War 1924; member, Simon Commission 1927–30; Chancellor, Duchy of Lancaster 1930–1; Postmaster-General 1931.

Baldwin, Oliver (32). War service, including Armenian army 1920–1; author, Labour MP (Dudley) 1929–31; eldest son of Stanley Baldwin.

Baldwin, Stanley (64). Conservative MP (Bewdley) from 1908; Financial Secretary, Treasury 1917–21; President, Board of Trade 1921–2; Chancellor of Exchequer 1922–3; Prime Minister 1923–4, 1924–9.

Balfour, Sir Arthur (58). Steelmaster; member or chairman of numerous government committees on industrial matters since 1913; member, EAC.

Barry, Gerald (33). Editor (Liberal-radical) of *Saturday Review* 1924–30, then founded *Week-end Review*.

Beaverbrook, Lord (52). Canadian company promoter; Unionist MP 1910–16; Baron 1917; Chancellor, Duchy of Lancaster 1918; owner of *Daily Express*, *Evening Standard*, etc.

Benn, Sir Ernest (56). Publisher; Liberal campaigner for private enterprise, retrenchment, free trade, individualism.

Benn, (William) Wedgwood (54). Brother of above; Liberal MP 1906–27; Labour MP (N. Aberdeen) 1928–31; Secretary of State, India 1929–31.

Betterton, Sir Henry (59). Barrister; Conservative MP (Rushcliffe) from 1918; Parliamentary Secretary, Ministry of Labour 1922–4, 1924–9.

Bevan, Aneurin (34). Miner, trade union agent; Labour MP (Ebbw Vale) from 1929.

Beveridge, Sir William (52). Social scientist and economist, expert on unemployment issues; Director, London School of Economics.

Bevin, Ernest (50). General Secretary, Transport and General Workers Union from 1921; member, TUC General Council from 1925; member, EAC and Macmillan Committee.

Blackett, Sir Basil (49). Controller of Finance, Treasury 1919–22; Finance Member, Government of India 1922–8; company director; director, Bank of England from 1929.

Bondfield, Margaret (58). Official of General and Municipal Workers Union; member, TUC General Council from 1918, chairman 1923; Labour MP 1923–4, (Wallsend) 1926–31; Parliamentary Secretary, Ministry of Labour 1924; Minister of Labour 1929–31. First woman Cabinet minister.

Boothby, Robert (31). Conservative MP (E. Aberdeenshire) from 1924; PPS to Churchill 1926–9; friend of Mosley.

Bradbury, Lord (59). Joint Permanent Secretary, Treasury 1913–19; director, William Deacons Bank since 1925; member of every official committee on the gold standard from 1918.

Brand, R. H. (53). Managing director, Lazards (merchant bank); advisor on international financial issues.

Bridgeman, Lord (67). Conservative MP 1906–29; Home Secretary 1922–4; First Lord of the Admiralty 1924–9; Viscount 1929.

Brockway, Fenner (43). Journalist, pacifist; ILP secretary 1928, chairman 1931; Labour MP (E. Leyton) 1929–31.

Brown, Ernest (50). Liberal MP 1923, and from 1927 (Leith); Parliamentary Secretary, Health Nov. 1931.

Brown, W. J. (37). General Secretary, Civil Service Clerical Association; Labour MP (W. Wolverhampton) 1929–31.

Buchan, John (56). Prolific journalist and author; publisher; Director of Information 1917–18; Conservative MP (Scottish Universities) from 1927, but affected non-partisanship.

Buxton, Noel (62). Liberal MP 1905–6, 1910–18, Labour MP (N. Norfolk) 1922–30; Minister of Agriculture, 1924, 1929–June 1930, when created Baron.

Chamberlain, Sir Austen (68). Unionist-Conservative MP (latterly, W. Birmingham) from 1892; offices included Chancellor of Exchequer 1903–6, 1919–21; Secretary of State, India 1915–17; leader of Conservative party 1921–2; Foreign Secretary 1924–9.

Chamberlain, Neville (62). Half-brother of above. Conservative MP (latterly, Edgbaston) from 1918; Minister of Health 1923, 1924–9; Chancellor of Exchequer 1923–4.

Chilcott, Warden (60). Businessman; Conservative MP (Walton) 1918–29; admirer of Mussolini; close to A. Chamberlain.

Churchill, Winston (57). Conservative MP 1900–4, Liberal MP 1904–22, Conservative MP (Epping) from 1924; various Liberal and Coalition Liberal Cabinet offices 1908–15, 1917–22; Chancellor of Exchequer 1924–9.

Citrine, Walter (44). General Secretary of TUC from 1926; member, EAC.

Clay, Henry (48). Professor of Economics, Manchester University 1922–30; advisor, Bank of England from 1930.

Clynes, John (62). President, General and Municipal Workers Union; Labour MP (N. Manchester) 1906–31; junior minister, 1917–19; chairman, Parliamentary Labour party 1921–2; Lord Privy Seal 1924; Home Secretary 1929–31.

Cole, G. D. H. (42). Reader in Economics, University of Oxford; prolific socialist theorist and polemicist; member, EAC.

Collins, Sir Godfrey (56). Publisher; Liberal MP (Greenock) from 1910; Coalition Liberal whip 1919–20; (Asquithian) Liberal chief whip 1924–6, removed by Lloyd George; member, Liberal Council; Simonite from 1931.

Crewe, 1st Marquess of (73). Liberal; Lord-Lieutenant of Ireland 1892–5; various Cabinet offices 1905–16; Ambassador in Paris, 1922–8. Tried to be aloof from Liberal quarrels.

Cripps, Sir Stafford (42). 2nd son of Lord Parmoor; barrister; entered Labour politics as Solicitor-General 1930–1; Labour MP from 1931.

Croft: see Page Croft.

Cunliffe-Lister [until 1924 Lloyd-Graeme], Sir Philip (47). Conservative

MP (Hendon) from 1918; junior minister 1920–1; President, Board of Trade 1922–4, 1924–9.

D'Abernon, Viscount (74). Banker, businessman; ambassador in Berlin 1920–6.

Dalton, Hugh (44). Reader in Economics, London School of Economics; Labour MP (latterly Bishop Auckland) 1924–31; Parliamentary Under-secretary, Foreign Office 1929–31. Close to Henderson; disliked MacDonald.

Davidson, J. C. C. (42). Conservative MP (Hemel Hempstead) 1920–3 and from 1924; junior minister 1923–4, 1924–6; chairman, Conservative party 1926–30.

Dawson [until 1917 Robinson], Geoffrey (57). Editor of *The Times* 1912–19 and from 1923.

De la Warr, 9th Earl (31). Labour; MacDonald protégé; Parliamentary Secretary, War Office 1929–30, and Agriculture 1930–1.

Derby, 17th Earl of (66). Conservative; Secretary for War 1916–18, 1922–4; held to represent Lancashire Conservatism; father of Lord Stanley and Oliver Stanley.

Dunnico, Rev. Herbert (55). Baptist minister; Labour MP (Consett) 1922–31; Deputy Chairman, Ways and Means committee 1929–31.

Edge, Sir William (51). Liberal MP 1916–23, from 1927 (Bosworth); Coalition Liberal whip 1922–3; Liberal whip 1929–30; Simonite from 1931.

Elibank, 2nd Viscount (54). Colonial servant; Conservative MP 1918–22; company director.

Elliot, Walter (41). Early socialist sympathies; Conservative MP 1918–23, from 1924 (Kelvingrove, Glasgow); strong coalitionist 1919; Parliamentary Under-secretary, Scotland 1923–4, 1924–9; Financial Secretary, Treasury Aug. 1931.

Eyres-Monsell, Sir Bolton (50). Conservative MP (Evesham) from 1910; junior office 1919–22; Conservative chief whip 1923–31; First Lord of Admiralty Nov. 1931.

Foot, Isaac (51). Liberal MP (Bodmin) 1922–4 and from 1929.

Forgan, Dr Robert (37). Labour MP (W. Renfrew) 1929–31.

Garvin, James Louis (63). Journalist; editor of *The Observer* from 1908; biographer of Joseph Chamberlain.

Geddes, Sir Eric (56). Conservative MP 1917–22; Cabinet minister 1918–21; chairman, Committee on National Expenditure 1921–2; chairman, Dunlop and Imperial Airways.

Gilmour, Sir John (55). Conservative MP (latterly Pollock) from 1910; Secretary of State, Scotland 1924–9.

Gladstone, 1st Viscount (d. 1930, aged 76). Youngest son of ex-Prime Minister; Liberal MP 1880–1910; Home Secretary 1905–10; Governor-General, S. Africa 1910–14; (Asquithian) Liberal organiser 1918–24; member, Liberal Council.

Gorell, 3rd Lord (47). Writer and publisher; chairman, Society of Authors;

(Liberal) Under-secretary, Air 1921–2; joined Labour 1924; disappointed office-seeker 1929.

Graham, William (44). M.A. degree in Economics; Labour MP (Central Edinburgh) 1918–31; Financial secretary, Treasury 1924; President, Board of Trade 1929–31. Admirer of Snowden.

Greenwood, Arthur (51). Former economics lecturer; secretary, Labour Party Research Department; Labour MP (Nelson and Colne) 1922–31; Parliamentary secretary, Health 1924, Minister 1929–31.

Gregory, Theodore (41). Professor of Economics (banking), University of London; member, Macmillan Committee.

Greig, Louis (51). Royal Navy surgeon, then RAF; stockbroker; Gentleman Usher to the King from 1924; friend, occasional personal financial advisor of MacDonald.

Grenfell, Edward (61). Partner, Morgan Grenfell & Co (merchant bankers); director, Bank of England 1905–40; Conservative MP (City of London) from 1922.

Gretton, John (64). Conservative MP (latterly Burton) from 1895; leader in the diehard rebellion 1920–2.

Grey, 1st Viscount (69). Liberal MP 1885–1916; Foreign Secretary 1905–16; president, Liberal Council; almost blind.

Grigg, Sir Edward (52). Private secretary to Lloyd George 1921–2; Liberal MP 1922–5; Governor of Kenya 1925–30.

Grigg, P. J. (41). Private secretary to Chancellors of the Exchequer 1921–30; chairman, Inland Revenue from 1930.

Gwynne, H. A. (65). Journalist; editor of (Conservative) *Morning Post* from 1911.

Hailsham, 1st Viscount (59). Barrister; Conservative MP (St Marylebone) 1922–8; Attorney-General 1922–4, 1924–8; Lord Chancellor 1928–9. Thought to be a possible successor to Baldwin around 1927–8.

Hankey, Sir Maurice (54). Secretary of Committee of Imperial Defence from 1912, and of Cabinet from 1916; Clerk to Privy Council from 1923.

Hannon, Patrick (57). Company director; prominent in businessmen's political organisations, including EIA; Conservative MP (Moseley) from 1921.

Hartshorn, Vernon (d. 1931 aged 59). President, South Wales Miners Federation; Labour MP (Ogmore) 1918–31; Postmaster-General 1924; member, Simon Commission 1927–30; Lord Privy Seal 1930–1.

Harvey, Sir Ernest (64). Service in Bank of England since 1885; Deputy Governor from 1929.

Hawtrey, Ralph (52). Economist; Director of Financial Enquiries, Treasury from 1919.

Hayday, Arthur (62). Vice-president, General and Municipal Workers Union; Labour MP (W. Nottingham) 1918–31; member, TUC General Council, chairman 1931.

Headlam, Cuthbert (55). Conservative MP (Barnard Castle) 1924–9, and from 1931; Parliamentary secretary, Admiralty 1926–9.

Henderson, Arthur (68). Trade union official and Liberal agent, then Labour MP 1903–18, 1919–22, 1923, (Burnley) 1924–31; chairman, Parliamentary Labour party 1908–10, 1914–17; secretary, Labour party from 1912; War Cabinet posts 1915–17; Home Secretary 1924, Foreign Secretary 1929–31.

Henderson, Hubert Douglas (41). Cambridge economist; editor, *Nation* 1923–30; Liberal candidate 1929; joint secretary, EAC from 1930.

Hilton Young, Sir Edward (52). Liberal, from 1926 Conservative, MP 1915–23, 1924–9, (Sevenoaks) 1929–31; Financial secretary, Treasury 1921–2.

Hirst, Francis (58). Liberal author, lecturer on political economy and free trade.

Hoare, Sir Samuel (51). Conservative MP (Ipswich) from 1910; leading anti-coalitionist 1922; Secretary of State, Air 1922–4, 1924–9; friend of Beaverbrook, attached himself to N. Chamberlain.

Hopkins, Sir Richard (51). Chairman, Board of Inland Revenue 1922–7; Controller of Finance, Treasury from 1927.

Hore-Belisha, Leslie (38). Liberal MP (Devonport) from 1923.

Horne, Sir Robert (60). Conservative MP (Hillhead) from 1918; Minister of Labour 1919–20; President, Board of Trade 1920–1; Chancellor of Exchequer 1921–2; declined Cabinet office 1923; successful City career.

Hutchison, Sir Robert (58). Liberal MP 1922–3, (Montrose Burghs) from 1924; chief Liberal whip, 1926–30.

Irwin, Lord (50). Heir of 2nd Viscount Halifax; as Edward Wood Conservative MP 1910–25; President, Board of Education 1922–4; Minister of Agriculture 1924–5; Viceroy of India from 1926.

Jenkinson, Sir Mark (51). Accountant; director of Vickers, etc.; prominent in industrial rationalisation movement.

Johnston, Thomas (49). Editor, *Forward*; Labour MP (latterly W. Stirlingshire) 1922–4, 1924–31; Under-secretary, Scotland 1929–31; Lord Privy Seal 1931.

Johnstone, Harcourt (36). Liberal MP 1922–3, (South Shields) from 1931; party organiser; member, Liberal Council.

Jones, Leif (69). Temperance reformer; Liberal MP 1905–18, (Camborne) 1923–4, 1929–31; member, Liberal Council.

Jones, Thomas (61). Deputy secretary of Cabinet 1916–30; secretary, Pilgrim Trust.

Jowett, Frederick (67). Bradford ILP pioneer; Labour MP (Bradford) 1906–18, 1922–4, 1929–31; First Commissioner of Works 1924.

Jowitt, Sir William (46). Successful barrister; Liberal MP 1922–4, (Preston) from 1929, becoming Labour on appointment as Attorney-General.

Joynson-Hicks, Sir William (66). Created Viscount Brentford 1929; Conservative MP 1908–18, (Twickenham) 1918–29; Minister of Health 1923–4; Home Secretary 1924–9.

Kennedy, Thomas (55). Labour MP (Kirkcaldy Burghs) 1921–2, 1923–31;
　Labour chief whip 1927–31.
Kenworthy, Joseph (45). Liberal, from 1926 Labour, MP (Central Hull)
　1922–31.
Kerr: see Lothian.
Keynes, John Maynard (48). Economics Fellow, King's College, Cam-
　bridge; editor, *Economic Journal*; Treasury official 1915–19; member,
　EAC and Macmillan Committee.
Kindersley, Sir Robert (60). Chairman, Lazards (merchant bankers);
　director, Bank of England from 1914.
Lambert, George (65). Liberal MP (S. Molton) 1891–1924, and from
　1929; chairman, Coalition Liberal parliamentary party 1919–21.
Lane-Fox, George (61). Conservative MP (Barkston Ash) 1906–31;
　Secretary, Mines Department 1922–4, 1924–8; member, Simon
　Commission 1927–30.
Lansbury, George (72). Labour MP (Bow and Bromley) 1910–12, from
　1922; editor, *Daily Herald* 1913–22; chairman, Labour party 1928;
　First Commissioner of Works 1929–31.
Lawrence, Susan (60). Trade union official; Labour MP (N. East Ham)
　1923–4, 1926–31; Parliamentary secretary, Health 1929–31.
Layton, Sir William (47). Economist; editor, *The Economist* from 1922;
　chairman, Liberal Industrial Inquiry; Liberal candidate 1929.
Lees-Smith, Hastings (53). Reader in Public Administration, London
　School of Economics; Liberal MP 1910–18; Labour MP (Keighley)
　1922–31; Postmaster-General 1929–31; President, Board of Education
　1931.
Leith-Ross, Sir Frederick (44). Deputy Controller of Finance, Treasury
　from 1925.
Lewis, Sir Frederick (61). Leading shipowner; bank and insurance
　company director, etc.
Lloyd, Lord (52). Conservative MP 1910–18, 1924–5; Governor of
　Bombay 1918–23; High Commissioner, Egypt 1925–9.
Lloyd, Geoffrey (29). Private secretary, from 1931 PPS, to Baldwin;
　Conservative MP (Ladywood) from 1931.
Lloyd George, David (68). Liberal MP (Carnarvon Boroughs) from 1890;
　Cabinet offices 1905–16 included President, Board of Trade, and
　Chancellor of Exchequer; Prime Minister 1916–22.
Lockhart, Robert Bruce (44). Diplomat, banker, author; journalist,
　Beaverbrook's *Evening Standard* from 1929.
Lothian, 11th Marquess of (49). (Philip Kerr until 1930). Liberal theorist;
　secretary to Lloyd George 1916–21, and advisor thereafter.
Lubbock, Cecil (59). Director, Bank of England (Committee of Treasury),
　Deputy Governor 1923–4, 1927–9; member, Macmillan Committee.
MacDonald, James Ramsay (65). Labour MP 1906–18, (latterly Seaham)
　from 1922; Prime Minister and Foreign Secretary 1924; Prime
　Minister from 1929.

McKenna, Reginald (68). Liberal MP 1895–1918; Chancellor of Exchequer 1915–16; chairman, Midland Bank from 1919.

Maclean, Sir Donald (67). Liberal MP 1906–22, (N. Cornwall) from 1929; chairman, Liberal parliamentary party 1919–22; member, Liberal Council.

Macmillan, [Hugh] Lord (58). Scottish barrister; (non-party) Lord Advocate for Scotland 1924; government advisor; chairman, Macmillan Committee; Lord of Appeal from 1930.

Macmillan, Harold (37). Publisher; Conservative MP (Stockton) 1924–9.

Malone, Cecil (41). Coalition Liberal MP 1918, joined Communist party 1920; Labour MP (Northampton) 1928–31.

Mander, Geoffrey (49). Liberal MP (E. Wolverhampton) from 1929.

Maxton, James (46). Labour MP (Bridgeton, Glasgow) from 1922; chairman, ILP 1926–31.

May, Sir George (60). Secretary, Prudential Assurance 1915–31; almost blind.

Melchett, 1st Lord (d. 1930, aged 63). Formerly Sir Alfred Mond; chairman, ICI, etc.; Liberal MP and minister, became Conservative 1926; co-chairman, 'Mond–Turner' talks.

Melchett, 2nd Lord (33). Formerly Henry Mond; heir of above; Liberal MP 1922–3, Conservative MP (E. Toxteth) 1929–30.

Meston, Lord (66). Indian civil servant 1899–1919; Lieutenant-Governor, United Provinces 1912–18.

Mond: see 1st and 2nd Lord Melchett.

Moore-Brabazon, John (47). Conservative MP 1918–29, from 1931; junior minister 1923–4, 1924–7 (resigned).

Morris, Sir William (54). Chairman, Morris Motors, etc.

Morris-Jones, Dr J. H. (47). Liberal MP (Denbigh) from 1929.

Morrison, Herbert (43). Labour MP (Hackney) 1923–4, 1929–31; Minister of Transport 1929–31.

Mosley, Sir Oswald (35). Conservative, then Independent MP 1918–24; Labour MP (Smethwick) 1926–31; Chancellor, Duchy of Lancaster 1929–30.

Muir, Ramsay (59). Historian, Liberal theorist; Liberal MP 1923–4; chairman, Liberal party 1930–1, and NLF from 1931.

Nicolson, Harold (45). Diplomat to 1929; author; journalist, *Evening Standard*, 1930–1.

Norman, Montagu (60). Governor, Bank of England since 1920.

O'Connor, Terence (40). Conservative MP 1924–9, (C. Nottingham) from 1930.

Page Croft, Sir Henry (50). Conservative MP (latterly Bournemouth) from 1910; National Party, diehard 1917–22; chairman, EIA.

Parmoor, Lord (79). Former judge; Conservative MP 1895–1914; joined Labour; Lord President 1924, 1929–31.

Passfield, Lord [until 1929, Sidney Webb] (72). Socialist theorist, etc; Labour MP 1922–9; President, Board of Trade 1924; Secretary of State, Dominions 1929–30 and Colonies 1929–31.

Peacock, Edward (60). Director, Baring Bros; director, Bank of England 1921 and from 1929 (Committee of Treasury).

Peel, 1st Earl (64). Conservative; Secretary of State, India 1922–4, 1928–9.

Percy, Lord Eustace (44). Conservative MP (Hastings) from 1921; President, Board of Education 1924–9.

Pethick-Lawrence, Frederick (60). Labour MP (W. Leicester) 1923–31; Financial Secretary, Treasury 1929–31.

Philips Price, Morgan (46). Landowner; Labour MP (Whitehaven) 1929–31; PPS to Trevelyan.

Phillipps, Vivian (61). Liberal MP 1922–4; chairman, Liberal Party 1925–7; secretary, Liberal Council.

Pigou, Arthur (54). Professor of Political Economy, Cambridge University since 1908.

Ponsonby, 1st Lord (60). Liberal MP 1908–18; Labour MP (Brightside, Sheffield) 1922–30; Under-secretary, Foreign Office 1924, Dominions 1929, Transport 1929–31; Chancellor of Duchy 1931.

Pugh, Arthur (61). General secretary, Iron and Steel Trades Confederation; member, TUC General Council.

Pybus, Percy (51). Businessman; Liberal MP (Harwich) from 1929; Minister of Transport from 1931.

Reading, 1st Marquess of (71). Liberal MP 1904–13; Attorney-General 1910–13; Lord Chief Justice 1913–21; Special Ambassador to USA 1918; Viceroy of India 1921–6.

Robbins, Lionel (33). Professor of Economics, London School of Economics since 1929.

Rothermere, 1st Viscount (63). Air Minister 1917–18; owner of *Daily Mail*, *Daily Mirror*, *Evening News*, etc.

Rowntree, Seebohm (60). Chairman of Rowntree & Co.; social investigator; Liberal political worker.

Runciman, Walter (61). Shipowner, bank director, etc.; Liberal MP 1899–1918, (latterly St. Ives) from 1924; Cabinet offices 1908–16, including President, Board of Trade 1914–16.

Russell, 2nd Earl (d. 1931, aged 66). Parliamentary secretary, Transport 1929; Under-secretary, India 1929–31.

Salisbury, 4th Marquess (70). Lord President 1922–4; Lord Privy Seal 1924–9; Conservative Leader, House of Lords 1925–31.

Samuel, Sir Herbert (61). Liberal MP 1902–18, (Darwen) from 1929; Cabinet office 1909–16, including Home Secretary 1916; chairman, Royal Commission on coal 1925–6.

Sankey, Lord (65). Judge; chairman, Coal Commission 1919; Lord Chancellor from 1929.

Schuster, Sir Felix (77). Director, National Provincial Bank, etc.

Schuster, Sir George (50). Colonial service; Finance Member, Executive Council of Viceroy of India from 1928.

Seely, General John (63). Conservative MP 1900–4, Liberal MP 1904–22, 1923–4; Secretary of State, War 1912–14; junior minister 1918–19; chairman, National Savings Committee from 1926.

Shakespeare, Geoffrey (38). Secretary to Lloyd George 1921–3; Liberal MP 1922–3, (Norwich) from 1931.

Shaw, Tom (59). Secretary, International Federation of Textile Workers; Labour MP (Preston) 1918–31; Minister of Labour 1924; Secretary of State, War 1929–31.

Shinwell, Emanuel (47). Labour MP (Linlithgow) 1922–4, 1928–31; Financial Secretary, War 1929–30; Secretary, Mines Department, 1924, 1930–1.

Simon, Ernest (52). Manchester businessman; Liberal theorist; Liberal MP (Withington) 1923–4, 1929–31.

Simon, John (58). Successful barrister; Liberal MP 1906–18, (Spen Valley) from 1922; Home Secretary 1915–16; chairman, Indian Statutory Commission 1927–30.

Sinclair, Sir Archibald (41). Secretary to Churchill 1919–22; Liberal MP (Caithness) from 1922; Liberal chief whip 1930–1.

Snowden, Philip (67). Labour MP 1906–18, (Colne Valley) 1922–31; Chancellor of Exchequer 1924, 1929–31.

Stamfordham, Lord (d. 1931, aged 81). Private secretary to King George V from 1910.

Stamp, Sir Josiah (51). Statistician, economist; chairman, London, Midland and Scottish Railway; director, Bank of England from 1928; member, EAC.

Stanley, Lord (37). Heir of Lord Derby; Conservative MP (Flyde) from 1922; Conservative whip 1924–9.

Stanley, Oliver (35). 2nd son of Lord Derby; Conservative MP (Westmorland) from 1924.

Steel-Maitland, Sir Arthur (55). Conservative MP 1910–29, (Tamworth) from 1929; Minister of Labour 1924–9.

Stevenson, Frances (43). Private secretary to Lloyd George from 1913; mother of his unofficial daughter, born 1929.

Stonehaven, 1st Lord (57). As John Baird, Conservative MP 1910–25; junior minister 1919–24; Governor-General, Australia 1925–30; chairman, Conservative party from 1931.

Strachey, John (30). Journalist; Labour MP (Aston) 1929–31.

Strakosch, Sir Henry (60). Banker; member, Financial Committee of League of Nations, and of Council of India.

Streat, Raymond (34). Secretary, Manchester Chamber of Commerce.

Sydenham, 1st Lord (83). Governor of Victoria 1901–4; secretary, Committee of Imperial Defence 1904–7; Governor of Bombay 1907–13.

Thomas, James Henry (57). General secretary, National Union of Railwaymen 1918–31; former member, TUC General Council; Labour MP (Derby) from 1910; Secretary of State, Colonies 1924; Lord Privy Seal 1929–30, Secretary of State, Dominions from 1930.

Tillett, Ben (71). Dockers' union organiser from 1887; chairman, TUC 1929; Labour MP (N. Salford) 1917–24, 1929–31.

Topping, Robert (54). Conservative party agent from 1904; Principal Agent from 1928.

Trevelyan, Sir Charles (61). Liberal MP 1896–1918, Labour MP (C. Newcastle) 1922–31; President, Board of Education 1924, 1929–31; Lord-Lieutenant, Northumberland from 1930.

Turner, Sir Ben (68). President, National Union of Textile Workers; chairman, TUC 1928; co-chairman, 'Mond–Turner' talks; Labour MP (Batley) 1922–3, 1929–31; Secretary, Mines Department 1929–30.

Tweed, Thomas (41). Chief organiser, Liberal party 1927–31.

Webb, Beatrice (73). Wife of below; social investigator, authoress.

Webb, Sidney: see Passfield.

Wedgwood, Josiah (59). Liberal, from 1919 Labour MP, (Newcastle-under-Lyme) from 1906; Chancellor of Duchy 1924.

Weir, 1st Lord (54). Industrialist, prominent in NCEO; Secretary of State, Air 1918; government advisor.

Wheatley, John (d. 1930 aged 61). ILP leader; Labour MP (Shettleston, Glasgow) 1922–30; Minister of Health 1924.

Wigram, Sir Clive (58). Assistant Private Secretary to the King 1910–31, Private Secretary from 1931.

Willingdon, 1st Earl of (65). Liberal MP 1906–10; Governor of Bombay 1913–19, of Madras 1919–24; Governor-General, Canada 1926–31; Viceroy of India from 1931.

Wise, Frank (46). Civil servant 1912–18; economic advisor, Russian Union of Cooperative Societies; Labour MP (E. Leicester) 1929–31.

Worthington-Evans, Sir Laming (d. 1931 aged 63). Conservative MP 1910–29, (St. George's, Westminster) 1929–31; Secretary of State, War 1921–2, 1924–9.

Zetland, 2nd Marquess of (55). Conservative MP 1907–16; Governor of Bengal 1917–22.

Sources

Unless otherwise stated, place of publication of printed material is London. Square brackets indicate abbreviations used in footnote references. The sources are arranged as follows:

PRIMARY SOURCES (unpublished and published)
    Private records (unpublished, and editions)
      Personal papers
      Government records
      Papers of parties and organisations
    Public material
      Contemporary publications and collected articles, etc., of individuals
      Autobiographies
      Official publications
      Publications of parties and organisations
      Journals and newspapers

SECONDARY SOURCES
      Unpublished dissertations
      Books, articles and essays

PRIMARY SOURCES

PRIVATE RECORDS

Personal papers

King George V papers, the Royal Archives, Windsor [RA GV]
Sir Charles Addis
    Addis diary and papers, School of Oriental and African Studies, London
Christopher, 1st Viscount Addison
    Addison papers, Bodleian Library, Oxford
1st Earl Alexander of Hillsborough
    Alexander papers, Churchill College, Cambridge
1st Lord Altrincham (Sir Edward Grigg)
    Altrincham papers (microfilm), Bodleian Library, Oxford
L. S. Amery
    Amery diary and papers, courtesy of the Rt Hon. Julian Amery

John Barnes and David Nicolson (eds.),
  The Amery Diaries 1896–1929 (1980) [*LSA* I]
  The Empire at Bay. The Leo Amery Diaries 1929–1945 (1988) [*LSA* II]
1st Lord Amulree
  Amulree papers, Bodleian Library, Oxford
Sir Norman Angell
  Angell papers, Ball State University, Muncie, Indiana
2nd Viscount Astor and Nancy, Lady Astor
  Astor papers, Reading University Library
1st Earl Baldwin
  Baldwin papers [SB], Cambridge University Library
Gerald Barry
  Barry journal and papers, British Library of Political and Economic
    Science
Lord Bayford
  John Ramsden (ed.), *Real Old Tory Politics. The Political Diaries of Sir
    Robert Sanders, Lord Bayford, 1910–1935* (1984)
Rear Admiral T. P. H. Beamish
  Beamish papers, Churchill College, Cambridge
1st Lord Beaverbrook
  Beaverbrook papers, House of Lords Record Office
Ernest Benn
  E. Benn diary, the Modern Records Centre, Warwick University
Lord Beveridge
  Beveridge diary and papers, British Library of Political and Economic
    Science
Lord Brand
  Brand papers, Bodleian Library, Oxford
1st Viscount Bridgeman
  Bridgeman diary and papers, Shropshire County Record Office
  Philip Williamson (ed.), *The Modernisation of Conservative Politics. The Diaries
    and Letters of William Bridgeman 1904–1935* (1988)
Sir Harcourt Butler
  Butler papers, India Office Library
Edwin Cannan
  Cannan papers, British Library of Political and Economic Science
Viscount Cecil of Chelwood
  Cecil papers, British Library
Sir Austen Chamberlain
  A. Chamberlain papers [AC], Birmingham University Library
Neville Chamberlain
  N. Chamberlain diary and papers [NC], Birmingham University Library
Sir Winston Churchill
  Martin Gilbert (ed.), *Winston S. Churchill vol.* v *Companion*
    Part 1 The Exchequer Years 1922–1929 (1979) [*WSC* v(1)]
    Part 2 The Wilderness Years 1929–1935 (1981) [*WSC* v(2)]

Lord Citrine
  Citrine papers, British Library of Political and Economic Science
Tom Clarke
  My Lloyd George Diary (1939)
G. D. H. Cole
  Cole papers, Nuffield College, Oxford
Martin, Lord Conway
  Conway diary, Cambridge University Library
Marquess of Crewe
  Crewe papers, Cambridge University Library
Sir Stafford Cripps
  Cripps papers, Nuffield College, Oxford
1st Lord Croft (Sir Henry Page Croft)
  Croft papers, Churchill College, Cambridge
William Crook
  Crook papers, Bodleian Library, Oxford
Lord Dalton
  Dalton diary, British Library of Political and Economic Science
  Hugh Dalton, *Call Back Yesterday. Memoirs 1887–1931* (1953) – diary
    extracts
  Ben Pimlott (ed.), *The Political Diary of Hugh Dalton 1918–40, 1945–60*
    (1986)
1st Viscount Davidson
  Davidson papers, House of Lords Record Office
  Davidson Indian papers, Bodleian Library, Oxford
Charles Dawes
  Journal as Ambassador to Great Britain (New York, 1939)
Geoffrey Dawson
  Dawson diary and papers, Bodleian Library, Oxford
Richard Denman
  Denman papers, Bodleian Library, Oxford
17th Earl of Derby
  Derby papers, Liverpool City Library
2nd Viscount Elibank
  Elibank papers, Scottish Record Office
2nd Viscount Esher
  Esher papers, Churchill College, Cambridge
H. A. L. Fisher
  Fisher papers, Bodleian Library, Oxford
J. L. Garvin
  Garvin papers, Humanities Research Centre, University of Texas,
    Austin
Sir John Gilmour
  Gilmour papers, Scottish Record Office
Viscount Gladstone
  Gladstone papers, British Library

Sir Louis Greig
　Greig papers, courtesy of Mr Carron Greig
H. A. Gwynne
　Gwynne papers, Bodleian Library, Oxford
Sir Malcolm Hailey
　Hailey papers, India Office Library
Elizabeth Haldane
　E. Haldane diary and papers, National Library of Scotland
1st Earl of Halifax (Lord Irwin)
　Halifax papers, India Office Library
J. L. Hammond
　Hammond papers, Bodleian Library, Oxford
1st Lord Hankey
　Hankey diary and papers, Churchill College, Cambridge
Sir Patrick Hannon
　Hannon papers, House of Lords Record Office
Sir Cuthbert Headlam
　Headlam diary and papers, Durham County Record Office
H. D. Henderson
　H. D. Henderson papers, Nuffield College, Oxford
Bishop H. H. Henson
　Henson journal, Dean and Chapter Library, Durham Cathedral
Sir Edward and Lady Hilton Young: see Kennet
Francis Hirst
　The Formation, History and Aims of the Liberal Free Trade Committee 1931–1946
　　(privately printed, 1947) – Hirst diary extracts
Thomas Jones
　A Diary With Letters 1931–1950 (Oxford, 1954)
　Whitehall Diary (ed. Keith Middlemas), 2 vols. (Oxford, 1969)
1st Lord Kennet and Kathleen Lady Kennet (Sir Edward and Lady Hilton
　　Young)
　Kennet papers, and Lady Kennet diary, Cambridge University Library
　Lady Kennet, *Self-Portrait of An Artist* (1949) – diary extracts
1st Lord Keyes
　Paul Halpern (ed.), *The Keyes Papers. Selections from the Private and Official
　　Correspondence of Admiral of the Fleet Baron Keyes, Vol. II 1919–1938* (1980)
Lord Keynes
　Elizabeth Johnson and Donald Moggridge (eds.), *The Collected Writings
　　of J. M. Keynes*, 30 vols. (1971–1989) [*JMK*]
George Lane-Fox
　Lane-Fox diary, courtesy of Mr George Lane-Fox
George Lansbury
　Lansbury papers, British Library of Political and Economic Science
Arthur, Viscount Lee and Ruth, Lady Lee
　A Good Innings, vol. III (privately printed, 1940) – Lady Lee diary extracts
1st Lord Lloyd of Dolobran
　Lloyd papers, Churchill College, Cambridge

1st Earl Lloyd George
  Lloyd George papers [LG], House of Lords Record Office
  K. O. Morgan (ed.), *Lloyd George. Family Letters 1885–1936* (Oxford and Cardiff, 1973)
  A. J. P. Taylor (ed.), *My Darling Pussy. The Letters of Lloyd George and Frances Stevenson, 1913–1941* (1975)
Lockhart, Sir Robert Bruce
  Kenneth Young (ed.), *The Diaries of Sir Robert Bruce Lockhart. Vol. 1 1915–1938* (1973)
11th Marquess of Lothian (Philip Kerr)
  Lothian papers, Scottish Record Office
James Ramsay MacDonald
  J. R. MacDonald papers [JRM], Public Record Office
  J. R. MacDonald (NLS) papers, National Library of Scotland
Malcolm MacDonald
  M. MacDonald papers, Archives and Special Collections, Durham University Library
Sheila MacDonald (Mrs Lochhead)
  S. MacDonald notes, courtesy of Mrs Lochhead
Sir Donald Maclean
  Maclean papers, Bodleian Library, Oxford
J. S. Middleton
  Middleton papers, Ruskin College, Oxford
Viscountess Milner
  Lady Milner diary and papers, Bodleian Library, Oxford
Sir Henry Morris-Jones
  Morris-Jones diary, Clwyd County Record Office
Herbert, Lord Morrison
  Morrison papers, Nuffield College, Oxford
1st Lord Mottistone (John Seely)
  Mottistone papers, Nuffield College, Oxford
Gilbert Murray
  Murray papers, Bodleian Library, Oxford
Harold Nicolson
  Nicolson diary, Balliol College, Oxford
  Nigel Nicolson (ed.), *Harold Nicolson. Diaries and Letters, Vol. 1 1930–1939* (1966)
Lord Noel-Baker
  Noel-Baker papers, Churchill College, Cambridge
Montagu Norman
  Norman diary, Bank of England
F. S. Oliver
  Oliver papers, National Library of Scotland
Lord and Lady Passfield (Sidney and Beatrice Webb)
  Passfield papers and B. Webb diary, British Library of Political and Economic Science

Margaret Cole (ed.), *Beatrice Webb's Diaries 1924–1932* (1956)
Norman and Jeanne MacKenzie (eds.), *The Diary of Beatrice Webb Vol. IV 1924–1943* (1985)
Norman MacKenzie (ed.), *The Letters of Sidney and Beatrice Webb Vol. III 1912–47* (Cambridge, 1978)
Lord Pethick-Lawrence
  Pethick-Lawrence papers, Trinity College, Cambridge
1st Lord Ponsonby
  Ponsonby papers, Bodleian Library, Oxford
1st Marquess of Reading
  Reading papers, India Office Library
  Reading Indian papers, India Office Library
Lord Reith
  Charles Stuart (ed.), *The Reith Diaries* (1975)
5th Earl of Rosebery
  Rosebery papers, National Library of Scotland
Seebohm Rowntree
  Rowntree papers, Joseph Rowntree Memorial Library, York
Walter, 1st Viscount Runciman
  Runciman papers, Newcastle University Library
Herbert, 1st Viscount Samuel
  Samuel papers, House of Lords Record Office
Sir Robert Sanders: see Bayford
Viscount Sankey
  Sankey diary and papers, Bodleian Library, Oxford
C. P. Scott
  Scott diary, British Library
  T. Wilson (ed.), *The Political Diaries of C. P. Scott 1911–1928* (1970)
William, 2nd Earl of Selborne, and Roundell, 3rd Earl of Selborne (Viscount Wolmer)
  Selborne papers, Bodleian Library, Oxford
John, 1st Viscount Simon
  Simon papers, Bodleian Library, Oxford
  Simon Indian papers, India Office Library
1st Lord Southborough
  Southborough papers, Bodleian Library, Oxford
1st Viscount Stansgate (Wedgwood Benn)
  Stansgate papers, House of Lords Record Office
Sir Arthur Steel-Maitland
  Steel-Maitland papers, Scottish Record Office, Edinburgh
Frances Stevenson
  A. J. P. Taylor (ed.), *Lloyd George. A Diary by Frances Stevenson* (1971)
H. L. Stimson
  Stimson diary and papers, Yale University Library (microfilm in Cambridge University Library)
George Strauss
  Strauss diary, extracts in Nuffield College, Oxford

Sir Raymond Streat
   Marguerite Dupree (ed.): *Lancashire and Whitehall. The Diary of Sir Raymond Streat*, Vol. I (Manchester, 1987)
Sir Louis Stuart
   Stuart papers, Bodleian Library, Oxford
1st Earl of Swinton (Sir Philip Cunliffe-Lister)
   Swinton papers, Churchill College, Cambridge
A. J. Sylvester
   Colin Cross (ed.), *Life With Lloyd George. The Diary of A. J. Sylvester 1931–1945* (1975)
Viscount Templewood (Sir Samuel Hoare)
   Templewood papers, Cambridge University Library
   Templewood Indian papers, India Office Library
J. H. Thomas
   Thomas papers, Kent County Record Office
1st Viscount Thurso (Sir Archibald Sinclair)
   Thurso papers, Churchill College, Cambridge
Sir Charles Trevelyan
   Trevelyan papers, Newcastle University Library
1st Lord Tweedsmuir (John Buchan)
   Tweedsmuir (Queens) papers, Queen's University Library, Kingston, Ontario
   Tweedsmuir (NLS) papers, National Library of Scotland
Sidney and Beatrice Webb: see Passfield
1st Lord Weir
   Weir papers, Churchill College, Cambridge
Sir Laming Worthington-Evans
   Worthington-Evans papers, Bodleian Library, Oxford

Government records

Files from the following series of papers, in the Public Record Office:

CAB 21	Cabinet: Registered Files
CAB 23	Cabinet conclusions [Cabinet]
CAB 24	Cabinet memoranda [CP]
CAB 27	Cabinet committees
CAB 58/2	Economic Advisory Council: minutes [EAC]
IR63	Inland Revenue: Budget papers
FO371	Foreign Office: General correspondence
PREM 1, PREM 5	Prime Minister's Private Office papers
T160	Treasury: Finance files
T161	Treasury: Establishment files
T171	Chancellor of the Exchequer's Office: Budget papers
T172	Chancellor of the Exchequer's Office: miscellaneous papers
T175	Sir Richard Hopkins papers
T176	Sir Otto Niemeyer papers

T188   Sir Frederick Leith-Ross papers
Files from the following series, in the India Office Library:
IOR L/F   India Office Records: Finance Department

Papers of parties and organisations

Bank of England
  G1, G3 Governors' papers
  G14   Committee of Treasury papers [BoE Cte]
Conservative party
  Conservative Research Department papers, Bodleian Library, Oxford
  1922 Committee minutes, Bodleian Library, Oxford
  National Union of Conservative Associations, Executive Committee and
    Central Council minutes (microfiche)
Federal Reserve Bank of New York
  FRBNY papers, including George Harrison papers
Labour party
  General Correspondence and Political Records (microfilm)
  National Executive Committee minutes [LPNEC] (microfiche)
  Parliamentary Labour Party minutes [PLP] (microfiche)
Morgan, Grenfell & Co. papers [MGC]
Political and Economic Planning
  PEP papers, British Library of Political and Economic Science
Trades Union Congress
  General Council minutes [TUCGC] (microfiche)

PUBLIC MATERIAL

Contemporary publications and collected articles, etc., of individuals (excluding
material found only in those journals listed below)

Beveridge, Sir William, *et al.*, *Tariffs: The Case Examined* (1931)
Boothby, Robert; Loder, John; Macmillan, Harold, and Stanley, Oliver,
  Industry and the State. A Conservative View (1927)
Chilcott, Warden, *Political Salvation* (1932)
Churchill, Winston, *Thoughts and Adventures* (1932)
  The Complete Speeches of Sir Winston Churchill, Robert Rhodes James (ed.)
  (1974)
Henderson, H. D., *The Inter-War Years and Other Papers* (Oxford, 1955)
Keynes, J. M.: see under 'Personal papers'
Laski, H. J., *The Crisis of the Constitution* (1932)
Lloyd George, D., Lord Lothian and S. Rowntree, *How to Tackle
  Unemployment* (1930)
Mosley, Sir Oswald, *Revolution by Reason* (1925)
Muir, Ramsay, *How Britain is Governed* (1930)
Nathan, H. L., and Williams, H. H. (eds.), *Liberal Points of View* (1927)

Percy, Lord Eustace, *Democracy on Trial. A Preface to an Industrial Policy* (1931)
Phillips, Hubert; Holgate, Arthur; Hughes, R. Moelwyn; Jones, T. Elder; Lloyd, Ifor; Menken, Jules and Sainsbury, Alan, *Whither Britain? A Radical Answer* (1932)
West, Gordon, *Lloyd George's Last Fight* (1930)

Autobiographies

Amery, L. S., *My Political Life*, vols. II–III (1953, 1955)
Bernays, Robert, *Special Correspondent* (1934)
Boothby, Robert, *I Fight to Live* (1947)
Brockway, Fenner, *Inside the Left* (1942)
Citrine, Lord, *Men and Work* (1964)
Croft, Lord, *My Life of Strife* (1948)
Dalton, Hugh, *Call Back Yesterday. Memoirs 1887–1931* (1953)
  Fateful Years. Memoirs 1931–1945 (1957)
Davenport, Nicholas, *Memoirs of a City Radical* (1974)
Davidson, J. C. C., *Memoirs of a Conservative*, Robert Rhodes James (ed.) (1969)
Denman, Richard, *Political Sketches* (Carlisle, 1948)
Grigg, P. J., *Prejudice and Judgment* (1948)
Johnston, Thomas, *Memoirs* (1952)
Kenworthy, J. M., *Sailors, Statesmen – and Others* (1933)
Macmillan, Lord, *A Man of Law's Tale* (1952)
Morris-Jones, Sir Henry, *Doctor in the Whips' Room* (1955)
Morrison, Herbert, *An Autobiography* (1960)
Mosley, Sir Oswald, *My Life* (1968)
Pethick-Lawrence, F. W., *Fate Has Been Kind* (n.d., but 1943)
Picton-Turbervill, E., *Life Has Been Good* (1939)
Price, M. Philips, *My Three Revolutions* (1969)
Rentoul, Gervase, *Sometimes I Think* (1940)
Samuel, Viscount, *Memoirs* (1945)
Shakespeare, Sir Geoffrey, *Let Candles Be Brought In* (1949)
Shinwell, Emanuel, *Conflict Without Malice* (1955)
Snell, Lord, *Men, Movements, and Myself* (1938 edn)
Snowden, Viscount, *Autobiography* vol. II (1934)
Williams, Francis, *Nothing So Strange. An Autobiography* (1970)

Official publications

The Board of Trade Journal
Parliamentary Debates: House of Commons [*HC Deb*]
Parliamentary Debates: House of Lords [*HL Deb*]
Committee on Finance and Industry, *Minutes of Evidence* (1931)
Royal Commission on Unemployment Insurance, *Evidence* (1932)

Parliamentary Papers:
  Select Committee on Procedure on Public Business, *Special Report* (1930–1
    (161) VIII, 203)
  Royal Commission on Unemployment Insurance, *First Report* (1930–1,
    Cmd. 3872, XVII, 885)
  Committee on Finance and Industry, *Report* (1930–1, Cmd. 3897, XIII,
    219)
  Committee on National Expenditure, *Report* (1930–1, Cmd. 3920, XVI, 1)
  Select Committee on Procedure, *Report* (1931–2 (129) V, 487)
Papers Relating to the Foreign Relations of the United States 1931 Vol. I
    (Washington, 1946) [FRUS]
Documents on British Foreign Policy 1919–1939, Second Series, Vol. II 1931
    (1947) [DBFP]

Publications of parties and organisations

Federation of British Industries, *Annual Reports* 1930–1
Friends of Economy, *First Annual Report 1931*
Labour Party:
  Annual Conference Reports, 1928–32 [LPACR]
  Labour and the Nation (1928)
Liberal Party:
  National Liberal Federation, *Proceedings*, 1929–32
  We Can Conquer Unemployment (1929)
National Farmers' Union:
  The NFU Yearbook, 1930–1
Trades Union Congress:
  Annual Reports, 1929–31 [TUCAR]

Journals and newspapers

The Economist
The Nation and Athenaeum
The New Statesman
The Nineteenth Century and After
The Observer
The Political Quarterly
The Spectator
The Times
The Week-end Review
Journal of the Royal Statistical Society
In addition, use has been made of newspaper cuttings preserved with
    certain collections of private papers, especially the extensive, classified,
    files in the Lloyd George papers.

SECONDARY SOURCES

Unpublished dissertations

Hart, Michael, 'The Decline of the Liberal Party in Parliament and in the Constituencies, 1914–31', Oxford D.Phil. (1982)

Janeway, William, 'The Economic Policy of the Second Labour Government 1929–1931', Cambridge Ph.D. (1971)

Short, Mary, 'The Politics of Personal Taxation: Budget-making in Britain 1917–31', Cambridge Ph.D. (1985)

Thorpe, Andrew, 'The British General Election of 1931', University of Sheffield D.Phil. (1987)

Books, articles and essays

Abel, Deryck, *Ernest Benn: Counsel For Liberty* (1960)

Ball, Stuart, 'The Conservative Party and the Formation of the National Government: August 1931', *Historical Journal*, 29 (1986), 159–82

   'Failure of an Opposition? The Conservative Party in Parliament 1929–1931', *Parliamentary History*, 5 (1986), 83–98

   Baldwin and the Conservative Party. The Crisis of 1929–1931 (New Haven and London, 1988)

   'The 1922 Committee. The Formative Years 1922–45', *Parliamentary History*, 9 (1990), 129–57

Bassett, Reginald, *Nineteen Thirty-One. Political Crisis* (1958)

Bennett, Edward, *Germany and the Diplomacy of the Financial Crisis, 1931* (Cambridge, Mass., 1962)

Bentley, Michael, *The Liberal Mind 1914–1929* (Cambridge, 1977)

Blaxland, Gregory, *J. H. Thomas: A Life For Unity* (1964)

Booth, Alan, 'Britain in the 1930s: A Managed Economy?', *Economic History Review*, II (1987), 499–521

Boyce, Robert, *British Capitalism at the Crossroads 1919–1932* (Cambridge, 1987)

Brockway, Fenner, *Socialism Over Sixty Years. The Life of Jowett of Bradford* (1946)

Bullock, Alan, *The Life and Times of Ernest Bevin. Vol. 1 Trade Union Leader 1881–1940* (1960)

Burk, Kathleen, *Morgan Grenfell 1838–1988. The Biography of a Merchant Bank* (1989)

Butt, Ronald, *The Power of Parliament* (1967)

Cairncross, Alec and Eichengreen, Barry, *Sterling in Decline* (Oxford, 1983)

Campbell, John, *Lloyd George: The Goat in the Wilderness 1922–1931* (1977)

Carlton, David, *MacDonald versus Henderson. The Foreign Policy of the Second Labour Government* (1970)

Clarke, Peter, 'The Politics of Keynesian Economics 1924–1931', in M. Bentley and J. Stevenson (eds.), *High and Low Politics in Modern Britain* (Oxford, 1983), 154–81

   The Keynesian Revolution in the Making 1924–1936 (Oxford, 1988)

Clarke, Stephen, *Central Bank Cooperation 1924–31* (New York, 1967)

Clay, Sir Henry, *Lord Norman* (1957)

Clegg, H., *A History of British Trade Unions Since 1889, Vol. II 1911–1933* (Oxford, 1984)

Close, D. H., 'The Realignment of the Electorate in 1931', *History*, 67 (1982), 393–404

Cole, Margaret, *The Life of G. D. H. Cole* (1971)

Cook, C. and Ramsden, J., *By-elections in British Politics* (1973)

Cooper, Andrew, *British Agricultural Policy 1912–1936* (Manchester, 1989)

Coote, Colin, *The Other Club* (1971)

Cowling, Maurice, *The Impact of Labour 1920–1924* (Cambridge, 1971)
   The Impact of Hitler. British Politics and British Policy 1933–1940 (Cambridge, 1975)

Crisp, L. F., 'The Appointment of Sir Isaac Isaacs as Governor-General of Australia, 1930', *Historical Studies*, 7 (1963–5)

Darwin, John, 'Imperialism in Decline? Tendencies in British Imperial Policy Between the Wars', *Historical Journal*, 23 (1980), 657–79

Day, J. Wentworth, *Lady Houston* (1958)

Dayer, Roberta, *Finance and Empire. Sir Charles Addis 1861–1945* (1988)

Deacon, Alan, *In Search of the Scrounger* (Leeds, 1976)

Diaper, Stephanie, 'Merchant Banking in the Inter-War Period: The Case of Kleinwort, Sons & Co.', *Business History*, 18, (1986), 55–76

Dintenfass, Michael, 'The Politics of Producers' Co-operation: The FBI-TUC-NCEO Talks 1929–1933', in John Turner (ed.), *Businessmen and Politics. Studies of Business Activity in British Politics 1900–1945* (1984), 76–92

Donoughue, B. and Jones, G. W., *Herbert Morrison. Portrait of a Politician* (1973)

Dowse, Robert, *Left in the Centre. The Independent Labour Party 1893–1940* (1966)

Drummond, Ian, *Imperial Economic Policy 1917–1939* (1974)
   The Floating Pound and the Sterling Area 1931–1939 (Cambridge, 1981)

Durbin, Elizabeth, *New Jerusalems. The Labour Party and the Economics of Democratic Socialism* (1985)

Eichengreen, Barry, *Sterling and the Tariff* (Princeton Studies in International Finance, 48, 1981)

Estorick, Eric, *Stafford Cripps* (1949)

Fair, John, 'The Conservative Basis for the Formation of the National Government in 1931', *Journal of British Studies*, 19 (1980), 142–64
   'The Second Labour Government and the Politics of Electoral Reform 1929–1931', *Albion*, 13 (1981), 276–301

Feiling, Keith, *The Life of Neville Chamberlain* (1946)

Freeden, Michael, *Liberalism Divided. A Study in British Political Thought 1914–1939* (Oxford, 1986)

Garside, W. R., *British Unemployment 1919–1939. A Study in Public Policy* (Cambridge, 1990)

Gilbert, Martin, *Winston S. Churchill. Vol. V 1922–39* (1976)

Gopal, S., *The Viceroyalty of Lord Irwin 1926–31* (Oxford, 1957)

Gore, John, *King George V. A Personal Memoir* (1941)

Graham, Thomas, *Willie Graham* (no date)

Gregory, Robert, *Sidney Webb and East Africa* (Berkeley, 1962)

Hamilton, Mary, *Arthur Henderson* (1938)

Hanson, A. H., 'The Labour Party and House of Commons Reform', *Parliamentary Affairs* 10 (1956–7), 454–68, and 11 (1957–8), 39–56

Harkness, D. W., *The Restless Dominion. The Irish Free State and the British Commonwealth of Nations 1921–1931* (1969)

Harris, José, *William Beveridge. A Biography* (Oxford, 1977)

Hearder, H., 'King George V, the General Strike, and the 1931 Crisis', in H. Hearder and H. R. Lyon (eds.), *British Government and Administration* (Cardiff, 1974), 234–47

Holland, R. F., *Britain and the Commonwealth Alliance 1918–1939* (1981)

    'The Federation of British Industries and the International Economy 1929–1939', *Economic History Review*, 34 (1981), 287–300

Howson, Susan, *Domestic Monetary Management in Britain 1919–38* (Cambridge, 1975)

    Sterling's Managed Float. The Operations of the Exchange Equalisation Account, 1932–39 (Princeton Studies in International Finance, 46, 1980)

Howson, Susan and Winch, Donald, *The Economic Advisory Council 1930–1939* (Cambridge, 1977)

Hyde, H. Montgomery, *Norman Birkett* (1964)

James, Robert Rhodes, *Victor Cazalet. A Portrait* (1976)

Jeremy, David (ed.), *Dictionary of Business Biography* (1984–6)

Kunz, Diane, *The Battle for Britain's Gold Standard in 1931* (1987)

Low, D. A., 'Civil Martial Law. The Government of India and the Civil Disobedience Movements 1930–34', in D. A. Low (ed.), *Congress and the Raj. Facets of the Indian Struggle 1917–47* (1977), 165–91

Lowe, Rodney, *Adjusting to Democracy. The Role of the Ministry of Labour in British Politics 1916–1939* (Oxford, 1986)

McDonald, G. W., and Gospel, Howard, 'The Mond-Turner Talks 1927–1933. A Study in Industrial Co-operation', *Historical Journal*, 26 (1973), 807–29

McKibbin, Ross, 'The Economic Policy of the Second Labour Government 1929–1931', *Past and Present*, 68 (1975), 95–123 (also in *Ideologies*, below)

    'Arthur Henderson as Labour Leader', *International Review of Social History*, 23 (1978), 79–101 (also in *Ideologies*, below)

    The Ideologies of Class. Social Relations in Britain 1880–1950 (Oxford, 1990)

Macleod, Iain, *Neville Chamberlain* (1961)

Malament, Barbara, 'Philip Snowden and the Cabinet Deliberations of August 1931', *Bulletin of the Society for the Study of Labour History*, 41 (1980), 31–3

Mallet, Bernard and George, C. Oswald, *British Budgets. Third Series 1921–22 to 1932–33* (1933)

Marquand, David, *Ramsay MacDonald* (1977)

Middlemas, Keith, *The Clydesiders* (1965)

Middlemas, Keith and John Barnes, *Baldwin* (1969)

Middleton, Roger, 'The Treasury in the 1930s: Political and Administrative Constraints to Acceptance of the New Economics', *Oxford Economic Papers*, 34 (1982), 48–77

'The Treasury and Public Investment: A Perspective on Interwar Economic Management', *Public Administration*, 61 (1983), 351–70

Towards the Managed Economy: Keynes, The Treasury and the Fiscal Debate of the 1930s (1985)

Moggridge, D. E., 'The 1931 Financial Crisis. A New View', *The Banker*, 120 (1970), 832–9

British Monetary Policy 1924–31 (Cambridge, 1972)

Moore, R. J., *The Crisis of Indian Unity 1917–1940* (Oxford, 1974)

Morgan, Kenneth O., *Consensus and Disunity: The Lloyd George Coalition Government 1918–1922* (Oxford, 1979)

Morgan, Kenneth, and Morgan, Jane, *Portrait of a Progressive: The Political Career of Christopher, Viscount Addison* (Oxford, 1980)

Mosley, Nicholas, *Rules of the Game: Sir Oswald and Lady Cynthia Mosley 1896–1933* (1982)

Nicolson, Harold, *King George the Fifth. His Life and Reign* (1952)

Owen, Frank, *Tempestuous Journey. Lloyd George, His Life and Times* (1954)

Peden, G. C., 'The Treasury as the Central Department of Government 1919–1939', *Public Administration*, 61 (1983), 371–85

'The "Treasury View" on Public Works and Employment in the Interwar Period', *Economic History Review*, 37 (1984), 167–81

Peele, Gillian, 'A Note on the Irwin Declaration', *Journal of Imperial and Commonwealth History*, 1 (1972–3), 331–7

Pimlott, Ben, *Labour and the Left in the 1930s* (Cambridge, 1977)

Pinder, John (ed.), *Fifty Years of Political and Economic Planning* (1981)

Pope-Hennessy, James, *Queen Mary 1867–1953* (1959)

Postgate, Raymond, *The Life of George Lansbury* (1951)

Ramsden, John, *The Making of Conservative Party Policy: The Conservative Research Department Since 1929* (1980)

Rodgers, Terence, 'Employers' Organizations, Unemployment and Social Politics in Britain during the Inter-war Period', *Social History*, 13 (1988), 315–41

Rose, Kenneth, *King George V* (1983)

Rose, Norman, *The Gentile Zionists. A Study in Anglo-Zionist Diplomacy 1929–1939* (1973)

Roskill, Stephen, *Hankey. Man of Secrets. Vol. II 1919–1931* (1972)

Sayers, R. S., *The Bank of England 1891–1944*, 3 vols. (Cambridge, 1976)

Self, Robert, *Tories and Tariffs. The Conservative Party and the Politics of Tariff Reform 1922–1932* (New York and London, 1986)

Skidelsky, Robert, *Politicians and the Slump. The Labour Government of 1929–1931* (1967)

Oswald Mosley (1975)

Stannage, Tom, *Baldwin Thwarts the Opposition. The British General Election of 1935* (1980)

Stevenson, John, and Cook, Chris, *The Slump. Society and Politics during the Depression* (1977)

Thomas, Hugh, *John Strachey* (1973)

Thorpe, Andrew, 'Arthur Henderson and the British Political Crisis of 1931', *Historical Journal* 31 (1988), 117–39

   The British General Election of 1931 (Oxford, 1991)

Tolliday, Steven, *Business, Banking and Politics. The Case of British Steel 1918–1939* (Cambridge, Mass., 1987)

Tomlinson, B. R., 'Britain and the Indian Currency Crisis'. *Economic History Review*, 32 (1979), 88–99

Weir, L. MacNeill, *The Tragedy of Ramsay MacDonald* (1938)

Williamson, Philip, '"Safety First": Baldwin, the Conservative Party, and the 1929 General Election', *Historical Journal*, 25 (1982), 385–409

   '"Party First and India Second": the Appointment of the Viceroy of India in 1930', *Bulletin of the Institute of Historical Research*, 56 (1983), 86–101

   'Financiers, the Gold Standard and British Politics 1925–1931', in John Turner (ed.) *Businessmen and Politics. Studies of Business Activity in British Politics 1900–1945* (1984), 105–29

   'A "Banker's Ramp"? Financiers and the British Political Crisis of August 1931', *English Historical Review*, 49 (1984), 770–806

   'The Labour Party and the House of Lords 1918–1931', *Parliamentary History*, 10 (1991), 317–41

Wilson, Trevor, *The Downfall of the Liberal Party 1914–1935* (1966)

Winch, Donald, *Economics and Policy. A Historical Study* (1969: 1972 edn)

Wrench, David, '"Cashing In": The Parties and the National Government, August 1931–September 1932', *Journal of British Studies*, 23 (1984), 135–53

Wrench, John Evelyn, *Geoffrey Dawson and our Times* (1955)

Index

All significant participants and witnesses are identified in the Appendix, to which references are not given in this Index.